Shrike

SHRIKE

Joe Donnelly

$\overline{C}$

Century · London

To Ken Smith for his fine argument
and tall tales on Monday nights

First published 1994

1 3 5 7 9 10 8 6 4 2

First published in the United Kingdom in 1994 by
Century Limited
Random House, 20 Vauxhall Bridge Road,
London SW1V 2SA

Random House Australia (Pty) Limited
20 Alfred Street, Milsons Point, Sydney,
New South Wales 2061, Australia

Random House New Zealand Limited
18 Poland Road, Glenfield
Auckland 10, New Zealand

Random House South Africa (Pty) Limited
PO Box 337, Bergvlei, South Africa

Random House UK Limited Reg. No. 954009

A CIP catalogue record for this book is
available from the British Library

ISBN 0 7126 58610

Typeset in Times by
SX Composing Ltd, Rayleigh, Essex
Printed in Great Britain by
Clays Ltd, St Ives PLC

Levenford is very like a town I grew up in, as it was then before the planners screwed up and took out its heart along with the other good bits. Because of the similarity, many of the names of the folk living there might be familiar to some people, but Levenford only exists in my imagination, and the characters are completely fictitious. Maybe the *Shrike* is too.   –   JD.

Shrike: *Lanius Cristatus*, the butcher-bird.
A creature with a very nasty habit.

Blair Bryden, *Levenford Gazette*

1

A murky night well into winter. The west wind had been blowing since morning, bringing dank drizzle in from the firth in dismal grey veils of rain. By six, the wind had strengthened, whipping the waves up to crash against the sheer basalt of the towering rock on the east side of the town where through the spray the lights along the castle ramparts flickered feeble and wan.

In the old centre of the town, River Street, now living up to its name, was more of an oxbow lake than the main thoroughfare, for the high tide and the higher wind had combined to back the river water up until it swelled over the quayside and flowed through the cobbled vennels and alleys to puddle under the street lights.

Just after eight, a car came slowly ploughing along the road, its driver gunning the engine high and slacking off the clutch with a whine. It shoved up a bow wave which washed its way into the doorways as the car made its way slowly along to the old bridge, turned and was gone.

The water seeped and slopped under shop doors. The old co-op would be awash again, for the tenth time in two decades. Benson's off-the-hanger suits would need to be sent to the dry cleaners. The floorboards of the old Woolworth's shop would be warped and twisted and Phil McColl's boys would have a hell of a job pinning them back down on the old joists.

Levenford huddled against the wind and the rain. On River Street there were few stragglers. A couple of boys on motorbikes came ripping through the street-long puddle. They mounted the pavement when the water got too deep on the road, almost cutting the knees from Mickey Haggerty, who was stepping unsteadily out of Mac's Bar on the corner of Kirk Street opposite the clock tower. He stood for a moment, wet and cursing, looked down the sodden length of the street, then shrugged his shoulders and started walking.

The road was higher at the far end, where it met the old bridge across the swollen river. Here, two alleys run down to the quayside. Brewery Lane is cobbled and narrow. Boat Pend is a covered alley, like an arched tunnel bored beneath the old facade of Cairn House, the town's oldest building. It stands gaunt and grey, four storeys high with a sagging, swaybacked roof covered in worn slates and red dragon's-back ridging. The windows are narrow, hardly more than slits. Near on thirty years ago the body of a thirteen-year-old boy had been found bound and gagged and two months dead in a back room of the old building which had been then a disused and empty third-floor surgery. According to the hushed rumour that had scuttled round the playground at Strathleven School, his hair had grown to his shoulders and his fingernails were two inches long.

So the rumour went and more besides. What was true was that the curious boy who broke into the old surgery and found the rotting carcass had been so horror-stricken that he'd never been the same again. He'd spent most of those past years in the care of Barlane Hospital on the outskirts of the town, only one step down from the State Mental Hospital where they kept the really crazy folk. He'd never got over it, but the old town had moved on. There were fresh rumours and new stories to tell in the playground and the story of Cairn House moved into history, for a while.

A quarter of a century on, the wind whistled and whooped, cold enough to keep all but the foolhardy or the determined off the streets. The damp seeped through to chill to the bone and there was a bite of ice too, a sign of a bad winter to come.

A figure came across the street close to the bridge just after the bikers had roared past, tyres hissing on the road. The street lamp outlined the shape of a man, huddled against the wind, staying close to the lee of the wall. He stumbled off balance as a gust of wind came shrieking up Brewery Lane and almost fell headlong, but recovered and staggered on.

He reached the dark entrance to Boat Pend, looked left and right, almost as if he was crossing the street, then moved inside. The darkness swallowed him in two steps.

At the far end of the Pend, where it gave onto a series of tight alleys and walkways, he stopped and twisted the old brass handle on a door set into the side of Cairn House. Inside, the coatstand in the short hallway was laden with wet coats now steaming in the slight warmth. The man took off his coat and scarf and rolled his flat cap tightly enough to squeeze it into a pocket. He turned and made his way up the narrow spiral staircase until he reached the third storey. He paused for breath, then lifted an ornate knocker and rapped twice on the door. It opened almost immediately and the man stepped inside.

'All here then?' the old woman sitting at the far end of the room asked. Her small eyes squinted in the dim light of a standard lamp in the corner of the room.

There was a low murmur of assent. There were six other people in the room, including the man who had just arrived and who was now using a white handkerchief to pat the rain from behind an ear.

'Could have picked a better night,' one of them mumbled and someone else agreed.

'Can't choose the night. Can't choose the time,' the old woman piped up in a clear voice.

Marta Herkik was a tiny woman, almost as big across as she was tall. Her black hair was caught back in a bun so severe that her pencilled eyebrows were arched high, giving her a perpetual look of surprise. The knife-straight white line that bisected her widow's peak showed the black was not natural.

She was dressed completely in black, except for a red stone in a silver brooch pinned to her collar, reflecting the soft light like a dying eye. She sat on a high-backed chair, small, surprisingly young hands flat on the surface.

'Well. I think we should begin.'

The six others shuffled themselves around the table, scraped chairs back and got seated.

'Hands please,' Marta Herkik said primly. They lifted elbows and hands from the black cloth which draped the table and she grabbed an end, slowly drawing it towards her across the surface. It made a soft hissing noise, like sand in an hourglass. The little fat woman folded the cloth neatly and dropped it to the floor beside her. Behind her, the fire sputtered and the blare of light from the hearth threw the shadow of the high-backed chair onto the far wall where it joined the ceiling.

Even in the dim light, the table shone and reflected the faces of the people seated around it, all eyes fixed on Marta Herkik. It was smooth as glass from years of polishing, and it was old.

It had six legs carved into the shape of arms, so well crafted that the individual veins followed the grain of dark hardwood, ending in hands clenched into knuckles. The table-top surface was a masterpiece of marquetry. On the border, six inches in from the end, nymphs and fauns cavorted in writhing, sensuous tangles, then beyond that was a circle, inlaid in white veneer cut so expertly there was no visible seam or join, a circle of tightly packed angular letters that almost resembled script but was not. Beyond that, in black, was a smaller circle which spelled the alphabet in odd, slanted lettering. Between the circles, close to Marta Herkik's edge, in similar black wood, the word YEA was cut in the same style. Opposite, just in front of William Simpson, the man who was last into the room, a single word. NAY. And in the centre, in a red wood almost the colour of new blood, an inlaid star of five points gleamed.

Close to the woman, a large book, leather-bound and faded with age, lay closed.

'I think we're ready,' Marta Herkik said.

She opened the book, using one finger to turn the pages until she found the right one. Each of them could see one passage had been marked off in black ink.

'Tonight, it is a special thing we do. We go further than we have gone before, because this is the time. We seek the guidance of the great one, who will open to us the future, to bring for some, a heart's desire, to others the knowledge that is also the power.'

She leaned over the book and began to read, though none of the others understood any of the words. The woman's voice came in odd conjunctions of hard consonants, flat vowels. She intoned the unmusical chant, turning the page when she reached the bottom and then carrying on for several minutes. Finally her voice trailed away. She lifted the book without closing it and laid it on a small table just within arm's reach. From the bag on her lap she drew a leather wallet which she snapped open and produced a set of large cards. Without looking she shuffled them swiftly, shaking the cards together. Every few seconds, she leaned forward and asked one of the group to touch the pack, each in turn, anti-clockwise. They waited until she had finished.

10

'The second part,' the old woman said, sliding her eyes across theirs. She put the pack on the centre of the table, face down.

'As before, each take three. They are your own keys.'

Janet Robinson stretched out a tentative hand, used two outspread fingers to pinch a wad of cards and with her other hand, took three. Each of them did the same. When they had all done so, Marta Herkik spoke up again.

'Keep these with you now. Do not look at the faces, for they are your hidden fortune. Put them away and hold them to you.'

Annie Eastwood and the other woman looked at each other. This was something different. The tarot cards were old, the writhing black patterns on the backs worn with use. Annie almost turned hers over to see what she had drawn, but Janet picked hers up and put them in her bag. Annie did the same. Each of the men put them in an inside pocket, wondering why they'd been asked to do this. William Simpson pulled back his lapel, made to slide the cards inside and glanced down at the nearest face. It showed a man suspended on a rope, and that surprised him. When Marta Herkik had dealt his cards before, it had been a different set. Then, the man had been dangling by one foot, the other crossed over. This one was a black etching of the Hanged Man. But the picture showed a rotting skeletal figure dangling from a gibbet on which perched five black crows. Eye sockets glared blindly above grinning teeth.

Marta Herkik broke the small silence. 'Do as I do, now,' she said and everyone leaned forward. They all had their reasons.

The small woman reached into a black bag on her lap and brought out something which she raised, then placed slowly in the centre of the pentagon forming the heart of the star. All eyes followed the movement. She drew her hands away and a translucent stone remained, so clear it could have been made of glass, almost perfectly round, though not quite, showing it had been formed from natural rock crystal. In its depths, only three inches away from the smooth surface, yet seeming far away because of the odd perspective within the curved stone, a small almond-shaped flaw caught the light and shone it back. Like the stone in the old woman's brooch, it gleamed like an eye.

Marta Herkik held her fingertips on the crystal dome. The others reached, some eagerly, some more hesitant, until they all touched.

11

There was a long moment of complete silence, then the woman spoke, this time very softly.

'We are gathered here to be granted the gift of sight and the gift of knowledge. We seek to know the un-knowable, to see the unseen, to go beyond the beyond. Open your minds and your hearts, because they are the channels. Empty your minds and let the power flow.'

On the woman's right side, Annie Eastwood, short brown hair still damp from the rain, felt a tremor under her hands, so soft she thought she might have imagined it, so slight it could have been the tiny pulse in the skin of her fingers.

She held her breath and waited. A divorcee for fourteen years, this was her fourth visit to Marta Herkik's back parlour. Her seventeen-year-old daughter Angela had gone out, against her mother's wishes, to a disco in Lochend, seven miles along the road on the south end of Loch Corran. She hadn't come home that night. Her boyfriend had borrowed his father's car and had taken Angela and his friend and girlfriend for a drive up the Shore Road past Linnvale where the scars of the summer's forest fire had left a black carpet of desolation. Not far past the turn-off, the car had gone out of control, hit a tree-stump and rolled. Angela had been thrown out of the car and tumbled fifty feet through the air to hit a solitary old oak tree a few yards in from the roadside. Almost every bone in her body had been smashed on impact. She had died instantly.

Annie Eastwood wanted to speak to her daughter. She had to know she was safe and happy. And most of all, she wanted her to know she was sorry.

To Annie's right Derek Elliot felt the shiver in the crystal and a half-smile formed on his face. He didn't really believe in all this hocus-pocus, he told himself. But he was curious. He was also young and he was ambitious. He'd failed his law degree four years before, but had talked old Harry Fitzpatrick at Levenax Estate Agents to take him on and he'd diligently worked his way into a junior partnership, though that meant doing all of the work while Harry played golf. In the past few months, Derek had been doing little private deals on the side, deals that would have made the old man throw a fit, had he known, but he did not know and Derek Elliot wanted to move on and up. He wanted Marta Herkik to tell him when. All he needed was a hint. Maybe a sign.

Next to him, Mickey O'Day had the look of a man who wants everyone to think he is on top. He was in his mid thirties and sported a loud tie and a louder checked sports jacket on which he'd pinned a carnation which clashed jarringly. Mickey was on his way out of the dark side of a bad run of luck. He still owed a small fortune to Carrick's bookie's shop. Mickey was a great believer in luck and that lady had written him a dear John. Eddie Carrick had sent his two boys along to the Castlegate Bar to leave a message. It was blunt and to the point: the old fella wanted his money by the weekend. Mickey didn't have it. He needed some help to get luck back on his side, just enough to make a favourite fall, to give an outsider a spurt, to get Eddie Carrick's big lads off his back. That was when he'd heard about Marta Herkik, and then his luck had started to change. Mickey felt the shiver under his fingers and gave a small smile that nobody else noticed. Maybe tonight, just maybe, lady luck would really smile on him and get him out from under, once and for all, put him back on top where he belonged.

Almost opposite Marta Herkik, William Simpson shivered in response to the tiny tremor under his own fingers.

He shouldn't be here. He knew that, and still he'd come. Exactly why he *had* come, he could not say, not to anyone. He was looking for something. Simpson was minister of Castlebank Church, preaching to less than a hundred souls every Sunday, most of them women, most of them old, and that part of his life was empty and hollow and as dry as the cellar beneath the crypt. More than anyone else in the room, he needed to believe in a life after death. And he needed that more than anything.

On his right, still going round the table anti-clockwise, was Janet Robinson, a thin, nervous woman with short fair hair and nervous eyes behind wide-lensed glasses. She was apprehensive, for a reason she could not name. She had been here before and listened to Marta Herkik's piping voice as she interpreted the tarot, but this was the first time she had sat with her fingers on the polished stone. Janet was a typist at the police station on College Street, a shy, timid woman. Her mother, a large, big-busted, big-voiced woman who had loomed like a shadow over her all her life, had died suddenly of a massive stroke that summer. Janet Robinson had been left with nothing to fill the vacuum. She didn't know what to do. Her mother had organised everything, every part of her life. For most of that life Janet had been afraid of her anger, had hated her dominance, but had succumbed until there was nothing much left of her own *self*. Now she wasn't sure what *she* wanted. But she knew she needed to lay her mother's memory to rest.

The last man at the table was Edward Tomlin, who sat with eyes fixed on the fingers sitting lightly on top of the shining stone. He was in his late thirties, slim and tense. He was a little bit frightened, though he did not know why. Tomlin was the caretaker in Castlebank shipyard, which had been the biggest industry in Levenford until the fifties when things had begun to go sour. Now he was in charge of a shell of rusting sheds and hangars, mouldering machinery and weed-filled slipways. His job was no job at all, for there was nothing to repair, or clean. He spent his time making sure the teenagers of the town were kept from using the old sheds as drinking dens, and that the younger children stayed safely outside the wrought-iron gates. The yard had died a long time ago, though one small section, close to the distillery, had been fenced off and it was there that the only heavy engineering took place, a stripped-down operation building spidery rig-sections for the North Sea oilfields. Occasionally Eddie Tomlin would stroll past the chain-link, listening to the harsh metal sounds, and hanker for the days when his father had been welding foreman, and when the big gates would open on a Saturday to spill the grimy men out into the street for Saturday football matches. More often he'd unlock the old tool room and open the box where he kept some of the things he'd collected over the years. In the quiet of the afternoon, he'd strip off his overalls and dress up in silk.

Marta Herkik pressed her small, smooth hand onto the glass. She gave a small smile of satisfaction when she felt the tiny tremor, and sensed the heightened perception of the people around the table. The rain beat a steady rap on the window, sounding like a backwash of sand on the shore, and the wind moaned down the chimney, flaring the coals to brightness in stuttering breaths.

'Here we are gathered,' she said in a low voice, almost a mutter. In her east European accent it sounded like *gattered*. 'To

14

make contact, yes? With those gone before us beyond the beyond. We each have the reasons. I am here to guide you and my guide will lead me through. May we bring to them peace and may they give peace to us.'

All eyes were fixed on the little woman's face. The stone on her shoulder winked red.

'We channel ourselves, our inner selves, together and through the crystal. A radio beam if you prefer it, sending our thoughts to the faraway, yes?'

They all nodded, slowly, like infants responding to a teacher.

'We begin now, please,' Marta said with a little nod. Under her fingers the tremor had become a vibration, slow and steady.

The woman closed her eyes and brought her eyebrows down as far as the pull of her tightly held hair would allow.

'We come to seek the help of he who holds the power,' she intoned, almost singing. It sounded to Mickey O'Day just like a bad piece of acting in an old movie, but even Mickey could feel the tension which seemed to twist from one to another in the circle around the table. There was an odd tingle of expectancy.

'We seek the knowledge, and answers to our questions. We seek the guidance from beyond to assist us,' Marta crooned. 'We are empty vessels into which can flow the knowledge and the power to see beyond. Come to us now, and answer our call. Bring us the knowledge and the sign.'

She took a deep breath.

Under their fingers, the smooth crystal trembled in a sudden hard vibration, strong enough to make it rattle on the table-top. Janet Robinson made a small noise, more an intake of breath. Edward Tomlin felt his heart give a double-jump.

'I ask it now,' Marta went on as if nothing had happened. Their fingers felt the thrum of resonance through the clear stone. 'We call you now to come to us.'

The rattle got louder, more urgent. Derek Elliot could see the flaw inside the crystal between his fingers. The movement was causing it to flicker and dance like a candle flame. Without warning, the movement stopped and a heavy silence followed. Annie Eastwood looked at the little woman, but Marta's eyes were fixed on the stone.

Then, again without warning, it moved.

15

There was no hesitation. It slid across the table to stop just in front of Marta Herkik. It made hardly a sound as it glided across the polished surface to plant itself right on top of the inlaid word YEA.

She smiled, just a twitch of her lips.

'Spirit,' she said. 'You have chosen to be with us, to journey from the far place. If we ask, will you answer?'

The crystal dome remained where it sat, right at the edge of the inlaid word. There was another momentary silence, then it began to shake again, just enough to drum on the polished wood.

'Very good. We shall now begin,' the old woman piped. 'The spirit is with us. I feel his presence and so shall you. Welcome him to yourselves.'

As soon as she said that, the fire flared then dimmed theatrically, and then, very slowly, the light on the lamp on the old dresser by the wall faded to red. The draught from the chimney swirled around the room. Each of them felt it. The hairs on Derek Elliot's knuckles stood on end, and Janet Robinson felt the skin between her shoulder blades pucker and crawl. The cold wind eddied from one to the other. William Simpson felt it waft through him, shivering him deep inside. Annie Eastwood drew in her breath, feeling the cold air spread into her lungs. It was as if the atmosphere had changed, suddenly tense and frigid, as if the wind moaning down the chimney had snaked right into their bones.

Marta raised her head and scanned the faces around the table. 'Which will be first?'

They all looked at her, then at each other, none wishing to make a move.

'Hurry now,' Marta urged abruptly. 'There is no time.'

'Give me a number,' Mickey O'Day blurted. What he really wanted was a name. A *winning* name. 'Give me a lucky number.'

The stone trembled again. Very slowly, it slid across the table, hovered in front of the NAY sign, then glided silently to stop briefly in front of Derek Elliot, sped diagonally across to tremble before Janet Robinson and then changed direction to flit down and stop between Marta Herkik and Annie Eastwood. As it moved their arms reached or drew back, still with their fingers on the stone.

16

'Six.' Mickey said, spelling out the letters. 'That's what it said, unless one of you's pushing the damn thing.'

Marta shot him a look which conveyed irritation and commanded silence.

'Just checking,' Mickey said with a grin. Already, in his mind, he was leaning on the railing at Ayr racetrack. Tomorrow, he knew, the going would be soft. There were fourteen runners. With the ease of the habitual gambler, he ran through the numbers. Red Crystal, a three-year-old untested colt, was among the bar runners at 33-1 in the day's major race. It was coming out of trap six. Mickey had hoarded his last win, though still in well over his head in credit bets. There were a few places who would take a ten or twenty, and if he spread his money around, it wouldn't attract attention. He smiled to himself, hearing in his mind the roar of the crowd at the post as his horse came through. Number six. Red Crystal. He looked down at the stone under his hands and saw the tiny flaw catch the light. Another sign. Another omen. For the first time in months he felt absolutely sure that his luck was going to dazzle him.

'That'll do nicely,' he murmured, strangely certain. Maybe, he thought, it would come up with a few more.

'Someone else with a question?' Marta asked.

Janet Robinson looked up, then dropped her eyes back to her hand.

'Yes, dear?' Marta encouraged. 'Don't be afraid. Ask what you want to know.'

For a moment, Janet was nonplussed. She didn't know *what* she wanted to know. She was trying to formulate a question when Annie Eastwood blurted: 'My daughter. Is she safe? I mean. . .' Annie looked straight at Marta. 'Is she happy? I have to tell her something. I didn't get the chance. I mean . . .' The words came out in a tumble. Before she could say more, the crystal moved so abruptly that Janet Robinson let out a little gasp.

It slid in a series of straight-line glides, halting precisely in front of the letters, its edge on the middle ring, jerking back and forth spasmodically. As it moved, the six people who had come to Marta Herkik's backstairs apartment silently mouthed the letters. Abruptly, the crystal came to a halt, in the dead centre of the table.

17

'Angela.' It was a whisper which was almost a gasp. Even in the dimness of the room, Janet Robinson could see the slackness in Annie Eastwood's face. The blood just seemed to drain away to below the collarline of her blouse. 'That's her name.'

A shiver went through their fingers again. This time there was no hesitation. The glass sped over the surface, pecking at a letter, diving off at a tangent, stabbing at another, coming back briefly to the centre to mark a pause . . . sometimes.

DARK it spelled.

Then: COLD.

Then: SORE. IT HURTS. IT HURTS. IT HURTS. COLD-DARK-COLD-PAIN O HELP O HELP OH NO OH OH OH MOTHERPLEASEHELPMEMOTHER.

Annie Eastwood squeaked, whether in fright or in pain, none of them knew. She jerked back and her hand flew from the crystal. A noise like a brisk handclap smacked the air and Marta Herkik's five other visitors felt their own hands thrown from the polished stone. The old woman's hand was the last on the surface. Another small noise, like an electrical contact, sparked under her fingers and her own hand was thrown upwards. It looked as if she had touched something hot.

'What?' she exclaimed, to no one in particular.

Just as the word was out, the crystal dome began to move again. It edged of its own volition to the NAY sign then back to the centre, then it was off again, flitting in a glowing blur, collecting its letters with each instant stop before it flicked to the next, criss-crossing the table in diagonal flashes.

TREEOSH it spelled out. Then OTHERES then EHORSET. Between each clump of letters, it paused and quivered. They all watched, mouths agape. Annie Eastwood's hands were shaking, balled into fists just under her chin, as if she was preparing to ward off the smooth polished hemisphere if it suddenly leapt at her. Mickey O'Day was sitting right back in his seat, staring at the stone as if it were a snake. Edward Tomlin, opposite him, had a knuckle jammed into his mouth, as if he were afraid he might make a sound. Marta Herkik's own face had sagged, as if even she couldn't believe what she was seeing.

Then William Simpson spoke: 'It's our initials. They're all anagrams.'

As soon as he said that, the stone rattled *hard* on the table-top, then went completely still.

'It was only our initials,' he said. 'But how did it do that?'

Without pausing, he shoved his chair back and bent to look under the table. He disappeared from view completely. Unconsciously Janet Robinson crossed her legs in an automatic movement as soon as his head bowed under the edge of the table. Five seconds later, he came back up again.

'There's nothing there. I don't understand this.'

He looked across the table to where Marta Herkik still sat, slack jawed, the hand that had been resting on the stone up close to her face, palm outwards.

'What's going on here?' he demanded.

Annie Eastwood made another little squeaking sound. She looked as if she might have a heart attack. Nobody else noticed.

'Come on. Tell me.'

Everybody turned to Marta. The old woman's mouth opened, then, very slowly, it closed again. Just as slowly, she closed her eyes and quite gracefully drew her head back until the tight bun was pressed against the high back of the chair. Her small reddened lips pursed and a frown of concentration knotted her pencilled eyebrows into a tight cupid's bow. She drew in a long breath through her nose, as if she was sniffing the air, expelled it the same way and drew in again, deep and slow. The hand that had been held up close to her face slowly dropped to her lap. The six people watched in silence. The woman's steady breathing continued for several moments, each breath longer than the last, each inhalation drawn out so slowly it seemed to take an age to reach its turning point.

Finally, Marta Herkik's head began to slump forward. She gave a little moan, hardly louder than the sound of her breathing had been, then fell silent. The rapping on the window-pane faded to nothing and the whistle of the wind down the chimney died away and the silence expanded. There was no movement, not the blink of an eye nor the twitch of a lip. The very air of the room seemed to be taut with a sudden expectancy.

'*Donuts.*'

Derek Elliot visibly jerked back in a start of surprise. Janet Robinson's eyes blinked rapidly three times.

Marta Herkik's head swung up and her eyes snapped open, staring straight into the smooth stone in the centre of the table. Her lips had not moved, but the voice had come from her.

'Donuts,' she said again. *'Hot. Icing. Sugar.'*

Still the woman's red lips were motionless. Her teeth seemed to be gritted together.

The voice which they heard was not a woman's voice, not the tones of an old woman, not the strong east European accent that Marta Herkik still maintained almost forty years after she had fled the Hungarian revolution and come to live with her brother in Levenford, just south of the highland line.

'Make me some hot donuts, mummy,' the voice piped up in the clear, singsong cadence of a small girl.

Beside the old woman, Annie Eastwood's face went through a startling metamorphosis. She stiffened, as if all the muscles in her cheeks and neck had gone into a bunching spasm, then, almost instantaneously, as if strings holding them tight had been cut, they sagged, giving her the vacuous look of someone in shock. Her eyes rolled upwards, the brown irises almost disappearing behind her eyelids. Even in the dim light of the embers it was clear that her face had gone sickly pale.

'They're my favourites, *mummy,'* the child's voice sang out.

Annie shuddered as if struck and the muscles of her face unslackened themselves in a galvanic jerk. She gave a little moan, very like the sound Marta Herkik had made. Her eyes flicked to the left. The old woman was sitting dead still, gaze fixed emptily on the curved crystal under her fingers.

'Angela?' Annie Eastwood's question was hushed. The tremble in her breath was audible. Everyone else stared at her. No one else spoke.

'Angie?' she said again, this time louder. In her mind a cruel playback ran its scenes in flick-flick motion. It had been Angie's fourth birthday, six months after Crawford Eastwood had packed a suitcase and disappeared, without leaving so much as a note on the mantelpiece, leaving her to bring up the baby on her own, leaving her, she later discovered, for a nineteen-year-old girl who had babysat on the nights Annie had been kept late stocktaking, while Crawford had been spending what little extra money they'd had down in the County Bar. She'd had to work hard then,

20

scraping and scratching to keep little Angie dressed and fed. There had been no money for birthday presents that year, not with the lawyer's fees and all, and she'd been too busy just trying to keep the house going at all to buy a birthday cake.

And little Angie had understood, even at four years old. She'd put her arms around her mother's neck when Annie had tried, bitterly and heart-achingly, to explain that there would be a cake at Christmas, and presents too, but – *oh God, I'm sorry, honeybun – I've nothing for you now.*

'Don't worry, mummy,' she'd piped up, hugging hard, trying to make the hurt go away. She'd *known*, even at the age of four, she'd known.

'Make me some donuts instead. Make me hot donuts with icing and sugar. They're my favourites.'

And Annie had got the flour and butter and moulded the donuts into rings, woman and small girl in the old high-ceilinged kitchen that she hadn't paid the mortgage on for four months. They'd dropped the doughy rings into the deep fat and listened to their spat and sizzle and she'd spooned the thick icing sugar on, letting it drip like sweet wax while they were still hot. They'd stuck four tiny blue candles on one of them and both of them had sung happy birthday, little Angie singing *happy birthday dear* ME while tears had clouded Annie's eyes.

That had been fourteen years ago. On that day, Annie had promised her baby there would be Christmas presents under the tree, and she'd promised herself too, that no matter what, she'd make a home for the two of them, come what may. And thirteen years after that, Angie had been catapulted out of a car and had broken all her bones and Annie hadn't even been given the chance to say goodbye.

The sound of the child's voice had brought that all back in one tidal wave of remembrance that swamped Annie Eastwood and dragged her under.

'*Don't worry, mummy. I'm a good girl,*' the voice cut through to the drowning woman and dragged her back. Her fingers tried to hook onto the smooth crystal dome, instinctively seeking purchase.

'Angie!' she managed to say again.

'*Yes, mother.*' This time, the tone was still that of a girl, but now a young woman rather than a child. Annie recognised it at once.

'Where . . .' Annie started. 'Where are you?'

'I'm here, mother. It's dark here. And cold. It's very cold and I can't get warm. I'm lost, mother.'

'But. . . .'

All eyes except Marta Herkik's were now fixed on Annie Eastwood. No one else spoke. William Simpson's mouth was set in a circle, as if he was sucking an invisible stick of rock. Janet Robinson's jaw had sagged down until it was almost on her chest.

'I'm all alone, mother,' the young woman's voice wailed. There was a panicky edge to it, a jagged ridge of fear. Marta Herkik's lips didn't move. Her mouth was still partly open. A pulse beat visibly in her neck under her chin, but her lips were motionless. Yet there was no doubt that the voice was coming from her.

'Angie. *Angela!*' Annie cried out. 'What's wrong? Where are you?'

'I have messages for people, mother. I have to tell them.'

'But Angie, *wait!*' the woman blurted, panicky, like a caller expecting the phone to be hung up.

Then the voice changed yet again. Marta Herkik's head came down in a slow nod. Her hands dropped equally slowly, and planted themselves on the table, one on either side of the YEA sign.

'A message. From the harbinger,' this new voice said. It had no accent at all. The words came out flat, like footfalls. It had no gender, no age. Marta Herkik raised her head and they could see the reflections of the small flaw in the crystal reflected in her eyes, like two smouldering points deep inside the wide pupils.

'A message for all of you. Hmm? From the other whom you have called.'

The old woman's jaw twitched, as if she was fighting back the words, *biting* back the words, but still her lips didn't move.

'A small payment for the summons. A little quid pro quo, hmm? You all want the future, all of you, and you shall have a future.'

'What's the old bugger going on about?' Mickey O'Day breathed. His eyes left Marta Herkik's rictus and flicked about the room, looking for something that would tell him this was a

22

recording. But the nerves rippling under the skin of his neck, like creeping fingers, told him this was a vain hope.

'Ah, the gambling man. A lucky number. The number of all luck. It is six, the number of my master's master.'

The short sentences came out in hard bites.

'Yea. It is six, and so shall ye know it. It is six times six times six. Test your luck, man of chance. Test the luck of the game.'

The old woman's head swivelled a fraction to the left.

'And you. Man of the cloth.'

Now the voice deepened. *'Shall I sing you a song? A hymn, perhaps. Suffer little children. It would be better for thee that a millstone be put around thy neck than corrupt one of these, my little ones. One of his little ones. More than one. You wear the millstone well.'*

'What the devil?' William Simpson almost choked on the rush of words. 'How dare you . . . I'll . . . I'll. . . .'

But the old woman's head had turned away from him, veering further to the left. The burning glint flared brighter.

'Mother's here, my dear. Watching over you, day and night, just as I shall guide you in the night.'

Janet Robinson shrank back.

'Oh, don't fidget. And close your mouth, or the wind will change and you'll stay like that, stupid girl. And remember. I'm watching you, all the time. I know everything.'

Janet's expression of fright changed immediately to a slack look of pure horror. She gave a strangled little coughing cry and then her mouth closed like a trap.

Marta's head continued its swing.

'Open the box,' the voice came. Edward Tomlin was locked in her gaze. *'The secret box behind closed doors, the Pandora's box of all your guises.'*

Tomlin shrank back, his eyes showing the fear of a man who knows his secret will be told. He held up a hand to ward off the words.

'If only they knew. The thing that you do. With the locks. And the box. And the doors.'

It came out in a singsong rhyme. A grating, sneering little ditty.

Marta Herkik's blazing eyes left him speechless. Her head snapped to the right and she glared at Derek Elliot.

23

'Ah, an ambitious man. A man with plans. With other people's money, hmm? A takeover? I accept your invitation to join the company. A welcome opening. In management, no less. Too many cooks. Of the books. Success to all.'

The voice stopped.

Everybody stared at the old woman, their faces frozen in expressions of fright or distress or outright shock.

There was a silence for almost a minute, while Marta Herkik began to breathe heavily again, each intake rasping, as if her throat was constricted, as if she was fighting for air.

Her fingers pressed down on the polished wood of the inlaid table, curved, and the knuckles stood white as she forced the tips down hard until her nails were pointed straight at the shiny surface. Then she drew her hands back, digging her nails in. There was a faint scraping sound at first, then as the hands drew towards her, a screech as the painted nails dug under the surface. Edward Tomlin saw a little corkscrew of veneer spiral upwards from under the end of her middle finger. Behind it, where her hands had moved, eight, almost parallel lines were gouged into the wood, ploughed furrows with jagged edges. Even as he watched he saw the long fingernail snap backwards right from the little half-moon quick at the base of the nail, with an audible *click*. Blood welled out from where it stuck out like a bird's beak and flowed into the lengthening groove. The old woman's expression did not change. She appeared to be grinning, but without humour. Her lips were drawn back from her teeth. Her eyes caught the flicker of light from the stone, but they looked blind.

Just as her fingers reached the middle circle, the stone began to move again, following a similar stuttering pattern to the previous zig-zag darting. Only Michael O'Day saw the movement. The rest of them watched aghast as Marta Herkik's fingers tore at the table.

'I think I've had enough,' William Simpson snapped. He shoved his chair back from the table. 'I don't know what on earth is going on here, but I'm leaving.' He pushed himself to his feet and took a step backwards.

Edward Tomlin's chair caught on the edge of a carpet and began to tilt. He stood up, eyes still fixed on the little stream of blood which was slowly oozing down its groove to the pentangle at the centre of the table. The path of the smooth stone had crossed over the trickle and had smeared a glistening pattern on its travels, a little thick blob where it had stopped at a letter and spun.

Marta Herkik breathed out violently, a cold hiss of air, strong as the gust of wind that had blasted out from the fireplace, but this time much colder. Even William Simpson, standing away from the table, felt it on his face. The cold invaded him again, made him shudder. The temperature of the room plummeted instantly. From the wall behind the woman's twisted shape, a ripping noise, like fine cloth torn apart, zipped down from the ceiling. A line of the heavy brocaded wallpaper simply peeled off the wall and flopped, snakelike, to the floor. Droplets of water beaded on the bare plaster where it had been pasted to the wall. Another rip and a parallel section unseamed and oozed wetly to pool beside the fireplace kerb.

The old woman's head was thrown back and her eyes rolled. The stone slowly swivelled in the centre of the table. Edward Tomlin's chair teetered, then crashed to the floor. The noise was enough to distract Janet Robinson and Annie Eastwood. They forced themselves back from the table, shivering with fright and the sudden glacial cold. Derek Elliot followed with a jerky movement as if he was afraid to be left behind. Michael O'Day was riveted on the lines of blood on the table. Cold fingers of revulsion and fascinated fear were trailing up and down his spine. The short hairs on the back of his neck were rippling in unison. They felt as if they were trying to crawl upwards.

Simpson reached the door, snatched at the handle and pulled it open. He turned to say something else and the door slammed shut with a loud clatter. He yelled in a strangely high-pitched voice as his hand, still on the handle, was twisted round in a sudden snap, wrenching his wrist. At the same moment, the fire flared and the flaw in the stone caught the light like a fanned ember. Marta Herkik's fingers were now dug into the wood at the end of the table. Her neck was arched back so far that her chin was pointing to the ceiling. She gave a strangled gasp.

Closest to her, Edward Tomlin heard a creaking noise. It reminded him of a branch bent to breaking point. Beads of sweat on the old woman's brow trickled down towards her ears.

25

'Somebody help her,' he shouted. 'She's having a fit or something.'

'Help nothing,' Derek Elliot said. 'She's nothing but an old faker. I'm getting out of here.' But the young man in the smart blue suit did not sound as if he believed a word of what he said.

He reached beyond William Simpson, who was still shaking his hand, and grabbed the door handle. He twisted it with some force and hauled. Nothing happened.

'Bloody thing's stuck. Another trick,' he said from behind clenched teeth. He braced himself and heaved.

There was a noise of wood splintering and the door opened an inch. Elliot grunted with effort.

On the table the stone started spinning, although only Michael O'Day saw it. Marta Herkik's head was bent so far now over the back of the seat that the bun on the top of her head was almost down at shoulder level. She was groaning now, rasping like an animal. Annie Eastwood took a step toward her, paused, then took two steps back. Her eyes moved to the old woman's fingers, stuck in the wood. Blood was flowing from the ends of them. All the nails were twisted off their cuticle beds.

'Oh, she's . . .' Annie began. In her head she could still hear her daughter's pitiful plea. Her mind was a turmoil, and she could feel her knees shudder as if they were about to give under her weight.

Derek Elliot heaved on the door and swung it open, helped by William Simpson, who managed to hook his undamaged hand round the edge of the heavy wood. There was another creak, then it slammed back against the wall with enough force to shiver the floor.

'Would you look at that?' Michael O'Day said, in a voice that held both fear and wonderment. Janet Robinson and Edward Tomlin couldn't help but look.

The glowing hemisphere of polished stone was whirling on the centre of the table. Tiny splashes of blood were flicked up and out in a Catherine-wheel spray. Marta Herkik sounded as though she was choking, yet nobody made a move to help her. In the flick of an eye, the whirling piece of quartz shot from the table and hit the stone fireplace behind the twisted woman with a noise like gunfire. Shards of crystal exploded outwards. One of them clipped Mickey O'Day on the cheek. Another raked Janet Robinson's calf.

But it was Marta Herkik who took the force of it. Her whole body stiffened, as if she'd been hit by a hammer, then her head whipped up and forward. The whole of the top of her head was crowned with sparkling pieces of glassy splinters. Blood drenched her hair.

William Simpson leapt through the doorway with Derek Elliot clawing at his jacket to get in front. Edward Tomlin almost knocked Annie Eastwood sprawling in his rush to get out. His shoulder hit the door-jamb and he spun, tumbled down three stairs before the turn and almost knocked himself out when his chin connected with the low sill of the stairwell window. Annie Eastwood's heel broke as she tripped over the sprawled man. Janet Robinson's didn't. She missed her footing, planted a high heel in Tomlin's groin and didn't even hear his squeal as the little metal edge punctured the fabric of his trousers and almost punched a hole in his left testicle. By the time she got to the bottom of the stairs she was almost gabbling in fright. Michael O'Day saw none of this. His eyes were riveted on the awful sight of Marta Herkik's head swinging up with its hair caked in blood.

One of the shards that had exploded out from the fireplace when the crystal had shattered was embedded in her forehead. That jagged shard, the biggest of them all, had contained the flaw at the centre of the stone. Now it gleamed and sparked like a third eye in the middle of the old woman's forehead. Her own eyes were rolled right back, still wide open, until only the whites glared out blindly. Her head continued to swing forward and her mouth moved in a series of spastic jerks.

Michael backed away, eyes wide, feeling his breath catch in his throat.

The voice grated out again, and Michael stared, transfixed, as the old woman's hands came up from the table, dripping blood. They flexed in front of her blind eyes, like ragged talons.

He started to say something, but the words wouldn't come. A nerve jumped under his knee and he thought for a moment he was going to fall to the floor, leaving him alone with the apparition still seated in the chair.

Then Marta Herkik started to laugh, but it was not the high, piping laugh of the old woman who had read his tarot cards only the week before.

This was a gruff, barking laugh. It sounded more animal than human. It started low, almost a growl, and quickly rose to a stuttering bark, like foxes in a dark wood. The woman's mouth was wide open. Her false teeth slipped out, bounced on her podgy chest and rattled to the table. The laugh continued and Michael O'Day couldn't move. The nightmare screech soared higher and higher, like a laugh on a speeded-up record, until it became the chittering of stoats in a gorse bush. Then it stopped abruptly, and old Marta Herkik's body arched backwards. There was a thin snapping sound as her legs pushed out. Her back curved and her head was thrown back in a sudden spasm.

Then she began to rise straight up from the chair, limbs spreadeagled, hands drooling blood. He watched aghast, paralysed. The woman's body reached the level of the high lintel on the fireplace and continued straight up. A hand scraped the wall. It moved, jittering, and smeared a line of blood on the bare piece where the paper had unseamed itself. The other hand stretched out, made contact with the bare plaster and scrabbled against it. Michael O'Day saw the smears become letters, the letters become words. Still nine, maybe ten feet in the air, and completely horizontal, her face pointing at the ceiling, the old woman's form began to spin slowly. It was so alien, so preposterous, that Michael O'Day felt a cold terror grip at the base of his belly. The spinning motion stopped and the woman coughed sickly, as if she was choking, and something crashed in the corner. His eyes flicked to the shadows where the walls joined just as a vase came hurtling from the gloom towards him. He didn't have time to move, but it missed him by a whisker, the wind of its passing riffling his black Irish curls. Beside it, a line of old books came whirring out, propelled by an invisible force, bulleting out into the room, slamming against the table, against the cabinet on the far side, pages fluttering and ripping. Above, one of the lightbulbs in the three-branched light imploded and a shower of tiny glass splinters rained down to the floor.

Michael's muscles unlocked. Enormous gratitude for the power of motion flooded him. He backed away towards the door, still unable to pull his eyes away from the woman who floated, fat

28

legs stuck out awkwardly from her drooping black skirt, close to the ceiling.

Then she dropped. It was as if a rope had been cut. She came straight down without a sound. Her head slammed against the stone edge with a soft *crumping* sound and her left arm was thrown forward into the red embers.

Michael turned and ran. He took the stairs three at a time, carooming off the walls of the staircase on the way down. He barged out through the doorway, almost tripped on something lying on the wet pavement and kicked it for three yards before he realised it was his coat. Without thinking, he snatched it up and ran through the rain across River Street and up Yard Vennel as the lightning flickered and the thunder rolled up the firth towards Levenford.

2

Down on Clydeshore Avenue, close to the shingle bank of the wide firth estuary, the thunderclap exploded overhead just as a jagged fork of lightning stabbed down from the black cloud, a sizzling stutter of energy which tore the air apart and speared the fork of a massive beech tree. The westward half of the tree simply peeled away from the main trunk and fell forty feet, flames licking up its entire length, to the ground below where the drenching rain instantly doused the fire.

The girl woke, wide-eyed, mouth agape, a cry trying to blurt from a fright-locked throat.

The lightning flickered outside, sending stroboscopic patterns through the chink in the curtain and on its heels, the thunder growled like a beast in the night.

Her hands were shaking, held up rigid and hooked in front of her face. Her eyes were wide and staring in the dark, blind to the flashes of light, seeing only the images of the dreadful dream unreel in her mind. Trickles of sweat ran cool fingers down between her shoulder blades and her heart was beating so fast, so hard, it felt as if it would punch through her ribs.

The dream was still running, rerunning, playing the scenes back for her, and the eyes, poisonous yellow-orange in the dark, stared through her, drilled into her very *self*.

Finally her lungs unclenched and the girl let out a moan of fear and anguish.

It had been a nightmare, a terrible dream. Someplace dark, where the very air felt as if it had been compressed by weight and heat. A featureless plain of blackness, seen from above. She had been floating over the desolation, knowing without seeing that this was no desert, that million upon million twisted and wizened and tormented things writhed far below, crowded so close together that they formed the surface. She could sense their suffering and their hate as she sped on, drawn forwards to the only feature, unseen in the distance, but sensed, somehow, the way it is in dreams, a looming foreboding, the certain prescience of the mindscape.

She finally approached a pinnacle of rock soaring up from the flat, a jagged tooth of stone, riven with crevices and saw-toothed ridges, black as night. On the almost vertical sides, she sensed more of the creatures, climbing ever upwards, falling back to oblivion among the masses, heard in her mind, their screams and shrieks of frustration and despair.

She rose up the face of the rock spire until she came level with the spiked top, and then she saw the shadow.

Blacker than black, deeper than night, it hunched, still as stone. It defied vision. There were no outlines to the thing which sat on the high vantage, yet her dream senses could perceive its malevolence. She tried to back away, but it drew her in towards it, an amorphous writhing shade within shadow. In the dream, she shook her head, denying its existence, tried to tell herself that this was a dream, but still its foul magnetism drew her on until she could almost have touched the slime-coated rock.

It turned, though she saw no movement, only felt it. Two eyes opened, enormous and sickly yellow, completely round and featureless. A baleful light speared her, reached into her and touched her very self. She tried to cry, to twist away from the touch of corruption and disease, but it held her.

Then the sound of thunder rolled over the plain. A green light flickered in the far horizon and the eyes closed.

'*Now, little one,*' a voice like scraping rock whispered inside her, '*we are together.*'

The shadow moved, a sensation of oily limbs, jagged joints, a spider-like, yet slithery motion, and the dark rose upwards from the rock towards a red-purple sky, changing to a sphere, fuzzing to a cloud. She was caught in the wake, dragged along in the turbulence. A crack appeared in the sky as she was blown through. . .

And she was in a strange room.

She was high, close to the ceiling, looking down on them as they sat around the table. The stone was moving, whirling faster and faster, jerking from one oddly slanted letter to the next. It happened in a flick-flick stop-motion sequence, out of synch. A man stood up, moved to the door. She saw, rather than felt, the

31

black cold wind whirl around the room, rattling the paintings on the walls, the quaint glassware in the cabinet. Two women getting to their feet, backing away. The old woman, bowed over the back of the seat.

All the time she felt the black presence of the thing that had dragged her from the hellscape through the crack in the sky. It was in the wind that shivered them all, it was in the stone. She saw it, a fuzzed and writhing cloud of darkness, narrowing down to a spinning cone and forcing its way into the old woman. She heard the grating tones as it spoke through her, sensed the sudden burgeon of fear in the women.

On the table the stone blurred in its spin then flew off to shatter against the fireplace and she heard the guttural laugh as the shards fountained outwards.

Run! Get away!

She tried to call out to them, but she could make no sound. She was locked in the dream, powerless to escape. The door opened, the men spilled out, the women at their heels. One man sat still, unable to move.

The old woman rose up from the chair, limbs twitching. The girl could see the black aura of the thing within and without her, heard its glut as it absorbed the fear and horror. Then the woman fell. The man now moving, strobe-effect jerks as the chair toppled. The terrible sound of broken bone and crushed flesh, and then, above it all, the shriek of mad laughter.

She tried to pull away again, but the numb lethargy still held her. On the ground, far below, the woman's dead eye flicked open and glared at her from a mess of damaged flesh. The lips moved, just a twitch at first, as if the nerves were finding new pathways to travel.

'Now it begins,' the grating voice said, so softly it was more menacing than the laughter. *'Wait and watch with me.'*

And she awoke sitting up in her own bed, shivering in the aftermath.

3

Jack Fallon stood with his back to the window, hands deep in the pockets of his coat. Ronnie Jeffrey was down on his knees in front of the fireplace, taking close-up pictures of what lay on the floor, half on the carpet and half on the stone hearth. The camera flashed twice in quick succession. When Ronnie turned, Jack could only see his eyes. The rest of his face was covered with a handkerchief knotted behind his neck, worn like a bank robber in an old Western movie.

'Right, Ronnie,' Jack said. 'That should do it.'

'About time too,' Ronnie said, his voice only slightly muffled by the mask. 'What a stink. She must have been here for days.'

'Maybe. Where's Ralph? I want him to start the prints. And watch your feet on that glass.'

'I'll ask him in.' Ronnie heaved himself to his feet and backed away carefully, unable to avoid the smaller shards on the floor under his heavy shoes. They crunched with a sound that grated in Jack's ears and tingled the nerves between his shoulder blades. The photographer got to the door and pulled the handkerchief down.

'Still stinks, even from here. Like a barbecue in a cemetery.'

'Could have been worse. Might have been summer,' Jack countered. He hadn't moved position since he'd taken up station at the window. His frame blocked off some of the light coming through the dusty pane, but not much. Outside it was cold and overcast. Implacable winter weather. If it *had* been summer, the stench in the room would have been overwhelming, stomach-clenching. The place would have been buzzing with bluebottles and the body would have been squirming with maggots wriggling under the skin.

'Thank God for small mercies,' Ronnie grunted as he left the room.

Jack stood for a while longer, eyes drifting almost lazily around the room, trying to shake off an oppressive feeling of threat that had been sparked off by the grating sound.

The place was a shambles. Three of the chairs which would have sat around the circular table were overturned, lying on their sides. A fourth was upside down on a low settee on the far side by the door. It looked as if it had been flung violently. The table itself, set solid in the centre of the room under a drop light, was deeply scored in grooves, freshly made, by the look of the places where the blood hadn't flowed. It was blood, Jack Fallon knew from long experience – too long, he sometimes thought – though it had blackened and caked in the runnels. He'd have known the smell anywhere, just as he knew the smell of burned flesh and decaying corpses. All three were here, present and correct, each clamouring for his attention and getting it. He felt the muscles of his throat twitch and he gulped back the reflex. He hadn't had breakfast, and that was definitely a bonus.

The old woman hadn't been covered up yet. An ambulance crew were waiting downstairs, and they'd have to wait a little longer. She wasn't going anywhere. Hadn't been going anywhere for a couple of days, maybe a week, Jack estimated, though Robbie Cattanach's pathology lab would give him a better guess, no doubt. He looked down at her. The sleeve and half the bodice of her black dress were burned away, along with her arm, which was stretched out right into the cold embers of the fire. They hadn't been cold, though. What stretched out from the woman's body was a twisted skeletal claw on a black, stick-like extension. The flesh had shrivelled and melted, causing the arm to warp. At the crook of the elbow, the tendons and muscles had bunched and torqued in the heat. On the floor just beneath, a two-foot wide greasy splatter had hardened on the floor. Jack knew it was the woman's body fats. They'd have sizzled out and dripped, like roast on a spit.

The fire hadn't gone far, maybe because there was little to burn on the woman. It hadn't made the leap over the kerb, or the whole place would have gone up. The room was a fire hazard. Old dry books lined the shelves on the wall, or at least some of them did. Most of them were scattered around the floor. Some were ripped apart, and a few single torn pages were strewn about the floor just at Jack's feet. On a shelf, a box filled with newspaper clippings. Lace curtains on the window, and dried flowers in vases. They had probably stood on every horizontal surface, but now they too were strewn about like weeds in a cut hayfield. It would have gone up like a torch.

He shifted his stance, allowing the weak light to filter through the net curtain onto the woman's face. Only half of it was intact. The side nearest the fire was wasted, burned almost away. The flesh was gone, exposing the animal-like clench of the jaw right up to behind the ear. The eye had shrunk, probably burst first, then dissolved into the dark socket. The other side of the face was still human, though the shrivelling of skin and muscle on the burned side had pulled everything out of shape, drawing that side into a strange plastic grimace. The skin on the unburned side was blackened with bruising. Blood streaks had hardened into thick scabs. The mouth, the half that was left, was wide open.

Almost on the terminator line, where the burned and puckered skin stopped and the untouched part remained, a piece of glass was wedged into the centre of the forehead. It glinted weakly like an eye, giving the corpse a look that was oddly alive. Above that, slender shards stuck up from the wasted scalp like shiny bristles. Slivers were strewn around the body, twinkling on the hearth around the blackened, contorted arm. Fragments of the flower vases were scattered like sharp confetti all over the floor. Down one side of the room, two lengths of the thick, old-fashioned wallpaper had been stripped from ceiling to floor and lay tangled and crumpled. Down the pillar-like lines, three yards apart, were two words, daubed vertically on the plain plaster in bold, dark capitals. That more than anything else raised a question mark in Jack Fallon's mind. It took his mind off everything else.

'She's been thrown all over the place. Hit with everything,' he said aloud into the dull room.

'What's that?'

Ralph Slater came in from the hallway. There was a streak of powder on his cheek. He was wearing thin rubber gloves which made his hands look artificial. All his gear was in the battered leather case.

'Nothing, Ralph. Just thinking.'

'Smell would stop a clock. Want a mint?'

Jack shook his head. He needed a coffee, strong and black, with three sugars. In the palpable air of the claustrophobic, ransacked room, even the thought of coffee was nauseating. He really needed a drink, but he'd been needing a drink for a while.

'No. Might as well get on. You know your bit. Ronnie's taken his snaps. I'll need everything from here.'

Ralph nodded. He put his case down on the old brocade settee, after making sure there was nothing there worth checking. There were enough smooth surfaces in the room to make the fabric of the upholstery hardly worth dusting.

'What about that then? Looks like a gang slogan,' Ralph said, nodding at the scrawled words.

'Not any gang from around here.'

Heteros. There was an odd slant to the letters on the bare space above the fireplace.

Etheros. The same twist to the right on the wall where the neighbouring piece of paper had been stripped.

The words, if they *were* words, started at the ceiling, at twice the height of a man. Whoever had written them must have used something to get up there, and then removed whatever he'd used. He must also have been confident that nobody would disturb him. Did that mean she'd known her attacker? That would make it easier, Jack thought.

Still it was too early to say. He'd got the call an hour before and had arrived ten minutes after that. A young policeman, just out of cadet school, had been standing at the outside door, one foot in a dirty puddle. When Jack had approached him, the youngster had turned and retched violently, obviously not for the first time. Jack dug into his pocket and gave him a fresh tissue. The constable had wiped his mouth vigorously before straightening up. His eyes were red-rimmed.

'They told me to wait here for you, sir. It's the third floor. Neighbours were complaining about the smell. Doors weren't locked.'

'Touch anything?'

The young man – he looked no more than a boy – gave Jack a look which declared he would have just as soon cut off his hand. He gave another shiver and tried to gag again, shaking his head all the time.

'There's a car on its way,' Jack told him. 'When it gets here, get back up to division and have a cup of tea. Then when you're feeling a bit fresher, write down everything you saw.'

The constable nodded, still wiping at his lips. Jack bypassed him. At the second level, he realised what the neighbours had been complaining about. Once inside, he wondered why they hadn't noticed sooner.

Ralph's two assistants came in and were going over the place, starting at the door and working their way in. They didn't seem badly affected by the smell. They were used to working with the dead. Jack could have done without it.

Oh, he could have done without it, nothing was surer.

He turned away and pulled the curtain to the side. The window faced north, across the main street up to the Barwoods behind the town. The clouds were dark and heavy, getting set to drop two days of clammy misery. After that, the weathermen said it was going to be cold. It was already cold out there. Down in the street, he could see the winking lights of the ambulance and the police cars, bright electric-blue flashes against the background of grey. People were walking past, heads down against the cold west wind.

Working with the dead.

Somebody had to do it. There was always somebody who *would* do it. Jack Fallon did not know if he was man enough for it any more. He wasn't sure he was man enough for anything any more. On the window, the smirr of rain had thickened to droplets which ran in jagged streaks, fuzzing out the grey outside, breaking up the winking blue lights. His mind started going back to another dismal day when he'd seen the same electric flicker through the rain on the windscreen of the unmarked car, and something had flickered through his mind, not like a light, but a darkness. It had come blaring in like a radio message with no source, over and above the hubbub of sirens and lights and real radio crackle, and a sudden surge of dread had made his stomach drop like a weight. That had been . . . that had . . . .

He turned himself away from the window before the vision came back to him, otherwise he would not be able to function. He shook it away with an almost savage twist of his body, gritting his teeth so hard he could feel them grind like stones. The memory tried to edge in, and he knew it would come back in force later on, when the work was done, when his mind wasn't focused, and then it would take him on the black dance again. But now, he had to think clearly.

Ralph's scene of crime team worked quickly and efficiently, dabbing here, collecting pieces there. The small tools of their trade were cutting and picking and probing around the room, watched by the dispassionate, drily blind eye of the dead woman, and the winking cyclopean shard set in the middle of her forehead.

'Any of you know her?'

'Name's Herkik. Polish or something,' Ralph mumbled back. His tongue was poking out between his teeth as he scraped a sample of the blood on the table, working with delicate deliberation.

'Hungarian,' Jack corrected. 'No, I mean, does anybody know anything else about her?'

Ralph shook his head. The two others made no reply.

'Right. We'll get it door to door. How long will this take you?'

'Another half an hour. Dr Cuthbert's made a prelim. The drivers can take her away when you're done.'

Jack crossed the room, careful not to stand on anything, which was difficult enough in the tight confines of the demolished room. He got to the door.

'Finished here?'

Ralph nodded, letting him know that he could touch the door. Jack closed it behind him and made his way downstairs, ignoring the old woman who peeked out, nose almost caught in the burglar chain.

In the street, the air was clean, but the drizzle made it a dirty morning.

John McColl was standing at the back of the nearest police car, using his big hands for emphasis as he spoke to two younger men in long raincoats and another three uniformed policemen. Jack reached him just as the others turned away.

'Bit of a mess,' the big sergeant said matter-of-factly. 'Got an idea or two from the neighbours, nothing much. They've had their heads up their arses this past week.'

John was a couple of inches taller than Jack Fallon's six foot, and another few inches wider. His hair had gone prematurely grey. He looked the senior officer of the two, but Jack outranked him by two levels.

'You're telling me.' Jack took a deep breath of air. He could feel the winter on the west wind.

He ran through the procedure. John McColl told him what the door-to-door team were doing, and what they'd got so far. He flipped open his notebook, turned against the rain and used a broad forefinger to point out the words as he spoke.

'Marta Herkik. Hungarian. Came to live with her brother. He's been dead about six years. Bit of a faith healer, the old lady, into spiritualism, that sort of thing. Fortune-telling and the like. Should have been able to see this coming if she'd been any good, eh?'

Jack nodded him on. John was a straight-talking, irreverent policeman who had little respect for authority unless it was earned. His father ran the family's three pubs in Glasgow, and John could have had an easy life if he'd chosen. The family wealth perhaps allowed him to forego the obsequiousness often demanded by superiors, but he liked Jack Fallon, and they had a mutual, easy-going respect.

'Neighbour below has been on night shift at the rig yard. Hasn't heard a thing. The one next door said there was a bit of a rumble on Saturday last week. Nothing much. She thought the old dear was shifting furniture. The walls here are two feet thick and the floors nearly the same. Built to last, this old place. Not much noise drift.' McColl closed the book.

'Any idea what killed her?'

'Just about everything in the place.'

'There was a case like that up in Creggan a few years back. Bastard got off on impeachment. Blamed somebody else and the jury was pulled both ways,' Jack mused. 'Right, we'll wait for the street teams. No point in jumping in. When Ralph's finished, let the ambulance crew go up. I'll be back at the office.'

'Taking the car?'

'No. I'll stroll it. Want to think for a bit.'

Jack shrugged his collar up higher against the rain. A hank of black hair had fallen down over his forehead and was trickling water onto his brow. He wiped it away with his hand and turned along River Street, took a left turn at Market Vennel, easing his way through the throng of umbrellas which stabbed at his eyes in the narrow lane, and out to College Street towards the station.

The sense of unease he'd felt in the house where the dead woman sprawled on the hearth stayed with him all the way.

4

The baby was crying in its pram. He'd been asleep most of the afternoon, waking only twice when the teething pains had stabbed hard in his gums, but he'd quickly fallen asleep again, wrapped up tight against the chill. Little Timmy Doyle had been running a temperature, and his mother had decided some fresh air would do him the world of good.

Cissie Doyle was in the kitchen preparing dinner for her husband, who would be home from the foundry in an hour. She heard the high-pitched cry as she stood peeling potatoes at the sink. The window faced west, and she got a glimpse of the sunset, a low-streaked sky of red and gold just beyond the Cardross Hills at Arden. The rain-clouds had cleared away earlier in the afternoon and now the darkening sky was clear as far as the eye could see. Cissie cocked her ear, listening again. The little cry had hiccupped to silence. She thought Timmy must have gone back to sleep again.

The Doyle household was ten storeys up, fourth from the top in a block of flats which had replaced some of the huddled tenements on the west side of the river, across from the yard. This part of town was still known as Wee Donegal, from the number of immigrant Irish who had made it an enclave before the turn of the century. The space between the old bridge and the rail crossing hadn't been enough to contain them all. The council had thrown up two cheaply built blocks to replace half the old slum, and to make sure the Irish stayed on their side of the river. They didn't know, or cared less, that a century on, the only difference between the old brownstone tenements with their single-ends and narrow stairways and the tower blocks was simply a question of age. There were people, but there was no *life* in Latta Court. All Cissie Doyle had, apart from an inside toilet and a single bedroom, was perhaps the most spectacular view in the town. She could see as far as the belt of crags up at Langmuir to the north-east, and right down the Clyde towards the Gantocks in the west. At that height, nobody needed a weather forecast. You could see the squalls coming up the river firth two hours before they hit. To the north, the Dumbuie Hills, close to Linnvale on the banks of Loch Corran, could be seen on a clear day, and much of the Loch itself, ten miles away, impressive and peaceful, the kind of thing they wrote songs about, the kind of scene people came the world over to see. On some days, the view was little comfort, especially when the lift broke down. Sean worked an extra two nights, Saturday and Sunday, to put enough by for a deposit on something closer to ground level. Something with a garden where wee Timmy would have the space to run and play in a couple of years' time.

She bent to peeling potatoes, lost in thoughts about a place with a garden, snowdrops in the spring, marigolds in summer.

The balcony where the baby slept was a hundred feet from the concrete at the base of Latta Court, and another forty from the flat roof where a single red light winked to warn low-flying aircraft of a high hazard. Up there, old Kevin O'Malley kept a pigeon loft which was the nub of a fierce wrangle with the housing authority. It was angled in against the lift-shaft housing and the ventilators, on top of which the communal television aerial reached skywards, Latta Court's lifeline to the outside world.

Timmy, six months and one week old, came awake some time later, the sky now darkening above to a deep cobalt where the three stars of Orion's belt were just winking into existence. What woke him was a heavy knock on the side of the pram.

The baby made a small noise, almost a sound of surprise.

Something banged against the pram again, making it rock on its springs. There was a low scraping sound and something moved, just against the railings. Way down in the engine-yard below, a cutting tool, amplified by the hollow metal structure of the boat-company works, sent a shriek of tortured metal up into the air.

The baby gave a start and his mouth turned down, the beginning of a wail getting ready to wind itself up and let loose.

Then a shadow flickered on the wall opposite the balcony rail. The shape was almost jet black against the light concrete. The motion caught the baby's attention enough to divert the wail.

Little Timmy turned his head, as much as the tight wrapping of blankets would allow. The movement stopped, disappeared. There was another scraping sound, this time from the other side. The little head swivelled. A dark shadow danced on the wall. The baby could only see the flickering shape. The movement bobbed and swayed, shortening and lengthening, weaving almost hypnotically. Little Timmy's eyes followed the movement. The shadow flicked to the side and was gone so suddenly that the baby's head swung back in puzzlement.

Then something dark loomed over the pram, blotting out the light. He heard a whispering rasp, words that in his baby mind made no sense, but made him shiver.

The baby felt something prod at him and he mewled in alarm. The shadow moved back, letting the faint light in again, then it came swooping down. Little Timmy's eyes opened wide in sudden fright. One of his tiny hands came free of the coverlet, wide open and shaking in the way that babies' hands do when they're crying sore. Timmy did not start to cry just then.

Something dark came looming from behind the hood and the pram was hit such a blow that it tipped over to lean against the wall. Inside, Timmy was rocked violently from side to side. He hitched in a breath and let out a squeal.

In the kitchen, Cissie Doyle used the back of her hand to wipe her brow and move a stray slick of brown hair which had fallen over her eyes. All four rings of her electric cooker were going at once. The potatoes were in the big pot at the front, while beside it, another pot, almost as large, was steaming away. Every few seconds, the lid would rise up, let out a puff of steam and the homely tang of minced beef, before plopping down again on the rim.

She'd been humming the chorus to a tune about a boxer playing on the radio in the corner, competing with the bubbling and popping from the stove, when Timmy had started to cry. She'd heard him give a little squeal just about the time the noise had blared up from the foundry, although the tinny metallic howl was the kind of sound she hardly noticed after three years in Latta Court. He'd whimpered a bit and gone quiet, then he'd let out a full-bodied scream.

'Good timing, Tim,' she gritted in annoyance. The dinner was almost ready.

Timmy screeched again.

'All right. I'm coming,' Cissie said. She turned to the far side of the kitchen and flicked open the wall cupboard and hooked out the ice-cream tub where the family kept the medicines. Timmy's teething gel was at the top, a flattened tube with hardly enough left in it to make a smear on his gums. Below that, three baby disprin rattled in their bubble packs. She popped one out into Timmy's bottle and poured some water from the kettle to help it dissolve more quickly, then added some cold water before forcing the teat over the neck.

Timmy's squeals got louder and more urgent from the far side of the other room.

'Oh, hang on a minute. I'm coming,' Cissie called out. *Poor wee soul*, she thought. She lifted the bottle to her mouth and sucked. The mixture was just warm enough, not too hot, mildly bitter. Just then the mince-pot lid lifted quickly and a stream of bubbles frothed over the side to hiss on the hot ring.

'Oh no,' Cissie snorted. She put the bottle down and lifted the pot from the heat. The lid settled down immediately. Beyond the kitchen door, Timmy screeched again, and the sound of it made Cissie freeze.

There was something in the sound that she had never heard before. It wasn't a cry of pain, not just teething pain. It was high and clear and wavering and it jarred on everything that made Cissie Doyle a mother. She was just in the act of lifting the lid on the pot, preparing to see the minced beef burned to the bottom, when the scream of her baby had scraped on the inside of her skull and snatched at the nerves in her spine. Then it stopped so abruptly that the echo of it rang in her ears. She dropped the pot with a clatter back onto the ring, spun round and yanked the kitchen door open.

Already a big bubble of dread was inflating itself inside her. She crossed the living room in five jittery-fast strides and almost fell through the half-open door that led out onto the balcony.

It was then that the bubble burst inside her, flooding her with cold shock.

Timmy's pram was angled over on two wheels, leaning against the rail surround. Its position prevented her from seeing inside. She snatched it back upright and bent over.

Her baby was gone.

Cissie stood there, holding onto the edge of the pram, unaware that her fingers were gripped so tight they had punctured the inside plastic fabric in two places. Her mind was shrieking at her in jumbled, yammering voices.

He's under the covers. He's rolled out. He's fallen underneath.

She scrabbled with the covers, heaving them right out. They were still warm with baby-heat. The pram was empty. Without thinking, she dropped to the concrete floor and hunted between the wheels, hoping against hope, hoping against dread, that he'd slipped out of the pram and rolled underneath.

And a little cold part of her brain was telling her: *He was strapped in. He* couldn't *have got out.* That same part of her mind was feeding the cold logic that a six-month-old baby could *not* have toppled his own pram.

He'd been buckled in. She knew that for sure. She *never* let him lie in the pram unless the harness was secured. Cissie hauled herself to her feet and pulled the carriage away from the rail. As she did so, the leather strap from the far side flipped out from the bottom and dangled beside her. The snap-hook was still caught around the eye on the side. But six inches from the catch, the leather was twisted and frayed. And the rest of the harness was gone.

Cissie's legs began to buckle under her as a ghastly thought struck her.

He's fallen over oh my god he's dropped.

She managed to get both hands on the top bar of the surround and leaned over

The world swooped away from her. The sheer sides of the tower block angled together in a dizzying parallax, making it look as if she was peering from the edge of an inverted cone. Down there, a couple of cars sat in the off-street park. Another was coming round the corner, headlamps swinging in an arc across the front of the neighbouring block like spotlights, coming to rest on the paved area a hundred feet below. Cissie's vision swam as vertigo drained the blood from her face. Hot bile rolled up from her belly as her frantic eyes scanned the ground in the light of the headlamps.

There was nothing. No scrap lying squashed to the concrete.

No smear on the slabs. The lights went out, dimming the parking area. A door opened, slammed closed, faint in the distance. Somebody got out of the car and came walking towards the door, right past where *anything* falling from Cissie Doyle's balcony must have landed.

The woman tried to cry out, tried to scream, but it was as if she was in a nightmare. Her mouth opened and closed as she willed herself to call out to the passer-by, to tell him her baby was down there, but her throat closed over. All she could manage was a clicking sound behind her palate. The door below opened and a brief light poured out then was shut off again.

Cissie shoved herself back from the railing, mouth still working and now emitting a strangled rasping sound which was more like an animal in distress than human speech. She turned to go back through the door, knees almost unable to take the weight. A slight scraping sound came from somewhere above her. Still moving, almost dreamlike, towards the balcony doors, Cissie's face tilted upwards instinctively. A shadow high overhead flickered against the wall and was gone. Cissie almost fell into the living room, and stumbled over a small footstool which Sean had bought for her after little Timmy had been born. She fell heavily, landing headlong on the thin carpet, then crawled and hauled herself to her feet. She made it down the narrow hallway, the animal rasping now a panicked, stuttering sob, threw herself out of the door and right across the landing where she battered desperately with the heels of her hands on the opposite door.

Nelly Maguire heard the thumping and the sound of a woman crying and hesitated a few moments before approaching her own door. She peered through the spyhole and saw Cissie Doyle's face distorted in the tiny lens, bloated and fishlike, her mouth opening and closing to complete the image. The door was shivering on its hinges. Nelly had three mortice locks and a burglar chain. It seemed to take forever to get them all opened. Finally she pulled the door back and Cissie Doyle fell in.

'Whatever's the matter?' Nelly started to say, before she was knocked backwards by the other woman's rush.

Cissie was now screaming hysterically. It took five minutes before Nelly could make out what her neighbour was talking about, although by this time, Cissie Doyle was shaking so

45

violently that she was almost incoherent. Her face was dead pale and her eyes were staring so hard the old woman next door thought they might pop out of their sockets and dangle on Cissie's cheeks.

Over and over again, the raving young woman kept repeating the same words: *My baby. My baby's gone.*

Jack Fallon got the call just after eight o'clock, half an hour after he'd arrived home. He'd put two slices of bread in the toaster and slung the contents of a tin of spaghetti into a saucepan. It wasn't much of a meal after nearly fourteen long hours going over statements, interviewing witnesses, and getting a blow-by-blow account from Robbie Cattanach, who had carried out the post mortem. He could have devoured a steak. He hadn't cooked one in months. Rae had had a way of doing a steak. She'd cut a pocket in the side of a slab of sirloin, making a beef purse which she'd stuff with blue cheese. Under the grill the juice would seep out and drip onto the mushrooms and tomatoes below the mesh. The thought of it made Jack's mouth water. The memory of the taste came back with such intensity he could feel the little creeping ache under his tongue. And hard on its heels came the other memory. Rae turning from the oven with the meat still sizzling, bearing the meal like an offering to a chief. Little Julie doing her Bisto-kid act, snuffling the aroma as she sat on the tall stool with her elbows on the breakfast bar. The scene came swooping back and hit him like a slap from an angry woman, almost rocking him to the side.

He recoiled from it, shunted it away. The toaster jangled in the corner and the two slices popped up, just overdone. Jack shook his head, again denying the memory. He took a plate down from the wall cupboard and placed the two pieces side by side, then poured the red mess from the saucepan over them. Some of the sauce dripped onto the table. It sparked another image in Jack's mind. There had been a trail like that on the slate hearth of Marta Herkik's fireplace, though that had been dark, almost black. There had been other trails like that, too many to think about, scrawled signatures of death.

He sat down and willed himself to eat, dodging memories on all sides. The tinned spaghetti went down easily enough, but it was hardly a man's dinner. He promised himself he'd get to the shops soon, get some real food instead of this stuff out of tins, to be snatched whenever time allowed, eaten in solitude. It was either that or simply move in with his sister and nephew who were the only family he had left.

He finished quickly, scraping the hot sauce from the plate with the spare crusts, then slung the plate in the sink, along with the coffee cup from the morning, which now seemed a lifetime away. He shook his head again, this time more ruefully. He should get himself together, as they said in the American films. He needed a dishwasher too. He shrugged his shoulders, and bent to the sink, running barely warm water over plate and cup, knife and fork. He dried them all and slung them back in the cupboard. The kitchen was small, and fairly neat, just enough for a single man. To Jack it was vast and empty, like a lot of his life. All that kept his mind focused was his work, and the occasional day out with Davy, which took his mind *off* his work.

Davy was five. He'd just started school in the autumn, and since Julia's husband had left, Jack had been cast into the role of permanent uncle. He took Davy to school in the mornings, and the two of them strolled up the Langmuir Hills together on good days. If anything had kept Jack sane, pulled him back from the brink, away from the neck of the bottle, it had been the irrepressible five-year-old boy.

Only last week, after the storm had tired itself out, he'd had the boy on his shoulders, down on the common ground close to the water meadow, where teams of volunteers had collected driftwood and old logs to build an immense bonfire to celebrate the eight-hundredth anniversary of the granting of the burgh charter. It had been a cold, crisp night, with the bite of hard frost in the air. The flames had roared forty feet high and the firework display had been impressive. They'd had sausages on sticks, baked potatoes from the ash-pits, and Jack had swallowed a fair mouthful of a good malt whisky from a flask miraculously produced by John McColl. Julia had taken the opportunity of having the house to herself, and on that night, tired and smelling of wood smoke, Jack had taken Davy back to his own place and let him snuggle up beside him. It was the first time he'd woken beside anyone else in a long time. The feeling of his nephew's small warmth beside him brought back sudden memories that he'd had to fight back. Now, in retrospect, he realised that it had been good for him. The wounds were still raw, still seeping, but the healing process might begin.

He went back through to the living room and moved the bundle of newspapers from his seat, then flicked on the television. A current affairs programme was rapid-firing news of unrest in a dozen different parts of the world, a ten-second-at-a-time catalogue. Jack used the remote to kill it all and reached behind him for his old guitar, a black and battered Fender. He ran his fingers up the strings, feeling the frets burr with the sound of a distant train, and automatically tightened the top string, which was always working slack. He slipped in the jack plug and reached a hand to jab the switch on the black amp. He heard the buzz of the base tone and turned the fuzz up just a little then strummed a chord. He'd played the old guitar since before he'd started shaving. Even now he could dredge up the old dream of playing like Hendrix, even playing like the Quo. There were times when the old guitar was the only thing that held him together, an anchor to the dreamy days of childhood. He hit a major and swooped it up the frets, fingers automatically tickling the strings in a rock-boogie, running into an absent twelve bars before dropping it down to fingerpick an old familiar tune about a boxer while his thoughts drifted on by themselves.

The telephone jangled shrill against the rolling notes, jerking Jack's mind back to the present. He turned the amp off and heard the bass note fade to nothing.

'Need you back in again, Jack.' The gruff voice broke in as soon as he'd announced the number. 'We've got an abduction by the looks. Or a murder.'

'That's all we need,' Jack said. 'Where is it?' He sighed and pulled the notebook from the other end of the table, using his teeth to take the cap from the ballpoint lying beside it.

'Alright, son, I know you've had a couple of days of it, but we need a look at this one right away. You'll want to take first shot.'

Chief Superintendent Angus NcNicol had said the same thing when the call had come in on the killing of Marta Herkik. Jack reluctantly took the compliment. He could have used eight hours straight tonight. His boss gave him an address, spoke for a minute more, then hung up. Jack let the telephone drop to the cradle and sat for a moment. Just as well, he told himself, that he'd left the vodka bottle unopened. Another half hour and he might not have been able to drive. Might not have been able to *walk*.

Five minutes later he was heading down the steep hill from Cargill Farm. The old farm building had long since gone, but the cottage was still there, the place he'd been born and raised in, and the place to which he'd eventually returned to lick his wounds when the whole world caved in. As much home as anywhere in the world.

On the way down the road, the car jouncing and jostling on the hard-rut, he thought about what Angus had said and about the events of the day.

The Herkik investigation was well under way. In a town the size of Levenford, you could expect a murder inquiry to be zipped up tight within twenty-four hours. There were domestics, drunken arguments and the odd stabbing. Most of them well witnessed and easily documented. Marta Herkik's killing was different.

Nobody knew a thing. Nobody had been seen leaving the building, nobody seen entering. All they had was a room that looked as if a tornado had blasted through it and a dead woman, half burned, beaten so badly she was unrecognisable.

Robbie Cattanach, the pathologist, had brought his report in almost a full day after Marta Herkik's body had been discovered. He'd come sauntering into Jack's office, wearing a distressed leather jerkin and scuffed jeans, looking exactly like the kind of youngster the beat men were locking up in numbers on Friday and Saturday nights. His casual appearance was a sharp contrast to the quick mind Jack knew ticked away behind the lazy brown eyes.

'Good news or bad news first?' he'd asked.

'She died of natural causes and we can wrap this up and walk away.'

'Nice try. No luck.'

Robbie was one of the few people Jack had much time for. He travelled, hail, rain or shine, on a big black Harley that Jack openly admired, and the two of them shared a regular pint, whenever Jack was in the mood for company, in the Waverley on the far side of the old bridge.

49

'It's a murder all right.'

'There's a surprise. So what killed her?'

'You name it. It's a bit like that old case in Creggan. John told me you'd mentioned it. I looked up the report. She's been hit by everything.'

He ran his eyes down the list.

'Skull fractured in two places. Lesions on scalp and forehead caused by impact of crystalline structure, common quartz, as a matter of fact. Seems to have been smashed first and *then* driven into her. There was a lot of force behind it. I'm not sure exactly how it was done.'

Robbie scanned the page again. 'Severe burns to left arm and left of face with carbonisation of muscle and bone. Two fractures of left femur, one on right, and a severe twist fracture of the pelvis. Jaw broken, right mandible driven into the base of the skull at the joint. Severe bruising to neck and upper torso. Black and blue all over, some of them skin ruptures.'

'So she's been beaten up. That's exactly what it looks like.'

'Oh yes. Beaten, hammered, burned. The lot,' Robbie said. 'But there's more. The inside story is just as revealing.'

Jack raised an eyebrow and the young doctor went on. 'Usual internal damage. Soft tissue stuff. Lesions on liver and spleen. Ruptured kidney. The right one was almost pushed through the muscle wall. That's the kind of thing you'd expect in a bad road smash, but here's the interesting thing.'

He turned the page and hesitated, scratching just above his eyebrow. 'I'll cut all the clinical stuff for the moment.'

'Let's be thankful for small mercies.'

'Well. The internal tends to be the qualification of the external. What we found was severe rupturing of throat, pharynx and trachea. Her windpipe was torn to shreds.'

'Caused by the strangulation?'

'No. You'd expect it to be crushed, sometimes it will flatten, but it's ribbed, like a vacuum hose, and it doesn't spring back. Hers was torn *apart*. Like from the inside. It looked as if something was rammed down her throat and pulled out again, very fast. But the lungs were just the same, and the oesophagus and the stomach wall.'

'What the hell would do that?'

'That's the bad news. It looks as if she was turned inside out. I've spoken to Walker up at the Western. He wants a copy of all of this. Nearly wet himself when I described it.'

'But what killed her?'

'Any one of these things. The blows to the head. The internal damage. Shock. All of it, except the burning. She was dead before that happened.'

'More thanks for small mercies, I suppose.'

'Oh, and there's one more thing. Her heart. We found that in the remains of the stomach.'

Jack thought back to the post mortem examinations he'd witnessed.

'Shouldn't be there, should it?'

'Up behind the ribs is where it *should* be. It sits in a sling of muscle and ligament, like a very strong harness. This old lady's heart had been wrenched out of its housing. Every artery and vein, and I mean the big ones, had been torn out.'

'Now what could do that?'

'Only one thing I've ever seen.'

Jack raised his black eyebrows again. He was trying to picture it and failing.

'You ever see the old Ridley Scott film about an alien?' Robbie asked.

'The one with that good-looking girl in it? Sigourney Weaver?'

'The very same. There's a scene in it where something bursts out of one of the crew. Comes out of the belly. Scared the living hell out of me when I first saw it.'

'Aw, come on, Robbie. You telling me this was an *alien*?'

'Don't be daft. That'll get me a holiday with the crazies in Dalmoak. No. What I'm saying, going only by the damage inside the old biddy, is it looks as if something was dragged out of her. I mean right from inside and out through her throat.'

Robbie gave him a grin.

'And thank the living God that it's not my job to find out who did that, or how or why. I just report what I find.'

'Thanks for that. Thanks a million,' Jack told him.

'Fancy a pint?' Robbie asked, still grinning.

'You must have the constitution of a horse. How the hell can you spend your day up to your arms in folk's insides and still drink beer?'

Robbie shrugged. 'Talent, I suppose.'

'I'd love to,' Jack said. 'But I'm up to the eyes. Even deeper, thanks to you. Oh, and before I search through all this, any idea of when it happened?'

'Friday to Saturday, maybe even the early hours of Sunday morning. Can't give you any closer than that.'

Jack nodded. 'That figures. She was seen on Saturday morning. Then there were noises in the flat later that night. On Sunday, nothing at all. That helps narrow it. We're talking about Saturday night.'

Robbie had left the report with Jack, who had spent half an hour reading through the catalogue of one old woman's destruction. When he'd first joined the police, too many years ago for him to want to count, the Creggan case had been fresh in folk's minds. There, an elderly and wealthy woman had been raped and then murdered. The killer had taken off all of his clothes, which was why there was not a speck of blood on him when he'd been arrested, ten hours later. Most of the woman's blood had been spattered on the walls and ceilings. She'd been hit with almost every movable object in the room. The killer had made a special plea of impeachment, accusing two other youths of the killing. At the end of the trial, the jury couldn't make up their minds. All three had walked free.

Jack hadn't been a policeman then, but he'd been young enough and keen enough to have read all the murder reports when he finally made it out of college. There was a similarity between the two cases, twenty years apart. Jack slung Robbie Cattanach's report on his desk and cupped his chin in his hand. Of one thing he was determined. Whoever did this would not walk away from it.

Dr Cuthbert had given Cissie Doyle a couple of pills. She was still coherent, but barely lucid. She had the look of a woman walking dreamily through a nightmare. Every now and then, she'd give a little start as if coming awake, and then the sleepy eyes would widen, allowing a little of the madness to come through.

Jack Fallon took it gently. Sean Doyle held his arm tight around his wife's shoulders, as if one of them would fall down if he let go. He just looked numb. The expression in his eyes told everybody he did not believe this was happening. It had not yet sunk into him that he was not going to wake up from this, that he was not imagining it, that little Timmy would not start to cry in his cot in the next room.

'So then what happened?' Jack asked.

The young woman continued where she'd left off, her voice a flat drone.

'I thought he'd fallen out. I looked under the pram. It was pushed over on its side, just sitting on the two wheels against the railings. I don't know how that could have happened. I mean, there was nobody *there*.'

Down below, right underneath the Doyles' window, half the night shift were searching the vacant ground. One of the police vans still had its blue light flashing. An open window on the neighbouring block was angled enough to catch the light and beam it across to the house where Sean and Cissie sat facing Jack. It looked like a winking blue eye in the winter darkness.

'I looked down to see if he'd fallen, but there was nothing at all. He'd just. . . .' Her voice slowed down as if an internal turntable had switched to long play. The last word came out long and slow. Her hands started to shake then, not just the tremor that had been running through them ever since Jack had been let into the house by the constable on the door. Now they were like the wings of a frightened sparrow, fluttering wildly. The woman's eyes widened again as she relived the memory of the discovery on the balcony. Jack reached across and took both hands in his. The trembling did not stop. He could feel it shiver his own hands. She didn't even notice him clench both tightly, turn them over and give her nails and palms a very quick examination. There was a small red mark just above the knuckle. She'd said she'd bumped the pot and some had spilled out. If she was telling the truth, he told himself, that would probably be a drop scald.

There was no reason for him to think that she might not be telling the truth, none at all, except for the fact that he had been in too many houses down the years, seen too many people who claimed they'd done nothing. Already Ralph Slater and his two-man team were working on the balcony and in the kitchen. They'd have checked the pots, just to make sure that smell was minced beef and not boiled baby. It sounded cruel, but it wouldn't have been the first time, not by a long chalk. This

53

woman, Jack told himself, was telling the truth. He could feel it in the tremor of her hands, see it in the blank look in her eyes. This was not a case of baby battering, post natal depression, teething trouble *snap*. Not unless Cissie Doyle was schizophrenic, and they'd soon find out if she was.

He patiently asked her the questions over and over again, checking every answer against the previous one until he knew exactly what steps she had taken, exactly how she had acted. Her baby had been strapped in its pram, and now it was gone. Now the real puzzle began.

He left them both in the company of the young woman in uniform who looked pretty and efficient in police blues, but hardly old enough to have left school. She'd made tea, hot and sweet, the way they recommended it, and was helping Cissie Doyle get her fingers around the handle when Jack went through the doors to the balcony.

Ralph Slater was leaning over the railing, dangerously far out. Below him the blue light still winked.

'Anything?' Jack asked.

'Nothing so far. We'll be quick as we can with prints, but I'll bet this place is clean.' Ralph heaved himself back up. 'I'm buggered if I know what happened.'

'You and me both. But the baby's gone. I don't think he jumped.'

'No, he didn't. The harness is ripped apart. Not cut. Somebody snapped it, and that took some doing. I reckon that's what caused the pram to tumble.'

Jack turned, leaned backwards over the wrought-iron balustrade, and looked upwards. The floors above stretched up into the black sky.

'You think somebody climbed?'

'Bet any money they did. Failing that, they'd have had to come through the house, which is possible.'

'But not to steal a kid. Maybe to rob. She had the safety chain on the door. You can see where she's pulled it too hard.'

'I agree on that. So somebody's come up or down. If we get prints to match from either balcony, we can say which it is. But I just can't imagine why. I mean, it's a hell of a drop. You'd have to be a rock climber to do it. They're all beards and folk songs. I can't imagine them stealing somebody's baby. Last three we had, two were young girls and the other a woman with a cot death. Never heard of a fella going in for it.'

'Always a first time,' Jack said. 'If somebody's crazy enough to climb this high, who the hell knows what he could do?'

He bent over the railing, as Ralph had done, but not quite so far as the scene-of-crime man. As soon as he leaned over from the waist, the cars far below started going in and out of focus. Jack felt the clench in his belly as vertigo flared. He was scared of heights. He pulled himself back in again and waited for his heart to slow down. Ralph Slater was saying something.

'. . . and there's something similar down there.'

'Hmm?' Jack asked.

'I wouldn't lean out too far if I were you,' Ralph told him, grinning wickedly. 'Not if you've no head for heights. You're white as a sheet, man.

'Anyway, I was saying, there's a set of scratch marks down there at the sill. Right on the concrete. You probably didn't notice for fear of falling.'

'No. I didn't, thanks,' Jack replied drily. Ralph was a good man, but Jack did not like heights. He didn't find them funny in the least.

'And up there,' – the other man indicated the sill of the upstairs balcony – 'there's more scrape marks. They're pretty fresh, as far as I can tell, and they've taken off the lichen scum. Concrete's dry underneath. I think we might have a climber sure enough.'

'Unless the baby did fall out.'

'That baby never snapped the harness, Jack. Neither did the mother. You and me would have a hard enough time. No. Whoever did this was a strong bastard. He's probably got a head for heights. Tell you something. If I was you, I'd check up Calderpark Zoo and see if they're missing a gorilla.'

Jack looked at him and began to smile.

'You've been reading too many Runyan books.'

'Maybe so, but I wouldn't like to meet whoever got up here without ropes and stole a baby.'

It was after two in the morning when Jack got back to the cottage, feeling like a wrung-out dishrag. He poured himself a large vodka, added a dash of fresh orange and carried it through to the living room. He took one swallow, put the glass on the coffee table by the arm of the chair, leaned back, and was instantly asleep.

The dream came some time in the cold, dead hours of the morning. It came creeping the way dreams do, the monster in child's clothing, in a simple scene from childhood. Young Jack Fallon down at the Garshake Stream, a wooden boat with a paper sail negotiating the rapids at the potholes, bobbing on the turbulence, a white flash on the green water then down over the lip into the froth of the deep pot. Young Jack following quickly, leaping from boulder to boulder, chasing to keep up, skittering on the edge of the falls, feet spread on the fork stones where the water poured in a solid rush. Down there the flash of sodden white sail and then the darkness of the deep water.

The change happened with that easy, lazy slow motion of dreams. The young Jack teetered on the edge, arms windmilling, eyes fixed on the deep water, the black whorls and eddies, feeling it pull and tug at him. Then he was falling. A shock of cold, a shock of dark around his head and in the dream he *knew* it was changing. He was going over the edge.

The *twist* came with that sinking wrench inside him. He was wet and cold. He was in a strange place. It was dark and musty, the air dry and metallic, rust-dusted. He could hear his own feet clanging along a metal walkway as he ran. Something was behind him. He could hear its feet, not so much a pounding, but a scraping scuttle sound, much faster than a running man. Whatever it was, Jack did not want to see it. He could hear a gurgling rasp of breath, so close behind him he could almost feel the heat of it on the back of his neck. In the dream he imagined a hand, or something not *quite* a hand reach out to snatch at his collar, to grab him by the neck. His feet clanged on the walkway. On either side, corroded railings whizzed past, blurred with speed, and then he came to the end of the platform. It stopped abruptly, with no warning. Jack skidded to a halt, one hand swinging to the side to grab the railing. His fingers touched hard metal, tried to grip and then he was over the edge for the second time. Behind him something made a noise that sounded like a laugh and Jack was falling straight down.

56

Lights flashed on his left side, sunlight or moonlight blinking through the holes in the sides of the shaft, and he was plummeting out of control. Below him, old and rusted machinery, spiked and spined, crouched at ground level, waiting to impale him at the end of the drop. He hit with sickening force. Instant darkness surrounded him. He was under water again, cold, gasping for breath, swimming up through the numbness towards daylight. He opened his eyes, and he was no longer impaled on the spikes, he was walking down a narrow street. Ahead, sounds of traffic, a horn blaring. He was walking out of the shadows towards the light, about to turn a corner when the premonition hit him low, grabbing at his belly.

He moved forward, knowing what would happen when he turned into the street. The car was hammering along on the wrong side, dodging the streams of traffic. Behind it, the blare of a siren. The lead car was red. There was a crumpled dent right along one side. The passenger window was smashed. Behind the windscreen, two pale faces, unrecognisable blurs. A mouth wide open. In the dream the sound of the siren faded away and the car continued on, weaving right and left, a tyre on the pavement then slapping down onto the road, the whole scene slowing down in the dilated timescape of the dream. On the pavement, people standing, mouths slack in surprise, in fright, as the red car rumbled towards them, its engine now a low roar. On the far side of the street, Rae coming out of the bookshop. He could see the bright yellow bag dangling from one hand. At her side, Julie, hanging onto her free hand, skipping around her mother, bright face angled up in question. Rae's head was turning, the smile disappearing from her face. Her eyes widened and she instinctively swung Julie off to the side.

The red car came swinging round, narrowly missing a delivery van. The tyres squealed, but in the stretched time of the dream, it was a low moan. The offside wheels came up as the driver fought for control, slammed back down onto the road again. The car leapt forward and smacked an old lady to the side. Rae was turning, Julie only a yard from her. The front of the car smashed Rae at knee level. She swung upwards, tumbling, broken. The yellow bag went fluttering off to the right. She hit the wall with a slapping sound and dropped to the pavement. The red car, its screen starred and dented where Rae's head had hit, came on, veering left, now slowing. It came in at the corner of the picture window. From where he stood, foot-rooted, paralysed in dream agony, Jack watched the edge of the window cave in. Little Julie staggering backwards, one hand raised for balance. Falling against the window as it crashed inwards. She flipped back, feet in the air. The jagged plates of glass jiggled themselves down like scales. There was a grinding sound, so low Jack could hear it in the bones of his spine. He was running now, running through a crowd of white-faced statues. The sound of slow glass shards rasping against each other, a sound of reaping scythes. Somebody screamed from the inside of the shop. The glass came down and down and down. Jack was running towards something red that flopped among the books.

His own hoarse cry woke him up.

He was sitting on the armchair, both arms outstretched as they had been in the dream, reaching for his daughter. In his mind's eye, he could still see her face, a little splatter of blood trailed across her forehead, her eyes puzzled.

He hauled himself out of the chair and made it through the kitchen door. He turned the tap on and put his head underneath the cold jet of water, willing the memory away, using the shock of cold as a shield. The image began to fade.

Jack came back through, face dripping. He reached for the drink he'd left. It was warm and a little stale, but he drank it down in one gulp, feeling the burn of the spirits down his throat. It made him shiver, but that helped shuck away the picture that kept dancing into his head. He eyed the bottle, sitting on the dresser in the corner of the room, seriously thinking about it, then shook his head slowly. He was hurting again, but the drink wouldn't help him tonight. Instead he reached behind the seat for his briefcase, snapped it open, and pulled out the copy of the preliminary report on Marta Herkik.

Outside, the wind rose, sending a cold draught under the front door. Winter had arrived. Jack Fallon would get no sleep. Instead he decided to concentrate on another death, to keep his mind in the present.

Three hours later, when the dawn was still a grey hint on the eastern sky, Jack shrugged himself into his coat and let himself out of the house. It was bitterly cold as he walked down the Cargill Road, past the turn that would have taken him to Julia's house and down along the curve of the hill towards the centre of the town. It was a miserable morning, but he hardly noticed it. Half an hour later, he was climbing the back stairs to Marta Herkik's house.

5

On the night Jack Fallon fell asleep in his chair and drifted into the nightmare, William Simpson opened the side door between the manse and the church and came quickly down the narrow alley to the iron gate that led to the boiler house. The key took two turns to slot the bolt back and the gate swung back with a groan of protest. The cold wind was gusting up the narrow space, but William Simpson did not feel it.

Inside his head, thoughts were sparking and sputtering, hot thoughts that made him hurry down the dry stone stairs. The green door at the bottom opened easily and he let himself into the basement directly under the old church. His knuckle hit the switch and a cone of light flickered down from the single bulb under the green metal shade. He screwed his eyes up against the luminescence, shying away from the light. In the past few days, he'd spent most of his time in his study, keeping the blinds drawn, hardly speaking to any but the most determined parishioners. Inside his head, the whispering, grating thoughts had prodded him unceasingly, as they did now.

Over in the corner, the boiler rumbled and sighed to itself. The pipes pinged and close to the basement ceiling, where an airlock always caught at the bend, there was a knocking sound, a witchety hammering in the cobwebbed shadow. Simpson ignored it. The bunch of keys jangled in his hands as he made his way forward. To his left, old pieces of the pipe organ, giant penny whistles, lay stacked against the wall, and beyond them, boxes of hymn books which hadn't been used in years were stacked one atop the other. Further back, a stout door, paint-peeled and cracked, stood bracketed by the red sandstone wall. William Simpson unlocked it, let himself in quickly and closed the door behind him before switching the low wattage bulb, letting its orange luminescence tussle with the shadows.

The old storeroom was his secret place. He had changed the lock nineteen years ago, not long after he had come to take charge of the Castlebank Church in the east side of Levenford. There was one key, and that remained firmly on the ring that he kept in his pocket at all times.

The room was small and clean. Against the far wall there was a double sink on which lay several flat photographic trays. Close by stood the circular drum of a drier, connected to a wall socket by a white cable. The light overhead shone dully, casting a weak glow over everything. Simpson sat down in the chair next to the wooden desk and opened the bottom drawer. He drew out a box, hand shaking with anticipation. Inside his head, the thoughts were sparking away like an overloaded fusebox, while behind them the ceaseless whispering goaded him on with incomprehensible promises. He felt hot and feverish.

The box had a small hasp. It opened easily on two brass hinges. The minister reached inside and drew out a small pink object which he placed on the rough surface of the desk. His trembling hand dived in again and brought out a tiny pair of panties, yellowed with age. There was a rip just under the elastic at the top, and an old stain down at the crotch. Simpson felt the texture of the flimsy cloth between his fingers and felt the hot anticipation rise. His breath came quicker and a slick of sweat beaded his brow. Outside the wind howled. In the other room the boiler sighed and gurgled and the spectral knocking came intermittently from the pipes. Simpson noticed none of these things. His hot mind was lost in the memory, unreeling the scene that he had played back too many times in the early years. Eventually he had all the objects laid out before him. The tiny briefs, and beside them a little lace handkerchief with two initials embroidered in a corner. A pink pair of small spectacles, the left lens starred with cracks. Next to last, was a fine silver circlet with a simple clasp, and alongside that the pink plastic hand and podgy-smooth arm of a child's doll. Simpson ran his hands over these things, feeling them, recalling the first time he had seen them, the first time his hands had closed over them, and he felt as if his brain was on fire. It had been a long time since he'd unlocked the drawer and opened the box, a very long time. Yet tonight, the cajoling voice in his head had driven him to come and touch them again.

His breath came quicker now, here in his secret place. Over

the years he'd made the storeroom into a darkroom where he would develop the family photographs, scenes of church picnics, the choir, the Sunday school. Some of the pictures he kept aside for himself, printing them out over and over again, waiting with trembling anticipation as the angelic face of a little girl would appear, faint at first on the blank sheet, watching it wax stronger until the lines were firmly caught on the page. His excitement would be like a pressure inside him as he watched the appearance, and then, his hand sneaking down past the waistband of his black trousers, he would watch while the photograph would overdevelop. The page would grow darker and darker until the child was swallowed by the blackness, overcome by oblivion.

He had told himself over many years that he was an evil man, and he knew that to be true. He'd thought of himself, at one time, as a man of God, but he knew he could not be that, despite the collar he wore and the sermons he preached. For inside him there was a need that he could do nothing but try to appease, though he had become cunning as the years went by. There were places in the church, under the choir loft, for instance, where he could stare between the knees of the teenage sopranos as they sang in practice. At Sunday School, a minister was always free to hoist a little girl on his knee and hold her tightly, feeling the heat of the little body, the flutter-beat of a baby heart. They trusted him, of course. At times he did not trust himself to hide the mounting pressure.

On this cold night, his wife was in the drawing room, with three of the women from the guild. He had heard their voices, each talking over the other, and the chink of fine china cups. His youngest daughter was upstairs, doing her homework. He dared not go up. The two older ones had left as soon as they were able. They had never said anything – perhaps they did not remember anything from when they were so small – but they had left home with no love in their eyes. Betty, his wife, tolerated him with cold politeness, Fiona with wary suspicion. Of course she knew nothing, but he sensed that she sensed something. Betty had used all her power to keep father and daughter apart. His was no longer a family of hugs and kisses. His was hardly a family.

But he had his darkroom, and she was content to let him potter around there, glad to have him out of sight. She went through the posture of the minister's wife – smiling as the congregation left the church on a Sunday, taking meetings of the guild, organising coffee mornings. But she had never forgiven him for the loss of her two eldest daughters and lived in fear of losing the third.

These thoughts did not occur to him on this cold night. His mind was strangely *alive*, crowded with bustling thoughts, urgent thoughts. He felt the old hunger well up inside him, the hunger he'd tried to deny over the years after the first terrible time. Despite having kept the treasures – a mad risk, he knew – he had lived with the guilt of it all. The burden had built up over the years, adding shame on shame, and yet he had been unable to change himself. Every time he had slipped his hand under a small girl's buttocks, every time he had sneaked into his daughters' rooms while they slept and slipped his hand under the bedclothes, he had been unable to deny the need. Yet afterwards, the guilt and shame had crowded in on him, dark shadows with long, accusing fingers.

He had gone to the spiritualist because there was something he needed to know. He had long since lost his faith in a forgiving God. The God he had wanted to dedicate his life to had made him a twisted thing inside his own soul, and if he had been a good and just God he wouldn't have done that. He had needed something to believe in when he had first taken those steps up to Marta Herkik's rooms. He had wanted a sign from the other side, from the dark or from the light, just a sign that would tell him there *was* another side.

What he wanted with that knowledge, even he did not know. It was a forked stick, barbed on both prongs. If there was a life hereafter, he might be consigned to a hell of his own for the things that had been done. If there was none, he had consigned another to oblivion in a moment of fine madness. But that thought did not occur to him now. He only remembered opening the door of the old woman's house, shaking his coat out in the hall. There was no memory of what had happened after that. Since then, he had very little memory of anything.

The day before he had left the manse in the late afternoon. Some time later, when it was full dark, he had found himself on the old chandler-yard road close to the bridge over the river.

How he had got there, or why he had come, he did not know. He had no recollection of what had happened after he had closed the garden gate behind him. All he was left with was a dull emptiness and a vague feeling of fear. And added to that was this new and strange sense of satisfaction, of unfathomable glee.

Now in the storeroom next to the old cellar, William Simpson's thoughts spangled and sparked. Old memories came rushing in at him, fresh desires welled up.

And again he heard the voice, scraping at first on the inside of his skull. It came as a dry, barely audible whisper, but it persisted, ever louder until he could finally make out the words from the gabble. It was telling him what to do.

After a while, the minister sat back slowly in the seat. The tremor of his hands had stilled. He closed his eyes and listened to the voice inside his head.

A quarter of a mile away, in the basement of the library on Strathleven Street, the girl was preparing to finish for the night. The words on the stock-list page were beginning to blur in front of her eyes and she yawned, stretching her hands up into the air, easing her cramped muscles. In the light from the overhead tube, her hair glowed the bright auburn of new chestnuts. She checked her watch, debated finishing the end of the list, then with a quick movement, snapped her folder shut.

From upstairs, in the main section of the library, she could hear muffled voices. Here, the basement was her own haven, a narrow room lined with stacks holding thousands of books, a wealth of words. The place was new to her, but she already felt at home in the dry cosiness of the stack room. She turned to lift her black bag from the floor by her ankle, when a sudden wave of dizziness washed over her. The shelves in front of her wavered and the light seemed to dim.

For a second she thought she would pass out.

Then from nowhere a picture came into her head and the stacks of books faded into the background, shimmered like a dusty veil and disappeared.

She saw the man climb onto the stool and watched as he tied something round his neck. His eyes were dead, though one of them had a strange blind sparkle.

There was an utter silence and then, behind her ears, she heard the whispering, the abrasive rasp that she'd heard before, though she couldn't quite remember when.

As soon as she heard that, a vast and overwhelming sensation of evil swept through her.

Here was an *evil man* and he was being urged on by an *evil thing*.

In her mind she heard a chuckle of glee. The man turned to look at her and his eyes glowed yellow-orange, the colour of pus. She shook her head. He was doing something with his right hand, showing her what he was doing. She tried to look away and he took a step forward.

The scene winked out. The stacks came wavering back into her vision. Above her the white light flared. She was back again in the library basement. The girl drew in air in a swoop, as if she had been holding her breath a long time. A small spasm of dizziness rocked her against the back of the swivel chair and then was gone, leaving her feeling drained. It left her with a shuddery sense of incomprehensible foreboding.

6

Two nights after little Timmy Doyle went missing from the balcony high up in Latta Court Jack Fallon was no further forward. Superintendent Ronald Cowie was piling up the pressure and in one vitriolic session Jack almost offered Cowie advice on where he could position the investigation with regards to his own person. He did not know what held him back, except for the fact that he had promised Angus McNicol he'd do his best, and he knew if Cowie was put in practical charge, then nothing would ever be solved. Cowie was a politician more than a policeman, a rubber of shoulders, a shaker of hands, and a lifter of the left trouser leg into the bargain.

Cissie Doyle was by now heavily sedated. Ralph Slater had been right about the fingerprints. There were none except those of the family on the balcony. The scrape marks on the concrete were a small mystery. They looked fresh enough, but could have been caused by anything, including the swing gantry of the maintenance machine mainly used by window cleaners, but not this week. That had been checked. The houses upstairs and below had been searched thoroughly by the teams organised by John McColl. Nobody had been able to object to that. The door-to-door men had uncovered half a kilo of cannabis, a full barrel of Ardenmill whisky – and how they had got that up in the lift nobody knew – along with the usual mix of stolen hi-fi equipment, televisions and video recorders. All of that was noted for future reference. Jack told the men not to waste time on peripherals. The baby was the object. A few folk in Latta Court breathed a sigh of relief, although the temporary owner of the half kilo was rushed to hospital four days later with blood frothing from a hole in his ribs after a stabbing down on Quay Street, possibly as a result of non-payment for goods delivered.

On the other side of town, not half a mile from where Jack Fallon lived in Cargill Farm Cottage, a group of women were on their third round of drinks in a terrace house on Overtoun Lane. Most of them were very merry by ten o'clock.

Lorna Breck was still red with embarrassment over some of the things she'd seen and handled in the past hour.

'It's all part of your education,' Gemma Conroy had said when she'd stopped giggling. One of the other women had shrieked with laughter. 'Once you've felt one, you've felt them all.'

'If they all feel like that, then I never want to feel another one,' Lorna replied in her soft Highland accent. This time everybody fell about. Somebody spilled a glass of wine down the front of her dress and went off into a fit of high-pitched hysterics.

'Don't worry, dear. Nothing's better than the real thing,' Mrs McCluskie had said, planting a beefy hand on her knee, and that really astounded Lorna. Mrs McCluskie, Gemma's next-door neighbour, was nearly sixty years old, and she looked as if the thought of such a thing would never have crossed her mind. The grey-haired woman had chuckled, sending ripples down her wobbly fat frame. She picked the plastic object up from the table, thumbed the switch and the peals of laughter started up again.

'If my Bert had something like this, maybe we wouldn't be in separate beds,' she announced.

'No. You'd be in a hospital bed,' somebody chipped in, and the squeals started up again.

Lorna felt her face redden again. The party had been fun. Gemma, her elder cousin, had organised it for the neighbours, the kind of party where men were refused admission. The girl with the case had opened it on the table and it had started with lacy nighties and silky briefs. Then, after a couple of glasses of wine, when everybody was feeling fine and dandy, she'd brought out the knick-knacks which had brought the house down as they had passed from hand to hand.

Lorna was the only one of them who wasn't married. She was twenty-six years old. She'd come to live in Levenford only nine months before, and brought with her the lilting softness of the west highlands. Living in a town this size had taken some getting used to, and she still found herself taking a wrong turn on the maze of alleys and vennels that radiated off River Street. It was different from the farm where she'd grown up, different from the small country town where she'd gone to school. She had a delicate, oval face and a childlike pert nose smattered with freckles, all framed by hair the colour of dark amber. The most

67

striking thing about her was her wide grey eyes, which on cold winter mornings took on the sheen of brushed steel, bright and sparkling under curved brows.

'Oh, don't let them kid you, Lorny,' one of the women said. Cathy Galt had her fair hair drawn up high on her head. She was a blowsy-looking woman who worked most nights down in Mac's Bar, a rough and ready establishment at the end of River Street, and was tough enough to throw any of the stragglers out through the swing doors and into the night. She had, however, a heart of gold. Lorna had treated her as an honorary aunt since she'd come down on the West Highland line to take up her new job in the library.

'If I ever saw a man with something like that, I'd divorce Campbell tomorrow and never let the fellow out of my sight,' she said. 'For the love of God, it's twice the size of anything I ever saw.'

'And you've seen plenty, I suppose?' Agnes McCann, Cathy's sister-in-law asked archly. As she did, Lorna gave a little start. She'd been looking at the woman and all of a sudden, she felt a small wave of dizziness shiver through her. For a second, the voices faded away, leaving her alone in a cocoon of isolation. In that moment, everything went still, except for Agnes. As Lorna watched, the dark-haired woman's eyes opened wide and her mouth opened wide, so wide Lorna could see the fillings in her back teeth. The colour drained away from Agnes' face and her hands came up and grabbed onto her hair. In the eerie, momentary silence, Lorna could sense that the woman was screaming. She jerked back, and the bubble burst. The voices came babbling in again. Lorna blinked and the expression on Agnes' face was back to normal, a lazy smile drawn on her face.

'I had my share before Campbell made an honest woman of me,' Cathy shot back. 'Though if I'd known then what I know now, I'd still be having my share.'

'I thought size didn't matter,' Gemma said.

'Och, it's only men who say that. I never heard a woman swear on that in all my life.'

Lorna felt herself squirm. The odd feeling had come and gone in the flick of an eye. Maybe it had been the wine, she told herself. Somebody laughed raucously and next to her somebody else grabbed the buzzing thing and flicked the off switch. Lorna gave a sigh of relief. She was not an innocent, though she was hardly experienced in these things. She had lost her virginity to James Blair only six months ago, and it had been a very nice experience, but nothing to shake the world. They'd managed it several times since then, when his mother was out of the house, and it had still been pleasant. Then when he'd talked about getting married, something she was certainly willing to consider, old Maggie Blair had put her foot firmly down. Despite the fact that James was twenty-eight years old, she was still the boss as far as his life was concerned, and while she didn't mind him having some hanky-panky with a farm-girl from the sticks, and a Catholic to boot, there was no chance of her becoming a mother-in-law to the lass. Maggie Blair was a firm believer in Protestant supremacy. She went down to Castlebank Church every Sunday and listened to William Simpson's sermons and then thanked God for not making her a papist.

The engagement was over in weeks. Lorna had sensed the coldness when she had gone round to James' house on a Friday night when they had planned to go to the cinema. Old Maggie had been abrupt, eying the girl from her position of authority, the big easy chair next to the fire. She'd been knitting her boy a thick winter pullover and her needles had clicked in staccato anger. On the way home from the film, Lorna had asked what was wrong and he'd blurted out his mother's views.

Lorna asked him straight out what he planned to do about it. He'd hesitated and looked blank, as if puzzled at the possibility that there was anything he *could* do.

'Like what?' he'd asked.

'Like leaving home? Or even just deciding what you want in your life.'

He'd turned to her, eyes still blank. She'd recognised the situation for what it was and immediately regretted losing her virginity to somebody who probably still got his mother to scrub his back. She'd turned on her heel, grey eyes flashing iron in the light of the street lamp, and she'd not seen him since.

Now, as she listened to the women talk about men, *their* men and just men in general, she recalled her own first time with a small feeling of regret. Certainly, James Blair had nothing to compare with the mechanical thing that had come out of the demonstrator's case. That had looked as if it had come from a horse. If she'd been presented with anything like that monster six months ago, she'd have screamed and run.

The demonstrator was packing up now, with all the orders clipped to a board. Lorna had bought a very pretty teddy, which was as bold as she could go in front of other folk, and even then, it had only been the cajoling of the older women that had made her do it. After the party rep had gone, somebody opened another bottle of wine. Old Mrs McCluskie had brought a half bottle of whisky out from her big black handbag and poured herself and Cathy a large measure each. She was telling her neighbour a particularly vivid joke about a man's anatomy, which Lorna heard with only half her attention until she realised it was *not* a joke. Mrs McCluskie was telling a story about herself. Lorna blushed again and wondered how women were able to talk so clinically about sex. She'd always believed that it was men who did that.

Cathy put on a tape and began pouring drink again. Somebody asked her what she had ordered from the rep and Cathy gave an exaggerated wink.

'Can't tell you, but it should put the old sparkle back into Campbell's eyes again.'

'If you can get him awake, that is,' Agnes put in.

'Oh, don't worry. I'll keep him awake all right,' Cathy said, laughing. 'My horoscope tells me it's my lucky week. I'm hoping it'll be my lucky night.'

'Well Lorna can tell you that, can't you honey?' Gemma announced.

Lorna looked up. Her glass was still half full and Gemma took it away for a refill before she could protest.

'How about telling our fortunes?'

'Oh, I haven't brought my cards with me,' Lorna said. Everybody in the room was looking at her, and it made her feel even more uncomfortable.

'What's this?' Agnes asked.

'Oh, Lorna reads the tarot. She's spot on.'

'It's just a bit of fun,' Lorna protested.

'And tea leaves too,' Gemma continued with hardly a pause.

70

'Is that right dear?' Mrs McCluskie beamed at her. 'Could you do mine? I went to that woman down at Lochend last week and it cost a fortune, and she didn't tell me anything I didn't know already.'

Lorna looked at her. The fat woman was beaming over the top of her spectacles. Lorna remembered the phrase she'd used only a few moments before and it came back in the clarity of total recall. *There was me with my legs up round his neck and him going at it like a sewing machine and then I sneezed and the wee bugger went flying off the end of the bed.*

Lorna felt a laugh building up inside her as she looked at Mrs McCluskie and tried to imagine her in *that* position. She bit down on the laugh but couldn't disguise the smile. To hide it she said: 'Yes, of course I will.'

Half an hour later she was swirling the dregs round in the bottom of a teacup. She upended it quickly, letting the tea drain away, then brought it back again. The leaves formed a complex pattern on the inside of the china. Mrs McCluskie drew herself closer, using her beefy forearms to jostle her large breasts into a comfortable position.

'What does it say then?'

Lorna took several deep, slow breaths, getting herself into the right frame of mind. She closed her eyes and let the darkness slide over her. Her breathing slowed a little further and then she could sense a little bit of the feeling that came when she concentrated. It always came with a tiny whine, like a bat squeak, just below the threshold of true hearing. It was a little pressure noise inside her heard. The noise got only a little louder then faded out abruptly, leaving her in a little cone of dead silence. Behind her closed eyelids, the dark swirled around her and then it began to clear. She opened her eyes to look into the patterns, reaching for the vague impressions that sometimes came when she tried really hard. The brown constellation of dark tea-leaves swirled and then something happened that Lorna had never experienced before. A picture came flitting unbidden into her mind and

she saw

A woman with a walking stick, the kind that has a strap to keep it firmly attached to the forearm. The woman turned, unstrapped

71

the stick and threw it into the air, turned again and came walking towards her, a big smile on her face.

flick

Two babies, a boy and a girl, side by side in a cot. Names came from nowhere. She knew who they were.

flick

A bundle of notes, too many to count, stacked on a table.

flick

A tall, tanned man with a white smile and thick greying hair coming through a door and into an old woman's arms. She knew his name.

The picture stopped without warning. The tea-leaf galaxy swum back into focus and Lorna blinked rapidly, bewildered, slightly shaken by the sudden sure knowledge, unable to comprehend just what had happened or how. She took a deep breath. All of the women sat looking at her, waiting expectantly.

'Well, what's it say, my dear?' Mrs McCluskie was leaning right over the table.

'You're going into hospital soon,' she began. Somebody at the far end of the room drew in a breath. 'But they will give you a new hip. You'll come out walking like a girl again.'

'Och, nonsense dear. It's just a wee bit of arthritis. Nothing to worry about. Too many exercises when I was younger,' she said, nudging Cathy.

'Well, it's going to be fine. And you're going to come into some money. Quite a lot. And your daughter Pauline's just had a wee boy *and* a girl. No. . . .' She paused and shook her head, eyes shut, remembering. 'No. She's *going* to have her babies soon. Boy and a girl. That's for sure. Both of them healthy too. One of them named after you.'

'Probably the boy,' Cathy said. 'That Pauline of yours isn't the full shilling.' Everybody laughed.

'And your son Benny. He's coming home.'

'What? My *Benny*? From Australia?'

'Yes. He's coming home soon. He's got a tan and grey hair,' Lorna went on. 'And he's got some good news for you.'

'My Benny coming home?' Mrs McCluskie asked again. She was snagged on that one point. 'After all this time?'

She put her hands up to her face, nudging her glasses upwards.

She drew them down again, and her eyes were sparkling. She glistened at Lorna.

'You wouldn't kid me on now, would you?'

Lorna raised her eyes, still puzzled. 'No. I don't think so.'

Gemma was looking at Lorna, eyebrows arched up in silent question. The girl fooled around with tarot cards and tea leaves and palm reading, always in a light-hearted way. Her predictions were always vague, never definite.

Old Mrs McCluskie was wiping her eyes. Beside Lorna another of the women was clamouring to have her fortune told. Lorna took the cup, turned it over, closed her eyes and took her breaths, trying to get herself down to that level again, where she could *see*.

The flickering scenes came in a rush, each a little vignette. The woman, a neighbour of Cathy, spread out on a carpet, morning sun streaming through the window. A shadow moving in through the door, the woman's face twisted in fright. . . . The same woman stepping out of a big car, an expensive pair of high heels clicking on the pavement. A man, the same one who had been beside her on the floor out on the other side. . . . The two of them in a pool beside a white house, two fair-haired girls splashing in the shadows.

Lorna started talking of good fortune, love and romance, wealth and sunshine. This time she kept it unspecified. She wasn't completely *sure* of what she was seeing when the patterns of leaves swirled out of focus. She found it just a little scary. Patricia Farmer, whose husband worked in the iron foundry and drank most of his wages on Friday and Saturday nights, tried to keep the smile off her face and failed. Everybody had seen the bruises behind the sunglasses. They all cheered raucously.

It was just at that moment when Lorna gave a little shiver. She had been reaching for Agnes McCann's cup when a strange inside-out sensation twisted through her. It had happened only twice in her life, when she was in her early teens, just before she'd started bleeding. She hadn't even taken her deep breaths to concentrate. This time it simply swept right through her and over her like a cold wave. She felt her whole *self* stretched this way and that. All sound disappeared. She was gone into the darkness.

Opposite her, Cathy said: 'What's wrong?'

Lorna had started to slide to the side. Her eyes were still wide open, almost alert. She fell against Gemma, seated next to her on the couch. A little gurgling sound escaped her throat.

'Hey, you nearly spilled my drink,' Gemma protested, feigning annoyance. Lorna did not respond.

'What's the matter with her?' Mrs McCluskie asked, just as Lorna slid off the couch and slumped to the floor. 'Oh my God, the girl's fainted,' the grey-haired woman said, pushing her seat back from the table.

Gemma got down beside her and raised her head from the carpet.

'Lorna? Come on! What's wrong?'

The girl's eyes were still wide, but now they were staring blindly, like steel bearings, reflecting the light on the ceiling. She made a little coughing sound and then her whole body went rigid, hands clenched tight shut, ankles together, and she was shivering, as if an electric current was sizzling through her.

A few seconds later the shivering stopped and Lorna's muscles went slack. Cath and Gemma managed, between them, to get her up onto the couch again. Cath had a hand to the girl's forehead. It was clammy and cold. She was about to say something when Lorna's eyes closed and then snapped open again.

'Timmy?' she said very softly. 'Has anybody seen my Timmy?'

'What's she saying?' old Mrs McCluskie asked.

'I left my baby lying here,' Lorna sang in a dreamy voice. 'And went to gather blaeberries.' She stopped, then began again almost immediately, speaking in a dreamy way. 'Fairies took him. Fairies took him away.' She turned, eyes bright and sparkling, yet oddly blind. 'Not fairies. Something stole him and he'll never come back again.'

She closed her eyes again and all of the women around her watched in silence. Finally one of them asked again: 'What on earth's wrong with her?'

'I don't know,' Gemma said. 'Maybe she's had too much wine. Can somebody get a cold cloth?'

Agnes McCann shifted in her seat, about to fetch the cloth, when Lorna's hand shot out and grabbed her just above the elbow. Agnes yelped. 'Ow. That hurts!'

74

Lorna's eyes flicked open again, eerily wide, glaring straight at Agnes.

'Ladybird, ladybird, fly away home,' she began, chanting, like a little girl in a schoolyard, skipping to the rhyme. 'Your house is on fire and your children are *gone*.'

She blinked very slowly and a big tear formed in the corner of one eye, bubbled over and rolled down her cheek.

'They're burning. They're dying. Oh my sweet Jesus Christ let them out, let them *go*!' Lorna's words came out in a rising torrent. They ended in a screech.

Beside her, Gemma jerked back. Her hand had been on Lorna's left arm, while the girl's right hand had been straight out in front of her, still grasping Agnes McCann's elbow.

All of a sudden, it had felt as if Lorna's skin was on fire. The heat had sizzled into Gemma's fingers, as if she'd laid them on top of a hot stove.

'The baby in its cot. The two wee boys in their beds. They don't know. It's coming for them, coming in the dark. And the smoke, it's thick and dark and they can't breathe. Oh God, it's hot. It's down the chimney. He's lying in the flames and he's dead, and it's coming for them and they're going to *burn*. Oh, please. Oh *mother of Christ!* They can't wake up.'

'Come on, Lorna,' Cathy snapped. She shook the girl by the shoulder. Under the dress she too could feel the heat.

'The girl's gone half daft,' Mrs McCluskie said, but her face was slack and sick-looking.

'No, it's an act,' Patricia Farmer said. 'Just to make us believe she can read our tea leaves.'

Just then, Gemma said: 'Something's burning.'

She sat upright and sniffed, then looked down. The fine fair hairs on Lorna's arm were beginning to curl. Her skin was a blotchy red, and a blister was beginning to appear down the length of her forearm.

'Oh quick. Get a cloth,' she bawled. Cathy dashed to the sink and ran a tap over a hand towel and threw it across. Gemma slapped the dripping cloth onto Lorna, covering her face and her arms. There was a hissing sound, like water steaming on a hot pan, and then steam, *real* steam billowed up from the towel.

Lorna jerked back as if she'd been slapped.

75

'What's happening?' she asked in a small voice. She looked groggy, as if still half asleep. 'What's going on?'

She looked round at the faces, all of them staring at her.

'Thought you were throwing a fit, girl.'

'And you're so hot,' Gemma said. She reached out a hand to take Lorna's in her own. The heat was gone, but the blister still raised its long mark on her arm. 'You were burning up.'

'Burning?' Lorna asked. Her eyebrows came down in a frown of concentration. 'There's something I must remember. Something. . . .'

She seemed to come completely awake. Her eyes swept across the women in front of her, then came to rest on Agnes McCann. Lorna opened her mouth, tried to speak, but her voice was snagged in her throat. She made a little hitching movement and the words finally blurted out. 'You have to go home, Agnes. Right this minute. It might not be too late.'

'What do you mean?' the other woman started to ask.

'No time, oh please, there's no time. Your babies. There's something wrong. There's going to be a fire.'

Agnes backed away, knocking the chair behind her.

'What's she on about? Is she trying to scare me or something?'

She looked at the rest of the women and they all looked back dumbly.

'My Pat's watching them tonight. They're all right.'

'Oh please, Agnes. Phone him now. Get him to wake up. There's something in the. . . .'

Just then, outside in the street window, a siren screamed, loud enough to rattle the windows and so sudden they all jumped. The sound wailed menacingly. They all heard the blare of the horn as the fire tender rushed past, wheels throwing up chippings as it turned down Overtoun Lane and up the hill towards Murroch Street. The sound dopplered down as the fire tender raced away, the wail like a demon in the night.

Lorna started to scream and Agnes McCann fainted.

The top of the old red sandstone building was completely gutted. The firemen fought the blaze for three hours, as flames licked a hundred feet into the night sky, turning the low clouds orange with the reflected glare. The family staying below the McCann house had managed to escape. Gordon Kennedy lowered his two sons down on a knotted sheet to where old Bob Cuthill had managed to get a ladder against the wall. Bob, who was seventy-two, risked his life to clamber up, despite the danger from red-hot falling slates that were whipping from the roof and whirring down like axe-heads. He grabbed the kids and hustled them away from the burning building. Gordie Kennedy got himself out of the window and along a three-inch ledge to the roan-pipe which was turning pink with the heat. The pain was unbelievable as the skin and tendons seared, but Gordie held on for ten feet until the downpipe pulled away from the wall and he fell a further thirty to the flagstones below, where he broke his left leg in two places and drove the ball of his femur through the socket of his pelvis. It took thirty titanium screws to put him back together again and he walked with a limp after that. He never got the full use of his right hand again, but his sons grew up to be men.

Agnes McCann arrived on the scene five minutes after the red tender had screeched past Gemma Conroy's house. When Gemma drove her and Cathy Galt round the corner, and they saw the flames blasting up to the sky, now half shrouded in a tower of dirty smoke, Agnes started to scream.

They helped her through the crowd gathered at the end of the street, tripping over hoses and splashing through the mucky leak-water and got to the second tender just as the whole of the roof caved in. A gout of incredible heat and a meteor storm of sparks blasted out from the windows of the McCann house. One of the window frames went tumbling away, whirling through the air, to land, burning furiously, on top of a parked car fifty feet away. Agnes screeched again, so high it disappeared beyond hearing, and her legs gave way. Cathy Galt couldn't hold her and the woman flopped into an expanding puddle.

Ten minutes later, the floorboards gave way and the whole of the inside of the tenement seemed to collapse into itself. The tall chimney stack, with its eight identical pots, teetered like a drunk, then fell with an amazing roar into where the McCann children had been asleep in their beds. The pots smashed with the noise of exploding grenades.

After that, it was only a matter of time as the fire ate everything that could burn. The firemen, leaning out from the snorkel gantries, poured thousands of gallons in a constant deluge over the inferno and finally, just after midnight, you could see they were beginning to win the fight. There were no prizes. There was nothing left but ashes and rubble.

All morning fire inspector Sorley Fitzpatrick and his team spent their time sifting through the rubble, dressed in their thick protective gear. The stone and brickwork was still sizzling hot to the touch, and in fact it would be another two days before the heat drained out of the masonry. They discovered the remains of the McCann family, but those remains were mere fragments. Pat McCann's lower jaw was almost intact and he was later identified by dental records, which was, all things considered, a piece of luck. He'd lost all of his top teeth years before and the plastic plate had melted to nothing. They found the complete skull of the elder boy, Jimmy, who was eight, where it had fallen and been protected from complete carbonisation by a pile of slates. A partial hip-bone identified wee Brendan, just turned six. Of the baby, nine-month-old Kerry, the pride of her father's eye, nothing was found in the smouldering rubble of what had been 46 Murroch Road. Sorley Fitzpatrick deduced that because of her size, and the fact that she'd had no teeth to speak of, her entire body had been consumed.

It was another week before the fire claimed the entire McCann family. Six days after the fire, Agnes McCann managed, despite the close attentions of a large tribe of sisters, aunts and cousins, to swallow the entire contents of a bottle of paracetamol pills in the middle of the night. By the time morning came around, her sister-in-law found her lying half out of the bed in her spare room. She was in a deep coma. By the time she arrived at Lochend General, she was dead.

Sorley Fitzpatrick's report came to twelve pages and at the end of it, nobody was any the wiser. Such was the destruction of the building, that the cause of the fire could not be determined with any degree of accuracy. There was just nothing left intact enough to be able to prove what had sparked off the blaze. Some assumptions could be made, however. From the initial reports, and from the progress of the fire as it was being fought, it was likely the ignition spot was somewhere in the family's living room and the fire had quickly spread from there to the other rooms. Perhaps a piece of coal had sparked a burning ember from the fire, perhaps the old wiring behind the skirting boards had burned out and set the dust and bone-dry timbers alight behind the lath-and-plaster walls. The speed of the spread was a puzzle, as was the fact that all of the occupants were overcome so quickly. In the end, the report left as many questions as answers. A fatal inquiry a month later determined the cause of death of Pat McCann and his three children was accidental. In Agnes' case it was judged that she had committed suicide while the balance of her mind was disturbed. But all of that was many weeks on, in and in the meantime many things were happening in Levenford as the winter nights grew longer and the cold began to grip the town where some people were just beginning to realise that things were not as they should be.

7

Jack had been back up to Marta Herkik's house again. He was convinced he must have missed something. Some tiny clue which would give him something of a lead. His mind was tugged in two directions, because of the Timmy Doyle abduction, and he could have done without that. Angus McNicol had insisted on him handling both cases, although Jack had protested that it would stretch his own resources too far, but there was no gainsaying the Chief Superintendent, who also carried the rank of Commander in the regional force. Jack was the man for the job, mostly because of his years of experience in the city's murder squad, and also because he was the best qualified man on the local force. Angus sidestepped the protests from Ronald Cowie, the second in command who technically should have been in charge of at least one investigation. McNicol did not rate Cowie's ability, and he did rate Jack Fallon. That was another problem, he knew, for the man now hunting a killer and an abductor who was also potentially a killer. Cowie had friends inside and outside the force. Angus hoped he wouldn't have to slap the man down. He also knew that Jack did not care a tuppenny damn if he made enemies or not. Everybody knew he had very little to care about except for his work.

For half an hour, sitting alone beside the table that still bore the black traces of dried blood, Jack sat, huddled in his big coat, trying to think, trying to imagine what had happened on the night Marta Herkik had been mutilated.

The clues were many and various, but their significance was obscure.

The killer, from all the evidence, must have had plenty of time to operate. He'd taken down two strips of wallpaper – a bizarre act in itself – so carefully the neighbouring strips hadn't been torn or scratched, and he'd daubed two words, both of them obscure, in that oddly slanted writing, smeared in now-caked blood.

Heteros: The Other. Straight from the Greek. Jack had found that easily by asking the classics teacher at Castlebank Academy. *Etheros*. That was more of a conundrum. There was no such word, not in any language. He'd checked with the languages department in the University. But there were pointers. It could, he was told, have something to do with *ether* as in air, or *ethereal*, like a phantom or a wraith. Or maybe, Professor Walker had pointed out, it was simply a misspelling.

'Anagram possibly,' the academic, who was a lot younger than Jack would have expected, said from behind a plume of cigarette smoke. 'Like in a crossword. I do the *Times* every morning on the train. Never finished it on the journey yet, but I'm still hoping.'

Jack smiled along with him.

'It's got all the same letters, so maybe they're just a jumble. Perhaps even the first one is an anagram of something.'

'Like what?'

The professor took another draw of his cigarette and scratched his head. 'I dunno. Maybe *The Sore*, or *The Rose*. It could even be a woman's name, Hortense.'

'That would need another letter,' Jack pointed out. Walker nodded amiably.

'Word blindness, that's my trouble. A real pain in a job like mine. Anyway, I can't see too many words you could form out of it. Just an idea. *Etheros* isn't quite a word, but if it's no anagram, I'd lean towards the phantom idea.'

'Any reason?'

'Just the fact that the first word means *an other*, or *the other*. Like in terms of something otherworldly. That's what you'd take *ethereal* to mean.'

'Could it be indicating that it's an indication of being heterosexual?'

'Could be anything. But if *etheros* means airy, it could indicate *fairy*. There's a million choices, well, at least a dozen, depending on how you look at it.'

Jack had sat looking at the words, wondering what had been used to write them. It could have been a finger, a very narrow finger, but there were no prints. There was nothing left behind that had been used to daub them. That meant the killer had taken it with him. He'd also taken whatever he'd used to strip the wallpaper. That was a real puzzle. Nobody yet, nobody in forensics, even at the central lab, had any suggestions as to how it had been done. There was no sign of commercial stripper, not even hot water or detergent.

He looked at the column of writing again, cocking his head to read the letters properly. Each was about equal in size, though obviously written in haste. They were all canted over on the right side. It looked to Jack as if the killer had started up high on the wall, but hadn't been standing upright. It seemed as if he'd been bent across, somehow perched horizontally to daub each letter. Jack couldn't figure how that had been done either, not without a ladder and a platform. If anybody had left the building with a ladder, or some scaffolding, no matter what time of night or day it had been, someone would have seen him, and no one had.

The scratch marks on the table were an easier proposition. They had been caused by Marta Herkik herself. The blood was hers and two of her nails were embedded right under the thin veneer, stopped at the ends of the grooves in the wood. She had done it alright, but why she had done it was a mystery. Possibly her killer had come up behind her and dragged her backwards. She could have tried to pull away, scratching at the table, been hauled back with her nails digging for purchase. He tried to picture it in his mind's eye, but the image wouldn't come. It wouldn't have happened like that. The instinctive reaction would be to pull the hands away, to twist and turn, not to plough up the veneer of the table.

There were several other options for some of the damage. One was that the killer had gripped her by the throat, which might account for some of the damage to the windpipe, no matter what Robbie Cattanach's report said. Perhaps she'd tried to get away, to *claw* herself away from the murderer. Or maybe the pressure on her neck had made her muscles go into a kind of spasm. Robbie had said that was possible, not likely, but he couldn't discount it.

If that had been the case, then the old woman had been slung against the fireplace. The crystal ball, or whatever it was, had been smashed and then the splinters driven into her head by some unknown means, and then the woman had been beaten with a very heavy instrument, breaking several of her bones and

82

rupturing most of her insides. The blunt instruments had also been removed from the scene.

Whoever had done this, Jack told himself, had taken plenty of time. That meant he was no ordinary killer, no opportunist. He had been in a frenzy, of that there was no doubt, but he hadn't been panicked. He had to be some kind of psychopath, and there hadn't been one of them around in Levenford for a while. It would make him even more difficult to catch.

Jack had spent days trying to get into the man's mind and had failed completely. He could find no motive. The method was clear enough, even if half the evidence was missing. Why anybody would have wanted to kill the old Hungarian woman, and then mutilate her so obscenely, was as yet beyond him.

The room was still lined with books, despite the number that had been torn from the shelves and shredded like confetti. Almost all of them had something to do with the occult. There was an old copy of Friel's *Ley Lines*, and a big illustrated edition, leather-bound and well thumbed, of Crowley's *Goetia* lying open on a small table next to the central one. Some of the paragraphs in the page had been marked off in black ballpoint, and there was a long pencilled notation in the margin. The other books gave explanations of tarot cards, instructions on the use of ouija boards, and there were old directories of palmistry and phrenology along with dozens on astrology. None of the books made any sense to Jack Fallon, though he thumbed through a few of them. Marta Herkik, he knew, charged a few pounds for palm readings and tarot divination, none of it declared on any of her tax returns. There were a few spey-wives around. The local newspaper even used one of them in its weekly star-gazing column. All of the advice was ambiguous. Jack considered them all charlatans, but harmless enough at that.

So she had been an old Hungarian woman reading fortunes. That was hardly a reason for dying like that. And she obviously wasn't so good at reading her own, or she might have seen this coming, Jack thought, remembering what John McColl had said.

There was no rhyme or reason. Nothing. Not even a *feel* about the case, except for a cold, baffling sensation of *wrongness* as Jack sat alone in the room where the woman had met her death. He did not jump at shadows, he did not believe in ghosts. In fact

Jack Fallon believed in very little and hadn't for some time – since his faith in anything had fragmented in the time it took a window to shatter. Yet there was something out of kilter about Marta Herkik's death. He told himself there was no normality about *any* killing, and he'd seen more than his share, but it was more than that. He attempted to dredge up what his intuition was trying to tell him, the little unseen observer inside his mind that managed to pick out seemingly random and unconnected facts and string them together like beads on a thread until he got the spark of an idea that would take him in the right direction.

Nothing came, except a cold shiver.

'Been sitting too long,' Jack muttered to himself. The case was going nowhere, and that angered him. He got to his feet, pulled his collar up, and with a quick motion swept back the hank of black hair that had flopped down over his brow. He opened the door and let himself out of the flat. The fresh air gusting up the circular stairwell was cold and sharp in his nose. He breathed deeply, clearing out the *death* smell, and started to walk down the stairs to the street door.

He crossed the road, feeling the bite of the west wind numb his left ear, and went into Dickson's newsagent's shop where the old fellow behind the stacked counter remembered him from his younger days.

'Heard you were back again, Jackie,' he said as he counted out the change coin by coin. 'Get fed up with the big city?'

'Something like that.'

Old Wattie Dickson looked him up and down. 'Grown about three feet since I last saw you. Bigger than your father was an' all.'

Jack smiled. His father had been a huge man with iron-grey hair cropped into short spikes. He'd been a sergeant for twenty years at College Street station and had never seemed to have any ambition to claw his way up the promotional ladder, though he'd been proud as a peacock over his son's progress. He had looked as hard as nails, a big craggy face on a mountain of a frame, but the looks had belied his true nature. John Fallon had been the fairest, most gentle and patient man Jack had ever known. He'd never once in his career used the black truncheon, and if there was a disturbance down in Mac's Bar or the Castlegate round at

84

the quay where Friday-night fights were par for the course, John could joke and cajole a violent drunk out into the street and persuade him up to the station to sleep it off. There was hardly a need for charging a hungover man in the morning, he always told his son. Jack had only seen his father fight once, when some of the Buist clan had come out of the bushes in Clydeshore Road, out for a reckoning over one of their number who had been banged up in Drumbain jail for three months over an aggravated assault, following an arrest by big John.

Jack had been seven years old at the time, on his way up the road with a jar full of small fish he'd caught in the tidal pools down on the foreshore. He'd turned the corner and stopped dead when he saw the six Buist brothers with their backs to him, all standing in an arrogant line in front of the big man in the dark uniform.

His father had spotted him the moment he'd come round the bend and had given a tiny jerk of his head, telling Jack to be off about his business. The boy had backed away, a little scared, but more curious, and then he'd crawled behind the thick privet hedge, peering between the branches.

'Right, boys,' John had said. 'I know you're a wee bit upset and all, but let's keep it peaceable now.'

'You put our Billy in the jail.'

'No, Bobby, he did that to himself all right. Let his temper run away with him, instead of taking a bit of breath first. Now, why don't you all just go home and take deep breaths yourselves, eh?'

'Why don't you take a flying fuck to yourself!'

'Now, now, boys. I'll ignore the language. But here I am keeping the peace on a nice morning.'

'You'll get no peace from us,' Bobby Buist slung back.

'Well, I'll have to caution you against anything you might be thinking of.'

'What, going to sling all of us in Drumbain?'

'Och, I don't think it should come to that. Not if you're sensible,' big John had said in calm and measured tones. The Buists were well known in town. They were of farming stock, but they'd come off the land. Now there was a squad of them, big, broad men with sandy hair and hands like hams. They operated on the fringes on the east of town. Odd jobs, scrap cars and the occasional pit-bull fight.

'It'll come to it all right,' Bobby Buist said, moving two steps closer. His two brothers and three cousins sidled out in a flanking motion. John Fallon stood stock-still, eyes still calm.

'So is it six to one, or are you Buist boys man enough to shorten the odds?'

'Like you did for Billy?' This from one of the men circling to the policeman's left. Without warning, he swung his hips and aimed a kick at John's crotch. The big man's hand snapped down on the ankle six inches before the toe of the boot connected. He took one step towards the man, stamping down hard with the edge of his policeman's boot to rake it down the fellow's left shin. The foot crunched the other man's toes and stayed there. In the same movement, John Fallon raised the attacker's right leg by the ankle in a swift jerk. From his hiding place, young Jack heard a sound like a greenwood branch twisted from the trunk. The man screamed and John dropped him just as the others lunged in. The policeman's fist shot out and slammed against Billy Buist's cheek and the man fell like a sack. The punch sounded like a mallet on wood. John took two steps forward. Gave a right and a left so quickly his immense hands were like blurs and another two went down.

The final pair stood hesitantly, fists raised.

'Now which is first, or are we going to have a peaceful morning?'

They had turned and run, tackety boots sending sparks up from the cobbles. On the ground around John, three of the Buist boys were rolling or groaning. Bobby Buist was out for the count.

John had straightened his tunic and rubbed a palm across his knuckles.

'Right, boy, you can come out now,' he called over to the hedge. Young Jack, with his jar of tiny fish, came slowly out from the lee of the hedge. He walked up to his father, admiration written all over his face.

The big policeman had bent down from an immense height, hands on his hips.

'Now, young feller. When I give you the nod to be off about your business, I mean it, eh?'

Jack had nodded.

'That way you don't have to see any of this nonsense.' He had

86

stuck out a hand and clapped it on his son's shoulder and walked him up Clydeshore Road, leaving the straggle of men on the road. Two years later, big John had dived into the Leven after a spring thaw when the river was in spate and had hauled out Tommy Buist, who was then ten, and the bane of Jack's life at school, risking his life for the son of one of the men who had ambushed him down the Clydeshore. That was the kind of man he'd been.

When old Wattie Dickson had told him he was even bigger than his father had been, the memory of that day had come back to him in a flash of real pleasure. Nobody had ever been bigger than his father. Despite his rank, Jack Fallon did not think he could truly fill his old man's boots. It was not a thought that concerned him unduly. He wouldn't even have tried.

'I read it in the paper,' Wattie said, indicating the stack of gazettes piled on the old wooden counter. Very little about the shop had changed since Jack was small, except for the fact that there were fewer home-made sweets in the sugar-dusted glass jars, and along the top shelf, there was a selection of glossy biological magazines positioned out of reach of the young.

Jack pocketed his cigarettes. He'd managed to give up a few years before, and had started again. He knew he shouldn't have, but the past while had not been easy. He fumbled in his pocket for change and took one of the papers from the pile.

'Sounds like a lot of trouble in the old town,' Wattie said. 'That poor old biddie across the road. Always came in every morning at eight for a bag of mints. Who would ever want to kill her?'

'I don't know, Wattie. There's a lot of bad folk around.'

'Aye, and more and more the older I get. They're all at the drug-taking up by Overwood. Wee kiddies of school age too. World's gone to hell if you ask me.'

Jack hadn't asked him, but he tended to agree. There had been a time, when he was young, when the local policeman would give a boy a boot on the arse, an experience likely to make the lad think twice before stealing apples, or hoisting a bar of chocolate from the counter when old Wattie had his back turned. Not any more, and the place was worse for it in Jack's opinion.

'Well, I hope you get the bugger who did this. He should be hung.'

'I'll do my best,' Jack promised him as he folded his paper and jammed it in the pocket of his coat. He crossed the road again, walked about fifty yards along River Street and took a right turn down Quay Lane to where somebody had opened a coffee shop on the site where the old brewery store had stood twenty years before. The bell clanged above the door when Jack walked in. There were two old women in hats sitting in the far corner. They looked up when Jack came in. He chose a seat next to the curtained window where a pretty girl with a short spiky haircut took his order for a coffee, and brought it a few minutes later. It was hot and strong and very, very good.

Jack unfolded the *Levenford Gazette* and saw himself staring out from the front page.

Triple Tragedy! The black headline didn't so much blare as shout at the top of the *Gazette*'s voice. Jack had spoken to the young reporter who looked as if he'd just left school, and, from the questions he'd asked, probably just had.

He read the story:

Levenford was rocked this week by three separate tragedies which claimed the lives of five people in four days.

On Monday, elderly Marta Herkik, a former bakery worker and amateur astrologer was found bludgeoned to death in her third-floor home in River Street.

A day later, nine-month-old baby Timothy Doyle was abducted while he slept in his pram on a tenth-floor balcony in Latta Court on Towpath Way.

And last night a fire claimed a father and three children in Murroch Street.

The town was in a state of shock at the death toll. Provost Stanley Moor said: 'I'm stunned. It is a tragedy.'

Jack smiled and read on. The young reporter managed to get as much shock, horror and drama into the story as he could. To a certain extent, it was no exaggeration, although as yet, Jack had seen no evidence of the townsfolk rocking and reeling. The young reporter had attributed Jack with a couple of words he hadn't quite said, but not enough to change the meaning. Police were investigating. The *Gazette* said they were working round the clock, which was fair enough. The picture of him had been one of the press office send-outs when he transferred from the city back to his home town three months before. It made him look five years older, and his hair was shorter. The caption read: *Inspector John Fallon . . . leading the murder hunt.*

The story went into the kind of detail small-town newspapers revelled in. Jack knew, before he even turned to it, that the back page would be a solid block of births, deaths and marriages. The police court section would be filled with dross, like drunks having a pee in public, drunks being locked up or being incapable, and drunks breaching the peace. Jack learned nothing new.

He flicked through the paper and got to the centre pages which showed some blurry photographs of the local theatre group strutting the boards, when his eye caught a heading and he began to read.

Cairn House: A History of Violence. The by-line named Blair Bryden, the newspaper editor. He'd been in the class above Jack at school, and they'd played football together in their teens. Jack had spoken to him several times since he'd come back to work. Blair was smart, and he knew his town. Jack read on:

History has repeated itself in Levenford's oldest known building, with the brutal death of Marta Herkik.

Older readers will remember a similar tragedy in 1965 when the body of a young man was discovered in a back room on the third floor of Cairn House. This was part of the apartment where Marta Herkik had lived for the past fourteen years, following the death of her brother Sandor, the well-known cobbler.

A mystery still surrounds the death of Neil Hopkirk, who had been missing for three months in the summer of '65. He was later discovered bound and gagged under the sink. Police at the time said he had died of starvation and thirst, although he too had been badly beaten and also sexually assaulted.

But even that was not the first tragedy of Cairn House, which records show was built in 1462, about the time of the extension to the Burgh Charter, and partially rebuilt in the eighteenth century, adding the upper storeys. The building was the original Tollbooth in town, where prisoners were jailed pending and after trial. Those prisoners who were guilty were hanged from a gibbet attached to its east gable wall, and records show sixteen such hangings in 1532 alone. After reconstruction, the house became church property for

89

two decades, until the minister, the Rev Andrew Scally, hanged himself from a beam . . . again on the third floor, in 1807. Three decades later, a bolt of lightning struck the chimney stack, which fell through the roof and crushed to death council leader Provost Thomas Latta and a seamstress who lived in a room at the rear of the building.

After World War I young officer Wallace MacNicol was found shot to death in the same room. Gazette *records show that he died of six bullet wounds in his head. This caused intense speculation, and the mystery of how he was able to shoot himself so many times – the gun was found in his hand, and the room was locked from the inside – was never solved.*

In 1948, another clergyman, the Rev Alistair Conn, who was visiting a young sick girl in Cairn House, fell to his death after crashing through a sash window into River Street. The girl, whose family later left Levenford, was never able to explain fully what had happened.

Now, the death toll of Cairn House continues. Professor Andrew Toye, head of the Department of Paranormal Studies at Glasgow University, said: 'These things could very well be coincidences. Some buildings do gather unfortunate reputations over the years. One wouldn't like to volunteer an explanation without more evidence.'

The story ran on for a few more paragraphs, and Jack smiled at Blair Bryden's quotes from Andy Toye, whom Jack knew from his law studies at the university. He had even considered calling on the professor himself, to get some hint of what might have taken place at Cairn House before the old woman died. He read on and something else caught his attention. It was a few simple paragraphs about a young girl who had foretold the fire at Murroch Street.

Jack raised his eyebrows and sipped his coffee slowly as he read the account of the librarian who had been reading tea leaves at a party. One of the guests, the paper said, claimed she had gone into some kind of seizure and then told another woman to get home because her house was on fire. It had turned out to be true. The girl named in the story had refused to comment on the matter. Jack smiled again. There was always somebody trying to make a few pennies, even out of tragedy.

He closed the paper, finished his coffee and left some coins under the saucer rim. The bell clanged again as he went out and turned into River Street.

8

As Jack Fallon walked out of the coffee shop down the lane, Lorna Breck was on her lunch break from the children's library. The library stood on the corner of Strathleven Street and had been built at the turn of the century with money from Andrew Carnegie's foundation. The children's section was half a landing up from the basement stack rooms, a dungeon of a place unlike the bright and well-lit extension that had been built upstairs for adults. Lorna thought they should have added something for the children, but instead, they had to line up by the wrought-iron gate at four o'clock until she came with the big bunch of keys to unlock the heavy old thing and let them down the narrow stone steps in single file.

There was atmosphere in the old place, but it was musty and claustrophobic. She had persuaded Keith Conran, her boss, to clear out a small store for the children to use as a reading room. The negotiations for that little improvement had taken months, but she had eventually won. Her next fight was to get a fire door somewhere. The little children's library was a deathtrap, with only one narrow door leading out of it. Lorna kept a big extinguisher next to her desk just in case.

It was two days since her terrifying experience at Gemma's party. The memory of it hung around her like the big black clouds now piling in from the west, heavy and sombre. She couldn't explain what had happened, and that frightened her. She could recollect nothing of what she'd said or done when she'd thrown the fit, as Cathy had described it, or whatever it was she'd had. She'd just opened her eyes with a terrible feeling of dread and an awful feeling of certainty.

It was only afterwards that Gemma and Cathy had told her what she'd said. She recalled nothing. She'd read about things like that. It could mean anything. What scared her was that it might be the signs of a brain tumour, and that scared her a *lot*.

Lorna's mother had read tea leaves at family parties and she had picked it up as she went along. She knew there was nothing in it, except that sometimes when she looked at the brown patterns, she got a little tickle of feeling, nothing more than a *shade*. It was fun. Or it had been. She had never, not *ever*, had any real sensation of prescience.

Under her sleeve, the strange blister itched. The swelling had died down within hours, leaving a tea-stain mark along her forearm. The downy hairs there were still curled, looking as though they'd been scorched. She couldn't remember any sensation of pain, no matter how she tried.

The story in the newspaper made her cringe with embarrassment. Keith, known to all the children as Conran the librarian, had asked her about it and she had avoided a direct answer. Some of the other girls who worked in the adult library tried to persuade her to read their palms and she'd abruptly refused. The thought of another episode made her recoil.

Lorna stopped outside the grocer's shop by the bakery, which at one time had been the cobbler's business run by old Hungry Sandy, Marta Herkik's brother. She put her bag down on the ground while she counted the money in her purse. There was a skirt in Peggy Mason's shop which she'd had her eye on for two weeks and she was hoping it had been reduced, as many of Peggy's clothes were after they'd hung on the lines for a while. As she bent over the opened purse the numbness flowed over her.

It was as if she'd slid without a sound, without a ripple, into a cold pool. The noise of the traffic in the street and the people passing by, the normal busy sounds of River Street just after noontime, faded away slowly, as if somebody had closed a door on them, leaving her inside a little personal bubble of space.

A high-pitched whine, like a summer insect, tickled deep inside her ears, above the faint sound of blood pounding. Lorna felt her hand slowly clench. The snap-clip of her purse closed over with the sound of a dull footfall. A bus passed by on the street, its engine a deep, almost inaudible hum. Somebody walked in front of her and looked at her, the passer-by a pale ghost moving with snail-like speed, like a body drifting in water.

The whine in her ears became a buzz and underneath it Lorna heard the whispering-chatter. It sounded at first like starlings on

93

a roof, the way they gather in flocks, whirring in black constellations in the air before settling to argue amongst themselves. She turned to the left, so slowly it took an age. The chattering got louder, like words which she could not make out. The numbness spread down her arms and rippled over her ribs. She turned and saw herself reflected back from the grocer's window. Somebody had put up a small blackboard offering prices of apples. Lorna could see her face, a pale imitation, wraithlike inside the glass. Her mouth was half-open, her eyes wide. She tried to think and the thought would not come. She felt as if she was wading through treacle.

Something spoke inside her head.

'I see you.'

'What?' she tried to say. All she heard was a rumble deep in her chest.

'Eyes to see. Ears to hear.' The voice was the scratch of fingernails on rough stone.

Lorna blinked. Inside the glass, her reflection did the same, a slow puzzled blink that looked sleepy in shady mirroring.

She saw her mouth open further. It was like watching someone from inside a dream. Something passed by on the street behind her and she saw the movement, then it was blotted out by a shadow in the blackboard, billowing in like a cloud. The glass wavered, or seemed to, and her reflection winked out. The chittering had faded inside her head, dwindled to a scratchy rustle. She dreamily felt as though she'd stepped out of the world, out of her *self* for a moment.

The blackboard disappeared in rippling shadow, like the surface of a river pool deep in a forest. The oscillations jarred, hardened and then with a weird, dizzying *twist* they stopped and Lorna saw

a street lamp. Orange light fuzzed by a hard frost. She shivered, felt the cold. Someone was walking down a narrow alley. The sound of heels on flagstones. She recognised the place, or thought she did. At least it looked familiar. As she turned her head, the scene swung with the movement, a cinematic pan. The orange light faded away. Up above a window opened and a faint voice, unintelligible behind a clatter of pots and pans, called out. The footsteps came closer. Lorna heard the whimper of a baby

94

crying, and in the waking dream, she turned, though she knew no muscle on her body moved. She was seeing this with her *mind*. A figure came walking towards her, passed by, hidden by shadows. A pale face turned to look at her. It was a girl, a young woman. In her arms, a baby held tight, close to her shoulder. Lorna saw a look of surprise, maybe curiosity, then the woman was gone.

A feeling of apprehension welled up inside her, bubbling like tar.

Something was going to happen. She *knew* it. Something *bad*.

The woman moved off along the alley, away from the light, turned beyond the hard stone corner of a building. From up above, Lorna heard a rough scraping sound, a scuttling noise, like stones being rubbed together. She raised her head and the scene swung dizzily. Up on the wall, a shadow flicked with spidery speed, disappeared into a deeper shadow. The noise continued, an abrasive scrabble that continued into the shadow. It reached the corner, elongated and then wriggled round and out of sight.

The anxiety twisted, tightened to sudden dread.

Lorna went down the alley, seeing the buildings tilt with the odd *mental* movement, reached the corner, turned it. . . .

And the shadow came down from the wall.

She heard herself scream, yet there was no sound. The woman was knocked to the ground by something that shot out from the shadow and struck her such a blow that she simply flopped. A dark shaped reached and grabbed. There was a jumble of movement and then a piercing cry, mirrored by an even higher screech. The woman scrambled to her feet, her screech of terror and anger reverberating from the narrow walls of the alley. She ran at the shadow. Something reached out again and smashed into the side of her face. She dropped like a stone, but this time she did not get up again. A dark pool quickly spread out from under her head, casting no reflection. The shadow shrank back into the wall, oozed into deeper shade and seemed to flow upwards in a liquid wriggle.

In a flickering moment, Lorna heard the sound of a baby crying, far above her head. She tried to look but she could see nothing. Her eyes were drawn back down to the alley. The black bundle huddled on the ground. Just beyond it, the pool was widening on the frosted ground, oozing far enough now to catch the orange light of the next street lamp. In the numb bubble of observation, Lorna's eyes looked up again. The shadow was climbing quickly, again with that spidery speed. It swerved away from the edge of a window from which light described a solid rectangle, then continued upwards. It turned and Lorna got the impression of eyes looking at her from within the oily darkness. She felt her whole being shrink back and as she did, the thick, gloomy shape simply peeled off the wall above her. Something that looked like a head turned and two eyes caught the orange light. They whirled, altering the colour to something that looked sick and suppurating. Lorna's fear screeched inside her, a wire wound up to breaking point. The scuttling sound came louder. Something small and white flopped inside the shade, like a broken doll. Another something else, wet and warm, splattered close by her with a small smacking sound. She felt a big scream try to force itself out of her throat, then realised with utter panic that no sound would come.

The thing, the shade, shadow, whatever it was, came down the wall, impossibly fast, jointed yet liquid. It hit the ground, bounced and leapt towards her. A face from a nightmare, worse than *any* nightmare, came looming up at her. A mouth opened and black spiked teeth glistened wetly.

Such was Lorna's terror that the scream building up behind her locked throat broke through in a sudden explosion of noise. The bubble of numb horror burst around her and the shadowed thing winked out in an instant. The scream went on and on and on.

The noise came from so close that Jack almost stumbled off the pavement as he walked quickly towards the street corner. It was high-pitched enough to vibrate the thick glass of the grocer's display window.

It happened just as he was almost past the fruit shop, like an air-raid siren let off only inches from his ear, but higher than that, the sound of a stone saw cutting brick. As he jerked round, a slight girl came wheeling towards him, her face drained so white she looked like a corpse, except for the wide open mouth and the incredible noise that came out of it. She barged into him, half falling, eyes gaping and so startlingly grey they seemed blind. Her mouth was stretched wide enough for him to have counted her teeth if there had been time. She stumbled and began to fall. Jack reflexively reached and caught her, twisting himself to make sure she didn't sprawl to the ground, and in the same moment knocked an old woman's trolley to the pavement.

The girl's scream stopped abruptly. Her face went completely slack and she sagged into him like a puppet with cut strings. All the strength just went from her and her knees buckled. Jack got a hand under her armpit and kept her upright, head swinging this way and that, looking for a place to let the girl sit, or lie down. The old woman whose trolley had been kicked to the far edge of the pavement retrieved a fallen turnip and a cabbage which had been inadvertently dribbled twenty feet down the road and then back again by passing feet, came up to him and squinted through rheumy eyes.

'You want to watch where you're going, son,' she said indignantly, then added: 'I hope your girl gets better.'

Jack nodded, putting an apology into the short movement.

'Take her into the shop, son. They'll give her a glass of water.'

The girl was shivering against him, as if she was racked by a fever, but against him she felt cold. He braced himself, swung her up with an easy movement and elbowed his way past the gawpers into the shop. The door swung back and he carried her straight past the queue of people waiting with baskets of fruit and vegetables, all staring with the blank curiosity of people who know something has happened that they've missed.

A woman behind the counter asked if she could help him. Jack said he needed a glass of water and a phone. He didn't stop, but continued through to the back of the shop. As expected, he found a sink cluttered with several cups. One or two of them were clean.

There was a seat in the corner. Jack was considering whether to try to balance the girl on it when the blonde woman came through the narrow door.

'What's the matter?' she asked brusquely.

'I don't know. Something wrong with this girl.'

'What? She faint or something?'

'Looks like it. Can you get a cup of water?'

The woman bustled to the sink, letting the door swing behind her. It was her busy hour and it looked as if she could have done

97

without the interruption, but she rinsed a glass quickly, let the water run for a while to let it get cold and turned towards Jack.

'Well, put the wee thing down then,' she said, her voice softening down. 'Oh my, would you look at her colour. Is she expecting?'

Jack shrugged. 'Damned if I know. I never met her before.'

The shopkeeper gave him a quizzical look and Jack eased the girl down to the seat. She was beginning to come round a little, but her eyes still looked blind and dreamy, as if she was coming out of an anaesthetic.

She gave a little hiccup and some colour came back into her cheeks. The woman handed Jack the glass and he held it up to the girl's lips.

'Here,' he said. 'Take a drop.'

He tilted the glass and let some water dribble between her slack lips. Some dripped onto the girl's lap, but enough got into her mouth. The lips twitched and the girl's throat worked spasmodically as she swallowed, then coughed. She came awake almost immediately, eyes blinking and watery, looking around, obviously bewildered.

'Where . . . ?' she started to say.

'It's alright, dear. You've just taken a bad turn. You'll be fine,' the shopkeeper said. Satisfied that this was not a life and death emergency, she gave the girl a smile, turned, and pushed her way back into the shop.

Jack held up the glass and the girl took another drink, this time deliberately. He kept tilting it as she demanded more and continued until she'd finished the lot. Her colour was coming back rapidly.

'What happened?' she asked, rubbing her eyes.

'I don't know. You let out a scream that would wake the dead and started to fall. I managed to catch you before you took a dive for the pavement. I had to carry you in here. Are you on any kind of pills?'

'No,' the girl said. She was looking down, eyebrows knotted in concentration. She still hadn't looked at Jack.

'I don't know . . . ' she started to say, paused, then changed direction. 'Something happened. I saw something.'

'Like what?' Jack didn't have a clue what she was talking about.

'It was in the dark. Something coming.' Her brows knit further, then she shook her head. 'Oh, I don't know. I can't remember. I thought I saw an awful thing and it gave me a fright.'

'You sure you're not on something?'

'No, I'm sure,' she said quickly and for the first time she raised her eyes. They were still the startling metallic grey they had been outside the shop, but now they held expression. As soon as she looked at Jack she flinched back and let out a small gasp. Her hand jerked up towards her face.

'What's wrong?' he asked immediately.

The girl was staring at him. Her eyes were huge, winter pools in a stormy sea. Her mouth opened slowly. She looked terrified.

'Are you going to faint again?' he asked.

She shook her head dumbly, and her mouth closed again. Her eyes were scanning him as if searching for something. She looked absolutely horrified, or terrified, though he couldn't decide which. For a second he returned her gaze. Then she seemed to snap out of it.

'I'm sorry,' she said. 'I thought I. . . .' She stopped again. Jack wondered if she ever finished a sentence. 'I don't know what I thought. Oh Christ, I don't know what's happening.'

'Do you want me to call a doctor? I can take you to the health centre if you like.'

'No thanks. I'll be fine.'

'You don't look that fine to me. Where do you stay?'

'Clydeshore Avenue, across the bridge,' Lorna said. 'But I have to get back to work.'

'And there's that?' he insisted.

'The library. Just round at Strathleven.'

'You sure you'll be alright?'

The girl nodded. She brought both hands up in front of her face and breathed in deeply, still looking at Jack over the tips of her fingers. He didn't know whether it was him or not, but the way she'd looked at him at first made him feel he must have developed some gross disfigurement, like leprosy. Now she looked at him with something that looked very like fear.

'Don't worry,' he said. 'I'm not going to hurt you. I'm a policeman.'

99

Lorna nodded. 'I know. It's not that. It's. . . .' She left another sentence hanging, then seemed to collect herself. 'Look. I have to go now.'

She got to her feet, stumbling a little. Jack reached out a hand and grabbed hers. As he did she jerked as if she'd been given a heavy jolt and her face snapped round towards him. Her big eyes had gone blind again, but this time they looked as if they were staring right inside him. She made another strangled little sound in her throat and pulled her hand away. As the contact broke, Jack felt a tiny physical *wrench*.

She brushed past him, murmuring her thanks, pushed her way out through the door, then past the crowd of people waiting to buy vegetables and out into the street. Jack stood for a moment, slack-jawed, wondering what on earth that had all been about. He followed her through, more slowly, his face a picture of puzzlement. By the time he got to the pavement she was gone. He looked over the heads of the passers-by, quite easily because of his height, but there was no sign of her. He hadn't even asked the girl's name. All he could really recall about her were those fathomless grey eyes and the look of fear in them when she'd glanced up at him. Jack was sure he didn't look that scary. He shrugged and set off along River Street.

Robbie Cattanach had said he'd meet him in Mac's Bar, which was a hole of a place as far as comfort was concerned and rough and ready as far as the regulars went, but it was close by and warm enough and the Guinness was poured slowly and allowed to stand awhile before Peter Hollinger, whose brother used to run the bar in Arden a few miles down the road, would set it down before a paying customer.

The young pathologist was not in sight when Jack pushed his way through the crowd of lunchtime drinkers. There were a couple of teenagers playing darts in the corner. Jack recognised the set of their shoulders and their shocks of sandy hair – members of the ever expanding Buist clan. One of them nodded to Jack, and the big man gave him a wink. The younger generations were settling down, he thought, remembering his father with a warm and slightly painful glow.

He ordered a pint and leaned his elbow on the bar, making sure he missed a puddle of beer. Hollinger, a bear of a man who ran a civilised, if occasionally boisterous bar – aided by his old shillelagh which hung beside the bottles on the gantry – let the black stout pour slow as tar.

Somebody came up behind Jack and clapped him on the shoulder. He turned, expecting to see Robbie Cattanach.

'Well, fan my brow if it isn't Black Jack Shelack.'

Mickey Haggerty made an exaggerated brow-fanning motion. He stuck his hand out and gave Jack a crushing handshake that was in complete contrast to the small man's wiry frame.

'How's it hanging, Jake? Long time gone blind.'

Jack remembered from childhood, and broke into a delighted grin. 'Yeah. Long time no see right enough, Mickey. How's yourself?'

'Fair to bloody awful, but we've not died a winter yet. Here,' – indicating the pint Peter Hollinger was laying down with magnificent reverence on the bar – 'let me get that.'

'Best offer I've had in a wheen of days,' Jack said, reverting back to his childhood slang. 'So, Apache Mick. You're getting more like Jack Palance every time I see you.'

'That's because I've had a hard life. I've a face that's worn out three bodies. Not like you fellas who get cushy jobs and get your names in the papers. The last time I got that I was up for drunk and incapable. I admitted I was drunk, but I've never been incapable. There's a dozen women of this fair town would swear to that, but they huckled me for it anyway. You wouldn't do that, Jake, would you?'

'Not if I was drinking with you. I carried you home often enough as I recall.'

'That's 'cause I'm just a wee *toaty* fella,' Mickey agreed amiably. Jack took a deep swallow of his beer, knowing he shouldn't but not caring much of a damn, and felt a warm glow from his chance meeting with a friend from the old days.

'Must be a couple of years since you were last in here,' Mickey ventured.

'Yeah. About that,' Jack agreed. 'It hasn't changed much.'

Mickey winked. He'd a cheerful, well-used face with prominent cheeks and a shock of boyish fair hair.

'Listen, I was sorry to hear about your wife, and all that. And your girl. Fucking awful.'

101

Jack nodded, his face placid. He was getting used to this by now. 'Aye, sure was.'

The two of them studied their pints for a moment of awkward silence, then Mickey, irrepressible at any time, chimed in.

'Anyway, it's good to see you, Commanche, no matter what. Life goes on, eh?'

Jack looked at him and felt a reluctant grin force its way across his face. Life goes on. Yes, he thought, sometimes it does. Sometimes it stops dead and sometimes going on is the hardest thing to do.

'So you're looking for the nutter that killed the old biddy?'

'Yeah. Not an easy one.'

'Well, I hope you catch the bastard. Nice old soul she was. My mother used to go to her a few years back. She was spot on. Told her she was coming into money, and the next week she took the roll-up at the bingo and came out with two grand. Bought me a new suit, in case I did something stupid and got married, but I pawned it and lost the money on a horse.'

Jack laughed for the first time that day. It was typical of Mickey. He'd been an engineer on merchant navy boats for years, travelling round the world, bringing home exotic tales to tell in Mac's Bar, and then he'd quit travelling. Now he drove a rubbish dump truck, a position he claimed was ideally suited to him because it came with absolutely no authority whatsoever, allowed him to take a day off fishing whenever he liked, and paid enough to get him from one weekend to the other most times. He was the most irresponsible, but probably the most genuine fellow Jack knew. He had two real hobbies. He played snooker to almost professional level, but not seriously enough to want to make the big time, with the added responsibility that would bring, and an abiding interest, for some reason, in American Indian culture. He'd been like that ever since he was a kid in Castlebank School, and nothing had changed.

'So what's the score with old Marta then? They say she was dead for a few days.'

'Yes. A week past Saturday.'

Mickey frowned.

'That was a bummer of a night. I nearly got drowned on River Street coming out of here. Tide was backed up and coming up the pends from Quay Street. You could have moored boats on the pavement. I'd a fair drink in me, 'cause I'd just won a double on two horses at Ayr. Blew the lot. It was too heavy to carry home.'

'You didn't see anything on your way home?' Jack asked casually.

'What's this, the third degree?'

'Save me taking you in for questioning,' Jack shot back, and Mickey laughed.

'Well, I saw two young fellas on bikes come up on the pavement. Graham Friel's boy was one of them. I remember he nearly couped me off my feet. The water was too deep round at the corner to get through. Looked as if they were on powerboats by the wash they were setting up.'

Mickey closed his eyes, thinking. 'I got a light off a bloke. Shuggy Thomson. He'd a fair skinful in him. Could hardly walk. The buses were diverted up College Street, so I had to go along to the bridge, and it was bloody freezing.'

He paused for a moment, frowning.

'Oh, here. Now I remember. Somebody passed by just at the old shoe shop. I can't remember the man's name, but he's a good punter. He was in the bookie's putting bets on the same day as me. Irish, I think. He's had a bad couple of hits on the horses, I can tell you that, but he keeps on putting the money down.'

Mickey stopped again. 'I crossed the road. Amazing what you can remember when you try hard. I went down Brewery Lane for a pee. That was murder, I can tell you. The wind was blowing a gale, and if you pee into the wind, you only get your own back.'

Jack looked at him, puzzled, and a second later he caught Mickey's drift and laughed again.

'That doesn't make me a suspect, does it?' Mickey asked, trying to keep his face straight, but unable to conceal the mischief in his eyes.

'Not yet. But I'll need a witness who saw you at home.'

'That might be difficult, for I never got home. I stayed with a lady. Her man's working on the rigs and isn't due back for two months, and I'm sure as hell not giving her name, and don't you be telling my sister either.'

Jack grinned again, but stopped when Mickey's brow drew down again in that furrow of concentration.

'Wait a minute. When I came up the lane I bumped into somebody. He was coming in the opposite direction, heading down River Street. Who was it now?' He took his chin between finger and thumb.

'I know. It was yon minister, Simpson. You know the man. Big in the masons. His mug is never out of the papers. Always looks as if he's eating shit, he's that torn-faced.'

'Can't say I do,' Jack said.

'Aye. He was scooting along the road in a big rush.' Mickey stopped again. 'Hold on. I stood and watched him. He never even said sorry for nearly knocking me on the face. He went down River Street and turned into Boat Pend.'

Suddenly Jack was all attention.

'You sure? That was on the Saturday night?'

'Dead sure. I was pissed, but I never forget. You never know when you'll need an alibi. It was definitely him. I remember thinking what a toffee-nosed bastard he was, and a bigot besides, but he never even looked the road I was on. Man of God? He would have left me lying in the gutter unless I was showing my left leg.'

'And this other man. The one from the betting shop. Did he go anywhere near there?'

'He was heading that way, but I couldn't be sure. I'll remember his name in a while.'

He took a big swallow of his drink, finished his beer and set the empty glass down on the bar. Jack offered him a refill, but Mickey shook his head.

'Driving all day. But if you're back in tonight, I'll take all you're prepared to buy.'

He reached up and clapped Jack on the shoulder. 'Hope you catch the bastard, Jake. Kick the shite out of them when you do.'

Jack said he'd think about it. He'd been thinking about it for the past few days. By the time he finished his own beer, Robbie Cattanach hadn't appeared. Jack toyed with the idea of another, then decided against it. What Mickey had told him was worth following up. He left Mac's Bar, turned the corner at Market Street, and headed up to the station.

Superintendent Ronald Cowie had left a message for him to come straight up to his office. The senior officer was sitting behind his desk and did not look up as Jack came in. Jack ignored the lack of welcome and sat himself down on a chair on the near side of the desk.

'I was hoping for a progress report,' Cowie said.

'No progress so far,' Jack replied. 'You've got everything I have.'

'And that's not very much.'

'You're right,' Jack agreed, keeping his voice steady, refusing to rise to it.

Cowie turned in his swivel seat and swung back again with a handful of newspaper clippings.

'One killing and one abduction. It's all over the front pages. It's been nearly a week and we've nothing to show for it.'

'These things take time,' Jack said. 'What we have are two separate incidents in different parts of the town. One a murder, and the other a possible murder. We have no serious witnesses. We've rounded up every peeping Tom and flasher. We've take two hundred fingerprints. We've had TV and newspaper appeals, and we've been round a thousand doors asking questions. We just have to keep on going. Something will show and then we can move.'

'I don't see any sign of progress,' Cowie said, running a paperknife between his fingers, trying to look like a hard man, which Jack knew he wasn't.

'There's not much, but I have a couple of things I have to check out.'

'And what's that?'

'Well, I've got one name of somebody seen in the area on the night in question, and I'm hoping for another. They don't sound like likely suspects, but if they were close to the scene, they might have something to tell me.'

'Who's the name?'

'A man called Simpson. He's a minister.'

'What, Bill Simpson? From Castlebank Church?'

'That's the man.'

'He's a friend of mine. A very good friend.'

Jack didn't doubt it. As soon as Mickey Haggerty had mentioned the masons, that connection had been an odds-on-certainty.

'He's also a church representative on the council. He's very close to the police committee. Do you really think we should bother him?'

Jack waved to the pile of press cuttings.

'I'll bother anybody if it gets me a result.'

'Well, I want you to take it very easy with Bill Simpson.'

'I'll try to get the handshake right,' Jack said wearily.

'What's that?'

'You heard.'

'I heard insubordination, that's what I heard.'

'No you didn't. You asked for a progress report. I gave you what I have. I'm keeping you abreast of the situation, which isn't very much at the moment.'

'I could have you taken off both of these cases, Fallon. Just like *that*,' Cowie said, snapping his fingers.

Jack stood up, and put his hands on the table. His black hair had fallen down over his brow. He towered over the seated man.

'Listen, Superintendent. You've not got your arse in Angus McNicol's seat just yet. I don't give a flying fuck if you can take me off this or not, but I don't think our boss would like it.'

'I should have been in charge right from the start,' Cowie said angrily.

'And have you wondered why you weren't?'

'You. . . .' Cowie started to raise his voice. 'Get out of my office, or I'll put you on report.'

'Yes. You do that. And let me get on with my job.' Jack gave the man a hard and utterly contemptuous look, then turned and stalked through the doorway, slamming the door behind him.

Despite what he'd said to his immediate superior, Jack had already decided to take it easy with Simpson. He went back down to Cairn House with John McColl and they knocked on all the doors again, asking the neighbours more questions. The young couple who lived directly below Marta Herkik's flat were quite definite. There had been noises on the Saturday night, around ten o'clock. They'd been watching a video at the time, a space movie about an alien. Jack recalled what Robbie Cattanach had said, and thought it was appropriate. It was definitely the Saturday night, because that was the only day either of them, both working in offices in Glasgow, ever got the chance to hire movie cassettes from the video shop. The girl, a plump, but pleasant-faced young woman – they'd been married for only three months – had gone to bed halfway through the film because she'd found it too scary and too gruesome. She had first heard the bumping noises from upstairs, but they'd soon stopped. There had been people on the outside stairs earlier on in the night, but that wasn't unusual. Marta Herkik often had visitors who came to get their fortunes told, but nobody had seen anyone on the stairs.

All of the neighbours told the same story, except for the lower dwellers, who hadn't heard the noises in Marta's rooms. None of them had had any visitors themselves that night. Only one had gone out, to pick up a Chinese meal from the takeaway on the far side of the bridge, but that was just after seven in the evening.

Jack left the building again, thinking. If the minister *had* gone down Boat Pend, there were few other places he could have been heading for. The alley went right down to the old quayside, but it was unlikely he'd be going there, for the whole of the harbour had been under a foot of water, thanks to the high tide and the backing gale sweeping up from the firth. There were no other houses easily accessible from the covered alley. There was a chandler's business attached to a fishing tackle shop, and the old bakery further along the quayside which was still operating, but wouldn't have opened until five in the morning. There was also the Castlegate Bar, a water-rat dive where no minister would have been seen dead.

No, he thought, it *was* possible that Simpson had been heading up the stairs to the old woman's flat.

And if he had, why had he, a man of God, been visiting a medium?

Despite the possibility, it didn't seem likely.

Jack picked up his car from behind the newsagent's shop and drove to the east side of town where the old buildings, sandstone tenements and a few detached houses, gave onto a more modern housing estate. The basalt rock where Levenford's hill fort had perched since before the pyramids were built, loomed against the darkening skyline as evening fell swiftly. The lights up on the ramparts were haloed yellow in the hard frost thickening the air.

William Simpson's wife Betty was small and silver-haired,

though Jack guessed she was a few years younger than she looked. When he introduced himself an odd, tight expression flickered on her face and then was gone. She invited him in and led him to the living room at the back of the manse. She poured him tea from a small china pot, a bird-like woman making fluttering motions. The cup rattled a little on the saucer when she handed it over to him. She did not appear overly nervous, but she gave Jack the impression of a woman with something on her mind.

'It's just routine,' Jack said encouragingly. 'I was hoping to speak to your husband.'

'What about?'

'Oh, I'm hoping he can help me. I'm counting on the fact that he's got a good memory. I'm in charge of the investigation into the death of Mrs Herkik. You'll probably have read about it.'

The minister's wife turned her lips down. 'The psychic. I don't agree with dabbling in that kind of thing,' she said.

'Me neither,' Jack agreed, quite untruthfully. He had no thoughts one way or the other on the issue. Spiritualism and fortune-telling was all mumbo jumbo to him, but then even established churches fell into that category. 'But I have to investigate, and I'm hoping your husband can help me there.'

'You think he had something to do with it?'

'Oh, no. It's just that somebody mentioned he might have been in the vicinity at the time.'

The woman frowned and shook her head, as if any connection between a minister and a medium was out of the question.

'When was that?'

'A week past Saturday.'

'No. Not possible,' Mrs Simpson said immediately. 'William always does his sermon after dinner, then he works in his darkroom most of the evening. Never comes out until late.'

'You mean he wasn't even out of the house?'

'Not the house. His darkroom's in the church basement.'

'I see,' Jack said agreeably.

'But you can ask him yourself,' the woman said, taking a small sip of tea. 'He's there now. He'll be in for his dinner any minute.'

Jack said that would be fine. Betty Simpson poured another cup for each of them into small china cups and sipped delicately, looking at the policeman over the rim. Upstairs, Jack heard footsteps, then louder ones on the stairs he'd passed on his way to the living room. The door opened. He'd expected the minister, but it was a girl of seventeen or so, taller than her mother. She had dark, plain glasses and frizzy hair. She looked at Jack curiously.

'When's dinner?' she asked. 'I've got a study group tonight.'

'Another half hour, Fiona. We're just waiting for your father.'

The girl nodded noncommittally and went out of the room again. He could hear her moving about in what he took to be the kitchen. Betty Simpson looked at the clock on the wall, checked the time against her watch, then called for her daughter again. The girl leaned into the room a few moments later.

'Could you give your father a knock? He's in his darkroom.'

Fiona pulled a face. Jack caught the expression and it struck him this was not a completely loving household, but that could have been said for half the homes he visited in the course of his work.

'Always pottering about down there. He's in the camera club,' she said, then added with a hint of dryness in her voice: 'as well as a few other things. He could have used the basement here, but he said the boiler room was much better for developing. I suppose it keeps him out from under my feet.'

They talked on for a few minutes more when a piercing scream launched Jack out of his seat. It was the second one he'd heard that day. This one was just as shattering as the first. He was at the door before he even turned to look at the woman.

Her face had gone ashen. She was sitting stock-still, with both hands clenched in front of her. Her eyes were fixed and glittering behind the half-moon glasses that had slid halfway down her nose, and they gave her the look of someone who knew something she had feared had just become a reality.

'Oh my God, what's he done to her?' she said through gritted teeth. Jack went through the doorway, almost knocking a coatstand over in the hallway. The scream continued, sharp as glass. He was round the side of the house when it stopped suddenly, then came back in a series of high-pitched barks, the kind of noise a fox makes when it is trapped in a den while the terriers growl and snap outside.

109

He ran past the wrought-iron gate before he realised where the sound was coming from. He stopped himself in mid-stride by grabbing one of the bars and swung himself around. Betty Simpson was coming out of the house, her small frame outlined by the light in the hallway. Both hands were now clamped up at her face. Jack skittered down the stairs, shouldered the door open and found himself in the basement under the church. The boiler threw off a lot of heat as it rumbled and gurgled in the corner. Off to the left, beyond the stack of organ pipes, a door in the wall lay open. The screeching cries came from there. He made it in three steps, went straight in and saw William Simpson hanging from a beam, his toes only six inches from the floor.

Fiona Simpson was backed up against the wall. Her eyes were bulging and pale behind the thick glasses. Her mouth was open so wide her jaw looked as if it had sprung out of the hinges. Jack moved forward, reached a hand up to the man's swollen face and felt under the chin for a pulse. There was nothing. The eyes were staring and the tongue lolled, almost black. The body was quite warm. He turned to the girl, blocking off the sight of her father dangling from the low ceiling. He tried to take a hold of her hand, but she snatched it away and then, quite surprisingly, started beating at him with both fists. The blows were flabby and ineffectual. Jack ignored them, and simply enfolded her in his arms, and all the jerking life went out of her. She sagged against him, her whole body shaking and then her knees gave way. Again, for the second time that day, Jack lifted a girl off her feet and walked. He managed to carry her out of the room, hooking the door shut with a foot, and then to the outside door and up the stairs. Betty Simpson was hovering at the gate.

'What's happened? What has he *done*?'

'Back to the house,' Jack said, brushing past her, the girl still flopped in his arms.

'But . . .' the woman started to say.

'Come on now. Do as I say. Get back to the house. *Now!*' he shouted, more loudly and harshly than he should have. He carried the girl to the manse, shouldered the door open again, walked straight into the living room and laid her down on the chintzy sofa. She flopped awkwardly, skirt rucked up over heavy hockey-playing thighs. He didn't notice. Instead, he turned to the girl's mother, who hovered in the doorway.

'Make sure she's alright. I have to use the phone.'

'But what's happened?' the woman protested again.

'I don't know yet. Just tend to the girl. I'll get the rest.'

He gently eased her back into the living room. Found the phone in the hallway and made two calls. Went back into the living room and told Betty Simpson to sit down. Then he told her that her husband was dead.

She went stock-still and then lowered herself very slowly onto the chair.

It was hard to tell, but to Jack, the expression that flickered on her face was not one of shock, as he'd have expected, but of relief.

In five minutes the first police car arrived in the driveway of Castlebank Church Manse.

Within an hour the body of William Simpson had been cut down and taken away, after all the photographs had been taken and the cellar checked out by Ralph Slater and his team, who were certainly earning their pay over the past week or so.

Jack spent another two hours talking to Simpson's widow. His daughter was unfit for any questioning. She had remained hysterical for half an hour before lapsing into a state of almost catatonic shock. An hour after that, she'd come out of the stasis and started screaming again. By this time Dr Cuthbert had arrived. He rolled up the girl's sleeve and gave her something which took about forty seconds to work and the girl's eyes rolled upwards and she fell asleep. Betty Simpson said she needed no pills or potions.

Jack Fallon had already been summoned to Superintendent Cowie's office, and he knew why, but he decided to let the man kick his heels for a while. What they'd found in the cellar under the church gave him too much work to do.

111

9

'I don't have to tell you that I don't want a word of this getting out yet,' Jack said to the assembled men in the room just down the corridor from his own small office. 'And that tape stays in the safe. Any bootleg copies and you'll have me to answer to, as well as the Court of Session.'

There was a general muttering. Some of the men turned to look at their colleagues as if protesting their innocence, protesting at the suggestion that they might even consider such a thing.

'We don't know if there *is* a connection, except that we're fairly sure he was seen near the scene of Marta Herkik's murder on the night in question, so I want you to get back round the doors and ask some more questions.'

Ralph Slater was sitting at the back of the room, his doleful face in his hands.

'Right lads, back out into the night, and see if you can bring me something.'

There was more general muttering as they moved out. Jack had managed to borrow four other officers, two men and two women from a neighbouring division, all of whom had worked or lived in Levenford at some time. It made it easier when the police knew the ground. It helped when you were looking for connections.

Jack motioned to Ralph Slater, who was at the tail end of the group leaving the room, then beckoned to John McColl.

'You wait on. There's a couple of things you might want a look at.'

Both men nodded agreeably and followed Jack back to the office on the corner. On the way, John paused. 'The Superintendent's looking for you.'

'I know that. I'm busy.'

'I'd watch him. He's a real bad bastard.'

'Not as bad as me when I make my mind up to it,' Jack responded with a tight smile.

'He could break you, you know. Just a word of warning.'

'I couldn't give a damn. He's as useless as tits on a bull.'

'Just thought I'd put my spoke in,' John said. 'The boys think you're okay, despite the degree.'

John was referring to Jack's accelerated promotion, something that had come almost automatically after he'd gained honours in criminology. The degree had helped in other ways. He'd made a very helpful range of contacts at the university.

'Thanks for the vote of confidence. Tell them I appreciate it. I'll tell them myself when I get the chance.'

He opened the door and let them in before him, then crossed to the television in the corner. A video recorder sat on top of the set.

'Looks like another bummer as far as immediate forensics are concerned,' Ralph said. 'I don't think there's ever been anybody in that room but him. We've not checked the prints, but the ones we have lifted seem to be from the same pair of hands.'

'You can tell that just by looking?'

'Been in the game a long time,' Ralph replied, taking the compliment.

'What did you think of the set-up?'

'Bloody weird. Looks like a right nutter.'

Jack went along with that, but there was more.

When the first police car had arrived at the Manse, Jack had left the young constables with the two women and gone back to double-check the body. Going back down the narrow staircase to Simpson's cellar, he'd had the same sense of *wrongness* that he'd felt in the Herkik house. It was nothing that he could put his finger on, just a feeling that prickled the hairs on the back of his neck and scraped on his nerves like nails on a blackboard. Maybe it was the sum total of many things.

The place had *smelled* like the Herkik murder scene. A mixture of blood and dust. The only difference was, there was no scent of charred flesh. The odour of faeces and urine had hung in the air like a dirty mist, an assault on the nose, and underlying that, a whiff of something rotten.

Simpson was turning slowly on the rope, his head to the side, swollen and turning black, jaw jutting to the left, making his lip pout like a man who's had a stroke. He was naked, apart from a pair of Argyll socks and plain black shoes. His clothes were neatly folded on the desk. Below him, saturated with blood, a pair of small plain panties lay crumpled on the floor beside an equally soaked handkerchief. The man's eyes bulged out from behind a small, pink pair of glasses that looked incongruously childish on the bloated face. One of the lenses was completely gone and through the empty frame Jack could see the dead man's eye socket was a mass of blood. At first glance it looked as if there was no eye at all.

Jack walked around the slowly turning cadaver. The stench was overpowering. There was a mess on the upturned chair and on the threadbare carpet on which it lay. The thick electrical flex had been tied with a simple knot to a screw-in hook which had been driven into the solid wood of the beam above. The noose was a simple hitch loop, not the kind a hangman would have used. As he moved around, Jack saw something pink lying on the floor. He hunkered down, careful to touch nothing.

He peered closer and saw the little fingers splayed out and his heart sank, his mind immediately conjuring up the baby picture Cissie Doyle had given him of her missing baby. He breathed a sigh of relief when he edged closer and saw that it was not a baby's hand. The light above glinted on the smooth plastic of a doll's arm, baby pudgy, its shoulder end red with congealing blood. He drew a deep breath, thankful it had *not* been little Timmy Doyle, though after five days, the hopes of finding the baby alive in any case were fading to zero.

After a moment, he stood up again and continued his slow walk around the hanging man. The desk, apart from the clothes, was completely covered in ten-by-eight black-and-white photographs, all of them showing children, some taken from odd angles. Over against the wall, there was a sink and a draining board bearing flat oblong containers. These two held pictures. Jack could smell the fixer fluid. One glance at the photographs floating in the discoloured liquid told him there was something else very odd about the Reverend William Simpson. He leaned over to have another look. The first picture was very clear, a little girl lying on grass. The second was, at first glimpse, a confusing jumble of lines and shades. He shifted, cocking his head to the side, and then the picture snapped into clarity. It was the same child, taken from a different angle, much closer in. Jack could tell by the position of the left knee, which was slightly raised out from the body. The close-up shot angled between the pale thighs to a glistening dark patch. As soon as the picture flicked into focus, Jack knew the dark patch was blood.

An instant flash of memory hit him like a kick in the belly, and on its heels a sudden surge of almost uncontrollable anger. He turned away from the developing containers, feeling hot bile rise in his throat and the muscles of his stomach clench and unclench. Simpson's one eye glared at him from behind the child's glasses. For an incandescent second he wanted to rip the corpse down and kick it and not stop until there was nothing left. His fists balled his knuckles white, but he pressed down on his anger, turning away, continuing the round.

It was then that he heard the whispering whirr from the filing cabinet directly opposite the hanged man. He moved forward carefully, making sure he stood on nothing, and leaned to the right. The lens of the video camera was like a black eye inside the hood. On the side of the camera, a small red light winked in the dark of the corner.

'Jesus,' Jack breathed. He was about to say something else, but then he realised that if the tape was running, everything that happened in the room would be evidence, faithfully recorded on tape. He thought back to his anger bubbling up and a sick feeling of relief welled up from the pit of his belly that he hadn't hauled the dead man down and kicked the shit out of him. That would have looked very bad in court.

He walked quickly past the blind eye of the lens, a blind eye that was taking everything in, then turned to Simpson. He was now facing straight at the policeman, head jerked to the side, face black, chest matted with blood which had streaked down a protruding belly and tangle in the grey pubic hairs. Between the legs, penis and testicles were grossly swollen, as black as the face was. Tightly wrapped around them was a black electrical cable.

And from the cable dangled the weight of an old pressing iron. It knocked like a pendulum against the dead man's shins, pointing to the ground like a ponderous arrowhead.

As Jack stood staring, footsteps thudded down the stone steps outside the basement. The door banged open and the footfalls,

115

now louder, clattered towards the storeroom. John McColl lowered his head to save banging it on the lintel, came squeezing through the narrow door, then raised himself up to almost his full height.

'Came as quickly as I . . .' he started to say, then saw the naked and bloody apparition dangling from the beam.

'Jesus fucking Christ, Jack,' he said before Jack could stop him. 'What the hell's going on here?'

Jack held a finger up to his lips. He was standing off to the side, away from where the lens was pointing. He jerked a finger in the direction of the camcorder and then made a sliding motion with one finger across his neck.

'What's that?' Big John asked. His eye took in what Jack was pointing at.

'Oh shite,' the policeman said.

Two hours later Jack sat beside Ralph Slater and John McColl facing the television in the office.

He used a remote control to switch it on, selected a spare channel, then used a forefinger to push the play button on the camera which sat beside it, an umbilical cable connecting it to the set.

'I've already had a look at some of this, but we'll take it right from the start. We'll probably need batteries before the night's out.'

'We've got a cassette adaptor. It lets you use these things in a recorder,' Ralph offered.

'That would help,' Jack agreed. 'Now, are you sitting comfortably?'

It was a poor attempt at levity, but the other two went along with it. For the next hour, they sat, horribly fascinated, as they watched the death of William Simpson in all its detail again and again.

It was the most appalling, most fascinating thing any of them had ever seen, and the most horrific Ralph Slater had ever witnessed, chiefly because he was always on the scene after a death, using his skills to work out what had happened. Now his abilities, he thought, were redundant. There was no doubt about what had happened to William Simpson.

It was not the worst thing Jack had ever seen, not by a long

116

chalk, because what was unfolding on the television screen was happening to somebody he did not know, or particularly care about. He cared even less after what he'd seen in the developing trays on the draining board.

The screen ran blank for less than a second, then flickered to life. Something blurred, casting a shadow, then pulled back, focusing in to become the hand that had been used to press the record button. The scene jiggled a little as the camera was moved slightly, then went still. The focus was clear and distinct and there was enough light from the overhead bulb to throw everything into sharp detail.

Simpson leaned back, staring into the lens. His face held no expression whatsoever. He stood like that, staring with dead eyes right at the three policemen, and raised his hands up to pull his dog collar away from his neck. The sound came crisp and sharp. They could even hear the rustle of the material. He turned and laid the collar and the black front bib down on the table, then removed his jacket and his trousers. He swivelled to face the camera again, standing in his shirt and a pair of oddly bright boxer shorts. He started undoing buttons then slipped the shirt from his shoulders. They were beefy and covered in hair. He laid it down with the rest of his clothes, taking his time to fold it neatly, bent, grunting a little, and removed the shorts before taking the belt from his trousers and cinching it around his paunchy waist. Then he turned to stare into the lens once again.

'Are you all sitting comfortably?' he said. It gave Jack a shiver. He hadn't watched the complete rerun. Simpson had said exactly what he himself had asked Ralph Slater. It was almost like *déjà vu*.

'Then I'll begin,' Simpson continued. He had a strong, quite deep voice, one used to preaching from the pulpit.

Just then, he smiled at the camera. The movement only encompassed his mouth. His eyes did not smile at all. They looked completely and utterly lifeless. It was like watching a rictus develop on a corpse.

The man turned to the desk, opened a drawer and pulled out a small box. He reached for his jacket, fished out a ring of keys, slotted one into the lock and snapped it open. The lid rose with a tiny squeal of protest. Jack thought it was like watching someone perform a religious ceremony. It reminded him of Catholic priests he'd seen at the occasional funeral or wedding. They always seemed to open something and bring out sacred objects. Simpson was handling each of the articles and laying them down with a certain degree of reverence. Jack recognised the little panties he'd seen lying wet on the floor. The white square of handkerchief followed, then the small pair of pink spectacles, then the doll's arm.

The minister lifted them all and placed them on a chair in front of the camera, laying the cloth objects over the back. The spectacles he slid over his nose, hooking the short, pliable legs behind his ears with some difficulty, then stuck the doll's arm under his belt, where it remained like a twisted pink handgun.

He moved away then returned, filling the screen. At first, none of them could make out what he had in his hands, then the man moved and they could see it clearly. The light glanced off the flat-iron and beamed coldly into the screen. Simpson carefully mounted the chair. They saw him first take the flex and loop it slowly around his testicles. The erection started immediately. Another loop spun round the rising penis, then three more, before, with a quick movement, the man tied a quick knot and jerked hard. They all heard the sudden groan of pain. The iron lowered slowly from his hands and jarred to a stop when it reached the end of its travel. The three of them groaned aloud, as Simpson had done, and simultaneously crossed their legs, imagining the excruciating pain they would have felt. The minister's mouth only twisted downwards a little, but his eyes remained expressionless, and that was the most awful thing about it. He looked like a man in a complete trance, like a walking automaton.

Everything at the man's crotch swelled hugely, until the three observers thought they might burst, although they knew that had not happened.

'For the love of God,' Ralph muttered. It was the first word any of them had spoken since the machine started to turn.

On screen the minister took the other piece of flex and tied it carefully, near the middle of its length, on the hook close to his head. The short end he roped twice around his neck, then tied the loose piece to the short length reaching to the hook, thus securing the noose. It was pulled so tightly he was hauled up onto the balls of his feet.

The back of the chair was just high enough for him to reach for the little panties. He picked them up and ran them over his face, snuffling at them like a pig rooting for acorns, like a dog checking a bitch. When he drew them down again, they watched as he slid his tongue over his bottom lip.

'Ha ha,' he said. It was not a laugh. It was a statement. Jack felt his hackles rise again. Beside him, John pulled himself back slightly. The flat sound the man had made was cold as ice. His eyes glared from the screen.

He rubbed the panties over his chest, then down his belly and finally to his groin. He held the material over his swollen organ and started to rub it slowly up and down.

'Suffer little children,' he said, in a voice that was a dreamy moan. 'Better for thee that they put a millstone round thy neck and cast thyself into the sea, than thou corrupt any of these, my little ones.'

Simpson grinned, though his eyes still glared, then the grin faded. The man started out from the flat screen and the eyes lost their hard, *mad* look. He reached out a hand towards the camera, still holding the little panties. His face sagged, like a child about to cry. They saw his lips move, trying to articulate again. He mumbled something.

'What was that?' Ralph asked.

Jack held up a hand and leaned forward to the screen, head half-turned to listen.

The minister whispered again.

'Help me.' They all heard the words. The man's eyes rolled, as if he'd just awoken and discovered himself in danger. Ralph looked at Jack, eyebrows raised.

Then in a flick, the expression changed again. The eyes went stony and flat, as if a film of ice had frosted them over.

'No help. No help. None for the wicked,' the hard voice, so different from the pained whisper, snapped out.

'To be, or not to be. That is the question.' Despite the constriction of the rope, the words came out clearly enunciated. 'That is the choice. Look at this vessel. This vassal. A man of calling. He has been called, and he knows not what he does.'

'What's that, the bible?'

Jack hushed him again.

Simpson snickered. There was no other way to describe the noise that came from behind his teeth. His lips stretched back in a grimace, but the eyes remained flat and dead.

He reached with his left hand and plucked the little doll's arm from where it stuck out from the belt and held it up just in front of his face. The policemen could see that his cheeks were dark red, dangerously purple. His temples looked swollen.

With a sudden jerk, he drew the arm down, shoulder end towards him. A little spike of metal, what had probably been a hook to hold the arm onto the rest of the doll's body, drove into the flesh on the side of his chest, just above the flabby man-breast. With a quick sideways movement which puckered the pale skin, he drew the thing across for a couple of inches. Blood immediately welled from the tear and flowed down in lines.

It happened so quickly that Jack had to replay the scene a couple of times. As he rewound, he could see the hand jitter and jerk spasmodically as the man used the spike to tear at his own flesh.

The cuts were not random. At the third viewing of that little splice of the scene which unfolded before their eyes, Jack was able to make out what was happening. Simpson was using the jagged metal to *write* on his own flesh.

Two words, now obscured by blood. Jack hadn't noticed them when he'd gone down to the cellar a second time. All he had seen was the sheen of red that covered the man's entire chest and belly.

Two words. *The rose*.

Jack stared. He remembered what Walker had said about the two words written on Marta Herkik's walls. They could have been an anagram. He'd plucked two out from the mix of letters. One of them had been just the words Simpson was scrawling on his own skin as the blood blurted, gouging the letters with quick rips and pulls in living colour, in dying playback.

When the man had finished, he reached behind him and plucked up the tiny handkerchief. He slapped it to his chest and immediately it turned dark red as it mopped up the fresh blood. He brought it away from his chest and held it up, squeezing it in his hand so that little scarlet drops dribbled from it sluggishly.

'And this is my blood, of the old and everlasting covenant, the mystery of faith which has been shared by many. I will take this and I will drink it, all of it so that sins may be revealed.'

'That's not right,' McColl said. 'That's not the words.' John McColl was a Catholic who attended St Rowan's Church every Sunday and even now still ate fish on a Friday.

Jack ignored him, fascinated, though repelled, by the action on the small screen.

Simpson held the bloody cloth up to his face and rammed it into his mouth. Gurgling, sucking noises issued out of the speaker. It had an eerie quality, like a ravenous dog wolfing food. The man drew the cloth away, showing his face, bloodied and smeared from nose to chin. He held the scrap up again, like a prize, then dropped it to the floor, where it flopped wetly.

'Let the contest now begin,' he said, then grinned again in that dead, cold rictus. Even his teeth were stained red. 'The summons is made, the vessel is empty. The challenge is thrown.'

McColl squirmed in his seat. 'Is this man a loony or what?'

On screen Simpson glared blankly at the camera, the deadly smile fading. He opened his mouth, his face now swollen and purpling like a beetroot.

'If I should die before I wake, I pray to hell my soul to take.'

Just at that instant, the flat expression left the man's face. The eyes rolled wildly. He shook his head, left and right, as if denying the words that had come out of his mouth. He raised a hand to try to grasp the cable that suspended him from the hook on the joist.

Then the chair flew away.

They replayed that few seconds over and over again, and none of them was able to say what had happened. The man was shaking his head, reaching for the noose, face turning black, when the chair simply kicked backwards and tumbled to the floor.

Simpson made a grunting sound, the kind of noise a man will make when he slips on ice, taken by surprise. The hand, which was still rising, up close to his face, jerked out spastically, almost rigid in a grotesque salute. The eyes bulged behind the little kiddie's lenses, then the hand came swinging back. The three of them were never able to work out whether it had happened deliberately, or if it was just the flailing action of a dying man's hand. Whatever it was, the arm snapped back and a thumb stabbed through the left lens and right into the eye. There was a faint crackle sound and a rubbery thud and blood spurted, forced by the pressure built up in the man's swollen head.

Simpson coughed. The hand came flying out again, leaving a ruined crater where the eye had been, then the whole body went into a paroxysm of violent shivers. The taut cable squeaked in protest. Just as that happened, the room went suddenly dark, not as if the lights had failed, but as if a cloud of dense black smoke had billowed from nowhere. The image fuzzed out on the screen, fading to grey and then to black. The squeal of the cable noose was like a mouse in the darkness, then, from the set on the filing cabinet, came a roar which at first sounded like static, then sounded nothing at all like electronic interference. Jack had heard it the first time he'd played back the latter half of the scene, but McColl and Slater rocked back in their seats.

The noise filled the room, a huge and utterly unnerving roaring sound. It was the noise of a vast and irresistible wind, the sound of an avalanche of rocks tumbling in a defile. It was the roar of an immense, hungry and maddened animal. It went on for several seconds, so deafening that Jack reached a hand to turn down the volume. Just as his fingers touched the control, the noise stopped and a dead silence rang in their ears. The screen began to lighten as the darkness, whatever the darkness was, cleared away like a mist driven by wind. As it dissipated, the shape hanging right in front of the lens became clearer until they could again see William Simpson hanging. The body was still trembling in tight little spasms as the nerves twitched and jumped. His right eye, still pale and bulging, was staring right at them.

The twitches continued for two minutes and then stopped. The feet, now dangling straight down, several inches from the floor, trembled a little for a while after that, then everything went still. The minister hung, slowly revolving, his head cocked to the side, while the blood began to congeal on his chest and face.

The video camera ran for another fifteen minutes. They sat and stared in fascination at the dead man suspended from the hook until a new noise came from the speaker, the light thud of feet somewhere in the distance, then the tap of heels on the floor beyond the door which was just out of sight until it swung open.

122

Young Fiona Simpson came slowly into the room. They could see the edge of the door when it reached its full swing.

'Daddy?' she said, almost hesitantly. She repeated it again, and came fully into the room, moving forward slowly.

For some reason, the dangling body did not seem to register with her. She moved behind it, glanced at the pictures in the trays, curiously at first, then her shoulders stiffened. She backed away, hands held up in front of her, pushing at air. She bumped into her suspended and bloodied father, turned round and her eyes registered it then.

Her mouth opened in an instant wide circle which showed every one of her top teeth. The scream went on and on and on.

It was the third time Jack Fallon had heard it. It didn't get any easier to listen to.

More sounds, thumping of heavier feet. Jack coming into the room, taking in everything with a sweep of his eyes. McColl watched his superior officer swing his head round, for the first few seconds, ignoring the piercing squeal after the first glance at the girl. His eyes registered the body, the blood, the bloodied scraps on the floor. He moved with an economy of motion, raising his hand as he passed the chair, automatically avoiding laying any prints on anything, his foot rising over the fallen chair lest he disturb it. His right arm came up and looped round the girl's shoulders just as the strength drained from her legs. He leaned her back, scooped her with his other hand, then backed out of the door, his gaze fixed on the hanged man. The tape whirred on.

Two minutes after McColl came in, the tape reached its end. The screen flickered, went black, then hissed with electronic snow. Jack reached forward and switched the machine off. John McColl let out a long, slow sigh.

'Excuse me, boss, but what the *fuck* was that?'

Jack flipped open his cigarettes, offered one to the other man, who took it in fingers that seemed to have been infected with the tremor that had afflicted Simpson in his last dying seconds. Both of them lit up and inhaled deeply. Ralph stoked up his pipe and sucked heavily as he left the room, shaking his head.

'That's the original snuff movie,' John said.

'That's why I don't want it out of the safe,' Jack told him.

'Make sure the guys get the message. Anybody making copies of that will be up for interfering with evidence. I don't want anybody else even watching it.'

'Can't blame you. I'm not sure I want to see it again, though I suppose I'll have to. Fair turned my stomach.'

Jack nodded. 'Shame about the girl. At least it's a step in the right direction.' He rewound the tape and let John watch it again.

Ralph came back some time later, still puffing on his pipe.

'I've got news for you. We can put Simpson at both locations.'

'Both?'

'Yes. Got dozens of them at the Herkik woman's. We got another partial from the hundreds at Latta Court. Would have missed it if I hadn't run through them again and got a match. Palm print, no fingers. From the inside of the broken lift.'

'You think it was him?'

'Sure it was him, though how he got up to the Doyle level I'll never know. He must have climbed somewhere. Maybe wore gloves.'

'He could never have come from the bottom. Not the shape he was in,' Jack stated.

'I agree, boss. But there's more. I got a fax from Jim Jackson at Lanark. Their files were all transferred to Regional HQ, but they dug them out for me. Simpson's prints match that case I was telling you about. The wee girl. Goes back a long time, but they still have the evidence in storage. They wired me the photographs and *bingo*. They've come up with the goods.'

Ralph lit up his pipe while the others leaned forward impatiently.

'We got a match on his prints from there. Plus the doll's arm. It's a match for the missing one from the doll they found. But more than that, the scene of death pictures are almost identical to the ones in Simpson's developing tray. The only difference is that the body had been moved. Can't say how far yet. But his happy snaps were taken some time *before* the body was found.'

He sucked hard on the stem and blew out a plume of blue smoke.

'I think that wraps it up, and it gets Cowie off your back.' He looked at Jack. 'I'd like to know one thing. What put you onto him in the first place?'

Jack tapped his nose.

'Contacts. Old friends.'

The two men left Jack's room. He rewound the video and forced himself to watch it again before he switched everything off and sat thinking. The unnerving scenes got no more pleasant with familiarity.

He should have been pleased, but he was not happy. They had enough to place Simpson at the two scenes. They had evidence to show he'd been at the scene of another, years ago, and that one had involved a small child who had been reported missing before being found raped and dead in a patch of scrubland fifteen miles south of the city.

Yet something nagged insistently at him. It was too pat, too cut and dry, and Jack had the experience to know that nothing was ever so easy.

And there were other things. The words that Simpson had gouged into his own chest. That had sent a *déjà vu* shiver right through Jack. The man had stared, grinning into the camera, as he'd done that. It was as if he was trying to tell Jack something, having a joke at the policeman's expense. There was too much of a coincidence with what the crossword-playing professor of languages had said.

And there were the words written on Marta Herkik's walls, daubed in those two paperless strips in the dead woman's viscid and congealing blood. There had been no sign of how Simpson had managed to do that, and Jack did not like that at all.

That Simpson had been a man with a terrible secret, he had no doubt, but what he *did* have doubts about was how he could have killed Marta Herkik so brutally, stripped the paper from her walls, ripped up dozens of her books and all without leaving any prints, except on the table, on the fallen seat and on the door handle.

He had doubts about how the man, in his sixties, corpulent and unfit, had managed to get to the Doyles' balcony on a cold winter's night, and without alerting anyone.

He flipped open Ralph Slater's scene of crime report, opened a folder which contained his own paperwork, and started to write. All they needed now was Timmy Doyle's body and they could close this case. Close it officially anyway.

Jack Fallon told himself it was all over bar the shouting as he wrote in his tight longhand. But the doubts crowded in like mourners at a funeral. He hoped it *was* all over bar the shouting.

10

Night fell abruptly and early. Thick clouds had piled in from the north-west, swept in on cold winds that had driven down from the north of Greenland, threatening snow and dismal hail. They had blown by after an hour of darkness, and the wind died. Overhead the sky was black, frosted with the stars, clear enough to make out the twinkling jewels of the seven sisters high over the Langmuir crags. There was no moon.

The hard frost crystallised out of the cold air to rime the windows and lay mirror-sheets of black ice on the roads out of Levenford.

On Thursday night, Jack Fallon was still in College Street station, going over the evidence reports again, still trying to knit together the puzzle which was growing in his mind.

Mickey Haggerty was on his third pint of beer in Mac's Bar, and enjoying every mouthful.

Robbie Cattanach was putting the finished touches to his report on the post mortem he'd carried out on William Simpson, the late minister of Castlebank Church. He hadn't needed a video cassette to tell him what he needed to know. Death was by strangulation. The other injuries were mere curiosities as far as he was concerned.

Lorna Breck sat with her feet curled up underneath her on the soft sofa in her small living room down by the estuary, trying to read a book, and making heavy weather of it. A small log fire flickered in the corner, the embers glowing red and sending out enough heat to make her feel comfortable on a cold night, yet she felt chilled *inside*. A sense of apprehension had been building up inside her since she'd left the library and crossed the old bridge, heading for home. It was vague, but getting stronger all the time, and Lorna couldn't shake off the sensation of foreboding. She turned the page and her eyes followed the words right down to the bottom before she realised she hadn't read a word of the story. The image of what she'd seen when she'd looked into the shop window kept coming back to her, faded not one whit by the passage of three days.

Just after nine o'clock, down on Quay Street, a shape moved along the pavement, indistinct at first in the frosty mist floating in from the river. In this old part of the town, the council had built a small walkway along the edge of the harbour, where an ancient boat repair shed had stood for generations until it had burned down three years before. During the day, in summertime, the clerks from the distillery and mothers with small children would spend a sunny hour throwing pieces of bread to the swans on the water, and losing most of it to the squadrons of screaming gulls who competed for the crumbs. Now, in winter, the swans were gone. The water was dark, the sound of its passage along the harbour wall liquid and urgent. It slapped against the small boats moored out in the deeper water midstream and made sucking, burbling noises as it swirled, out of sight, round the moorings and the old pier stanchions.

Shona Campbell needed the money. She was twenty-one years old and had a year-old baby girl. Eighteen months ago she'd had a good job in Cameron and Dunn's lawyer's office. Old Cameron had died twenty years ago and the practice was run by Roger Dunn, who handled most of the criminal work at Levenford Sheriff Court. In the old days, anybody banged up on a weekend drunk and disorderly would demand of the station sergeant: 'Get me Cameron.'

Now they got Dunn, so the joke went, done good and proper.

That was the position Shona Campbell found herself in, done good and proper. Two years before, she'd had an interesting Friday night at a party out by Eastmains, on the far edge of town, where she'd met Craig Campbell, known for some forgotten reason as Bunnet. He had looked good in his leathers, and better on the back of his big black Yamaha, and she'd agreed to let him take her home on the back of the purring machine. He was a barrel-pusher in Castlebank Distillery, the immense four-square building that loomed beside the curve of the river. She should have known better when he'd taken the half bottle of crystal-clear overproof spirit out of his inside pocket and taken a large swallow. She'd tried some, just a sip, and had shivered with distaste. He'd laughed, his fair hair falling over his brow, and his strong teeth white in the night, and he'd slipped a casual arm around her shoulder to kiss her goodnight.

She'd gone out with him four times, once to the pictures and three times roaring round the back roads on the big bike, and then he'd let the bike idle silently down the hill to Fetter Farm, where he'd sneaked her into the hayloft. She'd gone along with it, apprehensively at first, but when his cold hand had slid against the skin under her brassiere, she'd been unable to say no. He'd laid her down, taken off most of her clothes and some of his and then she'd come with such intensity that she gouged two stuttering furrows in the back of his leather jacket.

Six months later, they were married in a small ceremony conducted by the same Rev. William Simpson whose filleted and eviscerated remains were now glacial and blue in a cold-storage drawer in the old mortuary. A few months after little Kelly was born, Shona came quickly to the conclusion that Bunnet Campbell was a drunk and a waster, and by that time it was too late. They'd got a small, dingy apartment three up in a huddle of old tenements just off Quay Street and Shona settled down to watch the rest of her life drift by in a dismal haze of need and faded dreams.

She came round the corner onto the walkway. Ahead of her, a globe of light was haloed by the frosted mist. She could feel the icy air catch in the back of her throat, clean and sharp, and she drew the shawl tightly around the sleeping baby at her shoulder.

Here the walkway passed two low bench seats which had been there since the promenade was built and were already cross-hatched by initials and gang slogans. To the right, there was a high wall, punctuated by gateways which led into the alleys and back courts of the River Street shops. She passed the light, walking on quickly, her shoes clacking on the cold paving stones. About fifty yards on, Rock Lane pulled off up towards the main street, bisected by Barley Cobble, an ancient pathway which had once been the route of the old grain barrows when the distillery had been a family enterprise. At the end of this long, twisting and narrow alley, the Castlegate Bar, the oldest, and the dingiest drinking house in town, would be alive with noise and laughter and the occasional sound of snarling drunk men.

This was where Shona was headed. Bunnet Campbell would be

up against the bar, most likely sprawled across it. Thursday night was still pay night in the distillery. The men had threatened to walk out when the company suggested paying their wages direct into bank accounts, for two reasons. Firstly, few of them had bank accounts. But the main reason was that none of them, under any circumstances, wanted any evidence of how much they were paid for their week's work. The difference between their take-home pay and what actually *got* home was immense.

It had become a Thursday night ritual, a race against the drink and the devil, a bid to get some of the money before Tam Finch, the Castlegate's beefy owner, got the lot. Already, they were five weeks behind with the rent. Shona owed another two months on the hired television set, and there was a mountain of debt piling up, most of it to the Housemarket catalogue collector.

As Shona scurried quickly past the long wall, she thought about the good job she'd had in the lawyer's office and once again thought she'd been done. Good and proper.

Her shadow lengthened in front of her as she hurried, eyes smarting from the cold, until she got midway to the next street lamp. Beside her, an open gateway yawned, a dark blot of lightlessness. She was about to move on when a low moan came soughing out of the dark. The girl stopped and turned simultaneously, clutching her baby tightly against herself, feeling the child give a start at the sudden jar. The moan came again and Shona peered into the blank space, nervous lest something should leap out from the shadows. A shape moved, and the girl took a step back with a little intake of breath, but nothing leapt out. The gloom diminished a little as her eyes grew accustomed to it and finally Shona could make out the huddle against the swung-back gate. The low noise came again. A man moaning.

Shona took two steps forward and peered again. The man was lying in the shadows, back against the wall, beside a tumbled clutter of super-strength lager cans, the kind that were left there by the handful of drunks who hung around the quayside during the day.

'Are you alright?' she asked.

The shape stirred and a pale face swung upwards. Shona couldn't make out the features. She leaned closer and saw a thin man, one leg sprawled out in front of him, both hands up to the side of his face.

'Do you need some help?' On her shoulder, the baby made a little mewling sound and she automatically patted it to silence.

The man looked drunk. There was a rip in his trousers, a pale stripe against the rest of his leg. The young mother leaned forward and the man looked at her, or through her. He made the moaning noise again and some saliva dribbled down from slack lips.

His eyes were wide and vacant, mouth slack. Shona wondered whether to call an ambulance or a doctor or something. It was freezing down here and the sprawled, slumped man was only wearing trousers and jacket, no heavy winter coat. She began to straighten up, torn between her need to get round to try to snatch some of her husband's wages and her inability to let someone lie and die in the cold. Just then, the man gave a little jolt, as if he'd awoken.

'Go,' he said, very clearly.

'What?'

'Go. Gone. Go. Get.' The words came in a slobbery jumble, as if the man had little control over his mouth.

He raised himself up from the wall and stretched out a hand, so quickly Shona thought he was trying to strike at her. She pulled back, holding her baby even tighter.

'Go,' the man said, his pale face looming up from the shadows. 'Get out. Out of here. Go. *Get you!*'

He tried to heave himself to his feet, the one hand still outstretched towards Shona. He looked more than drunk. He looked *mad*, the girl thought. She backed away out of the gate. The shape loomed, then fell back with a crumping sound, a flaccid weight hitting the wall.

Shona hesitated again, wondering what to do, then the voice came out from the shadows, now more a shout than a moan.

'*Get you!*' This time it sounded like a threat.

That was enough for the girl. She turned quickly and clattered up the narrow end of Quay Street, turned at River Lane and jinked to the left along the alley that would take her to Barley Cobble.

Here the mist from the river had no breeze at all to dissipate its thick, pallid tendrils. They curled around the corners and scraped against the crumbling sandstone walls looming in on either side.

High on the stonework, old-fashioned lamps glowed dimly from within their orange halos. On her shoulder, the baby whimpered again and Shona clapped it lightly, drawing it in close to her body heat. The man in the yard had scared her. She shouldn't have stopped, she told herself, not to be threatened by some disgusting drunk.

She reached the cobbled alley and turned along it, through the swirling mist. Past a doorway she caught a glimpse of someone standing in the shadows and she jerked around, staring, breath caught. There was a dim shape there. At first she thought it was a girl of her own height, but then she twisted her head and the shadows resolved themselves into the shape of the old peeling door. There was no one there. She walked on for ten paces, not quite scared, but wanting to be out of the mist and home in her own little house, which, no matter how dingy and ill kept, was warm on a winter's night.

There was a noise above her. Still walking, she looked upwards.

A shadow came swooping out of the mist curling above her head and slammed her to the ground.

The blow was such a stunner that Shona Campbell's arm snapped just above the elbow. She hit the cobbled alley with a thud. Out of the corner of her eye, something black whipped backwards, lunged at her again. A searing pain screamed in her neck as her head was smacked to the side and above her, the orange light became two whirling fuzzy globes as her vision doubled. She rolled with the force of the blow, scraped her knee on a stone kerb, then fetched against the wall with a thump which socked her breath out in one loud, bewildered grunt.

Despite the pain and the shock, Shona kept little Kelly clasped tight against her with her left arm. She turned, gasping for breath, still unable to comprehend what had happened. Her vision was still swimming and she blinked back tears. Darkness wavered in front of her and she twisted away from it. The dark stretched out and grabbed the baby in one vicious snatch. The child wailed and Shona screamed. Her hand flew out and caught onto the trailing edge of the shawl, finger hooked in the wide crochet stitching, and she was dragged, wailing like a banshee, for several yards.

The tugging stopped and Shona managed to get to one knee, just at the corner of the alley where it gave into a small unlit back yard.

'My baby,' she screamed. *'Give her back!'*

She crawled, lurching to her feet. Just ahead of her, in the dark, she could make out the pale fluttering of the shawl and reached out.

Her fingers touched something cold and hard and rough. It moved under her fingers. She blinked again and her eyes cleared. Just above her head height, a snorting, rasping sound grated, like crumbling stone, and a foul stench of rot came wafting towards her.

'You bastard!' she bawled. 'Give her back to me!'

Under her fingers, something gave a wrench.

'Oh help! Somebody *help* me! It's got my baby!' Off to the right, a lamp blinked on, sending a long rhombus of light through the mist.

'What in the name's going on down there?' a querulous old voice demanded to know.

'Oh help me, mister. It's my baby,' Shona screeched incoherently. She grabbed at the movement, still unable to see anything in the darkness. She was wailing and screaming, scratching and scrabbling at the shadowy shape, when the black expanded again. Her arm was flung off with almost enough force to dislocate her shoulder. Something loomed in at her and she got a glimpse of two orange globes as a head swivelled towards her. There was a movement just above her. Her head snapped up, turning, and then the dark flicked out and hit her right down the side of her temple.

Her cry was cut off instantly. She smacked the ground with a wet *crump*.

There was a pain in her right elbow and a tight, ripping throb in her neck, but they started to fade almost immediately. There was no feeling down the left side of her face, which was now pressed against the cold cobbles. She tried to move, but her hands were trembling and she couldn't get them to stop. There was a wet feeling on her neck and a thick coppery smell. Her eye swivelled, automatically following a shadowy movement that scuttled and flowed, liquid yet spidery, up the wall close to her

133

head. Her other eye wouldn't move at all and that gave her confusing doubling of vision.

Shona's mouth opened and she managed a small croak. There was a warm smell of butcher shops, and Shona didn't know why she was lying in Barley Cobble. Very vaguely she thought she might have left the potato pot still bubbling on the old cooker and wondered if dinner would be burned before she got back again. She hoped little Kelly would be alright until then and she hoped the man lying in the dark behind the gate hadn't sneaked up to her flat and crept up beside Kelly's little cot. She wondered mistily about the darkness that had climbed up the wall with the fluttering white thing trailing behind it.

Her hands and arms and legs would not stop shaking. She tried to turn her head and managed to make it move. There was a wet, sucking sound as her face came away from the cobbles and the metal smell came warm again, clogging her throat.

The mist was getting thicker, crowding in on twists of gauzy white, and everything began to get cold. Her one good eye rolled and she saw a girl standing there in the alley, watching her. The girl was trying to say something and Shona tried to say something back, but she forgot what she was going to say and the girl started to fade away into the mist.

The corner of River Lane and Barley Cobble was silent for some time. Round the corner, less than fifty yards away, Bunnet Campbell was flopped over the bar, mumbling to Doug Mitchell, who was equally drunk, about the fact that his stupid wife couldn't run a piss-up in a brewery.

It was another half an hour before Shona Campbell was found lying in a pool of blood, limbs already frozen stiff, her face a ruin of sinew and bone. Of little Kelly Campbell, there was no sign, and it was not until the following morning that the baby's father sobered up enough to report her missing.

Later that same Thursday night, Jack Fallon was huddled over his kitchen table, which was littered with books and scraps of paper. He had cooked two pork chops, burned both of them but ignored the blackened bits and wolfed the lot, then he had made a pot of coffee and sat down at the table. He was on his fourth cup, which he knew was probably a mistake, because it guaranteed him little sleep that night. He almost smiled at the thought. Nothing guaranteed much sleep these days.

He'd got through a lot of work since he'd finished at the office. Robbie Cattanach's post mortem on Simpson would arrive on his desk in the morning and he expected no surprises. It was possible, he told himself, that the autopsy might reveal an exotic substance, like LSD or crack, or magic mushrooms or any other hallucinogenic substance, but Jack didn't think the minister was a likely candidate for turning on and dropping out.

He shook his head wryly. He had to stop pigeonholing people. Simpson did not seem a likely candidate for attending seances. He hadn't seemed the kind of man who would make a video recording of his own gruesome death.

There was no pigeonhole for that kind of thing, and that caused Jack more problems.

Oh, Angus McNicol had been pleased, not only at getting a name for Marta Herkik's murderer, but he also delighted in Superintendent Cowie's embarrassed fury. Cowie had been an elder of Castlebank Church. He'd been a lodge-fellow of the dead and dangling man who was now a twitching star of the small screen. Now the policeman was trying to dissociate himself from the minister.

'There was always something odd about him,' he declared to Jack and Angus. 'I could never put my finger on it.'

'That's why I went very carefully,' Jack said, trying to keep his face straight. Angus winked at him over the top of his whisky glass.

Cowie glared at him.

The big Chief Superintendent offered Jack another drink. He shook his head.

'No thanks. I've stacks of paperwork to get through.'

'No urgency now, is there?'

'I don't know.'

'What do you mean?' Cowie asked. 'I've released the name to the press. Told them our inquiries are at an end.'

'Yes, I saw that on the news,' Angus said.

'Might be a bit premature,' Jack said evenly.

'Nonsense. We've tied him into the Herkik place *and* Latta Court. What more do we need?'

135

'I don't know about you, but *I* need just a little bit more than circumstantial evidence.'

'Come on, Fallon. Simpson did it, and that's an end to it.'

'Well, I hope you're right. But so far we haven't got a body for the Doyle kid. And we've no motive for either. And the one person I would like to speak to is in the middle of a post mortem. On the receiving end, as we speak.'

'Well, that's hardly here nor there. We've got Simpson's prints from the Lanark case, and those photographs. That shows he was a killer in the first place.'

'It does tend to point that way. But I have to consider the near certainty that there were several people at Marta Herkik's house on the night she died. I don't know how many. I'd like to speak to them all.'

'To what end?' Angus asked.

'To make sure this wasn't a group effort. I don't mind nailing this to Simpson's door. The man was a walking shit-house. But if he wasn't the only one involved, then we could have a problem. Just think what the headlines will say if we close the file and then something else happens? I'd just like to make sure.'

Cowie turned to Angus McNicol, his eyebrows arched.

'Seems a waste of time, effort and public money to me,' he said stiffly.

Angus sat back and steepled his fingers, looking thoughtful.

'Oh, I don't see any harm in Jack here tying up loose ends if he can. I mean, it could have taken a long time to get Simpson anyway, so I think we're ahead on points. For the time being.'

He finished his whisky and leaned over the desk.

'Another couple of days, Jack. Just so we're sure.'

'Thanks,' Jack said.

Cowie left in an indignant bustle. When the door had closed, Angus asked him what he'd been getting at.

'Just what I said. There's something about this that doesn't sit square with me.'

'It would be better all round, propaganda-wise and from an admin point of view if we could leave it all with Simpson. It's neat enough for me.'

'But if it wasn't just Simpson, it could happen again. I don't think anybody wants that. We'll get egg all over.'

136

Jack had spent a full morning talking to the dead minister's wife. She did not know about the video and he had no plans to tell her just yet.

Her daughter Fiona was lying sedated in an upstairs bedroom of the handsome red-sandstone manse. Betty Simpson had refused all medication.

She offered Jack a sherry in a tiny cut-crystal glass, which he accepted. It was very bitter.

'I suppose you want to ask me some questions?' she'd said as soon as she'd poured a glass for herself.

'Yes,' Jack agreed. 'I do have a few questions.'

'About him. My husband.' The corners of her mouth turned down as she said it. It made her look as if she'd smelled something rotting in a corner. 'I've known for years,' she said.

Jack stopped in the act of raising the glass to his mouth. He put it slowly down on the table. 'Known what?'

'About him. About what he does.'

'And what does he do? Or did do,' he corrected.

'Girls. Young ones. He couldn't keep himself away from them. That's why my other daughters don't live here. Now he's dead I can say it. He *interfered*.'

'What, with your daughters?'

'With anybody's daughters. He was *sick*. But I couldn't stop him. I had to stay, to protect Fiona. To make sure he didn't go near her. He *was* sick, you know, and I hated him for it. I didn't know when we got married, but then I found *things*.' Again she made the disgusted twist of her mouth.

'Things?'

'Pictures. He'd taken them himself. Little girls, sometimes boys, but mostly girls. Disgusting pictures. And there were others. They must have come in the post. He never let me open any of his letters. Filthy pictures, but not as bad as the ones he'd taken by himself.'

'And did you ever tell him you knew?'

'I didn't have to. He knew I did. When that little girl was found in Lanark, I *knew*.'

'So why didn't you say anything?'

The minister's widow gave a little laugh. 'And who would have believed me? And if they *had* I would have brought shame on my

137

daughters. No. I said nothing for their sake, but now it's over, and he can't hurt them any more. He can't touch them now, and I'm glad.'

She raised her head and looked at Jack, pale blue eyes glittering like ice. 'I hope he burns in hell.'

The final word came out like a spit. The grey-haired woman smacked her hand down on the polished coffee-table and the thin stem of the sherry glass broke. Blood immediately dripped from the centre of her palm where the jagged edge had dug into the skin, but she hardly seemed to notice the pain. She wrapped a small handkerchief around her hand and continued to talk as if nothing had happened.

'I'd told him that if he touched me or the girls ever again, then I'd kill him. He never touched any of us after that. That was good enough for me. I just didn't think he'd go so far again, now that he was older.'

Jack sat back, listening to the stream of loathing from the small woman.

'Tell me. Why would he go to a seance?'

She looked at him, failing to understand.

'He was at a spiritualist meeting last week. A medium.'

'I don't know. He never said, but he never told me anything.'

'Did he keep a diary?'

'You can check his desk if you like. I couldn't say. Take everything away if you want. I never want to see any of it ever again.'

11

A biting north wind whistled round the straight edge of Loch View, which stood with three other high-rise blocks on the edge of town. The low pressure which had brought rain and sleet had moved off slowly into the North Sea and behind it, a ridge of clear high pressure dragged the freezing air down from the edge of Greenland, frosting the night sky as temperatures plummeted. The wind made the wires of the gantry moan as it plucked the steel braids with icy fingers and rocked the platform slowly back and forth halfway up the sheer side of the building.

Under normal circumstances, Jock Toner would have been mightily peeved that he was still up in the rig on a dark and freezing night. But the circumstances had changed. He'd been one of the team of bricklayers repairing the worn concrete on the side of the building, which had weathered away like hard peeling scabs under the weight of the winds. The gantry was suspended from a winch on rails on the flat top of the block, which allowed the men to be lowered and raised at the touch of a button on the winding motor.

It had been cold work all day. The wind hadn't stopped and even in the clear air, tiny ice crystals had whipped around the corner of the building, whirling in the turbulence, to sting the men's ears raw.

Ordinarily, Jock would have been home by now, probably dozing in front of the television, or maybe down in the County Bar for a couple of straight whiskies. He'd been the last man to leave the hut, and was just about to start up his battered old Ford when the council's clerk of works had shown up unexpectedly. He'd pointed out that the gantry had been lowered to the ground.

'What do you want me to do about it?' Jock had asked truculently.

'Basically, I want you to get it right back up the top again, where nobody can mess about with it.'

'My shift finished half an hour ago,' Jock argued.

'Well, you've got a choice. You can go home now and I can call the works manager and get him out in the middle of the night,' the fellow had responded easily. 'It's six of one to me. I'll let him know you insisted he got a call out. Either way, there's no way that thing can sit out for the rest of the night. Any kid could climb on and start the motor.'

He looked at Jock levelly, with a small smile.

'So, should I call the boss out?'

Jock let out a sigh of annoyance.

'No. I'll get the bloody thing,' he grated. To himself he swore he'd get Des Coleman, the rigger who should have stowed the gear.

The management man waited by his van until Jock was halfway up the side of the building before he walked to his car. Over the whistling wind, he could hear the whine of the motor as it reeled in the braided cables and the gantry slowly hoisted up and out of site on the dark face of the blocks. Jock saw the headlamps stab out and waited until the red tail lights had disappeared round the corner. The ice crystals, condensed out of the frozen air, were needling into his left ear and he cursed aloud. The gantry rose up slowly and steadily.

He was nine floors up, just rising past a lighted window, when the wind swung the platform to the right, and a movement inside the room caught his eye.

He had risen another nine feet before the image really registered and he hit the stop switch with a stab of his finger, then, with another jab, he thumbed the green button which reversed the gantry. He lowered it the nine feet, hoping the wind would hide the noise, then stood for a moment, holding on tight to the safety bars.

The rig swung gently away from the lit window and then back again and Jock was able to confirm what he'd seen. His face broke into a wide grin. It took three swings of the galley to identify the woman on the floor as he hung out as far as he could, one hand gripping the hawser, then about ten seconds to figure out why she was doing what she was doing with such obvious vigour.

Isobel McIntyre was spreadeagled under the collector from the

140

Housemarket Supply Company. Both of them were exhibiting great enthusiasm. The rep was fat and balding. Sweat was glistening between his shoulder blades and he had the hairiest arse Jock Toner had ever seen. His head was down on her shoulder and he was thrusting away as if his life depended on it. Isobel's eyes were screwed tight shut and her mouth was drawn back in a rictus of concentration. Even through the double glazing and above the whistling of the wind in the wires, Jock could hear the man's base grunt and the woman's high, animal snarl. He'd worked on the outside of buildings long enough to know that even if they had looked, the reflection of the light on the glass would hide him from the people inside the room.

He grinned again. Isobel was a distant relative of Jock's wife. She'd be shocked if she knew her second cousin's wife was doing it to a fine tune on the floor of her living room with the man from the HSC. Jock wondered just how much the woman owed on her weekly payments, for the supply company interest was extortionate. He also wondered just how many other women were paying their bills on their backs. As that thought struck him, he made a mental note to find out when the fat and hairy little man made his regular visits to his own house.

It was an hour after the clerk of works had disappeared in his van and Jock was still up on the gantry, halfway between the top of the building and the ground, enjoying every vicarious moment from his vantage point.

The wind had dropped and the spindrift crystals were no longer needling his ear. Up above the sky was velvet dark. There was no moon to light the thin snow-clouds that had built up to hide the stars.

Inside the room, the woman and the man had rolled on the floor for a while then he pulled her up onto the couch and after that he'd even tried to lean her over the ironing table, though their combined weight rocked it so much they gave up quickly. Jock was surprised that the spindly board had taken the weight and he thought to himself, one hand now working slowly deep in the crotch of his baggy overalls, that even if she was paying off debt, she was thoroughly enjoying the instalment terms. The grunting noises continued from the room as the rig swung silently, like a weighty pendulum, back and forth on the long cables, while Jock held on with his free hand.

The action changed and Isobel McIntyre crawled round to face in the opposite direction. Her fair hair was lank with perspiration and her whole body glistened. Jock knew she'd always been a looker, and now he could see that the reality was even better than he'd imagined. She had a long, slim body and pert little breasts that were lacquered with sweat. He watched her head bob up and down and his own hand started to move quickly. He couldn't remember ever being so turned on before. It was almost better, he told himself, than the real thing. He heard his own breath coming faster and faster as the woman worked away on the man, taking her own pleasure as she did, and in the cold night air, Jock's heavy breath fogged the window.

He leaned out, taking a risk by letting go his anchor hand for a moment, to rub the window with his elbow, when the gantry gave a sudden, violent jolt at the apex of its swing.

Jock Toner's heart lurched just as violently as he was thrown out over the railing.

'Oh Chri . . .' he squawked, in that instant not caring if the people inside the house heard him or not. By pure reflex, his hand shot out and hooked the cable just as his balance reached the point of no return, and hauled him back. The rig shook with the sudden movement. One edge scraped on the concrete facade with a metallic grinding noise. Jock's breath swooped in and he felt the blood drain from his face.

'What in the name . . .' he blurted aloud. For a moment he'd completely lost interest in the action through the pane. He held on tight to the railings while his heartbeat knocked on his ribs. His belly was quaking with the surge of adrenalin and his knees were jittering out of synch with each other. The gantry swung again, still oscillating back and forth, but now slowing down. Jock took several breaths to clear his head. He'd almost fallen straight off the edge, and he was still stunned by how close, how *instantaneous* it had been. His knuckles stood out white on the railing top.

The scene in the house momentarily forgotten, he leaned over the edge, peering down into the darkness below. A thin, ice-laden fog was swirling around the building, punctuated here and there by the dim lights behind curtained windows. Below the gantry, the braided nylon guide rope dropped away out of sight.

There was nothing there, though Jock knew *something* had hit the rope. He checked at his feet, where the braid was wound onto the plastic spindle. One end trailed away down into the mist and then looped back up again to where it was draped over the balustrade. At this height, Jock knew it couldn't reach to the ground, so that ruled out mischievous kids down there. He pondered the possibility that someone had opened a window and tugged at the guide, but it was hanging down from the far edge. Somebody would have to have long arms to reach that far.

The wind tugged the hawser again and made it sing a weird, mournful note. Jock leaned over again, peering downwards to see if there was anything that could have jolted the platform so heavily, but there was nothing at all. The cold mist was getting thicker. Down in the distance, away to the left, the orange street lamps were getting dimmer, haloed by fuzzy rings of luminescence.

He turned back and touched the wall to stop the to-and-fro motion of the gantry and then shifted his weight outwards, careful to keep a grip on the bar. The fright was gone, and his heart was already steadying down to a normal beat. The danger over, Jock Toner remembered the scene in the house. He leaned out as far as he could until his head was just beyond the window edge. Isobel McIntyre was facing in the opposite direction, astraddle the hirsute debt collector. She had a small tattoo on the right cheek, just above what Jock estimated would be the panty line. He watched the pink curves move slowly and felt the pressure rise again. Isobel had a superior way about her. He knew she would *die* if she thought she'd been watched doing it to a band playing with the man from HSC. His hand stole back inside his overalls again and the mist swirled thicker around him. His attention was nailed on the scene beyond the window.

Then something dripped on his shoulder just at the same time as he heard the scraping noise a little way above his head.

At first he thought it was a bird-dropping. Sometimes the starlings would flock in their thousands on winter nights, roosting on the high edges of the tall buildings. It was an occupational hazard for anyone who worked at a height, but Jock knew there were no starlings flying in the winter mist. He'd have heard their chattering, and up here, the night was silent apart from the moaning of the wind in the wires and the muffled, guttural noises emanating from Isobel McIntyre's living room. He looked up into the darkness overhead. The pulley wires were taut parallel lines which soared upwards but disappeared from view only a few yards higher than the level where he stood.

Something spattered again, catching him on the side of his head and dripping down his cheek.

At once he smelled the thick scent and his nose wrinkled in disgust.

'What the . . .' he grunted, again failing to finish a sentence.

Then something hit the wires with such force that it sounded like a base-string plucked hard. The gantry jumped about a foot into the air and bounced. Jock felt himself thrown against the balustrade again, but this time he was holding tight with his free hand.

He swung back while the platform was still moving and peered up again. A misty shape moved overhead, close in to the building, though the movement was obscured by the thickening mist.

Jock moved away from the window.

'Who's there?' he called up softly, not wishing to disturb the man and woman inside the house.

The scraping noise came again. It sounded like stone on stone, muffled by the night.

He was about to call out again when something white flickered wanly in the darkness. Beyond it, a black shadow elongated. Jock pulled himself up to his full height, eyes trying to make it out, when the shadow came suddenly *racing* down the side of the wall. It happened so fast that Jock Toner never had the chance even to open his mouth.

The shape, blacker than night, moved with astonishing speed. It came lunging with a liquid, pistoning motion, the white thing flapping alongside it. He got a glimpse of a jointed arm. Two huge orange eyes flicked open, and then something hit him so hard on the side of the neck he heard the harsh rip of muscles tearing above his shoulder. His grip was torn from the railing and he flopped against the outer edge.

The shadow came looming right at him. The eyes blazed again. Something cold and hard gripped him by the head. He could feel the clench of massive fingers on each temple and the bones felt as if they were simply caving in under the pressure. His arms shot out to ward the thing off. His knuckle hit blindly against the electric motor housing and accidentally jammed the yellow button. The engine whined into life as the gantry took a lurch and started to climb.

Even then, Jock Toner was aware of the foul stench which suddenly assaulted his nostrils. It smelled like rotting flesh.

Then he was falling. There was an abrupt twist and a searing pain as he was lifted in one jerking heave and thrown over the railing.

He screamed then, very loud and very clear as he plummeted through the mist. The force of the throw had sent him out from the building, much further than a man could have jumped. In that supercharged moment, jumbled thoughts and pictures flashed and fizzed in the man's brain. He was falling and he was going to die. He saw himself swoop down to the concrete flagstones below and saw himself splatter and bounce.

Then the nylon guide rope which had snagged around his calf as he went over the edge snapped him to a halt in mid-air as he reached the end of its drop. The force of the stall snatched his thighbone out of his hip socket and pain exploded inside him in a white flare. There was no time or breath for a sigh of relief, but in that instant Jock Toner realised what had happened. The pain was washed away in the realisation that he was not falling any longer, that he was not going to splatter and bounce wetly on the concrete below. Relief swamped him.

If Jock Toner had not been thrown out twenty feet from the side of Loch View, then he would have probably survived. But when he hit the end of the rope and felt his leg wrench out of its socket, he bounced like a weight on the end of a piece of string and came hurtling back in towards the building. He was spinning wildly as he tumbled back from the far end of the pendulum arc, yelling all the while, unable to control his position. The gantry was still making its automatic ascent of the building. Jock came flying inwards and spun just at the moment his head was below the top edge of Isobel McIntyre's window. The upward pull on the hawsers coupled with his swing ensured that his forehead connected with the sharp concrete with a muted crunching sound. A huge flash of white light seared through his mind and the circuits sparked and fizzled instantaneously in his brain as the concrete edge smashed a deep chiselled line into his forehead. Isobel McIntyre's window went red and opaque. A piece of Jock's skull lifted like a flap and went spiralling down through the mist to land with a crack on the concrete.

High up on the edge of the building, Jock Toner's body twitched and danced as it was drawn upwards, spraying his blood. The whole forefront of his brain was completely gone, but the brainstem just carried on as if nothing had happened. His heart still pumped and his nerves shook and shivered as he was hauled slowly skywards into the night. From the gaping hole in the front of his head, the blood came gouting out in a series of pulses.

Finally the engine reached the top and the automatic cut-out kicked in. The gantry whined to a stop. Thirty feet below it, Jock Toner's body quivered and spasmed, unseen by any human eye while his blood ran in rivers down the rough edge of the building, where it froze in long, dribbling streaks. Down below, on the concrete on the north edge of the building, it formed a thin slick which iced over in less than an hour.

Inside the house where he'd watched the two people grunting on the floor, Isobel McIntyre sat up.

'Did you hear something?' she asked.

'What?' the man asked, out of breath.

'I thought I heard a noise.'

'Probably me,' the hairy man said. He reached over to the seat where his clothes were crumpled in a heap and dragged his shirt across to wipe the sweat from his brow. 'What time is it?'

'Getting late. You'd better get out of here before my Kenny gets in.' Isobel got to her feet and came across to the window. She could see nothing out there. There was no light outside to show her the red coating on the window. She'd see it in the morning, along with the congealing scrap of flesh stuck to the roughcast edge just above her window and she would flee to the bathroom where she would be immediately and violently sick. The sickness would come upon her again one morning before the week was out, but there was another reason for that and it's another story.

146

Jock Toner's frozen and bloodless cadaver was not found until late the following morning by the team who came back to work to finish off the concreting. In fact, it was Neil Gunn, an eighteen-year-old apprentice, who noticed the shape dangling from the gantry an hour after he'd started work. He got such a fright that all he could do was hang onto the safety rail on the top of the block and scream for help from the foreman who was down in the hut. The ganger called the police and the fire brigade, who had to take one of the clattering lifts up to the roof and manually wind the gantry down to ground level where Jock Toner's body hit the ground like a log, frozen stiff.

At that time, everybody believed it had been an accident. All except one person who knew it was not.

12

The last thing Jock Toner saw as he spun on the rope before his head hit the concrete edge was a shadow rippling up the side of the building and into the mist. He had no time to wonder about the black shape.

On the other side of town, Lorna Breck saw the same shadow in a vision so terrifying she felt her heart freeze.

It was so vivid she could feel the sting of ice on her face and the bite of the wind which spun the crystals in flurries over the top edge of the building.

She'd been standing on a high place, watching the lights of the town twinkle dimly through the mist. Beside her a heavy metal frame hung out like a gallows and thin steel wires curved round the pulleys to disappear into the murk below.

'What's happening?' she heard herself ask in a voice that was more an echo. 'What's here?'

The words were swallowed up in the fog.

Lorna turned from the north-west edge, towards the pulley. Far across town a train lumbered out of the station, a slow beat at first, then getting faster as it picked up speed, unseen in the distance. From a little further west, a tortured squeal like an animal in distress came wavering over the rooftops as the crucible of iron in the foundry tipped its white-hot load into the pan and the strip wheels started their roll. This sound too was oddly echoed, as if it came from within a vast chamber.

Something drew her feet towards the edge, close to the pulley scaffold. She tried to pull back, unwilling to walk to the barrier that surrounded the flat top of the building like a small battlement wall, but the imperative overrode her own will. A sense of fear kindled inside her, an uneasy twist of foreboding. In her mind she could hear the scraping sound, like whispers in the dark, grating on the inside of her skull. It was like the sound of scrabbling nails; hard, chitinous claws in the distance.

She took another step forward, then another, until she

reached the barrier. It was a small wall, on top of which was a thick low tubular railing. Lorna shook her head, trying to deny the internal *push* and failed. She reached both hands out and clasped the metal. It burned cold into her palms.

'A dream,' she finally told herself, whispering against the wind. 'This is a dream.'

She knew it, but could not break free of it. Behind her, the wind whistled across the prongs of the tall television aerial, making it sing mournfully and the thin steel hawsers took up the dirge, moaning against the freezing winter night. The chill stole through the skin of her hands and spread up her arms like a frost in her blood, like sluggish river ice. She shivered and the cold flowed across her shoulders and down into her chest. Her skin felt brittle, as if it would shatter at a touch. Her bones were like glass.

She leaned over the edge, willing herself not to do it, unable to resist. She felt the creak of frozen muscles and her hands felt as if they had become part of the frigid metal. She bent her head and looked down.

The mist swirled in lethargic turbulence, tendrils of opaque white, limned by the streetlights to a dirty orange ochre. The hawser lines narrowed together in diminishing perspective as they disappeared from view into the haze. The shifting, amorphous form on the wall moved in a flicker of black and raced down the face of the building, a squat, spidery shade. The hawser twanged violently and the pulley roller squealed in protest. Lorna's eyes were locked on the turbulence below. The black reached the dim cradle. Something shot out from its squat bulk and she heard a meaty thud and a low, involuntary grunt.

Something cracked and then a shape flew off and away from the building.

'Please,' Lorna tried to say. The words came out in a little croak.

Then she heard the scream.

It came braying up the side of the building as the flailing figure launched out from the platform. Behind him a rope whipped like a tail. Beside her the pulleys squealed as they began to turn and the galley began to rise. Ahead of it the black mass came whizzing up the sheer face of the wall towards her. Ice flowed into her brain and the whole scene assaulted her senses in a series of stop-go frames. There was a deep, booming thud, the sound of a bowstring, and the man's flight stopped abruptly. Even in the distance, she heard the crack of muscle and tendon ripping. The scream died abruptly. The flailing form came catapulting back in towards the building. It tumbled and spun, obscured by the mist, then disappeared underneath the metal platform. A sickening wet noise crunched in the cold air.

And all the time, the black mass came flickering up towards her.

'Oh,' she heard her own voice gasp. Her nerves jittered in panic. She tried to back away but her muscles would not unlock.

She could hear the hard scrabble of claws on the stone and now a low, panting growl so deep she could feel it vibrate the bones of her skull.

It came rocketing upwards, incredibly fast, as if gravity had no effect on it. Its shape writhed and pistoned. She could not tell how many arms or legs the thing had. It seemed to possess no true shape at all, but it moved with frightening speed.

It reached the lip, just beside her. Something dark shot out and a hooked hand, or what might conceivably have *been* a hand, reached for the bar. It grasped it with a hard, clanging sound. The limb, or whatever it was, flexed and bunched, and the whole shape was hauled up to squat on the edge. It was like looking into a *hole* in the universe. There was only blackness. No sense of solidity, nothing to break up the shape and give it depth or real form. Even in the dream, in the terror that constricted her throat and made her cold blood feel like ice in her veins, Lorna knew that what she was looking at was *wrong*. Waves of complete and utter *evil* radiated out from the nightmare silhouette. Beside it, something white fluttered, but its lightness cast no reflection on the thing which squatted, its foul breath like grinding rocks in whatever it had for a throat. Something knobbly and shapeless turned just above what could have been hunched shoulders and two orange eyes opened, spearing her in baleful light, the only feature on the terrifying form.

Lorna heard herself gasp as the eyes lunged towards her, two malignant orbs. They were completely featureless at first, seemingly blind and mindless, then, in the centre of each, two yellow vertical slits in the orange opened with rasping clicks. It looked as if the eyes were burning with hideous flame. She could feel the heat of them and the hunger in them. She tried to loosen her hands from the rail and run. One palm ripped free with a pain that felt as if she'd left skin sticking to the cold metal.

The thing glared at her, still growling like a rabid animal. Then it moved. There was no fluidity then. A many-jointed limb suddenly reached out in the flick of an eye and held something aloft. It fluttered whitely. Lorna's eyes were drawn away from the sickening, hypnotic orbs and she saw what it held.

A tiny child dangled, caught up in a shawl which flapped in the wind. It made no sound at all. Its eyes were wide open and they were dead. Lorna could feel her vision waver in shock, but even as her knees started to give way, the thing moved again. The eyes blinked with another strange *click* sound. It did not even move its position.

Yet something black whipped out from its shapeless mass. It grabbed her by the shoulder with ferocious strength and flipped her off the edge of the building.

She tumbled over the lip, cartwheeling as she flew. Lights flickered as she passed the windows. She hurtled beyond something which hung below the gantry and fell in a nightmare swoop. The wind whistled past her and forced her breath back into her lungs and she fell and fell and fell and it seemed as if she fell forever.

Lorna woke with a thudding shock, incoherent with fright, gasping for air.

She was still whimpering fifteen minutes later as she sat on the overstuffed armchair close to the fire, sipping on hot tea held in a shaky hand.

'What's happening to me?' she asked aloud. Her voice trailed off into a sniffle. She reached for a paper tissue and blew her nose. The dream was still with her, vivid in her mind, as vivid as any of the dreams that had catapulted her out of sleep in the middle of the night, gasping for breath and damp with the sweat of night chills. And it had not just been at night either.

The visions had assaulted her at random, awake or asleep. It made her feel as if she was at the centre of some malefic whirlpool, at the mercy of dark undercurrents she could not control. In the past few days, her whole life had been turned upside down. She was scared to go to sleep, scared to stay awake. Down at the library, she'd find herself jumping at imagined shadows. Even during the day, the narrow aisles between the old Victorian bookshelves were dim, claustrophobic and threatening alleys where the narrow cones from the overhead lights could not banish the gloom. She would find herself looking over her shoulder, jumping at every rustle in the silence, and since the day she'd seen the shape in the reflection of the shop window, she hadn't dared to go down to the basement. A pile of books which had to be catalogued and covered in dust-proof plastic was still piled up behind her desk. Keith Conran, the head librarian, had asked her several times when she was planning to get the work done and Lorna had made excuses.

The library basement, two levels below the adult section, with even narrower walkways between metal shelving that were cluttered with old newspaper files, was dusty and dry and lightless. Every time Lorna thought of going down there, she pictured the slam of the door at the top of the narrow wooden stairway and the sudden blackness as the light clicked off. And in that imaginary scene, she would hear the scuttling claws of something even blacker than the blind dark snuffling and grunting its way towards her, getting ready to focus those appalling eyes on her.

It was only just after seven at night. Lorna hadn't meant to fall asleep on the couch, but she'd been exhausted. Her body was aching and her joints protesting. It felt as if she was picking up a virus, but she knew it was just lack of sleep, lack of *real* sleep. The aftershock of the dreams shuddered through her, making her hands shake so much she needed both of them to hold the cup. Finally she gave up and put it down on the kerb by the fireplace then held herself there, arms around her knees, holding herself tight, rocking slowly, as if the movement would ease the fear and bring her comfort. It did not help.

It had been almost two weeks since the first episode. That was how she had begun to think of them. *Episodes*. They were happenings. Occurrences.

They were *visitations*.

152

She hadn't written the first one down, though she could remember exactly when it had happened. It was before the night Gemma had asked her to come to the party, before the hellish vision of the fire. They had been in the old Bridge Hotel with some of Gemma's friends. They were all older than Lorna, but her cousin had been looking out for her since she'd come down to start her job in the library, especially after she'd finished with James Blair. Working in the library didn't give a girl much of a chance to meet new people, and Gemma had made sure she at least got out in company.

It was that night, after she'd come home and had her shower, that she'd had the next dream. She hadn't seen *it* then. Not the way she'd seen the shape since.

But in the dream she'd felt the presence and it had frightened her so badly she'd woken up unable even to breathe. She hadn't known what was happening. All she'd seen were the seven people around the table and then *things* had started to move and inside her head she'd heard the voice, scrapy as the claws on the side of the building in the other vision, telling her to *behold*. She had seen the old woman rise into the air, while the walls had sweated and the books had slammed from their shelves, sensed the terror in the other people who had fled from something they could not understand, but could sense with a primitive instinct.

The next time – and she *had* written this one in her diary – had been three days later when she was working down in the basement, sorting out the files. Keith had gone out for lunch while she had stayed to finish off.

The vision had hit her so hard that she'd fallen backwards against a stack of newspapers and had slid to the floor, blind to everything in the cellar while the dust had swirled up in a cloud and she was *outside*.

The baby had been in its pram. The door to the veranda was almost closed. Just one chink of light escaped the heavy curtains. She had heard the child's light snuffling breath. Overhead stars twinkled in the night air. Down to the left, the shriek of the forge was loud and she could see the glow heat through the holes on the side of the metal-framed building. Across town, where the night shift worked on the rig-construction, in the shipyard's engine room, something clanked several times, ringing flatly across the river. Three swans had come flying downstream, all in line, only feet above their reflections, ghostly images whooping through the air to disappear quickly from view.

The baby had coughed, then let out a little cry.

And the shadow had come racing down the wall with astonishing speed. It hit the pram with a thump which would have capsized it but for the close confines of the veranda balcony. It seemed to *flow* over it, almost hiding it from sight, then drew back. She heard clearly the ripping sound as the harness parted. The baby screeched, high and wavering and then it was gone, its thin little cry disappearing upwards, as the black shape scuttled in a diagonal to the far corner while she had stood watching from some vantage point – and she had no idea where she'd been standing – watching soundlessly, unable to scream a warning, unable to call for help.

Then, two days later, she'd seen the fire, and that was most shocking of all.

Because when that vision had assailed her she had *known* it was true.

She'd been staring into the tea leaves, and she'd focused herself as she'd done before and suddenly she had *seen* the whole thing. It hadn't been like a memory, or a mental picture. She'd been *there*. That had been the worst of it. She had been able to see it, to hear it. And to smell it.

The voices around her had faded. The last thing she'd heard was Gemma telling Mrs McCluskie to hush and then there had been a *click* inside her head, as if some little bubble had popped in a vein and the picture had come rushing up at her and she had gone swooping into it.

She had been standing in the corner of the room.

The man was slouched in a corner seat, feet stuck out in front of him, one crossed over the other. She could even see the hole in his carpet slipper. A newspaper was tented over his face as if he'd fallen asleep reading it. Beside him, a coal shifted in the grate and sent a small glow out from the hearth. As she watched, the side light beside the man's chair flickered then went dim. It was as if it was being lacquered with some filmy substance, layer upon layer which just caused the light to fade. It happened so smoothly and swiftly that at first Lorna was not aware of it. For a second she could see the orange glow of the filament then it winked out. The gentle radiance in the hearth was swallowed up in the darkness and then she heard the scraping sound coming from where the fireglow had been. There was the smell of smoke and soot and suddenly she was aware of something *else* in the room. It was pitch dark, but she could sense the presence of a *shape*.

The scene flicked again and she was in a small bedroom. From the other room there was a thudding sound. A man coughed or gagged and the sound stopped instantly. Tendrils of smoke came crawling in under the door. Two small boys were sleeping in bunks. The tousle-headed one on the top had his arm hanging down, fingers slack. In the cot, the baby was stirring. It rolled over and clumsily got to its feet, eyes closed, dummy hanging from the corner of its mouth. Sleepily the tiny girl struggled for balance as her feet sank down into the mattress. She had fair, downy hair. The smoke was coming thicker under the door. The baby coughed. The dummy flew out of her mouth and her eyes opened. The little girl looked straight into Lorna's eyes and held both hands up, mutely appealing to be carried.

Lorna couldn't move. Behind her, the door grew hot and the smoke filled the room. The baby coughed again. One of the boys turned in his sleep as the fumes thickened. Fire was roaring next door. Lorna tried to call to the boys to wake up, but again, she was dumb.

Then the door splintered open. Sizzling sparks exploded inwards. Something came past her so quickly the eye couldn't follow it. There was a high baby cry and then the window crashed outwards. One of the boys awoke with a start, screamed, and then a huge gout of flame, sucked in by the draught from the open window, blasted into the room. The boy's scream rose glassily. The smell of burning flesh assaulted her nose and then Lorna was elsewhere. She was on some dark place all alone and she could hear a small voice singing a song from childhood. The words were very familiar. They kept repeating themselves and then Lorna had been back in Gemma's house. Agnes McCann had been staring at her and Lorna realised the voice had been her own. Agnes McCann had a blank look on her face and suddenly Lorna *knew*. The smell of sizzling fat and

155

scorched skin and hair was thick at the back of her throat and she was looking at a woman whose children were dead and she was more frightened than she had ever been in her life.

Now she was still scared, but she was scared for herself.

'There's something wrong,' she mumbled, chin still on her knees, body drawn in tight. 'I think I'm going mad.'

But she knew she was *not* going mad.

She had read the reports. She had seen the news on television. The old woman dead in Cairn House; the baby missing from its pram in Latta Court. The suicide of Reverend Simpson, the babies and their father dead in the fire.

Three of these things she'd seen as they were happening, as if they were being shown to her for her disgust and someone else's pleasure. It was as if something was able to slide into her mind and show her the most terrifying, most sickening scenes it could find.

Yet one of these things had happened days *after* Lorna had dreamed them. She did not know what to do about that.

And worse. She'd seen the other baby, the one torn from its mother's arms in the alley down by the river. And this time she'd seen again the moving shadow which scuttled up and down walls and turned sickening orange eyes upon her, drowning her in their malevolent focus.

She'd seen the same thing on top of the high building where she'd never been, not physically, not in *real* life. She'd seen it clamber and flow up the sheer concrete side and pause only to snatch at a man and throw him to his death and then it had paused again to show her something, to take pleasure out of displaying what it held in a hand that was blacker than night.

Lorna Breck by now did not truly think she was going mad, but she knew that if the dreadful visions continued, then she surely would.

She had stumbled into something. Some part of her mind, some tiny crack somewhere, had opened up and was giving her glimpses of such monstrous malignancy, such shocking malevolence that she was unable to comprehend them.

Something inside her had opened a door into the future. Whether or not the shadowed, scuttling thing she could see in her dreams was real, she did not know, though something told

156

her that despite the impossibility of it, there was *something* that scuttered and climbed and snatched and killed. She had seen four things, four terrible things, and they had all happened. They had all come to pass.

Now she had seen two more things.

Lorna Breck was frightened to go to sleep, scared to stay awake. And she dreaded what she might hear if she turned on her radio, or opened a newspaper.

She did not want to hear of another death. She did not want to learn of a man hanging from a rope on the side of a tower block. She did not want to be appraised of yet another baby missing.

But she knew she would. In one or two or three days, she would learn it and she would be sickened by the horror of it and the sheer helplessness she would feel.

She felt as if she wanted to lock her doors and play music so loud it blotted out every thought, but even then, she knew, that would do no good at all.

As she sat there, still trembling, feeling the heat of the fire on her arms and legs and a terrible chill in her heart, Lorna Breck came to a decision. She would wait until she knew for certain that what she'd seen had actually *happened*, though she prayed to God that they would not. And if they did, she would have to speak to someone about it. She'd read the name in the newspaper. Lorna eased herself to her feet and took the phone book from the drawer on the sideboard and riffled through it until she found the number she wanted.

Jack Fallon picked Davy up just before nine and drove him to school. Julia was blocked up with the cold which had been building up for the past couple of days, and greeted him, still in her dressing gown, bleary-eyed and raw-nosed. Davy was ready with his schoolbag slung from a shoulder and a Thunderbirds lunch box. He was as chirpy as a robin, in stark contrast to his mother.

The heater was on full blast and the boy helped wipe the condensation from the screen, talking the whole time.

'Can we go up the hills again, Uncle Jack?'

'If I can get away.'

'If it snows, can we take the sledge up?'

'Sure.'

'You fell off last time. You hurt your head.'

'And it was sore. I scraped my face in the snow, 'cause I was holding onto you with both hands. Next time we'll find a place where the snow's thicker and there are no stones underneath.'

At the school, he promised the boy he'd try to get off at the weekend, though he knew it was far from likely. Taking Davy up beyond the trees and over the hills to the rugged Langmuir rockface would do everybody some good. It gave the boy some fresh air and time to scamper and explore. It gave Julia a break from looking after him on her own and it gave Jack some time to be with the only family he had left. He would have loved to say he *would* be able to take Davy out on the Saturday, but the previous night, Jack had got the call and all hell had broken loose. He'd been out until four in the morning and had managed less than four hours' sleep when he'd got home, and he was feeling blasted. It was going to be another long day and the weekend was going to be wall-to-wall heartache.

Davy waved from the gate at Crossburn School, a little figure in a pom-pom hat pulled way down over his ears and a woolly scarf wound round his neck a couple of times then tucked into the front of a padded jacket. He turned and disappeared into a melee of small bodies. Jack did a five-point reverse turn on the narrow avenue and headed down to the station, eyes grainy and feeling as if he could have used another ten hours' sleep.

Blair Bryden, who edited the *Gazette*, a tall, thin man with thick glasses and close-cropped hair, apprehended him on the steps.

'Hold on, Jack,' he called, catching up with him and taking him by the arm. 'You don't want to go in there.'

'You're right, I don't,' Jack said wearily. 'But that's what they pay me for.'

'No. What I meant is that everybody and his auntie from the dailies is waiting for you. Cowie won't say a dickie bird. He's going to feed you to the vultures.'

'I've been there before. There's not a bone they haven't picked,' Jack countered amiably.

'Also, it's my press day,' Blair added with a deprecating grin.

'Oh, I get it. Alright. Come on.'

He took Blair by the arm and led him round to the van park

behind the station then in through the back door. One of the young constables nodded to both of them, a quizzical look in his eye.

'Mr Cowie wants to see you right away, sir,' he announced.

'Soon as I can, Gordon,' Jack said and hustled the local editor along the corridor into an interview room.

'Right. Ten minutes, then I have to go and talk to them all. I'll give you another fifteen minutes' start and you can fax their offices and make a bob or two.'

Blair winked. The two men had known each other a long time. He drew out a spiral notebook, put it flat on the table, clicked his pen and looked up at Jack, his eyes pale and magnified behind the lenses.

'Is it a serial thing?'

'Don't know.'

'Opinion?'

'Not attributable, but it looks that way. Two kids gone. We have to believe the worst. Either that or it's somebody with an overblown maternal instinct who wants to adopt in bulk, but I don't subscribe to that theory. Not when the second mother is up in intensive care. It wasn't looking good at five this morning. I'm not expecting miracles.'

'You'll have to rule Simpson out on this one,' Blair stated.

'Best alibi in the world. He's on a marble slab.'

'And how about the Doyle baby?'

'Two ways. Either it *was* Simpson, and he was a right evil bastard if there ever was one, and there's something to link him with Latta Court.' Jack paused. 'That is definitely off the record. I mean it.'

'Don't worry. We never spoke.'

'Good man. As I say, it's a fifty-fifty at the moment. My instinct is that Simpson was *not* involved.'

'Which means we have a serial snatcher.'

'I reckon so. No serious violence in the first, but a lot on the second. I don't think it's a copy-cat.'

'Are you looking for a woman?'

'Possible, but not probable. Maybe somebody who's just lost a baby. Maybe a nutter who can't have any. Or maybe just a nutter.'

159

'This Campbell woman – where is she?'

'Intensive care in Lochend. She won't make it.'

'The father?'

'Sedated himself to the gills last night. We only got word on the baby this morning when he finally remembered. Useless bastard.'

Blair nodded. 'I know the family.' He looked at his neat shorthand notes. 'Any connection with the Herkik killing?'

'God, I hope not. I'm still up to my armpits on that one. Simpson was my best shot and I missed him by a hair.'

'So what else can you tell me?'

'That's about it. All we have at the moment are some screams in Barley Cobble. One of the old fellows upstairs heard a woman shouting, but there's plenty of that after a rough night in the Castlegate. She was found an hour later, close to ten o'clock, nearly frozen stiff. Bad head injuries. No sign of the baby.'

He put a hand up to his forehead. 'We've had door-to-door all night. Neighbours, relatives. I'm hoping for a lead today. Nobody can steal two kids and *not* leave some trail.'

There was a small pause, then Jack looked at the other man. 'Can they?' he asked.

'How about the other hanging?' Blair asked.

'You've got me there,' Jack admitted. 'What other hanging?'

'Up at Loch View. I just heard it on police band. Somebody found dangling from the side of the building.'

'Christ,' Jack breathed. 'That's all I need. You sure?'

'Course. I got a call two minutes later from a cousin of mine. She lives in the next block. Got a bird's eye view. I thought you'd have heard.' Blair snapped his notebook shut. 'I'm glad I got you then. Thanks for the few minutes' grace.'

'Any time,' Jack said. 'By the way, I thought you did a fair piece last week. I never knew all that about Cairn House.'

'It's amazing what you find when you look back the older numbers. I've got nearly two hundred years of history gathering dust in the back office. I thought I'd write a book on it some day. Like a ghost story.'

'Stick to facts, Blair. They're much scarier. Anyway, I've got to run. Better brief myself on this other matter before I meet your friends.'

'No friends of mine,' Blair said with a wide grin. 'They're the opposition. And by the way, you look like hell.'

'Thanks a million,' Jack said without rancour. Blair left the way he had come in and Jack went in the opposite direction, pondering whether to see Cowie first, or get a briefing from CID.

In the event, the Superintendent waylaid him on the way to the muster room and held his own office door open, inviting Jack inside. There was no way he could avoid it.

'Another fine mess,' he started.

'So I believe.'

'And what are we going to tell that pack at the front office?'

'The truth, basically,' Jack suggested. 'Either that or we could field them to headquarters, but that would get their backs up, and we might want them on our side.'

'I thought you might have been in earlier,' Cowie snorted, changing tack.

'If I thought you wanted a zombie, then I would have. But I thought it would be better if I got a couple of hours' sleep. I worked out a rota for inquiries. Slater and McColl have been coordinating through the night.'

'What about the other matter?'

Jack saw the look on the other man's face. It told him the Superintendent thought he had a card to play.

'You mean up at Loch View?'

Cowie couldn't conceal his surprise and annoyance. He nodded abruptly.

'Have to wait for the full works on that one.' He took a stab in the dark. 'I think it's an accident.'

'Too many accidents. Too many coincidences.'

'Oh, I think we have to separate the coincidences out.'

'Well, I think there's enough going on for us to handle. We're going to need better coordination on this.'

'You'll want to handle the press statement then?'

Cowie looked as if he'd rather kiss a snake. He was not backward about spouting to the media whenever there was good personal public relations to be harvested, but when, as they say in Levenford, the ball is on the slates, when there were two babies missing, a minister with a history hanged in glorious

161

multichrome, a mother dying in intensive care, and a Hungarian medium battered to death in her own home, there was little to say except the usual police standby: Enquiries are continuing.

That would not be good for the image. Cowie declined the offer.

'No. You're the man leading the operation,' he said coolly. 'For the time being.'

Jack did not miss the nuance.

'Right, I'd better get a quick briefing and then get about the business.'

He found John McColl in the room adjacent to his office. Craig Campbell was sitting opposite. Smoking a cigarette, looking ashen-faced and red-eyed. He gave the impression of a man who still had a way to go before he sobered up. Jack beckoned the sergeant into the office.

'How's it going with him?'

'He hasn't much of a clue. He's a drunk and a waster. I knew the girl. Friend of my daughter. Nice wee thing.'

'And what about the Loch View situation?'

'Oh, you heard?'

Jack nodded.

'Early word is that it's an accident. A scaffolder fell off a gantry.'

'Fell or jumped?'

'Looks like a fall. It's not a hanging. The rope was snagged around his leg. Hit his head off the side of the building. The place is a mess. I've two men knocking doors, but so far nobody's any the wiser. I called the fire brigade and Sorley Fitzpatrick's men got him down half an hour ago. Robbie Cattanach is doing the post mortem.'

'OK. Any other news?'

'Lochend General tell me the girl's in a bad way. They don't expect her to last the hour.'

'Oh, great,' Jack said. 'Now two murders. Two abductions. A suicide and an accident.'

'Not forgetting the fire up at Murroch Road.'

'Oh yes. We can't forget that. Life is one big picnic.'

Jack spent twenty minutes fielding questions in the conference room. The boys from the press were an unruly bunch, but they didn't give him as hard a time as he'd had in the past. There was little he could tell them to help them speculate. He stuck to the facts and refused to let himself be drawn to conclusions. There were enough simple facts anyway to let them go off feeling satisfied. Jack wondered how they'd feel when their newsdesks told them the local man had beaten them to the punch.

Robbie Cattanach did not take long to pronounce Jock Toner dead. For a start, his body was frozen stone hard as it twirled in the slight breeze, like a trussed fly on a spider's web. His eyes were open and iced over and his body was almost completely devoid of blood. The slick down the side of the building and the red ice-slide on the concrete paving testified to what had happened. At the slab, the young pathologist hardly needed the cutters to determine the cause of death. The crater on the top of the dead man's head was enough to give him the picture. He estimated the force with which Toner's skull had connected with the top edge of the window and came to a conclusion after he'd gone through a series of exhaustive tests which showed there had been no sudden stroke, no heart attack.

Later in the afternoon, he bypassed the normal channels.

'I thought you'd like to know,' Robbie's voice blared tinnily from the earpiece, 'in my view it wasn't an accident. Ralph Slater gave me a rough description of how the body was positioned, though I'll have a clearer idea once I see the pictures.'

'An idea of what?'

'If it wasn't an accident, we've got a jumper or he was pushed. I think he was pushed, and that gives you another murder.'

Jack's heart sank. He let the words sink in, then the questions marshalled themselves.

'That's the last thing I need. I'm hoping you're wrong. What gives you the idea?'

'Angle of concussion strike. If he'd fallen straight down, he might just have hit the lower edge of the windowsill, but probably not. There was some wind, but not enough to have much effect on fifteen stone dropping forty feet.'

'Go on,' Jack urged.

'And he hit the top edge, probably at more than thirty miles an hour, coming in at an angle with a last-minute jerk. I believe he must have gone right out from the building and come back again in an arc, travelling fast. The gantry must have been moving at the time, so the swing and the upward motion combined when he hit. Took the top of his head off. I've got almost total frontal damage, but nothing on brainstem. It's rare, but not impossible. His body functions continued for some time.'

'Explain that.'

'His heart kept beating, at least for a while. He was upside down, unconscious, certainly brain-dead to all intents and purposes, and gravity would have combined to account for the loss of blood. I estimate he'd lost nearly eight pints. That's almost the total body supply.'

'If the lift was going up at the time,' Jack began.

'Somebody started the motor,' Robbie finished. 'I don't think he would have started it himself. Pointless really. No,' he added emphatically. 'I think the fellow was thrown off.'

Jack thought about that for a moment. He had no reason to doubt Robbie Cattanach. The man was straight as a die, and certainly as good as any pathologist Jack had dealt with in the past. If it was murder, then there had to be a reason for it. Something else nagged at him and he chased it for a moment before catching the thought. It was a pattern. Not a clear one, not even a logical one. But if it was murder, then it was the second case involving a block of high flats. That might have been the only connection, but it was there. Even then, in Jack's mind, the separate incidents were not all conjoined. The only two which were almost certainly part of the one case were the missing babies, but the feeling that there was a connection, something *important* about the two incidents involving high places, struck a discordant note.

'Oh and another thing,' Robbie said, diverting Jack's mind. 'There were traces of blood on him.'

'And all over the ground as far as I've heard.'

'Yes. But there were drops of congealed blood on his cheek and shoulder, and on his jacket, which might just have come from somebody else. I'll be doing further tests. Maybe I can give you more of a clue later on.'

'I'd appreciate any clue right now,' Jack said with a drawn-out sigh.

Two abductions. Possibly three murders. A suicide.

Not a bad score, Jack thought, for just over a week. So far the only clue had led to one suspect, whom he'd found bloated and hanging in the cellar under the church. The rest of the inquiries had drawn nothing but more questions. There were no answers.

What Jack Fallon did not know was that there was another suicide in Levenford that day.

And the strange thing about it was that the man who had taken his own life was not dead.

13

Edward Tomlin stunned his family to silence when he told them he was going to die.

It happened on the Friday night, one day after Shona Campbell's baby had been torn from her arms by something which had leapt down at her from the shadows.

Tomlin was sitting at the head of the table in the kitchen in the semi-detached house in Eastmains, out on the far edge of town. When he sluggishly pushed his plate away from him, the sausage and egg was untouched.

'Are you not hungry?' Margaret Tomlin asked him. Between them, their two girls were feeding with obvious relish.

'I'm going to die,' he said. The words came out without a trace of emotion. Margaret picked up the tone immediately, though the girls missed it entirely.

'We're all going to die,' Christine piped up. She was fourteen and always in the top three in her class. She spread butter on a slice of bread as she spoke. 'It's a fact of life.'

'Oh, don't talk like that,' Trisha protested. 'I hate that.'

Margaret cut across them. 'What did you say?'

'I'm going to die.' He looked at her across the table, his face completely and utterly blank. Margaret Tomlin, who was a pleasant, plump woman with her faded fair hair pulled back in a ponytail, felt a slow coldness in her stomach. For the past week Eddie had been very withdrawn. He'd stayed out late, and as soon as he was home, he'd gone straight up to the loft where he kept the train set he'd owned since before they were married. The night before, it had been well past midnight when he came in and he hadn't said a word, though in the morning she'd found his trousers were scuffed and scraped and covered in mud from the knee to the ankle. When she'd asked him what had happened, he'd given her a blank look and had said nothing.

In all the years she'd known him, since both of them were at the school the girls now attended, Edward Tomlin had been a dependable man. Even boring, some might have said, and Margaret herself might have said it if she'd been pressed. Certainly, they led dull enough lives. The girls were quite well behaved and bookish. She worked as a clerkess in Castlebank. He patrolled the empty Castlebank shipyard. She knew nothing at all of the clothes he'd stolen from washing lines at night, the panties and stockings which he kept locked in the box behind the toolroom door, and which he wore in the hollow silence of the hull-shed.

He never forgot their anniversary and they always went out on that day for an Italian meal in Glasgow. He belonged to no club and rarely went out drinking.

In the past week or so, he'd been out without saying where he was going and when he clambered into bed beside her, she could smell drink on his breath. A couple of times she'd asked him if anything was wrong and he'd mumbled that there was nothing on his mind.

She thought about the possibility that he might have another woman and hated herself when she'd sniffed at the collar of his jacket for traces of perfume. On the Wednesday, when he'd gone out at night – *Just out, nowhere special*, he'd said vaguely – she'd gone up to the loft and checked through the desk he had there. There was nothing, no letters, no odd little gifts. She'd gone through his pockets while he was up with his trains and had come up with nothing. There were no receipts, no notes, no telephone numbers. Nothing except for the tarot cards. Two of them. The six of cups and the three of swords, old-fashioned cards with Victorian-style artwork back and front and the names of each scrolled on the bottom. Both of the cards were bent, as if they'd been stuffed in the pocket in haste. She knew next to nothing of tarot, didn't have a clue where he could have picked them up. She had put them back in his pocket and said nothing.

Now, on the Friday night, Edward turned round and told his family he was going to die.

'I've done something,' he said.

'Done what?' Margaret asked. She could hear the chill in her own voice, almost echoing the dead coldness in his. Both girls looked from father to mother, like spectators at tennis.

'Something. I don't know. It's too dark to see.'

'What are you talking about?' Margaret asked. She could feel a little tremor start in her left hand. She put down the fork and it rattled against the plate.

'I took something. I had to.'

'What's wrong, daddy?' Trisha piped up plaintively.

'I took weedkiller. Paraquat. I drank it.'

Margaret opened her mouth, closed it again, fighting the giddiness as the blood drained from her face.

'You did *what?*'

'Paraquat,' he repeated. 'I had to. It said so.'

'*Who* said so?'

So far his voice had been dead flat. No inflection, no cadence. The words came out and landed like cuts of meat on a butcher's board. Now Eddie Tomlin's eyebrows arched upwards, and a look of bewilderment came across his face.

'I . . . I don't know. Him. It. It said to.'

'Edward Tomlin. Stop it this minute.'

The puzzled expression faded, and the man's face went blank again.

'Too late. Can't stop it now.'

'I don't believe you,' she shot back, clutching at the straw.

He got up slowly and went to the back door. She heard the outside door, beyond the pantry, open with a clatter. He went outside and came back with a plastic bottle. She'd seen it before. He'd used it in summer to clear the weeds from the stone chippings on the narrow driveway.

'This is it. I drank it.'

For a moment he sounded like a little boy boasting.

'And I'm going to die.'

Trisha burst into tears. 'Stop it, daddy. I *hate* you speaking like that,' she bawled.

He turned to her and looked at her as if he'd never seen her before.

'Can't stop it. Not now. The clock is running.' Then he smiled, a ghastly smile which only moved his mouth, while the rest of his face remained expressionless.

'Time to go,' he added. He got slowly to his feet and turned away from the table.

The three of them watched him as he took four steps and then

168

started to slump when he reached the sink. His knees buckled and Margaret heard the thud as his ribs caught the rounded edge. He gave a little gasp and then she heard him retch violently. Liquid splashed into the basin and Trisha promptly vomited her eggs onto her plate.

'Eddie?' Margaret asked in a voice that was more of a gasp. '*Eddie*? Tell me it's a joke?'

He retched again. She could see his sides heave with the violence of it. This time nothing came jetting out of his mouth. He gagged twice then coughed, before bringing his head up. He turned and as he did, he began to sink slowly to the floor.

'No joke,' he said breathlessly. 'All over. All over now.' He hiccupped. His face had gone greenish white. 'Time to go now.'

He slid down against the cupboard door and sprawled on the vinyl. He tried to raise himself up on one elbow but failed. Margaret pushed her chair back and went to kneel beside him. He turned to his stricken wife, his eyes now wide and staring. A trickle of saliva dribbled down his chin.

'Got to go now. Only good thing for me.'

Christine was crying in a high-pitched continuous howl. Trisha was still trying to get her breath back. There was a hot smell of bile in the air.

Margaret Tomlin got herself up from her knees, her face as white as her husband's, and almost knocked herself out on the door in her rush to get to the phone. Within fifteen minutes an ambulance arrived to take Edward Tomlin to Lochend General, where Shona Campbell's body lay in one of the long, cold drawers.

A team of doctors began the hopeless fight to save his life. It took him six days to die as, inch by inch, the poison invaded his organs and one by one they began to close themselves down.

By the time Jack Fallon got home that Friday, it was nearly midnight and the cottage was cold. He slung his coat on the hook by the front door and poured himself a drink first, before putting the coffee on to heat. He was tired, cold and hungry, but didn't think he could eat.

It had not been a good day.

Shona Campbell had died, as the doctors had predicted, from blood-loss, exposure and the massive trauma. She had not

169

regained consciousness. This was a blow to Jack, who had posted a policewoman to sit by her bed in the hope she might, despite the devastating wound on her head, have been able to give them some answers.

Jack had spoken to Robbie Cattanach on the phone.

'A heavy instrument. Not quite blunt. Like a log with nails in it,' Robbie had told him. 'Tremendous damage to the left side of her head. It's a wonder she survived as long as she did.'

Jack urged him to go on. He knew he'd get the full report, but it wouldn't be until Monday.

'She put up a fight, that's for sure.'

'It was definitely a man, then?'

'Probably. I'd put money on it. Someone very strong. I gave some of the scrapings to your forensic people. She'd had a go alright, but that didn't do her any good at all.'

Ralph Slater and his team had gone over the scene for three hours and come up with very little.

'Whoever hit her was a fair size,' Ralph conjectured. 'It's definitely a downward blow. Caved in the side of her face. Not a pretty sight. There was a lot under the nails of her left hand. That's being analysed just now.'

'Footprints?' Jack asked.

'Cold night, boss. Freezing. Any prints are two days old.'

'What are the neighbours saying?'

Ralph handed over a manilla folder.

'It's all in there and not worth a damn. One old fellow heard someone yelling late on, but that's just normal for the area at that time of night. In fact, I get the impression it was quieter than normal.'

Jack had interviewed Craig Campbell, who had sobered up but made just as little sense in the cold light of day. He was no help.

Blair Bryden had managed to get the snatch on the front page of the *Gazette* and had a wing column devoted to Jock Toner's demise. It was quick work. He must, Jack knew, have written it all within an hour of leaving by the back door of the station and then got the printers to hold the Friday edition for a last-minute run. It was a fair enough piece, and Blair had the advantage of being a Levenford man born and bred. He knew just about everybody.

170

The story spilled onto the centrespread where the local editor had compiled wrap-up on the action over the past fortnight. Anybody could read the question between the lines. Two possible suicides, two child snatches. A woman killed. A father and his three children dead in a fire. While the *Gazette* did not say in so many words that there was a connection between all these events, its tone did suggest that misfortune had stamped into town and set up home.

Jack Fallon had to agree. It was a few weeks until the end of the year, and already a bad winter had settled on Levenford.

14

Over the weekend, the temperature plummeted. Saturday brought the first flurries of snow hitting in from the north-west, and by morning, Langmuir Crags were blanketed in white. Jack awoke at nine, later than he'd intended, and had a quick plate of bacon and eggs before shrugging on his padded jacket and stepping out into a world that had changed overnight. The snow was blinding under a clear, hard sky, and all the sharp outlines of winter – the bare black branches and the rocky outcrops at the edge of the muir cliffs – were fuzzed in white. Everything looked soft and peaceful. The wind had died and had drifted the virgin snow to soften the jagged edges. Jack walked carefully round to the back of the house where the land at the far end of the garden fell away steeply to the little stream that used to turn the wheel of Cargill Farm mill before Jack had been born. The water which normally tumbled down through the narrow gorge was now almost silent, just a musical tinkle. Icicles hung down from the lip of the falls, slender jewelled stalactites reflecting the low light of the rising sun. A robin whistled robustly close by and blurred red as it came to land on the fence post almost within arm's reach. It cocked its head to the side and fixed him with a sparkling black eye.

'And good morning to you,' Jack said.

The little bird, a bright red contrast against the snow, hopped onto the strand of wire, bobbed jauntily at him and piped a warbling challenge. If Jack had reached out with his hand, he could have touched the robin. It sat and glared at him defiantly, feathers puffed out, its beak a little dagger, spindly legs apart.

'Alright,' Jack said, with a laugh. 'I'm going.' The bird sang after him as he walked, feet padding silently in the soft snow, back to the house. He called the office to say he was going out to speak to someone and would be in later. It was a minor lie. He went back into the kitchen, took a handful of stale slices from the bread-bin and went back into the garden. The robin was now perched like a lookout on the garden fork that had been stabbed into the soil since October, when the last of the turnips were lifted. Jack ripped the dry bread into small pieces and scattered them onto the flat place where the short grass waited for spring. The robin flew down immediately and pecked. By the time Jack reached the house, the garden was teeming with sparrows and starlings. They were feeding hungrily, and the image took him back to the years when he'd sat at the back door, binoculars hard up against his eyes, identifying all the birds as they fluttered and squabbled over whatever he'd left for them. Here at Cargill Cottage, right out on the far side of town, there were still plenty of birds. Twenty years on, Jack remembered them all.

He walked to his car, brushed the snow from the windscreen and got in. He eased the car out through the gap in the hedge and started downhill, keeping in high gear, careful not to skid on the slope. A hundred yards down the farm road, he turned left onto Berry Avenue, which hadn't been there when he was a boy. Then it had been a jumble of old bramble thickets where mothers and kids spent September and October collecting enough to make jam and jelly to last the winter.

Julia lived at the far end, where the road came to an abrupt halt. Beyond that, a pair of sycamore trees stood like bare sentries to the path which led down the long slope to Langmuir Burn, a wide stream which drained from the bog way up in the hills and meandered down to skirt the town and empty itself into the Clyde near the Castle Rock.

Davy leapt about like an excited puppy when he opened the door to find Jack stamping the snow from his cleated boots.

'Can we take the sledge? Eh, Uncle Jack. Can we go down the hill?'

Jack ruffled his hair. Julia came out of the kitchen, still in her dressing gown, as she had been the day before. She was tall, and had the same jet-black hair Jack had. She was five years younger than her brother and under normal circumstances, she was a pretty level-headed and easy-going woman. She looked better than she had on the Friday morning, but as she leaned forward to kiss Jack on the cheek and say hello, he could hear she was still choked with the cold.

'Shouldn't you be in your bed?'

'Not with that wee tornado,' she replied with a watery smile. 'I've no energy at all, and he's been given an extra helping. Whatever he's on, I could use some of it.'

'Well, get back upstairs and I'll bring you some tea.'

'Oh, I'll be alright.'

'Do what you're told, girl,' he ordered with feigned severity. 'I'll take him out for an hour or so. I have to get to the office later, but I need some fresh air.'

'You want to get back to your childhood again,' she said and laughed weakly, then whipped out a tissue just in time to catch a sudden sneeze. Jack shooed her upstairs and put the kettle on. Davy danced around him until Jack confirmed they would go sledging, then raced off to get his snowsuit and boots. Ten minutes later, Julia was in bed with tea and a magazine. Jack and the small boy went out, dragging the old iron sledge behind them. It bumped over the roots between the old sycamores and beech trees of the bar-wood which separated Cargill Farm land from the small line of houses on Berry Avenue, then, when they were through the barrier, it glided smoothly on the virgin snow of the field.

The air was clear and nippy and the sun, now higher, sent slanting rays onto the hillside which bounced them back in millions of coruscating sparkles.

They reached the lip of the hill and Jack angled the sledge to aim it along the natural curve of a dip which swung as it descended to the flat pasture beside the stream. He had an old, battered, Russian soldier's hat with a stiff brim and flaps which covered his ears. He pulled it tight down onto his head, partially to shade his eyes from the glare and also to prevent a repeat of last winter's accident.

Wee Davy snuggled between his legs, both hands gripping Jack's knees, and then they were off.

The sledge moved slowly at first. They could hear the runners whisper on the dry snow as Jack pushed with both hands to get them moving and then they were down over the lip and accelerating. Davy squealed with excitement as they hurtled down the gulley, following the natural track. On either side, the snow was a blur and the runners sent up a fine spray of crystals as they shot along. Jack could feel the boy's fingers dig into the skin

174

of his legs as the slope dropped away from them for the final swoop down into the flat.

'Yee-hah!' Davy yelled, and Jack bawled along with him. They were hammering along, just hitting the level field. Here the cows had grazed the grass flat and only a few brown dockens and thistles punctuated the pasture. By luck, they passed them all without obstruction and were heading straight for the pool in the stream when Jack leaned his weight to the right and the sledge started to curve in its headlong flight. They veered parallel to the edge, slowing down now, when the left runner hit a molehill frozen hard as a rock. The sledge bounced. Jack made a grab for Davy, missed and the boy flipped up and over and landed in a drift with hardly a sound. The sledge bounced on, riderless as Jack was thrown to the left. He landed on his hip with such a jar his breath was socked right out, tumbled over the edge and slid down on his backside onto the ice on the pool, spinning as he skittered like a curling stone. He ground to a halt halfway out from the bank, head spinning.

He clambered to his knees, backside aching from slamming against something hard on his slide down the steep bank.

'Great, Uncle Jack,' Davy pealed. 'That was magic.'

The boy appeared round the side of a gorse bush, snow clinging like thick icing to his one-piece winter suit. His face was red with excitement and he was grinning from ear to ear. 'Can we do it again?' He was certainly none the worse for his fall. 'Come on, Uncle Jack. Can we go up to the top again?'

'Yeah,' Jack said. 'Just let me get my breath back.'

'How did you get out there? Did you slide all that way?'

'Sure I did.'

'Is the ice safe?'

'I think . . .' Jack started to say, just as an ominous metallic creak shocked the still air.

Jack felt the ice tremble under his feet.

'Uncle Jack, I think . . .' Davy shouted.

There was one monumental *crack*, and Jack dropped like a stone. The ice opened up and swallowed him. One second Jack was standing on the flat ice and the next he was foundering in the freezing stream, gasping for breath, snatching for something to grab hold of. Fortunately, by the time he realised what had happened, he was only standing in three feet of water. The ice had broken in the shallow end of the pool. Even so, it took him several minutes of splashing and spluttering to get to the bank, as every step of the way, the fractured ice kept giving way and he couldn't get his feet on anything solid.

All the time, he was cursing under his breath, and with every farcical step he could hear wee Davy break out into another burst of hysterics. When he finally made it to the bank and clambered up to the flat, his nephew was lying belly up in the snow, holding the said belly and laughing so hard he almost choked.

Jack walked towards him, feet squelching and jeans flapping wet and cold against his legs.

'Oh, so you think that was funny, do you?'

Davy continued laughing uncontrollably. Every time he tried to speak, he pointed at Jack, then pointed at the water where the broken segments of ice were now bobbing and clattering against each other, scraping and tinkling like plates of glass. When he did that he'd immediately double over so far his face was almost in the snow. Jack's feet were beginning to freeze.

He strode across to the boy, leaving big footprints.

'Laugh at your uncle, would you?' he demanded. He grabbed the small boy by one ankle and one wrist and swung him round, pivoting on his heels as he did.

'One . . . two . . . three . . .' he yelled when, for the third time, the lad was whirling towards the stream, still screaming with laughter.

And just at that moment, Jack's foot slipped. He went down on his backside again. Davy, who was at the apex of the swing, crashed down on top of him and the pair of them went slipping and sliding down towards the stream again. Jack managed to grab the boy before he disappeared under the ice, but went in again himself, feet first, backside next. When he ground to a halt, he was sitting in six inches of water and Davy was high and dry and still laughing hard enough to break a rib.

They spent another exhausting hour – exhausting for Jack, whose job it was to haul the sledge to the top of the hill after every run – until the cold water in his boots froze his feet to such an extent they began to hurt. Finally he had to insist, against Davy's protestations, on going home again. Ten minutes later, he was sitting with his feet in a basin of warm water, feeling his skin itch and burn as the circulation came back into them. Neither Julia nor her son could keep a straight face. In all, it was the best hour Jack had spent since the night of the bonfire celebrations.

An hour later he was down in the station. John McColl met him halfway up the stairs.

'Been trying to get you for ages. Superintendent's looking for you,' he greeted in a low voice. 'Looks as happy as a pig with piles.'

'So what else is new?'

'The boys think he wants you off.'

'He's always wanted me off. Want to work for him?'

'No fear. You're the devil we know. And he couldn't find his arse in the dark with both hands.'

Jack had, yet again, to caution John on respect for his superiors, which he knew was a futile exercise, but he couldn't keep the smile from his face. McColl wouldn't change, didn't care. What he said, however, was as much of a vote of confidence as Jack could expect.

'Got a few things you'll be interested in,' John went on. 'Ralph's in with the rest of them.'

Jack steered the sergeant into his own office and sat down on the chair by the window. Big flakes of snow were feathering down against the glass to pile up on the sill.

'Could have used this on Barley Cobble the other night. At least we might have had a footprint.'

John nodded as he handed over a sheaf of papers.

'What've we got?' Jack asked, flicking through them quickly, taking in just the headings.

'Initial forensic on the Campbell girl. Nothing great. A few nail scrapings that won't get us much further. Oh, and there's something from Dr Cattanach on the Toner case. You'll see that further down.'

'Yeah, I'll come to it later. What've we got that I can't get in the reports?'

'Good question. Ralph debriefed the night shift on door-to-door. Absolutely nothing. I think we've got a psycho.'

'It's always been a psycho, no matter what,' Jack asserted. 'There's a connection between the two kids, but the difference is that the second one occasioned violence. That means we've most likely got a shooting star. . . .'

'A what?'

'Somebody on burnout. Most psychopaths are very careful. They're not like your common or garden maniac. They're lucid and thoughtful and they tend to experiment with new things as they wreak their way along. You don't get sudden changes in method and style, more a gradual evolution. Then you get the shooting stars who get a taste for it and flare up out of control. I reckon that's what we have here. It's just a feeling.'

'Is that good or bad?'

'Good *and* bad,' Jack said after a while. '*Good* because they don't plan too much. They become opportunistic and they make mistakes and we catch them a little quicker. *Bad* because they can do an awful lot of damage before they burn out. Remember the case back in the sixties?'

'Before my time,' John claimed.

'And mine. But I read up on the paperwork. Place was in an uproar then. Five kids killed. I was at school at the time, just a nipper. But I never forget the feeling there was in town. Everybody was scared. That was a slow mover. He didn't burn out, at least not so far as anybody knew. He just disappeared. Everybody said he'd killed himself out of remorse. But I've had a look at the old pictures. *That* was a psychopath.'

'And?'

'With a psycho, there's no such thing as remorse.'

'You don't think it's the same one?'

'No. I don't. The kids called him *Twitchy Eyes*. I remember it clearly. One of the beat men went round all the classes telling the kids to watch out for a man with a twitch in his eye. That's going back more than thirty years. He'd be an old man by now, and I don't think an old man could have taken Shona Campbell's face off with a swipe, do you?'

'So what do you think?'

'We keep going round the doors. We have to find somebody who saw something. Anything at all. Unless we get one hint, then it's going to happen again, and then the shit's going to hit the fan.'

'I've got a feeling it has already,' John said. Jack nodded reluctant agreement.

The day shift were waiting in the muster room. Jack went over what they had. He hadn't had the time to go through the reports in the folder, but on first glance there wasn't anything earth-shattering that the team had to be told of.

In fifteen minutes, they were back out again, stamping the snow from their feet as they knocked on doors asking the same questions again and again.

Jack went back to the folder.

The forensic evidence provided more questions than answers. He brought out Robbie Cattanach's preliminary report from the autopsy. Robbie's few sentences were clear. The girl had suffered massive trauma to the left side of her face. Most of the flesh had been stripped from the crown of her head to her cheek and her occipital orb and cheekbone had been crushed inwards. Several small shards of bone had lodged in the brain and there was massive damage to brain tissue. Had she survived, Robbie said, she would certainly have been paralysed down the right side of her body and she would have been profoundly mentally disabled. What puzzled the doctor was the nature of the blow.

'Three deep indentations' his report continued 'descend from the temple to the chin. The parallel striations appear not just in skin and muscle tissue, but continue as grooves on the bone itself. The only similar groovings of this nature, as far as I recall, have come from injuries caused by large bears.'

At the bottom, in a personal note, Robbie asked: 'Have you checked the zoo in case they've lost one?'

Jack pulled his lips back from his teeth and sucked in air. He remembered only the previous week – though it seemed much further in the past than that – Ralph Slater asking him a similar question when they were going through the house in Latta Court. That time, because of the height of the veranda, Ralph had suggested they should be looking for a gorilla.

A gorilla and a bear. Both trained to steal babies. And one trained to kill a young mother with a cataclysmic swipe. Jack would have preferred it to have been either. An animal could be caught and captured quickly. It couldn't plan and it couldn't cover its tracks.

But Jack knew that was too much to hope for. He was looking for a human. A sick human, maybe. But a dangerous one who

179

would try it again. What concerned him, much more than anything else, was the certainty that the killer would strike again, and soon. He was not concerned about the bayings of the press. A double abduction made national news any day of the week. He couldn't care less about the backbitings of the likes of Ronald Cowie who saw every event as an opportunity for advancement or apportioning of blame. He only saw his job from the point of view of one who had to catch the killer before he took another life. He had to catch him and put him away. Somewhere in Levenford there were, he was sure enough to bet his life on it, two small bodies lying hidden. In this town there were too many nooks and crannies, too many sheds and huts and outhouses. There was the warren of derelict buildings out by Slaughterhouse Road where the land gave way to the marshes, and crumbling factories from the bad old days huddled round the west edge of Rough Drain, the local name for the extent of tangled wasteland at the east end of town.

There were places aplenty to hide two tiny bodies. There were places a killer could huddle and wait. All Jack Fallon and his overworked men could do was wait for a sliver of evidence that could act as a lodestone to point them in the right direction.

His own view had changed since the theft of little Timmy Doyle. Then, it could have been anyone, although there was nothing to show exactly *how* it had been done. The surmise was that someone had climbed up or down from balcony to balcony on the sheer face of Latta Court to snatch a baby from its pram. Yet there were no prints, no hairs or scraps of clothing to give any pointers. Worse, Jack Fallon could figure out no motive. This was beyond the range of anything he had dealt with in the past, and in the past he had dealt with many a baffling and confusing crime.

In his own mind, he had ruled out a woman. At first, there had been a tenuous connection – after a fashion – between both the baby snatch and Marta Herkik's brutal killing. But then Shona Campbell's baby had been wrested from her arms on a cold night and she had been hit so hard she'd died of it. This one could not be laid at Simpson's door, because he had taken his own gruesome way the day *before* the abduction.

Jack was opening the folder from Ralph Slater as he eyed the sequence graph on the wall. It displayed names and dates in his plain capitals, with arrows joining one set of words to another. There was as yet no clear pattern. Jack knew a pattern would help, but if one *did* develop, it would mean another killing, another theft of a child. That worried him more than anything.

Ralph Slater's report was badly typed, but clear enough. The dog handlers had come up with nothing. There was no scent trail to follow. From the position of the body – and the photographs in stark black and white under the glare of the flashgun left nothing to the imagination – it was clear that the woman had been felled by one tremendous blow to the head. She had dropped like a sack and she had stayed where she'd fallen. The pool of blood showed that beyond doubt. There had been some material under her nails, but it was not skin and it was not hair, as might have been expected from a mother fighting for her baby. Ralph had rushed this through the forensic lab at headquarters and come back with a riddle.

The preliminary report described the scrapings as *keratin*. Jack knew enough not to have to look the word up. He knew it was the substance which made up fingernails and horses' hooves and the scales of lizard skin. The stark and brief report came to no conclusions as to the source. Ralph's men had taken samples of a wet patch which had frozen on the shoulder of Shona Campbell's leather jacket. This too had only raised a conundrum. It was neither human nor mammal saliva. Whoever had analysed the substance – and there was only a scrawled signature at the bottom which Jack couldn't make out – said there had been some similarities between the sample and amphibian saliva, though the resemblance was remote. Also, he added, there were no antibodies nor bacteria, at least none identifiable or that he could culture, which was unlike any other known secretions. Another puzzle within the puzzle. There was nothing else to be gleaned from the report. Jack stuck it back into the folder and laid it down on the desk.

Craig Campbell's story stood up and walked. He'd been hanging over the bar in the Castlegate until close to midnight and could remember virtually nothing about it, but there were enough people who had some brain cells that were not numbed with drink who remembered him. Big Tam Finch confirmed that he'd escorted Campbell to the door.

'Legs like rubber, the daft bastard,' was what Tam Finch actually said. 'Seen it before with him. Getting set to boak all over the floor. Better he does it outside than have the cleaners scrape it up in the morning. He couldn't have put a nut in a monkey's mouth, but that's just the usual for Bunnet Campbell. His missus was down here regular every paynight to take his wages off him before he gave it all to me. Race against time every week. The man drinks at the gallop. Different story getting him out the door, I can tell you.'

Tam Finch could tell plenty. He ran the roughest, toughest bar on the riverside and kept a big, gnarled Harry Lauder walking stick hanging up by the gantry to keep order. What he said put Craig Campbell in the clear, though in Jack's mind, there was never any serious question that he'd murdered his wife. Jack had spoken to him only hours after the girl had been found and the man was too befuddled to realise what was happening. He didn't sober up properly until after she'd died and when he was given the bad news he took another dive right into a bottle to blot it out again.

The neighbours, as in the Timmy Doyle case, were next to no help. Apart from the one isolated scream in the shadows of Barley Cobble, nobody had heard or seen a thing. In both cases, there had been a quick strike and a fast and silent getaway. There were few clues.

By midday, the snow was blizzarding from the north again and Jack was up to his armpits in paperwork, collating the reports. It wasn't until then that he reached the note on Jock Toner. Robbie Cattanach had put it in a separate envelope.

As he scanned the few short lines, his eyebrows drew together, creating a furrow between them.

'Did a check on the blood on Toner's jacket. It is NOT his. Your forensic people will be able to tell, maybe. Toner was common O positive; the sample was Rhesus negative – same as the blood on his cheek and shoulder. Hope it helps.'

Rhesus negative. Jack sat still and thought about that. Robbie had already told him that he believed Jock Toner had not fallen from the gantry, because of the force with which his head had met the upper edge of Isobel McIntyre's window. The pathologist had suggested that he had jumped or been thrown.

Jack thought some more. There was a *different* type of blood on the man's clothing, and that meant there had to have been someone else there, unless of course, the man had had a fight with somebody on the ground first, and then hoisted himself up on the cradle. That did not ring true. Jack checked the notes on the interview with the clerk of works. Toner had grumbled about having to stow the gear at the end of his shift, but apart from that, he had seemed perfectly normal. That had been just after five at night. The body wasn't discovered until morning, and the preliminary investigation put his death at two hours after he'd last been seen, although that was merely a guess. It was hard to tell if the stiffness in his frozen body had anything to do with rigor mortis. A woman living in the second-top storey had told Ralph Slater that she'd heard the gantry winder go past her window just after seven, and that tended to back up the findings.

'So, what kept him up there for two hours?' Jack asked the empty room.

He stared at the snow flurries as they wheeled past his window.

Perhaps he was with someone, and they'd had a fight, Jack thought, but he shook his head. Jock Toner was used to heights but he'd have to be crazy to fight someone on a swinging pulley-gantry a hundred feet up the side of a building. Jack had been on the roof less than an hour after the body had been found, slowly turning on the rope in the freezing air. He'd looked over the side and he'd felt his stomach give that old familiar lurch of vertigo. It was a long way down. Mentally, he ruled out a fight, though stranger things had happened. There was something else in Robbie's note. Jack looked it over again, frowning all the while.

Rhesus Negative. The blood type. As had happened many times before, something *clicked* inside Jack's head and he made a small connection.

He rummaged through the pile of manilla folders, scattering them across his desk until he found the one he was looking for. He opened it and riffled through the few pages and discovered the sheets stapled together. John McColl had pulled the baby's medical files from the health centre. There was little to read. Forceps delivery. Seven pounds, slight jaundice. Blood type Rhesus negative. Slight factor eight deficiency. Two months after the birth, a bout of scarlet fever and a bad cough which turned

183

out not to be whooping cough. It was all there, what little there was of a baby's life catalogued in weights and illnesses.

Jack hooked the phone and called a number from memory.

A telephonist paged Dr Cattanach and he took a minute to come on the phone.

'I'm up to my neck at the moment,' he told Jack.

'Just a second,' Jack insisted. 'A quick question. I got your note on the blood traces.'

'Yes. Definitely not his.'

'I got that. Can you give me any pointers?'

'Narrows the field, Jack. Rhesus negative is not common.'

'How uncommon?'

'Very low percentage, if I remember my haematology.'

'That's a start. I just have to scan nearly thirty thousand to come up with likely suspects. Anything else?'

'Well, whoever it is. He's a bleeder.'

'Come again?'

'A haemophiliac. Didn't I mention that? There was enough blood to put it through the works. It's not surprising there was a fair amount of it. There's a lack of blood clotting agent, which means any cut continues to bleed. In severe cases, it just doesn't stop.'

'That should narrow it again. Hang on, Robbie.'

Jack put the phone down and crossed the room to open the door. John McColl came out when he heard his name bawled down the corridor.

'I need lists of local haemophiliacs,' Jack told him.

'Right away?'

'Day before yesterday.'

John rolled his eyes and went back into the operations room.

Jack lifted the phone. He was still frowning. Something else tugged at the back of his mind.

'Listen, Jack, I've really got to go . . .' Robbie began.

'One more thing. What's factor eight?'

'That's what I was telling you. It's the clotting agent in human blood. Without it a paper cut will make you bleed to death.'

'Shit!' Jack barked.

'What?' Robbie's voice came tinnily from the earpiece.

'Nothing. Last thing. How many people with that type of blood and none of the clotter?'

'Damn few. One in umpteen thousand, I suppose.'

'Just what I thought. I'll talk to you later, Robbie. And thanks.'

Jack slammed the receiver down and sat for the space of several seconds, staring at the roiling snow as the turbulence cartwheeled them past the window. A picture developed in his mind. He held it there while he shoved his chair back and bounded for the door again, calling for John McColl as soon as he snatched it open.

The sergeant came out of the other room, eyebrows raised.

'Just getting on to it, chief,' he said.

'Hold that result,' Jack said quickly. 'Get Ralph and tell him to meet me up at Loch View.'

John looked at him blankly.

'And I mean now,' Jack said.

The door opened and swung back with such force that it slammed against the wall. Janet Robinson saw her mother's bulk come ramming past the jamb, her cane in one hand, held up like a sword. In her other hand, a crumpled piece of paper was crushed in a fierce, white-knuckled grip.

'You slut,' the old woman hissed, and Janet realised that her mother was not *old*. She was a big-boned woman, heavy breasted and wide hipped, and she carried all the weight of authority that had dominated Janet's life since she could remember. Her eyes were slits between the clenched brows and screwed cheeks, but they glittered with that righteous anger.

'You dirty little slutter. You *whore* that you are.' Her mother came striding towards where Janet had been sprawled on the bed, but was now cringing against the head. The cane jerked with every word.

'Mother, I . . .' Janet squawked.

'Don't you *dare* call me *mother*,' the old woman said. Her short-cut frizzy hair seemed to stand up in a grizzled halo. 'I found what you've been hiding, and I've read it.'

She advanced two more steps, oddly bull-like for a woman.

'I've read it and it is *filth*.'

She raised the sheet of paper up and waved it with triumph and disgust.

'It's my letter,' Janet managed to say. 'You opened my letter.'

185

'And good thing I did, girl. Just in time to save your immortal soul.' She held the letter out from her and her knuckles whitened further as she crushed it to a tattered ball, then, with a little flick of her hand, as if she were ridding her hand of slime, she shucked it to the floor.

'I know what you've been doing. It's all there in black and white. You've been seeing a *boy*. And worse, you've been *doing things*.'

'No, mother, I didn't do anything.'

'Don't lie to me, girl. Don't you *dare* lie to me. I read what he said. You've been doing things behind my back. You've been doing things with a boy, you dirty little whore slut.'

Janet pushed herself back against the headboard. It creaked with her slight weight.

The big woman advanced, silhouetted by the light in the hallway, towering over the bed.

'I'll teach you to let a boy touch you.'

'But he didn't,' Janet protested in a voice that was almost a whimper.

'Did so. Did so. I read it. He wrote it. He *touched* you.'

'He only held my hand, mother. We were just walking. We were only talking.'

'And where were you walking? Out by the marshes where nobody could see. Out without telling me, eh? Where he could put his hand up your skirt.'

Janet tried to reply, faltered, then shrank back from the onslaught, but there was nowhere left to retreat. She was jammed up against the old wooden board, one hand drawn up to her mouth, the other held out in mute appeal, in dumb protection.

Her mother's shadow blocked out the light. The cane went up in the air, making a moaning sound through the air, followed immediately by a whistle as it came down again.

Pain sizzled on Janet's thigh and she jumped as if a jolt of high voltage had shot through her. Her squeal of pain bounced back from the ceiling. She twisted away and the thin whipping stick caught her on the upraised hand, driving down between her knuckles into the soft web of skin. It made a noise like a nutcracker and an unbelievable hurt lurched from her hand to her elbow.

'No, mother,' she shrieked. 'Oh *please!*'

The dark outline of her mother's arm rose quickly and came down in a blurred strike. The banshee whoop as it cut the still air ended in the crack of the bamboo on her back. Janet leaped in an involuntary spasm as silver pain cascaded from her shoulder to her hip. Her legs kicked out and she could hear herself screaming, though the sound seemed to be coming from far away, from someone else. Her mother's bulk leaned over her and her arm went up and came down again and again and all the time she was bawling at her daughter that she would never see the boy again, she would never see *any* boy again. With every blow the pain expanded exponentially until she felt her vision turn grey and clouded and the dark came and swallowed her mother first and then she herself fell into it and. . . .

Janet Robinson woke with a cry strangled in her throat. She was shivering with cold and with fright, and her face was beaded in sweat. The blinds were pulled and the curtains drawn over them, darkening the room to a gloomy grey. She groped her way to the side of the bed and fumbled for the clock, pictures still whirling up to the forefront of her mind, images of her mother's towering bulk leaning over her in righteous wrath, in holy hatred, punishing again for something the old woman had imagined she'd done. It was not the first time she had been wakened by her own screams and her own fear. It had happened every night since she had fled, panic-stricken, from Marta Herkik's room in Cairn House.

She shivered again, still able to feel the heat-strokes and the burning lines from where her mother had sliced at her with her cane, still quaking in the aftermath of her abject terror under the onslaught of her mother's anger. She held the clock in her hands, shaking her head to try to will the visions away.

It was one o'clock in the afternoon. She'd slept all the morning. Groggily, almost timidly, she eased herself out from the damp sheets. Her hands were trembling as if she had a fever, but she knew it was just the kick-back from the dream.

Her mother's image still shadowed the back of her mind. A big, domineering and hateful woman who had done everything in her power to cage her daughter and mould and meld her to her own use. She had succeeded. In her teens, the few boys who had expressed an interest never came back after the first secret meeting. Her mother had *always* found out and her rage had been apocalyptic. Since Janet had been old enough to remember, there had been only the two of them. The old woman never *ever* spoke of Janet's father. There had been the two of them, mother and daughter, the one determined to crush whatever individuality and whatever spirit the girl possessed, the other desperate to flee, frightened to make a move. And so it had gone on, into her lacklustre twenties, into grey thirties, while the old woman's bulk shrivelled in inverse proportion to the poison of her tongue, and finally she had died of a cancer that ate away at her belly and withered her down to a whispering rickle of bones and yellow skin, too weak to whimper, and Janet had been racked with guilt that she was *glad* her mother was finally suffering the pain she'd suffered as a child, as a girl, and as a woman.

When finally the old woman had rattled her last, Janet, now forty-five and conditioned to be completely dependent on the woman who had moulded her life in cruel hands, felt vast relief and terrible fear. Approaching an early middle-age, she ached for the chance to do things she wanted (although she wasn't really sure what they actually were). She had long since given up hope of forming a relationship with a man, and in actual fact, such was the enormous Pavlovian force of conditioning that she was almost overcome by nerves if she happened to speak to *any* man. But there were other things. She could buy the clothes she chose, instead of the shapeless, grey and hideously out-of-fashion *old woman's* garments her mother would buy and insist she wore. She could go to the cinema, might even buy a television. And most of all, there were women in the offices where she worked whom she thought she could become friends with. Real people whom she could maybe, one day, invite back to her own house, without the old vulture scaring them away with her razor tongue and her poison words.

That had been the hope, but the weight of her mother's memory had been so heavy that it still ground Janet Robinson down. It was as if the old woman lurked in every corner of her mind, scolding her whenever she had a rogue thought or any faint idea of self-improvement. She heard her mother's rasping voice, unrelentingly critical of her every move.

Then someone had told her about Marta Herkik and she had gone along with two of the women from the office to have their tarot cards read and the idea had come to her that she wanted to know that the old woman was really dead, really *gone*. She'd gone back, not just once, but four times, for consultations with the tiny Hungarian woman, and then she'd gone to the seance because by this time she believed that the little foreign woman could really confer with the departed. Janet Robinson hadn't wanted to confer. She just wanted to snap the bonds and to break free.

She'd gone to Marta Herkik's house, with the five other people and she had sensed *their* needs.

And then the terrible thing had happened in the apartment three floors up in Cairn House and they had run, hearts thumping in fright, while the nightmare noises in the room had followed them down the narrow spiral staircase.

Since then, Janet Robinson had heard her mother's voice every night in her dreams. There were days when she would again feel the glacial *cold* steal through her, emptying the warmth from her bones, and she would *feel* the presence of the old woman.

The awful, terrifying realisation was that she could sense her mother's presence, and it was as if the old woman was *inside* her, taking control of her own body, taking control again of her mind.

When Janet woke into the dark of the room on the Saturday afternoon, she waited until the fright and the shock of the dream had passed on, and paused until the trembling had ceased. Yet all the waiting in the world could not rid her of the growing sense that she was losing herself in her mother, that the old woman was taking her over from within.

She groaned softly and turned to the clock, still clenched in her left hand. The luminous dial blurred as she looked into the face and the dim light of the room faded to black.

15

On Saturday night, Jack Fallon was stamping the cold from his feet on the flat roof of Loch View. Beside him Ralph Slater was down on hands and knees, lightly scraping the powdery snow from the gritted surface with what looked like a shaving brush. Around the perimeter, his team had set up three floodlights on tripod stands, blaring white light onto the frosted roof. Off to the right, the elevator housing and the maintenance shafts stood black against the orange light from the main road in the distance. Above it, the red hazard light winked a warning to low-flying aircraft.

'There's more here,' Ralph said, angling his own heavy duty flashlight onto the scraped surface.

He squinted up to Jack.

'We didn't even look here,' he said, with a trace of embarrassment.

'No reason at the time,' Jack let him off the hook. He wasn't really in the mood for talking. Since the morning, when he'd fallen into the stream, his throat had tightened. It felt raw and made it difficult to swallow. 'Not for an accident,' he added.

'But what made you think of it?'

'Just a hunch,' Jack said with a tight grin. The snow had lessened, but the wind was whipping up little particles from the balustrade wall and sending them into his left ear.

'Aye, pull the other one. Any idea why there's blood here?' Ralph asked, while he delicately lifted samples of the dark and frozen stain to drop it into a fresh plastic sample bag.

'Another hunch.'

'And you'll be able to crossmatch it then?'

'Rhesus negative. Low on factor eight.'

'Sure it is,' Ralph said with heavy sarcasm.

'If it isn't, I'll buy you a bottle of Talisker. Believe me, I wish it wasn't.'

After the call to Robbie Cattanach, Jack had left the station, ignoring the message that the chief superintendent wanted a word with him, and had driven straight to Loch View. The gantry was still swinging from the high edge, frosted with snow. The rope from which Jock Toner had dangled, frozen and bloodless, was gone.

He'd waited at the top while Ralph's men unloaded the equipment. There was only an hour of daylight left. From his vantage point he could see the lights coming on in the town below. The Langmuir Crags were completely white, apart from the big fan-shaped cliff which overhung the scree below. Even in the deepest winter, snow never stuck to the face. As the lift whined, bringing the scene-of-crime team up to the top, Jack had made the mistake of wandering to the edge again, to where the metal gallows that held the gantry stuck out over the edge like lifeboat davits. He'd looked down through the light snow and felt the pull of the ground tug mesmerically at him. It happened every time he looked down from a height, every time since the last climb on Ben Nevis in his teens when a piton had pulled out and he'd watched the black shape plummet silently, without a scream, without a cry, and then reach the far end of the drop, with no thud in the distance. Yet he remembered the stomach-freezing red stain that scraped across the ice for thirty feet and he knew what had happened. Every time he looked down from a height like this, he got a flash of that cramping shock. The ground down there wanted to pull everything towards it. It dragged and tugged and hauled, not just on the body, but on the mind. Jack shoved himself back from the rail and turned away, waiting for his heart to slow down to a canter and for his breath to moderate. By the time Ralph's boys arrived, he was breathing almost normally.

He'd told Ralph what he was looking for. The other man looked at him askance, then shrugged and got on with the job. Jack couldn't blame the team for not looking last time. It had been a cursory job. A body bundled into a shiny bag and a long ride down to ground level.

It was seven, and without the lights and the hazard beacon it would have been pitch black by the time the roof of Loch View had been scoured. Jack put a rush on the lab order and the men packed up. He waited behind until he was once again alone on the roof.

'Must have been about this time,' he said to himself. He swallowed and grimaced as his throat clenched, and thought he really might be catching Julia's cold.

He walked slowly towards the edge. Little flurries of crystals were billowing from the edge of the wall, catching the orange of the street lights, taking on a noxious glint.

Jack knew what the lab would tell him. The blood would be the same type as that of the missing baby, and that would make it a certainty that it came from little Kelly Campbell. But who, he wondered, had brought her up here, and even more baffling, why?

Down to the left, heading due south, Barley Cobble was a fair walk away by the riverside. Off to the right, the two matching blocks of flats reared into the night, though Loch View was set on higher ground. This was the uppermost point on Levenford's north side. It gave a view right over the whole town under a darkly leaden sky.

Someone had either come up, or climbed down to where Jock Toner had been on the gantry, more than an hour after his shift had ended. Nobody knew yet why the man had spent so long up there on his own. All the doors in the building were now being knocked to find out. Jack considered the possibility that he might have had a woman here and had used the gantry as a surreptitious exit. It was a possibility, nothing more. It was also a possibility that they would find some irate and vengeful husband who had caught Jock using the exit. Jack would have been delighted if it turned out that way, but within himself, he knew it would not. Because an irate husband would not splash Jock Toner with the blood of a baby who had been snatched from its mother's arms, unless by sheer chance the said husband happened to be the abductor and killer. That would be too much to hope for.

He stood stock still, with the warning light blinking monotonously to his right, and tried again to visualise the scene. Images vied for prominence in the forefront of his mind, but none would settle. He needed more evidence, more of a hint. He wanted to know why a killer would bring a baby up to this height and then kill a man and then disappear.

Disappear he certainly had. The blood trail showed drips down the wall on the side where Jock Toner had cracked open his skull. They continued across the roof, away from the blinking light, and across to the other side, and then they stopped.

There were no marks across the balustrade to show that the man had jumped over, certainly nothing down there to show where he would have landed, and if he'd dropped from this height, there would have been plenty of evidence of that, spread for ten yards on the concrete slab. It was possible – and Jack was beginning to *detest* that word – that he had stuffed the baby into a bag or a sheet or inside a jacket. Ralph had found scrape marks on the concrete walls just below the lip on the gantry side and similar indentations on the east wall, but it was impossible to say what had caused the three straight and parallel lines. Possibly, he'd ventured, it was some tool the workmen used. In any case, it was unlikely, according to Ralph, that they had anything to do with this. When Ralph had mentioned them, something had tried to form a pattern in Jack's mind, but it had danced away elusively.

'Who are you?' he asked aloud. The wind whipped his voice away.

The picture tried to form itself, but though he concentrated hard, it refused to materialise properly. He did not have enough to go on, though there was more now than he'd had before. There was no doubt at all in his mind that little Kelly Campbell was dead, and that meant that Timmy Doyle was dead too. Six deaths. One suicide associated with the killing of Marta Herkik and a tenuous connection to Timmy Doyle. A suicide that turned out to have been a murder, at least almost certainly, and a connection with the one-hit killing of Shona Campbell and her baby. Two of them involving high places. All the deaths except for Simpson's suicide had happened at night.

The pattern was emerging, but it wasn't much of a pattern. Nobody had seen anything, not a thing.

Jack looked down at the lights spreading out below him.

'Where are you?' he asked aloud, gritting his teeth in the stinging ice crystals. His throat was burning.

In that moment, Jack made up his mind. There was a thread connecting all the killings. If he found one end of the thread, he would follow it to the other end. He was now certain that he was

193

dealing with a single killer, and eventually that killer would make the mistake he needed to catch him. Inside his pockets his hands clenched into fists as he walked towards the stairwell. He closed the door behind him and the winking hazard light was cut off.

Once in the car he called down to the station and ordered a house-to-house inquiry in Loch View and the two adjacent blocks. It would take a lot of manpower, but that was the way things had to go.

Ten minutes later, he was back in his office. He slung his coat on the hook and hunkered against the radiator to take the chill out of his back, thinking about the two phone calls he had to make. His feet were cold and his throat ached and he wondered if he had any paracetamol in his drawer. He was also wondering whether he'd been wise to take Davy on the sledge down by the stream at Cargill Farm. He was about to haul himself to his feet when there was a brief rap on the door, it swung open instantly and Ronald Cowie stepped in. At first he didn't see Jack hunched against the radiator, then the other man's presence registered.

'What the hell are you doing down there?' he demanded.

'Trying to get some heat into my bones.'

'I've been looking for you all day,' Cowie snorted.

'Have you? I didn't get the message. I've been out.'

'Yes. I heard. Complete waste of time.'

'You think so?'

'We're in the middle of a murder investigation, man. We don't have time or the manpower to have a whole shift out working on accidents or suicides. I suggest you get them back onto the priority work.'

'That's what they're doing,' Jack replied, then added: 'Sir.'

'That's not the way I see it,' the Superintendent said. 'Anyway, as of this afternoon, I'm in charge. Mr McNicol's laid up with flu. Some sort of virus anyway. So as of today, we do it my way.'

Jack made no response. Gradually he eased himself away from the radiator and got to his feet. He stared down at Cowie who glared back at him.

'Congratulations,' Jack said.

'You won't be saying that shortly. I want all the men pulled out of Loch View. That's obviously the wrong area. I want a complete ground search of every building on the south of River

194

Street. Two killings and an abduction in one area. I think that narrows the field, don't you?'

'It would, if the field had not expanded to suit,' Jack said calmly. 'We've already done a search, and a very thorough search, of the whole area, leaving aside domestic property. We'd never get warrants for all of them, not without good cause.'

'But every warehouse and every hole-in-the-wall shack down that side of the town should be gone over with a tooth comb.'

'And they have,' Jack retorted. 'You'll have read the reports. There's a file two inches thick.'

Cowie blinked. His thin grey moustache twitched. 'Then do it again. It has to be painstaking.'

'Oh, it will be. But I'd advise against it. If we pull the men out of Loch View, then we could miss something vital.'

'On an accident?'

'It was no accident. We found the baby's blood.'

'You *what*?' Cowie's face registered consternation. 'Why didn't you tell me?'

'Because I'm just back in. We found traces of blood up on the roof. The same type as was found on Toner. I believe it will match Kelly Campbell's blood.'

'Has it been analysed yet?'

'No. But there's a rush on it. The lab have promised it by morning.'

Cowie glared at Jack again. His moustache quivered and his eyes seemed to bulge in his face. Jack could tell he was not happy. He seemed about to speak when he abruptly spun on his heel and strode to the door, snatched it open and walked out, turning back only when he was right outside the room.

'This time I don't want to wait. I want to hear everything immediately. You hear me? *Everything.*'

Jack nodded. The door thudded shut and he smiled to himself, though he did not really feel like smiling. Under Angus McNicol, he would be allowed to work on this his own way. With Cowie in charge, he didn't know what spokes would be put in the wheel.

Mickey Haggerty, his friend from schooldays, was out when Jack called. His sister said he'd been up north for a week, staying with someone in Oban. From the tone of her voice, it sounded as though she might be a woman, and that wouldn't have surprised

195

Jack in the slightest. It was only on the way down from Loch View that he'd remembered the other part of the conversation with Mickey in Mac's Bar. He had cursed himself under his breath. Mickey had seen William Simpson the night Marta Herkik was murdered. He'd seen someone else near or at Cairn House, some Irish fellow whose name he'd forgotten. He'd promised to get back to Jack, who had made a mental note to give him a call, but then other things had happened and he'd simply forgotten. Netta Haggerty said her brother would be back in a day or so. She didn't know where he was staying. Jack thanked her and then put a call into the Oban Station. He knew a sergeant there whom he'd worked with in the city. By luck, Ian Nicholson was on duty. He took Mickey's description, a shock of fair hair and a lived-in face not unlike a young Kirk Douglas, and he promised to have a couple of men check the bars. That was the best he could do, and that was enough for Jack. If Mickey was in Oban – and he could have spun his sister any old yarn – then he'd be in a bar and easy to find.

'Do I lock him up or what?' Ian Nicholson had asked.

'No. He's a friend of mine. Drunk or sober, get him to phone me back.'

He had better luck with the second call. Andrew Toye answered at the third ring.

Night fell on Levenford at four o'clock. It was bitterly cold. The lights along the quayside were fuzzed to orange haloes by the creeping mist from the river. The water feeding into the firth was tidal for a mile upstream of the town and the river was low. There was no moon. The haar condensed in the cold air and the mist floated over the quayside walls and crept along the alleys, fogging the hard edges of the old buildings. For half an hour, the old bridge was thronged with children hurrying home from Kirkhill School on the west side. They hurried because of the cold and the dark and because of the sense of unease that had crept into Levenford since the killing of Shona Campbell and the taking of her baby. Until then, the townsfolk had not really been aware that something was happening. When little Timmy Doyle was snatched from his pram high up in Latta Court, there was shock. But it was one incident. Marta Herkik's killing was another shock, but the papers were full of such things. Old women got

196

mugged, and old women got raped and killed. It happened. It was terrible, but it happened.

Now, a second baby had been stolen and its mother killed, and while the killer *seemed* to be after babies, the community policemen had toured the schools warning children of all ages to be careful. Mothers reinforced the warning. Most children hurried home. There were few stragglers and the bridge cleared of its passing throng. An hour later, the bridge was busy again, this time with cars and a leavening of pedestrians hurrying home from work as the shops and offices closed. Up river, the engine works was still clanging and clanking and across the water, the high windows of the foundry glowed red and from time to time the spitting harsh cough of hot metal would tear at the still air, though by the time it crossed the river, the cat-screech was muffled by the mist. The foundry's massive brick chimneys towered over the building, their bases flickering pink in the flashes from the furnaces. In the old days, both would have belched smoke and sparks long into the night, but the new electric furnace had made one chimney obsolete. They towered into the darkness, a Victorian monument to the bad old days of hard labour and low pay and full employment.

Between Swan Street and Denny Road, in the heart of old Levenford, maybe two hundred yards from the river, there is a warren of old tenement buildings faced with dirty brown sandstone. They form a rectangle, dingy houses with narrow close mouths. Inside the rectangle, behind the facades, the back courts are a maze of old dustbin shelters and cluttered outhouses. Iron railings, peel-rusted and spiked, separated each individual tenement's territory. In the summer, the boys would climb the brick walls and race across the top of the shelters and leap from one flat roof to the other, bounding over the blank spaces, hurdling the lethal spikes. Ever since the blocks were built before the turn of the century, mothers had warned their children, on pain of dire punishment, not to climb the roofs and never to jump over the railings, and every generation of boys since then had risked life and limb and impalement, completely ignoring their mothers' threats.

The cold night air brought the river mist swirling through the closes. It oozed into the back courts and crept between the wrought-iron uprights.

197

Neil Kennedy was kicking a ball against one of the crumbly walls. He was eight years old, with a faceful of freckles and curly Celtic-red hair hidden under a knitted woollen hat. Upstairs, two floors up, his mother was cooking dinner. Neil felt his belly rumble and guessed the family meal might be ready in an hour. He didn't know if he could wait that long. The cold air carried the smell of the river, a wet and wintry smell of decaying reeds and bullrushes floating down from the upstream marshes. The distillery on the other side of town had done a malting that day, as everyone could tell by the cloying damp-towel odour that permeated everything. This was mixed with the smells of sausages sizzling, chips frying, and, as ever, the unappetising whiff of cabbage boiled beyond edibility.

Up above, the light from the uncurtained windows sent solid shafts of luminescence into the fog, occasionally flickering colour from the television sets behind the panes. Neil had wanted to watch cartoons, but at this time on a Monday night, his mother's favourite soap series was showing. She'd have the kitchen door open and the sound turned up and she'd occasionally lean back from the cooker to watch the latest, if thoroughly predictable act.

Neil kicked his ball against the wall, watching it bounce and then trapping it with casual deftness under his foot to repeat the action again and again. Over in the corner, a door slammed open and a corridor of light funnelled into the dim. Children's voices bounced from shelter to wall. Neil kept kicking the ball, communicating his presence by the dull thuds it made on the rebound.

'Hey Neilly,' a high voice called out. 'That you?'

'Aye.'

Three shapes flitted closer, resolving only yards away into three small boys, heavily muffled against the cold, squeezing themselves through a gap in the railings.

'Cold, innit?'

'Freezing,' Neil agreed.

'Had your tea yet?'

'No. I got sent out. The old man's not in yet.'

'Us too,' Gerry Murphy said. His twin, Patrick, nodded agreement. With them Phil Toner, six years old, whose Uncle Jock had been found hanging from the rope at Loch View, shivered. He lived across the landing from the Murphy boys.

'Want a kick-about?' Neil asked.

'Naw. Too dark.'

'And the ground's too icy. You could break your neck,' Phil said. Everybody had heard what had happened to his uncle, but from the perspective of small boys, it was a distant happening, not a thing to dwell on, nothing to spoil the immediate.

'Alright. What'll we do?'

'We could jump the dykes,' Phil suggested and everybody laughed. At the age of six, he couldn't have leapt the gaps on a summer afternoon.

'Aye, very good, Phil. What's your next joke?'

'No, really,' he protested and Pat gave him a shove.

'You'd never get to the top of the wall, never mind jump.'

'Kick the can?' Neil suggested.

'No,' Gerry said. 'The old man's on night shift. If we wake him up he'll lose the rag.'

It took five minutes of negotiations on the short list of options of things to do on a winter's night without much result. Somebody suggested going round to the old railyard two streets away where the spur line to the engine works had long since been disused. There was a ramp there, a concrete slope which led from the shunting point to street level. Earlier in the week it had been covered with frost. By now, Gerry suggested, it should be a sheet of ice.

'I'd better not,' Neil said. 'I'll get called up in half an hour.'

'Oh come on,' Pat said, giving him a nudge. 'You've got stacks of time.'

Neil let himself be persuaded with no further difficulty. The four of them went through the common close and into the street. Each end of Swan Street was fuzzed out by the mist. It was as if the world they lived in had shrunk to fifteen yards on either side. They moved along Swan Street, past Arden Lane before crossing Artisan Road to the old railyard entrance. The tall double gate was closed and padlocked. To the side, the gaunt facade of the crumbling warehouse and offices of the yard loomed upwards. Ferns, crumpled and brittle since the first frosts, clung to the damp patches behind cracked roan pipes and icicles formed fringes on the window ledges below the gaping blind eyes of the smashed frames. Here, closer to the river, the fog was thicker. It

199

caught in the throat and curled and coiled around the weave of the rusty chain-link fence where it had been pulled back in a tangled dog-ear by previous forays of small boys. They scrambled through the gap and walked four abreast along the disused tracks, avoiding the slippery sleepers, to the far side of the warehouse block. Set on the side of the crumbly brick building was a lone electric bulb protected by wire mesh. It glowed feebly.

The sloping ramp was completely iced over. In the weak light it glinted like black glass. Gerry Murphy tested it with a foot and almost fell on his backside, saving himself only with a flurry of windmilling arms.

'Like the cresta run,' he pronounced. They all stood at the top of the slope looking down at the straight swoop.

'Who's first?' Gerry asked.

'I want to try it,' Phil Toner piped up.

Pat and Neil laughed.

'Go ahead then,' Gerry challenged. Little Phil shoved his way to the edge where the flat surface leading to the old weighbridge turned downwards towards the high green gate at the entrance. He stood at the top of the slope, arms spread like a wrestler, one foot in front of the other. He swivelled his hips and launched himself, leaning backwards to prevent a headlong tumble. Behind him, the three boys watched as his arms waved out on either side. His scarf, turned inside out to form a hat, trailed behind him. Little Phil let out a wavering whoop and went scudding down the incline.

'Look at him *go*!' Neil yelled.

The small boy whizzed into the mist below. One moment a dark, teetering shape, then quickly greying to a blur before it was swallowed completely by the haar. They heard his shrill cry diminish with the distance until it stopped abruptly. A muffled thud came floating out of the mist followed immediately by a howl.

'Hey, Phil?' Neil shouted. There was no reply.

'Phil. Are you alright?' Gerry bawled. His voice, ghostly and faint, replied in a double echo as it bounced from the walls.

There was a silence for several moments, then from down below, Phil's voice floated up.

'I hurt my knee.' They heard him make the kind of noise boys

200

make when they are hurt but not injured and want to ward off tears. A minute later, the small boy came crunching towards them on the edge of the slope where piles of hard-core quarry stones gave enough grip to walk without falling.

'Banged it on the door. Didn't even stop 'til the bottom.'

'What's it like?'

'Really scary. Dead fast and you can't see where you're going.'

'I want to try,' Pat said. He braced himself and went off down the slope. Gerry followed, identical in size and clothing. Neil watched them disappear, hooting all the way, before he steeled himself, took a breath and launched himself down the slant and into the fog. Ahead of him the twins were yelling at the tops of their voices. There were two thumps, almost instantaneous howls of exhilarated alarm, then peals of laughter before Neil cannoned into the brothers and knocked both of them back against the door. Pat squealed while Gerry's breath was knocked out of him and he leaned against the high gate gasping for air. Just then, little Phil came careening out of the dark, sliding on his backside, and crashed into them, knocking their feet from under. They all collapsed in a giggling heap.

After the first slide into the unknown, the next was less scary and the third even easier. Pat found an old rusted coal-shovel without a handle and went skittering off, seated on the blade, using the pitted shaft as a grip. They could hear the metal rasp against the ice as he whizzed out of sight, then an almighty clatter as the shovel caroomed against the door. They all tried it, picking up more speed as the ice was smoothed out by their passage. Gerry found some cardboard boxes which they stacked against the door as a shock absorber to prevent real injury and they spent the next half-hour glissading down and trudging back up the hill, laughing all the while.

It was nearly seven when Neil realised he'd done it again. Since they'd found the ice-slide, his hunger had disappeared, but when he was under the single lit bulb by the side of the warehouse, he glanced at the plastic watch he'd got for his birthday and immediately the pangs returned, along with the sinking feeling he always got when he knew he was in trouble.

Pat and Gerry were preparing to skid down the hill together, with one twin on the shovel and the other sitting on his lap, when Neil told them he had to go back.

201

'I'll catch it if I don't get a move on,' he explained when they protested. He knew he'd catch it anyway. His mother had a habit of fetching him a skite on the ear and asking questions later. What was worse, she'd know he hadn't stayed in the back court kicking his ball as she'd told him to do, and that would earn him another skelp. His mother was small and thin, but when it came to open-handed slaps, she could strike like a snake and, according to Neil, she didn't know her own strength. Reluctantly he watched the twins skitter off downslope, whirling out of control as they picked up speed. He clapped little Phil on the shoulder and went back along the disused track towards the gap in the fence. Away from the light and away from his friends, it was darker and felt colder. He barked his shin on an old piece of railway track that angled out of the dead stalks of willowherb which clumped on either side of the old line, rimed with frost. Neil's feet crunched on the hardpack. His stomach rumbled again and suddenly he was really hungry. Ahead, one of the street lights gradually became visible as he approached the break in the fence. He crawled through, making sure his winter jacket didn't get snagged on the wires, and came out on the other side at the junction of Artisan Road and Station Street. He walked back the way they'd come, heading past the old warehouse. As he got to the front of the gate, he could hear the delighted yells of his friends on the other side as they crashed into the piles of boxes and for a moment he wished he could have stayed and had more fun with them. He passed the gate and set off along the decaying warehouse front when he came to the door in the wall. As he walked past, he heard a low voice and he turned, startled. The door was open.

Neil stood stock-still. The door was open. That itself was enough to spark off a dilemma for the eight-year-old boy. He knew he should be getting home, but the door had never been open before and any warehouse is a magnet to small boys.

The voice came again.

'You. Boy.'

A woman's voice. Quite soft.

'Hello?' Neil asked into the darkness.

'Can you help me?'

'Who is it?' he called out.

'Can you help me, please?' The woman's voice came from the darkness inside the building.

'What's wrong?' he heard himself ask.

'I need help. If you help me I'll give you something.'

Neil took a hesitant step forward and his foot crossed the doorstep. As soon as he took that step, a powerful feeling of foreboding quivered through him. It came so unexpectedly that the boy felt himself shudder and the hairs on the back of his neck tingled as they crawled against the wool of his hat.

He took a step back. Out from under the lintel, the feeling shrank away.

'Don't be afraid,' the unseen woman called out to him.

'I can't see you.'

'I need help. I've fallen and hurt myself.'

Neil leaned a hand against the brickwork at the side of the door. From inside he could smell mouldy wood and dampness and something else he couldn't identify. It reminded him of the pit out on Slaughterhouse Road where the flies would buzz around the discarded jawbones in summertime, but it was a wetter, colder smell.

'I'll get somebody,' he called out timorously.

'No, please. Just come and help me up. I'll give you money for sweets. I've got lots of money.'

Neil hesitated, still on the horns of his dilemma, but then, with simple childlike honesty, he realised that he could save himself a clip on the ear, get some money for sweets *and* earn some praise for helping somebody. His mother had always warned him about talking to strangers, especially strangers on dark wintry nights, but he had always taken that to mean *men*. Women did not carry the same threat, the same potential for hurt and badness, even if mothers could deal out swift and stinging justice. Women were *safe*. It took three seconds for this calculation to reach its conclusion in his eight-year-old mind. He took a step forward, pausing between the doorjambs.

The feeling of *threat* quivered through him when he took the next step into the gloom of the warehouse. Somewhere off to the right something dripped steadily, rapping damply on the wooden floor. Glass crunched under his feet as he went along by the wall, close to the open-treaded metal stairway that zig-zagged above

203

him. It was dark, but some light from the street managed to invade through the high windows. He could just make out a series of doorways leading off the one wall, while to the right, where the dripping sound came from, there was a wide space, punctuated by narrow pillars that stretched up to the dark ceiling.

'Where are you?' Neil called out.

'Here,' the voice, now weak and muffled, came from overhead. Neil stopped at the bottom of the stairs. He looked up to the turn at the top of the first flight. The treads were littered with scraps of paper and bottles and squashed and rusting beer cans.

'Up the stairs, and please hurry,' the woman called.

Neil went upwards, holding onto the corroded bannister with every step until he reached the top. Cold air and tendrils of frosted mist crept in through the smashed window. He could see nothing. He turned at the landing. Above him, some distance away, he could hear the woman sob softly. It did not occur to him to wonder what a woman was doing in a derelict warehouse at night. He moved on and up, and with every step of the way, he felt the tight fingers of alarm squeeze at him.

'Hurry, please hurry,' the broken voice called down urgently. Neil forced himself to move more quickly. He reached the second landing, where the light was even dimmer, and continued to the next.

Then suddenly, in the gloom ahead of him, he heard a rasping cough.

'Hello?' he asked into the dark.

There was no reply. Only a watery, choking sound. He inched forward, still holding onto the bannister, heart now racing. A dark shape was huddled against the railings at the turn of the stairs. A faint light managed to push through the layers of grime on the window, which was still intact by dint of being just out of range of small boys' stones. Neil approached cautiously, his breath now speeded up and coming out in quick plumes. He reached the huddled form and stood there, tense with apprehension, wondering what to do.

The thing moved, twisting towards him and suddenly Neil's heart was in his throat, punching away as if it was trying to

204

escape. A pale face lolled forward and the boy got a look at the woman. Even in the faint light, he could see her eyes rolling. Her tongue protruded, wet and slack from between flaccid lips, and a rope of saliva gleamed wetly.

She was sprawled across the steps, one leg angled out, her skirt rucked up. A pale moon showed where her tights had ripped at the thigh. There was a sour flat smell that again reminded the boy of the pit on Slaughterhouse Road, but here it was thicker, cloying and cold.

'What's the matter?' Neil asked tremulously, legs bent, prepared to run.

'Mother,' the woman moaned. Through the thick saliva, it sounded like *mudda*.

'What?'

'Oh . . .' another long moan, almost like a sigh, then the woman's head flopped. The smell grew stronger.

'Go. Now,' she said, though the words were hardly recognisable. Her face twisted towards the boy and her eyes seemed to come into focus. Her mouth opened again and just then, on the landing above, there was a small grating noise. The woman coughed, gagging, and her flaccid body convulsed. Just overhead something whimpered. At first Neil thought it was a cat, maybe a kitten, but the sound came again.

It was a baby.

The whimpering cry came clear from just above in the darkness. Neil knew all about babies. One of the reasons he'd been out kicking the ball against the wall was because his little sister, only three months old, and almost as much of a surprise to his parents as she had been to Neil, always needed feeding when his mother was making the dinner. She made the same wheedling cry when she was hungry.

'Up there,' the woman's strangled words came from beside him. She reached out a pallid hand towards him. Neil thought she was directing him upwards. The sense of apprehension diminished when the baby mewled again. He passed the sprawled woman, not noticing her shaking her head like a maudlin drunk. He came to the fourth turn, tripping over cans and boxes, heading upwards to where the darkness was almost complete.

There was a snuffling cry dead ahead. He scrambled up the

final six steps, almost losing his balance, eyes wide to try to see. Something whispered in his ear and he stopped dead.

'Get you,' it said. *'Catch you.'*

The words scraped and tickled, just loud enough to be heard. Sudden fear ballooned in the boy. The shadows seemed to close in on him, while the whispering voice, in his ears, in his head, chittered fast. Panicked, Neil turned, preparing to run back down the stairway, when the dark above came reaching down at him.

In that minute fraction of a second, that's exactly what it looked like to Neil Kennedy. He did not even have a chance to think about it. The dark simply rippled towards him, blacker than the gloom at the head of the stairs. He saw it rush at him and then it slammed him against the wall, knocking his breath out and smashing his nose with the ferocity of the strike.

Neil grunted in surprise and pain and fright. As he bounced, whirling from the wall, something whipped out towards him so fast it was just a blur. He felt a sharp, jagged pain under his collarbone and a corresponding stab at the top of his shoulder blade and then he was jerked off his feet with such violence that his head snapped back with a flare of pain which felt as though the muscles in his neck had been pulled apart.

The boy screeched as terror exploded inside him.

Beside him, the wall blurred as he was hauled upwards at shocking speed, pinioned by an enormous grip on his shoulder. He screamed again, a high and wavering sound that spanked back and forth from the walls of the stairwell as whatever had grabbed him and had him clenched in a ferocious grip raced upwards. The boy's heel hit off the bannister and his shoe flew into space, tumbling down the dark well, but he didn't even notice. The dark shape held him in a grip of such crushing intensity that he could feel the bones crack. Hot blood gushed across his cheek. He heard his own scream soar higher and higher and beyond it he could hear the rumbling grunt of the black thing that had him in its grip. He was jerked up in a stuttering series of lurches towards the roof where old beams criss-crossed one another. The thing paused momentarily. It snuffled and growled like a hungry animal, like a *huge* and ravenous beast, mindless and ferocious.

By the time they had reached the rafters, Neil Kennedy was almost unconscious from pain and loss of blood and sheer terror. He twisted spasmodically and felt the white fire rip through his neck. The black thing squeezed harder. There was a slight pop as something burst inside the monstrous grip. The boy felt himself flung round, legs whipping like a floppy doll, and his knee hit the edge of a beam. A loud crack clapped the air and a jolt of agony flamed in the boy's leg. The whipping motion snapped his teeth together, slicing through the edge of his tongue. The black thing drew him upwards in one final jerking movement and held him up. The boy's vision was fading fast. He saw two orange-yellow eyes open. A discoloured membrane flicked across them. The thing growled like a monstrous cat and brought its victim right up to its eyes. A mouth opened.

Neil Kennedy's heart stopped beating and he died, with those sulphur eyes drilling into his soul. The drips and splashes of his blood on the walls of the staircase began to congeal and solidify in the dark, shadowed place just under the roof of the old warehouse.

Only fifty yards away, behind the big double gate of the shunting yard, the three small boys played on, sliding down the ramp and crashing into the now shapeless pile of cardboard boxes. Their laughter and squeals of hilarity pierced the fog. Up in the roof-space, where dust-coated cobwebs festooned the narrow corners, a black shape with a smaller, lighter shape dangling in its grasp turned its head towards the sound, snuffling at the air. It moved in that direction in a liquid, insectile creep, then stopped and turned back. The sound had sparked off a barren hunger that could not be sated. Its eyes widened, glowing febrile and feral in the gloom. Wet drool dripped from the corner of a shadowed mouth. It began to move, away from the sounds, to the far end of the roof where a hoisting window gaped on the gable wall. Across the river, the foundry shrieked its night noises and a warm glow flickered on the base of the massive cylinder of chimney that jutted to the sky. The black thing growled again, so low the dusty windows rattled in their frames, and turned away from the light. After a moment, it moved on and out into the thickening fog.

The Murphy twins and their small friend lived to play another day. After almost an hour of excitement they trundled along the disused track, laughing amongst themselves, each aware that Neil Kennedy had missed some great fun. They agreed to meet the next day after school with anything they could use to slide down the ramp.

When Gerry and Pat Murphy got home, Neil Kennedy senior, a big angular man with the same Irish red hair as his son, was sitting on the arm of the chair in the living room.

'Where have you boys been?' Meg Murphy demanded to know. The twins looked at each other, one trying to read the other's expression, wondering what to say.

'Och, never mind,' their mother went on. 'Have you seen Neilly?'

The big man looked from one boy to the other.

'Yes, Mr Kennedy,' Pat said. 'He was playing with us at the slide.'

'But he came home for his tea an hour ago,' Gerry interjected.

'Well, he's not home yet,' Neil Kennedy said slowly. Already the look of a parent whose child is late on a winter's night was beginning to shade his face.

Half an hour after that, Gerry and Pat were standing side by side, answering all the questions the policemen asked them. They admitted being across in the old railyard. They were certain that Neil had gone home. Constable Bill McGurk took notes and then went outside to speak into his radio and within fifteen minutes, two police cars were parked at the junction of Artisan Road and Station Street. Neil Kennedy, too worried to have muffled himself up against the freezing fog, went with the policemen when the search started. They hunted all over the railyard, down the alleys that led to the river before it took its bend at the bridge, and in every back court between Station Street and the quayside. They did not find little Neil Kennedy that night.

Jack Fallon was woken out of a terrible dream at three in the morning and told the news.

For an instant, while his heart slowed down to a canter, he was glad to get the reprieve from the nightmare of flying glass and dripping blood, until he heard that another child was missing, and this time not a baby.

208

He was in his office on a freezing, dark and misty morning half an hour after the call.

Later that day, they found the body of a woman, frozen in rigor mortis and with the cold, caught on the anchor chain of one of the little tattered boats moored in the river. She was wearing one shoe, a brown lacing brogue, when they finally hauled her out of the icy water just below the weir downstream from the old bridge. When they got her to the quayside, her body, bent by the flow of water, could not be laid flat. When the diver placed her on her back, she rocked like an ungainly grey toy. They laid her on her side on the stretcher and she was taken to Lochend Hospital, where Robbie Cattanach carried out yet another post mortem. Apart from the lack of identification, and the fact of her being found floating in the river, there were no suspicious circumstances. The presence of dirty river water in her lungs showed beyond doubt that she had died from drowning.

The only odd thing, Robbie noted, was that both lungs were filled, which, in an ordinary drowning, is very rare, as the lungs normally react violently to cold water.

It looked as if she had walked into the river, taken a deep breath and held it in. The fatal accident inquiry might decide on it later, but Robbie Cattanach decided there and then that this was a case of suicide. As to the motive, he couldn't say.

16

Jack's throat ached every time he tried to swallow. It was raw and inflamed and felt as if it had been rasped with a burr file. He was in no mood for work, but of no mind to quit. Early in the morning he'd expanded the search and called in the dogs. The big Alsatians had hauled at their leashes, encouraged by the dog-handlers and by the unwashed school shirt that Neil Kennedy had worn the day before. Where the kids had played the previous night, the footprints were obscured by the tracks of boys and men from the search the night before. The late fall of snow in the evening had covered the scent and made it difficult for the big, panting dogs. Their broad pads made crisp pug-marks in the virgin snow on the old railway lines as they quartered back and forth, trying to pick up the trail of the missing boy.

It was late in the morning, while Jack was drinking hot blackcurrant to ease his throat and going over the interview reports, trying to pick out some tiny fact from them that would help in the hunt for the baby-killer, when John McColl came stamping into the office. His feet left a trail of slushy droplets on the worn carpet.

'Got another body for you,' he announced. He looked cold. 'They've just fished a woman out of the river. Looks like a swimmer.'

'Great,' Jack said, his voice sounding hard and gritty. 'Just what I need. Looks like the whole town wants to kill itself or get itself killed. Got a name?'

'Nothing so far. She's covered in all sorts of shite from the water. Nothing immediately visible. Looks to be in her forties. She was hanging over a mooring rope twenty feet out from the quayside, just up from the grain silo. Probably been there all night from the state she was in.'

'Suspicious?'

'Doesn't look like it,' John said, angling himself closer to the two-bar heater, still stamping his big feet.

'That'll make a change.'

'Anything on the kid?'

'Nothing from the search last night. Christ, John, we've had folk in every school and warnings in every paper telling folk to keep their kids in off the streets, and they never listen. Stupid woman sent her son out to play so she could watch television. We should lock the bitch up.' Jack put down his cup, then grabbed it up again as his throat reacted to the violence of his speech. He went into a fit of coughing.

'Aye. Maybe we should. But we'd have to lock up a thousand others. And I dare say she won't be feeling too happy this morning.'

Jack waited until the coughing abated and took another sip of the warm juice, letting it trickle down over the raw patches on the lining of his throat.

'Oh, I suppose you're right. But it's a bloody tough lesson to learn. See if we can get another bulletin on the radio this afternoon, just to drive the message home. I don't want to see any kids out of doors after dark.'

'You reckon we'll get away with a curfew?'

'It's not a curfew, John. Just scare the shit out of the mothers.'

'I don't reckon the Super will like it. He's getting a bit paranoid about the coverage.'

'Only because we're still in the dark. Once we get results, he'll be elbowing folk out of the way to get in front of the cameras.'

Jack started coughing again. John McColl looked over at him. 'You should see the Doc about that. The last thing we need is you laid up. With the boss off, that would leave us at the tender mercies of Mr Cowie, and that. . . .'

John's words trailed off as the door opened.

'Did I hear my name used in vain?' Ronald Cowie asked. He was tooled up in his best uniform, the buttons gleaming on his shoulder.

'Just saying I'm getting the paperwork ready for you on the body.'

'Oh? Which one's that?'

'Seems they fished a woman from the river this morning,' Jack said. 'Suspected suicide. John's on it.'

'I'd put that on the back burner. There's more important

211

things to worry about. I've been out to lunch with the Provost and Councillor Graham. He's on the police committee. They're getting very concerned over our lack of progress. The Chief Constable is showing a similar concern. It was a source of great embarrassment that I had very little to tell them.'

'That's because there *is* very little,' Jack said. John shuffled from foot to foot, clearly wanting to be out of the crossfire, but unwilling to get between his two superiors on the way to the door.

'Yes. Quite. You don't seem to have made any progress. And in view of Mr McNicol's absence, I've a mind to take over the handling of this case. Personally.'

Jack sat where he was, trying to keep his face impassive. In peripheral vision, he saw John McColl's jaw drop.

'Anything to say?' Cowie asked, one eyebrow raised.

'No,' Jack said. 'But it could set us back a day or two. Mr McNicol's view was that I should have a few days more. There are some lines of inquiry we are following up, and in view of the Kennedy boy's disappearance I think it's only fair to suggest a press and radio warning to parents. No doubt you'll want to make that yourself.'

He let that sink in, watching the obvious calculations going on behind the man's eyes. Jack decided to help him with the arithmetic.

'Naturally, the press will be keen to know what progress we are making, and we'll have to assure them that every effort will be made. As the man in charge, you can be sure of every assistance from me, of course.'

John McColl turned his body towards the fire, but not quickly enough for Jack to miss the wide smile creasing his face.

Cowie coughed into his hand. His eyes swung right and left. Talking to reporters was fine and dandy, as long as there was capital to be made from it. But if the only news was no news, he certainly didn't want to be the one associated with police failure.

'No. I don't think that will be necessary. At this juncture,' he said. It was all he could do to keep from spluttering. 'I had already decided to give you another few days. But I have to warn you that you'd better come up with something. I'll review the situation as and when necessary. But believe me, I'll have no hesitation in taking control if there's no progress. None whatsoever.'

'Understood,' Jack said, nodding curtly. Cowie stared at him and Jack let it simmer for a moment before he added very softly: 'Sir.'

Again, his superior looked as if his face was about to explode. Jack couldn't have cared less. The man had tried to cut him down in front of John McColl, and he'd been forced to back down himself. He deserved all he got. As he watched the retreating figure, Jack thought back to something his father had told him when he was just starting at the police college:

'Remember, there's always some jumped-up arse promoted beyond his capability. He's the one to watch, because he'll stand on you to keep his head above water. Never give him anything to hold onto.'

Jack thought his old man's advice fitted this moment precisely. He knew he'd have to step carefully or Cowie *would* move in and take over, and that, he knew, would be the worst possible scenario.

'You haven't made a friend there,' John McColl said, trying to keep the smile off his face.

'I don't make friends easily,' Jack replied. 'I've better things to worry about. Or worse.'

He looked down at the papers on his desk, brow furrowed in thought. After a few moments he looked up and raised a hand to sweep back the comma of black hair that had fallen down over his brow.

'This woman in the river.'

'Yes?'

'Dig a bit. Get me what you can, soon as you can.'

'Sure. But I think it's just a suicide.'

'Yes. So was Simpson, and we thought the Toner incident was a suicide too. But there was plenty more to them than met the eye. As of today, I want to hear about every death, when it happens, and the full works on each.'

John McColl looked at him, both eyebrows raised. Jack could read his expression easily.

'Yes, I know. It sounds like clutching at straws and jumping at shadows. But we can't afford to miss anything. Since the Herkik killing, there's been something not right about this town. I don't believe Simpson was the only one there. I've a feeling there was a riot of a party that night. I'm trying to find someone who might have been in the vicinity. We've got a tenuous connection between Simpson and the Doyle baby. Another serious connection between Toner and the Campbell child.'

'You think there's a link?'

'I'm coming round to that feeling, though I don't want it broadcast. Not yet.' He stabbed at the thickening file with his finger.

'Now we have a boy missing. Think about it. He was last seen across at the stockyard on the other side of Station Street. The yard carries on as far as the railway bridge over the river. And today we fish a woman out on the same side five hundred yards downstream.'

Jack spoke in short bursts, taking a break between them to ease the rasp in his throat. He took another sip of juice. It had gone cold, but it helped.

'We can't afford to overlook anything. I've got a hunch, nothing more, but the hairs on the back of my neck are beginning to crawl. The connections are only loose threads, but any correlation, anything at all, could be vital. That's why I want an ID on the woman toot-sweet. Match her prints with those from the Herkik place, Latta Court and Loch View, just in case.'

'We're not looking for a woman, Chief,' John stated. 'That's for certain, not unless she's an East German shot-putter.'

'Not directly. I agree with you on that. I just want to see where all the broken edges fit in. There's more going on in this town than anybody would believe, probably including me. I want to find out what was going on at the old woman's house, who was there, and why. And I want to know where they've been since.'

'What about Toner?'

'He wasn't there. The prints have been run through. But he was up to something and he was covered in the Campbell kid's blood.'

'Can I ask why you're so sure that the old woman's case has something to do with the others?'

'I'm not. That's the truth. I've just got a feeling about it. If I'm wrong, I'll admit it, but until I know for sure, I don't want to take anything for granted.'

John nodded. He moved away from the heater. A faint smell of damp clothes and singed cloth followed him to the door.

'I'll get you a name for the swimmer, hopefully by the end of the day.'

'I'd appreciate that,' Jack said. His voice had gone hoarse. 'Oh, and another thing. See if Sorley Fitzpatrick will lend us a Bronto today. The earlier the better.'

'A what?'

'One of their snorkel trucks. They can lift a couple of men up to roof level. If he can't spare it, check with the lighting department.'

'What for?'

'Yours is not to reason why, John,' Jack said, but he said it with a smile, even though the speaking was beginning to make his throat really ache. 'But I'll tell you.' He motioned the Sergeant across to the wall where a large-scale map of Levenford covered most of the space.

He indicated the points marked by red pins.

'Herkik. Doyle. Toner.'

'Yes?'

'Four storeys. Ten storeys. Eleven storeys at least.' Jack used his forefinger to punctuate each sentence.

'Whoever he is, he likes high places.'

'But Shona Campbell was killed on the ground,' John protested.

'Yes. I've been wondering about that. That's why I need the snorkel. I want the whole roof area of Barley Cobble gone over. We didn't find anything on the ground, and I just want to be sure. Can you fix it?'

'Sure. I'll get onto it right away.'

John closed the door behind him and Jack stood, staring at the map for a few minutes. When he'd been speaking to McColl, something had sparked in his mind, a connection half formed, that had wriggled away even as he'd tried to grasp it.

'Must be working too hard,' he said to himself. He swallowed and felt as if a marble had lodged in his throat. Jack put a hand under his jaw. The glands were swollen and tender, and he knew they'd be grape-sized by nightfall. He took an immediate decision, crossed to his desk and picked up the phone. The woman at the health centre told him she'd squeeze him in just before five.

Jack went back to the map, trying to resurrect the elusive thought that had died before it had been properly conceived. It wouldn't come, so he gave up. Instead, he went back to the phone and requested a sub-aqua team from headquarters. He knew Cowie would hate that, because of the attention it would bring, not to mention the expense, and the divers would hate it too, for the river at this time of the year would be freezing, filthy and dangerous.

Some hours later, and several streets away, in the basement storeroom of the old library on Strathleven Street, Lorna Breck sat hunched in a chair with her elbows on the table and her head in her hands. In front of her, the words on a catalogue file swam in and out of focus, and she had to concentrate hard to keep her eyelids open. She was desperate for sleep yet terrified to give up being awake because of the dreams that shunted in horrific procession, nightmare locomotives roaring and screaming through the dark.

They were coming constantly now, visions, dreams, illusions, apparitions, hallucinations. Lorna did not know what to call them. Like the terrible vision that had attacked and invaded her on River Street when she'd looked into the grocer's window, they came, even in sleep, preceded by the flat, oily smell of tomcats and a juicy electrical hum in the bones of her head behind her ears. As always, even in her sleep, she'd be aware of the dizzy numbness that stole through her, making her feel leaden and strengthless.

She could not evade them, could not avoid them, until the fear grew so great she would wake up, finding herself sitting bolt upright with the bedclothes knotted around her, damp with her own sweat, and she'd be gasping for a breath of clean air, black images of creeping shadows and scuttering blackness dancing in front of her eyes.

As she sat, trying to focus on the wavering print, she debated what to do. Keith Conran had taken her into his office and asked if anything was wrong. She'd shaken her head, telling him she had some sort of bug which she thought might work itself off. She wasn't ready to tell *anybody* about the things she saw in the

216

night, and more frightening, in the daytime. He'd suggested she should go and see Dr Bell, but she'd told him she didn't feel that bad. In fact she felt worse than she'd ever felt in her life, but she couldn't explain to a doctor why she felt that way.

Lorna propped herself up and rubbed her eyes. They were red and grittily sour. She'd been up since five in the morning, launched from sleep by an image so terrible she'd rolled over and retched helplessly and drily over the side of the bed, feeling the convulsions twist and jerk the muscles of her belly.

She'd known it was coming. She'd sensed it and smelled it and heard the sizzling hum in her head and the cold lethargy had stolen into her muscles in a creeping paralysis and then, with a bewildering *wrench* she was flipped out of a dream from childhood where she'd been picking brambles with her mother on a clear autumn day and slammed into darkness.

The cat smell faded and another scent, dry and musky and slightly rancid, came drifting over her. Birds. It was the smell of birds, like chickens, cooped up in an old timber shed. She remembered that smell from childhood and the days when she'd be out every morning for the eggs, shooing the fluttering birds from their boxes and rummaging in the half-light among the musty straw and feathers and half-dried droppings. Similar, but not the same, maybe another type of bird. The air also held the odour of dry rot. She was in a high place, looking down from an odd angle. She did not know where it was.

Off to the left, in a dark corner, dim shafts of light speared through holes – in the wall? the roof? – and showed a thick mist oozing creepily like grey searching fingers round oddly slanted beams. Something moaned nearby, off to the left. Close to the sound, something fluttered, a grey ghost in the grey swirl.

Pigeons, Lorna realised. Already she was in the grip of the dream and her heart was beginning to churn as the apprehension mounted. The thought of the pigeons, moaning and burbling in the dark, was somehow enormously frightening, though she did not know why. The place she was in was cold and dark, criss-crossed by the thick, mouldering beams.

Off in the distance, far below, she heard a squeak, mouse-like in the dark, then a creak, as if a door had been opened. A small silence followed, filling the hollows, then another sound, a woman's voice, muffled by the distance. A higher response, unintelligible, but obviously a question, a child's tones.

The apprehension changed, expanded and became fear. Lorna could not move. She could not speak and inside the numbness that gripped her muscles she could feel nerves jitter and jump, screaming out with her own need to scream a warning. It was a child. *Another* child.

Her mind yammered. *Getawaygetaway.* GO!

Down below, there was another murmur and a second high response. Footsteps on broken glass, hollow treads on old stairs. More voices, the child's hesitant sounds getting closer.

Up the stairs and please hurry. This time the woman's voice, rising in urgency, came clearly. At least the words were clear, but in Lorna's ears, there was an odd double phasing sound, a strange harshness underneath the words. It was as if someone *else* had spoken at the same time. The words rang up the deep stairwell towards her, reverberating from the peeling walls. Lorna's heart kicked twice. The echoes seemed to separate the woman's words from the underlying sound, and Lorna heard the other voice, a deep guttural sound that was as much a snarl as anything, but was still able to form words.

Her heart kicked again then seemed to stop dead in her chest. Lorna gasped for air, but could not catch her breath.

Down below, the child said something. There was another sound, like someone choking, a burbling, liquid *tearing* sound. Inside her head, but seeming to come from a great distance, she heard the scrapy whisper, almost unintelligible, jagged with threat, and her mind recoiled.

From her vantage point high in the rafters, Lorna saw the gloom of the stairwell instantly become black as night. Something slammed against a wall and all light was blotted out.

There was a sudden thumping sound, a series of raps, like someone knocking on the wall, followed by a savage slavering growl and a small cry of surprise and fright. Right on its heels came a scream of pain and terror, ricocheting up, soaring higher and higher until it was almost beyond the range of hearing, before it was abruptly cut off.

Lorna's eyes were still wide and her mouth wider as she panicked for air. Down below, the blackness expanded, billowing up towards her and the liquid snarl grew louder. She couldn't move. The shadow rocketed upwards, jerking from wall to wall in a series of lurching zig-zags, incredibly fast, appallingly menacing. It spurted up the stairwell, a rippling piece of pure night, until it reached the lower crossbeams. Something small tumbled within the blackness. She heard the crack as the small thing smacked against the bar with the sound of a green twig breaking. A foul, foetid stink assailed her and even in the dream she would have gagged if she'd been able to breathe. As the darkness drew towards her, pistoning from one perch to the other, she sensed the terrible *wrongness* of it.

Behind her, the pigeons, huddling together for warmth in the tight space where the roof beams slanted down to the wall, exploded in a panic of fluttering. The black thing scuttered past her and over the stench she got a hot metal whiff of blood. Something shot out from the moving shape and a bird detonated in a whirling puff of feathers and blood. Another came tumbling through the air towards her and hit the rafter with a dead thud.

The dark shape turned towards her. It had no definition, but it emanated force and badness and dreadful power. It sucked away all the faint light, like a living black hole. Even though she could not see its shape, she *knew* it had turned to face her, as she had in the other dream on top of the building. Two eyes flicked open, yellow-orange and poisonous as before, huge, protuberant, *alien* and utterly repugnant eyes, as blinkless as a snake. They turned towards her, malignant and engulfing and looked right into her. She felt the touch of that glance scrape across her like a bane, and in that touch she felt the derision of baleful glee.

The hunched shape sat there, glaring its malice, its breath a gurgling rattle, then it moved slowly. The limp thing that hung from it swung up and in the light of those poison eyes, she saw what it held.

The little boy's head lolled. There was blood on his nose and his cheek. Something dark dripped from his neck to splatter on the beam where the thing crouched. A white feather tumbled lazily in the air and settled on a splash where it stuck, trembling. The boy's legs hung downwards, one of them queerly twisted. He had one black shoe on one small foot. The other wore only a sock which had been almost pulled off.

The shape shifted, rippled and held the broken child out towards her, as if making an offering, a hunter displaying his kill. The orange eyes expanded and Lorna was filled with a shivering, sick loathing. She tried to back away, but she was hemmed in by one of the angled beams and her foot slipped from the timber. The thing turned, moving like oil, rippling its way across the roof-void in a series of undulations, so fast it was hard to follow. At the far end of the space, grey mist was billowing in through a rectangular gap in the gable wall. The thing flicked towards it, an impossible outline in the miasma, then it was gone. Lorna started to fall. She twisted and the stairwell opened up to swallow her. She plummeted downwards, unable to scream, and the hard stone floor at the bottom raced up as if to catch her halfway. Just before she hit she had an image of her broken and bloodied body lying unfound during the depths of winter.

And then she woke up, lungs screaming for breath, so scared, so dreadfully overwhelmed with fear that her whole body was trembling like a tuning fork. Then the nausea had thrown her to the edge of her bed and her stomach had tried to turn itself inside out, as if it could void her of the nightmare image by voiding itself. Nothing had come out except a trickle of sour bile.

Now, in the silent basement of the library, Lorna still felt sick, from lack of sleep, from the numb horror of the constant dreams, and from the dreadful fear of what the dreams were showing her. She shifted in her seat and brought her hands up to her eyes and knuckled both of them, trying to wipe away the sourness under her lids and failing. She bent to the figures on the register, making an effort to concentrate, and failing at that too.

The stacked storeroom was almost silent. Keith Conran had been working on the catalogues earlier in the afternoon, but he had gone upstairs to the adult section for the monthly meeting. In another hour, the schools would be coming out and the first trickle of youngsters, less now that the nights were dark so early and because of the warnings the police had spread throughout the classes, would come clattering down the old stone steps to hand in their books and have them stamped.

The old radiator on the wall, a heavy, cast-iron ribbed monstrosity, pinged and gurgled to itself as the antique heating system pumped water that was not quite warm enough through the maze of pipes that fed down through the ceiling. The faint hum of cars and lorries passing on Strathleven Street occasionally punctuated the wheeze of the heating system. On the far wall, the old clock with its fat black hands ticked sonorously, one second at a time, a sound that was so pervasive and so constant that Lorna had ceased to hear it. Apart from these sounds and Lorna's own light breathing, the basement was quiet.

She shook her head, feeling the short waves of chestnut hair feather lightly against her cheeks, and drew her eyes down the list, trying to match the delivery invoices against the books which had been ordered months before from the catalogues. It was far from easy. The words wriggled and wavered on the paper as she made the effort to focus tired eyes and tried to ward off the memory of the dreams. It was proving almost impossible, but she stuck with it, doing her best to concentrate. It was the only thing that kept the images at bay. She worked on for half an hour, making heavy weather of a routine job which should have taken minutes.

The seconds ticked by, like slowly dripping water, counted by the old wooden clock. It was half past three in the afternoon and outside a heavy dusk was gathering under low clouds when Lorna suddenly came completely awake.

Her head came up with a jerk and her eyes flicked wide open. She felt her breath catch in her throat. A pulse tapped just under the curve of her jaw.

The voice came again. A faint, gurgling rattle.

The girl stiffened. She could feel the fine hairs on the back of her neck creep in unison. Her skin felt tight and tingly.

'Who's there?' she called out softly. Her eyes were fixed on the gloomy corner at the far end of the racks where the heating pipes angled up the wall towards the roof. The faint sound had come from there and as soon as it had impinged on her consciousness, Lorna heard the rattling breath of the black thing in her dreams.

The sound came again, a little louder than before. Lorna shoved herself back from the desk, fighting off the paralysis of instant fright, eyes taking in the distance between the desk and the door on the opposite side of the stacks. She had her back to the one wall and would have to squeeze past the old storage heater to come round the front and get to the heavy door which hung slightly ajar on its brass hinges.

221

The sound came again, this time louder, and a palpable sense of *presence* locked into Lorna's perception. There was someone in the shadows. Some *thing* in the gloom at the far end of the narrow passage between the shelves and the dirty wall. She felt her hands shake as adrenalin kicked into her bloodstream, knotting her stomach and making every outline stand out in sharp definition.

Just then, the old clock clicked on the half hour and a harsh grinding noise of rusty gears and springs jarred the air.

Lorna's throat closed with an audible click and she started back at the sound. The clock had never made a sound before, apart from the monotonous tick. It was as if it had chosen that precise moment to come awake.

The girl pushed herself back against the chair. The fine hairs on her arms were now standing erect and the skin below them was puckered into gooseflesh.

From down in the shadows, the guttural rattle sounded like an animal in a den.

The clock chimed once and Lorna almost screamed. It was a low flat note that hung in the air for what seemed like seconds. It was only the chime of an old wooden clock, but the sound, an ordinary, almost commonplace sound (*although she had never heard the clock chime before*) filled her with an intense and inexplicable terror. The rubber grommets on the chair-legs juddered as they scraped against the vinyl floor squares, caught, and the seat toppled backwards. Hysteria fought for control as Lorna forced herself past the heater, feeling the seam of her jeans catch on the rough edge of the table. She was crossing in front of the stack of books when the door creaked loudly and slowly swung shut. The latch clicked home. Lorna stopped, frozen in the act of taking a step. Behind her ears, hot blood wheezed under increased pressure. Her throat clicked again as she gasped drily for air.

Then the light dimmed. It happened so smoothly that at first nothing seemed to be happening, then the bulb underneath the old green shade seemed to bleed power away. The yellow light dopplered down through orange to blood-red in a sliding graduation. It took less than two seconds, while Lorna's mind was still trying to take in the enormous fact of the door slowly closing by itself.

In those two seconds, gloom engulfed the basement.

On the ceiling, the filament of the bare bulb was still clearly visible, a red worm dangling in the dark, throwing off a weak effulgence.

Lorna hiccupped. It made a strange little noise in the thick air. Her legs felt as if they would give way under her flopping weight and that thought was what made her manage to keep on her feet. The idea of lying down here in the dark, behind the closed door, with something lying in wait in the now pitch-black corner was enough to kick another jolt of adrenalin into her shaking muscles, giving them just enough strength to stop her from sinking in a daze to the hard floor.

Her hand found the desk and her nails scrabbled on the wooden surface as she instinctively sought for purchase. The opaque glass of the door let in a wan glow from the outer office. It seemed a million miles away to the frozen girl who stood, terror-stricken, mouth slackly agape, holding onto the desk for balance.

Off to the left, where the shadows jostled at the end of the stacks, came another noise. This time it was not a rattle or a growl, but a whimper. Lorna turned, eyes wide, and in the act of turning, the narrow space between shelves and wall spun in her vision, suddenly wheeling in a spiral. Vertigo flooded her with sick nausea. For an instant, she could not feel her feet on the floor. The looping sensation of falling lurched in her belly and then Lorna was looking *down* into a black hole.

The darkness was absolute for several stretched out seconds, then Lorna saw a shape, and when she did, her heart scudded against her ribs.

The boy she had seen in her dreams was looking up at her. His eyes were rolled up so far that she could only make out the whites. There was a black splash on one cheek and a terrible gash on the other. Something poked through the skin, peeling it back in wet scraps. Even in her terror, Lorna felt herself lean forward, over the black pit, trying to make out what she was seeing. Something clicked inside her head and the thing sprang into focus. The little boy was dangling from a curved spike which had pierced the flesh under his jaw and come out through the side of his face. He was suspended in the pit like an animal in a butcher's

223

shop, mouth forced into a wide gape by the drag of his own weight.

For another long second, Lorna was frozen by the horror of what she was seeing. Beside the small boy, other shapes, even smaller, dangled in the shaft, pathetic, forlorn and limp. She tried to drag her eyes away but could not make them negate what she was seeing.

Then the boy's white eyes rolled down in their sockets. There was an audible creak as his head turned two inches to the right so that he was looking directly at her.

'Elf ee.'

She heard the high, strangled sound which gasped from the boy's twisted mouth as it worked to form speech. The words were unintelligible, but Lorna knew what they were saying.

'. . . op it.' An incoherent, yet eloquent appeal from a small dead boy impaled and dangling in a black pit.

Help me! Stop it!

The sense was unmistakable. In the midst of her fear, Lorna was swamped with pity for the thin little thing and those helpless dead things beside it. In the dark, despite the vertigo, she felt herself take a step towards the pallid face which was looking up at her, holding her with its dead eyes.

Then she heard the feral growl come rattling up from the depths. Beyond and below the dangling figures, she˙ sensed movement, eager, furtive motion in the black depths. Something was powering up towards her. She sensed it with every cell in her body. The thing was coming up the well, moving with that blurred speed. Her eyes widened and in the distance, two yellow eyes flicked open and glared, expanding like headlamps as they soared up to her.

Lorna snapped back from the edge. Panic burst inside her. Her throat unlocked and she screamed so loudly the glass panel on the door vibrated in sympathy. As soon as she screamed, the lights abruptly came back on. Without conscious thought, Lorna sprang to the door. Behind her, though the pit had popped out of existence when the light flicked on, she could hear the scrabble of nails on stone and the heavy, stuttered breathing of the thing in her nightmares. The muscles down the length of her backbone twisted and shrank in anticipation of a black, clawed hand reaching out to grab and rend. She made it to the door. The handle slipped, twisted, caught and opened. She threw herself out into the other room. A dark shape came looming in front of her and Lorna shrieked again. Two hands came up and grabbed her by both shoulders. She felt herself turn as enormous fear erupted and everything started to fade as her nerves finally gave up the fight. The blood drained from her head and Lorna collapsed to the floor in a dead faint.

Five minutes later, she gradually came dizzily awake sitting in Keith Conran's comfortable swivel seat. The librarian was patting her face with a damp cloth. Beside him, Nelly Coyle, who was in her late fifties and ran the reference section, clucked and fluttered like a mother hen. They gave Lorna a Hedex tablet and a drink of cold water, and a while later, though she maintained she was feeling fine (which was as far from the truth as Lorna could imagine) Keith insisted on driving her round to the health centre. Between himself and Nelly, they suspected that she might be pregnant, although neither mentioned their view. Lorna wouldn't hear of her boss waiting until the receptionist could fit her in and he left her seated, pale and shivering, in the waiting room where she had nothing to do but think about what she had seen in the darkness of the library basement.

In the other waiting room, Jack Fallon was flicking through a tattered copy of *Reader's Digest*, trying with difficulty to swallow, and wondering who on earth was interested in what somebody's spleen did.

17

Annie Eastwood saw her dead daughter again, and the familiar wrench of barren guilt and delusive hope twisted inside her. Since the night in Marta Herkik's house, since she had heard Angela's voice coming from the wrinkled mouth of the old woman, she had seen her daughter's face in glimpses and flashes, in reflections in shop windows, in faces in the lunchtime crowds on River Street, in the shadows behind the flaking, gaunt tombstones in old Clydeshore Cemetery.

She'd gone there many times since the bleak burial, but after the dreadful night in the old woman's apartment, when the walls had frosted and run with stone-sweat and the flawed crystal had spun on its own on the polished table, she'd come to the graveyard every day, dreading to see her girl's name etched on the new, polished granite, the words gleaming in the lights from the street just over the wall.

Angela Eastwood. Aged sixteen.

Her girl's life in four words cut on stone.

Make me some hot donuts, mummy. The high, clear voice of a little girl. It had frozen Annie's heart, chilled her soul. And the words the stone had spelled out, nudging each letter with dread certainty. *Cold. Dark. Hurt.* They had riven her like shards of ice.

Clydeshore Cemetery was cold and dark. Annie could recall the funeral, though she'd been so deadened by the drugs it had been days before the memory had risen to the surface of conscious thought. She'd been moving in a dream, in a nightmare. Since the seance at Marta Herkik's, when the cold breath had shivered through her, filling the empty place in her soul, she felt she'd been thrown back into that nightmare.

The dreams had started that first night, and they had tormented her every night since. Fearful dreams of dark and shadows, familiar places seen from unfamiliar perspectives. She awoke hands shaking, mouth agape, with the feeling she'd been seeing her dreams through the eyes of someone else. In the daytime, sluggish with sleeplessness, she'd find herself staring at some object for minutes on end, while the memory of her daughter's plaintive voice would be ringing in her ears. Annie Eastwood had not slept in the dark for more than a week. She kept on the bedside light every night. But still, in the small hours of the morning, the dreams stole up on her, stole through her.

The cemetery was old and cold and dark. Even the place where Angie was buried had been reclaimed from a cleared section close to the river where a bar of old, hoary trees had been excised after they'd died of Dutch elm disease. The small secluded patch of ground was punctuated by a handful of small, modern stone slabs which had been milled in Kirkland Quarry. To an extent, they were less eerie, less ominous, than the old Victorian monoliths which stood ponderous around the perimeter, half-hidden behind dark juniper and yew. The new-style stones, the kind decreed tasteful by the council, were typically bland and featureless, epitaphs more to the junk-food, tupperware era than to a human being's life. Hoar frost sheened the north sides of the old tombstones. Great grey blocks, mottled with lichen, names scoured almost flat by the decades of wind and rain; etched endorsements from days when God-fearing meant just that.

Ashes to Ashes, Dust to Dust. The Lord Taketh. Yea, though I walk in the valley of the shadow of death.

Old stones bore urns draped with heavy stone-carved cloth, Celtic crosses from a bygone day, carven angels, blind eyes glaring forever behind snail-trail fungus. In this ancient part of the graveyard, death stood bare and cold and final.

And yet as Annie Eastwood walked, shivering, through the wrought-iron gate, she could still hear the echo of her dead daughter's voice, clamouring for life in her memory. She slowly made her way up Keelyard Road and over the bridge. Below the stone arches the river tumbled black over the weir and already the haar-mist was beginning to creep ghostly over the lip of the harbour. The town was still busy, but most of the shops were preparing to close, and most of the passers-by were heading home from day shift at the distillery or from the oil-rig yard. She turned on College Street corner, up past the maze of vennels and alleys, and came out by the little park where the cenotaph to the

227

hundreds of dead in both wars and a few other skirmishes pointed at the cobalt sky. Here, the old bandstand sheltered in the lee of a thick patch of rhododendrons which had trapped most of the fallen leaves from the weeping ash trees. They rustled and whispered in the night breeze.

Annie's breath plumed in front of her as she walked past the bushes, heading into a small rectangle of darkness where the stand and the thick foliage cut off the street lamp.

It was there, in that little dead area, that she heard the dry whisper.

'I'm cold, mummy.'

She stopped abruptly, freezing as motionless as one of the dead-eyed angels. The thin nebula of breath dissipated like a wraith. Annie turned slightly, still without breathing, ears suddenly straining against the rubbery sound of the rhododendron foliage and the far-off traffic. Her eyes had instantly widened and she stared straight ahead at the black shadow in front. In the corner of her vision, the bushes shivered with a life of their own, as if something flitted through them.

'Cold, mummy.'

The whisper was like the rustle of dead leaves. It came from the gloom where the bush pushed forward onto the path, leaving a slight hollow where no light pierced. Annie's breath heaved and she felt the dreamlike panic begin to swell inside her.

'I'm here, mummy. I need you.'

The voice was no longer a whisper. It had gained in intensity, an echoing childlike sound which seemed to come from a distance, as if it were down a well, or in a cave. The wretched appeal was overlaid by that dry, rustling susurration of wind through a thicket.

Annie said nothing. There were no words to say, none that she was able to speak. Fright lurched inside her. She tried to pull herself away, to get towards the light. She had heard her daughter's voice only moments before she'd fled in abject terror from the suddenly menacing room in Cairn House. She had gone there in hope, wanting to find peace. And since that night, she'd had no peace of mind, only a gaping and cold emptiness in her soul and fear in her heart.

She tried to turn, tried to catch her breath properly, when

something came out of the shadows. Annie reacted as if a black dog had leapt for her throat. She gave a strangled gasp and threw one hand out in front of her.

'*Mummy. I need you.*' Her daughter's echoing voice came clearly across the three yards of darkness. A small shape came walking soundlessly towards her. Annie's vision swam as her heart fought to cope with the sudden pressure of the surge of dread. In that watery vision she got a glimpse of a pale face and fair hair streaming out. Two small hands reached for her. Despite her fear, she reached reflexively for them.

Something cold touched her skin, moved towards her, came into her embrace. She smelled the scent of soap, felt the silk of hair, and the wild *need* soared in her heart. Her daughter's face wavered in the shadows as Annie brought her in to hug her tightly, to cuddle the dead cold from the thin form. Yearning mother-love smothered her confusion and fear. Then the scent of soap and familiar girl-scent turned sour, became a septic scent which flooded her nose and mouth and the freezing cold flowed onto her, penetrating her pores, filling the empty space that had creaked open the night of Marta Herkik's seance. The abysmal chill invaded her. For a fleeting second, Annie Eastwood was overwhelmed by a ghastly sensation of violation and then the cold numbed her, froze her, stole the hurt and the sense and the self.

A short while later, Annie Eastwood emerged from the dark space behind the rhododendron patch, and moved on the path beside the bandstand, avoiding the light as much as she could, keeping to the shadowed places. On the strips of lane and alley where she had to come close to a street light, she twitched and averted her face. Down on College Path, a woman she'd been at school with and sometimes chatted to if they met while shopping, said hello and asked her how she was keeping. Annie Eastwood seemed not to have noticed, although, the woman thought, she couldn't have failed to hear her. The woman watched her wander off until she was lost to sight.

Jack met Lorna Breck in the chemist's shop just opposite the health centre. He'd been given, as he'd expected, a prescription for antibiotics. He'd had tonsillitis once, as a teenager, and he remembered the scary moment when, after the pain had built to

229

an extent that swallowing even water was impossible, he'd stood in front of a mirror, opened his mouth, and seen the fungus-like growths almost completely blocking his throat. As he stood, hands in pockets, waiting for the pretty assistant to measure out the pills, he grinned wryly at the memory. He'd thought, with rising panic, that he had a tumour. Those grey-green mottled swellings were just how he'd imagined a malignant carcinoma would appear. The penicillin had shrunk them to nubbins in one short night. He knew now he'd feel better in the morning and he was grateful he was not allergic to antibiotics, otherwise the ache in his throat would continue for weeks.

He looked around, nostalgically appreciating the fact that Burnett's apothecary had changed little since his childhood, defying the trend to become one of the plastic shopping-mall drugstores where drugs were the least available commodity. The walls were lined with crafted display cases crowded with oddly shaped bottles and jars filled with mysterious, tantalising liquids and powders. Most of them looked as if they'd been there since the beginning of the century, and possibly had. And most of them, Jack thought, were probably deadly poison.

Just then the door opened and the little bell over the lintel jangled tunelessly. Jack turned and saw the girl come in. He recognised her immediately. Her face was pale enough to make the smattering of freckles stand out like sepia ink-spots, framed by chestnut hair cut in a neat bob which curled like parentheses on her cheeks. She was looking down at the slip of paper when she walked in, absently letting the door swing closed. The other girl behind the counter reached for the prescription and took it from her without a word. It was only then that she realised she was not alone in the shop. She turned, looked up, saw Jack, and gave a visible start, as if she'd seen something grotesque.

'Something I said?' Jack asked lightly, though his voice had taken on a hoarse, hardened quality.

The girl looked up at him, eyes widening for a brief moment, then looked away. She gave a tiny shake of her head, and very quickly glanced over the counter to where the assistant was counting out Jack's capsules onto a scale. She looked scared and worried and uncomfortable all at once. Both hands fidgeted with the large black shoulder bag. Jack got the impression she would rather be anywhere than standing close to him.

'I hope you're keeping a bit better,' he tried again, just as gently.

The girl nodded, a jerky, mouse-like motion that was almost a tremble, but she kept her eyes down. There was something wrong with her, Jack could see that plainly enough. She looked as if she was held in so tight she was vibrating with the tension. He'd seen that often enough, sat with too many ravished women, bereaved mothers of newly dead children, the casual victims of an increasingly callous and careless society. He took in the contours of her face with the ease of long practice. She wasn't as small as she looked at first, nor as thin. It was just the clenched nervous stance, shoulders drawn in, knuckles standing out white that made her look frail, even gaunt. She was, he gauged, nineteen or so, and had the elfin look of a Renoir model, an innocent face which would have been unlined but for the worried frown and the way she had clamped her lips together in a tight line. Jack wondered what she would look like in repose. He imagined she might be quite lovely if she relaxed. With the dark rings under her eyes, she looked bloodless and ill.

The teenager in the white coat called out his name and he moved across to the desk, handing over enough for the antibiotics and a box of throat pastilles. The assistant smiled as she gave him change and a quick, measuring look, taking in his height and his hair and the presence of a ring on his finger in one sweep. Jack returned the smile and took his medicine, turned from the desk and almost bumped into the slight girl.

'Sorry,' he said automatically, and equally reflexively taking her elbow in his hand. Again she made that startled motion. He could feel the tenseness sing under his fingers.

'Who's done what to you?' he wondered, letting go almost as quickly as he had taken her arm.

The other assistant, this one older, fatter and myopic, called the girl's name just as Jack moved away, heading for the door.

'Lorna Breck.'

Something clicked in Jack's mind. He'd heard the name before. He pulled on the handle, wincing from the clang of the bell just above his ear, and let it swing back on its pneumatic absorber. Outside, in the cold, he scanned his mental file, trying to dredge up the memory. There was a familiarity that danced

231

away as he reached for it, but he knew it would come if he gave it time. The years of police work had honed his memory. The name would be in there somewhere. He pocketed the pills, opened the pastilles and stuck one in his mouth. The fruity juices watered under his tongue and eased the back of his throat. He sucked gratefully and walked along the edge of the small open space to where the car was parked under a winter-stark alder.

Behind him the bell clanged again. He didn't turn round, but kept walking. Footsteps tapped behind him, faster than his own. He was only yards from the car when he heard her speak.

'Excuse me.'

Jack took another couple of steps.

'Excuse me. Please.'

He stopped, turned. She came walking quickly towards him.

Jack raised his eyebrows, still saying nothing. She looked as if she would take off like a roe fawn in the gorse at the merest hint of reproof.

'You're Mr Fallon, the policeman?' She had a light, lilted way of speaking, every word clearly enunciated. She wasn't from around Levenford. From the highlands or islands, going by the accent.

'That's me.'

The girl looked left and right. She took a step forward, then another step back, as if considering an escape.

'You're in charge of. . . .' She stopped, bringing the bag close up to her body like a shield. 'In charge of what's happening here.'

'The very same. And you're Lorna Breck, am I right?'

'How did you know that?' A guilty look opened her face up. She had great grey eyes that widened appealingly.

Jack laughed, though it cost him a scrape of pain in his gullet.

'I heard the girl call it out in there,' he said, nodding back towards the chemist's. 'Don't worry. You're not on my files.'

But she was, he knew. He was still riffling through his mental notebook, trying to place the name. It still wouldn't come.

'Oh,' the girl said. She dropped her eyes again, then just as quickly looked up at him, spearing him with the intensity of her gaze.

'I,' she said, and stopped abruptly. 'What I mean is. . . .'

'Take it easy,' Jack said. 'I've got plenty of time.'

'It's what's happening. I mean in this place.' The girl swept her eyes around the car park.

'This place?'

'The town. Levenford.'

He raised his eyebrows again, willing her on.

'I need to talk to you. I have to talk to someone. I know . . . I mean, I *see* things.'

Jack took a step towards her, hands in his pockets.

'See things?'

She clenched the bag even tighter, hands pure white against the black, opened her mouth as if trying to speak, and then she burst into tears. It happened so quickly Jack was taken aback. She hardly made a sound, but huge droplets filled her eyes and spilled over and down her cheeks while her shoulders hitched up and down spasmodically. Her face was a picture of pure misery.

'Hey. Hold on,' Jack said uselessly. He went towards her, put his arm round her shoulder. She was shivering like a trapped bird. As soon as he touched her, she fell against him and all he could do was hold onto her while she quivered. He felt awkward and gauche.

It took a couple of minutes for the spasm of silent sobbing to subside. When it did, she tried to pull away, sniffing wetly, but he kept his arm around her shoulder until he was sure she wouldn't fall. Finally, he eased his grip. She snapped open the bag and drew out a wad of tissues and jabbed them in her eyes.

'Oh, I'm sorry,' she said, snuffling all the while, looking more than ever like a schoolgirl. 'It's just I need to talk to somebody. I need to talk to *you*.' She looked up at him and her big grey eyes were wide with mute appeal. 'I need help.'

'That's what I'm here for,' Jack said, keeping his voice level. He didn't have a clue what she was talking about, but there was something about the girl that made him want to listen. Maybe she had transmitted her sense of urgency, or maybe it was because she looked as if she was in serious trouble, but he thought if he said the wrong thing she'd be off and running.

'Hey. Come on and I'll buy you a coffee.'

She nodded, then looked up at him.

'There's nowhere open.'

'There's always someplace open.'

233

Just two streets away, the two women who ran Hobnobs coffee shop, a cluttered little place filled with mismatched tables and chairs, were cleaning up when Jack opened the door.

'Time for a quick coffee?' he asked. They were both friends of his sister, so he knew they'd let him sit for a while. One of them took in the girl by his side and gave a half-smile. Jack led Lorna Breck to a corner table. The coffees arrived, hot and steaming. Jack spooned three sugars into hers and smoothed cream onto the surface before shoving it across the table.

'Get this down,' he ordered, then started fixing his own, adding more cream in deference to his tender throat.

He raised the cup to his lips, savoured the heavy roast aroma, and took a sip. Just then the file in his head spat out the information.

'Lorna Breck,' he said. 'You were in the *Gazette* a couple of weeks back.'

She nodded slowly, face reddening a little. It did wonders for her.

'I remember now. It was something about the fire.'

'Agnes McCann's babies,' she said softly. 'They all died.'

'Terrible thing. The paper said you had a premonition or something.'

'Something like that.'

'Are you a what's-it-called? A clairvoyant?'

'A spey-wife? No. I don't think so. I read tea leaves now and again. My grandmother showed me. At parties and things. Just for the fun of it. It was only a little gift until now.'

'And now?'

'Now I see things.'

The words came out flat, like heavy slabs. Beyond the counter, the door leading to the kitchen was a clatter of noise and chattering women, but it hardly penetrated the little circle of silence that enveloped Jack Fallon and Lorna Breck at the corner table.

'You see things?'

She nodded again, keeping her eyes down.

'What kind of things?'

She lifted her cup and sipped through the cream, put it back on the saucer with a small *chink* sound, then raised her eyes again.

234

'There's something terrible happening here. I've seen it.'

Jack held her gaze. 'Seen what?'

'The babies. They've been taken. I saw them.'

'What? You *saw* them?'

'I did.'

'Where?'

'And there's more. There's a boy who's dead now. And the man who was thrown down from a height. I saw him. It's been in the papers.'

'And you *saw* it?' Jack repeated himself.

'Yes.'

'Where were you?'

'You don't understand. I saw them *happen*.' She tapped her temple. 'In my *head*.'

'You mean you imagined them.'

'No. I saw them. And I'm scared. It's terrible. It came and took the baby from its pram. It was crying awfully sore. And then the next time, it came down and hit the other baby's mother. It hit her so hard and she fell and even then she fought for her baby and it hit her again and all the blood. *Oh the blood*, it came running out of her and her eye was still open and she could see it carry her baby away.'

The girl's voice was rising with every word. Jack reached out and put a hand on her shoulder. She stopped talking immediately.

'Wait. Take it easy. I don't understand this.'

She looked at him, suddenly placid.

'What is it you don't understand?'

'Well, any of it. Where did these things happen?'

'I don't know. I've only been here since the spring. I'm not sure of the places.'

'Right. So how did you see them?'

'I don't know. Honestly I don't. It just started the night of the fire, or maybe before that. I've been getting bad dreams. But I saw the fire. I was looking into the tea leaves and then it came. I saw the smoke and something moving in the dark and I heard the babies in their beds and *oh, it was terrible*.'

All the words came out in a rush. She kept her eyes glued on his as she spoke.

'So you see all these things in the tea leaves?'

Lorna sat back, her eyebrows knitting down in an instant frown.

'No. They come all the time. Ever since the night of the fire. When I fell in the street, that's when I saw it again. It came down from the dark and took the baby away.'

'What did?'

'I don't *know*! It comes from the dark and I can feel its hunger. It's an *evil* thing.'

'Isn't that the truth,' Jack said. He didn't know what to make of what the girl was telling him. He readjusted his first impressions. Maybe she wasn't scared. Maybe she was downright loony.

'Why were you at the doctor today?'

'They sent me from work. I had another fright. In the library. I saw the boy.'

'What boy?'

'The one who's missing. He's dead.'

Jack put the coffee cup down very slowly. It made a clink sound as it rattled in the saucer.

'Say that again,' he said, slowly and softly.

'The boy you are looking for. I read it in the paper. It's the same one, and he's dead.'

'And where is he?'

'I don't know.'

Jack nodded, unable to conceal the dry sarcasm. The word *loony* flashed back into his head. It was a shame. In other circumstances the girl would have been attractive enough, even stunning. She looked clean and well groomed and despite the pinched, harried expression, she seemed, at first glance, to be intelligent. He lifted up the cup and swallowed the lot in one gulp. The interview, as far as he was concerned, was over.

'You don't believe me,' she said flatly.

'No,' he replied, equally direct. 'I don't play mind games.' This was not the entire truth. He'd had to play games with many people hauled into the cells after the cut and slash of a Friday night in Glasgow.

'It's not a *game*,' she shot back. He could almost visualise her stamping her foot in petulant emphasis. 'I saw it, and you have to believe me. I need your help. Somebody has got to stop this.'

236

'Alright,' Jack conceded. He sat back and stared at the girl. 'Tell me about the boy.'

'He's dead. It came down from above in the dark and just lifted him up. I could hear it breathing. It's like an animal.'

'What is?'

'I don't know *what* it is. You can't see it properly. It moves so fast, and it climbs.'

Jack started to say something, but she held up her hand. Her eyes were closed, screwed up in concentration, as if she was fighting to recall.

'He heard the woman. There was a woman there. She was in the shadows. I couldn't see her properly, not her face. Her leg was sticking out, and she had lost one of her shoes. Her bag was lying on the stairs.'

She paused and her frown deepened, making a furrow between her eyebrows.

'It was an old place. Broken glass and a smell of something. Birds. Yes. There were birds, fluttering in the dark. The boy called out and then it came down and took him. He didn't have time to cry out. It carried him up onto the rafters and the birds were fluttering about. His shoe came off too. I heard it. Something broke. I think it was his leg, and there was blood coming from his neck. The thing climbed up to the rafters and it was horrible.'

'And where did all this happen?'

'I don't know. It was an old place. Empty. Like an old factory or something. I remember pigeons and the rafters, and there were shutters on the windows and a door on the wall at the far side, like a hayloft door on the farm. For loading things.'

She stopped and looked at Jack.

'I *saw* it, but I don't know where it is.'

'Tell me about the woman.'

'She was on the stairs. It was dark, but there was light coming in. I could see her legs and her bag. There was something on the glass. *Stew* or something. Old letters on the glass. The woman called out to the boy and he came in and I couldn't tell him to run away, because it had already happened. He's dead.'

As she said that, her eyes filled up with tears again. They glistened, huge and moist, before she dived her hand back into the bag and hauled out a wad of tissues.

237

'And this thing. What is it? A man?'

'I don't know what it is. The woman brought it.'

'How?'

'I think they called it here.'

Jack was about to ask what she was talking about when one of the women came from behind the counter and lifted up both cups.

'We have to close now,' she said, balancing cups on saucers in one hand and brusquely wiping the table with a cloth in the other.

'Sure,' Jack said. He fished out some coins from his pocket and laid them on the table. She took the money and went back behind the counter.

'Where do you live?' he asked the girl. When she told him, he said he'd take her home. They walked back to the car in silence, and she didn't say a word all the way over the old bridge and down Clydeshore Avenue. She lived in a small converted cottage, not unlike Jack's own place, though more compact, down close to the tidal flats of the firth. The road stopped right on the shoreline walkway. Ahead of them, the estuary was slate-grey in the cold night air, lit by the flickering lights from the towns on the far side. A sea mist trickled around the rocks lapped by the incoming tide.

When the car stopped, she made no move to get out. Jack didn't have much to say. There were always cranks. He wasn't yet ready to give any credence to a girl who dreamed of murders days after they happened.

'You don't believe me,' she said, as if reading his mind.

'Well, let's just say I've been a policeman too long. My incredulity has had a tough apprenticeship.'

'But it will happen again.'

'Oh, I dare say it will.' The thought crossed his mind that he should take her in for serious questioning, but he quickly dispelled the notion. There was no way she could have been *involved* in any of what happened. He'd heard stories of clairvoyants before, but had never met one in the flesh. There were even tales of murder squads calling them in to help with difficult cases, but Jack had never considered that a possibility. He was a healthy sceptic. Facts did him fine. Recently, facts had been hard enough to come by, but he'd keep working until they turned up.

'It might happen again,' Jack conceded, 'though I sure to God hope it doesn't.'

'It will. It's an evil thing.' She didn't face him as she spoke. Her head was bowed and she stared at her pale hands. Jack turned round in the car seat. Her face was mostly in shadow, although some of the light of the street lamp sent a band of illumination across her eyes. They were glistening again.

'Listen, don't get yourself upset,' he started to say.

'It's too late for that,' she retorted, though her voice carried more sadness and despair than anger.

She reached and opened the car door, quickly stepping outside. She swung it back, paused, then leaned inside.

'You won't find the boy. It took him away. But it will come back again.'

The door closed with a click. He watched her cross in front of the car and push open an old wrought-iron gate. It squealed in protest, then clanged shut behind her as she disappeared into the shadows behind the hedge. Jack sat for a moment, thinking on what she'd said, before starting the car. He reversed up until the next driveway, turned in and drove back the way he'd come.

She was right in one thing, he thought. Whoever had snatched Timmy Doyle and little Kelly Campbell, and whoever had abducted young Neil Kennedy was rolling right along. He would most certainly try again.

Yet there was something else nagging at him as the headlamps drove twin cones through the pale mist on the way down to the bridge, and past the heavy Victorian gates of the cemetery.

There was *something* in what the girl had said. Disturbed she might be, needing treatment almost certainly. But she had said the killer had come *down* from the dark to smash Shona Campbell to the ground. Jack had asked John McColl to get somebody up on the roof at Barley Cobble because there had been no evidence on the ground. That tied in with Jack's thinking, especially in view of the coincidences of Jock Toner's death and the Doyle snatch.

It came down from above. That's what she'd said, not just about the Campbell killing, but about Neil Kennedy's disappearance. There was something in that. Jack pondered on it for a moment as he waited for a van to pass before getting onto the bridge and crossing back to the centre of town. There was something he should be remembering, but, like the girl's name, it stayed just out of arm's reach.

When he got back to the office, there was a stack of messages waiting for him. He called on John McColl and Ralph Slater first. Both of them appeared almost immediately at his door.

'Feeling better, Chief?' John asked.

'Not yet,' Jack said. He felt a bit guilty over spending the past half hour or so with the girl. Despite the nagging, unsummoned memory that she'd almost sparked off, he thought it had been a complete waste of time. He unscrewed the cap of the little brown bottle and dropped a couple of capsules into his palm.

'Thanks for reminding me,' he said. He swallowed both of the antibiotics with some difficulty. They seemed to expand to block his throat. There was a mouthful of cold juice in the bottom of the cup on his desk. He used it to ease the pills down.

'Right. Who's first?'

'Sorley gave us the lifter you wanted,' Ralph started. 'Came up with two things. Traces of cloth on the guttering and some scrape marks on the north side of the roof-slope. Plenty of moss-sheen. I've sent the materials to the lab for fibre comparison and a pic-man out to Latta Court to get snaps of the scrapes above the balcony at the Doyle place. I remember seeing something then. Didn't look significant, but if they match the roof down at the river, then we can be sure we've got a climber.'

'Good work. John?'

'Divers found nothing,' the sergeant said. 'But we got prints from the woman. She was definitely at the Herkik house. Robbie Cattanach gave us another preliminary. She drowned alright. Lungs filled with river water. Aged forty to fifty, no identification marks. No sign of violence. I'm getting dental records to see if we can get an ID.'

'How long had she been in the water?'

'Robbie says about twelve hours, give or take six. Harder to tell in the winter.' John leaned across the desk and laid down the buff folder.

'It's all in here. More to come later.'

240

'Fine. Keep working on it,' Jack said. 'And those marks could be very helpful. Once we find who the lady is, maybe we can find what happened to Marta Herkik. And once we find that out, I reckon we've got our man.'

The two policemen nodded and turned to go when Jack halted them.

'Hold on a minute. Anybody know anything about the second sight?'

'You mean mediums, that sort of thing?'

Jack nodded. The two others looked at each other.

'My wife does,' Ralph volunteered. 'She gets her cards read every other month. Says it really works, but then most women do. It's all hogwash to me.'

'No,' John countered. 'There's a lot of folk believe it. They use them to hunt for missing folk in the States. Why do you ask?'

'I just spoke to a girl who claims she sees things in dreams. Says she saw the Campbell snatch.'

'I'd haul her in for a going over,' Ralph said. 'We need every witness.'

'No. She saw it in a dream as well. Or so she says.'

'I'd bring her in on the team,' Ralph advised, trying to keep the smile off his face. 'But don't let Mr Cowie hear it, or he'll put you on sick leave.'

Jack shrugged and returned the grin. The others left the office, and when the door was closed Jack bent to the notes on his desk. There was a lot of technical data on the woman from the river. Still no identification though, which was a disappointment. Jack knew John McColl would get a name for her and quickly, but it might not be quickly enough.

He marshalled what was known. Things were beginning to piece themselves together, slowly, but surely. Simpson had been at the Herkik house. So had the woman. The dead minister had also been at or near the Doyle place. Now both of them were dead, both suicides. The Campbell baby had been taken some distance, up to the top of Loch View, one of the highest parts of Levenford, which mirrored the Doyle abduction.

There was a connection running through everything. Jack knew if he worked at it for long enough, he'd come up with the answer, but for the moment he felt he was wallowing in a welter of hints and near-facts. He was becoming more and more convinced there was more than one person, and that thought worried him. One lunatic, one psychopath was bad enough, hard enough to find. Two, or more, meant some sort of organisation, a group of perverted and malignant people who were killing for a purpose. He put the folder down, unopened, and picked up the white sheets of the various messages. Robbie Cattanach had called an hour ago. Andrew Toye from the University had returned his call only minutes after he'd left. At the bottom was a call from Oban police. Jack reached to pick up the phone. It rang under his fingers and he jerked his hand back in surprise before snatching it up.

'Hey boss, what's happening?' Mickey Haggerty bawled into his ear.

'I've been looking for you,' Jack retorted.

'You and half the police in the highlands.' Mickey sounded more aggrieved than worried. 'You have to help me. I'm a wanted man. They've got search parties all over Oban looking for me. I just got out ahead of the sheriff.'

'You're a popular man, Mickey.'

'It's no bloody joke. They've been asking after me in every pub. I don't know what the hell they want. I haven't been up to anything, except hustle these yokels for their wages.'

'Oh, calm down, Mickey. They were doing me a favour. I was trying to get a hold of you.'

'You?'

'Yes. Netta didn't know where you were staying.'

'Jesus Christ, Jack. You could have let me know. I've been ducking and diving up here.' Mickey's voice trailed off.

'Well, I'll call off the dogs and you can get back to playing snooker as soon as you give me what I need on that fellow you mentioned, the Irishman.'

'Him? But you've got that. I came in to see you last week, but you were out. I'd fixed up to come up here, so I left a note. Gave it to that boss of yours. The one with the face like a torn loaf.'

Jack cursed aloud.

'Oh come on, Jake. Don't blame me. I told you I'd get back to you.'

'No, it wasn't you, Mickey. Somebody just forgot to pass on

the message, and that's why I've had the Oban busy-boys combing the hills for you.'

'They'd never find me anyway. I'm shacked up with a pal of mine here. You'd like her.'

'So that's why Netta didn't have an address,' Jack ventured. 'She'll skin you.'

'Only if you tell her,' Mickey shot back, laughing. 'Anyway, you're looking for Michael O'Day. Lives out on Cross Road. He's Irish, from somewhere up north. Talks with an accent thicker than shit in the neck of a bottle.'

'What does he do?'

'Sells cars somewhere up in the city. Nobody knows where. But he's a heavy punter. Puts down a lot of dough on the horses. I heard he was down a lot of money to Eddie Carrick. Not a lucky man.'

Jack took notes while Mickey spoke, writing down everything in a tight hand. There might have been nothing in it, but he wanted to talk to everybody, hell, *anybody* who had been near Marta Herkik's on the night of the storm. Mickey seemed quite relieved that the Oban police were not hounding him for anything he might have done. He told Jack he'd expect a few beers for his trouble and Jack promised to call off the search.

The phone rang again as soon as it was on the cradle. This time it was Andy Toye, head of the Department of Parapsychology and Paranormal Studies at the university.

'Third time lucky,' the professor said drily.

'Been a busy man, Andy.'

'So I gather. You're having more problems, or so I hear on TV.'

'Too many,' Jack agreed wearily.

'Well, I've had a look at the material. The tarot cards are straightforward. Almost a full set of major and minor arcana. You can buy them in half a dozen shops, though these ones look very old. I could get an estimate on their age, I suppose.'

'No. I don't think I'll need that.'

'As for the other stuff. The photographs are very good. The table is a rather elaborate ouija board, as you'll know already. That looks quite old too, possibly made for a professional medium. It's for telling the future. They use a crystal glass to spell out the messages from the other side.'

243

Jack thought back to the scene in the shattered room. The old woman had been lying with her head on the kerb of the fireplace. Shards of crystal had been embedded in the top of her head.

'The other side?'

'Yes. The dear departed. Most mediums claim to have a spirit guide who takes messages and passes them across the great divide.'

'So this was a seance?'

'Sure it was. The whole room was full of spiritualist paraphernalia, and from different cultures. The old woman must have known her stuff.'

'Do they take it seriously?'

'Believe me, thousands of folk do. Everybody who reads a star chart in a newspaper has some level of belief.'

'And does it work?'

'There again, people think it works.'

'How about you?' Jack asked.

'Well, until a year or so, I was a healthy sceptic. Now I'm coming down on the other side.'

'You mean the other side, like in ouija boards?'

'No, the side of the believers. There's been a great deal of research into it. Automatic writing, poltergeists, that kind of thing.'

'And you believe in all that?'

'After what happened in Linnvale, I don't have much choice, because I believe the man who told me about it. That was real witchcraft, and it had real results.'

Jack was more interested in events at Levenford than Linnvale. 'What about the book?' He remembered the blood-soaked pages crumpled and scattered all around the body.

'Same again. It's occult. It took me a while to identify it, but we're a growing band, us paranorms. I've a friend in Winchester who identified it for me. He's got a first edition of *The Goetia*.'

'Now you've got me.'

'It's Crowley's book. One of his major works. *The Goetia* was his treatise on summoning spirits. It's a mite arcane and more than a little speculative, if you ask me. He claimed every spirit had its own name and that could be used in raising it up.'

'What sort of spirits are we talking about?'

'Oh, demons. Imps. That sort of character. Crowley's generally considered to have been the biggest charlatan of them all, but there's some folk believe he raised the Beast itself at Bolsekine House and again at Torbeck Estate way back just after the war. *The Goetia* was translated for him from allegedly ancient texts. It means necromancy. Crowley's own definition was *howling*.'

'Sounds like a horror movie.'

'Well, you did ask,' Andy said, but without rancour.

'So, this book. What would it be used for?'

'I told you. It's a guide on how to bring spirits into this world.'

'And folk actually believe it?'

'Don't knock it until you've tried it.'

'You think there was some sort of seance where they were trying to conjure up ghosts?'

'I can't say for certain. But it looks as if they were going beyond reading palms. It can be dangerous too.'

'It was dangerous for the old lady. Fatal.'

'Yes. But there's a lot of psychological danger in this kind of thing. You can't even buy a ouija board here any more. There's been too many documented cases of schizophrenia and psychosis relating to the use of the paraphernalia. I wouldn't recommend it.'

Jack thanked Andy and was about to hang up when another thought struck him.

'Oh, before you go, maybe you could help with something else.'

'Go on,' Andy encouraged.

'I was talking to a girl today. She says she's had visions or nightmares or whatnot about what's been happening down here. Tells me she's seen the events actually happen.'

'That's not beyond the bounds of probability. It's happened in hundreds of cases.'

'You mean you believe in this too?'

'I can't speak for the lady, because I haven't met her. But there's no reason to be a complete sceptic. I've had first-hand experience of telepathy. When you get violent acts, murders, accidents and the like, you often hear stories of people who've had some prescience of the event. It's far from uncommon.'

245

'So she might not have been spinning me a line?'

'Possibly. If you want me to have a chat to her, I'd be delighted.'

Jack said he would let him know.

'Well, you look at it this way. If she *is* telling the truth, then she'd be the best source you could hope for. I'd hire her if I were you.'

Jack put the phone down and thought about it, but not for long. It rang for the third time.

Robbie Cattanach was in ebullient mood, despite his occupation.

'Up to the armpits in gore, as usual,' he said when Jack asked him how things were going. 'Definitely a dead-end job.' Jack winced.

'So. Fancy a beer?'

Jack told him he was on antibiotics and couldn't drink.

'An old wife's tale. The new ones don't react with alcohol.' Jack allowed himself to be persuaded to meet Robbie in Mac's Bar in half an hour. The place was busy when he arrived some time after seven, just minutes before Robbie himself came in, buttoned up in his leathers, and with his black helmet under his arm. He accepted a pint and drank half of it in one gulp.

'Needed that,' he said breathlessly, putting the glass down. 'Clears the smell of formalin and worse. I did your lady today.'

'I know. Quick work. I've got the report to read up tonight. No surprises?'

'No. She killed herself. Only odd thing is the amount of water in the lungs. I reckon she walked in and breathed in hard. Normally there's still some air and carbon dioxide, but she was well and truly flooded. No other visible signs of trauma inside or out.'

Jack sipped his own beer slowly. His throat was easing slightly, though he didn't believe a word about modern antibiotics and alcohol.

'John McColl tells me you want to know about suicides,' Robbie volunteered.

Jack nodded.

'Well, there's another one,' Robbie went on. 'He's up in Lochend at the moment. And the remarkable thing is, he's not dead yet.'

'Okay,' Jack said, patiently. 'What's the punchline?'

Robbie looked at him with an expression of injured innocence.

'No kidding. He drank Paraquat. Definitely a goner. I should get him in the next day or two. Insides will be like a septic tank. He's been unable to tell the doctors a thing, but the toxics man tells me he's been raving about devils, poor soul.'

Jack's glass stopped halfway to his mouth.

'Have you got a name?'

'No, but he's in ward eight. At least, he was when I left. He could be down in the cellar by now.'

'Sorry, Robbie. I have to go. Thanks for the tip.'

Jack pushed his way past the startled pathologist, leaving his drink almost untouched. He reached the payphone at the far end of the bar next to the door and dialled the number. When it was picked up at the other end, John McColl sounded breathless.

Jack told him to stay in the office until he got there. It took him only a few minutes to get the car from the tight space at the back of the pub and scoot round to the station. John was waiting at the door and came across to where Jack had stopped, engine still running.

'Mr Cowie's looking for you,' he said. 'He's like a bear with a sore arse.'

'He'll have to wait. Get in.'

'What's the rush?'

'Another suicide,' Jack said. 'I want to catch him before he dies.'

He pulled out into the traffic and did not see the look on John McColl's face. If he had he might have laughed.

'This is the third dinner I've missed three nights in a row,' John said heavily. 'I was halfway out of the office when the phone rang. And now I've got to see a dead man who isn't dead yet.'

The man in ward eight looked as if he was caught in a surreal science fiction scene. Clear plastic tubes filled with different coloured liquids snaked from hissing, pumping machinery and wormed their way into the various orifices of the shape on the bed. The man was naked, apart from a small cloth over his groin from which a catheter looped its way into the harsh light from the overhead tubes. A plastic mask hid most of the man's face. A tracheostomy line plunged into a scabbed hole in the man's

247

throat. Electrodes suckered onto the bare chest and the wires fed off into an electronic monitor. The oscilloscope showed a very slow heartbeat.

'Impossible,' the toxicologist told Jack when asked if the man could be interviewed. He was a tall, angular man, with thick grey hair which looked as if it had been cleanly parted with an axe. He'd introduced himself as Charles Collins.

'It could be important,' Jack insisted.

The doctor looked at him levelly, then gave a disarming smile. 'Oh, I've nothing against it. I don't mind at all. It's just that he won't be talking to anybody any more.'

'You couldn't give him something?'

'I'd love to, but I've tried everything. There's nothing in this world that will keep him from the next. He won't wake up again. I estimate he's got between three and six hours. Damn fool.'

'What happened?' Jack asked. John McColl was standing off to the side, eyes fixed on the shape on the bed. The skin around the man's eyes was brown-tinged and flaking. The eyelids were bruised almost black. Down the length of the chest and the sides, the skin was a yellow, almost orange colour, obvious signs of liver failure. But for the faint hitching of the chest, he might have already been dead.

'He drank Paraquat. *Dimethyl-bipyridium*.'

'The weedkiller?'

'Yes. It's a non-selective herbicide. It doesn't choose what it kills. You could call it a *bio*-cide. His body has been shutting itself down since the first swallow.'

'Any idea when?'

'According to his wife, it was Friday night. He's lasted a lot longer than most. But it seems it was quite deliberate. I don't think he quite realised the consequences. He's been in intense pain for most of the past four days.'

'And there's no cure?'

'Never has been one. They invented this stuff for chemical warfare as a nerve gas and now sell it in every garden store, but they forgot to develop an antidote. It's amazing how few folk actually die from it considering its availability, but once swallowed death is a certainty.'

'Like taxes and nurses,' John McColl murmured absently, eyes still fixed on the wasting man on the bed.

'Quite,' Dr Collins said drily. 'Must use that at the next rotary dinner.'

He turned back to Jack. 'Paraquat is completely anti-life. The perfect final solution. We've had him on a ventilator since Friday. The lungs are the first to go. They'll be like soapsuds in there. There's hardly any tissue left to absorb oxygen. Kidneys are next. They've failed, so he's been on continual dialysis. Then there's the liver. That's packed up. He's jaundiced, of course, and his blood production has been disrupted. Marrow's going too, but that's a secondary issue. He's most likely got irreversible brain damage, both from lack of oxygen in the blood, and also because of the nerve tissue damage. I would say that by now he's beyond feeling any pain, though we've loaded him to the eyes with morphine.'

'So he won't talk?'

'As they say in the movies,' Dr Collins said, returning Jack's exasperated look with a smile.

'Any idea why he did it?'

'No. He was conscious for the first day. In a lot of pain and babbling when the painkillers wore off. After ten hours the lungs were too far gone for him to talk. He whispered a lot.'

'Can you remember anything he said?'

'Talked about the devil mostly. Said it was coming to get him. Maybe he was religious, what do you think?'

Jack shrugged. The shape on the bed was as still as death.

'His wife said he came in and told her what he'd done. He told her it was all over and then quite calmly said he'd drunk the Paraquat. I would have chosen something easier myself, maybe a bottle of brandy and some valium. That would give the devil a run for his money, and there's always a chance of a reprieve.'

Jack could tell the doctor had seen death in many of its forms. He was not making light of it. The best practitioners he knew were all as drily ironic. It helped them cope with the fact of it, let them make it a business and get on with the job, just like a policeman on a murder squad. Death was something you didn't get used to, but you learned to face it and not look away.

'Do you mind if we print him?'

The doctor raised his eyebrows.

'Fingerprints,' Jack explained.

'Be my guest. What's he done?'

'I don't know. I'm checking on all suicides, or attempted ones. I wish I'd heard of this earlier.'

'Wouldn't have done him any good.'

'Might not have helped me either, but at least I'd know.'

John McColl took only minutes to take the dabs, using a date-stamp pad from a secretary's office, carefully pressing each finger and both thumbs onto a clean page of his notebook. It was a strange experience, taking prints from a man who was completely helpless. As he reached for the wrist, he could feel the heat under the skin. The dying man was burning up inside, and John thought it was no wonder he was scared of the devil. He was already in hell.

It was after nine when they left, and closer to ten when Jack dropped the sergeant off at his house on the east side of town. They had stopped at the station to deposit the fingerprints, and Jack had picked up the reports he planned to read that night. John invited him in for a bite to eat, but he declined. He was tired and his throat was still sore, and he knew he'd be up early in the morning to interview Edward Tomlin's wife. He wanted to get home, have a long, hot bath, take another couple of capsules, and get to bed.

That's exactly what he did except that first of all he dropped in at his sister's house. Julia was looking much better than she had on Saturday, although her voice was still a bit husky.

Davy was in bed and Jack was reluctant to go up and wake him up. Julia subjected him to some sisterly reproof over the escapade in the stream, told him he deserved his tonsillitis for being an overgrown schoolboy, then told him how much her son had enjoyed his day out.

'Just wish I had more time,' Jack said. 'It does me a lot more good than it does him, I can tell you.'

She came up beside him, a tall woman, though her head only came up to his chin, and nudged him with her hip, putting an arm around his waist. The way she did it reminded him of Rae, and as soon as that image came, he shied away from it. He was too busy to get maudlin. Julia gave him a hug and asked him how the investigation was going.

'Not great. It's going to take a lot more work, so tell Davy I'll drop by and see him when I can, but tell him not to hold his breath.'

'He'll understand,' she said.

'Hope so. He's a good wee fellow.'

'Shame about his father,' Julia said, without malice. She'd been bitter when Malcolm had left, but time had smoothed the rough edges. It had been one of those things.

'Oh, and keep an eye on him, Jules.'

'I always do.'

'No,' Jack said. 'A close eye. There's something going on. I'd keep him in for the duration. And never let him out in the dark under any circumstances.'

'Fine, Jack. You just tell me how to raise my own boy,' Julia shot back, then instantly regretted it. Since he'd lost his wife and daughter, Jack and Davy had used each other for therapy, and that was a good thing. Each went a little way to replacing what was gone.

'Sorry,' she said, and dropped her eyes.

Jack shucked her under the chin.

'No offence, kid. Just humour me, eh?'

'Sure,' she said.

He let himself out.

Up at the cottage he had a quick glance at the post mortem report on the woman who'd been fished from the river that morning. It seemed as if it had happened days ago. The words began to blur in front of his eyes after only ten minutes and he started to doze off. The report slid from his fingers and landed on the floor with a slap.

18

Castlebank Distillery is one of the few places in Levenford which has night-shift working in winter. The demand for the export scotch whisky blend always soared before Christmas. There were orders to be shunted out and stacked onto the big containers that came and went at all hours heading for the docks in Glasgow for worldwide distribution.

Latta's yard just south along the bank was still noisy with the eerie buzz of the welders and sapphire lightning flashes sparked and flared along the length of the growing pyramid of steel which would be towed out of the estuary and up to the North Sea before the summer, all things going to plan.

The distillery is a square-set, brick-built eyesore of a building which towers over the south of the town, next to the tidal basin on the river. What it lacks in grace and style and visual appeal is more than made up for by the fact that it pays the wages of one in every four families and that alone helped generate most of the other business in the town. For that, the Levenford folk could put up with the stale-towel smell of the maltings and the cloud of steam which rose in a plume day and night. They could put up with the fact that ten per cent of the men had a drink problem because when a business involves millions of gallons of high-voltage amber liquid it is impossible to account for every drop. Without the distillery, Levenford could have rolled up its pavements and turned off the lights like many a similar sized town in Scotland had done in previous years.

It wasn't until much later that Elsa Quinn remembered seeing the woman in the corridor when she'd taken a break from the bottling line to get a drink from the fountain. She hadn't been paying much attention, mainly because she needed the water to swallow the tablets for the headache which had been building up for the past hour. Elsa was prone to migraines and when one of them started screwing its way in behind her eyes, her vision would waver and her tongue would feel thick and numb. She only recalled the woman in a vague way and couldn't put a name to her.

'I wasn't paying much attention,' she was to tell Jack Fallon. 'I had a splitting headache, but we don't get much time off the bottling lines, because they go too fast. I had to wait until a supervisor stepped in.'

The incident she was a witness to happened two hours after Jack had left Lochend Hospital and less than an hour before he'd woken up with a sudden and certain knowledge clanging alarm bells in his head. Then the phone had rung, two calls, one after the other.

Down in Castlebank Distillery the tea-break bell had rung, a harsh jangle of sound that grated on everybody's nerves. In the staff canteen, the plastic chairs were scraped back from the tables, cigarettes stubbed out into overflowing ashtrays. The dregs of strong tea were quickly swallowed or left to go cold as the lineworkers made for the exits and back to work. In seconds, the hubbub of noise had faded to the relative silence of the canteen girls clattering cups and saucers and sweeping the floor tiles.

Sixteen-year-old Carol Howard had worked in the building since August, when she'd left school with a diploma in typing and cookery. She was a pleasant girl with long dark hair which hung down her back in a tidy and quite elegant plait. She worked on the floor above the bottling plant, in the storeroom where the pallets of cardboard whisky cases were laid flat in library-stack lines and where boxes of bottle-tops and labels lined the walls, almost twenty feet high. Normally the storeroom workers and the bottling women had staggered work-breaks, but on the night shift the stores department operated on an emergency basis. If a box of labels was needed somewhere, or a fresh carton of tops, Carol would take the call, mark in the request on her terminal, and get one of the men to carry the delivery down to the floor below.

She'd spent the twenty minutes in the canteen with a crowd of girls her own age, three of whom had been in the same class at school. The talk was all of discos and boyfriends and how they all hated the job already, although Carol was quietly pleased about the fact that she'd landed an office job and didn't have to wear the sky-blue overalls which marked the rest of the girls as bottlers. Her nails were never broken, nor her hands scadded from the constant use of the washers and the incessant drip of whisky. The girls on the lines might have been paid more for their manual labour, but to Carol, working in an office gave her the edge.

When the bell had jangled, they'd all moved to the corridor, surrounded by the raucous laughter of the older women as they trailed back up to the third floor by the west stairs. Carol stood for a moment at the turn of the stairs, talking to two of the girls, making tentative arrangements for Friday night, when one of the supervisors called down to the two others, telling them to get a move on. One of them shrugged and both of them turned to follow the rest along the upper passage. Carol continued up the stairs and was about to enter the storeroom when she realised she'd left her bag slung over the back of her chair in the canteen.

'Damn,' she said under her breath, turned, and headed back along the corridor. As she passed the service elevator, she saw the woman leaning against the wall and continued past for several steps, before she turned. There was something about the woman's posture that caught her attention. She seemed to be sagging, as if she'd taken ill. Her face was familiar, but Carol couldn't place it. The girl came back towards the junction. The light on the ceiling beside the broad grey door had gone out. This part of the passageway was in shadow.

'Can I help you?' Carol asked the woman. There was no response. The woman turned her body a little, facing away into the shadow. The girl noticed there was a rip on her tights and scuff marks on what looked like sensible walking shoes. There was also a dark smear on the back of the woman's coat, as if she'd leaned against a wall.

'Are you alright?' she persisted, but still there was no response. The woman mumbled something, but it was too soft and low to make out.

The girl took another two steps forward, about to ask again, when the door at the far end of the corridor, round the bend from the elevator, swung open. One of the storemen popped his head out.

'Hey, Carol. They need some export labels on line six.'

'Right, Jim,' she called back. 'I'll be with you in a minute.'

The woman hadn't moved at all. Carol hesitated a moment, torn between concern for the stranger and the need to get down to the canteen for her bag before it disappeared. She also had to get back up and make sure the lines got their labels or she would get the blame for a break in production. She turned away and went down the stairs two at a time. As she did so, all the lights in the corridor went out.

She hurried to the canteen and opened the door. One of the cleaners was sweeping up close to where she'd been sitting at the far end. The woman was just reaching out for the small bag on the chair when Carol got there.

'Oh thanks. I knew I'd left it somewhere,' the girl said. A look of disappointment flitted across the cleaner's face. She shrugged and handed the bag over. Carol thanked her again, slung it over her shoulder and walked quickly back to the door, her heels clicking staccato on the tiles. She started to take the stairs again, then remembered the lights had gone out up on the fourth floor. The corridor up there was long and narrow, and at this time of night there was little activity. Carol was not scared of the dark, but she had a healthy regard for it. Instead of taking the stairs, she walked the ten yards to the service lift, hit the up button and listened to the whine and clank as the carriage lowered itself to the second floor.

There was a metallic thump and the doors accordioned open with a breathless hiss. Carol stepped inside, pressed button four and watched as the wall on the other side of the passageway shrank to a rectangle, a slit, then disappeared. The lift kicked under her feet and rose, rumbling upwards. She opened her bag to make a quick inventory, just to make sure nothing was missing.

Then the lights went out and the lift juddered to a halt so suddenly that Carol lurched off-balance. Her bag dropped to the floor and her knuckle rapped painfully against the side of the cabin, causing her to let out a little high squeal of hurt and surprise. Her voice echoed tinnily on the inside of the cage.

She was alone in the dark.

For a second, the fact of it failed to register as her mind tried to understand what had happened. Then the impact of it swooped

255

in on her. The lift had stopped and the lights had gone out and she was in the dark. There was not a sliver of light. Her eyes widened automatically as apprehension swelled to fright and then soared up to panic.

At the age of three Carol had crawled into the cellar under the house in Whiteford Road and got stuck behind a jammed door in the dark, cobwebby darkness. She'd been there for two hours until her mother had finally heard her panicked screams, and the nightmares had gone on for weeks after. Time had eventually healed the trauma. Yet the memory had lain dormant.

Thirteen years and five months after the childhood scare, something in Carol Howard's mind unlocked and the memory woke up and came racing like a black express train out of a tunnel, shrieking all the while.

Her heart did a jittery dance inside her, all out of step, and her breathing was suddenly all too fast, backed up as her lungs hauled for more air than they could hold.

The darkness was complete. The lights on the buttons had failed along with the overhead panel. She could hear her own breathing bounce back at her from the bare metal walls of the cage. Inside her ears, the fast pulse was a dizzying throb. Carol stepped forward and her foot snagged on the strap of her bag. She gasped as she tripped forward. For the second time her knuckle hit something solid, sending a shard of pain up to her elbow. She twisted and a long fingernail caught on the head of a rivet and ripped off to the quick. Underfoot something crunched. It sounded as though she'd trampled on a large insect.

Fear swamped her. Carol's mouth opened in an automatic scream but no sound came out. In her mind, she could hear herself screaming, but her ears heard nothing, and that made the terror balloon. *She was stuck in the dark and she couldn't call for help*.

With no visual point of reference she was completely disorientated. She took one step and something else crackled under her shoe. She lurched to the left and slammed against the wall of the hoist, sending a bolt of pain across her shoulder. The force of it unlocked her breathing and the girl screeched, as she had done in the cellar. Her outstretched fingers found the buttons and she stabbed and scrabbled at them, hitting none out of the ten.

Nothing happened.

Carol shrieked as loud as she could, hearing her cry shatter and fragment as it spanged between the walls and roof. She groped until she found the slit between the two sliding doors and hooked her nails in and tried to prise the edges apart. Another nail gave, pulling backwards with a burning twist of pain. The door remained shut.

The girl's scream played itself out, leaving her breathless and panting, both hands planted against the wall. In her mind she saw the women leave at the end of the shift. If the lift was slow in coming, they would just walk down the stairs. She didn't know if anyone could hear her from the outside of the double safety doors. There was no window onto the corridor.

The thought that she could be stuck in the dark all night, all alone in the lift shaft of an empty ten-storey building, sent another jolt of panic through her and galvanised her into another fit of hysterical shouting. She battered at the door with the palms of both hands, a rapid, urgent timpani which shook the metal cage and sent it clanking against the guide rails. The noise boomed up the shaft. The darkness squeezed at her. It felt tangible and thick. She couldn't see the walls, only feel the doors in front of her. The sides of the cabin could have been yards away, miles away, but in her fright, Carol could sense them close and getting closer, shrinking down to squash her in the dark. Her dread inflated, gripping her stomach, making her heart pound uncontrollably.

Then, miraculously, somebody shouted.

'Anybody in there?' The voice was muted, coming from some distance, or through several layers, but it was enough.

'Oh yes!' Carol squawked, suddenly flooded with gratitude. She still couldn't see a thing. She was still trapped in a metal box eight feet by eight feet, all on her own, but the very fact that somebody *knew* where she was was enough to swamp her with relief. 'Down here. I'm stuck. Please help.'

'Where are you?' the thin voice called out.

'I'm in the lift,' she yelled.

'Which floor?'

Carol stopped to think. Her heart was still beating fast. She'd come in on the second floor. She'd pressed for four and the lift had risen. *How far?* She couldn't recall. People had faith in modern lifts. They pressed the button and waited for the bumpy stop and the swish of the doors, trusting the machinery. Now it had failed and Carol realised she did not know whether she had gone up one or two floors. Or six.

'I don't know. Just get me out of here,' she called out in a jittery voice.

The instant balm was fading fast. It was still dark and it still crowded in on her as if it had weight.

Then up above, there was a thump and a heavy, ringing vibration which shivered the floor of the cab and sent it rocking again.

'What?' Carol cried. The floor lurched under her feet and she tripped forward again, arms out groping for the wall.

'. . . the hell was that?' the unseen man shouted. It sounded as if he was above her.

'What's happening?' Carol yelped.

Another booming vibration resonated down to the cage. It shivered as if it had been struck a heavy blow, and the cables thrummed like deep bass strings. Carol slipped to the floor and landed on her handbag. Something sharp dug into the back of her thigh and her teeth clicked together with a snap.

'Who's in there?' the man called out.

'Me. Carol Howard. Can you get somebody to get me out of here?'

'Alright, love, we'll get the serviceman.'

She sat in the dark, hoping the engineer would come quickly. There was always one or two men working on the lifts. She didn't know if there was anybody on standby at night. The thought of spending much longer in the narrow dark squeezed her panic tight.

Then right overhead, something hit the top of the cabin. The whole cage jerked and shuddered, rocking Carol onto her back. The sound was like a huge hammer blow. Carol squealed in fright.

'What's going on?' the man called.

Carol didn't reply. Above her, on top of the cage, she could hear movement.

Must be the engineer, she thought, grateful for the speed of the rescue. She knew there was a trapdoor somewhere on the top of the lift. That was how they'd get her out. She wondered if they would put a ladder down or just reach down and haul her up. She hoped the shaft wouldn't be too dirty or filled with spiders and cobwebs. They made her shudder, but she could bear the sight of them as long as she could get out of the dark.

The lift quivered violently again. Overhead there was a scraping sound on the cabin roof, then a screech of protesting metal.

'Hello?' she called out. 'I'm down here.'

There was no response.

Something moved. There was another metallic squeal and a thump. A splinter snapped off and clanged to the floor, followed by droplets of dust.

'Can you put the light on?' she asked.

The cables thrummed again and the lift lurched. Close by, she heard a grunt, then all of a sudden, the cage was filled with a foul, choking smell. Carol coughed, shuddering, and then her panic expanded on a bubble of dread. She felt the hairs on the back of her neck twist and shrivel as the skin puckered. A truly cold sweat soaked out of the pores under her arms and on her back. She felt her bladder give.

Above her, something snuffled like an animal scenting the air and then let out a low growl.

'Who's there?' Carol whimpered. She crawled backwards until her shoulder blades were against the door.

Something came down from the roof.

In the tight claustrophobia of the service lift, she could sense its presence. It forced its way through the hole in the roof, scraping against the metal sides. Something metal whirred in the air and tinkled on the floor.

She could see nothing, but her fear-heightened senses could pick out the presence like a biological radar. The putrid stench engulfed her, making her gag.

Something rasped again on the wall. She got a mental picture of a big scaly spider, then without warning she was hauled from the ground.

Just in front of her, whatever it was snarled, so low and menacing she felt the vibrations shiver through her.

259

Carol tried to scream. She tried to shout and holler, but as before, no sound came out. Something had lifted her with shocking force from the ground and she could not make a sound.

Dimly, far off, she heard the voice: 'It's alright, love. The engineer's on his way.'

The unseen thing wrenched her upwards. Her shoulder hit the edge of the trapdoor and she heard something crack under the skin. There was no pain, but there was an enormous pressure on her other shoulder. It felt as though it was trapped in a huge vice. Everything had happened so quickly that she didn't even have time to think, to consider what had come in the dark and snatched her from the floor. The tremendous fear had driven her mind into shock overload. Dimly she was aware of her blouse snagging on a jagged piece of metal, then, even more dimly, realised it was not her blouse, but the skin of her left breast. Warm wetness flowed to her waist.

The shape snuffled and grunted, the sound of a bloodhound, or a pig in a trough. It heaved her through the narrow opening with a violent jerk. She felt the skin of her leg peel off right down the outside of her thigh to her ankle. The sensation seemed very far away, as if it could have been happening to someone else.

The girl felt herself dragged upwards, swinging like a rag doll. Whatever held her leaped from one side of the well to the other. Her feet banged against the brickwork, sending off clouds of dust and pieces of loose concrete to rain on the roof of the elevator. For a second the motion stopped. Carol hung suspended in the void, her feet pointing down. She was lifted up slowly and something turned towards her. Two eyes opened and flared a poisonous yellow.

At that moment, Carol plunged through the other side of the shock paralysis. She saw the great eyes glare at her and suddenly she could see and feel and breathe. Enormous pain rampaged through her shoulder where the thing held her in an incredibly powerful grip. Her leg felt as if it was on fire and the side of her breast was a sunburst of agony.

The eyes glared at her with such hunger and hate and malevolence that Carol simply screamed.

Her ear-splitting screech cascaded and resonated all the way down the lift shaft, on and on and on.

Out on the corridor on level four, Peter Cullen shrank back from the door.

'What in the name of Christ was that?' Beside him, a crowd of women in their overalls instinctively reached for each other, moving close together.

The terrified screams came reverberating down the hole, magnified and amplified in the enclosed space.

Outside the door on the fourth floor, everybody heard the sound. It was more than a girl afraid of the dark. The shattering wails came crashing down from above, an incessant torrent of pure terror.

In the lift shaft, the thing moved and flexed. The girl felt the grip on her shoulder abruptly loosen. There was a popping sound as her skin puckered outwards and whatever had been holding her pulled out. Warmth drenched her back in a stream and under the noxious stink that filled the gallery, she could smell her own blood.

Suddenly, she felt herself fall, and just as instantly, she was jerked back. This time, the grip was on one thigh. She felt hard points drive into the thick muscle and a fresh pain detonated in her hip. The darkness swooped alarmingly. One second she was dangling feet down, and the next she was upside down in the shaft. The thing started to climb again, jerking from side to side on the walls of the duct, moving with ferocious speed. Carol's piercing screams followed it up into the dark heights.

Down by the lift door, they heard the ululating, echoing cries diminish. One of the women crossed herself.

'What's going on out here?' somebody barked from along the corridor. The stores supervisor, a stout man with thick bottle-end glasses, came waddling briskly towards the group.

'It's wee Carol. She's stuck in the lift,' Peter Cullen told him.

'So call for service and get her out, for goodness sake,' his boss said impatiently. Despite his officious appearance, George Hill was a kind enough soul.

'But she's not there anymore,' Peter continued as if he hadn't heard.

'What do you mean?'

'Something happened in there,' one of the women said in a tremulous voice. 'We heard her screaming. It was *awful*.'

261

Hill pushed his way through the crowd and leaned forward to put an ear at the line where the door edges met. He banged the flat of his hand on the panel.

'Carol. Are you in there? Are you hurt?'

A faint noise vibrated the door, a distant bang. The lift clanked against the rails.

'I can't hear anything,' he said.

'She was in the lift alright,' Peter Cullen declared. 'We could all hear her. Then there was a lot of noise. I thought it must have been the engineer going down the shaft. Then she started to scream. I think something's happened.'

'Right. Get some of the men out here and get these doors open,' George Hill snapped.

'Shouldn't we wait for the engineers?'

The portly little man turned towards the storeman and glared at him, magnified eyes widening impossibly.

'I don't care about the damned door. I'll take the responsibility. Just get in there and get that girl out.'

Peter Cullen and two of his workmates came back with a packing case crowbar just as the engineer came panting up the stairs. The four men wedged their way through the throng of women and George Hill had to tell the bottling line workers to clear a space. The serviceman used a punch-key to trip the door mechanism and he and another of the men managed to force one side open. The lift well gaped blackly. The engineer directed his flashlight into the void. Hawsers and cables dangled past the open door and disappeared into the murk. He swung himself carefully out, and shone the beam upwards.

'I see it,' he announced. 'It's between floors. I'll have to go upstairs and in through the top.' He turned to George Hill. 'Keep everybody away from here. It's a fifty-foot drop.'

Everybody stood back to let the man get upstairs. About fifteen minutes later, the serviceman was easing himself down to the top of the cabin, five feet below the sixth floor. In the beam of the flashlight, he could see the hatch was missing. There was some damage around the edges of the rectangular hole, but he didn't consider that then. His feet boomed on top of the cage and it swung under his weight, but that was normal. He squatted down, then dipped his head in through the opening, angling the light inside.

The box was empty.

He let himself through the hatch and hung by his hands before dropping the few inches to the floor.

The place stank. Later he remembered the smell and described it to the police.

'It was like something had been dead a long time. It was pretty bloody awful. I could feel it at the back of my throat. It made me want to boak.'

It was only once he'd cranked the elevator down to the fourth floor and stepped out into the corridor that he realised what the other smell had been, the warm and metallic scent that had thickened the air in the shaft. Both his knees were dripping with rapidly congealing blood from where he'd knelt on the top of the lift.

There was no sign at all of Carol Howard.

Somebody called for an ambulance. Somebody else called the police.

Jack Fallon had dozed off. He was tangled under the eiderdown when something snapped him completely awake, his mind suddenly alert.

'Shit,' he said.

He put both hands to his head, trying to hold the thought before it faded and fragmented. He'd been dreaming, or half dreaming, and something had come to him. He kept his eyes tight closed and tried to recreate the dream.

It had started quite normally. He'd been down at the quayside, at the stairs on the river end of Rock Lane, watching as they hauled the body of the woman out of the river. It didn't matter that he hadn't actually been there when it happened. He'd seen grey, clay-featured cadavers raised from the water before. It was not unusual for him to flesh out events in his dreams. He'd done that with little Julie, picturing her over and over again in the shop window in nightmares so vivid he could see every minute detail in clear focus, though he hadn't seen his daughter die. The dreams had come on the back of guilt and horror and shock and despair and whatever else lurked inside his head to spawn the black nightmares.

This dream had seemed real. The mist was spiralling off the surface as if it was heated by underwater pipes. Upriver, the

263

rigging of a small boat's mast clanged against a crossbeam. Cold water slapped against a hull, and up in the clear air, early seagulls wheeled and wheedled. The body was hauled out on two ropes which had been fed underneath. The woman was bent and rigid. One leg was sticking out, granite coloured, grotesque. Jack walked away, thinking about the grey foot without a shoe. He walked into the mist of the lane and came out round on Bankside Road, a geographical impossibility, but exactly the way things happen in dreams. Bankside Road was on the far side of the town centre, beyond the maze of alleys and vennels. Here the old shunting yards were hidden behind the green doors where Neil Kennedy had played. Though the snow had turned to ice on the pavements and crackled underfoot, in the dream, the snow was fresh and unmarked.

Two pairs of footprints led away from the green door.

There was something odd about them, though in the rationality of the illusion, Jack did not question them. The larger set, both left and right narrow like a woman's foot, were different in one respect. The left gave an imprint with wavy lines of a walking shoe. The right was a clear shape of a naked foot.

Alongside them, a small trail of a child's footprints were embedded. The left one bore the tyre-track marks of wellington boots. The right was a child's bare foot, each toe clearly delineated.

He followed the lines, his own feet making no noise. The air was suddenly quiet. The wind had stopped. No seagulls shrieked. It was as if he was in a cocoon of his own consciousness. He walked on.

The prints halted maybe three hundred yards along the curve where Bankside Street joined Artisan Road, close to the old engine works. There was an old building there. The redbrick Victorian railway-style construction of the warehouses.

They'd been closed even when Jack was a small boy. He remembered exploring every inch of them with Tom Neeson and Paul Hamilton when he was eight or nine. They'd been littered with broken glass then. The old shutters had been locked and barred, but there was always a way in through a window at the back, or the old cellar at the basement where a coal-hole gave access. They used to climb the stairs then scale up to the rafters

264

where the pigeons had their nests. Tom Neeson's father had been a pigeon fancier and Tom himself had started his own loft with the young birds they'd stolen from the line of dirty, shit-ridden scoops along where the ceiling sloped down to the rafters.

In the dream Jack walked inside, still on silent feet. He went along the narrow passage, turned and looked up.

There it was.

Bold letters in the old-fashioned fonts.

STEW.

Despite the dust on the window and the rime and grime of decades, the letters still stood out clear. Seen from inside, that was how they read, although the S was turned backwards.

He'd seen it before, all those years ago, and now it had come back to him.

He took the stairs slowly, one at a time, though the glass did not crackle and crunch under his feet. He scanned the whole lettering from just underneath, mouthing the words right to left, like a child.

West Highland Railway Company.

He stood staring at the antiquated window sign for some time, then turned slowly, retraced his steps, and walked to the rear of the building where the stock-room ran the length of the warehouse. From here, almost the whole of the gable wall was visible. At the far west end, heading towards the river where it curved on its way down to the estuary, there was a gaping rectangular hole in the wall.

The day they'd stolen the pigeons, they'd clambered down the rope which hung from the block-and-tackle pulley. As Jack stood in the echoing silence, the mist billowed in through the space on the wall.

Something moved in the mist, just out of sight, a dark outline, obscured and hazy. Jack felt his breath start to back up in his throat.

And he woke up hauling for breath, with the image of the swirling mist still reeling in the front of his mind.

19

Jack reached for the notebook under the pile of coins and keys on the table beside the bed. He flipped the pages until he found a clear one, still concentrating on the dream, holding it together before it broke up. He flicked the top off the pen, ignored it when it bounced on the table and rolled to the floor, and wrote quickly. When he had finished, he picked up the report from Robbie Cattanach on the drowned woman and scanned the lines until he found what he was looking for. One of her shoes had been missing when she was fished from the river.

He'd scanned the sentence just before he'd fallen asleep and had seen no significance there. Dead people in rivers were often missing shoes and boots. The current of the river sucked them away.

But in the dreamscape, the fact of the missing shoe had gained importance. He did not know what that importance was, but a piece of a complicated jigsaw had, as if by magic, fitted into another part. Now he knew where to look, though he wasn't sure exactly why.

Jack clambered out of bed, now completely awake. He shrugged into his old dressing gown and tied the cord tight around his waist. In the kitchen, he stabbed the switch on the coffee-maker and sat down, his mind a tumult of half-asked questions, half-answered responses.

The girl. Lorna Breck.

'He heard the woman,' she'd said. *'There was a woman there. She was in the shadows. I couldn't see her properly, not her face. Her leg was sticking out, and she had lost one of her shoes. Her bag was lying on the stairs.'*

The words came back to him with surprising clarity. The girl had scrutinised him with her glistening grey eyes, staring intently into his own. There had been something more than odd about her.

Despite the fact that Jack had seen her collapse in hysterics on

River Street, and the implausible tale she'd told about seeing the attacks on the children, she was still a conundrum. He remembered thinking of her as a loony. Yet there was something he realised only now that he'd missed.

In all the years he'd been a policeman, he'd seen hundreds, maybe thousands of cranks and crazy folk. Eventually, the trained eye was able to spot them. An odd walk, a twitch in the eye, something that set them aside from normal people.

Lorna Breck had looked worried and she'd looked sick, and the tale she'd told was preposterous.

But there was a strangely *reasonable* quality to her. And she'd said something which had sparked off a train of thought in Jack's mind when he'd dozed, and enabled him to come up with a picture that might be truly significant.

The warehouse. Jack recalled the sergeant on the dog team outlining the area they'd searched. The snow had made it difficult for the Alsatians. They hadn't found a trail to follow. The hunt had spread wider, but the police had only examined those empty buildings which had been open, or had an obvious entry. And they had been looking for a boy, nothing else.

Jack waited until the red light on the coffee-maker went out, sifting the few connected facts he had, weaving the scant threads together. He poured a cup, spooned three heaps of demerara into the brew and started to sip. It tasted wonderful, strong and thick, and in addition, the pain in his throat had subsided significantly.

He turned in his chair and reached for the phone, when it rang loudly. That, he thought, was happening too often. He picked it up, brusquely gave his surname, and a woman's voice said hello in a voice that was more a question than a greeting.

'Jack Fallon,' he said, unable to place the voice.

'It's me. Lorna Breck. We spoke today.'

For a second Jack was completely wrong-footed. He'd just been thinking about the girl, had decided he'd have to speak to her again, when she'd called him.

'Yes. We did,' he said, non-commitally.

'I had to call,' she said. Her voice sounded different on the phone, but despite the distortion, he could hear the tightness of distress.

267

'It's going to happen again. Or it *has* happened, and I don't know what to do.'

'Hold on. Back up. Start from the beginning,' Jack said, almost gruffly.

'I saw it, Mr Fallon. I saw it again. Tonight.'

'Saw it again?' he repeated.

'It was killing somebody. A girl.'

'Where?'

'I don't know. In a room. In a tunnel. Something like that. The girl was screaming. Oh . . .'

Her voice broke off abruptly.

'Now wait a minute,' Jack said, as gently as he could. 'Calm down a little and just tell me.'

There was a snuffling on the line. It sounded as if she was blowing her nose. When she started talking again her voice was cracked with strain.

'I wasn't asleep. It just came to me. It was in the dark. There was a lot of noise. Like drums, clanging sounds. The girl was screaming and it came down on the ropes and opened up the roof. She was terrified. I could *feel* it. And then it reached down and took her.'

'And you saw this?'

'Yes,' she said. She sniffled again, catching her breath.

'And then what?'

'I don't know. It lifted her up and she was crying all the time. It was just like the boy. It carried her up into the dark and . . . and . . .'

'And what?' he asked again.

'And she's dead.'

The words came out with heavy finality.

'You don't know where?'

'No.'

'Or when?'

'No.'

Jack sighed. He'd been right a few minutes ago. There was something more than odd about the girl. He didn't know whether to be suspicious, or dismissive. He had other things on his mind, but he was already on the horns of a dilemma. The girl had told him something earlier which he'd discounted and then a possible answer to part of it had come when he'd fallen asleep. He had to check that out before he did anything else.

'Listen,' he finally said. 'There's not much I can do about it at this time of night. But I'll speak to you first thing in the morning. Are you going to work?'

She said she'd been told to stay at home.

'Fine. I'll take your number,' Jack said. She gave it, and he said he'd call in the morning.

There was a silence on the other end which went on for several seconds, until finally she said, 'Please. I can't take much more of this.'

The telephone couldn't disguise the plaintive, almost despairing appeal in her voice.

'Leave it to me,' Jack said blandly.

He slung the receiver and let it hang on the phone for a minute or two while he considered what she'd said. Another killing, but she didn't know where or when. That was a big help. It was no help at all. First he had to investigate the warehouse.

The phone rang again and he snatched it from the cradle, expecting to hear her voice again.

'Mr Fallon?' A man's voice this time. 'Sergeant Thomson here.'

'Hello, Bobby,' Jack responded. 'What's up?'

'We need you down here. There's been another one.'

The words landed like thuds on Jack's consciousness. He didn't even have to ask, though for a vertiginous moment he experienced a strange rush of unnerving trepidation, as if he'd stepped out of reality for a moment and was floundering in a place where everything was out of true and out of step.

'Where?' he finally asked.

'The distillery,' Bobby responded matter of factly. 'We got a call half an hour ago. A girl's just gone missing.'

The weird *déjà vu* sensation washed through him again.

'What happened?'

'Christ knows,' Bobby said. 'Sorry, sir.'

'Don't worry, Bobby, just tell me.'

'She was in a lift. It got stuck between floors. When the engineer went in, she was gone. But there's blood all over the place. There's a few of the women taken to hospital.'

269

'Were they hurt?'

'No. They fainted.'

'Right,' Jack said. 'I'll be down in ten minutes.' He was about to hang up again when he told Bobby to hold on.

'Listen. While I'm here. Get Ralph Slater and John McColl in and then get a couple of men round to the old railhead warehouse on Artisan Street. The one next to the engine works. I want the whole place searched.'

'What are we looking for, sir?'

'Anything at all. Possible evidence of the Kennedy boy. I need it done now.'

He hung up this time and sat staring at the wall, feeling numb and disorientated. The second call, right on the back of the first, had thrown him off balance, leaving him with a weird sense of helplessness and scary confusion.

After a moment, he got up from the table and ran his cup under the tap, then bent and scooped cold water onto his face. The icy shock helped slow down his jumbled thoughts. It took him a few minutes to get dressed. He hadn't had time for a shower and as he ran his hand across his chin, he knew he was in dire need of a shave, but there was no time for it. He hauled his coat on, flicked his hair back from his forehead with an abrupt sweep of his hand, and went out into the cold night.

Ralph Slater was just arriving at the main gate of the distillery when Jack pulled up. A crowd of women stood at the door, huddled against the cold, with their heavy winter coats slung on top of their overalls. An ambulance light was winking in the covered area where the lorries normally loaded their goods. A patrol car was parked beside it, and just beyond, the bulk of a fire engine loomed against the brick wall. Already the mist coming off the river was thick and opaque, giving the buildings a dreamscape, fuzzy quality.

'What's the word, Jack?' somebody called from the corner. Blair Bryden started walking towards the car.

'Haven't a clue yet,' Jack told him. 'Give me a chance.'

'Her name's Carol Howard and she's sixteen. She went into a lift and never came out again.'

'Well, you know more than me.'

'My aunt works with her,' Blair said. 'She gave me a call.'

270

'Well, I'll have a word with her later. Give me some time to see what's happening and I'll have a chat when I come down.' Blair nodded. He was a conscientious editor.

Inside, Jack and Ralph took the stairs two at a time until they got to the fourth floor. The place was crowded with firemen. The elevator doors had been wedged open. Ropes trailed out through the space, disappearing up through the hole in the roof. Smears of blood had been trampled over the floor, leaving red treadmarks inside and out of the cabin.

One of the policemen came over as soon as Jack arrived.

'Nobody knows what happened yet,' he said. 'Apparently she went down to the canteen two floors below to get her handbag. This was about an hour ago, just after the tea-break. One of the storemen,' the constable flipped a page on his notebook, 'Peter Cullen. He said he heard a noise coming from the lift. The girl was calling for help. She seemed to be stuck in the jammed lift. A few minutes later, there was a great deal of noise inside the lift and the girl started screaming. There was nothing else until the engineer got the thing open. The girl was not inside.'

He closed his notebook.

'I'm afraid they haven't located her yet.'

Sorley Fitzpatrick, the chief fire officer, came bulling across, stepping over the lines of ropes.

'We've been right up to the top of the shaft. There's an air-vent on the housing which the boys say has been forced open. No sign of anything, Jack. If that girl was in the lift, then she's gone.'

'Have you checked down below?'

'Nothing there. Up above the cage there's a lot of blood. Smells like a slaughterhouse in there. I wouldn't recommend a visit.'

'Neither me, I suppose, but I'll have to take a look.'

He went across to the lift with Sorley and followed the man up the ladder set at an angle, reaching up into the space above. Somebody had rigged up a series of lights which clung to the rails on rat-trap crocodile clips. The lift rattled under their feet as Sorley pointed upwards. The shaft soared into the distance, getting narrower in distant perspective. Two firemen were lowering themselves down on the ropes. Ralph Slater eased his way through the gap to stand beside them, aiming his own flashlight here and there on the shaft walls.

'Christ, what a mess,' he finally said, then, without another word, he started scooping samples into the plastic wallets he took from his bag.

'There's more traces of blood, or what seems to be blood, further up on the guide-rail. Nothing on the roof, as far as I can tell, but I expect you'll want a look yourself.'

'Yes,' Jack agreed gloomily, knowing he would have to inspect the whole area. The idea of going up the shaft appalled him. He clambered down and into the building again. By this time, John McColl had arrived, looking a bit bleary eyed, but clean shaven. With him were two young detective constables. Jack asked the manager for a room and was shown to a tidy office. Inside, he started laying out instructions for the rest of the team.

An hour later, he found himself on top of the building, bracing himself against the cold west wind, as he had done on the top of Loch View after the strange death of Jock Toner. The parallel was not lost on him. As he stood in the centre of the flat expanse of roughcast he experienced another flashback.

'He's dead,' the girl had said. *'It came down from above in the dark and just lifted him up. I could hear it breathing. It's like an* animal.'

Like an animal. Whoever had taken the girl from the lift, leaving her blood to drip in a clotted pool, had to be an animal. A maniac. A psychopath.

'I don't know what it is. You can't see it properly. It moves so fast, and it climbs.'

It climbs. It *climbs*.

There was no doubt about that. He climbed, alright. Nearly to the top of Latta Court. And to the roof of Loch View, two of the highest buildings in the town. Now Jack was standing on the flat roof of the distillery, a towering block which overlooked the whole of the centre of Levenford. He turned to face south and could see right across the river, beyond the old cemetery on its promontory at the confluence of river and estuary. Across the firth, nearly eight miles away as the crow flies, the tiny lights of the south bank towns glittered in the fog like distant stars.

High places. Jack recalled his own words. The pattern had struck him before. There had been nothing but frozen blood on the ground on Barley Cobble where the battered body of Shona

Campbell had been found, yet on a hunch Jack had ordered a search of the roof and they'd found traces of thread. Of a sudden he was certain they would match the fibres taken that day from the baby's cot.

High places. Why?

He did not have the answer to that question, but now he was just as certain he was getting there, slowly and surely, and for some reason, a weird shiver ran through him. He did not know what he would find when he got to the end of the line, to the end of the questions. For a strange, almost panicky second, Jack Fallon did not want to get there.

He turned back from the south, sweeping his eyes across the town's night horizon. From where he stood, his view to the ground was restricted by the safety wall that lined the edge of the building, more than three feet high. Almost directly to the north, the ornate roof of the town hall, corbie-step gables and dragon's back ridging, nosed up behind the stand of elms on Memorial Avenue. Off to the right, the cranes and gantries of Latta Marineyard stood gaunt and prehistoric, ribbed and articulated. Someone had left a light on in the cabin of the giant lifting derrick. It glowed like a monster's eye. Beyond them, the black, towering sheds of the old shipyard with its own gaunt cranes, a conglomeration of metal, great slipway doors and winching gear, lying dormant until the need for boats came back again.

Then, just north of them, hardly visible, pointed the steeple of Castlebank Church, where William Simpson had preached to a congregation while hiding a dark and disgusting secret.

Swinging his gaze back, Jack followed the sightline. The tall poplars, mere shadows in the mist, along Slaughterhouse Road. The tower of the crumbling Provost's Hall, built two hundred years before by the ship-owning power barons who had ruled the town with God-fearing strictness backed by the oppression of vast wealth. To the far left, the dreary concrete blocks of Latta Court and its two neighbours huddled together, the winking red hazard light on the highest roof like an ember in a bed of coals. To the north-west, the black twin stacks of the old forge chimneys, rearing like gun barrels aiming at the sky, barely visible in the gloom. Out in the dark, the bells of St Rowan's Church plaintively tolled the hour.

High places.

Places above the sightlines, only truly seen from another high place.

'It climbs,' she had said. He could hear her voice, tight with distress.

'It climbs, alright,' he said aloud. The wind whipped his words away beyond the safety barrier.

But how did she know? Jack had dismissed the visions, or dreams, or whatever she cared to call them. He didn't believe in mumbo jumbo. That was for cranks and crazies and loonies, and thank Christ the majority of them were harmless. Despite what Andy Toye had said, that kind of thing was strictly out of the picture as far as police business was concerned. Facts, facts and more facts, they were what counted.

Yet what she had said nagged and tugged at him.

What did she know? That was more to the point. As he stood in the cold, he cast his mind back. She'd told him she'd seen someone – though she called it some*thing* – come down from above and smash Shona Campbell to the ground. Now they'd found the fibres snagged on the guttering.

She'd told him the boy was dead. There had been nothing in the papers about that, just that he was missing.

And tonight she had phoned him, in a blind panic, or so it sounded, to tell him that a girl had been killed.

She'd been right about that. There was no doubt in Jack's mind; no doubt in the minds of the firemen or the women who had stood outside the lift while the booming noises had echoed down the shaft and the screams had reverberated from above. The girl was dead.

So how did she know? And what did she know?

Jack turned and walked slowly back to the stairway which led back into the building. For some reason his feet had wanted to carry him to the edge of the roof, and he'd had to fight against the urge to look down. It was an odd compulsion and he'd felt it before, but he knew if he stood on the edge, he'd feel the tug of gravity, the insistent drag of the ground and its implicit invitation. The elevator housing, a squat, square construction, one of four which grew from the roof, was just beside the stairway. At its nearest side, the thick aluminium grid lay

274

buckled and twisted. Jack hunkered down to have another look at it. Ralph Slater's boys had already taken pictures from all angles and it had been dusted for prints. Nonetheless, Jack lifted it carefully, using his finger and thumb on a corner. It wasn't heavy. The thick mesh had been ripped and torn. He placed it against the hole where it had stood, and something peculiar caught his attention. The grille had been pushed *inward*, not forced out. He could see where it had bellied from the frame as if a considerable weight had been forced against it. The gridwork had snapped in several places. He took it out of the frame and held it up close to his face, peering at the broken ends of thick wire latticework. The edges were rough. They hadn't been cut. Furthermore, they were out of true, bent in towards each other as if they had been gripped by a powerful hand. He held his own hand up, but despite his own size, his fingers could not reach the span that would have been required to grasp the twisted pieces of metal.

He laid the grille down where it had been lying, and thoughtfully got to his feet. Somebody called his name from down below and he walked slowly to the stairs and back into the main part of the distillery.

'Absolutely nothing,' John McColl said. 'They're all saying the same thing. Plenty of noise and screams, then nothing. Scared the hell out of them.'

'Scares the hell out of me,' Jack admitted.

'Oh, by the way,' John interjected. 'There's been half a dozen calls for you. Everybody and their granny wants you to call back.'

'At this time of night?'

'Bobby Thomson wants you urgently.'

As soon as he heard that, Jack felt the familiar jolt as adrenalin kicked into his blood.

'What's he want?'

'You to call back. Yesterday.'

Jack took the steps three at a time. Nobody was using any of the lifts in the building. Sorley Fitzpatrick and the engineers were checking the other three, just in case. The distillery manager had sent the whole night shift home. Jack got to his car. Somebody had left a message tucked under the wiper. He snatched it out as he opened the door and eased himself in. It bore five digits. Jack

275

recognised Blair Bryden's number and gave a wry grin. He made a mental note to call the *Gazette* office in the morning, then reached for the receiver and called in. Somebody put him through to the desk sergeant and Bobby Thomson came on, his voice fighting through the static.

'The dog men are in, sir. I thought you ought to know.'

'And?'

'They found traces. A shoe. No, *two* shoes. A handbag. And there's possible traces of dried blood.'

'Shit,' Jack said vehemently.

'Sir?' Bobby's voice crackled. He'd heard that alright.

'Sorry, Bob. Expletive deleted.' Jack's mind was racing. There were too many options on what to do next. He closed his eyes and concentrated for a minute, ignoring the hiss of static in his ear.

'I'll get Ralph along as soon as I can. In the meantime, seal the area. Not a thing to be touched. No announcement.'

'Oh and Mr Cowie's looking for you,' Bobby came back.

'What's new?' Jack said to himself. Bobby chuckled and Jack realised he'd spoken aloud.

'Tell him I'll be along in twenty minutes.' Bobby acknowledged and Jack thumbed the off button. He debated sending the women patrollers up to Clydeshore Avenue to pick up Lorna Breck and bring her to the office, but then he dismissed the notion. He knew where she was. If he brought her into the station, the superintendent would only ask awkward questions for which Jack at the moment had no answers. He got out of the car and went back into the distillery. The crowds had dispersed in the cold, damp air. The ambulance light still twinkled blue starlight. There was an odd air of stillness about the place.

Jack contacted Ralph and hauled him down from the upper floors.

'We need another scene-of-crime operation,' he explained without any preamble.

'What, again?'

'Not a fresh scene. At least, I don't think so.'

He gave Ralph directions, told him he'd meet him at the old warehouse in under an hour, then went back to the car and drove back to the station.

At the desk, Bobby Thomson handed him a sheaf of messages which he snatched in passing and read as he strode along to his office, pausing only to waylay young Gordon Pirie, the fresh-faced recruit, and ask him to make a cup of tea. The boy looked over at the sergeant, who just nodded wisely.

There were two messages from headquarters, one from Criminal Records Office, the other from the forensic lab. He called CRO first, asked for an inspector he knew from the old days, and waited while the extension rang. Finally somebody picked it up. Jack gave his name and the inspector said hello.

'What've you got, Fergus?'

'Bingo on two counts. John McColl said this was a priority job. You've come up on both sets of prints. Tomlin was at scene of crime in the Herkik operation. We've twenty clear fingers and several palms, all with nine-point matching. It was him alright.'

'And?'

'The drownee. She was there too. We've got confirmation on all points. Nothing on the register on either of them, though, no previous. Unknown to the police on any list. If you can get me an ID on the woman, it will help.'

'I don't think that'll be long,' Jack said confidently. 'You'll get it as soon as I know it.'

'Okay. Best of luck,' the inspector said. 'By the way, what the hell's going on in your patch?'

'Damned if I know,' Jack said wearily. A sudden wave of tiredness swept through him. He couldn't remember the last time he'd had a full night's sleep. He ran his hand over his chin again and felt the rasp of an extra day's growth. 'But I'm working on it.'

'Your old pals are rooting for you.'

'And I'm rooting about down here,' Jack said. He thanked his fellow officer and went back to the messages.

At the lab, the sergeant who had left the message was off duty, but Jack was put straight through to the textiles and fabrics section. The young woman who answered was unfamiliar, but helpful. The threads of material snagged on the gutter on the roof at Barley Cobble, she confirmed, had been successfully matched up with fibres taken from the sheets of baby Kelly Campbell's cot, and corresponded to others taken from the

277

shoulder of her mother's coat. They were pure wool, dyed pink. The young chemist went into some detail about the composition of the dye and the cross-section thickness of the fibres, and Jack let her run on for a while, though he didn't need the technical information right at that moment.

It did confirm again, however, the conclusion Jack had reached earlier.

The killer was a climber. He liked high places.

Now he had a few other things to do. He had to find out why, and he needed to know how Lorna Breck knew. Did she know the killer? Was she involved? Was her story just an act to put him off the trail, or even a callous act of mischief-making? He decided she could wait, though not for much longer. The baby-faced recruit came in with a pot of tea and placed the tray on the table. Jack gave him an appreciative wink and the youngster blushed. As soon as he left, Jack dunked two of the biscuits until they were soft and swallowed them whole. He had just stuffed a third into his mouth when there was a knock on the door. Before he could speak the door opened and his immediate superior strode in. Jack swallowed too hastily and burned his throat.

'Didn't you get my message?' Superintendent Cowie asked.

'Yes. I was a bit tied up. I just had a couple of calls to make.'

'What's going on?'

'Another youngster. Seems to have been snatched.'

'Yes, I know all that, although I should have heard it from you.'

'No time. I went straight there.'

'Alright. But there's more. I didn't authorise extra men for another search. There's been three dog handlers brought back on duty. That's on top of the SOC's men. Can you enlighten me?'

'Well, acting on information received, I thought it best to enlarge the search area.'

'What information? From whom?'

'It's a bit vague at the moment, sir. I'd rather leave it until we have something more concrete. In fact it's more of a hunch really.'

'A hunch? We can't afford overtime on the strength of some vague intuition.'

'No. It was a bit more than that. But you did say you wanted immediate action, and that's what I'm trying for. I don't think headquarters will object to a couple of extra men on a night. It happens all the time in Glasgow.'

'That may be. But this is not Glasgow. We don't have the budget or the manpower.'

'We could put in a request for some more. I'm sure the divisional commander would look on it favourably.'

Jack knew what the reaction to that would be. Cowie would rather cut off his leg than put in such a request to head office. It would be an admission that he couldn't run his own patch. Jack himself knew there would be no shame in it. He'd been working on murders too long to care about who thought what. From his own point of view, he knew there was nothing to be gained from calling in the cavalry, at least not at the moment, despite the media pressure which featured the bizarre kidnappings on almost every teatime bulletin, and were certain to have a picnic and barbecue in the morning when news of the latest abduction hit the streets. There was nothing to be gained, and a possibility that an influx of officers who did not know the area might only muddy the waters. Jack needed just a little more time before he yelled for help, but he was pragmatist enough to know that when the time came, he would bawl his head off.

'Absolutely not,' Cowie said. 'The whole force is overworked and undermanned. We won't get any thanks for it.'

Nor the glory, Jack thought.

'So what do we know about the girl?'

'Nothing much. Bare details. I've sent a WPC round with John McColl to speak to the family.'

'Preposterous!' Cowie spat. His face was taking on that familiar red tinge. He looked like a man who wanted to be running things but didn't quite know how, which, in Jack's view, he was.

'You mean you think we shouldn't speak to them?'

'Not that. Of course we should. I want detailed statements from everyone involved. And I want duplicates of all reports.'

'Naturally,' Jack said, lying with a straight face.

'No. It's preposterous that girl should be snatched like that in a building full of people. Whoever is doing this is thumbing his nose right at us. The press will have a field day.'

'Probably. But at least you can tell them there are one or two developments.'

'I hope there are,' Cowie retorted. 'I sincerely hope there are.' He turned away from Jack and walked briskly to the door.

'Full reports, understand?' he barked, without turning round.

Despite himself, Jack grinned. He poured another cup of tea and drank it quickly. He wasn't sure when he'd manage to get another, for he felt a long night coming on.

It was almost two in the morning and he was now feeling utterly fatigued. He went down to the operations room and put out a call for Ralph Slater. When he came on the phone, he sounded just as weary.

'Just coming in,' Ralph said. 'No body, but plenty of circumstantial. Oh, I think I can ID the swimmer for you.'

'Bring it all in,' Jack said. 'I'll be here.'

Ralph took less than ten minutes to get round to the station. He looked blue and cold and his shoes and trousers were streaked with dust. Two of his team were carrying black plastic bags. The scene-of-crime boss told them to lay the material on the table and nodded gratefully when Jack offered him a cup of tea from the huge pot the new recruit had brought up from the canteen. The small gathering stood around, trying to get some heat into their bodies.

When the other two had left, Jack and Ralph went over what they'd found.

It was a pitiful collection. Two shoes. One a woman's, the other a child's training shoe.

Jack got a fleeting flashback to the dream. The prints had been clear. One bare foot and the clear marks of gumboots. It hadn't been accurate, but that hardly mattered any more.

'Definitely the boy's. We got a full description. It matches,' Ralph said over the rim of his cup. 'The other one's from the woman in the river. I can guarantee it. I could get the effects from downstairs, or even show you a print, but take my word for it.'

'Naturally,' Jack agreed. 'You're scene of crime.'

'Now the handbag is more interesting,' Ralph went on, speaking through a mouthful of biscuit. 'We found that on the stairs. Some blood drops on it. Much more on the upper levels and a fair puddle on the rafter boards, and I'll give ten to one it's the Kennedy kid.'

'No bets.'

The contents of the bag were in a separate wallet. There was a small purse with a few notes and change, a pen. Two combs and a lipstick.

Jack poked through it with a pencil.

'What's this?' he asked, looking over at Ralph. The two cards were face up, printed in fading pastel colours. The six of wands and the queen of wands, both of them old-fashioned, printed on linen board.

'I thought you'd find that interesting. They're the same kind as we found on Simpson. I think there's a tie-in.'

'Oh, there is. She was at Cairn House. Records have confirmed the prints.'

'But there's more.'

Jack raised an eyebrow. Ralph indicated the small pile of effects.

Jack nudged the cards out of the way, then he saw what Ralph had meant. It was a lapel clip, with a name on it beside a photograph of a woman with short, greying hair.

'It can't be,' he said through his teeth.

'But it is. She was covered in shit when they took her out of the river. Her own mother wouldn't have recognised her, but I'll take any bets that's who it is.'

'Janet?'

Ralph nodded. 'And Christ alone knows how she figures in all of this. She would never say boo to a goose.'

Jack scratched his head, perplexed. Janet Robinson had been one of the girls in the typing office. She was as quiet as a mouse, a young-old woman who kept herself to herself, but she was an excellent worker. She'd churned out dozens of reports for Jack in the past couple of months.

'That's all we need,' he said to Ralph, dropping the plastic card back into the pile.

He went back to the seat and eased himself down. 'Right. John McColl's out talking to Tomlin's wife after he speaks to the girl's mother,' he said. 'We might get something there, though I doubt it. I need somebody out to Cross Road to pick up a man.'

281

'Tonight?'

'Yes, tonight. I'll send two of the uniforms along. And there's a girl I have to speak to.'

'You and me both.'

'No, this one's got something to tell me. Ever heard of Lorna Breck?'

Ralph shook his head. 'Rings no bell.'

'She tells me she's been seeing the killings. Called me tonight just before Bobby Thomson phoned. She said it had happened again, to a girl this time.'

'Think she's involved?'

'I don't know. There's something weird about her. Under normal circumstances I'd say she was telling the truth, but I've been wrong before. I'll have another talk with her in the morning, but keep that to yourself. I'll have enough trouble explaining what was going on at Cairn House.'

'A seance, wasn't it?'

'Trying to raise devils,' Jack said.

Ralph gave him a nakedly sceptical look.

'You don't believe any of that crap, do you?'

'No, but they probably did. I think we're dealing with a bunch of weirdos. Some sort of sect, maybe devil worshippers or something. You've read the Orkney case, and the Yorkshire stuff. I think we might have a group of nutters who're taking it one step further than dancing naked round a fire and screwing goats.'

'You think they're killing folk?'

'I think,' Jack said, looking Ralph straight in the eye, 'I think they're sacrificing babies.'

Ralph Slater was in the act of swallowing a mouthful of tea. He choked and sprayed himself as he spluttered to get his breath. His eyes were watering and he snatched a tissue from his pocket and dabbed at them. Finally he turned back to Jack.

'Are you kidding?'

'No. I wish I was.'

'Cowie is going to love you. Are you going to tell him?'

'Not yet. Let's see what we can drag in. I can't keep him off my back for much longer.'

Later that night John McColl came back from Edward Tomlin's

house with something Margaret Tomlin had found in her husband's jacket. It was a tarot card, crumpled and lined, but there was no mistaking the pattern on the back. It was identical to the others that had turned up. On the face, it bore the picture of a heart impaled by three swords.

Edward Tomlin died in the early hours of the morning, when Jack was heading for home, almost stupefied with fatigue. His body was taken down to the mortuary, where Robbie Cattanach would open him up the following morning. Some months later, both Robbie and Dr Collins would collaborate on a paper for the *Lancet* on the remarkable physiological effects of Paraquat poisoning.

20

They found the body of Annie Eastwood in the morning while Jack was taking his nephew to school. He'd had five hours' sleep and had needed a blistering hot shower to get him completely awake. He'd dreamed most of the night, and when he'd awoken with a start at the buzz of the alarm, he'd been sitting upright on the bed, arms and shoulders goosepimpled, hands curled into tight fists. The substance of the dream had broken up when his eyes opened but he'd been left with a heavy after-sense of lingering gloom.

Julia offered him breakfast and when he told her he'd no time, she ordered him to wait for two minutes while she put the bacon she'd grilled for herself onto two slices of bread, wrapped them in tin-foil and jammed them into the pocket of his long coat.

'You look ghastly,' she said, concerned.

'Thanks a million,' he said, unable to keep the smile from his face. 'You're great for a guy's ego.'

'Look, you don't have to take Davy to school. I can manage.'

'No bother. It makes sure I get out of bed.'

'You need looking after,' she said, reaching a hand up to cup his cheek with affectionate gentleness.

'I'm doing fine, but now I've got to go,' Jack said quickly, breaking the moment, pulling away. Her concern was written all over her face, and he backed away from it. He would only begin to feel maudlin.

When he stopped outside the school gate, Davy leaned over from the back seat and gave him a kiss. Jack stopped him before he got out of the car.

'Did your mum tell you about staying in school all day?'

'Yes, Uncle Jack,' the boy replied gravely.

'And you wait for her or me to come and get you at home time?'

Davy nodded again.

'Well, you make sure you do,' Jack said, keeping his voice low and serious.

'I will. I'll stay in school.'

Jack ruffled his hair and let him go. He watched as the wee boy disappeared into a crowd of youngsters milling around in the playground. The school had doubled the supervision at intervals and lunch breaks. So far all the abductions – all the *killings* – had taken place at night, in the dark. But that did not mean the situation wouldn't change.

There was no problem in identifying Annie Eastwood, at least not from the effects she'd had on her person when she died. The difficulty in ensuring she was who her credit and library cards said she was lay in the fact that there was nothing left of her face, and so much damage to the rest of her body that it wasn't easy to determine at first glance that the mess on the rocks at the confluence of river and estuary was in fact human.

Ian Ramage, the full-time custodian of the old monument on top of the Castle Rock, had been woken in the early hours of the morning, while it was still dark and damply cold, by the barking of his Scots terriers. He had the tied house by the entrance gates, one of the oldest buildings in Levenford, older even than Cairn House. It was said that Mary Queen of Scots had been imprisoned there, as had William Wallace, the guerilla leader of the fourteenth century, before he was dragged down beyond the border and hung, drawn and quartered. The castle ramparts bordered the shoulders of the two-hundred foot high basalt rock, which, like Ardmhor Rock further down the firth, was the nubbin of a dead volcano, worn down by the ice and winds and rain of millions of years.

The rock towered over the east end of Levenford, black and massive, a hunched and looming presence which dominated the flat land where the river flowed into the tidal salts.

The ill-tempered yapping of the terriers roused an equally irate keeper from his bed in the upstairs room of the old stone house. The dogs were shoulder to shoulder at the window, paws on the sill, noses smearing the glass. They were barking furiously, ears pointing forward.

'Right, you two, hush up,' Ian snapped. The bitches stopped immediately, heads turned round towards him, before swinging back to stare out of the glass into the dark.

At this early hour of a freezing morning, it was unlikely that

285

any youngster had sneaked in through the gates, but Ian Ramage took his job seriously, though with more than a little ill will that day. He pulled on trousers and sweater over his thick pyjamas, wrapped himself in a worn duffel coat, grabbed his flashlight and then snapped his fingers at the dogs. They bounded from the window and followed him out onto the flagstone paths, their nails scrabbling on the cold slate.

Ian Ramage went down to the gate at the arched entrance. It was ajar, though only by an inch or so. Normally the keeper locked it at night, but in the winter, he usually relaxed the rule because so few people visited the ancient monument in bad weather. The dogs snuffled around the posts, then, moving together, went back towards the house, passed by the corner, still shoulder to shoulder, and scrambled up the first flight of stairs, yapping angrily. The keeper followed on, grumbling all the while.

There was exactly one stone step cut into the rock for every day in the year. It took Ian fifteen minutes to get to the top, where the basalt rose to a rounded dome topped by a flagpole and four ancient cannon facing outwards to the points of the compass. The balustrade wall snaked over the shoulder, twenty feet down from the summit. The dogs scampered down towards the dyke and simultaneously leapt up onto the flat top, each aggressively barking down into the dark below. Breathless, Ian followed them down and leaned on the wall, his eyes following the direction of their noses. Below him, down in the distance, he could hear the gurgle and splash of the water on the stones, like far-off conversation. He angled the powerful torch below the wall, but the beam was diffracted by the rising mist. There was nothing to be seen and no point in going all the way down to the rocky shoreline in the dark. He went back to his bed.

Four hours later he was explaining to a uniformed policeman what had happened.

The body was discovered by Geordie Buist. Though it was well out of season, he'd taken his spinning rod round the dark pathway to the base of the rock to haul out a few sea trout, which were starting their spawning run upriver. He'd lifted a two-pounder from the water after his third cast and had scrambled up the rocks to hide it in the lea of one of the forty-foot boulders

286

which had calved from the cliff. The silver fish, dead from a blow to the head, but still shivering and twitching, he stashed in a corner where the rock butted up against another. He turned, reached up to the stone side for balance, and his searching fingers grasped hold of a cold hand.

The sheer fright sent him staggering backwards to crack his head against the basalt with a sickening thud and he landed in a dazed heap. He lay there for fully five minutes before his head cleared enough to let him get to his feet again. Very cautiously he felt his way in the dark until he came to the spot where he'd stood before. He fished his cigarette lighter out of his pocket, and, with a shaky hand, flicked it alight and held it up.

The clawlike hand hooked down from above his head. The yellow light reflected back from trails of liquid running down the flat side of the stone. Two thick and shiny braids of what looked like twisted rope dangled from further up. Geordie held the lighter up higher and saw an eye staring at him from a pulpy mass above him. At first he thought it was an animal, because he could see a row of clenched teeth, more than a human ever showed, stretching back into the mass. Then he saw the thin string of pearls around the bloodied neck and he realised what he'd found.

Geordie Buist was a tough young man. He'd had his share of fist fights. He could gut and clean a rabbit or a fish or gralloch a poached deer with hardly a thought. But when the dead and broken face of the woman, her one impossibly protruding eye glaring from the red mess, registered on his consciousness, Geordie got such a fright that his bladder simply opened and hot piss gushed down the inside of his thigh. He stood there, frozen, hand upraised, for several stunned minutes, unaware of the warm flow down his jeans, until an eddy of wind snuffed out the flame of the lighter. The darkness which descended was complete. Geordie gave a gasp of alarm. The thought of being stuck in the dark with the grotesque, broken thing was too much for him to cope with. Whimpering all the way, he bolted out of the space between the big rocks, scrambled up to the path, and ran non-stop round the track at the base of the cliff until he came to the road. It took him twenty minutes to get to the police station and a further fifteen before the desk sergeant could get him to calm down enough to piece together sufficient information from the incoherent, almost hysterical babbling to realise what the ashen-faced young man was trying to say.

The police patrol who were sent to investigate found Geordie's rod and line along with the poached sea trout, but they were too busy that night to do more than give him a verbal warning. The following day, Sergeant Bobby Thomson enjoyed the fish grilled and smothered in a fine hollandaise sauce.

One of the policemen at the scene was Gordon Pirie, the young recruit who had made tea for Jack Fallon the night before. When he'd shone his beam on what lay on the rocks, he staggered back, slipped on the rocks and retched so violently and painfully that he thought he was going to pass out, and once he'd finished, he began to cry like a baby and couldn't stop.

Annie Eastwood was formally identified by Dr Bell, her own general practitioner, who recognised her appendectomy and hysterectomy scars and the small port-wine birthmark close to her hip.

But for these distinguishing marks, identification could have taken several days, because the fall from the castle ramparts, almost two hundred feet straight down, had broken almost every bone in the woman's body. The left side of her face had been stoved right in, crushing both cheekbone and jaw. On the right, all of the skin and muscle had been torn back to the ear, giving the face a doglike gape. As she'd bounced from one rock to another, her scalp had been torn off from forehead to crown and flung, like a bloody wig, ten feet from where the body sprawled upside down. Robbie Cattanach found four fractures of the spine and three compounded breaks in the left thigh alone. Her pelvis had sheared off three inches in from the hip-joint and a sharp edge of rock had opened her belly like a zip fastener and spilled everything in glistening ropes down into the void between the two huge stones.

One eye was missing and was never found. Somebody surmised that one of the rats that inhabited the nooks and crannies and fed on carrion from the shoreline must have eaten it. Two fingers and a thumb of the dead woman's left hand were later found further up on the rock, jammed in a small crevice, ripped off in the violence of her passing. One of them bore a ring set with amethyst stones.

The missing fingers were collected and used for prints. Later in the afternoon, Jack Fallon learned that Annie Eastwood had also been in Cairn House on the night that Marta Herkik had died.

Elsa Quinn, the only one of the women in the distillery who remembered seeing a stranger in the building the night before, was questioned again. The vague description of the woman's green coat was helpful. When a picture taken from Annie Eastwood's house was produced, it jogged Elsa's memory just enough.

'That's who it was,' she told John McColl. 'I never recognised her at the time. It's Angie Eastwood's mother. Angie used to work on the same line as me. But she died. It was a car crash about a year ago. It was terrible. We all went to the funeral, and that's where I saw her mother.'

'You're sure?'

'I am now. I had a terrible headache last night, so I didn't really look. I remembered thinking there was something familiar about her, but I couldn't place the face.'

'And where was she standing?'

'Beside the lift on the fourth floor,' Elsa said.

Jack brought John McColl and Ralph Slater into his office and closed the door.

'I want her house turned over,' he said when they were both seated. 'This is the first real tie-in we have to everything.'

'You don't think she killed the girl?' John asked.

'Christ knows!' Jack said sharply. 'No. Probably not. But she was there at the same time, and she was in the Herkik place. She's topped herself, or been thrown off the top of the castle. One way or another, she's in the middle of the whole mess. Get round there and give her place a spin, and send a squad round to Janet Robinson's place. I'm looking for anything at all. Books, diaries, letters, the lot. We have to know why she was at Cairn House and what was going on there. That's the crux of the matter.'

'Anything else?'

'Yes. Have you found this O'Day yet?'

'No. He's been gone for the last few days, according to his landlady.'

'Keep looking out. Get a warrant and turn him over as well. I'm fed up pussyfooting about.'

John went out and Jack turned to Ralph.

'This is getting out of hand. What can you tell me?'

'Nothing you don't already know. Looks like Eastwood jumped. She could have been pushed. According to the keeper there was some disturbance between four and five this morning. His dogs started barking. He had a check around, but didn't see a thing. If she'd been taken up there and thrown off, there would probably have been a lot of noise. Ramage says he didn't hear anything.'

Jack brought his hands up and ran his fingers backwards through his hair.

'I just don't understand it. You get a killing or an abduction – and these kids are dead, believe me – and then a suicide. Everybody so far, except Jock Toner, was at the seance in Herkik's room.'

'You reckon that's what it was?'

'Sure. I've got it on good authority. The Eastwood woman is the only one we can definitely place at the scene of one snatch when it happened. We don't know who she was with, if she was with anybody, but I don't think she could have taken that girl out of the lift on her own and hauled her up the shaft. No. We're looking for a strong bastard. A *crazy* strong bastard.'

'So we've got a tie-in, Jack. But I don't see where that gets us. We still haven't found any of the bodies yet. Not any of the kids.'

'We will.'

There were too many things to do at once. Around noon, Jack was tempted to capitulate and call in for some extra help, despite his superior's objections. He couldn't put off reporting to Superintendent Cowie.

'I've had the press baying at my heels all morning,' his superior barked as soon as Jack opened the office door. Cowie was sitting back in a high-backed swivel chair, both hands drumming on his empty blotter.

Jack held up a thick folder. 'I've got everything so far. So far all the suicides can be traced to the Herkik killing. I believe they are also involved in the abductions.'

'Nonsense,' Cowie snorted. 'You think this is some sort of kidnap ring? In Levenford?'

'Stranger things have happened. Everything is pointing that way.'

'Why?'

'Because they're all involved in some kind of devil worship.'

Cowie's eyebrows almost disappeared over the top of his thinning scalp.

'And you want me to announce that to the press?'

'Not necessarily, but they're going to want something.'

'I have to tell you, Chief Inspector, this is not looking good. And I'm losing patience.'

Jack said nothing.

'So what do you intend to do about it? I don't see any real progress. You're making us look like fools.'

'Actually I'm hoping to pick up someone who may be involved.'

'Oh?'

'Yes. His name is Michael O'Day. You'll have heard of him.'

Cowie shook his head.

'That's a surprise. An informant of mine said he gave you the information four days ago. O'Day was seen leaving Cairn House at the estimated time of Marta Herkik's death.'

The Superintendent gave another small shake of his head. His face was beginning to colour.

'Yes. He's been missing from his home for two days. Shame. Maybe we could have wrapped this up before wee Carol Howard was killed.'

'What are you trying to suggest?'

'I'm not trying to suggest anything. I'm just pointing out that I'm not making anybody look a fool,' Jack said, unable to keep the weary contempt from his tone. 'Now, if you'll excuse me, I've got a murder investigation to run.'

He stood up and left, closing the door behind him before the Superintendent burst a blood vessel.

Just as he got to his office, the phone gave a single ring. Jack lifted the receiver, listened for a moment, then answered briefly.

He went down the two flights of stairs to the front office. As soon as he got there, the waiting pressmen pounced. He held up his hands and told them to back off for a second while he spoke to the desk sergeant. Andy Toye was sitting in the waiting room. Jack told one of the uniformed men to take him upstairs. Just as he did so, Lorna Breck came walking in through the front door, between a woman and a man in uniform.

291

'Damn,' Jack said under his breath. He leaned across to the sergeant and told him to get the girl into the interview room as quickly and as quietly as possible. He turned back to the gaggle of reporters, using his hands to usher them away from the desk. The police officers walked right past them, and nobody seemed to notice the girl. Out of the corner of his eye, Jack got a brief impression of Lorna Breck's pale face turned towards him and then she was gone.

'Come on, Chief,' the thin man from the *Express* entreated. 'We've had nothing since this morning.' Somebody flashed a camera and Jack pointed a finger at the photographer.

'If that thing goes off once more in here, you're all out. No kidding.'

The cameraman shrugged apologetically.

'Okay, follow me,' he said, resignedly. He led them through a corridor and into one of the larger rooms near the cells, which was used for briefings. There were a few plastic chairs set in uneven rows. The group of pressmen jostled for a seat. Jack stood with his back against the wall and took out a notebook.

'Statement first. Questions next,' he announced brusquely, then checked his notes before beginning.

'We are investigating the disappearance of a teenage girl. It happened late last night in Castlebank Distillery. Witnesses say she became trapped in an elevator. By the time rescue services arrived, she could not be found. We are treating the case as abduction, possibly murder.'

'That's the fourth in two weeks,' somebody bawled from the back.

'I'm afraid it is. Our investigations are continuing.'

'Is there a link?'

Jack paused. 'That's a possibility we are looking into. I can't say anything further than that.'

'And you've got another suicide today?' the same voice asked.

'Possible suicide. The body of a middle-aged woman was discovered on the rocks on the west side of the castle in the early hours of the morning. She had injuries consistent with a fall. A post mortem is taking place at the moment. A report will be made to the fiscal and there's a possibility of a fatal accident inquiry later. We should have more details sometime today.'

292

'So what's happening here?'

'What's happening is that we are very concerned at recent events.' Jack did not enjoy using bland public relations speech, but he knew that one wrong word would catch the headlines. What was happening in Levenford was hitting the front pages of the national press too often. 'If I can use this opportunity to reissue our earlier warnings to parents to ensure that their children are not left unaccompanied after dark. I would also recommend that for the time being, no woman should be out on her own.'

Blair Bryden from the *Gazette* was sitting quietly close to the wall, writing in his notebook. Beside him another reporter piped up.

'None of the abductees have been found. All of them so far have been children, if you include the girl. Looks like there's some sort of pattern, wouldn't you agree?'

'We are investigating the possibility,' Jack said. A pattern was building up inside Jack's mind. It was becoming clearer – and yet also more confused – by the minute.

'You mean a serial killer?'

Jack paused and took a breath. He could see the headlines already.

'You know we don't like to speculate. I'm sure you will draw your own conclusions, but yes, that is one line of inquiry.'

He swept his eyes across the group of reporters. The photographer at the back flashed his camera blindingly. Jack blinked.

'Right, that's it,' he snapped.

'Sorry, chief. It was an accident,' the cameraman piped up.

'Apology accepted. Press statement over,' Jack said bluntly. Somebody protested, but Jack turned towards the door. Most of the gang followed him out, still firing off questions, but he ignored them. He turned right, went through the swing doors and headed along the corridor when a voice came from behind him.

'Thanks for the call, Jack.'

He turned. Blair Bryden, a slim figure in a long raincoat, had followed him through. Every policeman in the station knew the local editor. He was the only one who would have got beyond the door.

'Oh, damn,' Jack breathed. He stopped and leaned against the wall. 'Sorry, Blair. I forgot, pure and simple. I didn't get finished 'til very late, or very early. I can't even remember what time it was. My eyes were falling out.'

Blair shrugged.

'No problem. I managed to get plenty last night. Local knowledge helps. But there are one or two things that stick in my mind, thanks to my local knowledge.'

Jack raised his eyebrows.

'Like why you've hauled a spey-wife in on the act?'

'Eh?' Jack asked blankly.

'Lorna Breck. Two of your uniforms brought her in. You had her hustled away before anybody could see her. You must have forgotten I did a story on her only three weeks ago. The fire on Murroch Road, remember?'

'Oh. Right.'

'And Professor Toye was sitting out there this morning.'

'Well, that gives me a problem, Blair. I can't tell you at the moment.'

'But I can make a couple of guesses on my own.'

'Go ahead.'

'Andrew Toye is head of paranormal studies at the university. That's the tie-in to old Marta Herkik. She was some sort of psychic, which everybody knows. It's the professor's line of work.'

'Go on.'

'Lorna Breck. Five or six people heard her make some sort of prediction on the night of the fire. And it turned out she was bang on the money. So my guess is that she's been called in because you haven't a clue.'

'It's not quite that,' Jack said. 'I'd prefer if you kept this to yourself, at least for the moment.'

'You know you'll have to do better than that,' Blair said. 'They're both fair game, because I saw them, and as you said, we can draw our own conclusions. Furthermore, I don't think anything I could write about either of them would jeopardise the investigation.'

'But it could be wrong,' Jack stated.

Blair laughed.

'There's always that possibility. Now you, on the other hand, could put me right.'

Jack let out a long sigh. Blair was still smiling agreeably, and Jack couldn't help but return it.

'Alright. You want a deal.'

'That I do, chief.'

'Fine. I'll give you a couple of things right now, which you can feed to the nationals. You keep the professor and Lorna Breck out of print until Friday, and then you get first refusal on anything I can tell you.'

Blair cocked his head to the side, weighing the options. There were no options. He could write a speculative piece and wire it up to the daily papers and then have nothing but hearsay on Friday when the *Gazette* hit the streets.

'Done,' he said quickly.

Jack hauled his notebook out again.

'Names,' he said briskly. 'I'll have them confirmed later today, so don't send them out until then. Ann Eastwood. You'll have something on her already. Her daughter was killed in that accident up on the Corran Shore Road about a year back.'

Blair nodded, filing it away. He'd written that story as well.

Jack gave her address. He threw in Edward Tomlin. There was nothing to lose.

'So what's the connection?'

'Consider the fact that Tomlin poisoned himself last Friday. Now look at the dates of recent suicides and then check out what else has been happening on or around those dates.'

Blair closed his eyes for a few moments, then the smile came back to his face.

'You mean they're tied in to this?'

'That's a possibility we are considering at the moment,' Jack said, using the same tone he had at the press call. Blair laughed out loud.

'And you think there might be a connection then to Marta Herkik.'

'This is under investigation,' Jack responded blandly.

'That's why you've got Andy Toye. What the hell's going on here? Blood sacrifice?'

Blair was surprisingly quick on the uptake.

295

'No comment. And I don't want to read a word of speculation about that, or the deal's off.'

'Don't worry,' Blair promised. He scribbled something in his notebook, then looked up at Jack. 'Jesus,' he breathed.

Blair Bryden must have spent the whole day bobbing and weaving around Levenford that day. Every paper from broadsheet to tabloid splashed his story on the front pages on the following morning.

The operations room was empty when Jack brought Andy Toye along. The professor, a slight figure in glasses, looked around the walls, which were plastered with blow-up street maps of the town and cross-hatched diagrams with names handwritten in bold capitals beside photographs of the deceased.

'This is where it all happens?' Andy asked.

'All, or nothing. We do a lot of talking in here. The rest of the time is spent knocking on doors, or knocking our heads against brick walls.'

'I'm not sure I can really help you,' Andy admitted. He'd managed to find a cup of coffee from somewhere and had brought it along from the side room where he'd waited. He sipped it noisily.

'Neither me,' Jack agreed. 'But we'll never know until we try. John McColl will take you round to the Herkik place. It'll still be in a bit of a mess, but there might be something you'll notice that we've overlooked. I'm going on the assumption that there was a group of people there that night and they've got themselves involved in something. I don't know what it is, but if we can find out, then it'll be a great help.'

He looked down at Andy, who was finishing the last of his coffee. 'At least, that's what I hope.'

The professor walked across to a wall chart and scanned the names and dates, piecing it together for himself. 'The first child went missing almost a week after this alleged seance. Then the minister commits suicide. After that, the other baby is taken and his mother killed, followed by the attempted suicide of Mr Tomlin.'

'Actual suicide now. He's dead.'

'Then the boy goes missing, followed immediately by the woman in the river. Almost immediately, you have the girl taken from the distillery and another suicide within hours.'

'All of them connected to the Herkik incident, according to forensics.'

'For the life of me I can't see what's been going on. There's no occult sect I know of who've been involved in serial killings. Not in this country anyway.'

'All I want is for you to have a look around. We've found tarot cards in the possession of all the suicides so far. They match the ones in Cairn House. That can't be a coincidence.'

'No, but the abductions could be. Close involvement with the occult has been known to cause psychotic or schizophrenic symptoms in clearly documented cases. It's possible there was some sort of mass hysteria that is not linked to any of the abductions.'

'But Janet Robinson's bag was found at the place we believe Neil Kennedy went missing, and Ann Eastwood was seen, as near as we can tell, in Castlebank Distillery only minutes before Carol Howard was taken. That's no coincidence.'

Andy nodded in agreement. 'Well, I don't mind having a look, as long as you don't expect too much.' He pulled out a small leather-bound pad and began to copy some of the information from the chart. Just then, John McColl came into the operations room.

'We can stroll round now, if you like,' he said. Andy snapped the book closed. He gave Jack a little smile and went off with the sergeant.

Jack had called Ralph Slater in for the interview with Lorna Breck. She was sitting in the bare room, pale and slight, hands gripped on her black bag. A woman constable who was with her rose when the two men went in and closed the door behind her when she left.

The girl's eyes widened in recognition when Jack sat in front of her.

'I don't know why I've been brought here,' she blurted out.

'We'll try to make it as quick as possible,' Jack said. He had told Ralph nothing in detail about the girl. 'We just want to ask a few questions. Some of the things you told me yesterday are a bit puzzling.'

'Am I under arrest?'

'No. Not at all,' Jack replied, as lightly as he could. To himself he thought that she very well might be later on, depending on how the interview went.

He slotted a cartridge into the recorder, gave his, Ralph's and Lorna's names, stated the time, and left it running.

'What's that for?' she asked.

'Just to make sure we don't miss anything,' Ralph said, following Jack's lead.

'Right. Just relax,' Jack told her. 'I'll ask one or two questions, and you answer them as fully as possible. What do you know about Marta Herkik?'

'She's the woman who died at Cairn House, isn't she? I read about it in the paper.'

'Did you know her?'

'I hardly know anybody,' the girl said, eyes wide, slightly puzzled. 'I've only lived here since March.'

'And you never met her?'

'No,' she said. 'Like I said, I just read about her in the paper.'

'Do any of these names mean anything to you?' Jack ran down his mental list, reeling off the names of the four suicides. The girl reacted to Simpson's name. She'd heard it or read it, then she recalled the story about the minister's bizarre hanging.

'But you never met him. Never spoke to him?'

'No.'

He gave her the names of the three children and the teenager who had gone missing. She recognised the first three, having read of them and heard their names on television. The fourth drew a blank.

'Now, you told me that you *see* things.'

'That's right. I don't know why, and it's making me ill. I saw those babies and the wee boy, but I didn't know who they were until I heard their names on the news.'

'Can you tell me when this first happened?'

'It was the night of the fire, I think,' she said in a small voice, 'though I'd been getting bad dreams before that.' Clearly even thinking about it caused her some distress. Her big grey eyes opened wide, and both men could see she was putting herself back, remembering what had happened. She ran through the whole story for them.

'And this was the first time?' Ralph asked. The girl nodded, but then she stopped.

'Yes. No.' Her brow creased into a frown. 'It was the first time when I was *awake*. But before that, like I told you, I'd been having terrible nightmares.'

Jack didn't really want to know about nightmares. He'd had plenty of his own. They were not the kind of things people wanted to share, but he decided to go along with it in the hope that she might let something slip.

'Before the fire, I kept waking up. I didn't think about it until now.' She closed her eyes and they could see her trying to concentrate.

'They started before the fire. I couldn't understand them. I just felt there was something after me all the time. I couldn't really see it, but it was always there.'

She opened her eyes.

'And there was another one. Weeks ago. I don't know what it was. But there was a room of people, all sitting round a table. I couldn't hear what they were saying, but then the room went dark and there was a lot of screaming, people running, chairs being knocked over. I don't know what was happening, but it felt as if something awful was there in the room. The old woman was lifted into the air and then she was smashed down onto the floor. There was a terrible smell. I've smelt it again.'

Jack recalled the throat-catching stench on the inside of the lift shaft.

'Smell?'

'Yes, like something rotten,' she said, mouth turned down in distaste. 'Like sickness. Just awful, I think.'

Jack eased her away from the dreams. They were getting them nowhere, and Ralph was fidgeting, wondering what this was all about.

'Now, you told me you'd *seen* something when I first met you on River Street.'

'Yes. I don't know what happened. I looked into the shop window and everything went hazy. I saw the thing coming out of the dark. You can't see it properly. It moves too fast and the light doesn't show it. It came down and hit the woman and stole her baby.'

'And that was definitely on the day in River Street?' Jack asked carefully.

'Yes. It was dreadful.'

'That causes me a problem,' Jack said. 'Because the abduction of Kelly Campbell didn't take place until about a week later.'

'I know that,' Lorna said, suddenly quite definite, almost defiant. 'That's what I've been trying to tell you, but you won't listen.'

She looked straight at Jack. 'I don't know if I see the things *before* they happen or afterwards.'

'And last night, when you phoned?'

'It was happening *then*. I could feel it. The thing came down from the dark. It was banging on the roof and then it was inside and she couldn't see it, but she could sense it, and then the smell came and it scared her. Then it reached down and took her by the hair and pulled her up. It had her by the shoulder and there was blood coming down. The pain was terrible. She couldn't bear it.' The girl's voice got higher and louder as she went on at speed.

'How do you know she couldn't bear it?'

'Because when I see it, I'm in two places at once. I can see it happening, but I can see it from *inside* too. When it was happening to the girl, it was happening to *me*.'

She shrugged her shoulder quickly, letting the edge of her coat slide off. Underneath she was wearing a woollen sweater with a neat turtle neck. She pulled it down to the left, exposing a pale shoulder.

'Jesus,' Ralph mouthed.

There was no mistaking the bruises on the back and front. It looked as if the girl had been grabbed violently and squeezed brutally.

'Who did that to you?' Ralph asked.

'It's not a who. It's something I don't know. But if it doesn't stop, I think it's going to kill me.' When she said that, Lorna looked once again straight into Jack's eyes. There was no mistaking that what she was saying, as far as she was concerned, was the real truth.

It took the two policemen another hour to get the rest of the story. On each of the nights in question, Lorna had not been alone. She had a small diary in her bag which she brought out and referred to. Twice she'd been out with a friend from the library. Jack asked her where she'd been the night before and she told them she'd been baby-sitting for her cousin Gemma. He didn't bother taking notes. It was all on tape. He'd check out her alibis as a matter of course, but something told him they'd stand up.

Ralph arranged a car to take the girl home and when she'd gone, both men went back to the operations room.

'We should have brought her in here,' Ralph said. 'If she's telling the truth, she should be running this show. We could do with a psychic on this one.'

Andy Toye was still in the flat in Cairn House when Jack got there. He'd pulled up a chair and was hunched over the round table, which was still scarred and still scabbed with dried blood. In front of him was a large book with dull leather bindings. Beside it was the little notebook he'd used at the station.

He looked up when Jack came in and pointed to a seat, without saying a word. Jack sat beside him.

'This is *The Goetia*. Crowley's publication,' he said. 'Fascinating stuff.'

'I'll take your word for it. That was lying on the floor beside the kerb. Some of the pages were torn out.'

'Yes. I saw them.' Andy shoved his glasses up on top of his head and rubbed his eyes with his knuckles.

'I don't think they were trying to raise ghosts,' he said. '*The Goetia* is quite well known. I've spent the last hour trying to find a match for the names on the wall.' He looked up and pointed with his pen. The blood had dried to a brown ochre, the letters smeared on the old plaster.

'I was told they could have two meanings.'

'Yes,' Andy said. '*Heteros* from the Greek. It means an other, or the other. And *Etheros* suggests ethereal, or intangible. Or it could mean something else. I only noticed it a moment ago when I was looking at my notes. It could simply be the initials of the people who've been involved.'

He went down the list, reading them off. 'Herkik. Simpson. Tomlin. Robinson. Eastwood. If that's the case, there are two missing.'

'We're looking for somebody called O'Day. He was seen in the vicinity on the night.'

Andy grinned. 'Then all you need is someone whose name begins with an *E*.'

'You reckon?'

The professor shrugged. 'I don't know. It's only an idea, and it could be completely wrong. On the other hand, anything could be possible. I really don't know what was happening here. From the tarot cards and the ouija board, it could simply have been a fortune-telling session, but it may be that they went beyond that. *The Goetia* gives detailed instructions on how to raise spirits. It could have been some half-baked idea like that, and it could have gone wrong.'

'Like how?'

'Like mass hysteria. Psychosis. Something like that.'

'And the spirit angle?'

'Crowley believed it. Plenty of others have believed it too. But there's no real up-to-date documentation.'

'And what do you think?'

'In this world, anything's possible.'

Jack shook his head. 'I'd rather it was ghosts than some human.'

'Easier to catch a human,' Andy ventured. He snapped the book shut, and rose from the table. 'Where next?'

'There's a girl I'd like you to meet.'

Lorna Breck showed the bruises. She was sitting in the small front room of her house on Clydeshore Avenue. The road had been slick with ice on the way and Andy had held onto the dashboard, white-knuckled, as the car slithered and waltzed down the hill.

'It happened before,' she said in her soft voice. 'When I saw the boy. They faded next day, but I remembered the pain.'

'And this happens when you're asleep?' Andy was examining the dull marks on the girl's skin.

'Sometimes. But also during the day. I can't tell whether it's before or after.'

'Has this ever happened before?'

She shook her head. 'Never. I used to read tea leaves, but just for fun. Sometimes I would get a feeling about somebody. Just a tingly sensation. But then, on the night of the fire, I could *see* it happen. It was terrible.'

She pulled her sweater back over her bare shoulder. To Jack, she looked even younger than she had when he'd met her at the

302

chemist's shop. It came as a surprise when she'd told him she was twenty-six years old.

'I've seen pictures of *stigmata* before,' Andy said. 'It's believed to happen in cases of trauma, mind over matter, if you like. The power of the mind is sufficiently strong to create the haematoma marks on the skin.'

'But I don't want any of this,' the girl said, eyes wide and suddenly glistening. 'I just want it to stop.'

21

Out on East Mains, a small, modern housing estate not half a mile from where Jack Fallon lived, Derek Elliot had woken before dawn with a pounding headache. He was numbed from sleeplessness, for the night had been riven with the grim and morbid dreams that had assailed him for the past three weeks. In that time, the heavy-set man had lost three stones in weight. The girls in the estate agency had noticed the sudden weight loss, but had said nothing to his face. Elliot simply looked emaciated and ill. His annoyingly vapid moon-face had become gaunt and hollowed, his hail-fellow-well-met bonhomie had evaporated completely.

The dreams had begun after the night in Cairn House, when the cold wind had shrieked around the room scattering books and ornaments, blowing, it seemed, right through him, shivering his bones. He'd fled, like the others, down the narrow staircase and into the rain.

What had happened in there, he did not fully comprehend. He'd gone to Marta Herkik's house to have his fortune told, something he'd done several times now, every two months for the past year, ever since somebody had told him the old lady had a real gift for seeing the future. He hadn't believed it at first, though he'd wanted to. The first time he'd handed her two ten-pound notes, thinking it to be a waste of money, and then she'd sat him down on the other side of the round table and looked into the glass, and then she'd told him things about himself which had badly unnerved him.

Derek Elliot was twenty-six years old and, like many people, he was mildly superstitious. The first time he'd gone to Cairn House, he was on the horns of a dilemma. He was junior partner in Levenax Estate Agents, and for the past year he'd been incensed with ambition and anger, because old Harry Fitzpatrick, uncle of the fire station chief, spent most of his time on the golf course, letting him do all the work, for a fraction of the pay the old man took home. The Porsche, with its personalised numberplates, looked like a rich-boy's toy. Few people knew that it was leased, and the monthly costs were like a millstone around his neck. Marta Herkik had told him there were good signs as far as money and business were concerned. She told him he'd be successful in a plan he was making, and that someone close to him in business would take ill, opening the door for his enterprise.

He'd formulated the plan a few months before that. It was not complicated, but he couldn't put it into operation under old Harry's nose. Then the old man had suffered a mild stroke – making part of the old woman's prediction come true – and had been away from the office for a month and it was clear to everyone that it would be several more before he returned, if ever. That was enough to tip him over the edge. Derek Elliot spent the first few weeks cultivating Harry's contacts in the banks and building societies and then the right property had come up on the market. It was an old villa owned by a ninety-year-old woman who had died in an upstairs bedroom and hadn't been found for six days. Her niece, who lived in London, had no intention of living there. She contacted the estate agent by telephone and asked him to sell it immediately.

Derek Elliot did the survey himself, and wrote down a detailed report on structural faults, dampness and dry rot, all of which reduced the selling price by a huge margin and all of it a complete fabrication. He opened a bank account in another name, transferred some funds into it, put an offer in for the property, having forged half a dozen offers much lower than his own price, then, on the seller's authority, accepted his bid. The simple transaction netted him more than a year's wages when he immediately transferred the deeds to the next buyer. With this money, he bought up two houses on the east side of town under his assumed name, then arranged finance from building societies on hugely inflated surveys. When the money came in, he paid the mortgages for three months to allay suspicion, and then defaulted. The lenders sent agents down to Levenford to repossess the properties. Derek Elliot sympathised with them, said this kind of thing was happening too often, and went home to check his bank balance. In six months the deals had pushed his take to four times what he earned in a year.

305

Since then, he'd visited Marta Herkik's house every eight weeks or so. Each time she told him his planned venture would be a success, and each time he believed her. He'd come to rely on what she said as an omen for the future. If she ever warned him of danger, he'd rifle his account and take a plane to somewhere warm.

When she invited him to a special sitting, he was in no mood to refuse.

'Something different,' the old woman had told him in her sharp, crackling voice. 'Something that will show everything in the future.'

Since then, the dreams had come every night. Dreams of darkness and shadows. Unknown places where black things moved and the gloom was filled with the sound of screaming and the air was thick with the foul stench that had wafted over him at Cairn House. He could see eyes in the dark, glaring eyes swivelling right and left, hunting for him, and he spent his nights fleeing through alleys and runnels he'd never seen before with the snuffling of the black pursuer close at his heels, chasing him through the night.

On the morning that Jack Fallon took Andy Toye to Lorna's house, Elliot woke up from such a dream, shivering in fear, still hearing the guttural snarl of the thing that harried his heels. His back was lathered with sweat, and the cold perspiration only made him shiver more. The chill seemed to have got under his skin, making the blood sluggish in his veins. He dressed slowly and awkwardly, as if his coordination was failing, denying him the full control of his movements. The shirt collar hung down from his neck, made for someone much brawnier than he was now. He reached to put the kettle on, saw the blue veins like a raised road map on the back of a skinny hand, and instead, lifted the half-empty bottle of whisky. He twisted off the top, raised the bottle to his mouth and took a long swallow. The spirit burned all the way down to his stomach, but the glow faded almost immediately. He shook his head and grimaced. The drink, always his favourite, tasted foul. He felt his gorge rise, swallowed quickly and the roll of nausea subsided.

There was something wrong. He knew that now. Every time he closed his eyes he could feel the cold, rancid breath of the black

306

beast and he wondered if he was going completely mad. He didn't have the old woman to help him now. She was dead. He'd read about it in the paper and he'd been badly shaken, though, in himself, he'd known it all along.

Since that night, he'd struggled into the office, but he couldn't focus his mind on the deals. With old Harry Fitzpatrick still out of the way, he'd started going in late and leaving early. Instead of drinking with the crowd of young turks, the lawyers and accountants round in the Horse Bar on Station Street, he'd begun to take a bottle home with him at night, sometimes two. The drink did nothing to keep the dreams at bay, or the black thing in the dreams that got closer and closer until he could now feel it scrabbling at his heels in the night.

Things were going badly askew. In the last few days he'd had a visit from one of the building societies, who had wanted all the details on one of the properties he'd got the loan on. It was normal practice, but alarm bells had begun to go off in his head. He'd fumbled with the papers and stammered like a schoolboy. The rep had looked at him with a calculating expression, or so it seemed. Paranoia swept in like a vulture. Every time the phone rang, he jumped, startled. During the day, he'd begun avoiding places where people knew him. When he made it to the office, he went in and closed the door, sitting in the shade, away from the window. He put it down to lack of sleep, but the light was beginning to hurt his eyes.

Elliot put the whisky bottle back on the ledge below the curtained window and walked slowly, like an old man, into the darkened living room. Outside, a passing milk-float jarred on his ears as the bottles rattled in their crates. He winced and crossed to the seat beside the fire. The embers were still warm from the night before. He stoked them with the poker and they flared red, but the radiance did nothing to warm him. He felt as if he'd been invaded by a cold that would never heat up. Quite remotely, as if someone else was thinking for him, he considered the possibility that he might be dying. He was too tired to worry about it. There were enough things to worry about already.

It was just then that he noticed the cupboard door open. That was where he kept his fireproof box and the special bankbooks with the money he'd embezzled. He was sure the door had been closed when he went to bed. Alarm flared inside him, possibly the strongest emotion he'd felt for days. He crossed to the door and yanked it open.

The strong-box gaped. The papers and books he'd stuffed inside were lying scattered on the floor.

Derek Elliot's heart thudded painfully. He stood, slack-jawed, one hand on his chest, trying to comprehend what had happened. He'd heard nothing in his sleep, except for the fearful snarl of the unseen thing behind him. Immediately he thought he'd been burgled, then his jittery mind recalled the rep from the building society.

Had he been a detective? An investigator? His jumbled thoughts leapt this way and that, but his mind seemed to have no cohesion. He knelt and swept up the sheafs of paper and the passbooks, counting them out quickly. They were all there.

He opened the first. He'd made two deposits, using the name of someone he'd been at school with. It had been easy to get a travel-card with his picture as identity. The bank accepted that without a second thought.

The two tranches of money were written out on the left column, totalling forty thousand. There was a smaller amount in the same column showing the interest he'd been paid in the last six months. He let out his breath slowly. If anyone had seen these, then he was finished. He closed his eyes, opened them again, and his whole body shuddered.

Something was scrawled in red ink across the page, below the printed deposit amounts.

Debit. All sums forfeit. Account now closed.

The skinny young man lurched backwards and crashed against the chair. He snatched at the second passbook.

This time there was no writing, but as he stared at the page, the print began to fade from the bottom up. His total vanished as if it had evaporated from the paper, then, in moments, the figures above followed suit until the whole page was blank. He snapped it closed. On the front, just under the bank's logo, the name he had chosen had been written in ink. One by one the letters changed, right in front of his eyes. Raymond Caldwell, the boy he'd been at school with, was erased in seconds. In its place, in bold black letters, appeared two words: *Dead Account.*

Derek Elliot began to whimper. The third book was completely empty when he opened it, except for an old-fashioned block stamp, again in red. It slanted across both pages, just one word: *Debit*.

Now speechless, almost fainting from the shock, Derek Elliot jerked back and let the books drop to the floor. His eyes were glazed and staring. His weight seemed too heavy for his skinny legs and he slowly subsided to the floor in the corner close to the cupboard. He drew himself into a ball, his mind now so benumbed that he could think of nothing at all. Some time later, the postman came up the path and the letterbox clattered loudly as something was posted through the door. By this time, Derek Elliot's sanity had completely fragmented and he heard nothing. He crouched in the shadows in the corner, oblivious to everything except a whispered voice inside his head that he couldn't make out, but struggled to comprehend. Some time much later, when it was dark, the huddled figure uncurled and slowly got to its feet. The front door opened and Derek Elliot walked out into the cold night, heedless of the bitter cold wind blowing down from the snow on top of the Langmuir Crags. The whispering voice, now completely comprehensible, guided his feet.

Out beyond the town hall on Strathleven Street stand a couple of modern stores built of concrete and red corrugated iron in what somebody had described as recession-aissance style. The biggest is a do-it-yourself business which is always busy on Sundays, packed with hordes of women choosing wallpaper, followed by doleful looking men who are faced with the fun prospect of hanging it. Beside it, there was a carpet store that was doing badly, and next to that a car-parts business which sold everything from trailers and alarm systems to mountain bikes. A large car park dominates the yard and beyond that there's a stand of trees which borders a path beside Jinty Jackson's allotments where keen gardeners had a series of tight, well-tended plots crammed with vegetables in the summer months. In the winter, the little rickety greenhouses looked empty and forlorn. Each plot on Jackson's ground butted onto the Rough Drain, a mess of willow and reeds and tangled brambles, where every boy in Levenford was forbidden to play but which almost every lad on the east side of town used as an adventure playground. It stretched for almost a mile out towards Dumbreck Hill, another volcanic plug which marked the eastern border of the parish.

Jed Galt, whose mother Cathy worked nights in Mac's Bar, and who was one of the women who had witnessed Lorna Breck's strange seizure on the night of the fire, was leaning against a lightning-shattered trunk which had fallen over one of the water-filled runnels in the Rough. A cigarette dangled from the corner of his mouth. The three other boys sat on stones they'd rolled out from the brambles in a rough circle around the fire they'd made. Nobody came down to this part of town at night. It was truly rough and it was where the run-off water from the hills behind town finally drained before seeping down in a series of oily rivulets to the estuary on the east side of the Castle Rock. Thick, greasy smoke rose up from the flickering flames and filtered through the bare branches of a nearby tree, but there was nobody else around to see it.

Jed's father would be down at the Castlegate Bar with the rest of the drunks. What his mother made in one bar, Campbell Galt drank in the other. It had always been that way as far back as Jed could recall. His old man couldn't give a toss what his son got up to on winter evenings. The house could burn down and he'd never be the wiser until morning. Jed was seventeen. He was a tall, good-looking boy with an air of studied nonchalance about him. Inside, he bitterly resented his father because of the very fact that he, Jed, was down in the rough drain with the guys.

At the age of ten, Jed had shown considerable promise in art. He could draw horses and stags and peregrine falcons from memory. One of the teachers had shown him the basics of perspective and that had changed his whole outlook on his drawing. He'd spend hours, huddled over the kitchen table with a set of charcoal pencils his aunt Tricia had bought him, tongue hanging out of the side of his mouth, drawing the street scenes he'd seen on his way home. He'd shown promise, but his old man, in a drunken rage one night after an argument in the bar, had come home and swept the whole lot off the table and as an afterthought he'd mashed all the carefully stacked sheets together in his two big fists and thrust the whole lot into the fire. The charcoal pencils had followed and then he'd sent the young Jed sprawling across the room with a quick backhander.

'Bloody nancy boy,' he'd roared, eyes glittering and mean. 'Waste of fucking time. I catch you doodling about in here and I'll break your fucking arms.'

It was the last art lesson Jed Galt ever had and one of the most unforgettable lessons he got in life. Campbell Galt had reached base line. His wife struggled at a job which paid just enough to keep the house going with what she managed to hide away from her husband's romance with the bottle. From then on, Jed stayed out of striking distance of the old man's fists and boots. He contrived to be out of the house when his father was in and he ended up out of the house for most of the time. He lost interest in art and in schoolwork, and at the age of seventeen, he was out of school, out of work and had no prospect of getting a job. He knew he'd end up just like his father and that thought brought up a bile of bitterness over what might have been if he'd just been given a chance.

'We could go up the allotments,' Chalkie Black ventured. 'See what's in the greenhouses.'

'No point,' Jed said derisively. 'It's friggin' winter.' It had been different in the autumn when the nights were just drawing in with that mellow tartness that reminded folk of stolen apples and big, shiny horse-chestnuts. Then, some of the greenhouses had been bulging with black grapes hanging in great fists from the vines. Jed and his mates had jemmied one of the doors open and made off with their sweaters cradled out in front of them, loaded with the swollen bunches. They'd scoffed the grapes until the juices dribbled down their chins, feasting on them until they were sick.

'How about the school again?' Votek Visotsky piped up. He was a tall, pale-faced boy with light eyes and delicate skin. His grandfather had been Polish and Votek had inherited much of his looks. Unfortunately he was heir to less of the old man's brains. His father was manager of a car dealership in Kirkland. Votek could hardly manage to tie his high toe-tector boots.

'Not me,' Chalkie Black chipped in. His name was as much a contradiction as his appearance. Black he was not. His shock of pure white hair sat in tangles on top of his head, above a long, pale brow and equally white eyebrows almost hidden behind lenses through which his eyes looked tiny in the centre of concentric rings of corrective glass. He blinked in the light of the fire.

311

'It scared the living shite out of me last time,' Chalkie said vehemently. 'I'm not going back in there again.'

Eddie Redford nodded in agreement. It had been weird, going back to the place they had spent seven years of childhood. Even Jed Galt had been unnerved by the foray into their old school on Braeside Drive.

They had gone in on the day of the big bonfire on the common meadow out by Slaughterhouse Road. Votek had wanted to go see the firework display, but the others said that was kid's stuff and outvoted him. There was a space fiction film on at the Regal Cinema that they had wanted to see, but between them they didn't have enough money for even one seat in the front row and since the last time, when old Henry McLeish had shone his torch down the stairwell and caught Eddie pushing the bar to open the fire door to let the others in, there was no chance of a free night. The grouchy old bastard had put a chain on the bar to make sure nobody could get in. It also made sure nobody could get out and in the course of time that would prove to be a mistake of disastrous proportions, but that story is for another time.

The four of them had been strolling out by Cross Road, noisily kicking an empty beer can between them. Votek had taken a long-limbed boot at the can and sent it tumbling into the air over the old school wall. They'd scrambled over and into the low bushes, searching for the can, but in the dark, it was lost in the foliage. Jed had crossed the small playground and peered in the window of the cloakroom. It was too dark to see, but from memory he could conjure up a picture of the lines of coat-hooks and little benches. In the winter, there had always been a smell of damp from steaming coats and sodden shoes. The cloakroom was an extension built onto the ancient structure of the building, and more recently, it had been further extended to take in a toilet block which had replaced the old and filthy urinals along the far high wall of the yard where the boys used to climb on top of the roof and peer into the girls' section and occasionally pelt them with water bombs.

'Let's go in,' Jed had said, testing the downpipe for stability.

'What for?' somebody asked.

'Just for the hell of it. There's always something to lift. Maybe dinner money.'

Without another word, he shinned up the roan-pipe and onto the flat felted roof and moved easily onto the equally flat tarred surface above the cloakrooms. There were three translucent glass domes here, each more than a yard wide, which served as skylights to the long changing area. They were held in place by lead brackets and it took them two minutes to work the clips off one of them. The dome slid away from its mount with little effort, making a grainy bell-like sound.

Jed knelt at the edge of the circular hole. Down below, it was pitch dark.

'Who's first?' he asked the others, but nobody said anything. He eased himself over, sitting on the lip, then turned onto his stomach and lowered himself down. It was about ten feet above the ground, which meant that with his arms outstretched as he dangled, Jed would have nearly four feet to drop.

As he hung suspended in the darkness, with the three faces above him pale in the dim moonlight, a strange and scary apprehension shivered through him with no warning. He couldn't see below him. Already he could hear the quiet *school* sounds; the dripping of water in the toilets, the hiss of a cistern with a worn washer. The eerie chink of pipes.

In his mind's eye he saw something come out of the darkness to reach and grab his dangling feet in scaly hands. Right at that moment, a ten-year-old memory came zooming into the forefront of his mind. *Old Miss Walker*. She'd collapsed and died in the class next door when he and the others were six years old. Just like that, the other kids told him, snapping their fingers for emphasis. She'd clamped a hand to her chest and made a little moaning noise, and then crashed right across the table, stone dead. And after that, the older kids teased the younger ones with tales of how old Miss Walker's ghost, as white as a sheet, used to stand in front of the blackboard in the classroom at the end of the corridor. Jed's heart did a double beat as the imaginary picture, last thought of all those years ago, came flashing back, a long, bony white hand pointing out the ghostly columns of figures on the board. A long, white, bony hand down there in the shadows, reaching for *him*.

He could do nothing, hanging helplessly into the void. Abrupt panic flared and without thinking he started to haul himself back

313

up out of the hole. It was too late. His arms were too straight against the raised lip of the skylight. They couldn't bend properly to gain leverage. One hand slipped from the edge and he hung suspended for several seconds, every nerve cringing against the sudden lunge of the unseen thing that waited in the dark of the deserted night school. The fingers of his other hand slid slowly towards the edge. He hooked them frantically, trying to maintain his grip.

Then he was falling into the dark, no way out. His feet hit before he expected them to and the shock jarred up into his hips, toppling him sideways to crash against the wall. He spun round, cat-like, eyes wide, trying to see into the dark. From off to the right came a rhythmic liquid and echoing *plink* sound. Breathing hard, he swung his eyes left and right as the gloom resolved itself into the rows of coat-hangers separated by lines of mesh. In peripheral vision, shadows moved and danced, vanishing when he swivelled his eyes towards them. It was as if the place was crowded with half-seen, shadowy people waiting in ambush. He put both hands out in front of him and carefully stepped away from the wall.

And something came down out of the dark and crashed into his shoulder. Jed let out a whoop of pure fright and instinctively hit out at the thing.

'Ow. Watch it,' Chalkie Black bawled. His dangling feet were swaying back and forth.

'Stupid bastard, nearly killed me,' Jed yelled, trying to disguise the huge relief. All his childhood fears of the shadowy Old Miss Walker and things crouching under the bed or lying in wait in darkened cupboards had come shooting to the surface of his mind while he'd hung helpless over the well of darkness. Chalkie dropped to the ground, his white hair a weird, disembodied oblong in the dark. Votek followed seconds later, his heavy boots clattering on the floor. Eddie came last, rolling as he hit the ground, then the four of them stood in silence in the old cloakroom.

'Creepy, isn't it?' Chalkie said.

'It's only a school,' Jed retorted disdainfully. 'We spent years in here.'

'Aye, but in the daylight,' Eddie muttered. 'Now what?'

'Come on,' Jed said. 'Let's see what they've got.'

The corridors and stairwells had an empty and creepy echo. The sound of their footsteps boomed loud, no matter how softly they tried to walk. The headmaster's office, where on many an occasion each of them had stood, stony-faced and eyes downcast under the furious glare of Sister Bernadette, was locked. The secretary's room was not. The door creaked open and they crept in. The third drawer from the top held an old flat tobacco tin which rattled metallically. Jed slipped it into his pocket, then they found themselves in the classroom where Jed had learned to draw. Votek found some chalk and drew a highly stylised and disproportionate nude on the board and they all giggled. Eddie found a teacher's drawer open and a hoard of sweets she'd obviously confiscated. He filled his pockets. Chalkie picked up a good penknife. Votek kept the board duster after he'd rubbed out his masterpiece.

In a cupboard, Jed found a box of charcoal pencils. He drew them out and opened the carton. There were five of them, all different thicknesses, unused, their points new-sharp. A surge of nostalgia swept through him, followed by a sour bitterness. He almost threw them back on the shelf, but then, for some reason, he slipped them, before any of the others saw him, into the inside pocket of his scuffed leather jerkin. He was about to turn away when he saw the face.

'Hey look,' he hissed. 'It's Old Blackie.'

They all laughed. The little metal toy had sat on the teacher's desk for years. Its face was a parody of a black child, rolling eyes, wide, grinning lips, a hand outstretched. The children would put pennies into the hand, press a lever that jutted from the back and the arm would raise to flip the coin into the mouth. Money for black babies. Jed had often wondered, when he was still in the primary school, why the black babies would want to eat the money.

Chalkie reached for it. None of them really knew what happened next. It could have been that he nudged the little figure, forcing it against the back of the cupboard, making the lever move. Whatever, Old Blackie's hand moved up with a loud clink. The eyes rolled back in the head. Chalkie's hand came jerking back. The thing moved again and the hand dropped down, white and empty. The eyes swivelled back to where they'd been.

Chalkie stumbled back, coming down hard on Eddie's foot.

Then they were all scrambling for the door. Behind them, from the cupboard, the *chink* sound came loudly. Jed grabbed Votek by the collar and hauled him backwards, eager to be first. Votek sprawled, Chalkie ran right over him and then Eddie landed on top of him.

Somebody yelled in sheer panic. Jed got to the top of the stairs and ran down them, one hand sliding on the bannister. Behind him the thud of heavy boots told him the rest were behind him. He reached the ground floor and ran along the corridor with his pals behind him. Votek was whimpering because he was last. Jed slammed open the door on the bottom passageway that led to the cloakrooms. On each side, the massive doors of the old classrooms stood in opposite pairs. The boys slowed down here, getting their breath back.

'That wasn't fuckin' funny,' Votek complained. 'I nearly got trampled to death.'

'Just as long as Old Blackie didn't get you,' Chalkie snorted nervously. They had all seen the hand move on its own.

'Come on, you eejits,' Jed said. He just wanted out of the school. It had taken on a different, unnerving character at night.

They slowly crept along the final corridor. At the far end, the last classroom door was open. As they passed it, Chalkie peered in. The tall sash windows, the kind that needed a hooked pole to open, let in some light from the street beyond. They were crossing past the door-space when Chalkie's breath hissed in a sharp intake. They all turned, and they all saw it.

Just in front of the blackboard, motes of chalk-dust had billowed upwards in a faint cloud, maybe caused by a draught from the old ventilator grille beneath the board. Whatever had caused it, the pale haze swirled as they watched. The street lamp outside caught the dust motes as they floated.

'That's room seventeen,' Eddie hissed. They were all frozen in the act of passing the open door.

'Old Miss Walker's room,' Chalkie whispered back.

The cloud of dust eddied upwards and the light limned the edges and for a split second, something seemed to writhe there in

316

front of the blackboard. For that brief instant, the boys stared, eyes wide, mouths open. The shadow of the window bars rippled across the apparition and in the pattern of light and shade they saw the pale face, hollow eyes and a long dusty trail reaching out, pointing not at the blackboard, but at *them*.

'Oh my Aunty Jean,' Votek breathed. He backed away, bumping into Eddie, who stumbled right across the corridor and slammed against the opposite wall. Upstairs, far up in the gloom of the empty school, a door crashed shut with a resounding *boom* which reverberated down the stairs and along the corridor in a jarring shockwave of sound.

Eddie bounced off the wall, slipped to one knee and came bounding up. By this time the other three were haring down the corridor, Votek whimpering non-stop. Jed hit the door at the far end and it flew against the side wall with a hammer-blow crack. It was swinging back by the time Eddie straight-armed it and he almost dislocated his shoulder with the force of his passing. They scrambled, panic-stricken, through the cloakroom. Jed did not stop under the round skylight they had shifted an hour before. He headed straight for the far end, clambered up onto the windowsill, slipped the latch, swung the pane right out and dived headlong into the playground. He landed on the line of aluminium dustbins, which broke his fall surprisingly well, but the clatter of the trashcans as they scattered and rolled would have woken the dead. The other piled out after him, kicking the bins out of the way, and they all raced across the yard, scrabbled and scuttled over the wall and into the bushes at the far side. They did not stop until they had got to the edge of the Rough Drain, doubled over, hauling for breath.

'Bet that scared you,' Jed finally spluttered. He straightened up, spun Votek around and did a perfect imitation.

'Oh my fuckin' Aunty *Jean*!' he whooped and they all dissolved into hysterical laughter.

Five bizarre abductions and four equally grotesque suicides have rocked the town of Levenford.

The latest shock came with the disappearance of 16-year-old Carol Howard from Castlebank Distillery late last night. The young office clerk disappeared from a service elevator after it became jammed between floors.

Distraught fellow workers heard Carol screaming for help and made a desperate effort to prise open the doors to free her. But when engineers and rescue services arrived, she had disappeared, leaving a trail of blood inside the lift-shaft.

Police are treating the case as murder, the fifth murder, or suspected killing, to have stunned the town in the past three weeks.

Carol Howard, who had worked in the distillery for only a few months, was the eldest of four children. Her mother was being comforted by relatives, while police, led by Chief Inspector Jack Fallon, were organising a massive search of the building and surrounding area.

Only hours after the tragedy, the body of 45-year-old Mrs Ann Eastwood was found at the base of a cliff below the parapet of Levenford Rock, the site of one of Scotland's oldest and most historic castles. The grotesque find was made by an angler in the early hours of the morning. From Mrs Eastwood's injuries, police assume that she fell two hundred feet from the castle ramparts. It is the second tragic incident suffered by the family. A year ago, Mrs Eastwood's daughter Angela was killed in a horrific car accident on the Loch Corran Road. Like Carol Howard, she was only 16 when she died.

The story appeared in every national paper. Blair Bryden must have burned the midnight oil, quartering his area, collecting photographs and snapshots from friends and family, speaking to everybody at the scenes.

It went into detail on the missing Neil Kennedy, including a picture of the boy at a cub camp, looking bright and mischievous and without a care in the world. From somewhere, Blair had managed to get a christening picture of little Timmy Doyle and his parents and another snap of baby Kelly Campbell in her cot. A cousin had turned up a likeness of Shona Campbell when she was in fourth year in school. A black-and-white portrait of William Simpson, wearing his minister's collar and a long black gown, glared severely from the page. Edward Tomlin peeked out from his greenhouse in a grainy shot. From deep in the files, Blair had managed to find the snap of Marta Herkik taken only weeks after she'd arrived in Levenford after the Hungarian uprising. The picture showed a strong-faced, not unattractive woman, with piercing black eyes and dark hair.

The story quoted Jack Fallon accurately, though it did raise the question that the police were undermanned and had insufficient resources to bring to bear on what increasingly looked like the hunt for a mass murderer.

Blair Bryden had cleverly written a step-by-step account of how the murder of Marta Herkik had preceded the various abductions and suicides. He went into great detail about her reputed clairvoyant powers and managed to convey, between the lines, that some sort of sect might be responsible.

The tabloids carried five pages apiece, while the loftier broadsheets were more thrifty, but there was no doubt about it. What was happening in Levenford was now the top item on national news.

Jack read them all. It was fair coverage, though he thought it would probably do the investigation more harm than good. The only benefit, he decided, was that it would reinforce the warnings the community involvement boys had been giving round the schools and at every mother-and-toddler group in the area. Ronald Cowie was far from pleased. He stormed into Jack's office, waving a copy of the *Daily Record*, demanding to know who had released all the information. Jack told him it was just a matter of a good local man digging deep.

'I want that man arrested!' Cowie ranted. 'All of this is sub judice.'

'As a matter of fact, it isn't. Everything there is in the public domain. There's nothing we can do about it, and if we arrest him, the press will come down on us like a ton of bricks. They'll think we have something to hide.'

Cowie spluttered, and Jack made good use of the chance. 'And the crown office would have our guts. We can't arrest a man for stating fact or giving opinion. That's still not against the law.'

'Well,' the Superintendent said when he'd calmed down to a mere boil. 'We need results. Any result.'

'We're doing our best,' Jack said levelly. 'But I don't think that's good enough. I think this is getting too big for us. We need more bodies.'

'We've got enough bloody bodies. They're turning up under every stone.'

'I mean more officers to help with inquiries.'

'No,' Cowie said. 'Under no circumstances. It would make us even more of a laughing stock.'

'But it might save another life,' Jack protested, hearing his own voice rise. 'I want to make a formal request to headquarters.'

'Request denied,' his superior barked.

'If you insist, sir,' Jack said, forcing his voice back on an even keel. When he spoke, the words came out flat and cold. 'But as it is my judgement that such a request is not unreasonable, I shall put it up for you to make a formal decision. In writing, of course.'

Cowie froze. His eyes widened in anger and his cheeks began to quiver.

'Don't you dare defy me, Chief Inspector. I was a policeman when you were still shitting your pants, d'you hear me?'

'With all due respect to your length of service,' Jack said calmly, 'I am still obliged to follow regulations. I'm sure you would not want me to be involved in a breach.'

The Superintendent's hands clenched into fists. He looked as if he was about to step forward and throw a punch. Jack hoped he would not, if only for the fact that it would cause a mess which would be difficult to clear up. He stood head and shoulders taller than his superior, and he had almost twenty years advantage. If it came to a scrap, there would only be one outcome. Cowie glared and quivered some more, then turned and walked out of the office, slamming the door behind him. Immediately Jack wrote his request for an extra team of men and passed it through normal channels. Cowie would have to make a decision, then back it up with his signature. When he'd finished, Jack wished the man *had* taken a swing at him, just for the sheer satisfaction of knocking him to the ground.

It was a day for brutal slog-work, going over the statements gleaned by the teams who were out door-stepping. John McColl had got enough from Edward Tomlin's wife, including the tarot card, to show that the man had been acting strangely in the last week or so.

'He'd always been backward at coming forward. Hardly went out of the house,' John said. 'He'd a train set up in his loft. But Margaret Tomlin said he'd recently started going out to meetings every so often. He said they were train-spotters, or some sort, but she got suspicious. Went through his pockets, though she never came up with anything.

'Then the week before last, he came home late at night and went to his bed. She says he was ill with some kind of fever and kept yelling all night. The next day the fever was gone, but she says he was acting really weird. She heard him talking to himself when he thought he was on his own. Looks like he'd a change of character. Kept nagging at the girls to put the lights off all the time and during the day he'd sit in his room with the blinds drawn. She says she kept asking him what was wrong, but he'd just shake his head. Hardly said a word to her in the last week. Never spoke to anybody else as far as we know.'

A search of Janet Robinson's house brought nothing of note.

Apart from William Simpson, the suicides had all been normal people. Quiet, even solitary people who minded their own business. Nobody knew too much about them. On the surface they did not seem to be the stuff of strange sects. There was no history of violence, no rumour or speculation about odd habits.

Jack went through the list. Aside from the fingerprints on Marta Herkik's table and the added confirmation of the tarot cards, there was nothing to link them to each other. The only central connection was the old Hungarian woman herself and she was saying nothing.

Had the seance gone wrong? Had there been a sudden overwhelming surge of hysteria that had made them all turn on the little old lady? Jack had to consider the possibility, though while Ralph Slater's team had shown quite clearly, and the lab had confirmed, there was every sign of a struggle, there was nothing to show that any *person* in the room had been involved. There was no blood under Marta Herkik's broken nails but her own. No hairs or traces of fibres or skin flakes from anybody else.

It could have been that *one* of the group had stayed behind and brutally battered the woman to death. But that left another conundrum. Robinson, Eastwood and Tomlin. They had all been there, and they had all died – or started to die in Tomlin's case – just after an abduction. At first it had seemed simple enough. William Simpson had been bang to rights. He'd taken his own life and made a production of it, a theatrical, if grotesque confession. Or so it had seemed. That Simpson had been involved right up to

321

his recently strangled neck, Jack had no doubt. He had been an abuser of children, a pornographer, most certainly a killer of long standing, a sociopath or psychopath among other things.

Jack had had the feeling, on the day he'd watched the video of Simpson's death, that there was something too pat, too easy, about it. And he'd been right. The very next day, little Kelly Campbell had been dragged from her mother's arms and had disappeared into the cold night on Barley Cobble. Somebody had come out of the dark and had smashed the young mother to the ground with enough force to shatter the bones in her face. It had not been Simpson, not unless he'd come back from the dead to do it.

When that thought struck him, Jack gave an involuntary shiver.

Back from the dead.

That was what happened at seances. They tried to contact the spirits of dead people, to learn the future. Marta Herkik had died at a sitting, or just after one, from the scattering of tarot cards around her blasted room.

He shook his head wearily. *Too much listening to crazy folk*, he told himself. And if that included Andy Toye and Lorna Breck, then he couldn't help it. He did not have the time to go believing in goblins and ghosts. He was convinced he was looking for a crazed human, a clever and calculating human, but a crazy one nonetheless. And that human was bound to make a mistake sooner or later. He picked up the cup from the desk and threw the contents down his throat. The coffee was cold and tasted foul.

On the night they sat around the fire, Eddie Redford was adamant that it had only been a trick of the light.

'I'm not going back in there again,' Votek said uncompromisingly.

'Pissed his trousers,' Eddie said, and everybody laughed.

Nobody took the decision to break into Rolling Stock, the hardware store close to the allotments. It just seemed to happen. They'd come through a break in the chain-link fence at the edge of the garden plots and rummaged through the dump-skips behind the DIY store. There was a box of old lightbulbs which imploded with a satisfactory pop when thrown against the wall, and Jed and Eddie found two long fluorescent tubes Votek said looked like light sabres but when the two of them swordfenced, they shattered at first contact, showering each of them with fine glass dust.

Ten minutes later, they were round by the corner of the auto-parts store. Another developer was building an extension to the line of trading units, this one higher than the rest and corralled in scaffolding. Bricklayers had left a wooden barrow-ramp up to the first level. The four teenagers climbed this, then, without any spoken decision, ascended to the third storey. A big sign on the wall announced the planned opening of the town's first leisure centre and bowling rink. From there, the gently sloping roof of Rolling Stock was only a short climb. The four of them clambered up on the metal surface, feet ringing on the corrugated incline as they made their way to the peak. From there they could see across the hedge at the end of the allotments. Further in the distance, in the dark unlit mass of the Rough Drain, Jed could see the tiny red twinkle of the fire they'd made.

'I thought you'd put that out,' he accused Votek.

'I did. I pissed in it.'

'You couldn't have pissed hard enough. It's still going.'

Eddie was walking the ridge, arms out for balance. He stopped at the sloping glass skylight and levered it up.

'That'll be alarmed,' Chalkie said. 'You'll have the busies after us.'

Eddie kept hauling, swinging the frame upright, then laying it gently on its back where it stood up slightly against the ridge. Nothing happened. He leaned in and felt for the wires. They were still connected to the socket.

'Must have forgot to switch it on,' he said. They all crowded round the hole. Directly beneath them, there was a cat's cradle of rounded girders, like a kid's climbing frame.

'Whatdja think?' Eddie asked Jed.

The dark-haired boy looked around. There was only one entrance into the car park. Once inside, they could see any car approach through the big display glass doors.

'Aye. Let's go in.'

As before, Jed went first, easing himself onto the cross-braces.

323

There was some light from a quarter moon glimmering through the rest of the skylights, making some shapes visible below. It was not as scary as the school had been, and here, there were greater prizes. The others followed him along the spars until they got to the far wall where they butted into the breeze-block. From there, it was an easy descent of thirty feet down the gantry of metal shelves in the storeroom. Jed got to the ground and waited for the others to join him. He could feel the delicious tension twist inside him.

The place was a paradise, an Aladdin's cave of all the things they wanted but couldn't buy. A whole wall of car stereos, black and expensive, sat waiting to be hoisted. There were trailers and socket sets and shelves lined with expensive tools. And up at the far end, there were bikes in all shapes and sizes.

'I want one of them,' Eddie said in a quiet, covetous voice.

'We'll need to get a rope to hoist them up there,' Chalkie observed practically.

'There's tow-ropes all over the place. We could do it,' Eddie told him. He walked forward and ran his hand over the saddle of a sturdy looking mountain bike with thick treaded tyres. In the gloom, he couldn't say what colour it was. It didn't matter – already in his mind's eye he could see himself coming down the side slope on Langmuir Hill.

Votek had moved off down the aisles. Chalkie followed him while Jed fingered the precision tools.

He hefted a power drill and held it up like a gun when without warning a loud noise blared only inches from his ear. Jed jumped like a scalded cat, ears ringing, heart pounding.

Votek burst into hoots of laughter. He had reached across the low shelves and let off a car-horn right next to Jed's head.

'Stupid bastard,' he hissed at him. 'You'll get us all hung.'

Votek giggled again and let the horn drop to the floor. He found a row of spray paints and popped the lid on one, crossed to the bare wall close to the door and, with two quick sweeps of his hand, drew a *V* shape on the rough surface.

'Great thinking, moron,' Chalkie rasped. 'Just write your name and address and they'll come for you in the morning.' Votek shrugged, then filled in the space of the letter, made it a circle, then scribbled fuzzy lines all over it.

Up at the far end, Eddie had lashed two tow-ropes together and wheeled the bike across to the gantry. He was tying the rope round the cross-bar when the others found him.

'You really taking one?' Chalkie asked.

'Sure. They've got plenty.'

'Me too then.'

They all selected bikes, hauled them out of their stands and brought them to the wall. Jed clambered up, with the end of the rope between his teeth. Carefully he threaded his way through the girders, making sure he looped the rope under them when he crossed, so that it dangled down to the group below. Chalkie followed him through the wide skylight and then they braced themselves and began to haul. There was a rattle from down below and the rope rasped against the lip as he pulled, but once the bike left the floor, it came up smoothly. The handlebars banged against the edge and the two of them manhandled it through the gap.

Jed threw the rope back down, watching it snake like a pale worm into the gloom below. There was a tug, some jiggling, then another two jerks. They hauled this one up even quicker than before then repeated the manoeuvre until there were four new bikes lying on their sides on the slope.

'I'm going back in,' Jed said.

'What for?'

'They might have left money in the tills.'

'They'll all be locked.'

'No problem to a man of my caliper,' Jed told him, walking towards the skylight with an exaggerated limp. It was an old joke, but Chalkie laughed anyway. Jed climbed back inside and rather than wait out on the roof alone, Chalkie followed him through. They got to the ground and found Votek and Eddie both wearing bikers' helmets and giggling hysterically as they goose-stepped up the aisle. Jed went down the line and picked out a cordless drill. There were dozens of bits hanging from pegs. He slotted one in, tightened the mouth then squeezed the trigger. The tool was fully charged. It whined in his hand and he could feel the torsion bend his wrist to the right. He strolled down towards the cash-points and sat on the service shelf. The till-drawer was locked, as he'd expected. Jed aimed the bit at the key-hole on the side. The drill screeched and jumped in his hand as the point rasped at the metal.

Then the whole place went suddenly dark.

'What was that?' Votek called out.

'Wheesht, man. Just a cloud over the moon, or something.'

The dim light through the skylights had faded to nothing. Jed slid off the desk, jammed the drill down the front of his jacket and zipped up the front. He had just reached Chalkie at the bike stands when a huge booming noise thundered down from the roof. Jed's hand jerked away from the wall as a shock of vibration jolted up his arm.

'What in the name of . . .' he started to say and another ear-splitting crash followed on the first. It felt as if they were on the inside of a vast drum. The noise was so loud it made their ears ring.

'Oh Jesus, it's the cops,' Votek blurted.

'Shut up, wanker,' Eddie hissed at him.

The noise came again, like giant footfalls on the roof. There was a grating sound, like stone on metal, then everything went quiet.

'What's happening?' Chalkie whispered in Jed's ear. They were standing elbow to elbow, with the other two backed right up against them.

'Just wait,' Jed murmured.

There was silence for several minutes, and finally they began to relax a little, letting their breath out slowly.

'Probably kids throwing bricks up on the roof,' Jed said. It sounded reasonable enough. 'Is there another way out of here?' He moved away from the stack of shelves and crossed quickly in the dark to the far wall. The others followed him. There was a door there, but it was locked.

'We'll have to go back up,' he said, turning back to walk the across the floor again, when just above them, there was a scuttering noise on the wall. Something growled, low and guttural. Jed pulled back, and a dark shadow peeled itself off the wall and snatched Chalkie right into the air. The boy gave a gasp of surprise as he rose straight up above them. The others stood gaping upwards, in attitudes of complete bewilderment. Chalkie's white hair floated above them in the dark.

'Did you see . . .' Votek asked, incredulity plain in his voice.

Up on the wall, above their heads, the low, rumbling growl stuttered again. Chalkie said 'Oh,' in a very small voice. There was a crunching, tearing sound, a squeal of pain and then silence. Something splashed on Jed's shoulder.

'What is it?' Votek demanded in a shaky voice, then, uncharacteristically, he bawled out: 'Chalkie? Are you up there?'

Jed and Eddie were too stunned to move. It was as if time had suddenly stopped dead. The warm smell of blood was thick in the air. Votek took two steps forward, the rounded hat still strapped to his head.

'Hey, Chalkie. Quit messing about, eh?' He stood, looking up into the shadows where there was some indistinct movement. 'How did you get up there?'

Above him, the growling sound rolled out from the dark corner again. Jed lunged forward, started to call a warning, when a shadow moved down the wall with flickering speed. It elongated, stretched as it surged out from the surface. It hit Votek such a blow that the shiny plastic helmet was swiped clean off his head. It landed ten yards away with a heavy thump.

Jed stood frozen. Everything was happening too quickly, much too quickly. His mind was trying to sort out the different messages his senses were yelling at him. Votek was swaying on his feet. There was something wrong with him, though in the gloom, Jed couldn't make out what it was. Something splurted out from his friend and splashed to the floor. In those shattering moments, he could hear his own voice inside his head, repeating over and over again: 'Shouldn't have *thumped. Shouldn't have thumped!*'

Then it came to him with such a shock of realisation he nearly dropped into a dead faint. The plastic hat would have cluttered and rattled. It wouldn't have landed with that heavy thud.

Adrenalin jolted through Jed's veins. Up above, the shadow struck again, leaping off the wall. Votek was snatched forward soundlessly.

Jed jumped back. He grabbed Eddie by the collar and hauled him away, pulling him desperately towards the stack of shelves. Behind them, he could hear the snuffling, grunting sound the shadow was making. He didn't want to hear it, didn't want to see

327

what could be making such a noise. He did not want to know what kind of thing it was that looked like a shadow on the wall, but could reach out and knock the head completely off Votek's shoulders and leave him standing there in the aisles in his big toe-tector boots.

They made it to the far side. Jed started to scramble upwards, arms and legs snatching for hand-holds, feeling the terror scream through him. Below him, Eddie was standing, head down, both hands on the first shelf. Despite his horror, Jed clambered down to the floor.

'Come on, Eddie, it'll get us.'

His pal turned to look at him, his face just a blur in the dark.

'But . . .' he murmured. 'But I don't see . . .'

Jed slapped his face with a resounding clap. Eddie's head snapped backwards and hit the angular upright.

'Come on, you stupid bastard,' Jed hissed. 'Get up there. Fuckin' *move*!'

Eddie turned and began to climb like an automaton. Jed chivvied and shoved at him, forcing him up further, all the while expecting something black to come snaking up from below to smash them off the shelves like flies. They made it to the crossbeams and again Jed had to keep pushing at Eddie to make him move. They reached the skylight and Jed clambered out first, kicking the nearest bike out of the way. He turned and reached for Eddie's hand, bent his legs and heaved backwards. The other boy came on his belly over the ledge. He got one leg out onto the roof, shoved with his elbows and was bringing the other one out when his arms seemed to give way and he flopped down onto the sloping surface with a thump.

'Oh,' he said, just as Chalkie had done when he'd disappeared into the dark.

'Come on, Eddie, come *on*!' Jed bawled, not caring who heard him. Every nerve in his body was singing with utter dread.

Eddie tried to shove himself up. His face contorted with exertion. It lifted up from the roof and faced towards Jed. His eyes were opened so wide they looked as if they would roll out and dangle on his cheeks. Even in the cold night air, Jed could see the sudden and complete realisation on his friend's face.

'Oh, Jed. Oh Christ, Jed, it's got me.'

Jed stepped forward and grabbed Eddie's hand in both of his. His panic was telling him to run, to get off the roof and away from here and never stop running, but for some reason, he managed to squash the instinct down. His friend was hanging over the lip and it had *got* him.

'Come on, Eddie,' he cried, voice cracking. 'Oh, please, man. Come on, son.'

He heaved as hard as he could on Eddie's arm and something heaved in the opposite direction with such sudden force that Jed was almost catapulted right into the hole.

Eddie wailed. 'Oh Jed. Oh please. For *fuck* sake, Jed.' All the words came out in a liquid gurgle. Jed made a superhuman effort and his friend came up six inches. Eddie's free hand scrabbled on the corrugated metal of the roof, scratching like cat's claws. Then he screamed.

The sound shattered the night. A huge, high and piercing screech, like the night mail-train going through the junction at Bankside Road.

Jed almost let go.

There was a cracking sound from inside the lip of the skylight and Eddie screeched again. Jed started crying, fingers hooked into his pal's arm. Eddie looked at him again and his face had gone a sickly white.

'My fucking leg,' he said, very dreamily. Then, without any warning, there was an enormous jolt. Eddie's wrist slipped from Jed's grasp and the boy went slithering back through the skylight.

The lone boy on the roof stood frozen, his mind unable to comprehend what had happened. His hands and legs were shaking uncontrollably and his breath was coming so fast his vision began to swim.

He stood there, silent, shocked rigid, eyes wide, hair standing on end.

And a dark shape hauled itself out of the skylight, scraping the metal, growling so low it made the roof-plates shiver.

Suddenly something snapped inside the dark-haired teenager. His mind broke through on the other side of his terror. His hand flashed up and hauled on the zipper of his jacket. He reached inside and dragged out the drill.

'Right, you bastard. Come on.'

He dived at the gaping hole on the roof just as something heavy and oily black came scuttling out, limbs blurring fast. Jed jammed his hand forward, squeezed the trigger and aimed the whirling bit at shoulder height. Just as he did so, two enormous orange eyes opened with a snap that was audible over the shriek of the drill. His hand plunged forward and the whirling metal went straight into the poisonous orb. Something popped. A foul stench belched out. Liquid splashed onto Jed's hand and burned like acid, though he did not feel it then. The black thing grunted, recoiled. A piece of itself shot out and tried to grab at him, but the boy kept his arm rigid and his finger hooked on the trigger.

The shape roared like a vast beast in a den, almost knocking the boy off his feet with the ear-splitting blast of sound. It shook as if it had been jolted with a million volts, almost breaking Jed's arm. The drill whined and the foul mess splattered onto the front of his jacket. The drill kept on shrieking and the thing snarled and gurgled and roared, now backing off, heaving itself away from the biting metal. Filthy vapour had started to billow out from the obsidian surface, as if it was evaporating in the night air. It gave an almighty jerk. There was another pop as the twist of steel came out from the eye and then the thing twisted, still roaring, and disappeared back into the hole. Jed stood there, unable to move for some seconds. Under his feet he could feel the whole building vibrate like a bell as the thing, whatever it was, crashed along the girders and battered against the walls. Down there in the dark, it sounded as if the whole store was being wrecked.

Jed dropped the drill. Something was searing into the skin of his hand. He turned and ran across the roof to the scaffolding on the uncompleted building, scrambled down to ground level, then raced for the road at the far end of the car park.

Halfway along Castlebank Street, he collapsed in the middle of the road and was almost killed by old Wattie Dickson the newsagent, who was weaving his way home from East Mains Bowling Club. The old fellow saw the blood all over the boy's jerkin and bundled him into the back of the car. He reached Lochend Hospital in a commendable twenty minutes, much faster than he'd ever believed his ancient Wolseley car was capable of.

By the time Jed Galt was rushed into a cubicle on the casualty ward, he was incoherent with shock. A young registrar gave him a shot which should have put him to sleep in twenty seconds, but seemed to have no effect whatsoever.

The boy with the badly burned hand and face and the blood-soaked jacket kept screaming about a monster who had killed his friends. The registrar suspected he'd taken one of the designer pills all the youngsters were swallowing at discos these days. He gave him another injection which did what the first was supposed to do and then he began working on the burns. An hour later, while Jed Galt was still unconscious, he was transferred to the plastic surgery unit of a hospital on the north side of Glasgow where some of the best medical men wondered just what had caused an acid burn that had taken almost all the skin and muscle from the boy's hand, leaving white and pitted bones exposed to the air.

22

'It's happening again.'

'Eh?' Jack mumbled. 'What time is it?'

He was halfway out of the seat, one arm stretched, fingers fiddling for his watch on the side table. Papers were scattered on his knees and at his feet. The room had gone cold since he'd dozed off.

'I saw it,' Lorna Breck's voice, all shaky and urgent. 'It's *hunting* again.'

'Wait, hold on a minute. Slow down.' He brought the watch up, peered at the dial. It was nearly eleven. He'd only been asleep for half an hour, sprawled in the chair, but he'd been down deep. The jangling of the telephone had jarred him out of it, but he still felt as though he was swimming for the surface of wakefulness. He shook his head, tried to speak, but a yawn stretched out the first word and made it incoherent. When it was spent, he tried again.

'Yeah. Go ahead.'

'I saw it again,' Lorna Breck blurted. 'I wasn't asleep this time and I saw it. It's killing people. Or it's *going* to kill them.'

Jack broke through the surface and came completely awake. Oddly enough, his mind took a lateral step. *And we'll find O'Day tomorrow*, was the first thing he thought. There was no point in taking any chances, despite his scepticism of what Andy Toye called the *supra*-normal. Lorna Breck was clean. He'd had her checked out. Maybe, Jack thought, maybe she did get a buzz or a twitch, or some sort of second sight, and if she did, he would use it no matter what anybody said.

'Where?' he asked.

'I don't know,' she said, talking fast. 'In a big place. There were echoes. It came down through a hole and got them. I can still see it.'

'What do you see?'

'A big square hole on the ground. There's something lying

there. Like a bike. Yes. It *is* a bike. It went down through there. I can hear it, like an animal in a cave.'

'What else can you see?' he asked, not taking the time to be surprised at his question.

'A cellar. Somewhere big and dark. There's shelves. It has one of them. Two of them. Oh, there's blood all over, and the smell is choking.' She broke off and he heard a strangled cough, harsh and metallic in the line. 'I can feel its hunger. It hates them all. It *wants* them all.'

'What else?'

'There are two others. They're running away. Climbing back up on the shelves. I can feel their fear. Oh, they're terrified. They know it will get them. They're going up towards the hole. One of them is crying and the other is pushing him. Oh, Mr Fallon, they're only *boys*.'

There was a dead silence. Jack was about to urge her on. Lorna sounded as if she was talking in her sleep, or giving a scene by scene account of a war atrocity. He could hear the emotion squeeze at her voice.

'Now, he's outside. I can hear his feet. Like drums. The other one is coming. It's right behind him. Oh my. *Oh no*. He can't get out.'

She broke off again, but her breathing continued, rasping and panicky.

'Lorna, keep talking,' Jack ordered.

'It has him. The other one is trying to pull him out. But it has him. I can see his face. His eyes are looking at me. He *knows*.'

Then she wailed right into Jack's ear.

'Oh, please no. Oh God. It's pulling him down. He can't hold on. He's crying. The pain in his leg. It's tearing him apart.'

Jack was struck silent with the intensity of her running commentary. There was no doubt in his mind that she believed what she was seeing. On the other end of the line, the girl whimpered. He could picture her, eyes tight closed as she held onto the vision no matter what the cost.

'It's coming now for the other one,' she said softly, almost eerily slow. 'I can see it coming out.'

'What does he look like?'

'It's black. You can't see it properly. Just a shadow, but it

333

moves. Like a spider. It's reaching for the boy. He is stepping towards it. Oh, please!' Her cry soared up an octave and almost deafened Jack. 'Get back. Get away! Its eyes. *Don't look in its eyes.*' This came out in a screech.

Another pause, then she started again. 'There's something in his hand. Like a gun. It makes a noise. It's . . .'

Another silence. '. . . in its eye. He's hurt it. It's snarling. The boy, he hurt it. And it's hurt him. On his hand.'

Jack heard the sharp intake of breath. 'Now it's going back. He's beaten it and it's getting away. He's got to go. It will come back. It will come for him. I can feel it.'

Then she screamed at the top of her voice: 'Run! *Run away!* For God's sake, *run!*'

The cry was long and drawn out and rang in Jack's ears so loudly his hand jerked the receiver away from the side of his head. When he pulled it back, there was nothing but silence.

'Lorna?'

The silence continued for a while, then he heard her breathing.

'Lorna? Are you all right?' It was a stupid question and he knew it.

'Hold on. I'll come over. I'll be there in ten minutes.'

He clattered the receiver down on the cradle, brushed the rest of the papers onto the floor and shoved himself out of the seat. He was still wearing the clothes he'd had on all day and his hair was standing up in corkscrews, but he had no time to notice or care. He hauled his shoes on then reached for his coat, which was still slung over the back of the other chair, and shrugged his arms into the sleeves. A minute later he was easing out of the narrow drive and down Cargill Farm Road, heading for the other side of town. A harsh rime of frost had opaqued his windscreen and the wipers at full strength fought a game but futile battle to scrape it away, though there was just enough of a clear space above the wheel to let him see out. He shot a red light at the bottom of the hill where the road crossed over the through-town carriageway and gunned down towards Strathleven Street.

He had to knock on the door several times before Lorna Breck replied, asking tremulously who was there. The locks clicked and she opened the door a fraction. He saw one eye peer out then she opened the door fully. Her face was so white the smattering of freckles looked as if they were painted on, and she held a dressing gown tight round her as if huddled for warmth. He stepped into the house and as he went past her, the girl swayed and she started to droop as if the last of her strength had gone. He turned quickly, got an arm around her waist and held her upright. Against him he could feel the shivery vibration of her body, like a top guitar string wound up close to snapping point.

He eased her into the room, sat her down, then, without a word, went through to the kitchen and put the kettle on. In the two minutes it took for it to boil, she said nothing at all. He made two cups of instant coffee, spooned plenty of sugar into both, then took them through and made her drink one of them, holding the cup for her because her hands were shaking so violently she would have scalded herself. He waited patiently, sitting in the opposite armchair that he'd pulled across until their knees were almost touching, until she'd finished the drink, sipping his own coffee in alternate shifts. It did him some good and seemed to be helping her.

Finally, he put both cups down and leaned forward.

'You're alright now,' he said, wondering where to start. 'You're safe.'

'Nobody's safe,' she said flatly. Her grey eyes swivelled up towards him, glistening in the light of the side lamp. 'Not until they kill it. I don't know if anybody can.'

He took her through what she'd seen, and despite her reluctance, her repugnance, she went over it, again and again. One thing he knew for certain. If the killer had struck tonight, she had the perfect alibi.

'I don't know when, and I don't know where,' she said. 'I saw it on the top of the roof with something in its hands. It happened on the night before they found the dead man hanging from the rope. It threw him off. It just hit him and hurled him away. I now think I saw it *when* it happened.'

She drew in her breath in a stutter, the way small children do when they've been crying. 'But when I saw it on River Street, that was *before* it took the baby. I just don't understand it. There's no reason why it's *me* who sees these things, and I don't want any of this.'

'Take it easy,' Jack said, as soothingly as he could.

335

'I can't,' she snapped back. 'It's killing me too.' She looked up at him again, wide eyes brimming, and touched her hand to the centre of her chest. 'Killing me in here.'

He leaned forward and took both of her hands into his, kneading them gently. They were soft, and despite her shivering, surprisingly warm. But as soon as he touched her, she jerked back as if she'd handled a live wire. Her eyes snapped wide open and she drew in her breath in a sharp gasp.

'What's the matter now?' he asked, alarmed, wondering if he'd hurt her.

The girl's mouth opened and closed dumbly. No sound came out. She looked as though she was taking some kind of seizure. She held that pose for several seconds, looking like somebody kicked in the belly, before her breath came back. She let it out in a long, slow exhalation.

'Are you alright?' he asked again. She shook her head, very slowly, then raised her eyes up to him. They were huge and the swimming tears spilled out and onto her cheeks.

'She felt no pain,' Lorna said softly. Her hands clasped tightly on Jack's fingers.

'Pardon?' he asked, perplexed.

'The little girl. There was no hurt, no pain. There was no time.'

'What do you mean?'

'I saw it. I don't know why and I don't know how.' The whole tone of her voice had changed. Now there was no fear there, only a gentle compassion. 'It was your daughter, wasn't it?'

Jack's heart dropped into his belly. He could feel the skin crawl eerily on his back.

'I don't understand,' he said, trying to keep his voice neutral. The girl kept her eyes fixed on his, face placid behind the sparkling lines of her tears.

'You've blamed yourself for not being there. You keep seeing her over and over again. But it was not your fault. It was too quick for her and she felt no pain. Your wife and your daughter, they are at peace. I *know* it. You can let them rest.'

'How on earth . . .' he blurted, but she squeezed his hands in a strange reversal of roles.

'I don't know how. When I touched you, I could *see* it. I saw what you see, but there was more. I could feel them. I *can* feel them.'

She smiled at him, very gently and the pinched, harried look was gone. In that brief second, she was beautiful.

'They are with you, and forever. Not in pain and anguish, but in love. I can see them smiling at you.'

It was her turn to lean forward.

'They want you to forgive yourself. I can feel the heat of their love and the strength of their peace.'

Jack tried to pull away, horrified at the emotions which were twisting inside him, but she held onto him with surprising strength.

'I don't know how, and I don't know why,' she said softly, but insistently. 'Something has happened to me, something terrible. I see all these dreadful things and they frighten me because I know they are true and they are happening. But now I can see other things as well.'

She leaned back and drowned him with her eyes.

'If there is a bad, then there must also be a good, I think.'

'But it can't be possible,' Jack said. He felt as if he'd been hit a dull blow to the side of his head.

'I don't know what is possible. I've got this curse, but maybe part of it is a miracle. Maybe, if you help me to be brave, I can help you.'

Jack sat there, transfixed by the small slim girl with the lilting voice, completely thrown off balance. He didn't know what to think. She was either completely crazy or he was. And the crazy thing about it was, he wanted to believe she was completely sane. Because that would mean that everything she said was true.

The last train pulled in from the city at eleven-thirty. Kenny McIntyre, the one-man stationmaster, ticket-collector and occasionally porter, was down in the Horse Bar having a drink to drown his woes. His wife Isobel had told him she was three months pregnant and that was the last thing he'd wanted to hear. The odd thing about it was that he could not remember having done it with her for a while. She'd had a severe case of leg-lock for months as far as he could recall, and he'd wondered about the possibility that she might have found another man. Kenny, bull-necked, red haired and pot-bellied, had dismissed the notion. She was stuck up in the flat in Loch View all day. There was no opportunity for her to be getting a leg under anybody else, and anyway, she had never been that adventurous in bed. He eventually assumed that he'd knocked her up one night after a couple of hours and several beers in the pub. Maybe he couldn't remember, but he wished he had. He wondered how it had been for him. He also wondered how he was going to cope with a squawling kid in the tiny flat. That was going to make life hell, and it was just as well he was on night shift. His late hours also meant that he missed the violence of Isobel's morning sickness, which was a blessing. Of the hirsute and surprisingly athletic man from Housemarket Supplies, he knew nothing, even though she was still inviting him into the house and into her body every week.

The train came in, but Kenny stayed in the bar. At this time on a Wednesday night, there would be few passengers, not enough to worry about the odd one or two who might have skipped on a train without a ticket. There would be no inspectors to wonder about why he wasn't at his stall. The floor of the bar vibrated as the train pulled away. A few minutes later, two young men wearing football colours came staggering in, happy as larks, each holding the other upright. Obviously their team had won a midweek fixture. Despite their condition, the barman let them have a drink. Kenny McIntyre ordered another whisky and sat alone at the end of the bar, cursing his luck.

Up at the station, raised thirty feet above the road, Sandra Mitchell and Walter Dickson, whose grandfather ran the newsagent's shop on River Street, sat in the waiting room, entwined in each other's arms. They'd been kissing non-stop during the thirty-minute journey and had failed to notice the prim and elderly woman sitting opposite who had glared at them in reproof the whole time. They only came up for air when the train had stopped at Levenford and they had only just made it onto the platform before the doors scissored shut. It was a freezing night, and in the cold air their breath clouded out in front of them. Walter guided the girl into the waiting room, an old, redbrick building with a dirty fireplace which hadn't been lit in years and a stained wall the colour of bile which was hieroglyphed with graffiti. He pulled her down onto a slatted seat and jammed his mouth on hers, sliding his hand inside her coat and cupping his palm round the yielding warmth of her breast.

338

She gave a little moan, squirmed in half-hearted protest, then pushed herself against the pressure. The Lochend train came in ten minutes later, a clatter of sound and a flicker of passing lights as it headed, empty, back to the terminus.

Walter's hand eased out from the warmth and sneaked down to her knee. Without hesitation he brought it up the inside of her thigh, feeling the smooth nylon slide under his fingers. The girl stiffened, closed her legs and trapped his fingers. She pulled away.

'No, Wattie. Not here.'

'But there's nowhere else to go,' he protested. She had three brothers and a sister and parents who would kick up a stink if they thought she'd let Walter Dickson near her. He was an only child of parents who went to church every Sunday and would bring hell and damnation down on his head at the merest hint of anything pre-marital, and anyway, they did not approve of young Walter's choice of girlfriend.

'But we're still not doing it,' she said sharply.

'I've got something,' Walter responded earnestly.

'I don't care. Somebody might come.' She wriggled away from him and stood up to adjust her clothes. Inside she could feel the need begin to burgeon, but if she did it with Walter, then she wanted it to be nice, not on a slatted bench in a filthy waiting room which smelled of stale piss and smoke, and for some reason, freshly peeled oranges. He got to his feet and pulled her against him. She could feel him hard against her belly and the desire flared.

'No. Not here,' she protested, but it came out weakly, almost a whine.

'Where, then? We could go to Billy's.'

Billy was Walter's cousin, who lived in Miller Road, only two down from where young Neil Kennedy's family were existing in a miasma of grief and fading hope. He had a flat with a little boxroom. There was a possibility he'd let them in there for an hour.

'I don't know. I'd be embarrassed.'

'Don't worry. He'd never say anything. Billy's always got girls in there.'

She needed some more persuasion, so he kissed her again and

339

slid his hand inside the coat again, fumbling for the nipple. She stiffened against him, making little undulating motions with her hips. When he thought he'd worked at it enough he pulled back, still kneading with his right hand.

'How about it,' he said thickly.

'Alright,' she whispered back, voice now hitching with the rising urge. He gave her a quick hug that told her she'd made the right decision and they walked out of the waiting room onto the deserted stand. They made their way to where the exit ramp dived down in the centre of the raised area, between the two tracks. Out in the dark in the west, a train clattered in the distance. The couple were about to walk down the slope when a shadowy figure came towards them along the platform. Sandra heard the scrape of footfalls and twisted round, still holding onto Walter.

'What's that?'

Walter turned. A man was walking slowly, dragging his feet on the concrete close to the edge. He stumbled, caught his balance and came on.

'Just a drunk,' Walter said. 'Couldn't bite his finger by the look of him.'

The stranger came closer, lurching from side to side. They could hear him muttering to himself. Behind them the train rumbled louder as it crossed the bridge.

The man came staggering towards them and Sandra shrank back. Walter eased her to the side, leading her towards the exit.

'Nowhere else,' the stranger mumbled, weaving awkwardly. He looked as if he was blind. His coat flapped behind him and his clothes looked several sizes too large. His face was gaunt and haggard. 'Can't stop it. Nowhere else to go. Bastard.'

He lunged up towards the boy and girl, pale face agape.

'Bastard was *in* me.' The words came out in a blurt. 'Dirty now. Nothing left.'

'Get away,' Walter said. He held a hand up and pushed the weird stranger away. The man didn't even seem to notice. It was as if he hadn't even seen them.

'Don't want to,' he slobbered. 'Don't want to do it.' He stopped, swayed. 'Can't stop it. Nowhere else to go. Bastard.'

The train came roaring across the bridge in a rhythmic clatter

340

of wheels, the night mail from Mallaig away up in the north, nearing the end of its run down through mountains and moors on the West Highland Line.

In the cab of the diesel, Tom Middleton was leaned against the window, peering ahead through the viewhole, one brawny hand curled on the dead man's handle. The lights of the station hove into view. It was close on midnight and the lights were all on green as they should be. On the midday run, if he was driving, he'd hit the whistle to let the train scream through, but at night, it was against the rules, unless he spotted something on the track. The first lights of the platform flickered past, then something black fluttered right in front of the train. There was a very muffled *flump* and something flew past the window. A high scream sounded mutely then dopplered away as the train thundered past the station. The engine was well beyond the east slope of the platform by the time Tom reacted. He lifted his hand from the lever and the brakes bit. He could feel the wheels grind against the track, then his whole body was thrown forward against the plate and the cabin was filled by the screeching sound of distressed metal. The train shuddered on, the carriages slamming against the buffers, and careered in ever slowing progression as far as the automated signal box, almost a quarter of a mile along the track.

The scarecrow man had reeled away when Walter had pushed him, oblivious to his surroundings. He turned and they got a look at his face. It was completely devoid of expression, the slack, sagging face of a dead man. The night train had come thundering into the light behind him and an odd grimace had contorted the man's face.

His eyes opened wide and his wet mouth had closed. He turned away from them and took two faltering steps forward. The noise of the train was almost deafening, but Sandra clearly heard the man shout.

'No. I don't *want* . . .'

And then he was running forward on the edge, too close to the lip. He leapt out over the track, both hands stretched out at his sides like a figure on a crucifix, and the train smashed into him with a sickening sound.

Walter's hot desire collapsed. Sandra's urge evaporated in that single second.

Everything happened in slow motion. The man was in the act of leaping, coat flapping behind him, his white hands out as if to embrace a lover. The train caught him full on the body. Something flew off and tumbled into the air, whirling over their heads. The stranger was thrown forward. They followed his progress in the fragment of time it took for the train to rocket past. He was up over the platform, tumbling and twisting like nothing human, like a bunch of rags, then he was down. The huge wheels whirred on and over. They couldn't possibly have heard anything, but both of them later swore that when the wheels ran over him, there was a crunching sound. They heard it in their dreams for weeks after that.

The train crashed onwards with a rumble-and-thump as the wheels racketted on the joins.

'Jesus fu . . .' Walter said. He took a step forward, another two steps back, then went round in a complete circle, still holding onto the girl, who was completely rigid, both hands up at her face. Above them, something thumped onto the sloping roof. He looked up in time to see an object strike the old gutter then tumble to the ground. It hit the concrete with a solid thud.

'Did you see . . .' Walter began again. He turned to Sandra, who was still standing motionless, mouth open, eyes bugging out. 'He just jumped. Jeez . . . He bloody well . . .'

Sandra slowly started to move, like a sleepwalker coming out of a dream. Her hands turned, thumbs out, palms up and she swivelled her head towards Walter. He was still doing his weird little dance of complete and utter indecision when she finally spoke.

'Blood. It's his blood,' she whispered incredulously.

Walter took a step towards her. Her hands were still out, but they were shaking violently as if she had a severe case of palsy. She slowly brought them down and showed them to Walter. They were red with blood. Then she looked at her sleeves and the front of her coat. There were huge splatters all down one side. On her shoulder, there was a thick red gobbet of something the same colour, but which didn't look like blood at all.

'Walter,' she whimpered. 'Oh, Walter, I'm covered in *blood*.'

He seemed to snap out of his indecision. He reached out and took her by the arm, not wanting to get too close to all the blood,

342

not realising that the side of his coat was also saturated. He pulled her away from the platform, turning her round to go down the ramp to the exit, feeling the nerves kick and jitter behind his knees. He just wanted away from there. She allowed herself to be led meekly, still holding her hands out. They went round the pillar at the end of the barrier. The thing that had fallen from the roof was lying at their feet. He looked down and looked away before it registered, but Sandra's senses were tuned right up to perfect pitch. She stopped dead, mumbled something, then fainted clean away. He caught her just before she hit the ground, bending down to scoop her flopping weight up into his arms. When he was still crouched, his face was only two feet from the pale hand which lay palm up, fingers half-curled, still inside the torn sleeve of coat. In that instant of time, when the whole world had taken on the peculiar sluggishness and everything had gained the sharpness of supernatural clarity, he noticed the little bird on the end of the second hand, walking round the rim of the watch still strapped to the bony wrist.

'Woodstock,' he said, very clearly, though he could not remember the name of the dog in the baseball cap whose face was printed on the flat dial. He lifted the girl into a carry-hold and walked down the ramp, through the tunnel and out into the street. He made it across to the Horse Bar, shouldered the door open, put the girl down on the bench seat nearest the door, turned round to speak, and vomited the pizza with anchovies she'd paid for after the cinema.

The two drunks at the bar turned round and gawped stupidly.

'He's had enough,' one said to the other, and they both dissolved into a helpless fit of giggling.

Jack Fallon was in a state of complete confusion when he left Lorna Breck's house an hour after midnight. He was nonplussed, baffled, bamboozled. His mind was reeling from conviction to uncertainty and back to convinced certainty. He had to go and sit in the car for five minutes before he felt clear-headed enough to drive.

Their roles had reversed without any warning. She had been in a state of complete panic, bordering on collapse. Her whole body had been trembling and her face was slack and drained. Then he'd held her hands and it was as if something had jolted between

343

them and sent a shock wave through her nerves. When she'd started to speak, her voice had lost its brittle edge and she'd spoken to him like a mother comforting a child.

'I knew there was something when I first saw you,' she said. 'I didn't realise what it was. When you helped me in the street, I sensed something, but it felt like danger, like death. That's why I couldn't speak. I was so scared. I though you were a part of it.'

'Part of what?'

'Of what's happening in this town,' Lorna said, still holding his hands tightly.

'But I am part of it,' he said wearily. There were too many things going in. He felt like a circuit that was in danger of overloading. Thoughts were sparking and jumping, half formed, hard to catch. 'I want to stop it.'

'I know. I know now. But then I sensed something terrible from you, just for a second, but when you helped me into the shop, you were so gentle that I knew it couldn't be you.'

'I don't understand any of this,' he admitted.

'Me neither, but I'm trying to,' Lorna said earnestly. 'I really am. I can't help any of this. My granny said I had a better gift than her because I was a seventh child.'

'You've got family?'

'Four brothers. There were two more, twins, but they died at birth.'

'I've heard all that about seventh children. I don't believe it.'

'And neither do I. But I have to believe in this, because I can't escape from it. It's as if something is locked into my head, like a radar or something. I didn't realise until the fire that I'd been seeing it *before*.'

'Before what?'

'Before the fire. Those terrible dreams, really awful ones. I kept seeing those people in a room, all of them around a table. Not good people, *sick* folk. They were doing something and I didn't know what it was, but I knew it was wrong. Then the room went dark and something came.'

'Something came?' Jack realised he was repeating the last words of her sentences too often.

'That's the only way I can describe it. Something came into the room in the dark. They brought it. They called it up. I don't know what they did, or how they did it, but they called it up and it was inside them. It was cold, terribly cold, like ice inside them, because they had opened themselves up and called it.'

'And then what happened?'

'It's a bad thing. Evil. They didn't know what it was, and I don't either. But it came out and I could feel the bad in it. It was like sin. It was dark and the thing came and everybody started screaming and it was coming to get me and I was screaming too and we fled down the stairs.'

'Can you describe this place?'

'An old room. There were lots of ornaments and there was an old woman. She was small, with a funny accent, like German or something. They all took the cards off the table first and then they put their hands on a stone and the wind came blowing through them all and they brought the thing into them.'

In his mind's eye, Jack saw a group of people round the table at Marta Herkik's home. Was that how it started? As soon as he thought that, he realised he was starting to believe what the girl said, then realised he'd already started to believe it before now.

'And what you said before, about me. Where does that come from?'

'I don't know. It was like when I held hands with poor Agnes. It was like part of her came into me and then I could see it. Her children were dying and I could feel the fear and pain. I could see it there too.'

'You're saying this thing was *there*?'

She nodded placidly, eyes still fixed intently on his. 'I didn't know then, but I'm sure now. That was one of the first times I'd seen it. It was just a shadow, but it was moving among the smoke. The baby saw it and she started to scream.'

'So why didn't you mention this before?'

'I thought I was dreaming. I didn't know what I was seeing. And anyway, who would have believed me? I didn't even believe it myself.'

'And what you said, about my girl?'

'I don't know how that happens either, but it happens. It's from you. It's like you've got this big charge stored up inside you, like a battery. That's what it felt like, what it feels like now.'

She squeezed his hands in hers. The touch was warm and gentle.

345

'There's a big dam in your heart. You know it too. All the pressure has built up because you can't let the sorrow out. You've a good heart, Mr Fallon.'

'Jack,' he said, almost automatically. It was impossible to sit in front of this girl with her rumpled dressing gown, holding his hand, and having her call him mister.

'I know,' she said, with a hint of a smile. 'You've a good heart, Jack. It's the only good thing I've felt for a long time. But you have to let the pain go, and let them be at peace.'

'Tell me, then,' he said slowly. He suddenly felt very vulnerable, like a child faced with shadows in the night.

She closed her eyes, and stroked her thumbs down the space between his own thumbs and fingers. Her brow furrowed in concentration.

'Guilt,' she finally said in a whisper. 'Guilt and pain. The pain is yours. Jewellery. I see jewellery.'

'Jewellery?' he repeated automatically.

'Yes. No, jewels. Sparkly jewels, all bright.'

Jack's heart kicked over slowly.

'Jules. Sparkly jewels. I wrote that on her birthday card,' he said, voice catching. 'Her name was Julie.'

'And your wife. I see sunshine. You called her that?'

'Her name was Rae.'

She frowned harder. 'You have a picture in your head. You've carried it around with you all the time and you take it out and show it to yourself. But it's a trick. It's not real.'

Lorna's voice rose. 'It's not true. You could not have helped them. Nobody could. They didn't see it coming. And then there was nothing at all, only peace. They are at peace now, and you can let them go.'

Jack's heart did another lazy lurch inside his chest, as if it had held itself still and then did a double beat at once.

'They want you to be happy,' Lorna said. 'It's true. I trust you, Jack Fallon. You trust me.'

Close on one o'clock in a bitterly cold night, Jack gunned the car up the hill the whole length of Clydeshore Avenue, driving under the bare, spreading sycamores. He reached the top, changed gear and sped down the slope, past the old cemetery. The river mist lay in layers, like the set of an old horror film,

346

oozing round the ancient tombstones on the other side of the wall. Jack was going too fast. On the turn, his back tyre slithered on black ice and he felt the rear swing out. He drove into it, headed for the brick wall on the river side of Keelyard Road, then the tyres bit and he fishtailed the car back onto the straight before he slowed down on the dark road and stopped the engine. His heart was beating much too fast.

'Christ,' he breathed. His stomach had gone all shivery in the aftermath of the adrenalin hit. 'I must be off my head,' he said to himself.

He sat for a moment, started the engine, drove for twenty yards and a picture of little Julie's face came swimming out of the dark and danced in front of his eyes. She was smiling at him. The memory was hop-skipping on a sunny street, far from this chill winter, holding her mother's hand. He'd last seen them like that down on the shore, picking up shells. The vision was so strong that he almost waved to them. They were not lying in pools of blood, writhing in agony, cursing him for not being there, for not helping them.

They were smiling at him on a sunny day.

It was the first time since they'd gone that he'd seen them like that in his mind.

He stamped on the brake and switched the engine off. The picture faded from the forefront of his mind and Jack Fallon leaned his head down on his arms. He screwed his eyes up against the smarting of sudden tears, holding himself tight. He sat there for a long time, seeing the street lights through a wavery film as the pain and anguish and sorrow he'd held back, dammed up for all those years, suddenly breached the walls, and flooded out.

Some time after that, the headlamps of his car came on again, picking out the filigree of the winter mist, and his car came slowly over the old bridge and back into the centre of the town.

23

The station was awash with light when Jack got there. One of the patrol cars shot out of the exit, blue light flashing, though its siren was switched off. Jack parked quickly, went in the back door, and headed straight for the washroom, where he splashed cold water on his face until he felt as if he could face people again.

'You look as if you've got flu,' Bobby Thomson said when he leaned over the desk. 'Your eyes are all red.'

'Must be an allergy,' Jack replied, forcing a grin. 'Pollen or something.' Policemen didn't cry, and if they ever did, other policemen were the last folk to understand. 'What's happening now?'

'I was about to call you. You must be a mind-reader or something.'

'What?' Bobby Thomson's words immediately brought back a picture of Lorna Breck's earnest and gentle face.

'You coming in tonight. There's been another one.'

'What, a snatch?'

'No. Some nutter's been smeared by the mail train. Looks like a suicide. There's an ambulance heading round to the station, but the word is it's a hamburger job.'

'Bobby,' Jack said, with mock severity. 'A bit of decorum.' The sergeant grinned. He'd seen it all in thirty years.

The station was two minutes away, and it was quicker to walk than drive. As he turned out of the rear entrance of the station, Jack could see the electric wink of the emergency cars. He crossed the road, walking quickly to the old tunnel entrance and headed up the ramp.

Bobby Thomson had been right. It was indeed a hamburger job. Jack hoped that there was enough left of the body on the line to make identification possible, though it did not look as if it would be easy.

The ambulance teams were down on the tracks. One policeman was retching drily over the banister of the exit-slope.

He turned round and Jack recognised young Gordon Pirie, who'd thrown up down at the Castle when they'd found Annie Eastwood's corpse and had to be given a day off duty. He wasn't having a pleasant introduction to policing.

'Two witnesses,' the rookie's partner said. 'Sandra Mitchell and Walter Dickson. They said the man jumped in front of the train. They're still in the Horse Bar. Somebody's coming to take them round to the station for statements. Driver didn't see a thing. They're sending down a replacement to take the engine away when we're finished. Looks like it'll need a good hose down.'

Jack strode to the edge of the platform. Somebody had rigged a light and the white beam picked out everything in detail. The broken, slumped figure did not look like a man. The coat was spread out on either side, with a wide rip from hem to shoulder, and it glistened wetly under the lights. What Jack assumed to be a leg was pointed in the wrong direction, slanted over the man's chest, one shoeless foot resting on his shoulder. The face was a ruin of white bone and dark blood.

'Bet his name's O'Day,' Jack said. One of the men on the track turned up from the body.

'Don't think so, sir. We've got his wallet. Says he's a Derek Elliot. He's that bloke who runs the estate agents, according to his cards.'

Instantly Jack recalled what Andy Toye had said. The words on the wall could have been an anagram. Andy had that kind of lateral-thinking mind. He'd suggested he should be looking for people whose names began with the two missing letters, although the professor had been quick to point out it was only an idea.

'Elliot,' Jack said through clenched teeth.

If Andy Toye was right, the next man *had* to be O'Day.

The policemen on the track, helped by the ambulance team, managed to get the mess of the body into a bag, and hauled it onto the platform just as Ralph Slater came running breathlessly up the subway ramp.

'Sorry, Chief. Just got the call,' he said, gasping. He was toting his black scene-of-crime equipment case.

'I think we got the sixth one.'

'Huh?'

'From the Herkik case,' Jack said softly, keeping it between them. 'Looks like he took a dive in front of the Mallaig express.'

'Did a human Garfield?' Ralph asked. Jack grimaced.

'Got that one from John McColl,' Ralph said, grinning. 'He's got a way with words.' Despite himself, Jack felt a smile struggle through at the visual image the phrase conjured up.

'I'll speak to the driver. You confirm the ID and get the prints.' He turned away then came back to Ralph. 'That might help,' he said, pointing down at the dirty concrete close to the station wall. The young policeman was just levering himself upright when he turned and saw where Jack was pointing. Immediately he doubled over the safety barrier, sides convulsing in spastic heaves.

'He'll turn himself inside out,' Ralph said. He walked forward and picked up the hand which still lay palm up.

'Remarkable,' Ralph called over. 'His watch is still going.'

The young policeman moaned sickly.

Tom Middleton had nothing helpful to say. His face had lost all its colour and he'd the look of a man who's woken up to find a corpse and a bloodstained knife lying beside him. Anybody would have thought he'd made the train jump the tracks and had gone, hauling on the steam whistle, chasing after the man to grind him under the wheels. He kept shaking his head as if denying what had happened. One of the ambulancemen gave him something to drink and the engine driver spilled most of it on the way to his mouth.

'I saw him before he hit but I didn't know what it was,' the man said. 'It was only something black. Honest, I couldn't have stopped it. Damned thing takes three hundred yards at only thirty.'

'Did he jump?' the policeman was asking.

'Must have. Never saw anybody else. The whole train's in a mess. I thought he might have still been stuck there, but he must have gone under.'

The driver kept shaking his head in disbelief while the policeman took notes, then he seemed to come round a little and he grabbed the other man by the sleeve of his tunic.

'I've only got three weeks to go before I retire. I never had an accident in forty year, not one. I got certificates to prove it.'

350

'Yes, sir,' the policeman said patiently, easing his arm away, but Tom grabbed it and pulled it close, unaware of what he was doing.

'So why did the bastard pick *my* train?'

'I can't honestly say,' the constable said civilly. He didn't take offence, at least not while his superiors were watching.

Jack pulled his coat tight against the cold and went down the subway, crossed the road and into the Horse Bar, where a young woman constable sat with her arm round a younger girl who was snuffling into a crumpled tissue. Beside her, a boy of eighteen or so, with short cut hair slicked back with gel, was staring into the far distance just above the table.

He sat down and introduced himself. The boy nodded dumbly. The girl sobbed steadily, and for a second he was reminded of Lorna Breck, only an hour before. 'Give us some coffees across here,' he called out to the barman who was leaning against the gantry, boredly cleaning a glass.

'We're shut,' the skinny fellow called back. His hair was as black as Jack's, but it hung down in lank strings over his forehead.

Jack got up and walked to the bar. He put both hands on the surface and leaned across, towering over the man.

'I've got no time for any lip, and I'm in no mood for backchat,' he said, staring into the barman's eyes. 'Get some coffees. Now.' The man nodded. Jack went back to the seated group. The small man shrugged and hit the button on the coffee-maker.

The boy was quite lucid when he spoke, but his voice had the shaky hesitation of someone in shock.

'I thought he was drunk,' he said. 'He came along the platform, mumbling away. He looked as if he was on drugs. All starey-eyed and that. He came right up to us and I pushed him away. He was scaring Sandra.'

'You pushed him?'

'Yes. But not hard. He was saying something.'

'Like what?'

'He kept swearing. Saying "bastard".'

'At you?'

'I don't think so. I think he was talking to himself. Then he said he didn't want to do it.'

351

'That was exactly it?' Jack asked. The boy nodded.

'"Bastard was in me," that's what he said an' all. Said he was dirty now.'

Jack took a note of that. It didn't make much sense, but it seemed important.

'Then what?'

'Then he shoved past us. The train was just coming into the station. He didn't even stop, he ran out and jumped right in front of it. Jeez-o, you should have seen it. He went right up in the air and a bit of him came off. His hand. I saw it. Then he went down and the wheels came right over him. Sandra here just fainted. I had to carry her down.'

The barman brought the coffees across and set them down with a surly clatter. Jack spooned sugar into the four cups and shoved two of them across to the girl and the woman constable, who nodded her head and gave him a grateful smile. Walter picked his up and started to sip.

'What's that wee dog called in Charley Brown?' he asked vaguely.

'Snoopy,' the policewoman said.

'That was it. He was wearing a Snoopy watch, with the wee bird walking round the edges. It was still going. Even when his hand was off, it was still going.'

Big tears welled up in the boy's eyes and the girl started to cry again, great racking sobs that looked as if they would take a while to subside. The woman pulled her close, letting her lean against her uniform, and patted her shoulder comfortingly.

The mangled and eviscerated body was finally carried down to the ambulance. The ticket collector asked Ralph what he should do about the mess on the lines.

'Put some sand down,' was the only advice he could offer.

Back at the station mortuary, Ralph had the grizzly job of taking prints from the fingers of the dead man, including the five on the hand, now a pale grey, still in its sleeve. By the time Jack came back, it was getting on to two in the morning, and by then Ralph could confirm that yes, the suicide had laid prints all over Marta Herkik's table.

'So now we have to find O'Day,' Jack said. 'Send a team of people round to this guy's place. Usual statements from relatives and search the house for anything that will give us another connection.'

'Do you know what's going on?'

'I'm getting close,' Jack admitted.

'Want to let me in on it?'

Jack looked down at Ralph, who at six feet was a few inches shorter, though in his old tweed jacket and thick herringbone coat he looked almost as broad.

'I do, but I can't. You'd never believe me.'

Ralph gave him a searching look. 'I suppose it's got something to do with the Breck girl? Is she starting to talk sense?'

'She might be, but whether it really makes sense is anybody's guess.'

Jack walked off and went to his office, where he stood staring at a map of the town. After a while, he picked up the internal phone and dialled Bobby Thomson's number. There were sixteen men on night duty, plus the ones who were still out on the beat, and, Jack realised, that wasn't enough. He'd get operations to call them with instructions, and in the morning he'd fax a request to headquarters for extra men. The policemen trooped into the operations room and after a scuffling of chairs, sat attentively.

'I've a feeling it might strike tonight,' he said. He did have a feeling that it would, though he had an even nastier feeling, worse, a near-certainty, that it had already struck, after listening to Lorna Breck's anguished voice on the telephone.

'I need extra work on specific areas tonight,' he told the group. 'Forget about padlock rattling on River Street and the rest of the shops. If there's anybody breaking into places, then it's their lucky night. We'll catch them another time.'

He approached the large-scale map, showing the streets and vennels and alleys of the old centre of town.

'Concentrate on these areas,' he said, ringing them one by one.

'Latta Court and the nearby blocks. The Town Hall. Castlebank Church. The Distillery.' Each of the spots was punctuated by a quick, almost savage circling motion of his hand. 'Places where people come and go at night. Anywhere high. This bastard *climbs*.'

He turned round to face the men. They all gazed back.

353

'He doesn't like to leave traces, so he climbs up things. That's where we'll catch him. I don't want you guys racing around with the lights and sirens on. We'll have to do this softly-softly.'

When he'd finished, the men stood up and shuffled out and onto the streets.

Jack sat for another half an hour, trying to puzzle out, from the description Lorna Breck had given him, where the next killings would be, or had been. It would have been much better, despite her lilting highland accent which softened out her words, if she'd been a local girl. Then she'd know.

At the moment, nobody knew.

Jack cleared his desk and went home to bed, almost too tired to think.

24

The alarm woke him from a deep sleep while it was still dark. Thursday morning. Jack crawled out of bed, groping for his dressing gown, feeling drugged and dopey. The kitchen was cold and the glass on the window to the back garden was glittering with a latticework of frost. A faint sliver of moon on the horizon sent a glimmer of silver light onto the snow which had stacked up against the fence. The garden fork was still stuck into the ground, though only the haft was now showing. No birds sang.

Tea and toast was all he could face. Jack felt he could have done with another six hours' sleep, but at least he *had* slept some, and amazingly, the night had not been riven by the dreams for the first time in a long time. While he took a hot shower, he thought about what he'd have to do today. The patrols had picked up nothing, or he'd have got a call within the last six hours. As he soaped himself down, he was thinking about the suicides.

There was a pattern to them. They were all linked, so far tenuously, but definitely. They were connected to the murder in Cairn House that seemed to have taken place months ago, instead of mere weeks. They had all been there, which meant they were involved, to some extent, in the killing. Whether they had done it, either singly or in a group, was another matter. So far the deaths had come within days, even hours of abductions, strange deaths following the bizarre, incomprehensible taking of children, if young Carol Howard could be included as a child.

There were conundrums within riddles. Puzzles inside a maze.

The possibility of post-hypnotic suggestion crossed his mind. It had been the stuff of a thousand detective novels. The evil doctor and the mesmerised puppets ordered to do the evil bidding then instructed to negate themselves after the event.

But if that was the case, who was giving the instructions? And why?

And why had it all started with Marta Herkik? Jack decided

he'd give Andy Toye another call. There must be something missing from the puzzle. Some piece that would fit with everything else and connect all the other pieces and point the finger.

He came out of the shower and scrubbed himself dry with a crisp towel. The kettle had boiled and the toast was standing to attention in the toaster. He buttered some, made a cup of tea and discovered he'd developed a surprising appetite. He made another two slices, wolfed them down, and felt able to face the day.

'You're looking a lot better,' Julia told him.

'I managed to get some sleep. It works wonders.'

'You're overdoing things as usual,' she said with sisterly, almost motherly concern.

'That's because I've got plenty to overdo. It keeps me awake.'

'You should give yourself a break,' she chided.

'I will. I've promised Davy I'll take him up Langmuir Hills at the weekend. See if we can spot some mountain hares in the snow.'

'He'd love that. I hate keeping him cooped up all week.'

'Just so long as you do keep him inside. This thing will stop eventually, and then we'll only have the normal bunch of flashers and Peeping Toms to worry about.'

'Do you think you'll get him?'

Jack put his arm around her shoulder and gave her an encouraging hug.

'Course I will. That's what I'm overdoing.'

At the school, Davy went through his litany. Yes, he'd stay in school. Yes, he'd wait for his mother. No, he wouldn't talk to strange people. As he ran off past the pinch-faced mothers who were reluctant to leave the school gates, Jack felt a warm surge of love for the boy. He and Julia were the only family he had left.

Down at the station, there were no urgent messages. The sky in the east was showing a glimmer of dawn, and there was a slough of dampness in the air.

Both Ralph and John were in the operations room adding to the mass of information on the computers. Jack accepted a plastic cup of coffee, sat down and the phone rang. The day got worse from that moment.

Rolling Stock was supposed to open at nine, but Jim Deakin, the manager, who lived in Lochend, had a job getting his car started in the cold. It had finally coughed into life after he'd run the battery flat and had to push it forty yards to a slope on the road where it kick-started at the third attempt. When he got to the parts store, the rest of the staff were standing in a huddle outside the locked doors, swinging their hands under their armpits in energetic self-hugs, trying to keep warm.

'Sorry, guys, car problems,' he said, forcing his way through the small group of teenage girls and boys, jangling his bunch of keys. He slipped the lock, pushed the outer door, scooped up a small pile of mail and walked through to where an inner door kept the cold out. Everybody followed him through.

'Hey, it's freezing in here,' one of the lads who serviced the bikes piped up.

'Put the heating on, Doreen,' the manager told one of the girls. He opened the door to his own office and slid out of his heavy sheepskin car coat. He unlocked the safe and took out the rolls of change for the tills. The lights on the main store came on with a stuttering fluorescent flicker. One of the girls stuck a tape in the deck and loud music started blaring out of the speakers.

Jim Deakin brought the tray of cash round and started filling the register drawer. Doreen came back from the switch room, slid into her swivel seat and started putting on enough lipstick to last a week. She pouted into a small compact mirror and Jim thought she looked as if she'd eaten raw liver.

Just at that moment there was a shout from up at the back of the store. One of the lads, now in his sky-blue overalls, came pounding down between the aisles of oil cans and de-icer sprays.

'Hey, Jim. There's some bikes missing.'

'So find them,' the manager said, rattling coins into their doo-cots.

'No. They're gone. Three Raleighs and an Apollo.'

'How can they have gone? Are you taking the mickey?'

'Course not.' Donny Craig had left school at the same time as young Carol Howard. They'd even sat next to each other in maths, though she'd showed more aptitude than he had. His interest was bikes. He could repair and service them, change tyres and refit drive sprockets from dawn until dusk, which was what he was paid for. He was also very good at it, because he knew his bikes. 'They were there last night in their stands, and now they're away.'

He went back up the passage between the shelves. Deakin followed him, and after a few seconds, Doreen finished her morning make-up, slid off her seat, and came up behind them.

'Look,' the boy was pointing to the empty brackets. 'That's where they were.'

Doreen came up to stand beside the manager. She made a shivering sound. 'It's really cold in here. Where's that draught coming from?'

The manager turned round, about to tell her to go back to her post at the till, when the fuzzy daub of day-glo paint on the wall caught his eye.

'What the hell is that?' he barked, striding across past the spaces where the bikes had stood. Then he noticed something else further to the left, closer to the back of the shop.

'And that?' he said pointing. Doreen followed his pointing finger.

'Somebody's painted the bloody wall.'

Some distance from the yellow smudge of spray paint, the breeze-block facing was smeared and smattered in dark red. It looked as if someone had thrown several cans of primer right at the wall.

'Oh, for heaven's sake,' Jim said, standing hands on hips.

'Look up there,' Doreen said. Everybody turned, raised their eyes and saw the gaping skylight. A rope dangled down and looped itself round the cross-spars.

'Bloody hell,' Jim mouthed. 'We've been turned over.'

He strode briskly and officiously towards the wall where the paint had been splattered, taking small, annoyed steps when his heel skidded on a splash that stained the tiled flooring. His legs went up in the air and the manager came down with a thump, one hand sweeping a dozen aerosol cans from the nearest shelf.

Doreen tittered and Donny Craig was diplomatic enough to turn away to hide his grin. Jim Deakin got to his feet. There was a damp stain on his trousers from backside to heel. He glared at Donny then rounded on Doreen.

'What the hell are you laughing at?' he blazed. 'Go and call the police.'

Just beside him, one of the round children's helmets, as stridently yellow as the paint on the wall, lay on its side a few feet away. In a temper, the manager took a swing at it with his foot. Instead of the light plastic dome flying off like a football into the air, his toe connected with a solid crack. The helmet rolled a few yards towards Doreen. Deakin yelled out in surprise at the sudden pain flaring in his toes. He started to do a little hopping dance, cursing vehemently. He slipped again on the slithery patch of red and went down again with a clatter. His thick, heavy-rimmed glasses flew off and skittered away.

Donny Craig burst into helpless laughter. Doreen was holding her sides and bent double.

Then she let out a piercing scream which soared up to the roof and completely drowned out the noise the manager was making.

For a second the boy though she was hysterical with laughter. He was holding his knees with both hands. He looked up at her and saw, not mirth, but utter shock stretched across the girl's face.

Still giggling, he came across to her and reached out to touch her shoulder. She jumped back from him as if she'd been scalded. All the time, her squeal went on, an uncontrollable and incoherent babble of sound. She was doing a jittery little dance, as if she was standing in a nest of ants and trying to stamp them all to death. All the time she was pointing down at the floor.

Donny looked down and in that moment he felt the blood drain out of his head. There was a ringing in his ears and the whole store seemed to wobble around him.

A pair of light blue eyes stared up at him from inside the biker's helmet. The strap was snugged tight under the chin, keeping the mouth closed. There was not a mark on the face, but underneath it there was a stringy congealed patch of red from which a thin, ribbed tube protruded. It looked not unlike the plastic pipes which fitted on the little hand-pumps Rolling Stock sold for syphoning petrol, but instinctively Donny Craig realised it was not. Although he had never seen a human windpipe in his life, he knew exactly what it was.

He backed away, his face now paler than the grey one which stared at him with dead eyes on the floor.

'Ung,' he managed to say after several seconds. Jim Deakin

was standing on one foot, holding his other ankle in both hands, weaving for balance and still swearing comprehensively.

'Suppose you think it's bloody funny,' he said when the swearing stopped.

'Ung,' Donny repeated. His stomach was now going into spasms, trying to squeeze its contents upwards. The boy swallowed hard, took another two steps backwards and bumped into Doreen, who was now sliding sideways against a fortuitously positioned pile of car mats.

'And what's up with that silly cow?' the manager demanded to know. He came limping across to them. 'Look at the state of me. And I've probably broken my toes.'

'Jim,' the boy finally managed to say. 'Look.'

'What a bloody mess,' the manager was saying. 'Come on Doreen. Get on the phone and get the police round here. Damned vandals, they should all be hung.'

'No, Jim. You have to come and see,' Donny said. His voice had gone very soft, every word slow and dreamy.

'What is it now?' Deakin demanded. He hobbled across, Donny pointed, and the manager shoved his glasses onto his face with an irritated jerk. He peered down.

'What on earth?' he said incredulously. 'Is this some sort of a . . .?' He turned to Donny, looked at him strangely, bent down again as if to confirm what his eyes had shown him and came back up again.

Without looking back, he pointed at the helmet and the face inside it, wagging his finger in emphasis.

'It's a . . .'

Donny nodded blankly.

His boss turned and walked slowly down the aisle, shaking his head as if by denying it he could make the thing go away. When he got to the end of the aisle he turned and looked again. The helmet was still there. Donny was standing stock-still, hands at his sides. Doreen slowly slid the last few inches as the car mats gave way under her weight and they flopped to the floor with the girl on top of them.

Sadie McLean, a middle-aged woman with blue-grey hair in tight permed curls, came walking briskly out of the staff room. 'What's all the noise about?' she called out. 'I've just made the tea.'

Jim Deakin came walking slowly towards her.

'Want a cup, Jim?' Sadie asked brightly. He shook his head and continued to shake it as he walked past her. She watched him turn, shake his head again.

'You sure?'

'No.' He came slowly towards her. 'Sadie, there's been a wee accident. Could you call the police?'

'Accident? What? Where?' The woman turned around and saw Doreen lying on the pile of mats.

'What's happened to her?'

'Nothing. Just call the police, would you. Tell them there's been a break-in and an accident. Tell them it's very urgent.'

The squad car took fifteen minutes to arrive. Young Gordon Pirie, Levenford's newest recruit, should have gone off duty at eight, but he was grateful for the fact that there seemed to be an unlimited amount of overtime available in the last week or so, even if it meant being out at all hours of the night and attending gruesome scenes where the bodies were in pieces, not like he'd ever seen in all the real police movies. He was still a bit embarrassed about the night before, but in the cold light of day, he knew he could face anything. Policemen, he'd convinced himself, got hardened to that sort of thing. He drove into the spacious, almost completely empty car park, pulled up beside Rolling Stock and adjusted his helmet as he manfully shoved on the door.

The manager was leaning against the cash register, whey-faced. Close by, a woman was fussing around a young girl who was sitting on the floor, her shoulders heaving in violent, but strangely silent sobs.

'Good morning, sir,' Gordon said with brisk efficiency. 'What appears to be the problem?'

'There's been a break-in and a burglary,' Jim Deakin said lethargically.

'I see, sir. And when did you discover it?' Gordon pulled out his notebook and began writing.

'This morning.'

'Oh, tell him about the thing,' Sadie snapped.

'Oh yes,' Deakin said, nodding. 'I'll have to show you.'

Gordon put his notebook in his pocket and followed the small, portly manager up the space between the shelves. His eager policeman's eye noticed the daub of paint on the wall and the long vertical splashes above it.

'Wonder how they got up there,' he mused.

'Here it is,' Jim Deakin said, pointing down.

For a second, Gordon Pirie thought it was a plastic model, a mannequin's head, used to display the helmets. He lowered himself slowly to hunker down, stopped when he had almost got there, then jumped back up to his feet with a gasp of alarm. His foot slipped and his toe nudged the helmet, which rocked slowly back and forth, the dead eyes scanning the ceiling in an eternal stare.

Across from them, there was a door with a small stylised figure of a man stuck to the surface.

Gordon made it there in six big strides. He strong-armed it open, crashed through to the washroom and donated his breakfast to the sink.

Beside him a young man in dungarees was just rising from a leaning position, as if he'd been washing his hair. He heard Gordon's heavy splatter and sickly moan, and promptly dived his own head back into the sink and retched explosively.

Five minutes after that, Jack Fallon got the call. In ten minutes Rolling Stock was busier than it had ever been at that time of a winter's morning.

Ralph Slater was directing Ronnie Jeffrey's camera. There were two detectives up on ladders, taking samples of the splashes on the wall. A third was up on the cross-spars close to the roof.

'Looks like they came in here, sir?' he called down. 'That's a tow-rope. Two of them tied together.'

A wheaten-faced Gordon Pirie was taking statements from the staff. Somebody had put an empty cardboard box over the head in the helmet.

'What a mess,' Jack said. 'Maybe we should have done some padlock rattling last night.'

'I don't think we could have stopped this. The doors were locked. Nobody would have seen a thing.'

'And our men were looking in all the wrong places,' Jack said, feeling disgusted with himself.

From above, a voice called down.

'Sir, I think you should come up here and have a look.'

Jack went to the ladder they'd borrowed from the do-it-yourself store. It was a three-section affair, stretching up to the beams. He started up reluctantly and when he got halfway there, he felt the nauseous vertigo loop inside him. The ground was a long way down. For a few seconds he paused to settle his breathing, holding on white-knuckled to the uprights, then continued his ascent. It was difficult for him to scramble through the tangle of struts. From this height, the floor seemed impossibly far away and he tried not to look down.

'Over here, sir,' the detective said. He was standing on a beam with his head sticking out of the top of the roof. Jack reached him cautiously, held onto the lip and craned out. The roof sloped gently away. A few yards from the opening, where the window was lying back on its hinges, four bikes lay in a sprawl, wheels shiny and handlebars gleaming in the dawn light.

A big square hole on the ground. There's something lying there. Like a bike. Yes. It is a bike. It went down through there. I can hear it, like an animal.

Lorna's voice, sizzling with panic, came back to him with utter clarity.

A big square hole in the ground. It was a big square hole in the *roof*. No wonder she couldn't recognise it. Somehow, in that weird second sight she had, that sixth sense, she had *seen* this.

And she had seen more.

A cellar. Somewhere big and dark. There's shelves. It has one of them. Two of them. Oh, there's blood all over, and the smell is choking.

In the light of the early day, it was big but not dark. But there were shelves, going from floor to dizzying roof height. Jack closed his eyes and tried to picture this from the outside, and at night. It would *look* like a cellar. And oh, there was blood all over. Not paint, not car primer for rusty old jalopies, but thick, congealing blood which had dribbled in runnels down the walls. The smell was bad enough. It must have been throat-gagging.

The bikes in their forlorn heap angled their wheels up to the sky, thick tyres for bouncing along forest tracks and for whizzing along with the wind in your hair on sunny Sunday afternoons. Boys' things.

Oh, Mr Fallon, they're only boys.

While he stared out at the sky, Jack envisaged the nightmare scene. Four boys, Lorna had said. Whoever he was, whatever *it* was had come in, probably through the open skylight, the way the boys had done.

Who were they? He'd find out soon enough, no doubt.

He, it, the killer had caught one of them – the one with the helmet on? Then the next. *The others had seen it.* They'd panicked. In his mind's eye, he could see their frantic scramble up the sides of the shelves, no ladders, just angled metal bars to hold onto. One pushing the other, crying, screaming, bawling for their mothers in the dark of the big gloomy store, while someone, some *thing* came at their backs, still wet and slimy from the blood of the others. Their feet would have slipped on the edges of the shelves, their fingers scrabbled for purchase, fear freezing their blood, freezing their muscles to turbid slowness. They'd have crawled and clambered, whimpering, struggling to breathe over the pounding of their hearts. Out through the window, one turning to help the other, with their pursuer hot at their backs. He could imagine the feeling of the boy inside, desperately hauling himself upwards, the other one dragging at his jacket, imagining the killer coming for him, close behind, maybe clattering across the rails.

Had it been like that?

He could hear her words loud, desperate, in the telephone, as if she were calling him now.

It has him. The other one is trying to pull him out. But it has him. I can see his face. His eyes are looking at me. He knows.

The running commentary of a nightmare.

Oh God. It's pulling him down. He can't hold on. He's crying. The pain in his leg. It's tearing him apart.

She'd seen it, that was for sure. There could be no other explanation. Four boys, she'd said, down in a cellar, through a hole in the ground which was a skylight in the roof. The bikes were lying there as she'd told him. Who would think of mountain bikes on a roof? Nobody. Not even Chief Inspector Jack Fallon. He'd sent the men out last night to probe into high places, knowing within himself that there would have been another disappearance. But they hadn't checked *this* high place. As elevations went, it was so low as to be negligible, probably not even visible from the spot he'd stood up on the roof of Castlebank Distillery. But it had been high enough.

'Something here,' the policeman said. Jack pulled his head in from the fresh air. He could smell the blood again. Down below, the ground seemed to sway and he had to hold on tightly as he turned.

'Blood here,' the man muttered. 'And here and here.' He gestured with a finger.

'And what's this?' He held on with his left hand while he reached out over a space with what Jack considered casual foolhardiness and drew up a dark piece of cloth which had been draped over a spar.

'Saturated,' the detective said.

'What have you got?'

'Denim. Looks like a pair of jeans. Or the leg of one. It's been ripped off.'

He turned round, letting go his grip as he did, as if he was only two feet from the ground instead of nearer forty. Jack's stomach tried to do a quick somersault then steadied itself.

'Blood all over the place,' the constable said.

The two of them headed back across the girders. One of Ralph's men met them at the edge of the spars where the ladder leaned and there was a moment of lurching vertigo as Jack squeezed past the man, who had his forensics equipment case slung over his shoulder. Jack made it slowly to the ground. Ralph was just rising from his haunches beside the head in the plastic helmet.

'What do you think?'

'Damned if I know,' Ralph said honestly. 'This took a lot of strength. It's not a clean cut, not like an axe or a machete, but it's near enough. Something hit this laddie one hell of a blow. Probably a single swipe. It came from the left.'

Ralph carefully turned the helmet round. The glazed, drying eyes panned Jack with their infinity stare. The face was strangely peaceful, in repose. On the left, just above the ear, the plastic was caved in. There were three deep indentations. Ralph pointed them out with the tip of his pencil. At the base of each little valley, the plastic was scored right through to the skull beneath.

365

'I've seen these before,' he said.

'On Shona Campbell,' Jack said. Ralph nodded. 'Robbie Cattanach said it looked as if she'd been hit by a bear.'

'I'd like to see the bear that could have done this,' Ralph said drily.

'So how did it happen?' Jack asked. Out near the door, the two women were hugging each other and sobbing loudly.

'Beats me. Probably came in the same way as the young fellow, then hit him with something heavy and hooked. End of story.'

'There was more than one,' Jack said. 'Maybe as many as four.' He explained about the mountain bikes up on the roof. Ralph's assistant came forward with the soaked leg of denim now in a clear plastic bag.

'We've got a name for him,' the young man said. 'He'd a card inside his pocket.' He handed it to Ralph who flipped the little plastic folder open, then gave a dry chuckle which held no humour. He passed it to Jack.

It was a little red wallet. Inside was a tin picture of St Christopher stamped in relief and beside it a small card. 'In case of accident, please call Mrs Ena Redford, 52 Strowans Crescent, Levenford.' The card was signed: Edward J. Redford. Tucked into the plastic was a photobooth picture of a round-faced boy with freckles, grinning at the world.

'At least we can ID this one,' the CID man said.

'Not this one. This isn't the same lad.' Jack showed Ralph the photo. He held it beside the staring face.

'Not the same boy,' he agreed.

He got up and shook his head.

'So who's this?' he asked nobody in particular. 'And what in the name of Christ is going on?'

Jack left the scene of crime team and the rest of the officers in the hardware store and headed back for the car. He'd intended to go straight to Clydeshore Avenue, get Lorna Breck and bring her down here, no matter who saw them, but when he opened the car door, the radio was squawking. He thumbed the button and Bobby Thomson's gruff voice crackled out loudly. Jack got to the station in ten minutes.

The front office looked busy. Bobby Thomson was talking to a man and a woman and an elderly gentleman with a white moustache. Behind them a plump woman with faded red hair shifted nervously in her seat, while another couple sat together, holding hands, expressionless.

'This is Mr and Mrs Visotsky,' Bobby introduced. 'They've come to report their son missing.'

Jack's heart sank.

'Yes, it's our Votek,' the man said. He was tall and dressed in a smart blazer and slacks. His wife was slender, with mousy brown hair. She kept biting her bottom lip, and kept a firm grip on the crook of her husband's arm. The man said: 'I'm Karl Visotsky, and this is my wife Jean and my father, also Votek. Our son didn't come home last night.'

Bobby leaned over the desk. 'The others are with them too,' he said. 'Same problem.'

He lifted the flap, came round and brought the woman and the other two people towards the desk.

'This is Mr Fallon,' he said, offering no explanation. There were few, if any, in Levenford who did not know by now who was leading the hunt.

Mr Visotsky's light blue eyes scanned Jack's face, and right at that moment, Jack intuitively knew who the dead boy was. His father had the same pale stare.

'Come with me,' he said, leading them all into the interview room, keeping his face impassive.

They filed in, staying close, but keeping a distance from each other, as if each of the parents was afraid to be contaminated by what the others might have.

'I thought he was with Eddie,' the pale-faced woman with the silent husband said before Jack was able to say something.

'And Eddie told me he was meeting your Charles,' the plump woman replied, her voice shaking with tension.

Jack held his hand up.

'We'd best hear it one at a time. Now, if you just give me your names, I'm sure I can help.' Jack said that automatically, though he wasn't at all sure he'd be any help to these people. He was even more sure that at the end of the day he'd be no assistance at all. The man with the Polish name and the east-European eyes kept staring at him and a visual recollection transposed the dead eyes onto the worried father's face.

'I'm Ruby Black. This is my husband Angus,' the pale woman said. 'It's our Charles. He didn't come home this morning. We didn't worry last night, because he often stays out with his friends, but when I called Ena here,' she pointed at the plump woman with short hair that had been grey but was now a faded red, 'she said he wasn't there.'

'And Votek was supposed to be with the both of them,' the smartly dressed father said. 'They're just boys. They have nothing else to do but listen to records, and that sort of thing.'

Between them, they got the story out. They'd all of them called each other, and a woman called Galt in East Mains, but her husband, who had answered the door, unshaven and still in his rumpled boxer shorts, said he didn't know where his boy was, nor his wife, and at that time in the morning, he couldn't give a damn where they were. Jack took a note of the name and address. He picked up the internal phone, called through to the front office and asked Bobby Thomson to get a squad car out. He gave them the information and hung up. He turned back to the group again and the phone rang.

'That name you've asked for,' the desk sergeant said. 'I thought it rang a bell. There was a lad hurt on Castlebank Street. Old Wattie Dickson picked him up. They took him up to Lochend, injured, but not thought to be too serious.'

'Get onto them pronto. I'll want somebody to speak to him. Let me know the minute you've got anything.'

He turned back to the group. Mrs Redford was sitting off to the side, wringing her hands nervously.

According to the parents, their sons had been pals since they'd been at infant school. They had all left school together, none of them greatly qualified, and because of the lack of jobs, none of them was in work, although Votek Visotsky went along at weekends to clean the cars in the dealership his father managed. They stayed at each other's houses most nights, played football at weekends, and did nothing much of anything else. Just boys. None of the parents knew where their sons had been the previous night.

'They just go out,' Ruby Black said. 'They never say where they're going. You know what boys are like.'

Jack did. He'd been one. Even though he'd been fond of his

368

old man, seventeen and eighteen had been the years of minimal information, one-word replies, great secrecy even when there was nothing to keep secret. He'd stolen his share of apples and he'd scaled the battlements down on the Castle Rock and braved the undertow to swim across the river down at Keelyard Lane. He'd done a lot more besides.

'Haven't you heard the warnings? Read them in the papers?' he asked brusquely, a little unkindly. He regretted it as soon as the words were out of his mouth. There was one dead boy, two almost certainly, and if Lorna Breck was right, a third. There was a wall splattered with blood and a pool of the stuff on the floor, and a head in a silly day-glo yellow bike-bandit helmet rolling around on a tiled floor. Each and any of these parents might have lost a son that night. From the cheap plastic wallet in the sodden trouser-leg, Ena Redford had lost hers. What were warnings worth? In case of accident please call the police and the scene of crimes team, and then Robbie Cattanach down at the slab.

'But that's just for wee kiddies,' Angus Black spoke for the first time. 'Charles is a big boy.' Beside him his wife began to sniffle.

The phone rang again. Bobby Thomson told him the boy had been taken up to Keltyburn Hospital suffering from some kind of acid-burn. The hospital was famed the world over for plastic surgery.

Jack asked Bobby to get John McColl in as soon as he could, and turned back to the parents.

'We have had word of an incident,' he said, keeping his voice light. 'A boy slightly injured, possibly in a road accident. He's suffered some burns.'

They all sat up straight. Slightly injured. That was better than *injured*, and a whole lot better than the other words they used on the bulletins, like serious and badly and critical. Jack could see the hope in each of their eyes.

'Is it Charlie?' Ruby Black asked haltingly.

'No. I don't have details yet, but it seems to be Gerald Galt.'

The women visibly wilted.

'But this morning, we were called to another incident, a possible break-in. It is possible that two of the boys, at least two of them, were involved.'

'What? Are they under arrest?' This from the man with the Polish eyes.

'I'm afraid not, Mr Visotsky. I'm afraid one boy has been badly injured. He has not been identified yet.'

'Well, when will we know?'

'As soon as we do. Rest assured, we will be doing everything we can to locate the others.'

They all sat, none of them looking at each other, taking in what Jack had said.

Badly injured. He has not been identified.

Did that mean he was dead? The stark question was evident in all of their faces.

My boy? My Eddie? My Charlie? My Votek?

Jack hauled his eyes away from theirs, shoved his seat back and stood. 'If you could all wait here for a moment, I'll have somebody bring you a cup of tea. I'll be back as soon as I can. In the meantime,' he beckoned over to Karl Visotsky, 'could you come with me for a moment, sir?'

The man leaned sideways and patted his wife on the hand. The old man with them reached across to touch his son in a poignant moment of contact. Then Karl Visotsky followed Jack from the room.

'What is it, Superintendent?'

Jack let the mis-rank go.

'I'd like you to help me here. I've a difficult thing for you to do, and I can't be sure until you tell me. When I said in there that the boy had been badly injured, I wanted to spare the women's feelings, however briefly. In point of fact, one of the boys is dead.'

The man took a step backwards as if an invisible hand had pushed him on the chest.

'Is it Votek?'

'That's where I need your help. At the moment, no positive identification is possible.'

'Why? Has he been burned too?'

'Well, sir,' Jack put his hand on the man's shoulder and gripped firmly, the way a man does when he's telling another man to get strong and take it on the chin. 'No, he's not been burned. But there is another problem. Not all of the body has been found.'

370

'Oh my God,' the man said, jamming the words together in a rush. 'What's happened?'

'We don't know yet. I've got a whole team of people working on that just now.'

'Can I see him?'

'Yes,' Jack said, hating this even more. 'But you will have to prepare yourself, Mr Visotsky.'

The man nodded dumbly. Jack took him by the elbow, led him through the swing doors and down beyond the cells to the police mortuary. It was a small room with two Victorian tiled slabs and a harsh smell of disinfectant. There were three little arched windows close to the ceiling which let in little light. Somebody had pulled the old-fashioned cord mechanism which screwed the windows open on ratcheted iron curves, but the ventilation did nothing to clear the smell.

Along the walls, two filing cabinets of long drawers stood side by side. An antique freezer pump hissed and sighed.

'Is he?' the dazed father said, pointing at the rack, just as Robbie Cattanach came through the far door in a flap of white. He looked at Jack, who nodded, then introduced the man.

'As yet we don't know who this is. No matter what, it will be a shock,' Robbie said, keeping his voice low. 'I have to tell you, Mr Visotsky, we only have a part of a body here. You may recognise it and you may not.'

The man nodded quickly. His hands had started to shake. Robbie opened a drawer which rumbled on its travel, with the sound of the night-mail train clattering over the joins. Karl Visotsky moved forward with glacial slowness as if the air in front of him had become glutinous and thick. He put his hands on the edge of the drawer. Just as slowly, his head turned, though his eyes were still fixed on Robbie's face. Finally, with a dreadful roll, they swung down. His son stared up at him with those pale blue-green eyes.

He stood staring in utter silence for several minutes, a father carved in stone. Finally Jack reached forward and touched him on the elbow and the man jumped as if he'd been bitten by a snake.

He swung round and Jack saw the knowledge in his eyes. He himself had gone through that door to infinite understanding.

371

'Votek,' the man whispered, his head dropping in confirmation. 'This is my Votek.'

He turned away from the drawer, moving with senile deliberation. Robbie closed it quickly and as silently as he could and watched as the man reached the wooden chair beside one of the slabs.

'They took his body,' the boy's father said. 'They took my son's body away.'

He turned suddenly and glared at the two men. 'Who would do that to a boy? Eh? Tell me, who would do that to a big soft boy like my son?'

Jack had no answer to that. He was starting not to think in terms of who, but of what.

And what would do a thing like that to a big soft boy like Votek Visotsky, or to little Kelly Campbell, or to Carol Howard, screaming for mercy and her life in a black lift shaft, he had no idea at all.

He led the man away. Mr Visotsky moved like an automaton, as if he was battery powered and the cells had just run flat. In the space of the three yards from the freezer drawer and the door, the son of the old Polish man who had seen, and lived through, terrible things in the extermination camps of Auschwitz-Birkenau, aged visibly. Give him a moustache and white hair and he would have looked just like the man upstairs.

Ralph Slater was bustling in through the front door as Jack reached the ground-floor level. He had another set of plastic bags with his samples and scrapings. He came across with his eyebrows raised. Jack just nodded. He motioned to Ralph to wait there while he went back to the interview room. Over at the desk, the duty sergeant was taking notes while he answered the telephone. Jack heard him say something about a church. He walked through the doors behind the dead boy's father.

Karl Visotsky shuffled forward as if his feet were encased in cement and his wife read it all in his eyes. She came towards him and they met like slow-motion ballerinas in a tragedy. The other two women in the room looked at them, turned to each other, and Jack could see the dread begin to write itself on their faces. He crossed to Ena Redford and eased her from the seat. She pulled back as if he was a hangman, come to lead her away, but he gently drew her to her feet.

Ralph had put all the bags in the operations room, ready for the run to the lab. He came forward with a small bag in his hands.

'Mrs Redford,' Jack said, as gently as he could.

'You've found him,' she said blankly. 'Is he . . .?'

'No. I'm afraid we haven't found him, but I want you to take a look at this.' Ralph handed over the bag and Jack pulled out the little wallet. He opened it and handed it to the woman. She took it in trembling fingers, stared at it for a long time, breath hitching hard.

'For his confirmation,' she said. 'That's when he got that. He always had it in his pocket. It should have said somebody should call a priest, but he put my name there.'

'And is that Edward?' Jack said, taking the thing from her hand and easing out the little photograph. Eddie grinned dumbly out from the flat surface.

'Yes. That's Eddie,' she said, voice cracking. 'Where did you . . .?'

'That was found this morning, at the scene of a break-in. We don't know what has happened yet, but I'm trying to find out.'

'A break-in? When? Where? My Eddie wouldn't break in anywhere. He's not like that.'

Jack put his hand on her shoulder. There was nothing else to say at a time like this. As far as he was concerned, the boy was dead, but until he found a body, she would continue to hope.

'No. We're doing our best to find out what happened. I'll get a car to take you home.'

Mrs Visotsky was wailing when her husband and father-in-law led her out. Ruby Black and Ena Redford were silent, grey, and holding onto each other as if they might fall. Angus Black walked behind them, his face set and grim.

John McColl was in the operations room. He followed Jack out to the car and got in the passenger seat.

'Where to now?'

'Keltyburn,' Jack said. 'We might have a witness.'

He took the back road, avoiding the city traffic, hurling the car round the bends, straddling the centre line. John McColl looked at him uneasily.

'Are we in a rush?'

'We missed Tomlin.'

373

'By about four days,' John said. 'You'll never make that up no matter how fast you drive.' He checked his seat belt, just to be sure. They pulled in through the ornate wrought-iron gates of the hospital in twenty minutes.

Jed Galt was awake. His mother, a tall woman with big breasts and blonde hair piled up in a tangle, was leaning over the bed holding her boy's free hand. The other was held away from his body on a pulley. It was covered in slimy gel and had the colour and sheen of frog skin.

'He's had an anaesthetic,' the ward sister told Jack. 'He might not be much help at the moment.'

The two men sat down on the other side of the bed. Jack made the introductions and the woman let go her grip on her son's hand to shake theirs.

'We don't know what happened,' she said. 'I got a call from the hospital last night. I had to get a taxi.'

'Has he said anything?'

'No, but he's been sleeping most of the time. He was talking in his sleep, but it was just gibberish. The nurse said he might be delirious.' She reached forward and felt her son's forehead. He was a good-looking youngster, with jet black hair not unlike Jack's. His eyes were closed and he seemed to be asleep. On his cheek, there were two angry spots, shiny with gel.

At his mother's touch the boy stirred, and then drowsily opened his eyes. They rolled dopily for a moment, then seemed to come into focus.

'What's happening?' he asked tiredly. 'What's this place?'

'It's alright, Gerald,' Cathy Galt said. 'You've had an accident, but they're looking after you.'

The boy's dark eyes swivelled around and saw Jack sitting opposite his mother.

'Do you feel well enough to tell us what happened?'

He gave a little nod, then winced when it sent a vibration down his arm.

'I had a terrible dream,' he said, voice barely above a whisper. His eyes darted left and right. 'Where's Chalkie and Eddie? And Votek. Are they here?'

'No. They're not. You were found on Castlebank Street last night. It looked as if you'd been in an accident.'

'Accident?' The boy turned to Jack. 'No. I was . . . we were . . .'

Then his eyes flicked wide open and he came completely awake. He jerked back against the pillow and his mouth opened as if he was going to scream, but he just started gasping for air, like someone who had just run a marathon. His mother patted his hand and told him it was alright.

'No,' the boy moaned. He gave a little shudder and didn't seem to notice the vibration this time. His eyes were now staring up at the ceiling and his face had gone rigid. His left hand went into a spasm and gripped his mother's fingers so hard Jack could hear the knuckles pop.

'It was . . . it was chasing us,' he finally blurted through clenched teeth. 'It hit Chalkie. Hit him right off the ground.'

John McColl leaned forward to ask something, but Jack stayed him with a motion of his hand.

'It came down the wall. I thought it was a shadow. It went all dark and it came down the wall. It got Chalkie, but Votek didn't see it. He was asking Chalkie what he was playing at and the thing came down. It was like the *night* moving. So fast, Jesus. It reached out and hit Votek and his hat came off but it wasn't his hat, and Votek was standing there and the blood went all over the place.'

The words were getting faster and faster and the boy pushed himself back against the pillow, as if backing away from what he was remembering.

'It was coming after us. We climbed up the shelves. Me and Eddie. He couldn't move and I had to shove him and it was coming. I could hear it behind me, and *oh God* it was catching up on us. We got up to the roof and I got through first and Eddie was climbing up after me. He could have made it. I had him by the arm and pulled him and then it came behind him and pulled him back. Oh man I could hear it. He was looking at me and I could hear it break him and I couldn't hold him any longer.'

The woman on the other side of the bed looked at the two policemen in a state of confusion. Jack said nothing. The boy had revved up to full speed. There was no stopping him.

'He went down inside and it got him and then it came out after me. It was black and it moved so *fast*. It reached out and I got the

375

drill. I couldn't stop. It got Chalkie and Eddie and Votek and it was coming for me and I stuck it in the eye. I got that fucker right in the fuckin' eye. I thought it was a dream, but it wasn't. It was real, and it was going to kill me, so I drilled the bastard, and all this stuff came out of its eye and on my hand. I didn't even feel it until I came down. The drill was all bust. It was screaming at me. I could hear it inside my head, roaring and screaming.'

'Who was it?' Cathy Galt blurted out. 'Who did this to you?'

The boy seemed to jerk back to the present.

'What?'

'What was it? Who did it?'

'I don't know, Ma. It was too dark. It was black. It looked like a shadow on the wall, but you could hear it and it smelled like something had died. But I got it. I drilled it right in its eye.'

'You didn't get a good look?' John McColl asked.

The boy shook his head.

'It was black, and then it opened its eyes. Man, they were big. Yellow. That was all. When it looked at me, I could hear it, inside my head. It wanted to eat me.'

'So this man killed the others?'

'No. It wasn't a man. I don't know what it was, but it wasn't a man. It was a fuckin' *monster*.'

The boy twisted his head and started to cry, big tears rolling down his cheeks. He turned his face into the pillow, away from the two men.

'I'm sorry, Ma. We were just having a bit of fun.'

25

Jack called in on Angus McNicol on the way back from the hospital, and got a shock when he saw the Chief Superintendent lying in his bed, drawn and grey and showing three days' growth of white stubble. He told him everything that had developed so far, leaving out only Lorna Breck and the boy's description of the thing that had come into Rolling Stock when they were stealing bikes.

'So what next?' Angus asked hoarsely. He had lost a lot of weight. His wife brought in a hot drink and offered Jack a whisky, but he shook his head. He hadn't drunk whisky in a couple of years.

'Bloody ticker,' Angus had explained. 'I thought it was the flu. Buggered up the arteries. The doc tells me I need a bypass, and I'll probably get an early pension.'

'Surely not,' Jack said, dismayed.

'Nothing for it, so they tell me. Still, I'm told it's just a bit of plumbing. They do it every day of the week.' Angus gave him a half-smile. 'Oh, don't worry. They haven't written me off yet, but it'll be a while before I'm back on the size elevens. Should give me a chance to get the rose border in shape.'

Jack didn't know what to say to that.

'Oh, come on, Jack, it's not the end of the world,' Angus said. 'The only problem you've got is that arse Cowie. There's no way he's going any further, so you don't have to concern yourself that he'll get my job. But he'll put the knife in your back as soon as look at you.'

'That's what I wanted to ask about. I need more men on this.'

'I'll bet you do. I've been watching the news.'

'It's getting out of hand. But when I put in a request, Cowie turned it down.'

'You get that in writing?'

'Sure.'

'Good man. You cover your back. If there's reasonable cause, a concern for the community or a threat to it, you can repeat your request to headquarters. And I'll make a couple of calls to let them know what's going on. You'll get your men.'

Jack thanked him and left Angus propped up in bed with his book and a hot drink. He told him to get better.

'Better? Believe me I'll be running rings around you in a couple of months. You just get in there and get the job done and keep the place looking shipshape until I get back. And remember, watch out for Gridlock.'

'For what?'

'Gridlock. That's what they used to call your friend Cowie when he was in traffic. I got that from yon daft bugger John McColl. Now there's a man you can trust.'

Angus was as good as his word. In the early afternoon, Jack faxed his request to the central office and within half an hour he got confirmation that there would be another twenty officers at his disposal immediately. He got John McColl to work out rosters so that the incomers were paired with local men who knew the area. Despite the reinforcements, he didn't know how many men it would take to stop what was happening in Levenford.

If what Lorna Breck said was true, and if young Jed Galt, hands burned right back into the bone, was not raving about what had happened in Rolling Stock, then what he was hunting was something he did not comprehend.

A monster? A spirit? How did you stop one of them?

Jed Galt had said he'd stopped it with a drill. Jack had ordered an immediate search of the grounds around the hardware store, and within an hour of his arrival back at the station, they turned up a Black and Decker power drill lying under the scaffolding nearby. It was blistered and scored as if it had been sprayed with concentrated acid and the twist bit at the front was contorted and bent. Jack hefted it in his hands and called Andy Toye.

'You read my mind,' the professor said brightly. 'I was just about to call. I've been speaking to a few folk.'

'I've spoken to dozens,' Jack told him. He gave him a quick rundown on what had happened so far, including his talk with Lorna Breck in the late hours of the night.

'Oh, there's no question about her,' Andy said. 'I'd like to get

378

her in here some time and do some real tests. She does seem to have some sort of gift, but it appears to be random.'

'It also appears to be plugged into what's happening down here,' Jack interrupted. 'She saw it last night and she called me. She was in a right state. I haven't got any estimates on the time, so I don't know whether it was before or during or after the event.'

'I'd use her if I were you,' Andy advised. 'But on the other matter, I showed the photographs of the writing on the walls to a friend of mine in Leicester. He agrees that they are probably anagrams.'

'Certainly anagrams,' Jack said. 'We've found one of the other people. He jumped in front of a train. And his name starts with the letter you predicted, so now we're searching for this O'Day.'

'But not just an anagram of the names,' Andy said. 'That's why Crowley's *Goetia* puzzled me. It gives a list of what are allegedly the major netherworld princes, what you might call Satan's right-hand men, and it purports to show how they can be called up, although the details are very skimpy. Basically it's a potted biography of each, how they appear, and how to address them when they do.'

'And?' Jack asked.

'It's the rest of the paraphernalia. The tarot cards, the ouija-table and crystal. Carlsson at Leicester is more of an expert on the history of the occult. He's a palaeoetymologist.'

'That's going to need some explanation.'

'Studies ancient languages, most of them extinct. Came up with an interesting idea from the Magyar cultures of eastern Europe. Apparently they thought they could raise demons to tell the future, or do favours. It was a fairly complicated ceremony involving several stages and the final use of a crystal globe. The demon would appear within the crystal, trapped within it for safety reasons, and it would make the stone move to spell out the fortunes of those at the sitting. But it had to be called by name, because according to the lore, and also going by Crowley's book, each of the demons has a specific talent. Some of them are better for curses or bringing good luck, that sort of thing. In the first book of the *Lemegeton*, taken from the Hebrew, and supposed to be where Solomon got all his wisdom, there were four great

379

princes of the underworld, and about seventy earls. Beneath them there were supposed to be legions of other assorted demons and the like. Once invoked by name, they had to stay and do the bidding of the summoner until another rite sent them back.'

'To hell?'

'Yes,' Andy said brightly. 'To the netherworld. Hades. Whatever you like.'

'You think that's what they were trying to do?'

'I believe so. Something like that. Each of the people would have to bring the talismans from the previous telling. That's where, I imagine, the tarot cards come in. That's in the Magyar custom, related to some of the Sanskrit rites from the far east. But I think, and Carlsson agrees with me, that this particular invocation might have gone wrong.'

'How do you mean?'

'As part of the summoning, I told you that the particular entity had to be called by name. It is possible that first of all the special bindings had not been put in place, the ceremony needed to ensure the spirit or demon would be kept within certain parameters, to keep it from actually appearing in the real world.'

'Like a pentangle or something? From the movies.'

'Quite, though that's an old wives' tale.'

'It *all* sounds like old wives' tales.'

'Well, you did ask,' Andy said, not taking offence. 'The clue was in the anagrams. Almost certainly the words were made up of the initials of each surname. Carlsson feels that possibly, they were open at the time. By that, I mean that they had opened themselves up and invited the spirit, not into the room, but into *them*. If you recall *The Goetia*. There was a mark on the margin on one page.'

Jack hadn't noticed, but he said nothing.

'I wondered about that.' Andy started to quote, as if he was reading. Jack assumed he was.

'The twenty-ninth spirit is Astaroth. He is a mighty, strong Duke and appeareth in the form of an avenging angel, riding on a beast like a dragon. Thou must in no wise let him approach too near, lest he do thee damage by his noisome breath. Wherefore, the magician must hold the ring in his face, of pure iron or fine gold, or talisman blessed by consecrated hands, and that will

380

defend him. He can make men wonderfully knowing in all things.'

Andy paused and drew breath. 'Seems like a delightful character.'

'And that's what they were trying to raise?'

'Possibly, but I think it went wrong. It is possible they got part of the rite, but did not complete it. I don't believe it was Astaroth.'

'So what then?'

'That's where Carlsson was a help. He has an old text, an addendum to the *Lemegeton*, which purports to list the houses of the seventy-two princes. He checked on Astaroth, and discovered his lieutenant, right-hand devil if you will, was called Eseroth. Not a nice fellow. Let me read this to you.'

'For none may escape the hunger of Eseroth, the other one, the ravener of the night. Guard your children well in the dark shadows, and lock them away after sunset. For high nor low places will not hide them from the beast. He cometh in the shadow.'

Andy finished. There was a silence on the line which dragged on for several moments before Jack asked, 'That's it?'

'That's it. Etheros, a spirit of the air; Heteros, the other; and Eseroth.'

'Sounds like a devil with dyslexia.'

'But all the same letters, and the only one which fits the *Lemegeton* appendix. It fits with the mark on the book we found, or at least there's a close association. A ravener in the dark. Likes high places. Is known, among everything else, as *The Other*. And so far it has killed children.'

'And you think this can be done?'

'Believe me, there are more things than you'd imagine.'

'But what about this Magyar thing? Does it say how to get rid of it, supposing it actually exists?'

'Oh, it can be dismissed and returned, according to the addendum. Apparently that's not too difficult. But there would be one problem in this case.'

'And that is?'

'There's nothing to show that there were any bonds,' Andy said.

Jack thought about that for a moment. It was all too much to take in. He asked a final question.

'This Magyar thing. Is that some kind of religion?'

Andy laughed. 'Oh ye of little erudition, or even a certificate in geography. Did you never collect stamps as a youngster?'

Jack admitted that he had not.

'You would have known then. The Magyars are quite an ancient people. Originally they were part of the Indo-European migrations who settled in Eastern Europe. The word Magyar is what they call their country and themselves. We call it Hungary.'

When Andy hung up, Jack sat at his desk in complete silence. Devils and demons, things called up from the underworld. Despite how he was beginning to feel about what Lorna Breck had said, and from the description, garbled and hysterical, given by the boy in Keltyburn Hospital, he still wasn't ready to believe in ghosts and sprites and things that materialised in the night. Some form of ESP he could comprehend, but all of his work, every murder that he'd ever worked on, had been caused by people. Bad people, warped folk, but human beings. He'd wondered about child sacrifices, but only in the context of deranged, demented and sick people, not from the standpoint that there actually *was* a devil.

But then Andy had said one little magic word that somehow changed his viewpoint.

Hungary.

The professor hadn't known anything about the old woman, except that she was dead. Andy had made no reference to her nationality, and certainly Jack hadn't thought it relevant to tell him. But now he'd described some sort of ancient fortune-telling, devil-raising rite that had come from that strange and obscure country. Contrary to what his friend had said, Jack did have a certificate in geography, and though all the boundaries had changed beyond recognition since the Iron Curtain had rusted, he still knew where was where. He closed his eyes and pictured the globe. Hungary. East of Germany. North of Yugoslavia. Transylvania had once been part of the Hungarian empire. Tales of Vlad the Impaler, true stories from the Dark Ages that had spawned the legends of Dracula and the vampires. People had believed them, said they had been true. Could they not also be true of the old travellers who had come through the Khyber pass from India with their strange gods and cults and settled in the plains of Hungary?

Could they have raised devils? Could an old Hungarian woman have called up something from a dark place and let it out to steal children in the middle of the night?

Jack thought of Andy quoting from an old text. *The other one, the ravener of the night. Guard your children well in the dark shadows, and lock them away after sunset. For high nor low places will not hide them from the beast. He cometh in the shadow.*

It was stilted and pedantic. But, Jack thought with a sudden realisation, it fitted his bill. He was hunting a killer who came in the night and took children. A night hunter who climbed the high places. Was it all possible? And how did you get rid of a killer some old woman had brought up from wherever it was that devils lived?

Even more to the point, who the hell would believe him?

He put his elbows on the desk and laid his chin on his palms, trying to get his thoughts in order.

Later that morning Superintendent Ronald Cowie arrived in the station, saw the fax from headquarters confirming the extra officers to help with the investigation, and almost burst a blood vessel. Jack listened to him rant for half an hour, without taking in a word of it. He had other things on his mind.

He was still mulling over his conversation with Andy Toye when Bobby Thomson called up and told him there was a problem at St Rowan's Church. A man had locked himself up in the belltower and was refusing to come down.

'Just send a squad car, Bobby,' Jack said, irritated, wondering why the duty sergeant was bothering him with a nuisance. 'I'm up to my eyes.'

'We did. They've had no luck. The man says he won't speak to anybody but yourself.'

'Dammit, Bob. The world's full of eccentrics. He can stay up there until new year for all I care.'

'Well, he won't come down and he insists he's claiming sanctuary. I don't know what our rights are, but he's demanding to talk to you. Says his name is O'Day.'

383

Jack's mouth was open to stop Bobby in his tracks with a curt dismissal and it promptly shut with a snap.

'I think it's the bloke you've been looking for,' the sergeant added. By this time he was talking to a dead telephone. Jack had slammed the receiver down, turned, grabbed his coat and gone flying out of his office.

26

Some hours after the bodyless head of Votek Visotsky had been painfully kicked by Jim Deakin, Fergus Milby and Danny Cullen were nearing the top of the towering chimney next to the old forge just across the river from the old railway warehouses.

The twin stacks, a feature of the town's skyline, had been the subject of acrimonious letters in the *Gazette* for years. In the sixties, when the forge had shut down the primary furnace, it had been planned to dismantle the big stack which stood shoulder to shoulder with its twin, great shotgun barrels of brick aiming for the heavens. The outcry had been considerable. The Levenax Society had protested in lengthy denunciation of the vandalism to the industrial history of the town. It would destroy a landmark, they thundered. There was no concern for the tons of hot fumes that had spilled from the great stacks for years, not only polluting the atmosphere and covering the town in thick, flaky, sulphurous ash whenever the wind blew the wrong way, but also befouling the clean white bedsheets on drying greens all across town and as far as Barloan Harbour eight miles up the firth. There was also little said, landmark-wise, about the demolition of the tenements in Wee Donegal and the subsequent building of the gaunt and towering housing blocks, or the blast of smoke and steam from the vents in the distillery with their greasy overlay of malting barley.

The opposing faction who agreed with the demolition said it was an ugly old brick thing, an eyesore remnant of the sweated labour of the industrial revolution which made Levenford look like a dirty old mill town. The sooner it was gone, they countered, the better. Finally the town fathers decided to keep the stacks for their historic value. The forge owner, William Thomson, a second cousin to the desk sergeant in Levenford Police Station, shrugged his shoulders, happy enough that he would not have to pay a fortune to have the stack removed brick by brick. Explosive demolition was out of the question because of the close proximity of the other chimney which was still venting charcoal fumes from the secondary furnace. Ten years after that, Thomson had sold out, just before the bottom dropped out of the foundry industry. The business had kept going for another twenty years or so, hammering out great girders and beams for the rig yard and the diminishing building industry.

In the last couple of weeks, there had been some concern over the state of the north chimney. In the winter gales, a crumbling half-brick had come sailing down and had not only punctured a neat hole through the corrugated iron shed which served as an outhouse for the dozen or so foundrymen, but had punched its way right through the vitreous china pan, sending shards of jagged porcelain scattering like shrapnel in every direction. In the third trap along, old Bernie Maguire, who operated the charcoal hopper, was doing a crossword, hunkered over like a dying junkie, dungarees at his knees. Bernie should have been back at the hopper ten minutes before, but, being prone to constipation, he was trying, with some effort, to work out more than just the difficult crossword clues. The fact that his trousers were puddled around his ankles saved him from serious injury from the kniving porcelain flack. When the brick hit, travelling at enormous speed after a fall of nearly two hundred feet, it exploded like cannon-shot. Shards of china blasted out under the spaces of the door and the side walls. It tore Bernie's trousers to shreds and punched neat pin-holes through the thin cabin sides of the neighbouring traps. One small sliver sliced through a vein on Bernie's skinny calf and the resultant fine spray of blood was fifteen minutes in the staunching. The other men had come running out at the deafening noise and hauled the door open to find Bernie lying in a heap across the newspaper, pencil still in hand, the air pink from his spraying blood. They also discovered, to their disgust, that the falling brick had done the old fellow one favour. It had miraculously cured his constipation.

Two weeks later, another brick had come down, though it had blasted itself to powder, forming a quite spectacular sunburst pattern in Pompeiian red on the concrete a few feet away from the chimney. The manager of the English conglomerate which had taken over the forge finally got authority to bring in the steeplejacks to find out whether the stack needed a repair, or whether its time had finally come.

It had taken Fergus Milby and his apprentice Danny Cullen a week to get the ladders close to the top. It was dangerous, arduous and exhausting work, but the two-man team were the only steeplejacks in Levenford or any of the nearby towns. There was always work for them somewhere, and in the current job climate, the danger was worth it. To the untrained eye, the ladders looked flimsy, a delicate spidertrack up the side of the brick cylinder. In fact the light aluminium frames which locked one to the other could easily take the weight of six men. The major difficulty lay in the tedious task of raising each length to fit it in place, using the wire bands which travelled the girth of the chimney. It would have been less exhausting and less dangerous to hire a crane for the job, but it would have taken twice as long and three times the cost to erect one of the spindly jack-up jobs.

The original builders had placed metal slots between the bricks, which made the job easier, but still, it took them eight days to get to the top. Some time on the Thursday morning, while Superintendent Cowie was haranguing Jack Fallon in his office, attempting to browbeat him with dire but meaningless threats, they were putting the last section in place. Danny Cullen, eager to be first to the top, hooked his rope into one of the stanchions, making sure his safety harness was still attached with its anti-slip grip to the guide. He eased himself onto the flat surface, eight brick-widths thick because of the tapering of the construction, and carefully raised himself to his feet, sliding the guide over the edge with practised proficiency. He used the contraction hooks to hold the ladder in place, twisting the handles on the threads to bring the aluminium spars hard against the brickwork. Fergus Milby had told him there were two kinds of steeplejack, the slow or the dead, or as Fergus himself had put it, the careful ones or the stupid splattered bastards on the deck. Danny didn't want to join the ranks of the splattered. He stood up, avoiding a space where a brick had worked free and fallen off, and looked across the town from the top of the chimney. The view was quite spectacular. He could see the top of the blocks of Latta Court and its neighbours. Across on the other side of town, the great square red hulk of the distillery belched its perpetual plume of steam, like a slumbering volcano.

387

Up here there was almost dead silence, apart from the mewling of a seagull passing below, a grey kite far down, a bird seen from the wrong angle. There was no sound of traffic, except the very muted, toytown clatter of a train heading out from the station. Little model cars were silently crossing the old bridge in twos and threes, followed by a dinky little bus. Almost directly below, just out in the river, the boats looked neat and clean, like yachts at a classy marina, though Danny knew these boats were all paint-peeled and slimed with dirt and bird crap, half of them unpainted and the others only half-painted by weekend watermen. The distance gave a cleanliness and neatness to everything.

He strolled casually around the edge, a twenty-year-old boy gifted with a sense of balance and a natural affinity for heights. He looked down and saw Fergy Milby climb slowly towards him, unconsciously adjusting his safety clip with every two steps. His flat cap was on backwards, to keep the peak away from the steps of the ladder. Fergus was a careful mover who had instilled the slow-motion, moon-mountain climb into his apprentice. Danny stepped to the side. Steeplejacks did not give each other a hand. There were too many ways to lose your balance that way. The tradesman had regaled his assistant, ever since he had started three years before, with tales of men who'd taken a tumble down a chimney, or gone sailing off to convert themselves into the ranks of the splattered. Fergus was graphic if nothing else.

'Not bad, Danny-boy,' he said when he got to the top and sat, feet dangling over the drop. It was Fergus's joke on the younger man's Irish Catholic heritage. The steeplejack wasn't of the faith himself, but unlike many of his persuasion in the town, to whom religion meant little more than the colour of jersey a football team wore, it didn't matter a damn to him. He didn't watch football anyway.

Fergus opened his tobacco tin and rolled himself the customary crumpled cigarette, tamped the end on the nearest brick, lit up and drew in a deep breath.

'Haven't been up here since I was your age,' he said, gazing out over the toytown panorama.

'You helped build it then?' Danny asked, grinning at his own joke.

'Watch it,' the boss said gruffly, although he was used to the boy's comments. They worked well together, and in fact, the best compliment the steeplejack could make was that he felt safe with Danny Cullen. 'You want to become a *splatteree*?' he shot back.

The younger man sauntered around the rim of the chimney as if it were a wide path through a park. He automatically raised his feet to avoid the copper straps which snaked up over the sides and crossed the flat, each of them corresponding to the points of the compass. He was looking north, towards the mountains looming over Loch Corran in the distance, when something jarred him as being out of place. He turned back to Fergus who was contentedly puffing on his cigarette.

'What's happened to the conductors?' he asked.

'Eh, what's that?' Fergus asked, turning round with a casual, yet careful movement. He'd twisted his cap round so the peak shadowed his eyes.

'The lightning spikes – they're gone.'

Fergus followed the curve of the chimney. On the top flat, it was eight feet across the inner edges, and about three times that in circumference. The copper ribbons were stapled to the bricks with lead fold-over flaps. They travelled to the inner edge where the four-pronged steel aerials should have been, a precaution against bolts of lightning striking the inner surface and possibly travelling down to the furnaces below. From where Fergus was sitting, he could see the furthest one had been twisted right down inside the funnel of the chimney.

'I'll be damned,' he said, getting to his feet. 'There's something stuck there.'

'And here,' Danny boy said. 'What is it?'

He got to his knees and looked down the black hole. Something was snagged on the spike, which had been bent right down inside the shaft and then curled back up on itself. It looked like a bundle of rags, dirty and withered.

'Probably blown up and snagged in the gales,' he said. He reached down and hauled at the tattered bundle. It was stuck on the upcurved hooks of metal. He worried at it, holding onto the far edge of the chimney for leverage. The material ripped and the thing came free with a muted tearing sound. He drew it upwards and as he did, a foetid smell of rot came wafting up the funnel.

'Jesus, that stinks!' he said, face screwed up with disgust. He could feel the stench clog thickly in the back of his throat. He heaved the tattered mess up and onto the flat. A piece of dirty, mouldering cloth flapped back in the light breeze and a small brown round thing rolled out and clonked against the bricks.

'What in the name of . . .' he said, then let out a long breath of relief.

'It's a doll,' he said. 'For a moment I thought it was a kid. By God, it smells to high heaven.'

'How the hell did it get up here?' Fergus asked. 'We must have been the first folk up this height in twenty year.'

'I don't know. Must have been up here for ages.' He turned round and shoved the bundle towards Fergus. Just below him, another tangled mass hung from the spike nearest him, this one not much bigger. He stretched his hand down and worked at the cloth until it came free and drew it out of the hole. If anything this one smelt worse.

As he laid it down, something flopped stiffly onto the brickwork. It was dark and stick-like. It looked like a monkey's paw.

'It's another one,' Danny said. Fergus could hear his gullet work to try to keep the stench out of his throat. The apprentice was poking at a small torn hood. 'I think somebody's been playing a . . .'

He never finished his sentence. Fergus was sitting casually, with one hand behind him and a foot cocked on the edge while the other dangled over the drop. Unexpectedly Danny jerked backwards as if he'd been bitten by an adder. Fergus saw him scramble to his feet with alarming speed, the kind of speed people who work in high places have nightmares about. His boot snicked the inner rim of the chimney. A piece of brick crumbled off and tumbled into the dark well. Danny tilted to the side, suddenly off balance, arms windmilling. One foot was out over the shaft, while the rest of his body was teetering on the edge of the chimney. The mouldering bundle followed the pieces of brick and toppled into the chimney.

Fergus moved faster than he believed possible. Danny began to fall, and a cry of surprise and fright blurted out. His boss whirled, got to one knee and his hand shot out. He grabbed Danny by the belt, inadvertently knocking the wind right out of him with the force of the strike, and with a powerful heave, he swung him back from the edge and down onto the flat. Danny's backside hit the hard surface with a solid thud and he yelped again, this time in pain. He twisted to the side, almost went over the edge again, caught himself and then froze.

'Are you off your head?' Fergus bawled. 'Bloody idiot, you were nearly a goner then. What in the name of Christ's the matter with you?'

'It's *that*,' Danny bleated, pointing into the chimney. The mangy truss of cloth had slipped into the well, but had snagged again on one of the upturned hooks beside an even larger flaking bundle.

'What?'

'It's not a doll,' Danny murmured. 'It's a baby.'

'What are you playing at?' Fergus said. 'What would a baby be doing up here?'

'But *look*,' Danny insisted. 'It's a baby, and it's *dead*.'

Fergus's hands were still shaking from the sudden exertion and the terrible fright he'd got when he thought his apprentice was about to topple into the chimney. He lit another cigarette, with some difficulty, and took another long draw before letting his breath out in a stuttering sigh.

He got to one knee again and came close to where Danny sat, both hands firmly gripped on the brickwork. He followed the young man's eyes and stared at the small dirty pile. He reached a hand forward carefully and drew back a piece of mildewed fabric. Despite the care, the material tore in his hand with a whispering rip.

The small wizened face gazed up at him from blind crumpled sockets. Its lips were stretched back tight and dry, exposing gums which were bare except for two tiny teeth which protruded in the centre of the bottom of the jaw. The skull was shiny and brown and both little ears were like shrivelled autumn leaves. Fergus pulled the cloth back further and the foetid, sickly sweet stench blossomed like the scent of a poisonous flower.

'Dear God,' he breathed. With great gentleness, he pulled back the ragged cloth. Just below the neck, the small, fragile ribs were like wires pushing through a thin, tight membrane, and below them, there was a gaping hole. With the movement, something black and slimy dribbled inside the cavity and the stink was suddenly so bad the steeplejack found his own throat try to clamp itself shut.

He pulled himself back in revulsion and sat, staring at the dead face. Danny watched him, white-faced. Without a word, Fergus reached down and unhooked the other shape and hefted it out onto the surface. It came up easily, like a little pile of rags. He laid it gently down and unwrapped it from a dirty grey shawl. Danny heard his intake of breath.

The dead child had the wizened face of a mummy. He could see, under the parchment-like ochre skin, the zig-zag suture lines where the skull-plates joined and in the centre, a deep depression as if it had been struck a vicious blow with a club, but was in fact where the soft membrane of the fontanelle, where the bones had yet to form and knit, had sagged. The baby was so young its bones hadn't even had time to form. Below the little chin there was nothing at all of the throat. The skin puckered and curled on each side of a gaping wound in which Fergus could see the neck-bones push through dried muscle.

He laid the thing down, almost reverently, and turned away. His eye had caught the other things hanging from the lightning conductors, an arm's span below the lip of the chimney. He did not want to see any more.

'I'd better go back down and tell somebody,' he said numbly.

'I'll come with you,' Danny said. He edged away from the mouldering corpses and clipped his safety rig onto the cable which was suspended from the clamp.

'No,' Fergus told him. 'You'd better stay here. You're in no fit state to climb. Look at you, shaking like a leaf.'

'You can't leave me up here,' Danny protested, his voice rising. 'I'm not staying with these.'

'Och, don't be daft,' Fergie retorted.

'I don't care,' Danny whined. 'You're not leaving me up here with dead bodies. No bloody way.'

Fergus shrugged. He clipped his own lead onto the braided cable and started making the long climb down. Danny followed so close he almost stepped on his boss's fingers.

Five minutes later they were in the forge manager's office. Almost before Fergus Milby put the phone down, the wail of sirens started up on the other side of the river.

27

'Up there, sir,' the young policeman said, pointing to the hollow arched entrance of the belltower.

They were standing in the nave of the ornate church building which had been built at the turn of the century by a fiery monsignor from old Donegal for the greater glory of God. The Irish-Catholic families of the parish had been coerced, with threats of damnation, excommunication or years in purgatory, into donating money they could ill afford, because of the lack of work and their burgeoning families, to pay for the Italian marble altar, whinstone buttresses and beautifully masoned arches.

A monstrous crucifix with an appallingly bloody Christ nailed to a rococco cross hung suspended forty feet over the devout and worshipful congregation. The tough old monsignor, who saw himself cut from archbishop's cloth, and who wheeled and dealed without shame to have the parish promoted to diocesan status, had dreamed of building the most magnificent cathedral money could dictate. Certainly he had succeeded in building a church worthy of the name, but all his vanity and ambition were in vain. The Good Lord called him to a greater and everlasting position of worship within a year of the consecration of the building. The bells of St Rowan's church tolled for the solemn high mass of the monsignor's funeral and he was given pride of place in the new graveyard in the spreading grounds, after which everybody forgot about cathedrals and went back to church.

Father Liam Boyle, the incumbent parish priest, was a thin, grey-haired man with turned down lips who looked as if the milk of human kindness would go sour in his mouth.

He wore a long black soutane, faded at the cuffs and shiny with wear everywhere else, stained with grey blobs of candlewax down the length of the innumerable cloth buttons. He rubbed his hands together in a worried, nervous way, making them rasp against each other in a constant dry whisper.

'Must have been up there for days,' he said to Jack. 'There was a fault in the tintinnabula, or so we thought, but he must have done something to the mechanism up in the tower. The clock hasn't struck the half-hour for days. Our parish horologist couldn't get up there to check it. He opened the trap and somebody stamped it down on his head. He's lucky he didn't fall down the steps and break his neck.'

'So what's the position?' Jack asked the uniformed policeman.

'There's a man up in the belfry. He says his name is O'Day and he's claiming the ancient right of sanctuary.'

'Sanctuary, is it?' the priest snapped. 'After the vandalism that's taken place in this church, he'll have no sanctuary here. Sacrilege is what I call it. Only last week we had the altar broken into and a chalice stolen, full of consecrated hosts, and a rosary blessed by the Pope himself. No doubt our visitor can explain that to us all.'

'Yes, I heard about that,' Jack said. 'I'm sure the officers are doing all they can.'

'So what are you going to do now about this . . . this invasion?'

'Just leave it to me, sir,' Jack started to say.

'Father,' the priest corrected irritably. Jack acknowledged the correction with a dry nod.

He went across to the base of the tower, which was built, quite spectacularly, over the altar, resting on four arched buttresses that merged into the flanks of the walls. A narrow entrance, cut into the fine-grained sandstone blocks, led to an equally cramped staircase, which spiralled upwards for three turns before arriving at a wide wooden floor. Here, another uniformed policeman was leaning on a bannister. He straightened up when Jack appeared.

'Where is he?' Jack asked. The constable jerked his thumb upwards. Jack tilted his head. The narrow stairway, this one made of old wood, continued upwards. There was a smell of dust and bird-droppings.

'He refuses to come down,' the officer volunteered. 'We tried a bit of persuasion, but he's jammed something over the trap. He insists he'll only speak to you.'

Jack gave a weary sigh and started up the stairs after telling the constable to wait there until he came down. He wanted to take this on on his own. The treads had no risers and sank a fraction with every step. Almost every one of them creaked and the whole stairway looked too old and flimsy to take a man's weight. It turned, rose, turned again and continued upwards. The narrow lead-hatched slit windows gave little light. Jack kept a tight grip on the dusty bannister and wished he knew some prayers. He did not look down.

Finally the stairs stopped abruptly at a wooden ceiling festooned with the grey triangles of ancient cobwebs. Here, the smell of pigeons was much stronger and immediately Jack recalled the days out raiding the nests in the old warehouse where young Neil Kennedy had been snatched in the dark. It gave him a shiver. Something fluttered noisily off to the left where the spars supported the wooden floor above, hiding shadows in the corner. Jack took the last few steps slowly, paused for breath, then rapped on the wood above his head.

A muffled thumping sound came in instant reply. Jack banged again with his fist.

'Mr O'Day?'

'Who is it?' a voice replied, also damped by the wooden boards, but sounding only a foot or so away from Jack's head.

'Jack Fallon. You wanted to speak to me.'

'How do I know it's you?'

'What do you want me to do?' Jack asked impatiently. 'I've climbed up so far my nose is starting to bleed.'

'Get back from the door,' the man's voice ordered him. 'And no funny business, or I'll brain you, I swear to God.'

Jack took several steps backward, making sure his feet stamped hard on the stairs, though that caused a vibration that made him think they could give way any second. Above him, footsteps pounded the floorboards. The trapdoor at the head of the stairs opened a fraction, showing a thin line of wan light before a shadow blocked it off. Jack screwed his eyes up, trying to make it out, but could see nothing.

'Is that you, Mr O'Day?'

'Aye, it's me alright.'

'I've been looking for you.'

'That's no surprise. I've been waiting for you. You took your time.'

'Do you want to come down and talk about it?'

'Not on your mother's life,' the voice said. There was more

395

than a hint of a southern Irish accent there. 'If I move out of here, I'm a dead man, sure as you're born.'

'Oh, and why's that?'

'It's a long story, Mr Fallon, and I don't think you're about to believe it. I have to tell you it, though, but I'm not moving from here. It's the only safe place left.'

'Well, I want to hear what you have to say, but I don't fancy standing down here all day getting a crick in my neck. Can I come up?'

'No, stay there,' the man barked nervously.

'Oh, come on, man,' Jack said. 'I'm not going to hurt you. I just want to find out what's going on.'

There was a silence while the man considered it. Jack waited it out.

'Would you have a set of those handcuff things?'

Jack agreed that he did. He fumbled in his jacket pocket, drew them out and held them up for display. They jingled in his hand. The trapdoor opened wider. A pale face peered down.

'Right, you can come up. There's a post just inside the door. Put those things on your wrist and when you get to the top, put the other end round the post.'

Jack sighed again, but nodded in agreement.

'And I'm telling you. If you don't do what I say, I'll cave your head in.'

The door opened to its full extent, then slammed back to the floor with a gunshot boom which reverberated down the hollow length of the Gothic tower. Jack walked slowly up the stairs, snapping the cuff on his wrist as he did so. Warily, he clambered through the space until he could reach the bannister on the top side. He could see nothing, but sensed the man behind him. He reached forward and clicked the other ring around the upright and stopped.

'Right, I'm your prisoner. Now what?'

'You can sit down now,' the voice said from behind him. Jack turned and saw a scrawny man with a scraggy grizzle-grey beard that looked ten days from its last shave. He was emaciated and haggard. Jack recalled the dead man they'd found on the railway line. He too had been just a rickle of bones like the man who said he was O'Day. Without a word he turned and sat himself on the bannister. It felt solid enough.

396

The man came towards him, blue eyes rimmed with red. In both hands he hefted a metal bar. On the other side of the dusty room there was a set of levers and pulleys. The spar looked as if it had come from there. That probably solved the mystery of why St Rowan's bells had stopped clanging the half-hour. He wasn't concerned about the weapon. The man looked as if he would blow away on a breezy day, and though there was a frantic, wildly haunted look in his eyes, Jack knew he could get the weapon off him, even with one hand tied behind his back.

'Nice to see you at last, Mr O'Day. I've been concerned about you,' Jack started.

'Not near as concerned as I've been,' O'Day said. He stole a quick glance to check Jack's handcuffs, then seemed to relax a little, although his whole body looked tight as a banjo string.

'You're on the murder hunt, aren't you? The boss?'

Jack nodded.

'That's what I have to talk to you about. I don't want to kill anybody, and I don't want it to get me.'

Far downstairs, something dropped with a clatter and the noise boomed up the hollow. O'Day jerked round like a cat, raising his lever like a club.

'Don't worry. They won't come up unless I tell them, and I'm not going to tell them. You've got a promise on that.'

Michael O'Day's shoulders slumped. He was wearing what had been, until now, a smart and probably well-cut suit with a light blue shirt. Now, suit and shirt looked filthy and creased, as if they'd been slept in for a week, and they hung on him like drapes. His neck was thin and scrawny and his face was so wasted his cheekbones stuck out like knuckles and the skin was drawn in as if he was sucking on something bitter. Very slowly, he lowered himself down to the floor where he'd spread a dark blue winter coat that had also seen better days, some of them recent. On the coat, a silver chalice with an ornate lid topped by a small cross stood gleaming in a stray shaft of light. At its base was a set of prayer-beads with a crucifix that seemed to be worked in gold.

'Can't eat, can't sleep,' he said in a voice that sounded close to exhaustion. The dark rings under his eyes deepened as he lowered his head. 'It comes for you in your dreams.'

'What does?'

'Whatever it is the old woman called up. Honest to God, I never meant anything like that to happen. She only said it was a special night. I don't know about the others, but I just wanted my fortune told. I needed the luck, for it's been out this past couple of months. Big Eddie Carrick's boys have been hunting me for weeks. Ha! That's a big worry. He's Mother Theresa compared to what's been after me.'

'You know about the killings,' Jack said levelly.

'I know about them alright. I was there when the old woman died. I was the last one in the room and I thought I was going to die as well. After that I locked myself up for a while. I heard about the kiddies, on the news, but I didn't connect it, even when that bigoted bastard Simpson topped himself. He deserved all he got. There was something slimy about that one, I can tell you.'

O'Day's voice was beginning to rise. Jack held out his free hand and made a calming gesture. The man stopped and took a breath.

'When the other baby went missing, and you found the woman, I started to suspect, because by then I was getting the dreams. Terrible nightmares. By the third one, when you got that woman in the river – did you know she worked at the police station?'

Jack said he did. 'I thought you would,' the man went on with hardly a pause. 'Quiet girl, wouldn't have harmed a fly, but I'll bet you all that's changed. I don't know what she was doing at old Marta's place. It was after she topped herself that it came to me, clear as day. I never read anything about the Tomlin fella, or Mrs Eastwood, but I've got a feeling they've gone too.'

'And Derek Elliot,' Jack interjected. O'Day gave a start.

'Him an' all? That makes me the last one. And that's why I'm staying here.' He reached and grabbed the chalice. 'This is all I've got. It can't get me as long as I've the sacrament with me. Are you of the faith?'

Jack shook his head. 'Not any,' he said.

'Well, you should be, because it'll protect you from what you're after.'

'And what is that?'

'I'll tell you in a minute. But first of all I have to tell you about the night in Cairn House. Did you know they found a boy there way back in the sixties? Dead for months and murdered?'

'Yes. I was just a kid at the time, but we all heard about it.'

'Before my time an' all. But she told me, the old woman did. It gave the house a special power, she said. I thought that was a whole heap of shite myself, but she believed it, and she knew her stuff I suppose. She said the forces gathered where something terrible had happened, like it was a crack between here and wherever, and she was right about that. You have to know what you're up against, and then God help you. Look at me. How old would you say I was?'

From the look of the man, Jack would have guessed fifty, but he said nothing.

'I'm thirty-six years old, for Christ sake. Last week my hair was as black as yours. And now look at what's happened to me all because of that old Hungarian witch.'

'So what happened?' Jack asked softly.

Michael O'Day's shoulders slumped. He sat there on the dirty coat, one hand on top of the chalice. He looked dazed and ill. Finally, after a few minutes, he began to speak and Jack Fallon listened to the most bizarre story he had ever heard.

'I'd been up to her place a couple of times,' Michael O'Day began.

'I'd heard she could tell fortunes, and that's just what I needed. Some good fortune. You ever back the horses? No? Well I've been punting them most of my life and I've had some big wins, I can tell you.

'But I hit a bad patch, and I was down to Eddie Carrick nearly eight grand before I knew it. Big Eddie was putting the bite on, and I couldn't pay him. Anyway, I heard about the old Hungarian biddy and went up there.

'Some of the others were there on that first night, all sitting round a table. She took a twenty for a reading. It was near enough all I had. She gets out a chart, like a calendar with all the dates on it, and gets me to hold her hand while she runs a finger over it. Every now and then she'd give my hand a squeeze and when that happened, she stuck her nail into the paper. After that, she takes out a pen and makes a ring around the dates. It was four weeks in October.

'"These are the best days for you," she says. "Avoid all the others." After that, I had to wait three days. On the first day, it was a Thursday, I went up to Lochend and I just picked the first numbers that came into my head. Every horse was on the nose, and they all came in. I couldn't believe it. I came out with three hundred in the one afternoon, and I can tell you, it was a fight not to go straight back in again the next day. I had to wait for nearly a week, and it was hard. My guts were all twisting up inside, the way you get when you need a drink, but I stuck it out. On the Tuesday I was up at the bookie's again with a wad of notes in my hip pocket. I walked out of there with nearly a grand. I was walking on air. I hit Eddie Carrick with the lot and he called off the dogs for the moment, though I was still down a huge pile. I kept to the dates and most of the time the horses came in. I took a couple of dives, but things were looking better and at the end of the month I went back to the old lady. By November, I had Eddie's slice down to five.

'Then at the end of that month, I got an invite through the door. No postmark or anything, just a card asking me to come up to a special sitting, and that's when it happened.

'The rest of the folk who were there before had turned up. When I got there, most of them were waiting. The minister fellow, Simpson came in last. I don't know what he was doing there, him a man of the church, but I didn't care. I was curious like. The old woman had said she wanted us all there to do something different, something that would let us see into the future. After the two months I'd had, I didn't want to miss out.

'We all sat round and she brought out some old cards and asked us all to pick three. She tells us they're all symbols of fortune. Then she produced a sort of crystal thing and put in on the table and asks us to put our hands on it. I remember it felt cold. The old lady starts going into the mumbo jumbo routine, all about opening ourselves up because she is calling on a very powerful guide who can tell us everything we want to know.

'All I wanted to know was the winners.

'Then the stone starts to shiver, right under our hands. I could feel it and at first I thought it was a trick, maybe one of the others moving it, but it kept on going. Then it slid right across the table and stopped at a word.

'Old Marta, she says one of us should ask a question. I asked it for a number, and sure enough, the stone moved right across, one side to the other and back again and spelled out *six*. It did it twice. I thought somebody was pushing it, but then again, I had this really *weird* feeling in me as well. I could see the numbers in my head.

'Then the other woman piped up. Something about her daughter and before you could wink, the stone's off and running again. It started sliding across the table, every which way, spelling out the words and then all the hairs on the back of my neck started walking. It started spelling things like *cold* and *hurt*. I remember it because right at that moment, the room started to get cold, as if somebody had opened a window. You could hear the wind, though I don't know where it was coming from, and all of a sudden I was frozen stiff. The woman who asked the question, Eastwood her name is, or was, she started to cry, but before anything happened, the stone started spelling out jumbles of words and the minister bloke, Simpson said it was spelling out our initials.

'I looked at old Marta and she was sitting staring at the thing with a big smile on her face, like she'd won the sweepstake. I can't tell you how, but I suddenly got the creeps, and when the wee woman started speaking, I nearly *shat* myself. I mean, it wasn't her voice at all. She sounded like a wee girl.

'She started talking about doughnuts and Mrs Eastwood nearly threw a fit. The woman kept talking in this kid's voice, all high and squeaky and none of the foreign accent neither.

'Right at that point, I wanted to get my arse right out of there, but I couldn't move. I don't know if any of the others noticed it, but the room had got colder than a witch's tit. She kept on talking, but her voice was changing all the time and then it got really deep and started talking to us. I mean, it *couldn't* have been coming from the old woman. It was a *man's* voice. It sounded like he was inside a tunnel.

'I could tell everybody was scared. You could feel it. The old woman was staring at us all, but it was like it wasn't *her* at all. Then she started to breathe, as if she was choking, and that's when it started to go wrong. Her fingers were dug into the top of the table. You could hear them scraping into the wood. I think one of her nails broke, but I was watching her face. I couldn't take my eyes off it. The light in the corner flickered and then it went out. There was a fire going, and all I could see was the light reflected in the stone. I was all for getting out of there when out of nowhere there was a fuckin' hurricane in the room. The fire blazed up and all the books started flying out of their shelves, like somebody was throwing them. Then the fire went down and I could *feel* the wind. Not blowing *at* me, but *through* me. It was freezing cold, colder than you could imagine, like I had turned to ice inside. I swear to God that I've never been warm since then.

'The others got off their mark, running for the door, but I couldn't move. I wanted to go, believe me, but I just sat there. The old woman's head went back and her neck was pressed against the bar of the seat. She sounded as if something was strangling her. Then the glass went shooting off the table and hit the fireplace. It made a noise like a bomb going off and smashed to bits. I got cut on the cheek, but most of the glass got the old lady. It nearly took her head off.

'They all made it out of the door before the old lady turned round. She swung round and her head was covered in pieces of glass, right into the skin and bone. She looked at me and she started to laugh and I tell you, I nearly died on the spot. My legs were shaking, but I couldn't get them to move. I think it was then, it could have been earlier, there was a tearing noise up on the wall and a whole sheet of paper came peeling off and then another one came down.

'I managed to get out of my chair when she said something, though I know now it wasn't her that said it.

'"Go now and wait for me. You who have named me are my vessels. I am within you and without you, and now I claim my first."

'That's exactly what it said. I didn't know what it meant then, but, God help me, I know now. The old woman fell backwards. I could see her twisting about down there, like she was still alive, but like all her muscles and bones were breaking. The horrible voice started roaring again, but it wasn't like a voice any more. It was like an animal. I was trying to move when she rose into the air. She went way above my head and there was nothing holding her up, I swear on my mother's grave. Then she dropped and hit the fireplace with a god-awful noise, like an apple under your foot. That was when I started to move. I thought my legs wouldn't start, but I got them out from under the table. The old woman was rolling about in the fireplace, but there was something else there too. I couldn't see it because all the lights were out and the fire had died down. I only saw a shadow, and it wasn't the old woman, that's for sure. It was something else. It was black and it was hunched on top of her and it sounded as if it was eating her.

'I got out of there and ran down the stairs into the street. The others were gone. All the time I could hear that voice telling me I had to wait for it coming.'

When Michael O'Day stopped talking, the silence that followed was almost deafening. He sat and stared at the floor for a while, then he reached out and lifted the lid of the chalice. From where he sat, Jack could see it was half-filled with white discs. O'Day dipped his hand in and lifted one out, very carefully, despite the tremor of his fingers. He lifted the wafer and placed it on his tongue. His mouth worked drily and then he made an exaggerated swallowing motion.

'The difference,' he said, 'between heaven and hell is that nobody believes in hell. Look at me. I'm between both of them and headed for one. It's all mumbo jumbo, isn't it? Except that it works. It can't get me in here, you know. This is the only place I can be and not hear that voice in my head. Now I know what it meant.'

He looked up at Jack, a wasted, unkempt figure sitting on a dirty coat.

'The whispering started a few nights later. I thought I'd left the television on, or maybe the radio, but it wasn't that. It was as if somebody was talking in another room, just out of hearing. But it got louder and I could make out the words. I kept having these dreams. You know what happened at the race? It came in, that horse. A big grey out of trap six. I took six grand from bookies all over Glasgow, and I tell you, I should have stayed there. Maybe if I hadn't come back, everything would have been alright, but I was pretty much mixed up at the time.

'Then I started having the dreams. Terrible dreams, and I was cold all the time, as if that wind was still blowing through me. I couldn't eat and I couldn't sleep. I felt as if I'd stepped right out of the world. The voice would whisper to me at night, but it was coming from inside me. It got that I was scared to lie down at night, just in case it came when my eyes were closed, but I knew it was coming when I read about the others. It said it would use us. I don't know how it does it, but it used them, and they're dead, all of them.'

'And what is it?'

'It's nothing on earth. Nothing *from* this earth. It was blacker than pitch and it was moving. That's all I saw in that room, but I could *feel* it.' O'Day tapped the side of his head. 'And I can hear it, in here. It wants me, it wants me to do things, to come out in the night. I think it needs us during the day, maybe somewhere warm to live, I don't know. It whispers at me and tells me things. It *shows* me things. It sits up in high places, where it's dark and I can see what it sees. It eats at night. I see it, but it's like it's showing me what *it* sees. It goes back up there at night to feed. But it won't have me. It can't come in here.'

'Why not?'

'Because it's a church, consecrated ground. The old woman, I don't know how she did it, but she raised a ghost, or a devil or something. It's used the others to take those wee babies. Now it wants me to do the same, and when it's finished with me, I'll go the same way. That's why I have to stay here.'

He sat up straight. 'I'm claiming sanctuary.'

'You can't stay here forever,' Jack said quietly.

'I'm telling you,' the man said with surprising strength. 'If you take me out of here, then it'll get me. You can't stop this thing. If it gets me, then it'll make me do the things it wants. It just wants to kill.'

Jack spent two hours up in the belltower with Michael O'Day, going over the story again and again. O'Day was consistent, telling it the way he remembered it. Finally, feeling drained and a little numb, he told the man that he could stay in the belltower, though he'd probably be back to ask some more questions. O'Day agreed with that. He got to his feet, moving like an old man. With a quick motion he snatched up the prayer beads and held them up. The carved gold cross gleamed in the dim light. 'Here,' he said. 'You should take this. If you're looking for that thing, then you'll need it. I don't think there's anything else can stop it.'

He slung it across and Jack caught it with his free hand and stuffed it into his pocket. O'Day watched warily, holding the rusty lever up in front of him while Jack unlocked the cuffs and put them in his pocket, but Jack merely turned and backed down the stairs.

At the bottom, the two policemen were standing with the priest.

'Is he coming down then?'

'Not for the moment,' Jack told him. He wanted out of the church, into the fresh air, somewhere he could think. 'He's got the chalice. It's not damaged.'

'Well, aren't you going to bring him down?'

'I'm afraid I can't do that,' Jack said. 'He's claiming sanctuary.'

'Sanctuary?' the priest said angrily. 'I want him out of my church.'

'Unfortunately, the law still stands,' Jack told him, making it up as he went along. He hadn't a clue whether there was still a law, or if there had ever been one outside of a film. 'A citizen claiming sanctuary cannot be forced out of a church against his will.'

He turned and left the priest standing open-mouthed in the aisle.

There was little time to do any thinking. Jack went back to the station and straight into Superintendent Cowie's room, unannounced. Ron Cowie was dunking small biscuits in a cup of coffee, though he sniffily made no move to offer one to Jack.

'You must have plenty of time to spare,' he said with heavy sarcasm, 'if you can afford to waste it on trespassers.'

'Just the one trespasser, and, coincidentally, the very man I've been looking for.'

There was nothing for it but to tell Cowie exactly what O'Day had told him. The response was entirely predictable. The Superintendent told him it was both claptrap and balderdash and that he was derelict in his duties by wasting so much valuable time.

'So where is this idiot?'

'He's still up there. He's claiming sanctuary. I told him he could stay there for the time being. He's going nowhere.'

'Nonsense, you can't have people stealing religious relics and then disturbing the peace. Even it it's only the Catholics they're disturbing. Just send somebody over there and get him out.'

'I think that would be a mistake. I promised him he could stay. It's the best way to get cooperation. Whether anybody believes what he says, it's obvious that O'Day believes it. He's as secure up there as anywhere.'

Cowie opened his mouth to say something, but just at that moment there was a knock on the door. A young policewoman popped her head through.

'It's a call for you, Mr Fallon. Sergeant Thomson says it's urgent.'

Jack left Cowie spluttering over his coffee.

28

Young Danny Cullen was sitting on the ground just outside the gate when Jack and Ralph Slater got to the forge. His face was ash-grey and he was puffing continuously on an unaccustomed cigarette. Fergus Milby was talking to a man in a tweed jacket and a loud tie who was wearing a bright yellow hard hat that made both policemen think of Votek Visotsky's head rolling along the bloodied tiles on the floor of the car accessory store.

'It's the bodies,' Fergus told him. 'Me and Danny found them. Just wee babies, and the smell would kill you.' The words came tumbling out. He did not look quite so ashen as his apprentice, but you could tell he'd had a shock.

Jack took it a step at a time. He got the men's names first of all and then he asked what they'd seen and where.

'Up there,' Fergus pointed. 'They're in the chimney. Four of them at least. It gave young Danny a right turn. Nearly pitched him off.'

Jack looked up and his heart sank. *High places*. There couldn't be anywhere higher than that in the whole town.

'Shit,' he said, not quite under his breath. 'How the hell do we get up there?'

'Oh, it's all right. We've got ladders up the side.' He pointed out through the gate and Jack took a few steps outside to see where he was indicating. The spindly aluminium steps hugged the bricks all the way to the top, narrowing ever closer in the distance.

'Oh great,' he muttered. 'Bloody terrific. You'll have to come up with us.'

The man nodded. Jack took off his coat and slung it in the back seat of the car. Fergus Milby gave him a webbing belt harness, showed Jack how to clip on the safety catch and explained that it would move up along with him, but would lock if he dropped. Jack remembered it all from his teenage days, the last time he had climbed with a rope. A jittery nerve danced behind his knees and for a second he felt physically sick.

407

'Don't worry,' the other man tried to reassure him. 'That cable can hold three tons. You'll be as safe as houses.'

Fergus went on up the ladder, taking light, easy and confident steps. Jack stood at the bottom, took several deep breaths and began to follow him, keeping his eyes fixed on the brickwork inches in front of his eyes, not daring to look elsewhere. About forty steps up, he was sweating so badly his shirt was soaked and beads of salt water were dripping into his eyes. Despite that, he slowly climbed upwards, unable to force his hand off the rung and wipe his eyes, risking only the quick movement needed to grasp the next one up. At just over a hundred feet, though as far as Jack was concerned it could have been two miles, all noise below faded away to a faint hum. There was a slight wind and the metal treads, chilled by the breeze, were cold under his hands. Beneath him he could hear Ralph Slater's laboured breathing. At that moment, Jack knew that even if he decided to quit, he couldn't get back down beyond the scene-of-crime man. There was nothing for it but to continue upwards towards the top of the chimney.

Finally, without any warning, the brickwork in front of his eyes disappeared and a fresh cold breeze blew into Jack's eyes, causing them to spark with tears. He blinked them back, still gripping tight to the rungs of the ladder. Out of the corner of his eye, he could see the river snake away to the north, a silver band between the grey banks, and for a second the world zoomed in and out of focus while he rose the crest of a rush of vertigo.

'No bother,' Fergus Milby said. He had unclipped his safety line and was standing with incredible casualness, halfway round the chimney. 'Come on up.'

Jack heaved himself onto the top edge. For a second his hand refused to relinquish its grip on the rung, and it took a great effort of will to make it move. Finally he reached and grasped the edge of the bricks, feeling the tips of his fingers try to dig right into the hard surface. With infinite care and with enormous, gut-wrenching trepidation, he eased himself onto the top and sat, holding on with both hands, one leg inside the chimney, the other out, each heel jammed against the sides for extra purchase.

Then the smell hit him and took his mind off the appalling height.

'That's the first one we found,' Fergus said. He hunkered down beside the little tatter of cloth and pulled a piece back. The baby's parchment-like face seemed to be screwed up against the cold. Jack knew it was just desiccation. The fluids had leached out of the body and the wind had done the rest.

He risked a sideways turn and looked down the shaft. The afternoon sunlight only illuminated about ten feet then faded to blackness. It looked like a huge well. On the opposite side, he could see a piece of metal which had been bent down then pulled up again to form what looked like a butcher's hook. Something larger than the two bundles was suspended from one of the spikes. Even from where he sat, Jack could see the matted hair and the outline of a chin. A grey hand hung down there just in the twilight between daylight and shadow. Below it, he was not sure, but he thought he could make out a leg.

Ralph clambered up beside him and patted him on the shoulder.

'What a view, eh?'

Jack nearly fell off.

'Bloody hell, Ralph. Take it easy,' he bawled.

'Okay, Chief,' Ralph replied cheerily. 'You'll have us both off if you don't relax.'

Jack did not reply. He merely pointed at the thing hanging down from the spike.

'Oh dear Lord,' Ralph said softly, but with great feeling. 'How in hell did they get up here?'

Jack sat motionless, looking at the body on the far side and the smaller one close by, hanging next to a small thing that looked like a shrivelled skinned rabbit, but which he knew was not. The sickening dread of falling had been replaced by an entirely different emotion. For a while he forgot that he was perched nearly two hundred feet above the town on the huge chimney stack.

Five pitiful bodies. Three babies and a young boy and a teenage girl.

High places. Lorna Breck had been right. Michael O'Day with his mad eyes and his stuttering voice and shaking hands had not been wrong. This was one of the high places. This was where it had brought them. As he sat there on high, with the wind now

409

blowing across his face, Jack Fallon stopped thinking of *who*. There was no face to be put on this killer, no prints, no previous convictions, at least none that were on any police computer. Whatever had scaled this tower with no ladders, hauling the dead and bleeding bodies of these babies and children, could not, surely, have been human.

Jack slowly eased himself round on the flat. Across the roof of the forge was the green open space on this side of the river where the three housing blocks stood shoulder to shoulder. Latta Court had been the first. Little Timmy Doyle had gone missing from there. Whatever had scaled the wall of the block, climbing up from the ground or down from the darkened roof, had brought the little baby down from that height and come scrambling up here with its victim to impale it on an old lightning spike. Out beyond the flats, where the river took its turn past the tidal basin and swung into the saltwater estuary, the bulk of Castlebank Distillery loomed close to the rock where the castle sat. Carol Howard had gone up in the lift shaft, dragged up by something that had made her screams echo up to her workmates outside in the corridor, terrible screams that had made women burst into tears and grown men shiver. Just beyond it hunched the Castle Rock, where Annie Eastwood had walked the parapet and dived to spread herself on the butcher's blocks of the basalt rocks below.

Across the river, beside the railway bridge, the old warehouses huddled, derelict and shabby. Jack could see the square opening on the gable wall where the hoist had still worked when he and his pals had stolen pigeons. The jig still jutted out, though the pulley rope had long since rotted to tatters. Lorna Breck had seen it, the night Neil Kennedy had gone missing. She'd seen something come down from the dark and snatch him up like a rag. In that nightmare vision, she watched the thing scuttle in a black blur towards the opening in the wall. Jack tried to visualise the scene at night. Had it clambered across the railway bridge? Swung on the electricity gantries? It had brought them here, the five of them.

Something jarred at his memory. He closed his eyes to concentrate, and it came right to him. The three boys who had gone missing from the parts store were not here. He did a quick

410

count. Five bodies. Three babies, a child with matted and dirty red hair peeling in strips from a dented skull, a girl hanging from a spike that had impaled her under the jaw and come out at the temple.

Jack rhymed them off in his head. Carol Howard, Neil Kennedy, Timmy Doyle. Little Kelly Campbell. All present and correct, battered, bloodied, torn, but all here. And one other. One more little scrap, dangling down into the maw of the chimney, spiked through its skinny little chest so that it was hunched and contorted.

There hadn't been another child. Nobody had reported one missing, and in the last two weeks, every mother whose boy was five minutes late in coming home from school or who dawdled on the way back from the corner shop was on the phone to the station, half hysterical with worry. A third baby meant another huge problem among all the rest of the troubles which crowded in on him like melancholy mourners at a funeral.

As he sat and stared at the suspended shapes, Jack suddenly got a picture of Julie, lying among the shards of glass in the shop window, blood pooling out underneath her, eyes glazing over, motionless, lifeless. He saw in his mind's eye the spike of glass she'd landed on, driven through her back, through her heart and out in the centre of her chest, just under her breastbone. She'd been impaled, just like these dead and mouldering children.

No pain, Lorna had said, and of a sudden, Jack Fallon believed her completely. She'd seen it, seen it through him when she'd taken his hand in hers.

And what would she say now? Had these babies felt no pain?

He thought not. Little Timmy Doyle, wrenched from his pram so violently that the leather straps had snapped. Tiny Kelly Campbell, snatched from her mother's arms by something that had come down a wall and hit her so hard it had smashed the bones of her face. And she'd fought for her child, fought with the desperate ferocity and courage of a mother against something so powerful it had killed her with a blow. Neil Kennedy, whose blood had been found in congealing puddles, slowly soaking into the dry wooden beams of the old warehouse. It had come down and taken him like a spider does with a fly on the web. It had plucked him from the stairs and *climbed*. Had the boy felt *no pain*? And Carol Howard, screaming in the lift, her shrieks of anguish and terror diminishing as she was hauled up the shaft while her blood had sprayed over the cables. Pain and devastating terror were what she had felt. There was no doubt in his mind.

And there was also no doubt, right in that instant of clarity, that he would find it. No matter what it was, man, beast or goblin or whatever, he would catch it and he would stop it. He would catch it as an offering to these babies, these children, who were hung up like sacrifices in the well of the old forge chimney.

Then it came to him in a flash, the mental picture he'd formed when she'd described where the thing went. Looking down into a well, with the fires below. This was the place, this was the well. Down there, even in the gloomy winter-afternoon daylight, he could see the flares of the forge glowing red through the windows. No wonder she didn't recognise this place. At night, looking down, it would be like a vision of hell.

Fergus Milby went back down the ladder for a length of rope and some bags. It took him half an hour to get back, and the light was beginning to fade quickly. Ralph took as many pictures as he could, crouching on the lip of the chimney with a casual ease that alarmed Jack.

'I don't understand it, Chief,' he admitted. 'How the hell did they get up here?'

It climbs. The words seemed to echo in Jack's mind, repeating themselves over and over again.

'And why here? What's the point?'

It feeds. That's what Michael O'Day had said. It had brought these bodies up here and hung them up, like tidbits in a hellish larder. The little form lying on the flat had been savaged. Something had ripped it from the neck, and below the jagged gash, there was little left but strips of torn flesh. The other one, a very cursory appraisal had shown him, had been gutted. Strips of skin peeled back from a gaping space where the belly had been.

Jack did not want to tell Ralph any of what he was thinking. He regretted telling Cowie about O'Day. That had been a tactical error. It had taken *him* long enough, too long, to begin to come round to believing that what he was hunting was not human, but something conjured up, however it had been done, however preposterous it sounded, on the night that Marta Herkik had held the seance in Cairn House. Cowie had gaped at him as if he was mad. Even a reasonable man would have shied away from the notion.

Now Jack's problem was in deciding what to do about it. His choices were limited to one.

Fergus Milby popped his head over the edge. 'They had to get this rope from the post office,' he said, slightly out of breath. 'The engineers use them for pulling cables through the pipes.' He clambered onto the lip, unslung a big haversack and started pulling a plastic bag out. For the next half an hour, the three men wrapped the bodies, the babies first, into the bags and lowered them down the side of the chimney. Jack watched as the black trussed shapes diminished from view to the waiting people who milled like ants at the base; beside the winking blue lights. Finally, with some effort, they freed the body of Carol Howard. It was a hideous task. Both Jack and Ralph had to work to free the head from the spike, twisting it this way and that until they could draw the limp weight upwards. The smell was thick and poisonous. Finally the metal hook drew out with a wet, scraping sound and they laid the girl down on the bricks. One of her legs was gone. A ragged mess of blood, gristle and bone shards lay in the crater where the girl's hip had once been.

The two of them quickly wrapped her in a plastic sheet, tied the ends and looped the sling of rope around her. They dropped her over the edge. It took a long time for her to reach the ground.

The journey from the top of the chimney stack was less nerve-wracking than the ascent. The hot anger twisted inside Jack and cauterised his fear of heights. He'd seen murder victims aplenty. He'd been there on the moors when they'd dug up the bodies of drug dealers, and he'd been to many a low-life tenement in the city to find a glare-eyed corpse in a pool of blood and vomit or trussed like a chicken in a bath. The anger had come on him then, many a time, but not the way he felt it as he slowly lowered himself, rung by rung down the spindly ladder on the great forge chimney while the winter wind snatched at his jacket and the watery light began to fade from the sky. The pitiful bodies, hung like carcasses in a butcher's shop, torn and mutilated, had brought up emotions he'd been holding down for a long while.

413

For the first time he felt a strange mixture of pity and admiration for Lorna Breck. There was no doubt now that she was seeing these things. For some reason he could not quite understand, she was tuned, like a radio, to the thing that was taking children up to the high places to spike them on the old lightning forks. They had died from this, and she was living with it.

He was halfway down the chimney when a thought from the far past came back to him, way back in the sixties when he was just a small boy in short trousers, catching sticklebacks in the mill-burn that drained out of the water meadow into the river, or spearing flatfish down on the salt flats in the estuary.

Twitchy eyes. That's what they'd called him, the crazy man who had killed the boy in the back room of Cairn House all those years ago. He'd abducted a girl in East Mains, raped her and left her for dead up beyond Corrieside where there was a tree-filled glen, now long since cleared to make way for the encroaching housing schemes. The memory brought a strange twist of apprehension in Jack that had been long dormant. Then, in that hot summer, every child was scared of the man with the twitchy eyes whose crudely drawn image had stared, like a character in an old murder movie, from the posters in every school. He'd taken another small boy out on Westerhill where the trees tangled down the hill towards the shoreline and he'd smashed his head with a half-brick and kept on hitting him, so the story went, until nobody could recognise him as human. All summer there were organised picnics and play schemes, something the town had never had before. Mothers banded themselves into child-watching teams. Many kids were kept in and around their homes until the schools went back.

Then it had simply stopped. Police found an old couple dead and fly-blown in a croft house up on Blackwood Hill on the far end of town. They'd been shot at close range with a twelve-bore shotgun and left to rot in the tiny front room. That was the last of the killings in that year. The tracker dogs had scoured the moors up as far as Langmuir Crag, but the killer had long gone. He never killed again, as far as anybody knew. Later on, when Jack had been in his teens, his father had told him he thought the man had probably wandered up into the tarns of the moor where there were floating bogs which went down forever. Maybe he'd fallen

414

into one of them, or maybe he'd gone up into the hills and blown his head off. The killings had stopped, but Jack Fallon remembered the strange feeling of threat he'd felt when any stranger looked at him in the street. He remembered the wrench of anxiety as he scanned the stranger's face to ascertain whether this one had *twitchy-eyes*. Whether this was the one who would reach out and grab him and hit him with a half-brick until nobody could tell if he was human.

He remembered it and his anger grew. There were enough dangers for children. There were trees to fall out of, things for kids to swallow and stick in their throats. There were pans of boiling soup to scald them and fires to burn them. There were cars to run out of control and smash them through shop windows to impale them on knives of glass. These were the hazards, these and many more.

But it was different when someone, or some-thing, was out there, deliberately stalking children, snatching them away from their mothers and their homes and carrying them off to impale them in dreadful ignominy in a dirty chimney tower. He thought of the families whose lives had been ruined, the mothers and fathers and the brothers and sisters, a whole chain of anguish and choking misery, and he felt the heat of the anger boil inside him. By the time his feet touched the ground, he was almost speechless with rage at this *affront*. He didn't even supervise the loading of the trussed parcels into the wagon. He left that to the squad of men who had arrived. He got straight into his car and drove away, hands gripping the wheel in strangle-grips.

Lorna Breck called from behind the door when he rapped the knocker. When she heard his name, she opened it almost immediately. She looked up at him and gave him a tired smile, then held out her hand. He took it and she led him through to the kitchen.

'You're worn out,' she said.

'No,' he replied with some irony. 'I'm as fresh as a daisy.'

She let go his hand, but kept smiling. Her wide grey eyes looked him up and down appraisingly.

'You've had that same shirt on since the last time I saw you, and your trousers are covered in dust. You need a shave and a shower.' She wrinkled her nose as she spoke, and he felt uncomfortable under her scrutiny.

'And you have something important to tell me.'

'I do,' he agreed. 'And I will if you make me a coffee, hot and strong, but first I want to ask you something.'

'Of course I will,' she said, crossing to thumb the switch on the kettle. 'As long as you don't mind instant.' Jack shrugged.

'Tell me. The other night when you were describing the place it goes – could you tell me again?'

Lorna's face sagged. She came forward and leaned her hands on the back of the chair on the other side of the table.

'You've found them, haven't you?'

'Yes. By sheer luck, if you can call it that. They could have been there for years.'

'In the tunnel, or the well?'

'In a chimney. One of the two on the other side of the river.'

'Damn!' she hissed. 'Damnation. I didn't think. Yes. That's it. I can see it now. But who would have thought?'

'I know. I couldn't think either. You gave me a clue once, when you told me about the Kennedy boy. I remembered it from my childhood. If you'd grown up here, you would have known where it was.'

'It's all unfamiliar to me.'

'I know. It's not easy,' Jack said. 'You were also right about the bikes. It took three boys last night. I should have called you, but it was very late.'

'You should have called anyway. What happened to the boys?'

'They broke into a hardware store down near the allotments at Rough Drain. It must have been there, or come in after them. One of them got away.'

'The one who hurt it?'

'Yes. He put a drill in its eye. He told me it wasn't human.'

'But you know that,' Lorna said intensely.

'I'm finally beginning to believe it.'

'So what are you going to do now?'

'I don't have a clue. But I think I'll need your help.'

416

29

It was after six when Jack left Lorna's house down on Clydeshore Avenue. By this time it was dark and flurries of snow were whirling past the trees on the dark street, borne on a bitter north-west wind. Jack pulled his collar up as he walked towards his car, feeling the ice crackle under his feet. When he got to the station, both Ralph Slater and Robbie Cattanach wanted a word with him. He went down to the mortuary, where the young doctor was becoming a familiar presence.

'I'll have to transfer all of them to Lochend for a proper post mortem,' he said briskly. Normally Robbie was a cocky young fellow with a mischievous sense of humour, but when he worked, he was all business.

'But I have done a preliminary investigation. You've a girl of between fourteen and eighteen, a boy of about seven or eight, and three infants, two female, one boy. Ages range from approximately one to two years.'

'Cause of death?'

'Far too early to say. There's an incredible amount of damage, but at first glance I would suggest most of it has taken place after death, and I mean *long* afterwards.'

The three tiny forms, stripped of their rotted clothes and the plastic sheets, lay side by side, crosswise across one of the tiled blocks. The girl was spreadeagled on another. From ten feet away, Jack could see the devastating injuries on their bodies. The girl's one leg stuck out awkwardly. Her face was badly distorted where the spike had forced its way through her cheek. She was not as badly dried out and withered as the other small forms, but it was clear that in the cold and dry atmosphere of the chimney, her body had begun to lose moisture. It was lopsided and elongated. The ribs on the right side of her chest pushed up in corrugated lines, topped with a stiff flap of shrivelled skin which had once been a breast. On the other side, the ribs had been caved in, or pulled out, but Jack couldn't tell which.

'Robbie, I've got a problem here. I only had reports of four children. We've got one too many here.'

'We've got five too many, Jack. One's more than enough.'

'You know what I mean. There's a child here who's unaccounted for. It must be one of the girls.'

Robbie walked across to the slab and Jack followed behind his flapping white coat.

'Girl one. Approximately nine months.'

'That'll be Kelly Campbell. That's the one with the blood type.'

'Yes, I remember. The other is approximately two, going by the number of teeth.'

The little form was stretched out, head stiff and off to one side. A gaping hole just under the collarbone showed where the hook had forced through the skin and then, in time, torn upwards with the weight of the small body's suspension. The child had been disembowelled. Inside its abdominal cavity, the spine was clearly delineated.

'This one is in a more advanced state of decomposition than most of the others, except for the infant boy,' Robbie said matter-of-factly. 'At first glance, I would say this was one of the first.' He lifted up a stick-like arm. Something dangled loosely on the wrist. It was a small silver bangle. Robbie eased it off slowly and held it up.

'This might help,' he said, handing it to Jack, who turned it round to let the light catch the surface. One word was engraved in an amateurish script.

He turned to the phone and called through to the front counter. Sergeant Thomson came to the phone.

'Bobby, look out the file on that fire on Murroch Road about three weeks back. Get me all the names of the victims.'

He stayed at the phone, tapping his foot impatiently. Finally the duty sergeant came back. Jack could hear the pages flick over while Bobby Thomson muttered to himself.

'Got it. That was the Sunday night. Yes. One Patrick McCann, also dependents James, Brendan and Kerry. Tragic case, sir. Mrs McCann took an overdose several days later. I can look up the details if you like.'

Jack told him it wouldn't be necessary. He made another call,

418

this time asking for an outside line, and got straight through to Sorley Fitzpatrick at the fire station.

'Sure, Jack,' Sorley said agreeably. 'I was there that night and most of the morning after. A lot of damage. Took the whole top storey and collapsed it down through the lower floors. Not a damned smoke alarm among them. You'd think people would learn.'

'What about the victims?'

'All dead, I'm afraid. The heat was pretty fierce. We got some remains, about enough to fill a biscuit tin. Your folk identified the father and one of the kids. The other couldn't be positively identified, and we couldn't find the baby at all, but that's not surprising. Soft bones and baby teeth, they don't hold up too well if the temperature's high enough. It's rare, but I've seen it happen before. I estimated we got a complete disintegration on the baby, poor wee soul.'

There was nothing more to ask. Jack thanked him and placed the receiver down. Again Lorna Breck had been right. She'd seen the fire happen, from a quarter of a mile away, just when it was raging through the McCann house. She'd touched Agnes McCann and had gone into a trance, and that strange, nightmare gift of hers had transported her right into the house. Everybody had believed it had been a fire, pure and simple, but Lorna Breck knew it had not been, and now Jack Fallon knew it too.

He held up the tiny silver bangle, a little hoop just big enough to slip over a baby's wrist, and read the engraving again. *Kerry*. A child who was supposed to have died in a fire, had now turned up in the chimney of the old forge, found completely by accident because a brick had fallen down and nearly brained Bernie Maguire while he sat on the pan. Jack calculated backwards. The blaze at the McCann flat had come only two days after Timmy Doyle had been snatched from his pram, and William Simpson had died two days after that. He could have sent a team up to knock on all the doors with a picture of the minister to get conclusive proof that he had been in the vicinity at the time, but he immediately decided against that. He did not need it any more. The fact that Kerry McCann had been found with the other bodies was enough for him. If there had been any doubt left in his mind, then it was completely overwhelmed by the facts.

419

He remembered the old quote, was it from Sherlock Holmes? *Whatever remains, no matter how improbable, must be the truth.*

However improbable, however *impossible*, was the idea that a group of people had gathered in the room at Cairn House and conjured up some kind of monster? It was the stuff of horror films, and bad horror films at that. In this day of computer games and video recorders and international conglomerates, where did a notion like that fit in? Yet it was also the day of ritualised rape and ethnic cleansing and death squads and innumerable evils that could make the world an annexe to hell.

Whatever remained, however impossible, had to be the truth.

And the truth was that something hideous scuttled in the dark in the high places of the ancient town of Levenford, something that had been brought up from another place in a strange and incomprehensible rite and given a kind of life. And it had rewarded those who had called it up with death.

'I don't think we have to look any further,' Jack said. 'She's Kerry McCann, aged about two. We thought she'd died in a fire.'

'That's the one in Corrieside?'

Jack nodded. 'They thought she'd been burned to a cinder.'

'Might have been better if she had,' Robbie said. 'I'm just looking at the damage to the bodies. These kids have been torn apart. Look here.' He leaned across the stiff and withered form nearest him.

'That's a bite there,' he said, indicating a crater the width of a handspread just under the ribs. 'But it looks more like a shark-bite. I'll do some sums and work out a radius, but you can take it from me that whatever did this has a mouth like a gin-trap, or it's somebody using some kind of tool. You can see there, where the flesh has been torn. The skin has been sliced in a bite and then ripped off. It's taken away the horn of the pelvis too, which indicates great crushing strength.'

He turned to the girl on the other table, sprawled in ungainly and grotesque stiffness. 'The leg has been bitten off. I thought at first it was a tear, but if you look here . . .' He quickly turned the body over. It kept its position, as if it was made from wood. 'You've got the same type of injury. Powerful incision through the skin, then tearing to the underlying muscle and crushing of bone. Something bit in here then twisted, like a crocodile.

'And if you look at her shoulder,' Robbie shifted his position, 'you'll see an odd thing.'

Jack looked. There was a great deal of damage on the girl's back. It meant nothing to him.

'Bruising and lacerations. Consistent with being dragged along a rough surface. But there,' he said, pointing with his pen. 'Two indentations, four inches apart. They've punctured the skin and muscle and left severe pressure bruises. They're exactly the same on the other side. That's how she was lifted.'

'And that's a bite?'

'No,' Robbie said flatly. 'Definitely not a bite. It's a grip. Something grabbed her with extreme violence, enough to break her collarbone, and as far as I can see, put a hole right through her shoulder blade. The odd thing is, there are marks of only four digits. Like an owl?'

'Go on,' Jack said, unsure of what Robbie meant.

'An owl sits with two claws at the front and two at the back. Ideal for perching and also for snatching prey.'

'So I should look for an owl?'

'No. You should be looking for something with a handspan about a foot wide, with four claws on each.'

'So what do you recommend?'

'Nothing on this earth,' Robbie said with a grim smile. 'Remember what I said when I examined Shona Campbell's body? Somebody had hit her with the strength of a bear?'

He looked at the stiff, blackened shape lying on the table.

'It certainly wasn't a bear. If you want to get something that's close, I would suggest the museum of natural history. The only thing I can imagine is one of the dinosaur raptors, and they've been dead for sixty million years.'

Jack left him making preparations to transfer the bodies to the lab at Lochend. It was too early to call in the parents of the dead children, though he knew he'd have to, all except Agnes McCann, who had decided life without her family was not worth living, and Shona Campbell, whose corpse was still in cold storage waiting for release by the sheriff. The identification of the bodies would be a nightmare for all concerned. What father would recognise his daughter, or mother her son, when they had been left hanging up like meat, bitten and chewed and mutilated?

Ralph Slater had taken fragments of clothing from each of the bundles and had sent them to the central forensics lab for analysis along with fibres he'd collected at the scenes of the abductions.

'I don't know what the hell's going on,' he said in frustration.

'You and me both,' Jack agreed with him, not telling the entire truth.

'So what next?'

'I've got the extra manpower from head office. We go back over every scene. I want you to work with John McColl and try to get a central location. Work out a progress map for me, times, dates, the lot. And put in elevations as well. There must be a pattern.'

Even though he said it, Jack was not convinced there would be any pattern. His only hope, he realised, would be for Lorna Breck to use her special talent and see it in action again, and he would hope against hope that she recognised something in time. What he would do then, he hadn't a clue.

'I don't know,' Andy Toye said in answer to the question. Jack had managed to get him between lectures, but he would have hauled him out of one had it been necessary.

'There's a lot of speculation, of course, but no recent documentation. The old texts say how to summon a spirit, but then it's supposed to be confined within a container or by some other means. You could try holy water, or maybe a stake through the heart.'

'Like a vampire?'

'I'm just taking a shot in the dark. I just don't know.'

'What about the instructions you read out? Something about a talisman or whatever?'

'Wherefore, the magician must hold the ring in his face,' Andy quoted from memory, 'of pure iron or fine gold, or talisman blessed by consecrated hands and that will defend him.'

'Would something like that work?'

'I don't know. Nobody does. You could give it a try, but don't come to me if it doesn't work.'

'I won't,' Jack said, drily.

'Can I take it you're beginning to take this seriously?' Andy asked.

'I have to take it seriously. I've got eight murders so far and six suicides, plus two boys missing presumed dead. I've got a regular Armageddon on my hands down here, and the only clues I have are from a delirious seventeen-year-old who says he stuck a drill in its eye, and from a Highland girl who's got some kind of ESP.' He paused to draw breath. 'And I've got a pathologist friend who tells me I should be looking for a dinosaur with feet like an owl, the strength of a bear and a bite like a crocodile. Yes, I'm taking it seriously.'

'I think the girl's your best hope,' Andy said. 'I do think she's got a gift.'

Jack came down from his office and through the swing doors just as a commotion broke out right at the desk.

Three uniformed officers were scuffling with a man who was bent over the front desk with an arm up his back. He was desperately kicking out in all directions. A lucky toe caught young Gordon Pirie right in the crotch and he went down like a sack of potatoes, hands jammed between his legs, groaning in pain.

Jack continued walking. One of the other officers slammed the man down hard on the desk, making his head thump the polished surface. The fellow yelled, squirmed round and saw Jack.

'You bastard!' he bawled at the top of his voice. Two old ladies who had come in to report a lost purse shrank back, shaking their heads and tut-tutting in genteel disapproval.

'You swine that you are!' the man shouted. 'You said you'd let me stay in the church.'

Jack stopped in mid-stride and spun round just as one of the policemen clamped his hand round the man's throat and forced him back to the desk. Michael O'Day spluttered and struggled, displaying surprising strength despite his scarecrow build.

'Promised me, you cheating lying shite,' he screeched, feet still flailing. 'Let go of me, you swines.'

'What's going on here?' Jack barked. Everything went quiet.

'Bastard,' Michael O'Day spat at him.

'Hold on, you,' Jack ordered. 'And stay still.' He walked up to the constable who was holding the skinny man in a death grip. O'Day's jacket was torn at the pocket and the collar of his shirt, already crumpled and dirty, was sticking up at an angle. A light dusting of snow was melting on his shoulders.

'What's happening?' he asked again. 'What's this man doing here?'

'Superintendent Cowie told us to get him down from the church,' the policeman said. 'He nearly took my head off with an iron bar. Damned maniac. He's in for it now.'

'Just hold on. Mr Cowie told you to arrest him?'

'Yes, sir. Breach of the peace and theft, but now he's up for resisting arrest and police assault.'

'You promised me, you lying swine,' O'Day grated bitterly. He was struggling against the big policeman's grip and making no progress. One of his shoes came flying off and rolled under a chair.

'Just wait here until I get to the bottom of it,' Jack said. 'And stay quiet, or I'll throw you in the cell myself.'

He stalked off back the way he had come and shouldered his way through the swing door. At the Superintendent's office, he bulled his way in without knocking.

'What's this all about?'

Cowie looked up.

'I beg your pardon?'

'O'Day. You've had him arrested.'

'Of course I did. He was causing disorder, and according to you, he'd already admitted theft,' Cowie said smugly. 'We can't have people like that running around, and we can't have policemen making deals and condoning such actions, especially when they have more pressing and serious matters to attend to.'

'But I told him he could stay there.'

'I know you did, and I overruled you. Listen, Chief Inspector, I don't know what you're playing at. You came to me with a fairy tale about seances and devil-worship. Now I don't know about you, but that doesn't strike me as going by the book. I think you've overstepped the mark, and I've cut you down to size.'

'O'Day is crucial to my investigation,' Jack said as calmly as he was able.

'Oh really? A mad Irishman who thinks he's being chased by ghosts? Up in a church belltower? I can hardly see how that figures in your investigation. I really don't know what sort of investigation you are conducting, but so far it's produced nothing except delusion. Let's see, you've had how many murders? Eight so far? Nine? Half a dozen suicides. And what have you got? An Irishman who says he claims sanctuary and has you convinced he's been conjuring up devils.' Cowie smirked. 'Not the most impressive result of an investigation, is it?'

'But I need him,' Jack protested, almost speechless with anger.

'No, mister. You need to get results, and so far you've come up with big fat zero. You've made yourself look a fool, and by God, you won't make me look like one. You've gone over my head and I don't like that.'

'I went by the book on that one. We need more men.'

'I make the decisions around here, and you'd do well not to forget it. The Chief Superintendent, as far as I can gather, won't be back, at least not for some time, and when he's gone, I'm in command. You'd do well to remember that too. I want this place running properly and that includes the murder investigation. So far your attempts have been abysmal.'

'I already told you I was following up a lead in connection with O'Day, and I told you it was important to leave him where he was. At least he's talking.'

'Talking gibberish, yes. And if you believe a word of it, you're a bigger fool than you're beginning to look. Now he's in our custody and you can talk to him all you like, but I warn you, *Chief Inspector*, I don't expect you to waste any more time. You've got a madman out there who, as far as we know, has killed eight people of this burgh. I must stress to you as strongly as I can that I am far from impressed with your lack of progress, your attitude and your conduct of this operation. One more such lapse, and you will be off this case. I have that authority, and by God I'll use it.'

He smiled up at Jack, favouring him with a triumphant self-satisfied narrowing of his eyes.

'Now, if that's all, some of us have important work to do.'

Jack spun on his heel and stalked out of the office.

The front office was empty, apart from the two old biddies who were huddled together at the desk, giving a bored looking young policeman their details. Bobby Thomson cocked his thumb in the direction of the cells. Jack went downstairs, passing the mortuary as he went. The wasted and mutilated bodies, covered with white sheets, were being carried out of the rear door for the short trip to Lochend and the pathology lab.

Michael O'Day was sitting in a corner, huddled up inside his badly wrinkled coat, feet drawn up beside him on the low bench-cot and arms hugged around his knees.

'Bastard,' he hissed when the young turnkey opened the door and let Jack inside.

'For what it's worth, I didn't agree to this. I had already told them to let you stay where you were.'

'You expect me to believe that? Eh? Listen, you, I'm a dead man. You're looking at a corpse.'

'You'll be safe enough in here,' Jack said reassuringly, but it didn't work.

'Safe? You think I'll be safe? Are you mad or what? I told those cretins to leave me alone. The only place I was safe was in the church. Now it'll come for me. I can hear it already.'

The emaciated man cocked his head to the side, as if listening.

'It's back in my head. I can hear it. You've killed me, don't you see it? Jesus help me. It's coming for me. It'll make me do whatever it wants.'

'No,' Jack said, though he knew he was on unsteady ground. 'We'll give you protection. I can't put you back in the church. It's an order down from upstairs and I've got to go along with it.'

'Protection, is it? And what protected Janet Robinson? She worked here, for God's sake. Did that protect her? Listen, man, you can't stop this thing. It's not human.'

He stopped and cocked his head again.

'Fuck off, you bastard,' he said, staring right at Jack, but his eyes were focused much further away. 'Get out of my fuckin' head,' he screeched.

All of a sudden, the man on the cot began to cry. His eyes were still open, still wildly staring.

'It's coming for me,' he wailed. 'Oh, holy mother forgive me. I didn't know.'

30

Mutilated bodies of five children have been found by detectives leading the biggest ever murder inquiry in Levenford's history, the story blared from the front page of the *Gazette*.

The gruesome find was made by steeplejacks working on a disused venting chimney at Thomson's Forge.

And the discovery follows the macabre abduction of two teenagers and the brutal slaying of another in a car-part store in the early hours of Thursday morning.

The latest violent death was discovered yesterday when staff at Rolling Stock in the commercial centre just off Strathleven Street opened for business. The horrified shop assistants discovered part of the body of a young man, and evidence of a violent struggle in which, it is suspected, two other teenage boys have been injured or killed.

The dead boy has been identified at Votek Visotsky, whose father Karl is the well-known manager of Kirkland Automobiles and secretary of the Round Table. The shocked parents were too distressed last night to speak of the tragedy.

The missing boys are Edward Redford and Charles Black, both of East Mains, who have been missing since Wednesday night. A blood-soaked piece of clothing, bearing a wallet identified as belonging to Edward Redford, leads police to suspect he was involved in the incident. His whereabouts are subject to a massive police search of the area around the Rough Drain on the east side of the Burgh.

Police are also investigating an incident involving a fourth youth, known to be a friend of the other three, who was found badly injured on Castlebank Street in the early hours of the morning by local bowling club secretary and newsagent Walter Dickson. Mr Dickson took the boy, believed to have been burned, to Lochend Hospital from where he was rushed to Keltybank Hospital, the world-renowned plastic surgery unit, where he is still undergoing emergency treatment.

The bodies in the Thomson Forge Chimney, one of the town's major landmarks, were discovered by Fergus Milby and his assistant Daniel Cullen moments after they scaled the 200-foot tower in a routine maintenance operation.

They told the Gazette *that the dead children had been impaled on the spikes of lightning conductors and were hanging inside the chimney. Mr Milby described the scene as being 'like a butcher's shop'.*

Police are working on the theory that the dead children include the bodies of babies Timothy Doyle and Kelly Campbell, both of whom were abducted two weeks ago. Mrs Shona Campbell was killed in the barbaric attack. Two of the others are believed to be those of Neil Kennedy, 8, who went missing from his home in Miller Road on Monday night, and Carol Howard, 16, who disappeared from an elevator in Castlebank Distillery on Tuesday. The identity of the fifth child is unknown at the moment, raising yet another riddle in this series of tragedies. Police have confirmed that they have had no further reports of missing children so far.

The horrific slayings, which began with the murder of elderly Marta Herkik in her home in Cairn House on River Street, now thought to have been the beginning of the series of deaths and abductions, have been paralleled by a bizarre succession of suicides.

Blair listed them at length.

The man heading the murder and abduction inquiry, Detective Chief Inspector Jack Fallon, has appealed for any information concerning the deaths.

Mr Fallon and scene of crime officer Inspector Ralph Slater were first on the scene at Thomson Forge where the bodies were found, and again affirmed the warnings to all parents. Because of the public outcry over the series of horrific killings, Regional Headquarters have confirmed the temporary transfer of a significant number of officers to help in the inquiry.

Mr Fallon said he had to weigh the balance between causing a public panic and ensuring public protection.

'I have to say protection comes first,' he told the Gazette: *'Every parent should by now be aware of the danger to children. This person, or persons, has so far taken babies, a boy, and a teenage girl, and possibly three youths. All of the incidents have happened at night, but this pattern may change. We cannot say.*

'Every parent should be made aware of the dangers. Children must be watched at all times, and they should under no circumstances be out after dark. Any woman, young or old, should avoid dark or isolated places where there are no people. At night, all windows and doors should be locked. Deserted areas must be avoided.'

Provost Stanley Moor, leader of the Labour administration on the District Council, however, last night hit out at the lack of police success.

'What are we paying them money for?' he asked. 'They've got people out stopping drivers with broken tail lights and giving out parking tickets, while there's some maniac running around our streets and killing our children. This town is under siege, and I wasn't voted in here to sit back and take it. I will be speaking to the Chief Constable first thing in the morning to demand immediate action.'

Provost Moor declined to offer any advice to the murder squad detectives, or to suggest what action they should take.

The story continued on pages two and three and the centre spread. Blair Bryden had again burned the midnight oil and he'd gone knocking on the doors. There were interviews with relatives and friends, pictures of white-faced shop assistants at Rolling Stock who were far from shy about describing in detail what they had found in the early hours of a cold and frosty morning. Blair had been circumspect about his own descriptions. An old aerial shot of the town had been hauled out of the files and spread across the centre pages, with every location outlined with a black circle. It looked as if Levenford had been used as a target by a giant hoopla-player. They crowded on the page like a scattering of malignant haloes. On the wing column of the spread, there was another article.

OCCULT DETECTIVES?

Chief Superintendent Jack Fallon is remaining tight-lipped about the involvement of two alleged psychic experts who have both been interviewed at Levenford Police Station and are believed to be helping with inquiries.

The experts are Andrew Toye, professor of paranormal studies at the City university, and librarian Lorna Breck, who recently

429

featured in these pages after a tragic fire on Murroch Road which claimed the lives of four people.

Professor Toye is a well-known authority on the occult and a veteran psychic investigator. Last year he was involved in the Blackhale mystery where a young girl was thought to have been the focus of a poltergeist-style haunting. Professor Toye is also respected for his expertise in Celtic Studies.

Lorna Breck, of Clydeshore Avenue, who recently came to Levenford to work in Strathleven Library, is reputed to have foreseen the disastrous fire which claimed the life of Patrick McCann and his three small children, James, Brendan and Kerry.

Though Miss Breck makes no claims for any psychic capability, Mrs Moira McCluskie, a friend who was present during the 'episode', told the Gazette: 'It was amazing. I've never seen anything like it in my life. Lorna was reading the tea leaves, and we were all having a bit of fun. Nobody took it seriously, at least I didn't.

'But then she went all funny and started telling Agnes to go home. That was the mother, poor woman. She said she had to go home because her house was on fire, and it was true. When we went downstairs, we could hear the fire engines in the distance and by the time we got along to Murroch Road, there was nothing left of the house.'

Both Professor Toye and Lorna Breck have refused to comment on their involvement.

However, it is known, or suspected, that the first in this terrifying spate of murders happened during a seance in Cairn House, the tragic history of which has been revealed in previous issues of the Gazette.

Mrs Herkik, a Hungarian refugee, was a well-known psychic or spey-wife who held regular seances in her fourth-floor rooms. Police are working on the theory that she may have actually been killed during the progress of such a sitting.

A further, and more disturbing theory is that she may have been at the centre of a cult of devil-worshippers or occultists.

At St Rowan's Church, Father Liam Boyle said: 'This kind of blasphemy is dangerous and a sin against the Holy Ghost and the first of the commandments. People who are involved in these practices are in danger of losing their immortal souls.'

Chief Inspector Fallon has so far refused to confirm the involvement of either Miss Breck or Professor Toye, but other forces in England have, on numerous occasions, sought the help of so-called psychics in the search for missing persons. But the fact that a paranormal expert and an alleged fortune teller have been discussing the issue with the murder squad detectives suggests that they had been called in for advice on both the mysterious and brutal killing of Marta Herkik and the whereabouts of the missing children.

Mr Fallon would only confirm that none of them are suspected of any involvement in the horrendous crimes which have terrified the people of Levenford.

The discovery of the five dead children in the chimney of Thomson's Forge may indicate that their involvement has been helpful.

It is not understood how, or why, the children were taken to such an inaccessible place and hung on the spikes. The awful find, reminiscent of the cache of the Shrike, *or butcher-bird, which impales its prey, has sent shock waves of fear and anxiety throughout the community. On Friday, Fr Boyle is to hold a special service of prayer for the victims and for an end to the spate of killings.*

'What the hell is this?' Cowie said, throwing the newspaper down onto his desk. It landed with a loud slap.

'It's a newspaper,' Jack said, blandly. 'Is this what you called me in for?'

Jack had managed to get up to Julia's house where she cooked him the first real dinner he could remember in recent weeks.

As he wolfed a steak pie, Davy sat beside him while Julia eyed him askance.

'So he's not happy?' she asked.

'He'll never be happy. Dad told me about folk like Cowie, promoted above their station. The handshake still counts for too much, even these days.'

'Dad would have killed you if you'd joined them.'

'I would have killed myself,' Jack said through a mouthful of pastry. 'There's too many damned secrets without having a society to start new ones.'

'Uncle Jack said a bad word,' Davy piped up gleefully, nudging

Jack just under the ribs. 'Just like he said when he fell in the water.'

'Now Davy,' Julia told him, though she was looking at Jack with her eyebrows raised. 'Don't tell tales.'

'Explosive expletive,' Jack said, trying to keep his face straight. 'I didn't think he heard.'

'Are you going to catch the bad men?' the boy asked, eyes wide and serious.

'Bad men?' For a moment Jack was nonplussed, then the coin dropped. 'Oh yes. I'm going to catch them.'

'We had a policeman round today again. We can't even get out in the playground any more. We all have to stay in.'

'That's the best thing. When I catch the bad men, you can all get out to play again.'

'Good,' Davy said brightly. 'I told my pals you would get them. They all said it was a monster that caught people and ate them. Some of the girls were crying, but I wasn't. I told them you'd catch them and punch them on the nose.'

'That I will,' Jack said. In himself, he was wondering how he was going to catch whatever he was hunting. Somehow he thought a punch on the nose would not be standard operating procedure.

He'd toyed with the idea of going back up to Lorna Breck's house, again, but after his run-in with Ronald Cowie, he'd decided against it, because he was still tense with anger. A sister was different, especially one like Julia who'd already been through the wars of a divorce. She knew how to handle him. Her house, just round the corner from Cargill Farm Cottage, was the one place he could sit and let the tension ease out. There was another reason, one that he'd just begun to realise when he'd thought about making another trip across to Clydeshore Avenue.

She was a strange girl, Lorna Breck. The first time he'd met her, she'd been in a state of hysterical collapse. The second, she'd looked not much better. But since then, since he'd got to know her a little better, and once he'd made the enormous mental leap of actually believing what she said, he'd seen her in a different light. He'd thought of her short chestnut-shiny hair and her wide, innocent grey eyes as they fixed upon him and he had felt the stirring of something he hadn't felt for so long he thought he'd

432

forgotten how to feel it. Sometimes in the past couple of days, without even consciously thinking it, he'd noticed what a stunner Lorna Breck was. Maybe he'd bodyswerved the notion, shrugged it off as soon as it started in his head, but when he considered his reasons for going back up to her house in the early evening, he couldn't really think of one, except that he wanted to.

So he came to Julia's house instead and had dinner with his sister and his nephew and tried not to think about Lorna Breck at all.

That was where Ronald Cowie's assistant found him after telephoning several numbers.

'The boss wants you in here pronto,' the voice said.

'Why, what's happened?' Jack asked. Davy was over at the table by the window doing a jigsaw puzzle he'd asked his uncle to help him with. Julia was on the armchair, legs curled up underneath her, looking across at her brother with muted concern.

'I don't know. I haven't heard anything. He just wants you to report to his office immediately.'

It was pitch black when Jack got into his car. Davy waved from the window as he pulled away and went back down to the station.

Cowie looked up at him when he came into the Superintendent's office and threw the paper down with an angry slashing motion.

Jack picked it up and read Blair Bryden's front page piece.

'Seems about right,' he said.

'Oh no, it's not alright,' Cowie snorted. 'Are you responsible for that information?'

'Some of it, not all. He's a digger. Knows his area.'

'And what about the rubbish on the centre pages?'

Jack flipped through and held the wings of the paper up in front of him. He gave the aerial shot a cursory glance. He'd his own picture from the air, and huge grid-maps besides. He already knew where everything had happened. He scanned the quotes from Doreen Sweeney in Rolling Stock, flicked over the tremulous statements gleaned from Sandra Mitchell, who had watched the crazed Derek Elliot being ground to a pulp under the train, and skimmed over the colourful description of the find in the chimney as told by Danny Cullen.

433

Then the headline on the other side of the page caught his eye and he felt himself sag.

'Witchcraft?' Cowie barked. 'Is that what we're down to? I thought it was bad enough with that Irishman, but this really takes the biscuit.'

'Sorry,' Jack said as levelly as he could. 'I'm not with you.'

'You had better believe that,' Cowie said, his voice rising in indignation. 'I want to know what you're playing at. I was told nothing about these charlatans. What the hell are they doing on a murder case?'

'They're helping with inquiries.'

'You'd better explain that,' Cowie grated.

'Certainly. Professor Toye is an old acquaintance of mine from university. I brought him in for an expert opinion on the Cairn House murder. He's an expert of parapsychology and the occult. Assuming that Marta Herkik was involved in some sort of seance at or around the time she died, I thought his advice might be helpful.'

'And this Breck girl?'

'That's a different kettle of fish,' Jack said, extemporising. He was loath to tell Ronald Cowie exactly why he'd been dealing with Lorna Breck. Certainly Blair Bryden had worked something out for himself, and Jack could not blame him for running the piece in the *Gazette*, no matter how unhelpful it was to him. He'd promised to keep it out until Friday's edition. Jack had forgotten that the bi-weekly paper was printed on a Thursday night. Cowie had got an early copy.

'She's reputed to have some sort of extra sensory perception. Professor Toye believes she'd be helpful.'

'And that's why you have made this whole station a laughing stock?'

'I don't quite see it like that. Lorna Breck was able to give us a specific pointer to the warehouse where the Kennedy boy was snatched. Based on that, I feel that she might be crucial to this operation.'

'Mister Fallon,' Cowie hissed through clenched teeth. 'Must I remind you that this is a murder inquiry? The fact that you have brought in so-called psychics and fortune tellers makes you, and every man in this station, look like a fool, and I'm not going to

434

have that. The people out there,' he said with a sweeping gesture, 'expect solid investigation, and that's what they are going to get. They do not expect you to consult the stars, or witches or whatever you care to call them. They want this thing stopped, and if you think star-gazing is going to do it, you're very much mistaken.'

'I brought them in for sound reasons. They are also in addition to the investigation. I've had people out all over town every minute of the day since this started.'

'And come up with nothing, as I predicted. Now it's your day of reckoning. The reputation of this force and the safety of the people of this burgh is much too important. As you told me earlier, you believe this man O'Day was at the sitting which ended in the death of Marta Herkik?'

Jack saw what was coming, but he could not tell a lie on this.

'Yes. I believe he was.'

'He admitted this to you?'

Jack nodded.

'And you left him up in the belltower, despite your knowledge that he had broken into the church and stolen valuable religious objects.' Cowie snorted with derisory laughter.

'So, you have a witness to a murder. All the others believed to have been present are dead, and you let this man stay free? Didn't you stop to think that this man is not only a witness but a prime suspect?'

'I don't think so,' Jack said. 'In fact I know he is not a suspect. He couldn't have carried out the killings.'

'I take it you got that from the stars, eh?'

Jack said nothing, and Cowie blustered on triumphantly.

'Gross dereliction of duty. Criminal dereliction as far as I'm concerned, and I suspect a few others will see it my way. I am now formally taking over this case, which, if you had done your job properly, you would realise is pretty much cut and dried. I have instructed Inspector Slater to formally arrest Michael O'Day for the murder of Marta Herkik and complicity in the killings of Doyle, Campbell, Kennedy, and Howard with others unknown. I believe his already admitted links with the suicides will reveal more than you have so far found.'

Cowie leaned forward and put his hands on his spotless desk. The buttons on his shoulder gleamed in the overhead light.

435

'Have you anything to say?' he asked, with what could only be described as a sneer.

'I think you're making a huge mistake. O'Day did not kill any of those people. Look at the state of the man. He can hardly stand up. If you speak to Dr Cattanach, he'll tell you. The marks on those bodies were not made by anything he's ever seen.'

'Oh, you haven't considered the possibility of ritual torture and mutilation?'

'You think he climbed that chimney and put the bodies there?'

Cowie faltered a little, but then came back strongly.

'That's neither here nor there. You have a man who admitted he was there when the Herkik woman was killed and who has admitted his association with all of the others suspected of involvement. I think that wraps the case up nicely. Now, if you'll excuse me, I have some serious police work to do. And you, my university educated friend, will be the subject of a report to headquarters. As far as you are concerned, I think you can count your days on this force as numbered.'

Jack stood there, towering over his superior, almost unable to breathe because of the tight anger building up inside him. It took a great effort of will to force the words out of his mouth without shouting.

'Listen to me, you crazy shit. If you think this is over, you've got another think coming. And if you stop this investigation now, then you'll be responsible for what happens next. This is *not* finished yet. If somebody else dies, then you'll have blood on your hands.'

Cowie smiled brightly. 'Oh, I don't really think so. And by the way, I'll be adding this conversation to my report.'

He flicked a hand towards the door. 'That will be all. I believe you are off duty now. I understand you have several days owing, so as of tonight, I must insist you take them. You look a little over-tired.'

Jack found the door handle and it took another major effort not to wrench the door from its hinges.

He found Ralph Slater and John McColl in the operations room. They looked up as he came in and he could see their discomfiture as soon as he opened the door.

'Sorry, Chief,' Ralph started. 'There was nothing we could do.

He came down and insisted I make up an arrest sheet on O'Day. The poor bastard didn't understand a word when I read him his rights. He's down there going mental. Gibbering like an idiot.'

'Do you think O'Day did any of this?'

'Oh, I think he's crazy enough at the moment, but he's scared out of his mind, and it's not us he's frightened of. Says something's coming for him. I reckon you've got a better idea of what he's talking about than we have, but no, I don't believe it. There's not a pick on the man. He looks as if he hasn't eaten for a fortnight, and he's scared witless.'

'Is that fool Cowie closing the case?' John asked.

'I'm afraid he is. I'm off it, in case you didn't hear the jungle drums. That only means he'll make an announcement tomorrow, get a bloody great pat on the back, and then all the kids will come out to play again. Then another youngster will get killed. I told him it's not over yet, but he wouldn't listen.'

'Man's a buffoon,' John said. 'Batteries not included. So what do we do now?'

'I've got a problem. I've been told to take time owing. I can't refuse it. But I would appreciate it if you kept me in touch.'

He scribbled three numbers down on a sheet of paper and handed it to Ralph.

'I'll be at one of these if you have to get hold of me. Stay close to Robbie Cattanach and get his post mortem results as quickly as possible. And Ralph, if you can get a rush on those blood samples from Rolling Stock, they'll tell us who was who. The search for those lads will need top priority, but for God's sake, have a word with the Community Involvement boys. No matter what Cowie says tomorrow, and he'll probably send a fax up to HQ tonight, I want them all round the schools in the afternoon. We can't afford a stand-down on that, or we'll lose more children.'

He stood, hunched over with his hands in his pockets, the familiar slick of straight black hair hanging down over his eye.

'We're going to lose more anyway,' he said with utter conviction. He opened his drawer and took out a flat folder which he stuffed inside his bag, then left without a word.

This time he did go to Lorna Breck's house. Again she called out from behind the door, but when she heard his voice she opened it quickly and gave him a wide smile. Jack's heart did a strange little flip and he mentally berated himself for a fool. Lorna reached out and took his hand, pulling him over the threshold. He dropped his bag in the hallway.

'I was hoping you would come back,' she said.

'Why's that?'

The girl shrugged. She was wearing a pair of light jeans and a baggy pullover that made her look even younger than before.

'Oh, I don't know. I've been thinking, maybe we can work together on this. I feel safe when you're with me.'

Jack's heart did its little thump again. He wasn't sure he liked this.

She led him through to the kitchen still holding his hand. 'I've got some wine in the fridge. Want some?'

Jack hadn't had wine in as many weeks as he'd missed hot dinners. He decided he'd really like a glass or two, or ten. She handed him the bottle from the fridge. It was red, but he didn't care. It would taste just as good cold. He pulled the cork while she got the glasses and poured two manly amounts. She told him to sling his coat and jacket over a chair and they both sat down opposite each other.

'Something's wrong,' she said.

'You got that from holding my hand?'

'No, silly,' she said and then she laughed for the first time in Jack's recollection. It was surprisingly throaty and very feminine and Jack took a drink from his glass so he wouldn't notice if his heart did it again. 'I can see it on your face. You look as if you want to do somebody an injury.'

'Oh, I do. I've just been pulled off the case by a pompous, ignorant, incompetent fool of a man.'

'Why?'

'Because he read the *Gazette* today. They've speculated about you and Professor Toye.'

Lorna coloured. 'But I didn't say anything to them. Mr Bryden phoned me and I told him I didn't want to comment.'

'So did Andrew Toye. It doesn't matter. That's not the real reason. My Superintendent thinks he can get a feather in his cap by telling the world he's arrested the killer. He's hauled Michael O'Day down to the station. He's been up in St Rowan's belltower for the best part of a week. All he's eaten and drunk are holy wafers and holy water. He couldn't put a hole in a wet tissue.'

438

Lorna looked at him intently. 'That means he'll stop the hunt, doesn't it?'

Jack affirmed that with a look.

'So it will keep on going. It will kill other people.'

'That's what I told him, but he's hungry for the fame and the kudos. And by the way, he called you a charlatan.'

Lorna's eyes widened instantly and it was Jack's turn to laugh.

'Oh, what the hell,' he said. 'Let's have a drink, then a think. I've got one or two friends who have promised to help me.'

'And another one,' Lorna said. Jack looked across at her and she smiled again, her eyes crinkling. 'You've got me.'

Jack took another gulp of his wine. He sat in uncomfortable silence for a few moments until Lorna spoke again. 'I do want to help, but I'm scared.'

He reached across the table and engulfed her small hand in his. The skin was warm and soft. 'Me too, and working blind. I want to try something, see if I can use you as my eyes, but first I'll tell you what O'Day told me, and what Andrew Toye thinks.'

He explained about Michael O'Day's appeal for sanctuary.

'He says it can't get him as long as he's on hallowed ground and has the sacraments to protect him. So far, as far as I can see, he's been right.'

Jack reached for his coat and fumbled in the pocket. He drew out the cross which O'Day had handed to him up in the tower. He'd forgotten about it until that moment.

'He said I should keep a hold of that. Thinks it can protect me. I suppose I should give it back to the church.'

Lorna reached across and took the crucifix in her hand, hefting it.

'No. I think you should keep it until this is over.'

He shook his head. 'Maybe O'Day believes, but not me.'

She held onto the golden cross, rubbing the surface with her thumb. 'Now that he's out, what will happen?'

'I don't know. My folk have promised to keep a special watch on him. I think he'll be safe enough where he is. Nobody can get in and he can't get out. The man's hardly got the strength to walk. He told me about the seance in Cairn House, and I believe him. The rest of them didn't turn on Marta Herkik. They were involved in some kind of ritual and he says something came into the room. Like a scene from *Poltergeist*.'

439

Lorna raised her eyebrows, asking a silent question.

'It was a film. Great special effects. O'Day says this was no trick. Andy Toye goes along with it. It's hard to take it all in, but I'm prepared to go along too. O'Day says whatever it is, it's been using the people who were at Cairn House. I don't know why and I don't know how, but he seems to think it needs them for energy or food or something.'

'Where does it come from?'

'God alone knows. Andy has some old books which tell how to raise demons. Call it hell or the underworld or another dimension, it doesn't matter. I've got to find it and I have to stop it, though I don't have the faintest idea how to do either. That's why I've come to you for help. I want you to try to see it for me.'

Lorna's face paled. 'I thought you might suggest something like that. I don't know if I can.'

'You don't want to?'

'No, I don't, but I will try,' she said in a small, resigned voice. 'But I don't know if I *can* do it. This isn't a voluntary thing, you know. I've been trying *not* to see it for weeks, and I've failed miserably.'

Jack poured another glass of wine for both of them. Already he could feel it heat him up inside. He changed the subject and for the next hour or so they pretended to forget about why he'd come. Lorna told him about her childhood on a farm up on the north-west coast. He told her about his own, in Levenford, running wild up in the Langmuir Crags, catching newts in the bomb-craters which had been left since the war, guddling trout in the streams which ran down off the hills. She made some cheese and toast and they had another glass, almost finishing the bottle, and then they both went through to her small cluttered living room and sat side by side on the sofa. Jack fetched his bag, drew out the folder and produced a sheaf of photographs.

'These might help,' he said. 'I know the town, but you might recognise something in them.' He laid them down on the floor, overlapping the prints until eventually he had a jigsaw picture of the town spread on the carpet.

Lorna turned the lights down and sat, staring at the pictures which were barely illuminated. Jack sat in silence, hoping she might spot a landmark, seen from above, that she would recognise. It took a minute or so before he realised that she'd closed her eyes. Her breathing deepened, the only sound in the quiet room.

He was about to speak when she shivered violently and then gasped sharply.

'Oh,' she moaned. 'It's dark. Cold.' Her shoulders drew upwards and her hands crossed themselves to rub her forearms before she twisted and drew herself into a tight hug.

'Cold,' she said again. 'I can *feel* it.' The words were slow and drawn out, like the speech of a dreamer. Jack felt a crawling sensation trickle under the skin at the back of his neck.

'I see stone. A wall. It's dark in here and cold. The wind is blowing through. The smell. I can smell birds. Dead. Dead birds. No noise.'

She stiffened. 'It's *there*. I can feel it. Oh, it's there in the dark. He hurt it. Oh, the pain,' she wailed, slapping a hand to her eye, 'and anger.'

He started to say something, but she held up her free hand to forestall him, even though one eye was covered and another closed tight.

'Wooden beams again. Old boxes. I see an elephant. A round hole with chicken wire to stop the birds, but it's torn. There's a smell of paper, and something else.'

Lorna shivered again. 'It's blood. It's all around.'

She dropped her hand, eyes now wide, but somehow unfocused, as if she was searching in the dark. She turned slightly, head swivelling.

'I see them. Oh my. They're hanging there.' Her voice shuddered in horror. 'Dead. All of them. Hanging on the pipes. It can see in the dark. It is moving out from the corner where the roof goes down to the beams. Like a shadow. I can hear it breathing, like an animal. It is hungry, and it has pain. It's going up to the pipes and it's. . . .'

Lorna let out a loud cry. Her body arched back as it uncoiled violently and she fell against the back of the couch. She lay there, head lolling, gasping for breath. Jack moved across to her and put his arm around her shoulder, drawing her up to a sitting position. She fell against him and he held her tightly, trying to deaden the tremors with his own body.

'Come on,' he said softly. 'You're safe.' He smoothed her hair with his other hand, holding her head in at his neck, almost under his chin. She smelled warm and clean. It took a few minutes for the trembling to die away and he still held her tight. Finally, she began to raise her head and he shifted position. She looked up at him and her eyes looked huge in the gloom, dark puddles against her pale skin.

'I saw it,' she said, faltering, trying to keep from sobbing. 'It was *feeding*. There was a foot hanging down. I could see the shoe, like a trainer. It came out of the dark and it reached up. They were hanging down from the pipes. Three of them. The feet almost touched the floor.' She stopped, drew in her breath in a quick hiccup. 'No. It was *one foot*. There wasn't another one.'

'Do you remember where it was?'

She shook her head. 'I don't know. It was in a roof. I could see the beams sloping down to the floor. Dead birds. I could smell them. And boxes of paper. All stacked high. It was behind them, in the corner where it's dark. It doesn't like the light. And there was an elephant on the boxes. A funny kind of elephant.'

A memory tried to form itself in Jack's mind, but it was too vague. It was an odd thing to say, an elephant, but there was significance to it. He concentrated hard, and it came to him.

The elephant with the castle on its back. It was the main motif on the old burgh's coat of arms. It appeared on every signpost on the edges of the town. It was the stylised image of the great double humped rock of the castle beneath which Annie Eastwood's body had been found. Jack closed his eyes and tried to visualise the old house inside the castle ramparts where Ian Ramage, the keeper, lived. He'd been down there half a dozen times with Davy on weekends in the summer. It had a pitched roof, as Lorna had described, but he could not remember a circular hole where birds, or anything else, could get in or out.

'Could you see anything else?'

She shook her head. 'It was *feeding*. It turned and looked at me. Its eye opened. The other one's been hurt, but it looked at me and then it *smiled*. At least I think it did. It's too black to see. But it was looking at me and it *knows* I was watching it.'

Her whole body shuddered powerfully.

'It knows about me,' she whimpered.

442

31

Gordon Pirie's shift had been over for an hour, but he stayed around the office after midnight talking to a blonde policewoman who worked on Ralph Slater's team and who was three years older than he was, wondering if he should ask her out. He was too new to the job to realise that she was surreptitiously involved with Sergeant Thomson, whose divorce papers had come through only a month before. She recognised and even appreciated the young recruit's interest and chattered to him amiably while she typed up her reports. He took the hint when she pointed out that he was getting unpaid overtime and should either be home in his bed or in the back room of the County Bar, whose rear alleyway door was always open, no matter what the hour, to off-shift policemen.

He got his hat from the stand and adjusted it self-consciously, struggled into his still-new coat and went down the corridor towards the fire-door which led to the front office. Before he pushed through, he could hear raised voices out at the reception desk and when he opened the door, a barrage of noise erupted. Close to the front entrance, a man was bawling at the top of his voice, while two policemen were trying to calm him down by the time-honoured method of getting him in a head-lock and bending him forward, one arm up behind his back, so that his head almost touched his knees.

At the desk a woman in a faded grey coat was screaming as loudly as the pinioned man was, her shrewish face screwed up and red from the effort. A drop of saliva spat out from a mouth which showed long, stained teeth. She was using words which Gordon Pirie had heard many a time, but had rarely used himself. Beside her, two small children in dirty, fake-fur lined anoraks were crying almost loud enough to drown their mother out.

'That's the last time I bail you out,' she screamed. 'Ungrateful shite! Just you wait 'til I get you home.'

443

'Aye, well just don't bother your arse next time, bitch that you are,' the man bawled back, still struggling against the two policemen. 'And get your fuckin' hands off me, you shower of bastards.' He lashed out with his heel and kicked fresh air, but on the back swing, his heel caught one of his captors right on the shin. From where he stood Gordon heard the crack and he winced in sympathy.

'Get off me, you swines,' the man snarled.

'Aye, leave the wee bastard alone,' the woman shrieked. 'He's not worth the bother.'

'See you, you ugly bitch. You're nothin' but a po-faced shrew like your mother.'

'Don't you bring my mother into this.' She turned to the snivelling children. 'That's your granny he's talking about, God rest her soul. Have you ever heard the likes? Just don't yous listen to him.'

Gordon stood bemused, watching the tussle as the small man in the greasy donkey jacket and outsize navvy's tackety boots writhed and twisted like a cat in a sack while the two big policemen tried to get a firm grip of him, one of them still hopping on one foot. Bobby Thomson, behind the desk, was trying to keep the smile from his face.

'Domestic bliss,' he remarked jovially, whereupon the woman rounded on him.

'Just you shut it. He never did anything wrong,' she hooted, diverting her wrath at Bobby, who merely shrugged and failed to keep his face straight.

Just at that moment, from down the other corridor, another blast of noise erupted. The sound of a man shouting hoarsely came reverberating up the passage, followed by a loud, violent banging. Gordon turned round just as the man's voice rose to a yammering scream.

'I thought this would be a quiet night,' Bobby Thomson said with a long-suffering sigh.

'I suppose that's another one you've been kicking lumps out of, you big bastards,' the woman yelled.

Down at the cells, the shouting rose to a crescendo and the furious hammering on the door resounded up the passageway.

'Here, son,' Bobby said. He reached behind him to the green

board and unhooked a tangled bunch of keys which he slung onto the desktop. 'Away and see what's eating him. Tell him if he doesn't shut up and get to sleep I'll come down and give him something to shout about.'

'Aye, that's typical of you lot,' the woman shouted. 'Folk that never did you any harm. You should be out looking for the nutter that's killing those bairns, instead of picking up decent folk just because they've had a wee drink.' She turned to the ongoing struggle at the door.

'Hey Hughie, stop your nonsense and get yourself home before I take my hand to your face.'

Gordon stood with the keys in his hands, wondering what to do. Bobby glared at him and told him to get moving.

'But I'm just going off . . .' Gordon began to protest, but stopped when the sergeant simply stared him down. Bobby's moustache was beginning to bristle. The young man turned and went down the corridor towards the cells where the racket was almost deafening in the enclosed, narrow space. He followed the sound and stood outside the metal door.

Inside, hardly muffled by the thick steel, he could hear the prisoner screaming incoherently. There was a loud thump and the door quivered on its hinges. The young policeman flipped back the cover on the peephole and put a wary eye up close to the door.

There was nothing to be seen. The cell was pitch dark, but the man's screams soared upwards in a harsh cacophony. Something hit the door again, making it ring like an anvil. He rattled the key in the lock and gave it two turns to the right. The mortice snicked back and he pulled the door open.

At first there was nothing to be seen. The overhead light, which should have been on continuously, was out. The hard cot against the wall was empty. In the corner next to the reinforced window-grate, the prisoner was bawling dementedly, and from the sound of it, he was thrashing on the floor.

He kept the door open with his foot, letting the wan light from the corridor shine against the wall of the cell while his eyes accustomed themselves to the darkness. He snaked a hand onto the outside wall and checked the old brass switch. It was in the on position.

'What's going on?' he called out.

'Keep away from me,' the man screeched, the first coherent words Gordon had heard from him. 'Keep away for the love of Christ.' Something moved in the far corner and rolled in the gloom towards the cot. There was not enough light to see what it was, but he got the vague impression of a man's form writhing on the floor.

'What's all the noise about?' the young policeman asked, stepping forward. He crossed to the wall and hunkered down beside the hunched shape. As soon as he touched him, the man lashed out with a fist and caught Gordon a sharp crack on the cheek.

'Keep away from me. Get!' the man squawked. He was kicking and struggling. One foot hit the side of the cot with a thud and his head rapped against the cold tiles of the wall. All the time he kept repeating his demands to be left alone.

'Hey, hold on,' Gordon said. The blow on the cheek had made his eye water and he could feel the flush of heat spread round to his ear. 'Come on now. Get a hold of yourself.'

Behind him, the heavy door swung very slowly until it clanged against the post. The light faded to a deep gloom. Through the thick and dirty glass on the cross-hatched window, there was hardly any light at all from the nearest street lamp. Gordon groped forward in the dark and felt the man's shoulders. They were shivering violently as if a shock of high voltage was running through him.

'Come on and I'll help you up.'

He pulled at the man, who jerked back as if he'd been scalded.

'No. Oh please, no,' he screamed. 'Don't touch me. Keep your filthy hands off me. You're a fucking devil.'

'No, no, it's alright. I'm a policeman.'

Gordon hadn't heard about the arrest that day. He didn't know why the man was in jail. He assumed he was a drunk who'd been hauled in from the street or one of the benches at the Cenotaph grounds. He also thought the man might be suffering from the DT's, although he'd never seen that happen, only heard about it. He wondered if he should go back and tell the sergeant.

Ignoring the man's frantic writhing, he grabbed him under the armpits. 'Come on, man, get up.' He tried to lift the fellow, bending right down over the slumped form, when a foul smell suddenly filled the cell. At first Gordon thought the reek was coming from the man on the floor and he drew back, disgusted, throat gagging.

'Dirty bugger, have you shit yourself?' he gasped through the throat-puckering stench.

He let the man fall to the ground and turned away, almost retching.

Beneath him, the man was moaning and blubbering. By now the words were all jumbled up and incomprehensible. Gordon dived a hand into his pocket and pulled out a handkerchief his mother had pressed into a neat square. He clamped it over his face.

Then the room got colder. It wasn't like a draught, or a breeze from an open window. In one quick moment of time, the temperature of the cell simply plummeted. Gordon breathed in through his mouth and he felt the sharp glacial air catch in his lungs.

'What the hell?' he mumbled through the handkerchief. The cold was so intense it was already numbing his fingers and nipping at his ears. He straightened up, eyes widening, trying to see in the dark, when something moved in the corner just to the right of the door.

'Eh?' he said. For some reason he couldn't quite understand, his whole body was instantly *singing* with unaccountable tension. He whirled round, trying to make out the movement. Just at his feet, the man whimpered. Gordon took two steps.

'Don't!' the man blubbered. 'Stay away. Oh please, get away from here.'

Gordon thought the prisoner was talking to him. He half turned towards the man when his peripheral vision caught a sudden movement in the gloom. The blackness just reached out to him, a shadow that simply expanded out of the darkness. Before he had time to flinch, it elongated with rippling speed and seized him by the neck with such force he heard his own larynx collapse.

A muted squawk of sound was forced out of his mouth as the pain tore across his throat.

Then he was in the air. His feet came right off the ground as he

447

was thrown backwards by an immense force. The darkness whirled around him, cutting off every dim ray of light. The grip on his throat was so fierce he couldn't breathe, and he felt his eyes begin to bulge with the unbelievable pressure inside his head. The hot metal taste of blood filled his mouth. Something else popped in his neck and a jagged pain danced down to his shoulder, followed by an immediate warm, wet flow.

The young policeman's hat flew off and hit the wall and his handcuffs sailed from his pocket to jangle to the floor. The heel of his boot struck the man on the floor on the side of the head, but the policeman did not notice that. He was still travelling upwards in the dark. He felt himself turned, still in mid-air, and something else took hold of him by the chest and a vast pressure squeezed at him. It felt as if he was being gripped in an enormous, relentless vice that was squashing him flat.

Everything went in ultra-slow motion, on the crest of the sudden tidal wave of fright-induced adrenalin flow. Gordon heard the door close with a low *clang* so deep it was like a vibration of a monstrous gong. Just in front of his face, unseen in the perfect darkness, something snarled, low and feral and guttural. He was still rising through the air, too frozen to struggle, when he was slammed against the wall. His head went whiplashing back against the glass and one of the tiny, inch-thick panes in the heavy grid cracked. A sickening nausea swelled and rolled in the back of his head and an unbelievable ripping pain tore into his back between his shoulder blades.

The force of the blow expelled the air from his lungs, squeezing it past the enormous pressure on his throat to come out in a cough of blood which spurted down his nose and sprayed from between his teeth.

The pressure on his neck vanished and he felt his body sag downwards. The grip on his ribs squeezed once, with ferocious, incomprehensible force, then let go.

Completely dazed, Gordon hung there in the dark, twisting in a sea of hurt which swelled higher and higher, gaining in intensity. Beneath him, his legs kicked out in a palsied frenzy, though, bewilderingly, he felt no pain there. Their spastic dance, however, raised the white-hot pain in his back to an incandescent flare. There was something else wrong, but he couldn't

448

understand what it was. Something terribly wrong which he was unable to fathom in the shock of the violence and pain. In front of him, something moved with a scuttering sound. The darkness expanded again and in that dark, a huge bare eye flicked open and stared into his. Even through the blood which clogged his nostrils, he could smell the putrid breath as the darkness exhaled in a ravening growl so deep it shivered the walls. The eye fixed him with its dead stare and he felt as if he was being sucked into it as it grew closer and larger.

The shrieking hurt in his back rived right through him. He couldn't breathe. His chest twitched helplessly and every hitch sent a knife of pain through his chest. The young man's whole body went into a spasm of trembling and he shuddered uncontrollably, up against the wall. He felt the rending *tear* of skin and flesh inside him. Gordon's hand came up reflexively, inadvertently brushing against something that was hard and slickly smooth, protruding from between his ribs. His hand scrabbled there on the wet fabric of his tunic, his mind reeling in confusion while inside his brain synapses and dendrites were sparking away with urgent, unbelievable messages.

He was impaled on the wall. Something had come out of the dark and lifted him up and hung him up on a spike.

In that strange slow-motion, stretched-out instant of time, he realised what had happened and the enormity of it dawned on his stunned mind.

The dark had moved. It had shoved him on a spike and put it right through his body. The realisation of imminent death washed over him in a flow as cold as the air of the cell. In that moment his brain stopped its jangling dance and an icy calm spread through him. Beneath his waist, his nerveless legs, cut off from the command centre at the top of his spine by the curve of metal driven through from shoulders to breastbone, continued to dance and quiver on their own. Already the pain was beginning to fade, as Gordon Pirie, brain starved of oxygen because of the enormous loss of blood, began to lose consciousness.

'I'm dying,' he heard his own voice, as if from far away, though the words were inside his head. His shattered larynx and the crushing force on his windpipe had made breathing almost impossible. His abdomen still bellowed jerkily and he could hear

449

the hiss of air escape through the gaping hole in the front of his soaked tunic.

I've only just started my job and I'm going to die, he thought distantly.

Just in front of his face, the enormous, putrid yellow eye glared at him with a light of its own. The absence of any pupil made it look eerily blind, but the young constable, dangling there in the dark, could feel the frigid malevolence in its stare.

It continued to watch in utter coldness as the life faded from the boy's eyes.

The last things Gordon Pirie heard were the odd drumming of his heels against the wall, the steady, hoarse animal sounds of the dark thing's breathing and the whimpering gurgle of the man on the floor.

The thing continued to watch, glaring right down behind the young rookie's eyes, searching for the crossover moment when all life became extinct.

For a while there was complete silence in the cold dark. Very slowly, the dark shape pulled itself down from where it hung on the wall. The great eye closed. The shadow flowed back from the cot in a strange liquid motion, and oozed towards the man on the floor.

Michael O'Day screamed in panic. He was not quite sure what had happened. Something had hit him on the head and the blow had knocked him against the wall, giving him the merciful respite of a momentary daze. He blinked his eyes, feeling the cold steal into his bones, and then the dark came rolling towards him.

'No,' he said. 'Get away. Leave me alone.'

He shrank back against the wall, eyes wide and terror-stricken. The shadow flowed over his legs, swelled, then shrunk. Michael O'Day opened his mouth to shriek his fear and the dark elongated towards him and flowed between his lips. He tried to clench his teeth shut, but his jaw was forced open so wide he could hear the muscles creak. An intense cold, even deeper than the now arctic chill inside the cell, flowed into him, a glacier of ice. Michael O'Day gagged, twitched violently just once, and was still.

The dead silence fell like a weight while the man lay, hands held up like claws in front of his face, eyes staring, face contorted in a frozen gape. He lay like that without a sound, without a movement, for quite some time.

But after a while, in the dim light of the cell, Michael O'Day's pale Irish eyes blinked once.

He grunted as he turned and shoved himself to his feet. Without a sound, he crossed the cell to the door and pushed it open. The feeble light, a single bulb overhead encased in a heavy mesh, briefly illuminated the wall at the far end of the small room.

Gordon Pirie was hanging against the wall. His lifeless eyes stared out from above the spattering of blood at his nose and chin. His tunic was tented out in the front of his chest, forcing his radio to twist to the side on his lapel. From a gash in the fabric, the upward-curved ratcheted spine of the window opening protruded like a blunt sabre. The young man's police boots dangled two feet from the floor. His eyes were unfocused, but they seemed to be peering into the far distance.

The thing that wore the body of Michael O'Day closed the door and locked it with a quick turn of the key. It turned, staying close to the wall, avoiding the light, until it got to the mortuary. The door was open, and in the shadows, it slipped inside. A moment later, there was a jangling of keys and a quick snap. The door opened at the back of the station and a dark shape let itself out into the huddle of outbuildings. Down from the station, past College Walk, the shape merged with the shadows of the rhododendrons of Cenotaph Park.

The pale eyes glinted with an inner light which gave them a yellow tinge in the deep shade. It remembered this place. It had been here before.

She woke with such a start that her cry of alarm catapulted Jack out of sleep. For a second, there was a rush of disorientation.

'Whassamatter,' he blurted. Lorna was struggling in his embrace, squirming in panic. He tried to move but his arm had gone to sleep and was caught between the girl and the back of the couch. He shifted position and pulled free, still dozily confused. Immediately pins and needles sparked painfully down the length of his arm.

The effort of Lorna's attempt to use her unwanted perception had exhausted her and the effect had appalled her. She had

451

slumped back in the settee, rigid with panic and he'd put his arm round her to hold her close again. She hadn't said a word for more than twenty minutes and he waited until the tuning-fork vibration of her body had faded and she'd started breathing slowly again. He still held her close, gently rubbing her arm with his hand in slow, soothing strokes. She mumbled something and he bent his head only to discover she was fast asleep.

Jack wondered whether to carry her into her room and tuck her up in bed, but dismissed the notion on the grounds that she might wake up while he did so and wrongly suspect his intent, and because of the possibility she might wake up and get another fright when she found herself alone. Her breathing deepened and she snuggled comfortably into him. A few moments later Jack dozed off.

When her cry woke him, he didn't know where he was. His eyes were gritty and the back of his throat dry. The pins and needles were stinging under the skin of his arm and his shoulder was stiff. Lorna was writhing to pull free.

'What's happening?' he asked again.

'Get away. Oh *please* get away from me!' Her cry was deafening, so close to his ear. Jack twisted round and despite the numbness in his arm, he took a hold of the girl by the shoulders. The shivery vibration transmitted itself to him. She was staring straight ahead, eyes wide and unblinking.

'No. Get away,' she cried again.

'Hey. Calm down,' Jack soothed. 'It's alright.'

The girl jerked back and her eyes blinked, then fluttered quickly, as if she had just noticed his presence.

She shook her head, obviously bewildered, still shuddering with powerful emotion. 'Where? What?' she asked in quick succession.

'It's okay. I think you were dreaming,' he said softly.

'Dreaming?' she seemed as confused as he'd been when he woke. Then her eyes widened hugely again.

'Yes. I *saw* it. I saw it again, Jack.' She drew her breath in a backwards gasp. 'It's hunting again. Oh, it was terrible.' She turned into him and grabbed the front of his shirt.

'It's killed someone. It threw him against the wall. Oh, he was in such pain. It got him and lifted him off the floor and he hit the wall and the pain went right through him and he's dead.'

The words came out as if she was living the scene, *feeling* the pain.

'Where was it, Lorna? Did you recognise anything?'

She closed her eyes, trying to *see* back into her dream.

'It was dark. Not high. The man came in. There's a heavy door and the walls are white. But the door closed and it was dark. Too dark to see. It's a place I've never seen before. Oh, it's awful, I don't know and I can't tell you. I'm *useless*.'

'No you're not,' Jack said, though in truth he wished that if she *did* have some special perception, it would be a little more helpful. 'We'll get there.'

Lorna eased herself out from his embrace, first loosing her grasp on the front of his shirt. Her grip had been so strong that she'd torn one of the buttons off the fabric. It fell between them and slid into the gap between the cushions.

'I must have fallen asleep.'

'Yes. You were sound. It's getting late. Maybe you should go to bed.' Jack bent to scoop the scattered photographs together and jammed them in the folder. He stood and reached for his jacket.

'Where are you going?'

'I'd better be off. It's pretty late, or early, depending on your point of view. You've had a rough day.'

'Please don't go,' she said, pushing her way out of the settee to put herself between him and the door. 'Please stay with me. I'm frightened. It knows about me. I can feel it. I've got nobody else to help me.' Her eyes were wide again and glistening with the promise of tears. She looked so slight and childlike as he looked down at her that Jack felt a powerful, and very masculine surge of appeal.

He hesitated, but only for a moment. 'Okay, sure. It's not as if I've got work in the morning,' he said. She took his hand and held it tightly in a meaningful gesture of thanks and pulled him down to the settee. Then, quite impulsively, she leaned forward, tilted her head and kissed him quickly on the cheek. Just as quickly, she flushed furiously. Quite taken aback, Jack felt his own colour rising and he grinned stupidly, feeling for the first time in a long while like an awkward schoolboy. Lorna pulled away and went into the kitchen. He heard the click as she

453

switched on the kettle. He took the opportunity to use the telephone and spoke to Ralph Slater for a few minutes, giving him what little information he had, convinced it would be no help at all. A few minutes later, she returned with a tray of milky coffee and some biscuits.

Then, without hesitation, and with surprising calmness, she told him exactly what she had seen in her nightmare.

It was close to two in the morning when the two-man squad pulled up outside the front door of the station and the second drunk of the night was hauled in, a big, belligerent and red-faced man who roared even louder than the previous miscreant and took a swing at one of the policemen, though he only succeeded in knocking his hat off.

'Hanging off the edge of the quay,' the policeman said. 'Can't get a word of sense out of him. He'd have drowned if we hadn't huckled him.'

The two-man crew pinned the big fellow up against the desk and, with deft expertise, they unbuckled his belt and drew it through the loops.

'Gerrof,' the big man spluttered. They held him tight.

'Alright, McFettridge,' Bobby said. 'Another free room for the night and your wife crying her eyes out in the morning.'

He reached behind him absently, to unsnag the keys from the hook, but his fingers only scrabbled against the baize on the board.

'Where did I put them?' he asked nobody in particular, scratching his head before he remembered.

'Damn, I gave them to that new boy. Idiot must have gone home with them in his pocket.'

The first stramash at the front counter had taken a further ten minutes to resolve. It had almost resulted in the small, dirty and aggressive man being hauled back to the cells, but finally his wife had taken him by the scruff of the neck, after giving Bobby Thomson and anybody else in the vicinity the rough edge of her particularly scabrous tongue, and led her husband off into the night, with the two sniffling children trailing behind.

The duty sergeant cursed under his breath, swearing he'd give the new recruit a real going over in the morning. He unlocked the cabinet and fumbled about in the mess of odds and ends until he found the spare set, and handed them to one of the men holding up their captive, who now looked to be in a state of drunken collapse.

'Sling him in four,' he instructed. 'I've got his particulars from the last time.' The men started towards the cells with the man slung between them.

'Oh, while you're down there, check in on number six. The weirdo was making a right racket earlier on.'

He bent down to fill in the drunk-and-incapable form while the others dragged the drunk down the corridor.

Stuart Bulloch, who had been showing Gordon Pirie the ropes on the morning they'd been sent round to the pathway beneath the castle's balustrade and had come across the body of Annie Eastwood on the rocks, helped ease the man down on the cot. All the fight had gone out of him and as soon as his head touched the cold tile roll which served for a pillow, his snores reverberated round the cell. Stuart turned the lock, flicked the spyhole just to make sure, then slapped it closed. As he turned down the corridor, his regular partner asked him if he wanted a cup of tea, but didn't wait for an answer and headed for the muster room.

The light was off in the opposite cell when Stuart checked the peephole, a natural precaution in the case of potentially violent prisoners, and in his experience, they could *all* turn out to be fighters.

He popped the lock and shoved the door open. The dim light shone against the shape on the wall.

At first, Stuart thought the prisoner was standing on the cot, trying to peer out of the almost opaque glass.

He walked forward.

'Come on down,' he said, when something *clicked* in his brain and the reality of what he was seeing hit him like a blow.

Gordon Pirie stared into infinity. His mouth was sagging open. Blood saturated his sagging chin and there was a great dripping wash of it down the front of his tunic. The curve of metal from the window jutted out and up.

Stuart's mouth opened and closed several times. He was trying to say something, but no words would come out.

He backed off slowly until his backside came up hard against the wall and he got such a fright he jumped almost a foot into the air. Without a word he turned round and dashed out of the cell, using the doorpost as a fulcrum to swing him up the corridor. His shoulder jarred against the far wall, though he would not feel any pain for another hour at least. He battered the swing door open and came hurtling out into the front office.

Bobby Thomson looked up.

'Is he okay?'

Stuart Bulloch stood there, still unable to make his mouth say the words, pointing behind him like a pale-faced mime artist.

'What the hell's up with you?' Bobby asked him irritably. 'I've had enough fun and games for one night.'

Finally Stuart got his voice back. 'It's that new fellow. Gordon,' he blurted.

'Aye, him that's going to get my toe up his arse in the morning.'

'It's . . .' Stuart started, stalled, tried again. 'He's . . . oh fuck, sergeant, he's dead.'

The fun and games went on all night.

Jack Fallon got a call from John McColl at three in the morning. It was the second time he'd been jarred awake that night. His neck protested creakingly as soon as he moved. Lorna was huddled at the far end of the couch, snug under the eiderdown she'd brought through from her bedroom. She was snoring very softly. His duvet had slipped to the floor and his back ached from the twisted position he'd assumed sometime in the past hour. As he reached for the phone, to answer it before she woke, he was trying to hold the thought that had sprung to his mind in the split second before sleep vanished.

'I tried your sister. She gave me an earful for waking the wee fellow,' John said.

Jack rubbed the sleep from his eyes. 'She'll blame me. What's up?'

'This shit's hit the fan, Jack. Yon Irishman's just killed that new boy.'

'Hold on, John. What are you talking about?'

'That O'Day fella. The one from the church tower? He's escaped. Bobby Thomson's in an awful state. He sent the rookie down to shut him up. There was a bit of a stramash at the front

456

counter with a couple of drunks and by the time it was sorted out Bobby forgot about the boy. Gordon Pirie, that's his name.'

'I remember him. Nice lad. So what happened?'

'Ralph's down there at the moment. The place is a bloody shambles, a real slaughterhouse. Young Pirie's hanging on the window. Christ alone knows how he got up there, but he's got a bloody piece of metal from the window right through him. Cowie's down here and he's going berserk. He put out a note to HQ that he'd got the killer. Now he's lost him.'

'So where's O'Day?'

'Who the hell knows? He's not here. The cell door was locked. I reckon we were wrong, Jack. O'Day didn't look as if he could blow his nose without falling over, but it had to be him. How he got that boy up on that spike is anybody's guess, but believe me, it went right through him. It's sticking out of his chest.'

'No, John. It wasn't him. Believe me, it wasn't, but you have to find him.' Jack remembered what Lorna had told him. A dark place with white walls and a heavy metal door. Where else could it have been but the old cell down at the station? He cursed himself for not seeing it.

But he had seen something else.

'Listen, John, I'm still grounded until I hear otherwise. But it doesn't mean I'm crippled. As soon as you get clear there, find the keyholder for the Town Hall. I need him round there, and I'll need you to come team-handed.'

In the split second between sleep and wakefulness, when the phone was ringing somewhere in the distance, Jack Fallon had got a flash of his own extra sensory perception. He'd been unable to dredge up the information before, but again sleep had unlocked the filing cabinet of his brain, and the picture had come clear. He'd grown up in this town and he'd seen every building from every angle. The elephant and castle coat of arms had helped direct his mind to the place Lorna had seen when she had closed her eyes and used her weird power. It was a place with a circular window high on the gable wall, with wire mesh over it to keep the pigeons out.

Lorna was still asleep when Jack hung up. He debated whether to wake her, decided against it, and instead wrote a quick message on a page of his notebook and left it on the coffee table

457

next to the settee. He washed his face quickly with cold water from the kitchen tap, then put on his jacket and coat, knowing he must look rumpled and scruffy. He also needed a shave, but that was the last thing on his mind. Just as he went out the front door, closing it as quietly as possible, Lorna turned over in her sleep, mumbled something, then wriggled into a more comfortable position. She did not wake up.

She was still asleep at five when Jack got back from the Town Hall. The caretaker had been very ill-tempered about being woken in the small hours and even more irate when John McColl told him he'd have to accompany the officers round to the old sandstone building on Kirk Street. Grudgingly, he opened the front door. The night was cold and overcast. No moon or stars were visible and a bone-chilling wind was whipping round the corners and moaning in the telephone wires. Jack arrived just as the caretaker turned the key. John McColl had brought six policemen, who stood around in the cold, swinging their arms and blowing into their hands. They nodded to Jack, but said nothing.

Inside, the elegant marble staircase with its carved wood bannister swept up to the town chambers where the councilmen debated with strenuous argument the minutiae of the burgh's business and still managed to louse everything up. Jack ignored that and went past the provost's office and through a back corridor to the disused police court where, as a nervous rookie, he'd first given evidence in a breach of the peace case. Beyond that, there was an even narrower back staircase which twisted upwards. At the top, an old green door barred further progress. John McColl took the keys from the grumbling caretaker and told him to go back downstairs. The man protested some more but all eight policemen stared him down and he clumped back down the stairs, muttering under his breath.

The door creaked open and immediately Jack smelled old paper and mouldering feathers. He and John McColl moved in first and Jack felt a twist of tension as his body prepared itself for a fight. He clicked the light-switch down and a fluorescent bar on the storeroom wall stuttered fitfully before coming on. It was covered with the dust of years and its light struggled to chase the shadows. The room was filled almost to the ceiling with boxes

458

bearing stickers with the town's fanciful coat of arms. A narrow passage between the stacks led away towards the gable. John asked one of the uniformed men for a torch and sprayed light in front of him as he followed the lane.

Beyond the boxes they found a fairly large space where a storeman of old had come to have a fly drink. A couple of dusty vodka bottles stood against the far wall where the circular air-vent had been barred with wire mesh which was now jagged and torn.

The body of Chalkie Black, his white hair like a dim halo in the wan light, hung motionless, his one trainer trailing close to the floor, brown with dried blood. His head was twisted to the side by the piece of electrical cable conduit that had been torn and bent out from the staples which held it against the wall, and spiked through his neck, just under the jaw. Beside him the two others were suspended in the same fashion, except that Votek Visotsky had no neck to impale. The steel tube went through his left shoulder and jutted out on his back close to his spine. One of his arms was missing.

32

Blair Bryden's story had coined the phrase and it stuck. Newspapers prefer it when the crazed and the criminal have tags to hang their stories on.

SHRIKE!

The tabloids and the broadsheets blasted the name from every front page.

SHRIKE: Teenage Victims Impaled. Shrike strikes in Police Cell: Policeman Brutally Murdered.

NIGHT SHRIKE: The town which lives in fear!

And because most people hadn't the foggiest clue what a shrike actually was, they wheeled on a famous naturalist and bird watcher who had already been thrown off three Scottish islands because the farmers objected to his protection plans for the geese which were eating them out of crop, field and homestead.

'The *Shrike*,' he expounded on every networked news programme, 'is a little bird with a very nasty habit. It feeds on lizards, frogs and often helpless nestlings of other birds, which it impales on the spines of a thorn-bush which it uses as its larder.'

A photograph of a neat little bird flicked up on the screens, a bright-eyed, sparrow-sized and quick moving thing with an elegant red back, a black stripe covering its eye and beak with a delicately fearsome, almost hawk-like curve. The picture immediately flicked to a filmed scene of a bird with a small naked nestling still wriggling helplessly in its beak, forcing the blind wingless creature down onto a blackthorn spike. The baby bird squirmed as its outsized head was forced down onto the sharp thorn. The shrike bobbed its head vigorously, hammering down on its victim, and the spine came forcing up between the bulbous closed eyes. The nestling wriggled a little more then went still.

'*Lanius cristatus*,' the popular ornithologist said, 'is an efficient predator and carnivore which revels in its nickname, the *Butcher Bird*. It is such a successful hunter that many of its impaled victims are uneaten, and decompose where they hang.' The picture panned left, showing an array of pitiful little bodies, feet dangling groundwards, some of them shrivelled and dry.

Massive Hunt for the Shrike, the papers shrieked, and that was true enough. Two busloads of policemen drawn from divisions all over the region had been drafted in to comb every inch of the town. Every school in Levenford closed its doors at two-thirty and squad cars followed the clusters of pupils home, while it was still light. Some mothers kept their children at home all day. At night, the streets cleared quickly as workers, men and women, hurried home, casting quick glances to the side when they passed a darkened close mouth or a narrow alley, jumping in alarm if the wind rustled the needles of the evergreen trees lining the edge of the park.

A heavy pall of fear descended on the town. It was as if the people of Levenford were under siege.

A roadworker just finishing a job on Denny Road, close to where Neil Kennedy had lived, was shovelling the loose rocks from a surface awaiting tar infill where the electricity engineers had dug a forty-yard trench, and got the fright of his life when scratchy footsteps came up behind him. Something growled and before he had time to think he had whirled round in an absolute panic and, with one blow of his spade, smashed the skull of a friendly black labrador whose owner had let it out for a piss. The dog dropped like a sack, without so much as a whimper, its brains leaking onto the hardcore surface.

A mother of three, who like Shona Campbell had gone down to the Castlegate Bar to salvage some of her husband's pay packet, was coming along Rope Vennel up to River Street when a shadow loomed into view, a bulky silhouette which clumped jerkily towards her. She backed against the alley wall as the faceless shadow stumbled forward. It lurched to the side, heading straight for her, and she screamed so loudly she was heard by two patrolmen, who came running down River Street at full tilt and thundered down the alley. By the time they had got there, however, the Castlegate Bar had emptied and the screams of pain and fear were echoing from the narrow walls. They found, under a press of bodies and flailing fists and feet, the battered and semi-conscious form of a seventeen-year-old

461

amateur footballer who had twisted his knee at a five-a-side match that very night and, far from attacking the petrified and still screaming woman, had merely slipped on a patch of ice while limping home. At Lochend Hospital doctors stitched a nasty gash on his forehead and strapped up three broken ribs. They put dressings on his multiple bruises and contusions, and then they examined the boy's knee. It needed no treatment. A week later, his dental bill cost him three weeks' wages.

Out in East Mains a stranger seen talking to two teenage girls was chased for his life.

In Corrieside a burglar shinned up a roan-pipe to break into the fourth storey of a tenement building. He came silently down the pipe half an hour later, with a haversack containing a video recorder slung over his shoulder, only to find a waiting group of men in ambush behind the privet hedge. They beat him half to death. The men, hyped up with the fear and alarm that had spread through the town, then went on the rampage in what was one of the rougher areas of the town.

There were two houses in Corrieside which had become regular pharmaceutical dispensaries. Neighbours had complained to the council and to the police about the needles and syringes picked up by their children on the verges by the side of the street. There had been a couple of raids, but the occupants had reinforced the doors and by the time they were battered down, any evidence had been flushed down the toilet.

The fathers of Corrieside took the law into their own hands and required no evidence but what they already knew. One of the homes was on the sixth storey of a squat block of flats. One of the men used a sledge hammer to smash the door off its hinges and they stormed in. A sleepy, unshaven and skinny man, known until then as something of a hard-ticket and who already had done two stretches for grievous bodily harm, came diving out of a bedroom with a plastic bag in one hand and a wickedly curved sheath knife in the other. The hammer came down in a swift arc. The man's wrist shattered and the knife whirled down to the floor where it stuck, quivering. In the bedroom a woman started screaming as the man was forced back inside. The group of men battered the skinny fellow all round the walls, each of them punching, kicking and gouging until he was a bloodied

462

scrap. Then they threw him through the window to tumble forty feet or more to the ground, where he broke his other arm and fractured his skull. They dragged the woman out of the house and down the stairs where they beat her to a pulp and left her naked on the pavement before moving in a determined posse up the road to the third-floor home of two brothers who were selling pills and worse to schoolchildren.

One of the boys escaped through the window and suffered only a prick from a needle in the grass which later gave him hepatitis and a nasty infection which turned gangrenous and caused him to lose two fingers and a thumb. He never returned to Levenford again. The other brother was kicked senseless and his legs were broken so badly that it took fifteen hours of surgery to make them look like legs again, though they never worked like legs after that.

The men went home to their houses with the feeling that they had hit back against what was wrong with Levenford that winter.

The town huddled in the grip of the cold and the crazy fear that hunched at the back of everyone's mind. The people of the burgh battened down the hatches and waited for it to be all over.

Superintendent Cowie ordered the printing of a set of posters which were stuck on every wall and lamp post, bearing a picture of Michael O'Day culled from a passport photograph which had been taken three years before. It showed him as a chubby-faced, dark-haired smiling man, with light blue Irish eyes, and bore no resemblance whatsoever to the wasted, haggard, grey-haired wretch Jack Fallon had spoken to in the belltower of St Rowan's Church.

For two days nothing else happened. The huge and painstaking search turned up nothing, no sign, not a hair of Michael O'Day. Jack spent his time between his sister's home and Lorna's house. On several occasions, Lorna tried to go into the kind of trance-like state she'd demonstrated before, but she could see nothing. For those two days, her hopes were beginning to rise that it had gone. Jack even suggested the possibility that O'Day had died, because he'd looked far from healthy the last time he'd seen him, or, like the others, had committed suicide and remained only to be found. He offered the suggestion that because O'Day had been the last of the people who had been at Marta Herkik's seance, then the whole thing might be over.

463

On Monday, the wind veered northwards and brought a freezing blast of air straight from the Arctic. At five o'clock in the morning, Graham Friel kicked his motorbike to a stuttering start and came down the Arden Road from Westerhill on the far side of the town. He had to wipe the icy crystals of snow from his visor as he turned over the old bridge and into the centre of the deserted town, heading for Riverside Bakery just off Barley Cobble. The bakehouse had been producing fresh bread and well-fired rolls and traditional mutton pies for more than two hundred years. Graham had worked there since he left school, and within a year he'd be a fully fledged master-baker, a title which caused not a little hilarity among his friends.

He throttled back on the turn on River Street, careful of the black ice on the morning-cold road, and made his way past the deserted shop fronts. When the river had burst its banks and flooded Benson's Tailors, Woolworths and the other shops along the row, Graham Friel had been one of the two boys who had sped on their bikes over the flooded tarmac and along the soaked pavements, sending up bow waves and almost knocking the feet from Mickey Haggerty as he made his way homewards on the night of the storm, the night Marta Herkik had died in Cairn House.

Now he was keen to get into the bakery and lean with his back against the hot brick of the oven to take the cold out of his bones. The icy air, colder in the wind-chill of his speed, numbed his lips and bit at the enamel of his teeth as it whipped under the edge of the visor. None of the shops was open and the place had that ghost-town emptiness of the early winter morning.

Graham moved slowly along the main street, slowed further as he came up to Rock Lane which parallelled all the other alleys leading down to the riverside, turned and dropped a gear to drive down towards the bakery. Inside, he unstrapped his leathers and put his helmet down on the bench. Gregor Christie had fired up the ovens and when Graham stepped through to the bakehouse a delicious flour-dusted breeze of heat enveloped him. His boss nodded from under his white hat, a big-bellied jovial man who was already up to his elbows in white dust. The slow egg-beater paddles in the kneading churns were dancing around each other as they stirred the dough.

464

Graham leaned against the bricks and felt the heat banish the cold. He stood there, spreadeagled, flattened against the surface for a few minutes, the most enjoyable of any winter's morning, and then got to work. The two of them manhandled the tub to the table and with deft expertise, they heaved the dough out onto the board, flattened it with their palms and sliced it into strips which they balled into small ovals and laid on the trays. Working steadily, Graham used his long paddle to slide the bake-trays along the grooves on the oven sides, enjoying the fiery scorch when the door was opened, until he'd loaded the first batch of rolls. When the hatch clanged shut the heat died immediately.

He made tea for both of them, while Gregor prepared the bread for the stores along River Street, then when the timer rang, he started unloading the first bake. The rolls were hot and light and mouth-watering.

'Where's the milk?' he called over to Gregor. 'I've buttered the rolls.'

'Good man,' the baker said, squeezing the last of the dough into the high silver pans. 'There's a bottle in the bag. Where did I put it?' Gregor scratched his head, then raised a finger.

'I must have left it in the car. It'll be behind the front seat.'

Graham pulled a face at the thought of going back outside into the dark and chill morning. Gregor ignored it and chucked the keys over to him then turned to start loading the second oven, whistling merrily. The younger man went out of the bakehouse and through the storeroom, jamming his hat down on his head. As soon as he opened the outside door, a draught of frigid air leached the heat from his face. He shivered and bent his head as he hurried down the unlit narrow space between the storeroom and the wall of the neighbouring building. He quickly opened the car, reached behind the seat and found the bottle of milk in Gregor's tote bag. Graham slammed the door, locked it and turned back up the gap. Just before he got to the end of the passage, where the double doors of the gate faced onto the alley, hiding the loading bay and the little space where Gregor parked his car, he stopped, listening.

Above him, the noise came again, a rough scraping sound, just audible over the moan of the wind which rattled the tall gates.

Graham half-turned. Already the cold was draining the warmth from his bare arms. He looked up to where the roan-pipe on the wall disappeared into the early morning dark. For a moment, he thought he saw a movement, and he stood puzzled. Nothing happened and he turned back towards the car. The noise came again, a rapid scuttering of something hard rasping on the stonework. He turned again, looked up, and the dark simply rushed down towards him.

In the bakehouse, Gregor Christie slammed the oven gate shut with a resounding clang and put his paddle against the wall. He yawned mightily, and strolled towards the table to where his breakfast, two hot and crusty rolls dripping with butter, awaited. Graham had poured the tea, but it was still black. Gregor sat down heavily on the seat, grabbed a roll and jammed it into his mouth, tearing off a gargantuan bite. He lifted the tea, despite its lack of milk, and took a sip just as the frantic howl shattered the dusty peace of the bakehouse.

Gregor jerked back and spilled half a cup of tea right down his front, scalding his considerable belly from breastbone to crotch. He let out a whoop of pain and went stumbling back from the table, dropping the rest of the cup onto the wooden surface while he hauled the burning cotton away from his skin. Outside, in the narrow gap between the building, Graham was bellowing incoherently.

Despite the pain on his belly, Gregor stumbled to the door, pushed his way through the storeroom and pushed the exit-bar.

'Oh, get off,' Graham screeched, though the words were hardly intelligible. 'Oh Jesus. *Gregor!* It's got me it's got me it's oh help me for chrissake I'm. . . .'

The babbling screech soared up so high it sounded like a woman's shriek and then cut off abruptly.

Gregor bulled his way out into the back alley.

'What the hell's going on?' he bawled, peering down the gap. There was no sign of Graham.

Up above, there was a scraping noise, like stone rubbing on stone. Gregor looked up. For an instant he thought he saw something light in the shadows, but it disappeared as soon as his eyes focused. He scratched his head and hurried down the passage, squeezing his stout frame between the stacks of plastic

466

baskets to where his car sat in the shadow. Graham was nowhere to be seen.

A pale pool of milk spread out on the concrete of the bay and shards of glass were scattered all around. Graham's hat was lying upside down in the middle of the puddle.

Gregor took a step back. For some reason his legs were shaking and his heart was pounding and he was suddenly very scared. He did not know what had happened. He stole a glance at the double gates and saw the padlock still on the chain. Graham had locked it, as usual, after parking his bike, a precaution against opportunists who might sneak in while they were busy. There was no way out of the yard, except back the way he had come. Graham hadn't been in the alley, and his desperate and scary screams had come from outside.

Gregor backed away from the pale pool of split milk. Every nerve down his back and arms was jittering and jumping as a huge and nameless fear shivered through him. He took one quick and very nervous glance up at the dark space between the two buildings, and then he skittered up the alley like a fat and frightened cat, barged through the door and slammed it hard behind him. He got to the bakehouse and flopped down on the seat and sat there for several minutes until the distressing and dizzy pounding of his heart slowed down enough for him to reach for the phone. The police arrived within five minutes and it took another half an hour to get any sense out of Gregor Christie. The mug of tea which Graham Friel hadn't had a chance to drink went cold.

At five past six Laurie Liddell jumped off the back of his milk float and scurried up Yard Vennel, only four hundred yards from Christie's bakery, with two eight-bottle crates rattling in his hands. The scaffolders who had set up their frame for the sandblasting operation on the Ship Institute, an old Victorian pile from a bygone era of commercial and maritime wealth, started early and they started on gallons of tea. Laurie was fourteen, and despite the warnings on every poster, he had not thought for a moment of quitting his job. It paid too much, despite the hours.

He ran on, head down, past the metal bars on the side of the building, when he heard a noise a few feet above his head. He

467

glanced up and something snatched him clean off the ground so quickly he didn't have a chance to utter a word. The crates of milk went flying forward, tumbling as they went. The bottles flew out and shattered on the cobbles in a series of glassy explosions.

The milk-float driver moved on another forty yards while the two other boys darted up the alleys, hurrying to keep warm.

'Hey, where's Laurie?' one of them asked when he got back into the warmer cab.

'Is he not with you?' the driver asked.

'No. He did the delivery for the workies. He's not down yet.'

'Och, away and tell him to get a move on,' the driver growled. 'We can't hang about here all morning.'

'He's probably taking a piss!' the boy protested.

'I don't care if he's having a shit and a haircut. We've a run to finish. Now get back and haul him out of there.' The driver jerked his thumb over his shoulder and bent to his tally book.

Colin Jamieson, who was Laurie's cousin and older by ten months, jammed his hands in the pocket of his heavy jacket and huddled against the cold as he scampered back towards the institute. He rounded the vennel at a trot and ran to the far end where the workers had their storage hut.

'Hey, Laurie, come on. He's spitting bullets.'

There was no reply.

He stuck his head round the side of the hut, expecting to see Laurie hunched against the slatted wall, a cloud of steam rising from a spreading puddle. There was nothing there.

'Hurry up, will you?' he called again into the dark, but there was no reply.

Puzzled, the youngster went right round the back of the hut, next to where the scaffolding rig clambered up the black side of the old building. His foot kicked a piece of glass and it tinkled against a brick. He looked down and saw the pool of milk, just as Gregor Christie had done on the other side of River Street.

'Aw Laurie, he'll murder . . .' he started, but did not finish. Something struck him on the back of the neck with such colossal force he went flopping to the ground. One second he was standing there, gawping, and the next he was face down on the cobbles. Dazed, but still conscious, he managed to raise himself to his elbow when a grip clamped on his head and lifted him straight off the ground. The shadows of the scaffolding swung and somersaulted in his vision as he was flipped upwards. A terrible pain cracked in his neck and everything started to go dark. The last thing he saw was a single yellow glow, like a poisonous moon, right in front of his face as the thing that had hit him, then picked him up like a rag doll, watched as the life drained out of his eyes.

At six-forty it was still dark and bitter cold. On Swan Street, just round the corner from Cenotaph Stand, in one of the oldest parts of town, Lisa Corbett went upstairs to check on her grandmother, who lived in the little flat above in the old and crumbly tenement. The old woman had applied for a sheltered house because the worn stairs up to the fourth floor were getting too much for her, though she knew she'd miss being so close to her daughter's family. Lisa was nineteen and worked an early shift on the lines at Castlebank Distillery. In the mornings, she always went upstairs to make her gran a cup of tea and find out if there was anything she wanted from the shops.

She closed the door behind her. The light on the stairwell was off, which wasn't unusual, because most of the tenants would rather wait for the council to fit a bulb than spend the money themselves. It mattered little. The teenager had been up and down the steps almost every day since she could walk. She took the first flight, and was turning to the second, past the sash window which looked down onto the back courts, when a gust of freezing wind came blasting in from outside. She turned automatically, reaching to slide the frame down, when everything went dark. A sickly smell of rot filled her throat and she screwed her face up in disgust. Then with such speed that the girl had no time to blink, she was dragged right out over the windowsill. The skin of her leg peeled down from knee to instep as she was whipped over the edge against the sandstone. She never made a sound.

Half an hour after that, the old woman, who had been expecting her grand-daughter because Lisa was as regular as clockwork, went to her front door and peered down the stairs. Something lay on the flat landing in front of the window. She toddled down the flight and picked it up. It was Lisa's handbag.

At eight, still wintry dark, the wind had picked up. It tugged at George Wilkie's heavy coat when he opened the front door of the old college, which was now used as the town planner's office. The milk, he noticed, hadn't been delivered, and the janitor knew there would be complaints from the pen-pushers when they arrived at nine. He shivered in the cold and closed the door behind him before going downstairs to switch on the old boiler to get the heat running through the ancient pipes. He could have done with a hot cup of tea himself, and muttered grumpily. He lit his pipe and blew out a plume of smoke on his way to the back door where the black plastic bags were leaning against the wall. The rubbish would be collected by the cleansing department later in the morning. He shoved the door open and started hauling the bags out into the little quadrangle at the back of the building where the planners, now that the building was a no-smoking area, would huddle for their morning cigarettes. He'd hefted the last of the bags outside and dumped them against the wall, and was just turning back towards the building when the wind whooped fiercely into the confined space, picking up pieces of paper and cigarette packets and whirling them together in a dust-devil circle. Something rasped on the wall above his head and he looked up. Something black fluttered against the wall. For a moment he assumed it was an empty bin-liner caught by the wind.

Then it dropped down on him so blurringly fast he didn't have a chance to even open his mouth. A tremendous blow hit him on the top of his head and the force snapped his teeth together so hard the stem of his pipe was broken cleanly in two, and the upper plate of his dentures broke into three pieces. Sparks of burning tobacco fountained out and were whipped upwards by the blustering wind. Old George, who was due to retire in February, was slammed to the ground and then, without warning, lifted up again. The force of the blow had detached the retina of his left eye. The other, still blurred, was vaguely aware of the old, dusty windows passing by, although he did not know why they were moving. When he reached the level of the guttering, George was hauled onto the slates beside the corbie-stepped gable. Something black opened an eye and stared into his. Still dazed, it took him some time to realise that an

470

inexorable grip was squeezing at his neck. He gasped once as the pressure built up inside his head, then the vision of his good eye just faded out. The yellow orb glared until the life-light drained away, then the thing turned and began to climb, dragging the old man like a bundle of rags.

33

Jack drove down Clydeshore Avenue towards Lorna's house at seven on Monday morning. He'd spent the weekend alternating between there and his sister's house, and thanks to Superintendent Cowie, he was able to keep his promise to Davy, though all the time he'd been in a turmoil of agitation following the death of young Gordon Pirie and the find of the three bodies in the town hall's attic store. When he'd suggested that O'Day might have killed himself, Lorna had just shaken her head slowly. That, in itself, was possible, though try as she might, she sensed nothing, but she insisted to Jack yet again that what had killed the children in Levenford was *not* human.

Despite his preoccupation, Sunday afternoon turned out to be the best Jack had spent since the firework celebrations of Burgh Charter Day.

It had been icily cold, but the skies had been clear with the kind of pale frigid blue of deep winter. Davy had met him at Julia's front door at eleven, bundled up in a jacket that was several sizes too large and with a tasselled hat pulled down over his ears. They had strolled up the full length of Cargill Farm Road, past the old mill with its ice-locked wheel and then crossed the fence to get beyond the trees and onto the hillside.

Langmuir Crags were white with snow that had drifted to five feet in places when they arrived, panting at the top of one of the gentler slopes. Davy had insisted on rolling a snowball, though Jack did most of the work until he had a thick disc a yard high, then, with much laughter and cheers, they had sent it rolling down the long swoop, watching it grow as it travelled. Fifty yards downslope, the snow-wheel hit a rock and collapsed into itself in a crump of hard-pack. Davy whooped with glee and it took some persuasion to dissuade him from building another. They breasted the edge of the flat plateau and trudged through the heather. Jack lifted his nephew onto his shoulders when the snow got too deep and they walked on over the hill and down the next depression where Loch Murroch lay flat and iced over. Up here the wind picked up the little shards of ice which had frozen to the heather bells and sent them tinkling in a musical whisper over the flat white expanse of the hill-loch. Overhead, high in the clear air, a buzzard mewed plaintively as it wheeled on broad wings, hungry for the meals that had tunnelled under the snow or had changed their colour to perfectly match their surroundings.

Davy had spent two hours skittering and sliding on the ice. Most of the time he was on his backside, or sliding on his front on the clear patches where the wind had brushed the ice to polished black smoothness.

The pair of them had watched as a mountain hare, greyhound fast, and completely white bar the twin jet spots of its long ears, came streaking down the hill and onto the flat surface, legs blurring and kicking up a trail of ice crystals. The animal had sped right out into the middle of the lake, dashing past them until it hit the slick clear surface. It had spun twice, like a character in a cartoon, rolled, found its feet with miraculous agility, and raced for the far side of the narrow loch. They watched until it hit the sloping snow-bank in a puff of powdered snow and disappeared.

Up here, in the clear winter air far above town, the destruction that had taken place in Levenford seemed far away. From the slopes of the rolling plateau, the town was well hidden from view. There was no sound but the moan of the wind through the runnels and gulleys, the call of the bird high overhead, and the crunch of snow underfoot.

Loch Murroch has a waterfall at its westermost point where it overflows to drain down into the Langmuir Burn, a winding stream that cuts through the soft, layered strata of ice-age deposits on its tortuous route to the estuary. The falls were silent but for the steady drip of water from a portcullis of icicles which dangled from the lip, some of them waist-thick and dropping twenty feet to the iced-over pool below. Jack eased Davy down the incline next to the falls and let the youngster break off a sword of ice. He chose another and they fenced until their weapons shattered into rainbow-sparkling diamonds.

They followed the stream down the hill until they came to another, deeper pool where Jack sat the boy down on a flat rock and opened the sandwiches Julia had prepared for them. The walk had given them ravenous appetites and they demolished the food in minutes. As they sat there, Jack pointed out the dark shapes moving in the sluggish water which was moving just enough to keep the deep pool ice-free. Every now and then, there would be a bubbling turbulence on the surface as a sleek shape would dart up from the depths and turn with a flash of silver. Jack had come up here when he was not much older than Davy was now, trudging up the slope in winter to the redds where the salmon and sea trout gathered to spawn. As a youngster, he had used a loop of twine strung across a forked branch to snare one of the fish by the tail before hurrying back down the hill, watchful for old Dan Leitch the gamekeeper, on his way home with his prize. He'd thought about those days many a time since, not least because his own father had been a policeman who had never raised a disapproving eyebrow about his son's poaching of fish, and had always tucked into the fresh salmon with relish.

They watched the fish for almost an hour while Jack gave a running commentary and answered all of Davy's questions as best he could, before they started heading down the hill. Already the sun was heading for the horizon, though it was still early. Halfway down the long meander of the stream, Davy began to tire and Jack hoisted him back on his shoulders for the last two miles to the trees.

Twilight was setting when he got the boy back home and after a bath, Davy was so tired from his long romp in the fresh air that he fell asleep on Jack's knee, halfway through a story about dungeons and dragons. He carried the boy through to his bed and tucked him in while Julia made coffee.

'You're good for him,' she said when she poured cups for both of them in the kitchen.

'And he's good for me,' Jack said, grinning at the recollection of rolling the boy in a drift as Davy's childish laughter pealed across the snow.

'It's about time you got yourself a good woman,' Julia said in that direct sisterly way that always made Jack smile.

'You're one to talk,' he retorted. 'You've been on your own too.'

'Yes, but I've got David,' she said. 'You need somebody to get you out of yourself. You've been working too hard. All work and no play, Jack. You'll get dull.'

474

'Oh, don't worry about me,' he said. 'In fact I'm seeing a girl tonight.'

Julia looked at him quizzically over the rim of her cup, so he told her about Lorna Breck. She listened while she sipped her coffee and let him talk, gauging his tone. Jack told her about the girl's strange gift, and how she had been instrumental in finding three of the bodies and the place where Neil Kennedy had been snatched. He only talked about her in relation to the case, but his sister had known him a long time.

It was what Jack did not say that made her smile.

He had taken Lorna to Barloan Harbour where the old canal emptied into the estuary. At one time, the canal had been a busy waterway, but since the war it had fallen into disrepair until a couple of years back when someone had taken the notion to open it up as a boating marina. It was still in the early stages yet, but the old buildings and storage yards had been converted into chandler's shops and fancy outfitters for the modern seafarer and there was also a neat little restaurant built into the disused railway arches which crossed over the locks beside the basin.

He had asked her on a whim and had been surprised when she readily agreed.

The food was French and expensive and quite superb. During the meal they tried not to mention the one thing that had brought them together, though it sat silent and invisible between them. They talked about everything else. He discovered she'd once been almost engaged to the son of a wealthy farmer and had broken it off when he'd stated quite flatly that she would have to leave work in the local library and take over looking after the chickens and milking cows at five in the morning.

'I decided there were better things to do with my life, though I haven't done them,' she said. 'Maybe I should have gone along with it,' she said with a quick laugh.

He noticed she'd laughed a lot during the meal. When he'd picked her up, she still looked almost as worn and drawn as she had the time he'd met her in the chemist's shop, but once they passed the burgh boundary, heading east, when the town was behind her and they were driving through farmland close to the banks of the estuary, it had been as if she'd walked into sunlight, although the sky was already dark.

He told her a few stories from his past, some of the cases he'd worked on, picking out a few of the funnier ones, though in fact there were too few in his line of work. Eventually she asked about Rae and Julie and for the first time in a long while, he was able to speak about them without the twisting ache in his belly and the heavy weight of loss on his shoulders. He talked about his daughter's birth, the most momentous experience of his entire life, and how she was a perfect cross between him and Rae, with his black hair and her brown eyes. Lorna reached across the table and used her two small hands to cover his in a gesture of understanding.

Finally, despite their avoidance, the matter that had brought them together intruded.

'It's strange,' Lorna said, still holding onto his hand. He did not pull away. 'This is the first time I've been able to think about it without panicking. It's as if I'm safe here with you.'

'I think it's because we're out of the town. There's an atmosphere you can cut with a blunt knife. People are just coming to terms with what's been happening. I'm praying that it's over.'

'I don't think it is. It would be a miracle. I could get on with my life, but I don't think so. I've had a bad feeling about it, even though I can't sense it any more. I really don't believe it's gone.'

She looked at him earnestly, searching his eyes.

'What if I'm right?'

He shrugged, keeping his face impassive, and trying not to show his own budding feelings as he met her grey gaze.

'If you're right, then my boss has certainly blown it. He'd already made an arse of himself, sending a fax to headquarters telling them he had the killer. John McColl told me the other night he'd sent the same telex to every newsroom. They had the story on their front pages and then that poor youngster got it. The second editions made Cowie look like a fool, which, of course, he is.'

'You'd rather be back in there, wouldn't you?'

'Of course I would. I'd like to think that it's gone with O'Day, but I have to be honest. You've been right so far. If you say it's still there, then, yes, I'd sure like to be back. My immediate superior is as useful as a bull with udders and thick as two planks. If you're right, I *should* be back in there.'

476

He'd taken her home, travelling on the back road that went way round the edge of Langmuir Crags, a narrow snow-banked country lane which dipped and turned. It took an hour longer than it would have if he'd taken the main road, and both of them knew he was just delaying taking Lorna back into Levenford. He came in for a moment, checked her windows and told her to snib the door behind him. She stood at the door as he went down the path and when he got to the gate, he wondered if he should have kissed her. Jack wasn't sure any more about body language. He'd been out of circulation too long. On the way back to the farm cottage, he began to wish that he had, and then suffered the pang of guilt for thinking that thought. When he got there, the place was cold and too many unwashed clothes were lying around. He put them in the washer and absently played his guitar until the cycle was over. When the shirts were in the tumble drier, he went to bed and slept until six.

As had happened so many times in the past, when he awoke, he had an idea of what he should be doing. It had come to him sometime as he slept, although he could not remember dreaming. If Lorna Breck's extra sensory perception worked better when she touched someone, maybe it would improve if she came with him to Michael O'Day's house, to see if there were any vibrations or sensations that might trigger off her second sight. It was a long shot, but his enforced absence was already chafing. If she found nothing, no shivery sense of premonition, then it might allay her fears, and that would certainly quieten his own.

At seven, still dark and bitterly cold, he parked the car outside the gate and pulled his collar up against the wind driving up the firth as he walked quickly up the path.

There was no response to his knock. He tried again, twice, but Lorna's now familiar voice did not call out from behind the door. He checked round the side of the building. There was a light on in her bedroom, though the curtains were closed tightly. There was no sound of running water from the bathroom, which was in darkness, and for a moment Jack hesitated, wondering if she'd perhaps fallen asleep with the light still on, then recalled she'd already told him she was scared of closing her eyes in the dark because of the visions that would crowd into her mind. It was early enough for her to be still asleep and he decided against waking her. He turned back on the path. Across town the sound of sirens wailed eerily and the ululating sound, so early in the morning, triggered the shivery sensation down his back. He was about to head for the gate when he heard the faint cry from inside the house.

He stopped, holding his breath to listen. The wind rattled the bare twigs on the elm tree at the side of the road and the whine of the siren faded in the distance. Nothing happened, and he began to think he'd imagined it, when the sound came again, faint, almost like a moan.

He hurried round to the front door, crouched, and jammed two fingers to open the flap of the letterbox. The narrow hallway was dim, but there was a line of light from the bedroom which formed a bar on the floor and up the wall. In that band of illumination, a bare foot stuck out through the doorway on the floor. As soon as he recognised it, Lorna moaned, a long, drawn out, quivering sound of distress.

Jack banged hard on the door, rattling it on its hinges, but there was no response from inside, except the shuddery cry. It sounded like an animal in pain.

He stepped back, now suddenly worried and scared that she'd been hurt. He was about to raise his foot and stomp his heel just below the lock, when he stopped. She was a country girl, raised on a farm, far from any major town. He turned, and in the darkness, felt along the wall beside the door where he'd seen the plant-pots in daylight. He lifted the second one and his fingers found the key. In seconds he had jammed it in the lock, twisted it, and pushed the door open so hard it banged against the wall.

Lorna was lying on the floor of her bedroom. When he reached her, his heart did a double thump when he saw her eyes, wide and staring. She was spreadeagled with her arms drawn up at the side of her head. They were trembling violently. A trickle of saliva dribbled down from her half-open mouth and her whole body was jerking in a series of violent spasms. He threw himself down beside her and took her face in his hands, calling her name. The tremors made his own arms shake.

The moan abruptly stopped and the girl began to pant like an animal. Powerful, heaving gasps shook her and her shoulders came right off the floor as she fought for breath. All the while her eyes were staring blindly.

He drew her up to a seated position, wondering what to do. It looked as if she was in the middle of a fit, and if that was the case, he should turn her on her side and make sure she didn't swallow her tongue.

Just as he made to move her, she twisted violently against him and drew a hand up to his face, as swiftly as a cat's strike. He felt her nails rake down his cheek and he drew back, breath hissing with the burn.

Lorna came half off the ground, panting like a dog. Her face twisted savagely, though her eyes were still wide and frantic. He caught her by the shoulder and pulled her against him. She struggled viciously, and with such surprising strength that he was thrown against the wall with a jarring thump.

Then she screamed like a cat. There were no words, just one long shriek that soared so high he could hear it crackle in his ears. He moved quickly and gathered her in his arms and smothered her with his own strength. She struggled against him, still screeching, but he held on tight, wrapping his arms around her and locking his muscles. He held the position for several minutes while her screams rattled the windows in their frames and then, without warning, without any slow trailing away, the noise stopped. Lorna sagged in his arms like a puppet whose strings had been cut and lay limp.

Jack didn't move for another few minutes, wondering whether to carry her to her bed or take her through to the living room where he could phone for a doctor, but then she gave a start against him. He drew his head back to look at her. She blinked, looking dazed, and then simply burst into tears. The sobs racked her from head to foot. It was as if a dam had burst inside her. Huge tears welled up and spilled down her cheeks to soak into his shirt. He held her tightly, rocking her gently, until finally, the sobbing began to subside. She sat still for a little while longer, then moved against him, wiping her cheeks on his already damp shirt.

'You want to tell me what happened?' he asked softly.

She hiccupped, tried to speak, then hiccupped again in the aftermath of her tears.

'It's killing again,' she finally blurted thickly. She sniffed and shivered again, almost as she had done when she'd been lying rigid on the floor.

'I saw it, Jack. It's not gone away. It's still here and it's angry. I could *feel* its hate. It showed me everything and it knows I can see. It's killing *now*.'

'Where?'

'Everywhere. I couldn't stop it. It's as if it wanted me to see it all. I *know* it wanted that. I got up to get a drink of water, and I saw it, right in front of me.'

'Here?'

'No,' she said. Her shoulders hitched as she swallowed a sob. She tapped the front of her head. 'Here. It was worse than before. Oh, it was much worse. I could see everything. It's on the rampage and it's killing so many people.'

Jack held her tight, trying to calm her. Slowly, he eased her to her feet and reached to the side where her dressing gown had slipped to the floor. With the difficulty of long-lost practice he helped her into it, pushing her arms into the sleeves the way one does with a small child. He drew her to her feet, tied the cord firmly around her waist and led her into the kitchen. He made an instant coffee for them both, making hers thick and strong and sweet and urged her to drink it, holding the cup to steady it in her fluttering hands. He waited until she had finished, made her drink another, then started to ask questions.

'Show me the pictures,' she interrupted.

He went through to the living room and picked up the folder from the table where he'd left it. He drew up a chair beside her and spread the photos on the table, then drew her forward with his arm around her shoulders. She slipped her hand round his waist. It was still shaking, but warm against his side.

'The first one. It came down between buildings. He heard it and looked up.'

'Who did?'

'The boy. He had a white hat. Something in his hand, a bottle maybe. I could smell cooking. He looked up and it came down so quickly he didn't have a chance to move. It took him by the shoulder and climbed the wall with him. He was screaming and crying, and his feet were kicking against the wall, but it went back up into the dark. It was playing with him. It threw him onto the roof and then it took him by the neck and looked into his eyes until he was dead. It was looking into *my* eyes, and it was *laughing*.'

'How do you know that?'

Lorna turned her eyes on him. 'Because I do,' she said slowly. 'Because it wants me to know. I don't know why, but it does, and it's like a disease.'

'Did you recognise the place?' he asked.

She shook her head. 'I could hear the gulls, and a clanking sound. And the smell of something cooking.'

Lorna closed her eyes and actually sniffed, as if she was scenting the air.

'No. It wasn't cooking. It was *bread*. Fresh bread like my mother bakes. It was coming from a door between the two walls.'

Jack reached for the remainder of the folio of prints and searched through them. He selected one and held it up. It showed a warren of alleys down by the river.

'Was it there?' he asked, jabbing his finger. 'There's a bakery here.'

She took the picture and he watched as her eyes narrowed in concentration. She was trying to convert what she had seen in three dimensions to the flat surface of the picture which had been taken from several hundred feet in the air. Finally she nodded.

'I think so. It might have been the place.'

He pushed his chair back from the table and got to his feet. 'I have to phone Ralph Slater,' he said.

'Wait, Jack. There's more. It hasn't stopped yet. It's angry now. It's like it wants to kill everybody. It's like a nightmare. I was there and I saw it take two boys, just little ones.' She held her hand out to indicate a height. This time she flicked through the pictures herself.

'It's somewhere I've seen before, an old building with scaffolding on the side. The first boy was carrying something. It rattled. Milk bottles, maybe?'

Jack let out a long sigh. The warnings had been in every paper and on every screen. Yet every morning, hours before daylight, young teenagers, boys not even in their teens, were out in the dark, scurrying up alleys and tenement closes to deliver the town's milk. Lorna drew out a print and this time she pointed.

481

'There. He went up there and it came down the scaffolding, swinging from bar to bar. Oh, it's so fast. It took the boy by the head and lifted him up and it *stuck* him up on the bar. The other boy came round and it watched him. I could see him from up there. It was *showing* me. I tried to call out, but it laughed inside my head. Oh, Jack, it's filthy. It's like a *sickness*.' She leaned into him and the tears started to trickle down her face again. There was nothing he could do to stop them.

After a few moments she started again, telling him about the old man. She did not recognise this place, nor the stairwell where she'd seen the girl being dragged from the window. But in every case she told how it had swung its victim upwards and held it there until the soul fled, watching the life-light fade from the eyes.

'It *is* like a disease,' she said. 'It's foul and it hates everything here. It makes me feel unclean.'

Jack made his phone call and Ralph's wife told him her husband had been out since almost five, two hours before. He managed to get Bobby Thomson at the station, who accepted Jack's request for urgency and relayed a radio message to the scene of crime officer. Ralph called him back within two minutes.

'Christ almighty, Chief. We need you down here.'

'No time to chat, Ralph. Drop what you're doing and get round to Christie's bakery.'

'How did you know?' Ralph said incredulously. 'I'm just back from there. Listen, Jack, the shit's hitting the fan down here. It's a fucking slaughterhouse. There's a baker missing from Christie's place. His boss heard him screaming outside the bakehouse. He's gone, but the walls are covered with blood. Next we get a bloody milk-float driver telling me he's lost two of his lads. They went up the alley by the Ship Institute.'

Jack closed his eyes, picturing the place. The alley was exactly where Lorna had pointed out on the grainy print.

'No sign?'

'Nothing but broken milk-bottles. No blood, nothing.'

'Anything else?'

'We've just had a report of a girl gone missing round on Swan Street. I've just sent a squad car round there.'

'Well, there's another one. I don't know where it is, but there's an old man gone. It took him at the back of a building. Somewhere with railings, like a back court. I don't know exactly where, but I reckon it's in the centre of the town.'

'Jesus, Jack, I've got my hands full down here,' Ralph bawled down the phone. He sounded helpless. 'And anyway, how the hell do you know? How did you know about the bakery?'

'You'd never believe me,' Jack said. 'Listen. Hold on down there. I'm coming in.'

'Cowie won't like it.'

'Cowie can shove it up his arse,' Jack retorted vehemently.

Back in the kitchen, he told Lorna he'd have to go. She looked up at him, the disappointment evident in her eyes.

'I'm sorry, but I really should. Ralph is down at the bakery. You were right, of course.'

Lorna nodded dumbly. 'I know,' she finally said. 'I wish I didn't have this thing. I wish it was somebody else.' She stood up and came towards him and put her hands on his hips. Without thinking he drew her forward by the shoulders. She tilted her head and without thinking, he kissed her gently on the lips. She tasted of woman and sweet coffee.

As soon as he did so, she jerked back as if she'd been scalded. For an instant Jack was taken aback, completely wrong-footed. Her hands suddenly gripped the side of his shirt and her fingernails dug into the skin just below his ribs. Her eyes were huge and suddenly terrified.

'No,' she gasped.

'I'm sorry,' Jack stuttered. 'I didn't mean to. . . .'

'No,' she repeated. 'It's not . . . oh Jack. It's you. I can *feel* it.'

He tried to take a step back, but she held on desperately, shaking her head, her face a picture of shock and dismay.

'It's you it wants. It knows about you, and it wants you.'

'Me?' he asked stupidly.

'I can sense it. The thing's in my head. It knows you're the man who understands what it is. It knows you've been hunting it, and it's coming after you.'

He laughed, though he knew it sounded shallow and forced. Cold fingers began to scrabble their way up his spine.

'Well,' he said, 'it'll have to be a big mean bastard then. I've been around a long time.'

'No, I mean it, Jack. Please be careful.'

He pulled back, but she leaned against him, as if she'd lost strength, then raised her hand to the back of his head and pressed him against her. This time she kissed him properly, forcing her mouth against his with a kind of hungry desperation. Jack could do nothing except respond, though his mind was awhirl. They stayed together for a long moment.

Finally he pulled back. She was looking up at him and her eyes were filling with tears again, making them huge and lustrous.

'Promise me you'll be careful,' she said quietly, holding him tight.

He promised.

34

Ralph Slater had been right. Everything was hitting the fan by the time Jack got to the station. Even as he crossed the old bridge, screeching over the curve in second gear, recklessly ignoring the black ice on the brow, he could hear the urgent wail of sirens way down on River Street. On the turn towards Artisan Road two police cars sped past, cutting in front of him, lights sending blue strobe flashes bouncing off the glass doors of the Regal Cinema.

Bobby Thomson only raised his eyebrows when Jack came hustling in, letting the door slam behind him. He watched in silence as the other man strode past the desk and took the stairs three at a time, coat flapping behind him.

Ronald Cowie's secretary half rose in her seat as he came barging through and raised a hand to forestall him, but he ignored her, twisted the handle on the office door and stormed inside.

'This damned stupidity has to stop,' he snapped without pausing for breath. 'It's a slaughterhouse out there and you've got me kicking my heels. I've had enough. As of this moment I'm reporting back for duty.'

'And why not?' a voice said from behind him. Jack whirled and saw a tall, grey-haired man in a herringbone coat standing with his hands in his pockets. 'Where've you been, Jack?'

Divisional Commander Hector Nairn came walking towards the desk, his eyes shifting from one man to the other. Cowie was still seated behind his desk, his mouth hanging open.

'Is there something I should know?'

'Chief Inspector Fallon had to take some time owing,' Cowie started to say.

'That's a lie. I was ordered out, and if you'd have let me handle things my way, you wouldn't have half the force out on the streets this morning.'

'Ordered out?' Nairn looked from one to the other again, then

485

swivelled his eyes back to Jack. 'I think there is something I haven't been told, and I think I should hear it right now.' He turned and pulled up a swivel chair and lowered himself slowly into it. He'd been head of the murder squad in the city when Jack had joined. The two of them had worked on dozens of cases together.

Jack hauled another chair from the far side of the office and sat down heavily.

'Office politics, and I'm bloody fed up with them,' he said. Mentally he took his gloves off and prepared for a bare-knuckle fight.

'We've got a serious situation here,' he began.

'Now there's an understatement if I ever heard one.' Hector snorted.

'And getting more serious by the minute. We shouldn't have lost young Gordon Pirie. If we'd let O'Day stay in the church, then he'd most likely still be alive, and those kids wouldn't be dead this morning.'

Jack turned to the Divisional Commander. 'I've wasted the last few days doing nothing but being kept out of the way while we announced we'd got the killer. But I knew we didn't have him, and we won't get him unless somebody sits up and takes notice.'

'You went off duty,' Cowie protested, his face red.

'With respect, Superintendent, I was ordered to take my leave. I have a duplicate copy of my objections to that order, and my protest over the arrest of Michael O'Day.'

'Is that right, Ron?' Hector Nairn asked softly, but there was an iron undertone. 'Did you order Jack off the case?'

Cowie began to bluster. His mouth opened and closed. He started to say something, but the senior officer held up his hand.

'You tell me, Jack. And when you've finished, I want to hear an explanation of everything I've been reading in the newspapers.'

'It's simple,' Jack said. 'I was told to stay away on Thursday night. That's the night the tele-message claimed that we'd got the killer. I objected to that and to the arrest of Michael O'Day because I didn't believe he should have been in a cell.'

'But he'd stolen religious artifacts and he confessed to being involved in the Herkik killing,' Cowie interjected.

'Yes, he had admitted to taking the chalice, and for a reason which was explained to you.'

'Mumbo jumbo is what I heard,' Cowie rasped, but Hector Nairn merely held up his hand again.

'That's enough, Ron, I want to hear it from Jack and I don't want to waste another minute, okay?'

'But the man had not admitted to killing Marta Herkik,' Jack continued. 'He only said he was in Cairn House on the night it happened, and he was perfectly safe up in the church tower. He was asking for sanctuary.'

'A bit archaic,' Hector observed.

'Yes, maybe, but he was safe, and he was going nowhere. I'd been looking for him for some time, and if I'd got the message from an informant on time, then perhaps we could have resolved this case a week ago. But I didn't get the information from Superintendent Cowie until it was too late, and my request for extra manpower was denied. I am not into playing politics. I'm a policeman and my job is to catch this thing.'

'Oh, I agree with that, Jack,' Hector said with a humourless smile. 'So what's the juju I've been reading about?'

'Devils and monsters,' Cowie interjected. 'It's absolute rubbish.'

'I won't tell you again, Ron,' Hector said icily. Cowie's mouth closed like a trap.

'That's speculation in the press, but there is a basis to it. Marta Herkik was killed in the middle of some kind of seance. That's why I brought in Professor Toye. He's an expert on paranormal studies, and I know him. He has given us valuable advice.'

'Yes, but what about this spey-wife?'

'Every source helps. She's been helping me. Basically, as far as I can tell, she's got some kind of extra sensory perception. She's seen some of these killings as they happen. Sometimes *before* they happen.'

'And she's not involved?'

'No, she is not. I've been there when it's happened. She's clean.'

'And you believe all this?'

'I have to believe it. I was with her this morning when she told me about the boy in the bakery and the milk-boys. We're not

487

looking for missing persons, I can tell you that. We're looking for corpses. And if we don't get our fingers out there will be a lot more, I can tell you.'

'It's a bit of a mouthful to take in all at once,' Hector said gently.

'I agree. I was too long in arriving at it myself, but everything has fitted so far. I want to continue to use Lorna Breck, no matter how it looks, or whatever it costs us in public relations. Our image doesn't matter a damn. It's the kids in this town who matter.'

Jack stopped talking for a moment to gather his thoughts and while he did, Hector Nairn asked him to tell him the full story right from the start. Jack wasted no time. He took him through it, from the killing of Marta Herkik, to his conversation with Andy Toye about what might have actually happened on the night of her death. He told him about Lorna's premonitions and his initial incredulity, then the finding of where Neil Kennedy had been snatched, and her visions of baby Kelly Campbell's mother being smashed to the ground on Barley Cobble.

'What did it for me was when we found the bodies in that chimney.' He turned to Cowie. 'Check Robbie Cattanach's report. There was one extra body. I told you this before. That was the baby from the fire on Murroch Road. That's the one Lorna Breck saw when it was actually happening. Sorley Fitzpatrick – he's the firemaster – said he thought the baby might have been completely destroyed by the heat, but Lorna Breck told me she saw something take the baby from the cot. I know it's far-fetched and it doesn't sound like straightforward police work, but I can't deny her as a source, and at the moment she's all we have. She's the best we're going to get.'

'So who are we looking for?'

'We're looking for Michael O'Day, initially,' Jack said, not wanting to tell anybody exactly what he was looking for.

'So he'd been the killer all along?'

'No. Something, or some-one has been using these people. And it all started on the night of the seance.'

'So what is it?'

'I don't know. But I'll find out and I'll find it.'

Hector sat back in his seat.

488

'It really is a bit much to take on board, Jack,' he said.

'I've had longer than you. But I'll get nowhere if I'm twiddling my thumbs. Michael O'Day saw something at that seance that scared the hell out of him, and he believed it. He locked himself up in the belltower to get away from it.'

'And you think this Lorna Breck is genuine?'

'I know it. I don't know how she does it, or why, but I've seen it happen. If I don't use her, then we can all walk away and let children die. It's as simple as that.'

'So what are we looking for here?'

'Damned if I know. Seriously, I just don't know.'

'It sounds as if you don't think it's human. Not the kind of thing I want to tell the Chief Constable.'

'Frankly, that's the least of my problems. Tell him we're hunting a deranged escaped prisoner, which is the truth anyway, because somebody took O'Day out of the church. It could be an influence which has *forced* these people to do what they've done. Michael O'Day was convinced he'd be safe in the church tower, and I think he was right. He told me he did not want to kill anybody, but that he'd be compelled to if he was taken out of sanctuary. I believed him then, and I believe him now. It doesn't matter what you call it, and it doesn't matter what it is. It's a killer, and it has to be stopped. Let's say it's some psychosis brought on by the seance. I just want to stop it killing anybody else.'

'Well, you've got my backing on that. As of now, you're in charge of the case,' Hector said. 'Use whatever resources you need, and ask for anything else you want.'

He turned to Ronald Cowie, who hadn't said a word for some time.

'I want you to understand that Chief Inspector Fallon has my fullest confidence. There will be no interference in this case whatsoever. From you I want a full report of why a senior investigating officer was taken off duty in the middle of such a serious case, and it had better be good, though, frankly, I doubt it will be.'

Cowie did his goldfish act again. Hector heaved himself from his chair and walked to the door, Jack followed him out. Beyond the anteroom, the divisional commander stopped him.

'I can't say I honestly believe a word of what you've just told me,' he said. 'I think we're looking for a nutter, or a group of them. But in the meantime, I'm going to rely on your judgement, no matter what. Just don't make me look like an idiot.'

'I'll do my best,' Jack promised him, though in his own mind he wasn't sure what that best would be. He didn't even know where he was going to start.

He was only in his office five minutes when Robbie Cattanach knocked on the door and popped his head round.

'I heard you'd been sent home,' he said. 'Then I got a whisper you were back.'

'Word travels fast,' Jack said.

'Listen, I know you're busy, even busier than I've been, if you can believe that,' Robbie began. 'But I have all the reports on the bodies in the chimney and the others ones from the town hall. The baby is definitely Kerry McCann. There's a great deal of desiccation of the tissues, caused by the cold and the dry atmosphere at the height of the chimney, but the blood tests are fairly conclusive. There is not a shadow of doubt about Kelly Campbell, again because of the blood tests, and the others have been positively identified as Neil Kennedy and Carol Howard. We suspect the fifth to be Timothy Doyle, but identification has been hampered. There are no distinguishing marks and sufficient putrefaction as to make it very difficult. His own mother hasn't recognised him, and to tell you the God's honest, there isn't that much left.'

'I know,' Jack said. 'I brought him down.'

'As far as the other three are concerned, you can call off the search for Charles Black and Edward Redford. Votek Visotsky we know about. The missing part matched.'

Jack pulled a disgusted face.

'I know,' Robbie apologised. 'It sounds callous, but what else can I say?'

Jack shrugged.

'Cause of death?'

'Blood loss and shock in all cases, more or less, though we can't be too sure about the three infants. However, it does point that way. Partial strangulation on Charles Black, and severe

490

trauma in Redford's case. His leg was pulled off at the hip. That would kill anybody. Visotsky died from a single blow to the side of the head.'

Robbie stopped and looked over at Jack.

'I'm more interested in the secondary wounds. Mutilation describes it better. In every case, they occurred after death, and in some cases long after the event.'

'How do you figure that?'

'Without being too technical, generally we can tell by the condition of the skin close to the wounds. The integument dries out quickly in the open air, making it more liable to rip. There's no elasticity and it pulls away on either side of a cut. But that's neither here nor there.'

Robbie reached into his black case and brought out a set of ten by eight prints. He shuffled them onto Jack's desk.

'I've burned the midnight oil on these, and I can tell you, my freezer room's filling up too damned quickly. We don't have room for any more cadavers and I'd be pleased if you could catch this loony and give me a break.'

He leaned over the prints, without waiting for a response, and jabbed his finger at several of them in quick succession.

'Every one of these injuries is post mortem. You can tell by the tearing of the underlying muscle and ligaments that this is exactly what it was, a tear. To get this kind of damage, we're talking about considerable force. Something very powerful. You get this trauma in mechanical accidents, where people have been dragged into machinery, but that's not what happened here.'

'So what did happen?'

'I'm coming to that. Just bear with me. Just remember what I said when I looked at Shona Campbell's body. I've a set of pictures in a book which show the aftermath of a bear mauling. The damage is similar to this, wrenching of muscle and ligaments, twisting of joints in the socket. It's what you'd expect when you have a powerful animal dismembering a carcass.'

'We've ruled out animals.'

'I know you have,' Robbie said. He leaned over the spread of prints again and used his finger to stab here and there.

'Look at this. These are certainly bites, and it's got a radius you wouldn't believe. I've worked it out that it's got a gape

491

about seven inches across. This was not, repeat not, caused by a human. Something has been eating these children after they were dead.'

'You know anything with a bite like that?'

'Ever watch *Jaws*?'

'Get out of here,' Jack said. 'We're looking for no shark.'

'I know that. I just don't know *what* you're looking for. This doesn't fit anything I've ever come across. I've been through all the books, because the fiscal's ordered full inquiries into each of these cases, and I just don't know what to tell him.'

'Neither me,' Jack said. He didn't know what to tell Robbie Cattanach either.

'Welcome back to the cuckoo's nest,' was how John McColl greeted Jack when he made it to the operations room. Ralph Slater turned round from the grid-map and gave him a tired grin.

'You should have stayed away,' he said. 'It's a madhouse in here and out there.'

Jack didn't bother with the explanations both of them were expecting. Instead he crossed to the map and told Ralph to give him a briefing. Ralph began with the call from the bakery and went on non-stop for fifteen minutes, pointing out the by-now very familiar parts of town.

'We've a report in on the girl. Lisa Corbett. She just disappeared from the stair landing. Somebody found her handbag on the stair between the third and fourth floors, but there's no other sign.'

'How about the old man?'

'Nothing so far. Nobody's called it in. What I'd like to know is where you're getting this from?'

'Later. As of now, I need you to organise a special team, all local boys, to do a search of every place that's higher than forty feet.'

'That's a lot of places.'

'I know that, but we have to do it. Forget outbuildings and garden huts. This thing doesn't operate on the ground. Remember where we found the bodies? And Jock Toner? It came in the skylight at Rolling Stock. It's a climber and it leaves them up high. That's where we'll find the bodies, and that's where we'll find it.'

492

'So you think it's bodies again?'

'Certain of it. It hasn't left one alive so far. Also, it operates in the dark, so it has to hide somewhere during the day.'

'You keep calling him *it*,' John McColl said. 'I thought we were looking for O'Day.'

'We are,' Jack replied. 'He'll be holed up somewhere. If we can find him and lock him up before dark, then we've got a chance. After dark, then it's anybody's guess. Whatever's controlling him can do what it likes then.'

'You mean like hypnosis?'

'Something like that,' Jack said, though he didn't explain what he really thought. Ralph and John looked at each other, but said nothing. Ralph picked up the phone and made a call, and ten minutes later, Jack was briefing the patrols. The search went on through the day.

At three o'clock, while it was still light, but already turning to dusk, Keith Fraser, who ran a television repair and installation business from a small workshop behind Wattie Dickson's newsagent's place, was on top of Denny Court, the second grey monolith of high-rise council housing by the river next to Latta Court where Timmy Doyle had been snatched from his pram. Keith had been an electrical engineer in Castlebank Shipyard until Korean shipbuilding had all but obliterated the Clyde from the forefront of marinecraft and made it just a memory with only gaunt black cranes on the skyline as a reminder of the boom days. Now he was in a growth industry, and spent much of his time on roofs and up ladders installing the satellite dishes which were beginning to proliferate like mushrooms on walls and houses throughout the town.

Despite the wail of sirens in the frosty morning, and despite the shocking spate of murders which had cast a pall of unease and trepidation among the townsfolk, the residents of Denny Court on that day were more concerned about the fault in their television reception. They flooded the council with complaints and Keith Fraser, who was working in Lochend that day, eventually had to head back into town and check out the problem before the good people of Denny Court started a riot over the loss of their daytime quiz shows and soap reruns.

The elevator, smothered in graffiti and stinking of sweat and

493

bad cooking, took him to the ninth floor and refused to go further. He had to trudge up the final five flights with his toolbag until he got to the roof where he used his pass-key to get out onto the flat.

He spotted the problem with the communal aerial immediately, but it took several moments for the gruesome truth to dawn on him.

The aluminium prongs of the antenna were bent out of line by two small bundles which dangled down from the spidery rig. At first Keith thought that one of the housewives from the teeming block of flats had come up and hung her washing on the aerial, but as soon as he crossed the asphalt roof, he realised what he was seeing and took several slow steps backwards, shaking his head all the while, eyes fixed to the sightless and staring eyes which twinkled red in the glow from the hazard-light dome.

Keith made it all the way to the ground, shunning the elevator the whole distance, and reached his van parked fifty yards away before he remembered that he had a portable phone in the pocket of his jacket. As it was, it took him seven attempts before his shaking fingers managed to press the numbers for the police emergency service and even when he got through to the operator, he could not speak for fully three minutes.

In the station, Ralph Slater got the call and made it across the bridge to Denny Court in seven minutes, followed by two patrol cars with sirens squealing.

Young Colin Jamieson and his cousin Laurie Liddell had both been spiked under the jawline on the aluminium spines, which made their towsled heads twist grotesquely. From the amount of blood under the body, it was clear that Laurie had still been alive at the time. His bloody prints on the spike above his head showed his desperate yet futile efforts to free himself. Ralph could visualise the squirming youngster trying to raise his body while the pain tore into his neck. His agony must have been extreme. From what he could see, the youngster would have been trying to scream for help as his struggles weakened, but no help came because nobody would have heard. The spike of metal had been driven right through the boy's larynx. His cousin, a small, slight shape dangling close by, had probably died before he was hung up like a carcass in a butcher's shop. His

494

eyes still glittered, kept moist in the cold air, and the hands hanging limply at his sides were blue with the lividity of blood draining down into them. The spike had taken him on the left side of the jaw, causing only a small puncture hole, but he had been driven down upon it with such force that it had rammed right through his temple on the other side.

Keith Fraser produced a hacksaw and cut through the metal and the boys were loaded into bags which were too big for their small frames, while Ronnie Jeffrey took pictures of everything for posterity.

Just before darkfall, on the coldest night of the year so far, the body of Lisa Corbett was spotted by a teenage boy. The only surprise was that no one had seen it earlier. Sorley Fitzpatrick sent his biggest ladders from the fire station, but they couldn't get high enough up the steeple of the old parish Church at the crossroads of River and Kirk Streets, and eventually they had to call in the Sea King helicopter from the submarine base further down the estuary to come and lower the frail, limp thing down from the golden weathercock where it had been swaying in the gathering breeze. The massive cast-iron weather vane had easily taken her weight. The girl had been pierced through the shoulder by the six-foot long stylised arrow and had swung with the northening wind until her foot had snagged on the compass-point. There she had hung all day, leaking drops of blood to the far pavement in the strange secrecy of height and familiarity before a schoolboy had casually looked up and wondered what the flapping shape was. He'd pointed upwards and his friends, on their way home from school early, had gathered around. Passers-by had stopped to rubberneck and finally a policeman had chanced along. Even he hadn't recognised the shape, but he knew of the find on top of Denny Court, and called it in just in case. John McColl had to go back to the station for a pair of binoculars and when he twiddled the focus ring, the dead girl's pale face, jaws so wide the back teeth were visible, had sprung into awful clarity.

The body of Graham Friel was found a week later pinned to the guard-rail of the gas tank on the east end of town. It might have gone undiscovered for a while longer, but because of the freezing winter, people were using more gas than normal to heat their homes and when the huge cylinder sank as the fuel was drawn off, the bloody body of the bakery worker was found lolling on the curved roof. An arm and most of the shoulder were missing and were never recovered again.

Old George Wilkie, the caretaker at the planners' office, had simply disappeared. It was not until May, when the buds on the trees had exploded into green, that his rotting carcass slipped off the overflow pipe on the roof of the old masonic hall and tumbled into the valley gutter, blocking the flow of early summer rains. The water backed up behind the body and seeped over the lead flashing and into the old hall where the brothers met in secret conclave, ruining a display of memorabilia from the boom-town bygone age. Keith Fraser's cousin George, a mason who also ran a roofing firm, got the ladders up to check the blockage and found the corpse of the old man, though, by this time, it was only his coat which held him together over the drainage gutter. The flies had had the spring months to get to work and when George grabbed a hold of what he thought was a bundle of rags, a pile of squirming white and bloated maggots came spilling out of a sleeve, along with a skeletal arm which had been picked almost clean. The stench was awesome.

On the day the bodies of the milk boys and Lisa Corbett were found, Blair Bryden worked overtime to get the story on the wires and his story blared from every networked news channel. The name he'd coined for the killer had stuck.

Blair himself managed to get in front of a camera in a live broadcast from the crossroads at River and Kirk Street, pointing up to the night sky where floodlights illuminated the needle-spike on the old church steeple.

'This,' he said, 'is where the *Shrike* brought his latest victim.'

He gave a brief and eloquent summary of the ghastly events which had rocked the town in the space of three short weeks, and managed to slip in a barbed comment about Jack being taken off the case by Superintendent Ron Cowie, whose picture was shown, carefully chosen by Blair, one suspected, to catch a shot of him with his eyes closed and mouth open. He added that O'Day had escaped from the cell after Jack got his marching orders. Blair speculated as to where the *Shrike* would strike next and painted a picture of a town shivering with fear, which was closer to the truth than the viewing public beyond the burgh boundary realised.

Next morning, his story made the front page of every newspaper, but by then it was all over bar the shouting.

35

The wind had veered again and was blasting down straight from the north when Jack left the station and headed up to his sister's house. The night was blistering cold and the frost sparkled like diamonds on the windward sides of the trees and lamp posts. Jack hadn't stopped, hadn't slowed down all day. Robbie Cattanach had had to request extra storage space for the cadavers at Kirkland Hospital and the fiscal had drafted in another pathologist to help with the autopsies which were becoming monotonously, if horribly similar. In every case, the cause of death was either by devastating blood loss, massive trauma or both. Every one of the bodies in the storage freezers had been mutilated in one way or another. Robbie had been able to establish that the bite marks all had the same radius and similar shear-lines. Each of the dead had been gripped with enormous pressure, sufficient to cause dreadful bruising and in most cases, skin rupture. The pathologist was able to show, in a series of quick diagrams, the spread of the grip and the strange, two-digit claw marks on either side. Robbie Cattanach was not now prepared to put down on paper any speculation as to what on earth could have caused the marks. As far as he was aware, nothing living could have inflicted such damage.

Under John McColl's direction, the teams had hit the high spots and searched as much of the town's skyline as they could before nightfall. That search continued after dark in a town that had become strangely silent, eerily empty. Few cars moved on River Street. The cinema simply shut its doors and the bingo hall posted a sign saying that they were sorry, but they were closed for alterations. Under normal circumstances, this would have caused a riot among the blue-rinsed brigade, but there were few grannies who would risk venturing out in the dark just to test their luck. All early morning milk deliveries were cancelled and Castlebank Distillery stopped its night-shift bottling operation after acrimonious but very speedy negotiations with the union representatives. There was little else to be done when the entire bottling line failed to turn up just after seven o'clock. Latta Marineyard stayed open, working round the clock to finish the oil-rig platform just at the south of the tidal basin beside the old shipyard. The floodlights blazed down onto the maze of metalwork and the sizzling electric flashes of the arc-welders continued through the dark. Apart from that, and the constant passage of police patrol cars, the town had simply locked its doors. The townsfolk huddled behind them and waited.

On the other side of town, somewhere between the looming brick megalith of Castlebank Distillery and the volcanic rock where the castle perched at the junction where the river ran into the firth, something moved in the dismal dark of the old shipyard. The great sheds, where some of the ships that had made the Clyde great had been fabricated, were silent and empty. There were four massive structures, all connected and constructed of iron beams and corrugated iron, blackened by dirt and grime and the smoke of a bygone age. From the giant shed nearest the castle, a slipway which still had launching tracks embedded in the stone swept down towards the tidal basin where the hardy wrack which could survive in the brackish water floated on a greasy surface. Inside, out of the wind, it was like a huge and dark cavern. Somewhere high, water leaked from an aged tank and dropped fifty feet or more into a rust puddle with a metronomic, almost metallic sound. High on the sides of the launch bay, a fretwork of metal stairs and ladders soared up into the utter blackness above.

It was not silent here. Apart from the steady drop of water, and the echoing chink of a rusty chain which hung beside the pulley door and was stirred by the harsh wind, the fine ice particles blown from the trees across the river abraded the outer surface with the sound of glass splinters and the wind itself whistled through the narrow gaps where the corrugated iron had peeled away. Beyond, closer to the distillery, the whine of machinery and the harsh sizzle of arc-welding came over the wall from the rig-yard.

Inside the gaunt and towering shed, something stirred in the darkness. It moved slowly, but with little care for silence, out from the shadows underneath the stairwell against the far wall. A

499

little light, not much more than a glimmer, was reflected up from the oily water in the basin, just enough to catch the figure of what had been a man shamble back into the shadows.

If anybody had seen Michael O'Day they would have recoiled in disgust. There was hardly an ounce of flesh on the man's bones. His once-smart coat was in tatters and covered with whatever filth he'd been lying in. The scarecrow figure turned and his eyes, now sunk deep under grizzled white eyebrows, closed quickly against the pale glimmer of light, screwing themselves up in obvious pain. O'Day's thick hair, once black but now white, had all but gone, save for a few lank strands which fell down behind his ears. One hank, greased with oil, swung down over his eyes. On his shoulder another clump had stuck to a patch of engine grease and fluttered there like moulted sheep wool. His face was so emaciated his cheeks appeared to be black holes and the bones were ridged out, giving his face a skull-like, fleshless look. The skin of his forehead was scabbed and peeling, and a suppurating sore seemed to be eating into the side of his nose. As he shambled back from the door, an incoherent mumbling sound came dribbling out between his cracked lips along with thick and ropy saliva which swung with his jerky movements to add to the damp stains on the front of his coat.

He took several steps, swaying like a drunk, then stopped, shaking his head.

Something that was almost like words, but was still unintelligible, came out in a guttural stream. The man's body jerked left and right, then he started walking again, feet scraping the stone floor, kicking aside rusty nails and rivets. He got to the far corner and reached the other space beneath the stairs and began to crawl into the darkness.

For a while, he stopped moving and simply huddled there on his side.

Then he began to twitch. It started with a twist of his neck, an involuntary spasm, then his whole body began to shudder. A hellish scream echoed round the vast chamber of the shed, reverberating from one dark wall to another, but no one heard it. Michael O'Day's scrawny form writhed uncontrollably and his heels drummed against a metal plate which had been left under the stairs, banging a rapid drum-roll before they stopped

500

abruptly and went limp. There was an instant of silence and then something moved out of the shadow. It was blacker than black and it moved with spidery speed. It flowed up the side of the stairs, clinging to the outside of the bannister, then leapt without pause to the first level of the side-wall platforms, reached a long limb upwards with eerie liquid grace and began to climb.

When it got to the top, high on the side of the shed, it paused, making a throaty, rumbling sound. Until now it had not opened its eyes, but when it froze to complete stillness, they flicked open, two caustic yellow orbs, blind looking, and the left one puckered and scarred, yet both searing in their intensity. The thing swivelled its head.

Here, out of the sickly warmth where it had spent the hours of light, the air was cold and somehow alien, yet despite the emptiness of the shipyard, it sensed life, abundant, hot and fluttering life all around. Its head flicked to the side and cocked up to the left, a mantis-like motion of alert menace. Up in the high beams, it sensed the warmth of the starlings which had flocked and wheeled like bees in the dusk and now huddled in uneasy clusters. Its unearthly perception discerned the shiver of alarm which rippled through the roost as the birds sensed its own presence. It was too dark for them to fly. Instead they nervously fluttered, each small bird crouching tight as the unseen but strongly felt presence of the black thing touched them.

On the old iron stairway, the black gargoyle creature turned its head down with that same insectile flick and the birds were forgotten. Out there, beyond the towering metal walls of the boatshed, there was warm life aplenty, a surfeit of it, a storehouse of vitality, cowering from the dark, waiting to be reaped. It closed its eyes and *sensed* way beyond the walls. It scented the fear and the unease, like the fluttering consternation of the little birds in their roost, but much stronger, much more powerful. They tossed and turned and they worried, all of them giving off the sweet emotion that filled its senses with a potent spice. The obsidian lips parted and a drool of saliva slithered in a wet braid to splash on the metal tread where it sizzled and boiled in the freezing air. It held itself stock-still and forced its senses outwards, beyond the nearest buildings, past Castlebank Church and over the centre of the town, keeping a grip on its own clenching hunger.

Soon it would have nowhere to shelter, unless it found welcome warmth, unless it *invaded*. Time was running out. Here, in this place of light, where the minds and souls were throbbing with savoury life, it had almost outstayed its allotment, unless it found a nest to shelter from the burning radiance of day. Anger, glowing and feral, boiled up inside the thing as it hunched, still as stone, on the metal ledge, while it outreached with its baneful mind over the town beyond the shipyard.

Finally its perception focused and found what it sought. The strange *other* mind it touched was filled with flickering thoughts, wheeling emotions, and under it all, the dark bubbling fear that all prey possesses. It dipped into the mind and sipped on the emotion, nurturing the fear, sampling the jittery thoughts, and then, as quickly as it had entered, it withdrew, leaving hardly a trace of its presence.

Out on Clydeshore Avenue, Lorna Breck shuddered, as if a chill wind had blown through her. Somebody must have walked on my grave, *she said to herself.*

In the old shipyard, the thing turned its mind away and pushed outwards, following the skein of thought it had invaded. It dipped here and touched there, a cold, unseen presence.

After a while, it began to move, flowing like oil up to the roof of the massive shed. A starling chirruped as a shadow deeper than night passed by. An eye gaped in the dark and the bird died instantly. Its small body tumbled, fluttering to the ground far below. When it hit, there was hardly a sound.

It was after eight when Jack knocked on Julia's door. Davy opened it, flashed him a big smile and then bounded away to watch whatever was on television. Julia was in the kitchen, sitting at the table with her big electric typewriter in front of her and a pile of papers on the side.

'You've been in the wars, I hear,' she said, pushing her chair back. She crossed to the sink and filled the kettle.

'It's a long campaign,' Jack said wearily. 'I just need a wash and a clean shirt and a quick bite.'

Julia reached up and rubbed his cheek.

'And a shave. You look totally disreputable.'

'Always the one with compliments,' he shot back.

She slapped his jaw lightly.

'I told you to get a good woman who'll do your shirts for you.'

'I've got one, and you're a marvel. Just tell me where they are and I'll be out of your hair in ten minutes.'

Despite his obvious agitation to be gone again, Julia made him sit down and have a cup of tea while she rustled up a sizeable grill of bacon and eggs and hot toast, then sat down and watched him until he'd finished the lot. She asked him about the case and he responded almost unintelligibly between mouthfuls, but she gleaned enough to get the picture.

'This girl, what's she really like?' she asked.

'She's okay. I thought she was a bit of a flake at first, with this mental thing, but I reckon she's straight,' Jack told her. 'She's got auburn hair.'

Julia's eyes crinkled over the top of her teacup.

'Do I detect a note of interest here?'

'Oh, don't be daft. She's too young for me.'

Julia smiled again. She knew her brother, probably better than he knew himself.

Davy's programme finished and he came charging into the kitchen, narrowly missing the fridge. He pushed and squirmed until he was on Jack's knee.

'I'm off school tomorrow,' he announced. 'Can we go sledging again?' The boy was bouncing around on Jack's knee with unconcealed enthusiasm.

''Fraid not, pal. Too much work. But maybe at the weekend. No promises, but I'll do my best.'

Davy took a sausage from his uncle's plate, slid down to the floor again, and went pattering out of the kitchen. Jack watched him, unable to keep the smile from his face.

'He's as fly as a bag of monkeys, that one.'

'He's picking it up from you,' Julia told him with mock reproof. She leaned over the table and took his empty plate away. 'As you heard, you don't have to come for him tomorrow. They've closed the school on the pretext of in-service training. The kids are having an extra week's holiday.'

'Silver lining for the wee ones. I wish I could say the same for the rest of us.'

'Are you going to catch him?' Julia asked. Like every mother, the enormity of what was happening in Levenford had seeped into her. She was afraid for her child.

'Sure I will, and damned quick. We're getting closer now. It's just a matter of time. You just look after Davy until the weekend, and it'll be over. That's a promise.'

He reached across and ruffled Julia's hair, the way he'd done when they were both teenagers. Then she had screamed in protest, now she just came close and leaned her cheek against his shoulder.

'I'll be praying for you,' she said.

After the huge meal, the hot shower went a long way to making Jack feel he was able to face the night ahead and the plan he'd been working on. He stood under the cataract of water, letting the heat soak off some of the tension which had crept under his skin. His thoughts danced at random while the steam fogged the tiles. He closed his eyes for only a moment and all thought wavered away, drifting into the mist of vapour. A few seconds later, Jack gave a start, as if coming awake. He ran a hand through his hair, pushing it back from his forehead, and knuckled his eyes. Without looking, he reached out and yanked the shower handle, twisting it far over until it pointed to the blue marker. The hot water switched to a jet of cold. He endured it for ten seconds, feeling his skin pucker as it froze, then, when it became unbearable, he stumbled out of the shower, gasping for breath. While he shaved, he remembered Julia had asked him to run the bath for her. He jammed in the plug and let the bath fill noisily while the steam misted up the mirror, making the shaving more difficult. He rinsed off with a sharp splash of cold water and ran his fingers backwards through his hair again, knowing it would fall back over his forehead once it dried.

Downstairs, Julia had placed a fresh shirt over the back of a chair close to the fire and he savoured the momentary crisp warmth as he buttoned it. Davy was perched on the arm of the seat, eyes fixed to the screen where Bugs Bunny and Daffy Duck were perpetrating enormous wrongs on each other. Julia had got into her dressing gown.

'Come on, young man, it's time for your bed,' she told her son, who immediately protested that he was off school the following day, and using Jack as a back-up, he wheedled his way into staying up for half an hour.

'I've run your bath,' Jack said, stretching an arm into the sleeve of his coat.

Julia looked up at him.

'I hadn't planned one 'til later,' she said.

'Oh, I thought you asked me to,' Jack said, brows knitting in puzzlement. He'd been sure she had asked him to fill the bath.

'Must have been some other girl,' she said, smiling. 'Are you sure there's nothing I should know?'

Jack patted her backside.

'Go on. Get up and soak before the water gets cold.'

Julia hadn't planned on an early bath, but for some reason, and despite the oddity of her brother telling her he'd imagined she'd asked him to run the hot water for her, the idea of a quick warm soak appealed to her.

Davy gave his uncle a hug and tried to elicit a definite promise for Saturday. Jack ruffled Julia's hair again at the bottom of the stairs before she went up for her bath, then, impulsively, took her in his arms and squeezed her tight, silently showing his love and appreciation before he walked out into the cold. Down the path towards the gate, the wind moaned through the bare branches of the rowan tree and cut into him like a knife.

He'd parked the car up at the end of the road and the fifty-yard walk drained the heat from him, despite the thick wool of his overcoat which he'd buttoned up to the neck. Ice had already started to rime the windscreen and had clogged the keyhole enough to make it difficult to turn the lock. The engine started first time and Jack eased the car onto the hill and carefully steered it down the slope towards the centre of town. It was only when he was halfway down Kirk Street, when he raised his hand to check his watch, that he realised he'd left it at Julia's. The radio spat and he thumbed it on. Bobby Thomson told him there was a message to call Lorna Breck. Jack told him he was heading that way anyway. He switched off and accelerated over the crossroads.

The cartoon had ended just after Uncle Jack had left. Davy flicked through the channels, but there was nothing of interest for a seven-year-old so he hit the button and watched the picture disappear to a dot. Upstairs, he could hear the watery sounds of his mother in the bath and he knew that in a few minutes she'd be down to tell him to get into his pyjamas and go to bed.

He picked up a toy car lying on its side close to the fireside

505

kerb and trundled it along the top of the fireplace, making a noise he thought was a close representation of a racing car. The kerb was warm on his stockinged feet as he edged along, feeling the heat of the coals against his legs. Just at the end, before he turned the car to retrace its route, he found Jack's watch. Davy dropped the car and carefully lifted the timepiece. It was heavy and silver and had two little faces inside the big one and a picture of a thin sliver of moon rising beside the quarter hour.

He turned and scampered across to the window. He peeled the curtain back and leaned up against the glass, raising his hand to cut out his own reflection. He hadn't heard Jack's car outside, as he normally did when his uncle came to visit. He peered out. Specks of snow danced up against the pane then veered away, gusted by the wind. Further along the road, an orange street lamp winked as the branches of the chestnut tree swung in front of the glow. Jack was nowhere to be seen.

Davy pulled back and thought for a moment. If the car wasn't there, that meant it was probably parked outside the cottage, and that was only two minutes away across the back gardens behind the house. It was dark out there. If he told his mother, she'd tell him just to leave it. Davy sat down and thought. He closed his eyes for only a moment and when he opened them again, it was as if he had just woken from sleep. He rubbed his eyes and then turned to pick up the watch.

Take it.

The thought came from nowhere, like a distant whisper, and the decision was somehow made. Without further pause, the boy hauled his shoes from under the table and jammed them on his feet with the wriggling motions children use when they haven't opened the laces. His hooded jacket was still slung over the back of the chair and he pulled it on quickly and did the zipper right up to the neck. At the bottom of the stairs, the heavy watch clenched firmly in one hand, he paused for a second. Upstairs his mother was still splashing in water. Any second now, she'd pull the plug and he'd hear the gurgle as it flushed through the pipes.

It would only take a minute, he told himself.

He reached for the front door handle, then stopped again. If he followed along the road, then Jack might get to his car first and drive away. There was a quicker way, the kind of route Davy and his small friends knew intimately because of the hours they'd played in each other's gardens. He went down the hall, through the kitchen and eased open the back door. Here, in the lee of the wind, it was cold, but not bitterly so. Davy pulled the door closed and twisted the handle to make sure it made no sound, then scampered down the steps and across the crisp, frosted grass of the drying green.

At the far end, the small rockery gave enough height to scramble over the lattice fence and into the neighbour's garden. On the corner, beyond the onion patch, there was a gap in the privet hedge which was used as a short-cut by most of the kids in the street. It led through to the stand of tall pines which bordered onto Cargill Farm Road.

Davy had never been in the barwood at night. Beyond the protection of the fences and privet hedge, the unhindered wind tugged at his jacket and pulled the hood back from his face.

The track between the trees was hard-packed and solid with frost. The boy's feet thudded noisily as he scurried between the gaunt trunks. Overhead, the dry pine needles scraped and whispered and up there in the dark, two trunks sawed noisily against each other with a shivery squeal, like an animal in distress. In the dark, he held his hands out in front of him and his eyes were instinctively open wide to catch as much light as they could in the gloom. Here was a strange world of shadows and eerie sound. Twenty feet in from the edge, the far-off light from the window of the nearest house faded to nothing and Davy was alone in the gloom.

He stopped, hands still outstretched to protect against the knife-edge twigs that jutted in spikes from the conifers, momentarily lost.

Just ahead on the track, or what he assumed was the footworn path, a small juniper bush reached out a fuzzy branch just at head height. It waved lazily, almost threateningly, as the cold wind whipped it into motion. Davy shrank back, and bumped against a tree. A broken branch jabbed against his spine and when he twisted, he felt the material of his jacket rip.

From just ahead of the juniper bush, a twig snapped and suddenly everything went quiet.

For a second there was no sound at all, not even the whine of the wind above. It was as if a heavy door had silently closed, trapping him in still air. The wind, for some reason, had stopped. Davy stood frozen, heart now beating faster. He held his breath, ears straining to listen, but no sound came.

Very slowly, he raised his foot then put it down in front of him. It happened almost without volition, because as soon as the twig had snapped, the kind of sound a twig would make if something heavy had stood upon it, his first thought was to turn back the way he had come and scramble through the hedge and over the lattice fence and back into his own house.

Instead his foot moved forward. He took another step, then another, heading for the far edge of the wood opposite Jack's house.

He made it past the waving arm of the juniper bush, feeling with his feet to keep them on the bare path.

Something rustled nearby in a patch of dead brambles and a small unseen thing scuttered out and dashed into a scraggle of rhododendron. Davy's heart skipped a beat and he gasped involuntarily. This stand of trees was a different place at night. For a small boy, it was like a different world.

He waited until his heartbeat settled again, though it was still beating fast, before he moved again.

Ahead, maybe forty yards away, he thought he could see a patch of light from the street and made his way towards it, easing his way past the dark trunks.

Halfway across the belt of trees, there was a depression where a big pine had come crashing down in a winter gale. Most of the tree had been cut away and burned in the neighbourhood fireplaces. All that was left was the fan-shaped root system and the dip in the earth where it had been torn free. Here Davy and his small friends had played adventure games, using the great roots as a gang hut or a fort or a space-station, whatever the game dictated. At night, however, the spiked semi-circle glowered like the skull-frill of a monstrous dinosaur. In his mind, Davy could picture the dead tree in the warm light of a summer day, but now, in the dark, it had changed into a threatening mass, something with a life of its own. The boy veered away from it, moving right off the pathway and into a closely planted section of pines.

Without warning, the wind came gusting between the trunks again, more ferociously than before. It whipped at Davy's hood and he raised a hand to snatch the drawstrings. Uncle Jack's watch was still held tight in one small fist.

He felt his way between the trees until he came to a dead end where the rubbery rhododendrons crowded together to bar any progress. Immediately a sensation of being trapped in the barwood swamped him. It was as if the bushes had *eased* themselves, roots and all, out from the edges and right across the track. Davy's breath locked in his throat and he back away again as he had done when he'd seen the juniper branch beckon to him. He turned, groping his way in the dark, every nerve now jittering with the awareness of the motion of the forest, mentally conjuring up dread movement behind him where the bushes were thickest. He banged his shoulder against a tree, swerved to the right and reached an open space where he stopped, panting for breath.

And in that moment, he knew he was not alone. He did not know how he knew. Yet suddenly, something in the dark had changed and that change had been picked up on an instinctive level, received by wire-taut senses, gathered and sent to his brain along jangling nerves. He was in the dark, among the night-strange trees and there was something there with him. He froze.

Up above him the wind shrieked through the icy needles and far off the two trunks screamed frictive protest. A shivery fear tingled up and down the bones between his shoulder blades. Davy swung his head from side to side, beginning to panic, wondering which way he should go, not even sure now of how to get back, in the dark, to the safety of the privet hedge crawlway.

Then something came crashing out of the dark towards him.

It happened so suddenly that he didn't have time to think.

All he saw was a black shape, blacker even than the trees over his head. He'd been standing there swinging his wide eyes from left to right when the movement had flickered in peripheral vision. His neck had jerked round towards it so fast he felt a painful wrench in the neck muscle under his jaw. Ahead of him, between the trees, but high up from the ground, there was a loud crash as something leapt from one trunk to land on another with a thump strong enough to shiver the roots. At that very moment,

Davy heard the grunting sound, a noise so hard and deep and fearsome that he simply turned and ran. It was the kind of sound a dinosaur would make in the dark of the forest. The noise of something that would open preposterous jaws lined with curving serrated teeth and snatch a small boy from the ground and snap him in two with one savage crunch.

In that instant, he heard the voice in his head.

'Get you. Catch you.'

It was like a creak of wood against wood, the rasp of stone on stone. It was a voice so cold and so deadly it sent wild fear sizzling down his back.

'Catch you kill you, catch you eat you.' The voice in his head jabbered in malignant glee.

Davy took off. He ran like a startled rabbit, jinking past the jagged saw-tooth trunk of an old pine as he scooted along the track, legs pumping fasts, lungs bellowing air.

Behind, high and off to the right, the thing smashed through foliage, hit another trunk with a smack and wrenched a small branch loose in its passing. Davy heard the scrabble of claws on bark and a rip-tide of terror surged through him. He opened his mouth to let out a scream, but all he managed was a whimper. His uncle's watch was still clutched in a death-grip in his hand as he blundered through the trailing strands of brittle bindweed, while all the time the dreadful voice was screeching in his mind.

Something hit the trunk above his left shoulder and Davy immediately dodged to the right. As he did so, his foot snagged on a root just at the edge of the depression where the tree had blown down and the boy went sprawling headlong. He saw the dip yawn in front of him. His left hand went out in a reflex action. The ground fell away from him and he felt his body twist as his legs swung up and over. The spiked branches in the gloom of the hole were waiting to impale him and he could do nothing as he flipped in the air towards them.

Then something hit him a shocking blow on the shoulder. The ground, only inches from his face, swung away from him with dizzying speed. He felt himself thrown upwards and something under his shoulder blade ripped with an actual tearing sound and a searing bolt of pain arced across his back.

Again the boy's mouth opened as the hurt twisted through

him. His eyes were still wide open, but the dark world of the trees whirled and spun. His shin scraped across rough bark and scored a flare from knee to instep. The grip on his shoulder was so enormous that he couldn't breathe and the big scream boiling up from deep inside simply came out in a bubbling wheeze.

In a matter of seconds, the boy was up in the canopy of the pines, hauled and jolted along as whatever had grabbed him leapt from trunk to trunk at bewildering speed. Davy could smell the noisome stench which surrounded him and he could hear the guttural, mindless snuffling of the creature every time it flexed itself for the next leap. Needles tore at his face and twigs poked at his eyes. By the time he reached the end of the line of trees on Stockyard Street, Davy was barely conscious. He felt himself drawn upwards, even higher than before. Out on the road a car's headlamps flickered briefly, though the sound of its engine was just a low drone, almost drowned out by the now-sluggish thudding of blood in the boy's temples. Whatever held him gripped him harder still and he felt the last of his breath expelled from his lungs. Little green lights sparkled in front of his eyes and then everything faded away to complete darkness.

The thing that had snatched the small boy in the belt of trees did not pause. Using the trees and the darkened sides of buildings as its own skyway, it skirted the low land on Rough Drain until it crossed Castlebank Street over the old spur line rail-bridge and disappeared into the high warren of deserted sheds in the shadow of the rock where the castle perched.

Lorna was wrapped against the cold in a thick wool jacket and a knitted tam-o-shanter hat with a big red pom-pom. It made her look more childlike and innocent and the paleness of her skin made her eyes huge and luminous, but the pinched, fearful tightness of her face contradicted the illusion of youth.

'Ready?' Jack asked, and she nodded, not trusting herself to say anything. She was so frightened she thought she might be sick.

When they had discussed the possibility, in the cold light of day, she had readily agreed. It was a long shot and she knew that Jack knew it too but at least it was a shot. Lorna had been willing, almost desperate to do something, anything that might rid her of the terrible visions that were ripping her apart. But now, in the cold dark of night, as she eased herself into the passenger seat, the slumbering fear in the pit of her belly had woken up and was twisting and writhing like a rat in a corner.

It had seemed simple then. Jack had wanted to use her as a direction finder, some kind of psychic sonar. That was how he'd described it and she'd laughed then, a girl from a farm on the edge of a village in the back of beyond, picturing herself with a dish aerial on her head, trying to pinpoint a source. The pictures, he'd explained, were no use to them, because Lorna didn't know enough of the town, not the way Jack knew it after a childhood spent exploring every alley and shack. She'd laughed then, but she was not laughing now. Even before he'd arrived, the cold twist of fear had started to roil in her stomach and she could not fight it.

'We'll just drive around,' he'd said. 'If you get anything, anything at all, let me know, and we'll try to find it.'

She'd agreed to that. 'And don't worry,' he'd told her. 'You'll be with me all the time, and you'll be in the car. If we can find it, then I'll call up the cavalry.'

Lorna hadn't worried then. As long as she was with this man, she was safe. When she'd collapsed into his arms, the sense of sureness and strength and honesty had come radiating out from him. Behind it, as before, she felt the bleak empty space that had not been filled, had not healed over, since the deaths of his daughter and his wife, but in that moment she'd known that she could trust him implicitly. Whatever faultline had opened in her mind and let in the nightmare visions of terrible death had also allowed another perception. For some strange reason, she felt closer to Jack Fallon than to any other person. That thought had warmed her, but not enough to douse the embers of fear.

Now, despite the closeness, despite his protective presence, she was dreadfully scared, though she tried to hide it. She nodded again and he started the engine and they pulled away from the house. Neither of them heard the muted ringing of the phone in the empty house.

He drove up the slope of Clydeshore Avenue and down the run towards the old bridge, both of them peering through the windscreen at the fine salting of frozen mist which rolled and tumbled in the headlamp beams. He slowed down at the turn and was about to pull out when Lorna cried out so loudly his foot automatically stamped on the brake pedal and the car fishtailed right across the junction. Jack swung the wheel, guiding the nose into the skid, found purchase and eased it to the far side and slowed to a stop. Lorna was thrown right back in her seat. In the wan orange light he could see the pallor of her face. Her eyes were wide and staring, both hands up at her face with her fingernails dug into her cheeks and she was moaning incoherently.

He reached over to her and grasped her shoulder. Under his fingers he could feel the tuning-fork vibration that told him every muscle in her body had locked in tension.

'What's wrong?' he asked, shaking her almost roughly.

She opened her mouth and he thought she was about to speak, but all that came out was a low moan.

'Come on, Lorna,' he said, more urgently. He shook her again, even more strongly. Her head rocked back against the headrest, and a lock of hair which had been tucked under the rim of her hat fell down over her eye. She gasped, then started hauling her breath in, like an exhausted swimmer who's battled an undertow to reach the surface.

'What is it?' Jack demanded, his voice now loud.

'Catch you kill you, catch you eat you,' Lorna jabbered, the words tumbling over each other in a rush. It didn't even sound like her voice, not the sing-song highland lilt that gave her the air of innocence. Her tone had dropped to a harsh rasp, almost a growl. Jack felt a chill crackle through him.

He took both her shoulders in each hand, leaning right across the seat, and grabbed her tightly, pulling her roughly back and forth. Her eyes were staring straight ahead, and her pupils were so wide they were like blind, black pools. Her breath was rasping in her throat, so fast it sounded like a dog panting. He pushed her hard against the back of the seat, slamming her roughly against the fabric. It seemed to work. Lorna blinked twice. Her breath caught in her throat and then she let out a shuddery wail. Jack pulled her in towards him and held onto her as she shivered against his chest, mewling continuously. He rocked her, the way he had soothed Julie when she'd been teething, waiting until the spasms passed, then finally pushed her back. Her face was still

513

deathly pale, making the freckles on the bridge of her nose stand out like sepia ink-blots, but her vision was back. She knew where she was.

'It's out again,' she said, with difficulty. Her voice was cracked and uneven.

'What happened?' Jack asked simply.

'It came down from the trees,' she said. 'I could hear its *thoughts*. There was a boy. It was telling me what it was going to do.'

She paused, seeming to cast around, looking for the right word. 'No. It was telling me and it was telling *him*. Oh, it's evil. It's like a disease in your head. It wanted the boy to be frightened. It was leaping from tree to tree, jumping through the branches. It moves so fast. It came rushing down and took the boy. Oh, Jack, I could feel his fear, it was like glass inside me. He didn't have time to scream.'

'Where was it?'

Lorna shook her head.

'Trees. That's all I could see. I don't know where. It took the boy up into the trees and carried him along the branches. It's dark in there.'

Jack was now beyond any semblance of disbelief.

'What in Christ's sake is a kid doing out in the dark? Eh? Do the stupid bloody parents in this town have no fucking idea?' He felt the hot and futile anger rise inside him again in the certain knowledge that another child was dead.

'It's still moving,' Lorna butted in. 'It's gone beyond the trees. It crossed over on a bridge and then up a wall, away from the light.'

'Where, for Christ's sake?' Jack demanded, voice too loud.

She shook her head.

'It wants me to see, but I don't know where. I think it's a railway bridge, but it's too dark.'

She sat back, hands over her eyes, concentrating. She held her pose for several seconds, then jerked up.

'The boy. He's still alive. Oh, but he's hurt. It still has him, but he's broken something. He's so small.'

Her eyes flicked open.

'I can *sense* the boy, Jack. There's something wrong here. It's important, but I don't know what it is.' Lorna's voice rose higher. 'The boy is special to it, but I don't know why. I can feel it laughing. It's like poison.'

'Just as long as we find out where,' he told her. 'That's what we need to know.'

36

Julia came downstairs, towelling her hair briskly. Her dressing gown was wrapped tightly and cinched at her waist, accentuating her slimness, though the huge black and white slippers with the Snoopy faces on them just looked ridiculous. They'd been one of the birthday gifts from Jack, who had obviously taken Davy with him when he'd bought them.

She pushed open the living-room door, expecting the usual barrage of noise from the television, and was pleasantly surprised to find it was turned off. Davy was nowhere to be seen. He'd even put away his winter jacket, which had been slung over the back of a chair. She still had the after-bath glow, an almost lethargic sense of cleanliness and well-being as she moved into the kitchen. Normally at this time of night, the surface next to the cooker would be a mess of crumbs and jam-splatters from Davy's enthusiastic attempts at making his own supper, but the place was clean. She poured some milk into a cup and put it into the micro, pressed the setting for two minutes, and fished the jar of cocoa down from an overhead shelf. Her hair, still slightly damp, clung to her temples in a dark mop of ringlets. Julia absently draped the towel over the radiator.

From the kitchen doorway, she called upstairs.

There was no reply. Julia walked down the narrow hallway and turned up the flight, her ludicrous slippers scuffing on the edges of the treads. Jack had bought Davy a little personal stereo and a handful of story-teller tapes which the five-year-old favoured instead of books, though she knew this would probably change. He was probably up in his room with the earphones on and the sound up to full volume. She got to the top of the stairs, turned past the bathroom which still smelt of bath oil and warm water, pushed open Davy's bedroom door and stopped dead.

The room was empty.

Julia's heart did a slow and easy flip, like a sleeper turning over in bed.

The coverlet on the bed was still stretched up over the pillows and a scattering of toys, most of them grotesque robotic things depicting characters from the last science fiction romp he'd seen with Jack at the cinema, lay in a cluttered heap on the floor. The little stereo was on the shelf over the bed, neat headphones dangling down like a futuristic wishbone.

She crossed quickly to the closet and pulled the door open. Davy's jacket was not there.

Her heart flipped again, squeezing inside her chest as if gripped by a cold hand. Julia backed away, taking two steps, then spun quickly and almost ran out of the room. She pushed her way into her own bedroom and swept her eyes round. He wasn't there. She got to the top of the steps and whirled herself round on the newel post, descending so quickly one of her slippers came off and tumbled behind her. She jerked open the cupboard door under the stairs, flicking on the light with her free hand. A jumble of brushes and mops stood silently.

For the first time since she'd stood at the bottom of the stairs, Julia called out again. Her voice bounced back towards her from the tall wall at the top of the stairs. There was no reply.

Panic lurched drunkenly and the bathtime legacy of lethargy simply disappeared.

'David!' she yelled again. His name faded away. For a second, she thought he might be hiding, behind the settee, under the table. No. He was gone.

Julia strode to the window and yanked the curtain aside. In the glow of the street lamp outside, she could see the ice particles swirl in the rising breeze. She checked under the table again where she'd last seen his shoes. They were gone too.

She sat down heavily, one hand going automatically to her forehead where a tension headache was already beginning to pulse above her left eye.

He must have followed Jack.

As soon as that thought came, indignation piled itself on top of the panic.

How *dare* he, she hissed aloud between gritted teeth, motherly anger bubbling up inside. She'd told him a million times, since he was old enough to understand, that he must never ever go out of the house without first letting her know. Now he'd slipped on his shoes and his heavy jacket and followed Jack out into the night. She didn't know why, but she'd find out as soon as her brother brought the boy back, and then she'd tan his hide good and proper. Even as she thought that, the idea of the small boy out in the dark on a winter's night in Levenford made her heart thump heavily again and her instant motherly wrath winked out.

Davy was out there in the dark. He was out there alone, a seven-year-old boy on his own. While whatever was stalking and hunting children in Levenford might be out there with him.

Julia's stomach clenched so tightly she thought she was going to be sick. She gulped back against the gagging sensation and reached the phone in three strides, snatching up the receiver even as she began to stab at the buttons.

The earpiece clicked as the numbers registered, then burbled softly as Julia stood, shifting her weight from foot to foot.

'Come on, Jack,' she bawled into the thing. 'Please pick it up.'

It rang softly, double chirrups overlain by static. Her thoughts were racing ahead. Had he gone to Jack's house? Of course he must have. She tried to recall whether her brother had the car with him, whether she'd heard the engine start up, or the door slam, but nothing came.

Meanwhile the earpiece was purring insistently in her ear. If he'd been at home, he'd have picked it up by now.

Julia's heart did another lurch as the next thought hit her like the night mail-train. If Jack wasn't at home, then where was Davy?

She dropped the receiver with a clatter and sat down heavily on the arm of the chair. All the strength just drained out of her in that one moment. Her mind was a whirl as the panic gripped at her. She put two hands up to her temples, pressing hard, trying to make the unwelcome thoughts stop, striving to clear her mind and think. Finally all the wheeling pictures in her mind slowed down, ground to a halt and she concentrated. It took only a second to decide what to do. She grabbed the phone again, dialled the station number. Bobby Thomson recognised her voice as soon as she spoke and started to say something.

'No time, Bobby,' she snapped at him. 'I have to speak to Jack right away.'

'Sorry, Julia, he's not in yet.'

'I thought he was coming straight to the station,' she said. A wild whoop of hope surged inside. Maybe Jack was on his way back to the house with David shivering and shamefaced in the back seat. Jack would have torn him up for being out of the house alone. He was more paranoid about the killer, the one they were calling the shrike, than anybody. Even as the hope flared it died. He lived only two minutes away by car. He wouldn't have stopped to read the boy the riot act. He'd have brought him straight back, and *then* kicked his backside good and proper.

'I can give you John McColl,' Bobby offered.

'Sure, but when Jack comes in, tell him to call me right away.'

The phone clicked. A gruff voice spoke into her ear.

'Operations.'

'John? Julia.'

'Who?'

'Jack's sister.'

'Oh, hello. Haven't seen you in a while.'

'Sorry, John. I don't have any time. Any idea where Jack is?'

'No. He said he'd be in later, but I don't know how late. He's out with the search teams at the moment, I imagine.'

'Well, I have to speak to him right away. Can you contact him and get him to call me?'

'Sure,' John promised. 'I'll give him a shout on the radio. He'll get back in a couple of minutes.'

Julia thanked him and hung up. She dropped the phone and went striding in her now-bare feet through the hallway and snatched her coat out from the cupboard next to the kitchen. Her old gardening shoes were lying on their edges and she shucked them on, ignoring the sandy grit rasping against her soles. She belted the coat tightly over her dressing gown and opened the front door, about to step out when she stopped.

The smirr of ice-dust, too fine to be called snow, had frosted the front step and dusted the flagstones leading down to the gate at the bottom of the garden. The cleated imprints of Jack's shoes were clearly delineated on the flat surface, a single trail of wide exclamation marks, but they were the only footprints there. Davy hadn't gone this way. Immediately she realised what had happened and dashed for the back door. As soon as it swung open, and the outside light came on, the evidence leapt at her. Davy's prints, the zig-zag soles puckering up the spindrift, angled down the steps and across the drying green towards the rockery in the far corner.

Julia's stomach clenched again. He'd taken the short cut through the trees. Without stopping, she ran across the short grass, not even hearing the crackle of the frosted grass underfoot, leapt up on the rockery and clambered over the fence. She knew the route the children took, though it was less easy for her to squeeze through the gap in the privet hedge. As she pushed her way through the cold foliage, she cursed herself for a fool. She should have told somebody, Bobby Thomson or John McColl, that David had gone round to Jack's place. She should have got one of the patrol cars up here to look for him. She'd left the house with only a coat, no flashlight, nothing of any use in the trees. She hadn't even told either of the policemen that she needed Jack to call back immediately, and even if he did, there would be no reply. Julia debated going back to the house and calling the station again, but then mother instinct took over. Her son was out in the belt of trees. Maybe he'd gone beyond them and reached Jack's place. She wanted to find him *now* before he took another step.

She made it through the hedge and took the few steps it needed to reach the belt of trees. As soon as the branches overhead loomed dark, cutting out the faint glimmer of the stars, she started calling her son's name.

Up above, the wind plucked at the twigs and pine needles and the few dry leaves left clinging to the fine branchlets of the beech trees, sending their whispery paper rustle down to her, and the darkness closed in.

There was no reply. Julia stumbled on, her heart now thudding hard enough to make breathing difficult.

'David,' she shouted at the top of her voice. Behind her, just out of vision beyond the edge of the trees, a light came on in a house, sending a faint glow of illumination and sharpening the shadows. Far off to the right, up Cargill Farm Road, a dog barked throatily. Julia ploughed on, ignoring the brambles which snatched and tugged at her bare legs, beating her way between the trees. A few yards further in, the faint glow from the house

520

faded to nothing and she was walking in darkness, panic fluttering inside her, clogging her throat, rasping her breath. She reached the small clearing in the middle of the barwood, but now the darkness was so intense that she could see nothing. She blundered on, hands held up in front of her face, towards the old root-fan of the fallen tree.

Behind her, the wind moved the joining branches and they screamed loudly in frictive protest. The noise was so sudden and unexpected, so eerily *human* that Julia jerked around, still walking. She did not see the deep pit left by the ripping roots of the fallen tree and she simply crashed over the edge in a dizzying tumble. She landed with such force all the breath was punched out of her lungs. Something sharp speared her on the hip and an awful pain ripped across her pelvis. She bounced, rolling forward, and in the dark, something hit against her forehead with a sickening crack. The dark broke up into a spangle of flashing blue lights. Davy's face wavered among them and she tried to call out to him, but then he faded away and the lights went out and Julia felt herself fall slowly into oblivion.

On the other side of the river, Jack was about to start the engine again when the radio coughed. He thumbed it on, gave his call sign and John McColl's voice tried to break through the heavy static. Jack heard the words sister and call, but little else. He asked John to repeat it. There was a flare of interference then the sergeant came back, a little more strongly.

'Julia wants you to give her a bell. Sounded important.'

'Can't do it right now,' Jack said. 'I'm heading over the bridge onto River Street. I've got an idea, so tell Ralph to wait for my call. Give Julia a ring and see what she wants.'

Jack didn't know if using Lorna would work, but he had an odd feeling of anticipation, and exhilaration, as if *something* was getting ready to happen. Overhead, up in the murk, the clouds were gathering, whipped in on the thundery low pressure that was playing havoc with the radio, and despite the deep chill, there was a tension in the air.

'What's your intended route?' John asked.

'No details as yet. I'll come back first chance.' He clicked the radio and the static died. The engine coughed then ran smooth. He pulled out and drove over the bridge. They turned right along

521

River Street. Lorna sat silent, fingers curved and pressed against her temples. Her eyes were closed. Every now and again, Jack would glance across at her, and when they passed under the overhead street lights, her face, in the brief flash, was tight with concentration.

They travelled a hundred yards or so when Lorna's head snapped upwards. Jack eased the brake down and stopped.

'Something,' she said. 'I felt something.'

'Like what?'

'I don't know. Just a bad feeling. We're close, but it doesn't feel right.'

She peered out through the windscreen, shading her eye against the lamplight, eyes screwed up, then she shook her head. Jack prepared to pull out again when she turned and looked over her shoulder. He looked towards her and saw her eyes widen.

'There,' she said, pointing out of his window. He turned and followed the direction of her finger.

Cairn House loomed taller than the rest of the buildings, a great, grey and worn facade, with the maw of Boat Pend a dark tunnel running through its centre at ground level. No lights shone from the tall and narrow windows.

'In there?' Jack asked, feeling the anticipation wind up inside.

'No,' she stated flatly. 'Just a bad feeling. That's where it came in. Something terrible happened in that house. Many terrible things, from long ago.'

'That's where Marta Herkik died. Cairn House.'

'She should have left it alone,' Lorna said in a surprisingly hard voice. 'And they should knock that place down. It's like a sponge. All the badness is soaked up in there. That's why it was able to come in.'

'From where?'

'From somewhere worse. That place is an abomination. It's an evil house. I can feel the badness, like leprosy. Like a cancer. They should burn it to the ground.'

'Maybe another time. Should I go in and look?'

Lorna started back. 'Don't go in there,' she said, voice sharp. 'Not ever.'

'I mean, should I call in the reserves and search the place?'

She shook her head. 'It's not in there. I would know.'

'Sure?'

She nodded slowly and sat back out of the light. Her eyes were like pits in the shadow.

He pulled out on the quiet street and started along. Just past the bakery where young Gordon Friel had been dragged to the roof by the thing that whispered inside his head, a patrol car passed by, driving slowly. The driver flicked his lights in recognition and moved on past. There were no pedestrians.

They continued to the cross and turned left up Kirk Street, heading past the masonic temple and on towards the town hall. At the turn, they passed the church steeple where John McColl had gazed up at the flapping body of Lisa Corbett, and Lorna shuddered as a bleak picture flashed into her head and faded. Another shiver rippled through her as they slowly moved past the masonic hall, but this time there was no image, just a sense of foulness and rot. She turned her head away, feeling sick. Jack drove on.

Pain was hammering into the centre of Julia's forehead. It seemed to drive through her brain and ricochet from the back of her skull. She twisted, not knowing where she was, and the movement caused her to roll further into the hole. Something sharp twisted against her pelvis and a glassy agony sang in her hip.

The movement cranked up the pain in her head and again little orbiting lights flickered and danced in her vision, though it was so dark she couldn't tell if her eyes were open. For a long moment, she was completely confused. Thick nausea stirred at the back of her head, just above her neck. She turned and the pain in her hip corkscrewed viciously, launching a squeal from her open mouth. Dopily she wondered what had happened, why she was lying wherever she was and why the pain was so bad. She raised herself up on both hands, feeling her palms press against jagged splinters of wood. The pain flared again in her hip, so fierce that a white light seemed to flash inside her head, then something pulled free with a revolting wrench that came from right inside her.

David.

His face danced across the forefront of her mind and for a second the pain vanished.

Something wrong. Something wrong!

523

Something about David. She clawed for it, fought against the dizziness and nausea and the cloud of oblivion that was trying to billow over her.

Gone.

And it all came back in a lightning flash. She'd followed him through the trees because . . . because he'd *gone.*

She remembered stumbling through the undergrowth, hands up in case she bumped into a sharp branch, and then she'd fallen.

How long ago? She tried to think, tried to force back the terrible hurt in her side that came sweeping back in a red riptide. Seconds? Minutes? Hours?

Julia cried out aloud, against the pain and against the sudden and terrible dread.

He could have been gone for hours. The thought got her onto her feet. The darkness spun around her, shapes and shadows fluttered in front of her eyes and she took a step forward. Wet warmth drained down her thigh as she clambered up the ridge of frozen earth, panting for breath. She made it over the lip and stumbled forward. Something hard hit against her side and the pain there blossomed like a poisonous orchid. She bit against it, breath hissing between her teeth, too scared to stall, too desperate to faint. She did not know how long it took to reach the edge of the barwood, fighting the exhaustion and pain and sick apprehension. At the privet hedge, she stopped, close to collapse, panting like an exhausted animal. The wet had now soaked into her shoe, making a soft squelching sound with every step. She dragged herself through, made it to the back door of the nearest house, crawled up the stairs and when she banged on the door, she didn't even realise she was screaming at the top of her voice.

Old Miss Loch, who made cakes for the local youngsters, but went into an apoplectic rage if she caught them using her herb garden as a short-cut, opened the door just as the lights were beginning to come on above the doors of the houses nearby.

'Whatever's the mater?' she asked tremulously, easing the door open a fraction, peering over the safety chain.

'Help me,' Julia blurted. 'Oh, please. I have to get to a phone.'

The old woman, hair done up in bright pink rollers, squinted down at the woman on the stone steps. She seemed about to close the door again, then she recognised Julia. She undid the chain and came out, reaching to help her up.

'What's happened? Are you hurt?'

Julia lurched against her and smeared the old woman's nightdress with a vivid splash of blood. Miss Loch jerked back, aghast.

'Oh my!' she gasped, planting a hand on her flat chest.

'Phone,' Julia mumbled, pushing past through the kitchen. She got to the hall, where the telephone sat on a neat doily on a small occasional table and fell to her knees. Despite the pain, she called Jack's office. John McColl picked it up on the third ring.

37

She could sense it like the sub-audial chitter of bats, a tingling whisper felt, rather than heard, at the base of her skull where the messages from her brain shunted down the length of her spine. It was like the stealthy scrape of chitinous nails on stone, the rustle of dry winter leaves on a forest floor.

Jack had eased the car up Kirk Street and then along past the station, following the line of the tracks as far as the old warehouses, using his own mental map of the places where the killer, the *Shrike*, had struck.

He stopped and turned the car around just past the old green door of the derelict building, recalling for himself the dull sense of hopelessness when they'd found the boy's boot lying face down on the cluttered treads. When the lights swung across the crumbling facade, they picked out the words Jack had seen in the dream when a piece of the pattern had locked in place: *West Highland Railway Company*. Beside him, Lorna let her breath out sharply.

'I saw it here,' she said flatly. 'That's where it took the boy. It was using a woman then, I think.' She shuddered, lips pursed tight. 'But it's not there now. I can feel the echo. Pain and hurt and fear.'

He reached across and gripped her forearm in a silent gesture. The shiver subsided.

'Not here,' she said. 'I have to get away from this.'

Beyond the warehouse, on the other side of the river, the twin stacks of the furnace chimneys loomed up into the night. Whoever or whatever had killed Neil Kennedy must have crossed the water on the railway bridge. He tried to picture it in his head, a man or a woman dragging the flopped body of a small boy, feet smacking up and down on the sleepers, then the strange, preposterous climb on the bare face of the flue, and the grotesque impalement on the twisted lightning rods.

Why had it happened? There was no answer to that. There was no semblance of reason.

Jack spun the wheel and retraced his route to the junction of Strathleven Street where the old library stood on the corner. Overhead, the sky was black, but the clouds beating in from the west on the quickening wind had obscured the stars completely. There was a change in the air since the afternoon, an electric tingle of a gathering winter storm. The spindrift of ice was beginning to change to flakes of snow, blown horizontal and spiralling in the turbulence round the corners of dark buildings. Jack thumbed the radio to call in his position, but all he got was a burst of static.

'Where now?'

Lorna shrugged, a small movement he didn't see, but felt nonetheless.

He followed the road past the entrance to the commercial estate where the new do-it-yourself stores and garden centres crowded up against the old factory buildings which were being renovated to compete for business.

'That's where it got the boys,' he told her.

She swivelled in her seat and the light from the street lamps reflected back at him from her eyes as she looked past him.

'It came across the roof,' she said, as if picturing the scene again in her head. 'Down through the hole. I didn't know it was a roof, not then.'

'But we all know now,' Jack said. 'Don't blame yourself. Nobody knows anything. The town's gone crazy.' He clamped his free hand on her arm again and she gripped his fingers. Her own hand felt soft and warm and somehow welcome.

'Anything yet?' he asked.

'Closer,' Lorna muttered. 'It's waiting somewhere, and it knows we're coming. I'm sure. But I don't know where. Keep going this way.'

'How do you do it? What does it feel like?'

'Like sickness. As if it's touching inside me as well. I don't know why it picked me. It knows something, something bad, but it's hiding it from me. That's the feeling I get. Like being pawed by something filthy.'

He kept travelling west, past the line of scraggle-willows which staggered unevenly on the banks of the small stream bordering the Rough Drain before taking a twist and disappearing into the overgrown acres of withered hogweed and tangled hawthorn. At the far end, he turned and headed straight south, down the long road which led to the castle, taking it slowly while the wind fluttered the flakes against the screen. The radio coughed twice just then, causing Lorna to jerk back in her seat, but when Jack picked it up again, it only hissed at him.

Castlebank Church loomed on the left, and as they passed, Lorna gripped his fingers tightly.

'What is it?'

'It was there,' she said, voice hollow. 'But there was badness there before it came.' She leaned forward in her seat, looking up at the grey spire of the church, then across the stone to the buttressed sides. 'It used the bad there, because it was weak and dirty. Because it was easy.'

She drew back, mouth turned down.

'I don't want this,' she whispered. 'I don't want to *feel* these things. I don't think I'll ever be clean again.'

'You're doing fine. Take it easy now,' he said, twisting his hand palm upwards to snare her fingers in his. 'We have to find where it's gone, and then it'll stop. That's a promise.'

She gave a small nod, hardly a movement in the dark of the car, and he moved on, right down the length of the road towards where the volcanic rock hunched like a sleeping monster on the bank of the firth where the river flowed into the estuary. Far down the water to the west, lightning stuttered and flickered in the squall whooping towards the town.

'This is where Annie Eastwood came,' Jack said, prompting. 'She fell off up there.'

Lorna followed his pointing finger. Up high on the second dome of the rock, she could just make out the shadowy outline of the balustrade wall. She got a faint residual sensation of black despair, a strong and recent echo of bleak emotion, and beneath that, images of violence and terror.

'It's old. There's been badness here too. So much of it, and for so long. The stone is steeped with it, like that terrible house.' She closed her eyes and from nowhere came a string of images, men in skins crooning round blazing fires while above them, in wicker cages, things, people, squirmed and screamed in agony as the flames crackled. She saw men in cloaks and with broad swords

528

come running down the stairways cut into the stone, hot with exertion, stinking of fresh blood. She saw skulls on pikes along the parapet, pecked by squabbling crows, mouths agape, sockets blind to the sky. The pictures scuttered in rapid sequence across the forefront of her mind, as if she was remembering something she herself had seen. She blinked, shook her head and drew back.

'Not here,' she said. 'We have to go back.'

Jack said nothing. He reversed, spun the wheel and drove away from the castle. They reached the junction and turned left, slowly cruising towards the oil-rig yard, when Lorna gripped his hand so tightly it caused his knuckles to grind together painfully.

Just at that moment, the radio sneezed again. Jack pulled his hand away and grabbed the receiver.

'Fallon here.'

'Jack?' Static hissed and sparked around his name. 'John McColl. You'd better. . . .'

'Say again.'

'Your sister,' John started, voice fragmenting in the electronic hiss. 'You'd better get back. She says your nephew's gone missing.'

'She what?' Jack bawled, jamming his foot on the brake.

The radio spluttered and wheezed. John's voice disappeared into it, each word broken up and scattered. Jack opened the car door and got out, walking several yards to get a clear signal.

'Julia said he went . . . trees . . . hurt.'

'Forget it, John,' Jack shouted, trying to overcome the interference. 'I'm coming in. Give me three minutes.'

He clicked the thing off, jammed it in his pocket and ran back to the car.

'Come on. We have to get to the station. It's my nephew. He's gone missing, I think.'

Even while he spoke, the images were whirling around his head. He hoped he'd picked the message up wrongly. The static on the radio had left plenty of gaps, yet Jack knew that something was badly wrong.

He gunned the engine and took off with a shriek as his back tyres spun on the iced road, following the curve where the brick wall of the old woodyard abutted the pavement. He came to the end of the road, turned left again with hardly a glance for traffic, hauled hard on the wheel and sped towards the gaunt black frame of the derelict shipyard. He was doing nearly fifty, just passing the wrought-iron gates when Lorna flew forward, both hands up against her temples and screamed so loudly that Jack almost let go of the wheel.

'Stop. Oh *God* I see it.'

He floored the brake and both of them were thrown forward as the car's nose almost crunched on the road. The tyres whined for several yards before everything ground to a halt.

'What in the name of . . .' he blurted, but she cut him off.

'There,' she barked. 'It's in there.'

'Where?'

She pointed out of the nearside window.

'There. In that place. It's waiting for us. Oh Jack, I can feel it inside my head.'

She rocked back again, hands still pressed to the sides of her head.

'No. Oh please no.' The words came tumbling out almost incoherently. 'Get you out of my *mind*.'

'Jesus, Lorna, I have to get back to the station,' Jack started, but quick as a striking snake, she turned and shot out her hand and grabbed his in a fierce grip.

'No. It is showing me what it has. The boy is in there, and he's alive. He's dreadfully hurt, but it hasn't killed him. He's saved him to bring you here.'

She turned right towards him, eyes incredibly wide.

'That's what it wanted. It wanted you to come. I don't know why, but it wants you.'

'But Davy's gone missing,' Jack protested, but before the words were even out of his mouth, it dawned on him. 'It's got him?'

She nodded, face slack.

'Oh sweet mother of Christ,' Jack spat. He grabbed the radio again, thumbed the switch, and started bawling into it. The flare of static hissed around them. Way to the west, but closer than before, the lightning danced in the clouds. He slammed the receiver down, while the images spun and swooped in his mind. Davy out in the snow. Julia in her bathrobe, a towel over her shoulder as she went up for her bath. Then from nowhere, little Julie's smiling face turning towards him as her mother spun her round on a summer's day. He tried to think past the images, tried to banish them so he *could* think.

'I can't get through,' he finally said. 'I need back-up.'

'No time,' she said. 'The boy needs help.'

She closed her eyes and for the first time, she deliberately thought *outwards*, reaching beyond herself instead of passively waiting for the terrible images to flood her senses.

Beyond the gates, the air was different, somehow thicker, murky. She concentrated harder, stretching her touch beyond the gates and through the gaunt corrugated iron sides of the huge empty building. She could feel the bleakness, the blackness, like a poison cloud.

'It's high,' she whispered. 'Up in the dark. It likes the pain, feeds on that. I can feel its hunger and emptiness. It is not like us, Jack, not like people. It's just evil. Bad and corrupted.'

She opened her eyes again.

'It's waiting.'

Jack let out his breath and the indecision vanished.

'Right. I'm going in there. You keep trying the radio and tell them we're at Castlebank Yard. Tell them I'm going after it, and for Christ's sake tell them to send everything they've got round here.'

'I should come with you,' she said, though the very thought of going into the empty shipyard appalled her.

'No. If it's in there, I'll find it. If Davy's there, I have to get him out. I'm putting all my faith in you, so you have to trust me.'

He reached into the glove compartment and rummaged until he found the flashlight.

'Give it five minutes. If you can't raise them, get round to the station and tell John McColl what's happening.'

'But I can't drive.'

'Oh great,' Jack said harshly. 'Bloody fantastic.'

'I'm sorry. I just never learned.'

'Forget it. Just stay in the car. Keep the doors locked and keep trying the radio.' He opened the door and turned to get out when she reached forward quickly and took him by the lapel of his jacket, levering herself upwards to kiss him quickly, pressing her

531

lips hard against his cheek. As soon as she did that, a picture of Julie's smiling face flashed in front of his eyes then faded away slowly. He eased himself away, got out and closed the door.

The huge gates towered three times the height of a man, rimed with frost, and on the sides of the iron spars, the thicker snow had been glued by the wind. The air was freezing cold and the gusts whined through the barbed wire tangles fixed to the top of the wall. Far-off thunder rumbled as the storm powered up, like a big animal looking for a quiet place to settle. The gates were locked, but there was enough play in the padlock chain to allow Jack to push them inward and squeeze through the gap. They groaned in rusty protest, an eerie, almost human sound, then clanged back together. He walked forward, into the shadow of the towering black building. The light from the nearest street lamp was cut off by the outside wall and he was left alone in the dark. He jabbed the flashlight button and a weak cone of light spread out in front of him. There were no other footprints in the dirty snow but his own.

Back in the car, Lorna flicked the radio button on and off, but there was no coherent sound over the electronic froth. All of her senses were wound up to sizzling tension, and the strange *other* sense was like a scream inside her head. She had reached for the thing and she had touched it with that part of her mind.

And it had laughed at her.

It was hunched there in the dark, still as stone, not far from where the boy hung from a hook on the wall, small feet dangling and lifeless. The sense of deep pain radiated out from the frail form, but dulled by unconsciousness, body pain which juddered along damaged nerves and tried to scream messages at a brain which had closed itself off.

The black thing had sensed her own self and had let her approach, showing her images of blood and rot, teasing her with its foul mirth.

Again she saw the fire in Murroch Road, saw the shadowy thing move among the smoke, clutching the little bundle. She heard her own voice mimicked with foul sarcasm: *Ladybird, ladybird, fly away home.*

It turned its thoughts and she saw the baby in the pram, jolted awake by the violent blow, and smelled the fetid odour wafting in the air. Sleepy baby eyes swivelled and saw the strange shadow, then a bewildered, uncomprehending innocent mind was touched by the filth of its thought and hunger. Instinctive panic welled inside and a scream bubbled up.

Too late. Too late. The scream was cut off.

. . . And Lorna was in Memorial Park when Annie Eastwood's dead daughter came out from the shadows of the rhododendrons and glided forward to embrace her mother, to squeeze her mother, to ooze inside and *invade*.

She blinked her eyes, breath caught in her throat and the image winked out.

It was *showing* her. The thing that had come into the world in the back room of an old house where bad things had been done down the decades, down the generations, was letting her in on its secret.

It was mocking her, showing her how it made people do the terrible things that had ripped her from sleep at night, or even slammed into her consciousness while awake, and she knew she had been right all along. This thing was not human and it was utterly evil. It could take people and get inside them and corrupt them for its own baleful use.

She thought of Jack walking into the dark and deserted shipyard where the gantries and stairwells climbed in a web of tangled metal to the soaring roofs and she realised he could not face this thing on his own. He did not even know what manner of thing he was hunting, did not know that *he* was the prey.

He would not sense it. It would come down from the heights where it sat like a black gargoyle. It would come for him with such speed he would have no time to react.

And then it would take him.

Horror flooded her at the thought of the creature inside Jack, changing him, forcing him to do obscene things, making him sin again and again, and finally twisting his mind and forcing him to the ultimate degradation.

She reached for the handle and pulled the catch. Nothing happened. She'd locked the door as instructed when he'd left. Quickly Lorna flipped up the button and wrenched the door open. Cold air swooped in, bringing a flurry of snowflakes. She got out, closed the door behind her, and crossed to the gates.

533

Using all of her strength, she managed to move them forward the distance necessary to part them then shoved her way into the shipyard grounds. As soon as she stepped beyond the protection of the wall and the street light as Jack had done only minutes before, she heard the cold chuckle of laughter inside her head. It was thick and oily and filled with vicious glee.

A primitive fear opened inside her and Lorna thought she was going to be sick.

Jack got in through a small door on the side of the vast shed, like the entrance to a goblin's cave on the side of a mountain. He had to brace his foot against the metal wall and heave hard before it creaked open on rust-frozen hinges, and then suddenly it swung back against the surface with a deep booming sound which reverberated and echoed around the man-made cavern.

He stepped in while the noise slowly diminished, a vast and fading drumbeat, angling the flashlight in front of him and cursing himself for not replacing the batteries after the last night's search. As soon as he was inside the shed, where great ships had been conceived and built and launched down the slips into the tidal basin, the sharp wind was cut off. A few flakes of snow eddied in beside him and sparkled in the feeble light. Behind him the door slowly swung to and fro in the gusts of wind.

Inside it was deeply dark, a monstrous hollow place. The torchlight picked out a length of chain, each link thick as a man's chest, scaled with rust, coiled like a metal anaconda. Jack was not given to flights of fancy, and his mind was on finding Davy – his belief in Lorna's strange perception was now total – but when the wind through the doorway ruffled the rust-flakes on the hauling chain, for one brief moment he thought it had moved and his heart kicked against his chest so hard it hurt.

He swung the light towards the heavy coils, forcing his breath to calm down, damning himself for an idiot scared of the dark. Jack walked past the massive links, still creepily wary lest the thing did actually move (*and if it did, oh what then?*) and moved deeper into the vast space of the building shed.

The air smelt thick and oily, and underlaid by other smells. Somebody had lit a fire in here some time ago, off in a corner somewhere, and the scent of charcoal and burned wood mixed with the other odours. Dusty rust, flaking paint, rat droppings.

Bird shit and birds' feathers, the throat-clogging smell of a busy winter roost. Jack walked on past a massive block of old machinery and a stack of acetylene cylinders, giant ant cocoons scattered in a heap.

The empty place was not silent. The wind was rasping grains of ice against the high roof and the westward side of the building, scraping the corrugated metal with the sound of shingle on a deserted beach. Far off to the left, where the big hangar doors were wedged shut, a light chain dangling from a crossbeam clanged like a cracked bell against a stanchion. Somewhere close by, a rodent made a sound like a squeaky shoe then pattered away unseen. Up above, out of sight, nervous starlings twittered and chirruped. He took a step forward and his foot kicked against an old rivet which tinkled across the oily floor and struck an empty paint-tin with a hollow clunk. Beyond the perimeter fence, outside the yard altogether, the screech of tortured metal in the fabrication plant shivered the walls. The men who worked round the clock there on the new rig laboured on, unaware of the drama in the deserted shipyard.

The place was empty, but it was alive with odd noises and unseen life.

Somewhere in here, the killer had Davy. It was waiting for him. Lorna had said it would be high, though he already knew that. Somewhere, he knew, there would be a stairway, something the old shipwrights had used when they built up the immense hulls of the craft. He'd have to climb again, and the thought twisted at him. But he'd climbed the chimney, reliving his own nightmares, and that was just to find the emaciated, torn bodies of the missing children. If Davy was up there – and he knew he was – he'd have to grit his teeth and find him, no matter how high he had to go.

He followed close to the wall, skirting an old milling machine and a pile of wooden boxes mouldering under a torn tarpaulin, when a clatter of noise erupted far overhead. Something solid hit one of the steel spars with such force it sent a vibration right down the framework and into the ground. Up in the dark, the starlings screeched in panic. They took off, flying blind, so many of them in flight that their wings roared in the air, like a predator bursting from cover. Jack stopped, startled again. He could hear them, fluttering and screeching up there, then there was a cascade of noise, a series of hard drumbeats. For a moment, Jack was puzzled, then he realised what had happened. The little birds were crashing into the sheet metal sides of the shed. They were so terrified, they were flying in the dark, unable to navigate. On the east side, a dirt-encrusted array of skylights showed a flicker of lightning and a cloud of birds fastened on the brief light. They smashed against the glass, punching into the thick panes, killing themselves as they darted for freedom.

Another loud boom spanged the air and the birds started to fall. Jack jerked back as one of them hit him on the shoulder with surprising force, a bunch of meat and feathers. The bird made a little squawking sound as the air was driven out of its tiny lungs, but it was already dead. Another one fell just two feet away, bunching, a puff of feathers in the dim light, then another and another, bird rain, drumming on the empty cans and steel benches.

Way up in the darkness a hellish screech ripped the air. Something crashed against the roof, fast and hard and powerful. The noise of the starlings was cut off instantly. Whatever was up there, jarring against spar and beam, was moving fast, crossing the whole width of the shipyard shed. Jack felt the hairs on the back of his neck prickle in unison. When the noise reached the far side, in a matter of seconds, the birds started to fall again, but not in ones and twos as before. This time the flock, thousands of them huddled for shelter on every cross-tie, came dropping, stone dead, to the ground. They hit off Jack's head, smacked against his chest. One struck his wrist and knocked the flashlight right out of his hand. It landed on its face, glass tinkling, then winked out. He stood in the darkness, all alone while around him the tiny bodies of birds thudded as they hit until finally the downpour ended. He warily walked forward, feeling his way with hands in front of him, while his feet could not avoid crushing the soft little bodies underfoot. He found the torch and shook it until the batteries made enough contact to coax a wan light.

He could not turn back, despite the appalling sense of wrongness that shivered through him at the thought of the cataract of dead birds. This was something different, something unexpected and alien. Even at that moment, no matter what he'd thought before, he was still really expecting to find a man in the vast hangar; a crazy man, obsessed or possessed. What kind of thing could have scuttled across the girders and wiped out the winter flock of starlings, he could not comprehend. It could not have been human. He was in here, alone, trying to find that thing. Had it not been for the certainty that Davy was in here with it too, he might have turned back and run.

He forced himself forward until he came to the cat's cradle of stairwalks set onto the far wall. His knuckle rapped against the bannister and a small pain flared in the bone. The torchlight was all but useless, but it was all he had. He angled the faint beam upwards, but it could penetrate no further than the first turn. Beyond that was pure blackness. The shivery fingers were still crawling down from the nape of his neck, spiders down his spine, but he ignored them as best as he could, put a foot on the first tread, pointing the flashlight ahead of him, and began to climb. He reached the turn and something happened to the air. It was as if it had suddenly become charged, somehow more solid than before. He paused, taking a deep breath, and a sickening scent of rot enveloped him. His throat clamped against it, cutting off the reflexive urge to vomit. This was worse than the bodies in the chimney, more putrid than mere fleshly decay. It was a stench of utter foulness. He tried to hold his breath, realised the futility of that, and carried on. The reek abraded the soft membranes in his throat and his nose and made his eyes water glassily. Still he kept climbing.

And far overhead, he heard something chuckle in the dark. It was a sound so coldly gleeful that he actually felt the skin on his shoulders pucker and cringe. It was waiting for him.

'Bastard,' he hissed.

Jack reached the first landing and swivelled left, gripping the rusty bannister with his free hand. The torchlight was fading fast to a rosy glow and as he turned, the connection failed and the light went off. He shook the thing again, trying to worry the batteries together, when he heard a faint noise behind him. He spun, almost losing balance, and a hand clamped round his elbow. Huge fright exploded in the pit of his stomach. He jerked back, raising the heavy torch to slam it against the thing when Lorna said:

537

'It's only me.'

Jack had to throw himself backwards to prevent the flashlight cracking her skull. A surge of cold relief flooded through him, followed by hot anger and dismay. His legs suddenly felt weak.

'Jesus God, you scared the crap out of me,' he finally managed to say.

'I'm sorry, I didn't mean to,' she said, reaching out to take him by the elbow again.

'I thought I told you to stay with the car?'

'I couldn't. The radio isn't working and you can't find the boy by yourself. I can.'

'No,' he said, shaking his head, though she couldn't see the motion. 'There's something in here. It's too dangerous.'

'I know it's here. It's up there,' she said. He knew she was pointing in the darkness. 'It's waiting for you.'

'And that's all the more reason for you to be out of here. I haven't the time to keep an eye on you. Now will you get back to the car and let me get on with this?'

'No, Jack. You won't find the boy, and even if you did, you can't get him out. Not with that thing in here. I can find him and get him out if you can keep it away.'

He stood in silence for a moment, thinking. It was wrong, he knew. It went against everything he was to allow the girl to stay in the black shipyard shed while the thing (*not a man*) that killed children and could slaughter a flock of birds in an instant was somewhere up in the high gantries lying in ambush, waiting for him to climb to it. Yet she was right. It had brought Davy here as bait to lure Jack inside. All that mattered was getting the boy out of here, and it would surely try to stop him. But if he could deal with the killer Lorna might somehow get Davy to safety. He shrugged and reached for her hand.

'Right, but stay close to me,' he whispered. 'Really close.'

He pulled her towards him and she put a hand around his waist, brought him close and pressed herself to him in a spontaneous gesture of solidarity. In the brief contact, he could sense her tension and fear and he wondered at her courage in coming into this metal cavern in the dark to face the thing that had driven her close to madness since the night Marta Herkik had died.

538

'Come on,' Lorna said. 'We have to climb.'

Very carefully, they followed the narrow metal staircase, level by level until they came to the crosswalk close to the top of the hangar. Above them, the dirty row of skylight windows flickered in gauzy rectangles as the sheet lightning of the approaching storm lit the sky.

'Where now?' Jack asked.

'Up further. He's close, and so is the other. It's waiting.'

'Well, I'll be ready for him, don't you worry,' Jack said, though he wasn't sure he was ready and his intestines felt knotted with anxiety. He groped around, hoping to find another flight of steps, but there were none. Instead, in the dark, he fumbled until his fingers clamped around the first cold rung of a ladder set against the wall. His heart sank.

'You wait here,' he told Lorna.

'No. I have to come with you,' she protested, but he put his hand on her shoulder and squeezed.

'No chance. Two of us on a ladder gives us no room to manoeuvre.' He thought of the birds flopping in their hundreds, the powerful smack of a solid form hitting the corrugated walls. 'If anything comes up, or down, then we're stuck. You wait here. I'll find him and bring him down, and then we can take care of whatever else happens.'

Lorna said nothing. Jack turned and started to climb, biting down the looping vertigo, holding tight to the rungs. There were eighteen steps in all to the first catwalk. He counted them all, through gritted teeth, and at the top he gingerly stepped out onto the scaffolding planks. He followed the skyway, gripping the bannister carefully, shuffling his feet so as to maintain contact with the beams until the next ladder, which would take him almost to roof level. Men had walked and worked here, when he'd been a boy, welding and riveting the mighty hulls of ships which still sailed the Atlantic. They'd worked in the light, not in this gloom. He climbed the narrow ladder slowly, feeling the sides of the building vibrate under the onslaught of the west wind against the bare wall, until he reached the final level just under the crossbeams.

He paused to get his breath back and something moved above him, close to the slant of the roof. Even in the dark he could

539

make out the quick, scuttling motion. Lightning flashed again and he got a glimpse of a shape scrambling with spiderlike speed on the metal ties. It spun on one long limb, grabbed a spar, flipped over and landed with a violent thump which jolted the wooden planks under Jack's feet and almost tumbled him over the edge of the narrow gangway. He clenched the safety barrier with both hands, head and chest leaning out into the void. He couldn't tell how high he was and the blackness below looked as if it went down and down forever.

Forty days and forty nights.

The words came in a whispery scrape inside his head. Even as he gripped the rail, white-knuckled, centre of gravity perilously close to the point of no return, a part of his mind wondered where the phrase had sprung from.

And they fell from the light to the outermost darkness where there was weeping and gnashing of teeth.

The thought scrabbled on the inside of his skull, a hideous invasive abrasion.

'What on earth . . .' he blurted aloud, heaving himself back from the edge.

Not of earth, fool.

Ahead of him, in the dark, a deeper darkness, a pure blackness so profound it seemed to suck the rest of the gloom into itself, hunched just above head height. A sensation of dreadful cold and awesome malice radiated out from it, a chilling aura which made the skin of his scalp crawl.

Down below, Lorna called up, her voice echoing in clean, clear tones from the walls.

'Be careful, Jack. He's close. He's coming.'

Too late, he thought, holding himself dead still.

Too late, too late, the voice in his head chanted, and then the voice changed, became a grating chuckle that was more like the growl of a hungry animal than a laugh.

'Who are you?' Jack thought, or asked, although he did not quite know which. He jammed his thumb hard on the button on the flashlight, willing the thing to work, but nothing happened. The darkness and the oppressive malevolence flowed over him.

I am the other. I am the spirit. I am that which is Eseroth. I am what AM.

540

'Where's the boy?' Jack asked, this time aloud, and all the time wondering why he was asking, why he was perched up on the skyway, talking to a shadow.

In the blackness, two eyes flicked open with an audible *click*. Poisonous orange orbs swivelled towards Jack and speared him with a blind gaze. He felt the blind-sight crawl over him like the touch of a leper.

Come into my parlour, little man. Come eat of the flesh and drink of the blood and do this in memory of me.

'Go take a flying fuck to yourself,' Jack bawled back at the eyes, anger suddenly sparking hot enough to wrestle the fear. Lightning stuttered stroboscopically along the line of skylights and the eyelids closed with a meaty slap. The flickering luminescence danced for several seconds and for that time, the weird greenish light illuminated the central part of the huge shed, throwing harsh shadows from the cross-hatched girders against the walls. Jack blinked against the sudden glare and inside his head a blare of pain stabbed from temple to temple. Through blurred vision, he saw a dark shape scuttle back away from him.

'Light,' he whispered to himself as the alien *other* pain faded. Realisation sparked in a duplication of the lightning. 'It needs the dark.' He didn't even realise he had stopped thinking of this killer as *he*.

He turned back along the gangway, past the ladder he'd climbed, feeling his way carefully, quickly as he could. The walkway turned abruptly at the corner and followed the far wall. He called Davy's name, hearing the word ricochet from wall to bulwark, breaking up on the high girders. The wind shrieked through the holes in the thin steel plate and rattled the corners of the roof in a sudden cacophony of sound which reverberated round the hangar.

'David! Davy! Can you speak to me? It's Uncle Jack.'

The wind whooped in response. 'If you can hear me, Davy, make a noise.'

'You're close, Jack,' Lorna's voice soared up. 'He's near to you.'

The metal plates clanged together as the wind slammed against the west wall. The sound faded away, then Lorna's voice ripped through the dark.

'*Move*,' she shrieked. 'Jack, it's coming!'

He heard it behind him. Something clattered across the girders, each contact causing them to ring out like gongs. It came from the left, swung straight to the right, leaping an impossible twenty feet, slammed against the wall behind him. Jack started to turn, disoriented in the dark.

Just out of the corner of his eye, he saw the dark move with the speed of a striking snake and land with a jarring thump on the platform just ahead of him. In the corner the thing merged with the shadows, and he had only a fleeting impression of something squat, limbs elongated and oddly jointed, blacker than coal. Chittering sounds crackled in his ears and then the scrapy voice came scratching into his mind.

And he took him to a high place and showed him all that lay before him and offered it all, if he would fall down on his knees and adore him.

The words grated with sly menace. Jack stood his ground, trying to make out the shape squatting on the walkway.

All of this, it rasped, like stone grinding on stone. A picture flashed into Jack's head, completely unbidden. Julie's face wavered just in front of his own, beside her mother. They were staring at him oddly. Completely bewildered, Jack opened his mouth and closed it again.

They were covered in blood. He could see the great jagged shard of glass poking out from the front of Julie's dress, and the red river splurted down the flowery pattern, making it glisten slickly. Rae's eyes were wide open and glaring.

'You should have been there, Jack,' she said, though her voice had that same scratchy undergrowth rustle he'd heard before.

'But you can come with us now,' she said and then she smiled, but it was not her smile, not the lazy smile of gentle humour he remembered. It stretched into a leering, hungry grin. She reached out her hand. Julie did the same, her small blood-slathered fingers splayed out. Despite the sudden wave of horror and unbalancing loathing that surged inside him, Jack felt himself reach. He took a step forward, felt the edge of the parapet under his sole and reflexively snatched for the safety bannister. His hand groped in the air, clenched on nothing. He felt himself begin to topple and instinct took over. The grotesque wavery

542

vision winked out. In a panic, he swung his hand to the side, found a stanchion and grabbed at it just in time.

Raucous laughter yammered in his head.

He pulled himself back to the platform, gasping for breath.

'Bastard,' he hissed, turning round to face the squat thing, and just then, another image was forced into his mind.

He saw Davy hanging on the side of a wall, his little body twisted to the side, eyes glazed and drying, a trickle of saliva and blood dripping from his slack mouth. Beneath him, Lorna Breck was lying spreadeagled and naked on the perforated metal of the skywalk. Her head was thrown back and her legs splayed while between them, the wizened figure of Michael O'Day nuzzled and slobbered. He could see her writhing, mouth agape, making little jerking motions. Revulsion squeezed at him. He closed his eyes, wishing the sight away, but it persisted, dancing at the forefront of thought. O'Day lifted his head up and his eyes locked on Jack's own. His emaciated face was skull-like and his skin was peeling. His mouth was open showing two blackened teeth. Blood was smeared round his mouth, and a wet piece of red flesh trembled at the corner of his lip.

Jack shook his head, eyes tightly closed. O'Day began to laugh and he could hear the lecherous, manic madness in it. He pushed away from it.

'No,' he bellowed into the dark. 'Get out of my head!'

The surge of anger and adrenalin was so powerful that the picture disappeared instantly, leaving him standing on the gangplank, chest heaving, heart pounding.

The force of his anger drove him forward, towards the black shape. It leapt to the left, bounding right over the safety rail, hit a spar which clanged in resonance, spun, tumbled in the air and crashed against the wall behind him. He half turned and something hit him on the back with such enormous force that he was catapulted forward towards the corner of the wall. His cheek hit against a support beam and he heard the bone crumple just under his eye.

Very far off, he heard Lorna Breck scream, then the sound faded away. Little whirling lights danced in front of his eyes and as they began to fade, Jack realised he was losing consciousness. A dreadful sleepy numbness oozed through him. Somewhere in the distance, he heard a series of metallic booms, like sounds heard in a dream. How long he'd lain crumpled on the skywalk, he had no idea, though it could only have been a few seconds while his brain struggled against the creeping lethargy. He rolled over, groaning as his cheek scraped against the floor. As he turned, the flashlight flickered on and at the far edge of the beam, a shape jinked behind a cross-tie.

His vision faded again and he slumped to the floor, fighting the fuzzy clouds of dizziness. A loud noise thudded behind him. He tried to turn, couldn't make the effort and a second crushing blow slammed into his back. A dazzling white light flashed in front of his eyes and a purple after-image swallowed it and he felt himself falling into complete oblivion.

38

Two levels below, Lorna heard the booming clatter. Jack said something she couldn't make out and in her own mind she heard the grating response. She shrank back from it, trying to close her mind off against the metal onslaught. It was as if something had reached inside her head, scoured her brain. Revulsion flooded through her and she shuddered violently as a tide of nausea swelled.

An appalling perception of corruption washed over her and she bit back the cry that almost blurted out.

Then from somewhere close by, a white-hot flash of child-pain came ripping through the mental barrier, so fierce and sharp it shattered the images that were beginning to form in the dark in front of her eyes. An augur of pure pain drilled into her shoulder, twisting her body to the side, and an involuntary gasp hissed between her teeth.

It was as if her mind was being torn and stretched in every direction. The boy's pain lanced through her, overlaying Jack's horror and disgust, and beneath it all, scuttering like poison scorpions, the malignant mind of the alien thing scratched and grated. She fought against it, tried to ignore Jack's anguish, and held onto the child's hurt, drawing it into herself, experiencing its agony. It was like a light in the darkness, pure physical sensation, a beacon she could orient by.

Up above, Jack shouted something, maybe a curse. His voice shattered on the corrugated roof and reverberated across the wide empty space.

Lorna closed her eyes and ignored the pain shrieking in her back, concentrating on the source overhead. She found the ladder where Jack had ascended to the next level, and clambered upwards.

Off to the right, over her head, something hit a support pillar with a massive thump that shook the entire roof and caused the ladder to thrum under her fingers. Jack bawled incoherently again, but she could not afford to listen. She reached the first level, groped until she found the next set of rungs and climbed quickly, blindly, drawn towards the blaring beacon of the boy's pain. At the topmost level, where the roof slanted towards the west wall, she turned away. Off to the right, something was moving fast, but away from her. A light flickered briefly, a weak circle of luminescence. Jack groaned aloud.

Lorna made it to the end of the gangway, letting the blast of pain wash through her, feeling it intensify with every step.

Davy was hooked onto a twisted bracket, one foot dangling limply, the other jittering with involuntary nervous motion. His eyes were open, though she could not see them in the gloom. His mind was awash with pain.

She came to the end of the skywalk and stopped at the retaining barrier.

Six feet away from her, impaled on the stanchion, the boy hung well out of her reach over the black emptiness.

He was too far away. Even if she swung out over the void, she would never reach him. Despair and anger clawed with each other. Lorna groped out along the wall, trying to find a beam or a spar which would give her enough purchase to ease out over the drop and drag the boy back to safety, but in the dark, her fingers only rapped against the rusting metal sides of the hangar.

She pulled herself back, exhausted and defeated, and behind her something sniggered. Lorna spun round. It crouched on the beam over the walkway, a shadow inside blackness, a contorted thing, limbs spread, each of them hooked onto a spar or a rod, oddly elongated, strangely jointed. In a tumble of impressions she thought of an insect, a reptile, a spindly crab, but she knew it was none of these.

The thing sniggered again, a guttural gurgle of sound that conveyed chilling glee and frightful contempt, and a sudden terrible realisation broke on her.

It did not want Jack. It cared nothing for the boy. It had tricked her.

The thing Blair Bryden had named the *Shrike* wanted only one thing. It needed a warm place to stay, a hot, living place to wait out the daylight hours. It had used the boy to bring Jack, knowing that he would use her to find his nephew, and that's what it wanted.

546

Step into my parlour.

The mental invasion made her recoil in revulsion. It was like a rotting necrosis inside her skull. Behind her, Davy's pain flared. The boy whimpered and his heel drummed against the steel wall, a soft booming sound which twisted the hurt and made it scream. The blast of agony was powerful enough to fade out, if only for a moment, the foul touch of the fiendish thing hunched on the cross-ties.

She shook her head, trying to negate the pain, attempting to deny the knowledge of what the thing wanted. Lorna staggered backwards until her back thumped against the safety rail.

'No!' The word blurted out of its own volition.

The faultline in her own mind, the one which had opened up on the night she had dreamed of the terrible thing in Cairn House, was what it needed to get inside her, to invade and take her over. In that instant of clarity, she sensed its own desperation. Its time was short. Its human havens had been used up, were almost gone, and it had nowhere else to go except back to where it came from, unless it could invade her own mind.

Another image bloomed in her mind. She saw a place of unfathomable depths, a place of dread cold and dark where scaled things with spiked tails and gaping mouths filled with glass-shard teeth roiled in their obscene legions. She sensed the reek of the place and the barren emptiness, felt the hunger and the hate and the overpowering radiation of pure evil. This was where it had come from, she knew instantly, drawn from this festering abyss to a world of life and plenty. It had feasted here, glutting itself on the hot emotions of fear and despair, sucking the life-light from the eyes of children. It had been called, by accident or design, into the bodies of the people who had sat round the table in Marta Herkik's house.

And unless it found shelter, it would have to return.

Ask and it shall be yours.

The voice wheedled.

Lorna tried to back away, shaking her head, huge fear twisting in her belly. She saw herself like the others, forced to creep from hole to shadow, carrying the evil inside her.

Be one with me.

'No,' she managed to gasp.

The thing moved then, limbs reaching out to the slope of the roof. She saw its humped form clamber onto the corrugated sheets, creeping upside down, head twisted impossibly on a reptilian neck, eyes now open and fixed poisonously on her, glaring right into her soul. She could see the puckered dark spot close to the bottom of the left one, like a ragged pupil where the orb had been punctured. The thing reached the support pillar, twisted itself round until it was head down, and descended like a black mantis to the walkway. She could hear its gurgling breath and smell the reek of putrescence.

It reached out a long limb, holding it low, a gesture of harmlessness. Even in the dark she could see the hugely elongated fingers and the curve of claws.

'Get away from me,' Lorna hissed.

It took two steps forward, spearing her with those venomous eyes. It laughed again, with the sound of crushing stones. The long limb stretched towards her, came up in front of her face. There was no escape.

Lorna found her willpower draining away. The darkness deepened and a dreadful numbness began to steal slowly up from her feet, turning her legs to ice, freezing her belly. Under the glare of those mesmeric eyes, she was an exhausted swimmer fighting against the undertow of a riptide. She struggled desperately, in a futile attempt to push back the force of the thing's will. She felt the faultline in her mind give under the pressure. A coldness pushed in on her and she felt her own sense of self fragment and dissolve. Something hard and scaly touched her just under her neck. Just as the blackness closed in on her, she felt a wrench as the front of her winter jacket was ripped away in one violent jerk, exposing her pale skin to the winter cold.

Jack coughed and a gout of bloody bile spurted from the back of his throat, leaving a filthy acid burn in his gullet. Somewhere in the distance a pain was throbbing and his ribs felt as if they'd been squeezed in a crusher.

Consciousness returned in rolling waves. His head was throbbing, felt as if it was twice its normal size. Inside his ears he could hear the slow pounding of his pulse. His eyelids opened slowly, pulling back across eyes which felt as if they were popping out of their sockets. Dizziness spun at him, then the pain screamed in his thigh.

For a moment he was completely disoriented. It was too dark to see. A warm wetness trickled across his chest, flowing up towards his neck.

A grunt escaped him as he tried to move, and the augur of pain twisted in his thigh, causing him to cry out in the dark.

He was upside down, and he was stuck on something. He could feel a sharp shard brutally tearing into his muscle. He was impaled, pinned like an insect over a black void.

Sudden recollection, instant realisation, came back to him. He recalled the shadowy thing, impossibly agile, spider fast, leaping from gantry to beam to cross-tie, a blur of black on black. It had hit him and he'd fallen and then it had slammed into him again.

David.

He had to get the boy. He was still alive. It hadn't killed him. And as soon as that thought came, another one batted it away.

Lorna.

What had happened? How did he get here? The thoughts blasted over the terrible hurt in his thigh.

Numb despair squeezed at him. It had them both. Like a fool he'd played the hero and come up here with a faulty torch and no weapon and it had taken him in the blink of an eye.

And now it had Davy and the girl.

He twisted again, trying to raise his body, fell back, tried again, reaching out in the darkness, trying to overcome the molten lava searing through his body. His fingers jarred on a spar and automatically clenched. He got his other hand onto it, every movement causing a pain in his chest or a river of agony in his leg. He pulled and felt something scrape wetly inside him, close to his hip. His teeth snapped on his tongue, but there was no pain there. It was all in his leg and on his ribs. He groaned against it, hauling himself slowly, excruciatingly off the metal spike. Something twisted. He felt skin and flesh drawn outwards, then there was a sudden jerk, a soft ripping sound and he swung free. His legs swung out over the emptiness and he hung on desperately, feeling his strength fail. The rusty spar dug into the curve of his hooked fingers, threatening to sever them from his hands. The thought of that summoned up a cold wash of

549

resolution. He couldn't fall, not now. He had to find a way back to the skywalk, had to find Davy, needed to find Lorna. With desperate slowness he heaved himself upwards, feeling his shoulders quiver with the effort of raising his own weight onto the beam. Finally he got his chin onto the metal, ignored the pain as the sharp edge ground on his jawbone, hooked an elbow over, then his undamaged leg, pulled himself up and lay panting, only inches from the roof.

Sweat ran down the black comma of hair and into his eyes and he blinked it away. Close by, one of the grey skylights flared into a rectangle of light and in that brief flash, Jack saw the thing on the gangway, thirty feet away from him. Even when the light was gone, the image, which was so sharp, stayed with him.

Lorna Breck was backed up against the rail. Beyond her, something small and pale hung limp against the wall. In front of her, something built with impossible geometry had reached out and drawn a long, deformed limb down from her neck, ripping her clothes open. Her breasts had jutted, soft and terribly defenceless.

The after-image faded to orange and purple. Without further thought, he clambered along the beam, ignoring the urgent messages of pain which seemed to come from all through him, reached the end gasping for breath, jittery with need for speed, and lowered himself to the platform. When his feet took his weight, exquisite agony surged from his ankle to his groin.

The smell of the thing was like a thick cloud in the air. He could sense her fear and futile struggle and panic welled up. He groped for the torch on the fretwork of the footplate, thought he'd found it, but it was only a scaffolding bar. He dropped it, heard it clang, cursed incoherently to himself. It couldn't stand the light. That was the blazing message right at the top of all other thought. If he could use the light, he could make it back off, at least until he got Davy down from the height, at least until he dragged Lorna away.

The flashlight was gone. Sour rage bubbled up inside him. The torch must have fallen, tumbled all the way down to the unseen floor below. The anger flared even hotter than the pain. He bent, gasping with the effort, scrabbled for the scaffolding bar. It needed two hands to heft its weight. He raised it up, ignoring the

550

noise he made and turned, staggering along the narrow walkway to the hideous black affront reaching its other hand to Lorna Breck's face.

Her mind was caving in from the pressure, unable to resist any longer. Somewhere else, behind her and in front of her, she could feel *other* pain, child suffering, man hurt, throbbing through the wave of darkness that pressed in on her. She tried to hold the pain, a lifeline to her own world, while the relentless frozen force of the thing's will pressed in on her like a black glacier. Her volition crumpled, imploded. It reached her *self* through the faultline and began to flood into her, a crawling, obscenity, filthy as rot.

She dimly felt the heavy cloth rip down and the cold wash of icy air, then her whole body jerked upwards and back, almost throwing her off the platform as a hideous mental blast seared through her. Suddenly the mind-force was gone, shattered. Her eyes flicked open and she saw the fuzzed outline of the fiend shrinking back, its elongated scaly arm twitching back to merge with the rest of its black mass. Its malignant mind was blaring in agony, so powerful she could feel it in her own body. The shape lurched back, eyes now clamped shut, shrinking away from her. She felt a warmth between her breasts and glanced down. A faint blip of lightning flickered somewhere high and picked out the plain shape of the cross on the rosary, lying between her breasts. In the weird green flicker, she thought she saw it glow.

Exultant hope bubbled up inside her. She freed her hand from the barrier, reached up and grasped the heavy gold crucifix, gripping it tight, holding it up the way she'd seen folk do in the old scary horror films. This was no vampire she faced, no creature of this world, yet instinctively she sensed the power of the talisman and felt the creature's anguish.

It had power, this cross, power maybe enough to beat this devil. Jack had given it to her, laughing his disbeliever's scorn. He'd told her O'Day had believed it protected him from the thing that stalked Levenford. He'd told her jokingly that it wouldn't harm her to wear it, and she'd kept it and later she'd slipped the beads around her neck. It had been an inert lump of metal then. Yet now, in the sudden flare of hope, of lack of *despair*, it seemed to be riven with power.

551

She held it in front of her, praying for another flash of lightning to add to the holy force. She took a step forward and another while inside her head she could hear the jittery screech of the thing.

She walked another two steps then something came lurching along the gangway. At first she thought it was another one, a second gargoyle creature, and the surge of hope evaporated. Behind her, Davy whimpered, a little shuddery noise among all the commotion. She turned involuntarily, forgetting the crucifix, cutting it off from the thing and as she did, the monster leapt for her. She heard its rush, froze. . . .

And Jack swung the scaffolding bar. The six feet of heavy steel came whooping round in an arc and smashed into the humped, misshapen back.

The force of the contact jarred right up his arm with such force it numbed his fingers and almost made him drop the weapon. It was like hitting solid stone. A huge clang rang out and scattered amongst the girders. The black creature fell forward, hitting the walkway with a solid thump. In the blink of an eye it was up again, spitting in fury. It whirled like a black tarantula, shot out an incredible arm, grabbed a spar, hauled itself forward and launched straight at him. Jack twisted his body, pulling the hollow bar back, gauged his moment and swung with all his strength.

The thing blurred up and over the club, faster than the eye could follow. An arm, piston quick, jabbed out and caught him a massive blow on the chest. The scaffold-bar whipped out of his hand and went tumbling away. Jack was thrown backwards. The back of his thighs hit the rail, unbelievable pain exploded in his leg, and then he was over the edge and tumbling.

Lorna screamed. She saw him topple and tried to call out to him, but all that came out was a screech of anguish. His feet disappeared from view and the thing spun, incredibly fast, and came clambering along the railing, a demonic tightrope walker, a grotesque spider on a web, straight towards her.

Jack flipped over. His ankle hit a crossbar and something snapped there. His hands were in front of him as he fell. In a brief instant, he saw Julie and Rae smiling at him in a summer garden and he knew he was about to die.

Then something smacked into his belly. His breath punched out in one instant whoosh and he bounced, flopping over. Some basic instinct made him reach in the dark. His hands grabbed the chain which ran from the wall to a pulley-wheel. One hand slipped, hooked up again reflexively, found the old chain, and he hung suspended over the well of the shed.

Up and to the right, he heard Lorna scream. Sick pain pulsed up from his ankle, but he ignored it. He pulled himself several feet along the horizontal chain until he came to the pulley and risked letting go with one hand while he made a grab for the vertical drop of links which descended to the floor far below. As soon as he gripped it, he swung his other hand over, then wrapped his undamaged leg around the pulley chain. As soon as he did so, he felt a lurch, and a harsh grating sound.

'Oh shit,' he grunted.

He dropped five more feet. Something squealed in protest ten feet from where he hung. Without even trying, he spun on the down-chain and a long line of light came into being right in front of his eyes. He had no time to think, he was just trying not to fall, suspended close to the far wall of the hangar. The chain rattled and he plummeted his own height and the line of light became a blazing rectangle.

Up above, a ferocious caterwauling sound ripped the air, so loud it rattled the metal roof and made his ears ring. Jack dangled, swinging and revolving, gripping the rope so tight it burned. The chain rattled again and the service door opened even wider, rolling back on its wheels, protesting all the way. His weight on the chain, along with the counterweight which swung in the darkness along the wall, was just enough to drag the massive door open.

The night floodlights from the rig yard across the fence glared in through the gap, sending strange cross-hatched shadows on everything, dazzling Jack where he hung. He screwed up his eyes against the blinding light and dropped another four feet to the next level. He could now see what he was doing. When he came level to the platform, he swung his weight back, biting down the tide of pain running from shoulders to feet, got himself close enough to the rail to get a grip and hooked a hand round the bar. Very carefully he hauled himself over, slipped to the walkway with a crunch of pure hurt and lay gasping.

553

On the top deck, Lorna watched the thing come for her, limbs pistoning, a blurred monstrosity. She cringed back, half turned, forgetting the cross in her hand.

Then the metal had screamed in protest and a miraculous pillar of light had seared the gloom.

Instantly the thing skidded to a halt. Its monstrous eyes thudded shut and a shriek of agony brayed out in a high, ululating shudder.

Lorna's own eyes flooded with tears. She wiped her sleeve across them, shaking her head to clear her vision. Then she saw it in the light.

It was a nightmare creature. Its squat body was humped and warted. Oddly bent bones like deformed ribs poked out against a taut reptilian skin. Its shoulders were wide and upwardly curved and from them, two impossibly long arms stretched out on either side, hooked spatulate fingers clenched on the rail. Its head was large and ridged with nobbled scales. Leathery eyelids squeezed shut over popping eyes. Its face was almost flat, and there was no nose, just two ragged holes which flickered spasmodically. Below them, its mouth gaped open, drooling green ropes of saliva.

It hung on the rail, shivering in agony, and as she watched, its whole shape began to crumble. Lorna stood frozen, mesmerised, as the edges of the creature began to blur and run. Its skin bubbled, wavered, started to evaporate in black wisps.

It made an obscene growling sound from behind its amphibious lips, so deep the metal vibrated in sympathetic resonance.

Inside her head, Lorna felt its panic and pain and a second wave of exultation overtook her. The door opened wider, allowing even more light into the vast covered yard. The thing screeched, a devilish animal caught in a trap. Its warty hide frothed. Murky clouds of vapour started to trail off, fuzzing its outlines. It scuttled back, heading for the corner. Droplets of its skin, or pieces of flesh, hit the steel walkway and sizzled there, sending up orange puffs of mist. Metal creaked and the great door swung even wider, sending the light into every corner.

The thing howled, then took off. It leapt out from the corner, swung on a beam, then hit a pillar, head down. Without stopping it scrambled downwards, bunched itself then sprang for the stairway, trailing a grey-black cloud around itself.

It passed close to Jack, screeching all the while, as he was getting onto his sound foot. He straightened up, his whole body a world of hurt, and saw the thing coming straight at him. Its mouth was agape, a huge maw, barbed with row upon row of shiny teeth.

He flinched back, expecting it to leap at its throat, but instead it shot out an arm, hooked an upright and spun down the next flight. Its thickening cloud of vapour clung to it as it moved. It reached the third level, tumbled and hit the landing with a crash. Jack followed its motion, unable to take his eyes off the thing as the lights boiled it away.

It got to the second level, scrambled over the bannister, dropped fifteen feet to the first, then crabbed along the flat. By this time, it was hardly solid at all. At the bottom, he saw a rolling black cloud, pulsing with motion, but boneless and limbless, roll down to the foot of the stairs to disappear into the faint shade.

For several moments, he stood there, transfixed. Up above, he heard Lorna call out his name. Jack slowly forced himself to move, gasping with the enormity of the pain, and hobbled up the stairs.

He found her at the end of the skyway. She didn't seem to notice that her breasts were bared to the light.

'He's here, Jack,' she cried, pointing behind where she stood. 'I can't reach him. Oh, he's so hurt.'

Jack made it to the far end. Davy's eyes were open and his mouth was moving, though there was no sound. He was stuck to the wall, one foot still shivering as if the nerves had been cut. Jack got to the rail and leaned over. Way down there, jagged piles of machinery, old boxes of rivets, rusty spikes of metal awaited to kill anybody who fell.

He estimated the distance, measuring the gap between the barrier and the first of the roof spars. He still had one good leg and two working arms. Jack got himself over the first obstacle, leaned out until he could grip the spar, then swung himself over until he got his foot on a support beam on the wall.

Davy's eyes followed him. Tears were streaming down his face, but he still made no sound.

'It's alright, Davy boy,' Jack whispered as he edged himself closer. He reached the boy and felt the pulse in his neck. It was fast, too fast, but strong. He eased a hand behind his nephew's back, edging it up against the metal wall, and found the hook of steel. The thing had punctured the corrugated sheet and torn back a spike of flimsy metal. It impaled the boy just under the shoulder blade. Jack could not understand how the youngster could be alive, never mind conscious, hanging there like that. His hand worked its way along the slithery coagulation of blood. He eased himself closer, got his arm right round the boy's chest, and gently lifted him off the spike. Davy sighed, then his eyes rolled upwards and his head flopped to the side.

Very carefully and very slowly, Jack retraced his steps. It took ten minutes to edge back to the skywalk. When he got there, Lorna reached out over the drop and took Davy from his hands and swung him to the relative safety of the gangway.

The movement had caused the gash in Davy's back to bleed freely again. Jack fished a handkerchief from his pocket and jammed it against the ragged hole. Between the two of them, they managed to carry the boy down the stairs, flight by flight until they reached the bottom. Lorna stayed close on the last short section, ready to support Jack if he stumbled. They reached the bottom, turned towards the door, and something came lurching out from under the stairs.

Lorna yelled in fright. Jack hadn't even seen the movement. He turned, put his weight on his broken ankle, bellowed in pain and began to topple.

The apparition that had been Michael O'Day came staggering towards them. The white hair was almost completely gone from the narrow head. The eyes were shadowed pits. Two emaciated hands, the fingers elongated and skeletal, reached out, groping, towards Lorna.

Jack twisted as he fell, trying to keep Davy up, then hit the floor with a jarring thump, hard enough to clash his teeth together. Davy tumbled out and rolled.

The thing that O'Day had become lunged forward and clamped its hands around Lorna's neck. She made a loud gulping sound.

Jack turned over, unable to take his eyes off the scene. He groped for anything on the floor and by a sheer miracle found the scaffolding bar that he'd used up close to the roof. He used it to get to his good foot, hopping awkwardly, then swung it under and then over his shoulder.

Lorna was struggling, pulling away, trying to kick out at the thing. She made a horrible gurgling noise as the fingers squeezed on her throat. Jack pivoted and brought the hollow steel pole down in a scything arc. It hit O'Day just above his ear with a pulpy thud. The crazed man's hands flew out to the sides, then he flopped like a rag doll, hit the ground and was still.

Overhead, lightning flashed and thunder cracked in a simultaneous burst. In seconds, huge hailstones bulleted down to rattle on the metal roof in a deafening roar.

'I think you killed him,' Lorna said.

'I hope to Christ I did,' Jack replied wearily.

He hobbled to where Davy lay, eased himself down to get his arm around the boy, then gently lifted him up off the ground.

They got to the door just as one of the workmen from the rig yard came walking towards them, swinging the beam of a powerful torch in through the opening.

'Hello?' he called out. 'Is anybody there?'

39

He came swimming up from the dark, reaching for the surface, trying to break through from the dream.

It had come after him again, up in the high gantries, racing towards him with preposterous speed. His feet were glued to the skywalk, hands gripped on the rail, unable to loosen. His breath was locked in his throat. It came like a black spider, limbs pistoning, jerky yet frighteningly fluid. He could hear the scrape of its claws on the metal, the feral bass growl erupting from its toadlike mouth. Its eyes were like sickly orange headlights, spearing him with fearsome blight.

Beside him, on the wall, Davy and Julia writhed, stuck on shards of glass. Behind him, his dead daughter whimpered in pain and begged him to help her. On the metal gangplank, Lorna lay sprawled in a pool of blood, eyes wide and blind and dull.

The thing came racing on, angular yet sinuous, solid yet fluid, an ever-changing black mass, transforming and mutating as it grunted and gurgled, slobbering its malice.

He backed off, came up against the wall. It jerked forward, blank amphibian eyes wide as saucers. Its mouth opened, yawned enormously. Rows of glassy teeth reflected light.

Then he was out of it. The membrane of the dream broke and shattered and he was through, back in the real world again. He hauled for the breath that had refused to come, drawing cool air into aching lungs. He came fully awake, sitting up in bed, slathered in sweat, shivering from the horror of the image.

For several moments, he sat, trying to keep the muscles in his arms and legs from twitching, attempting to calm himself, to hold onto the reality that it was only a dream. He switched the light on, banishing the shadows. Very slowly he turned round, expecting to see her curled up, auburn hair fanned on the pillow, snuffling warmly in sleep.

She was sitting bolt upright.

Her hands were held up in front of her face, palms out, as if she was shoving something back from her, warding it off. As soon as he turned, he could feel the tremble in her body, a taut shivering, tuning-fork fast. Her head was shaking from side to side, small, jerky movements, little spasms. He reached for her, touched her shoulder, felt the deep shudder ripple through her. She was cold as stone, every muscle under his fingers bunched and contorted. Her eyes were wide open, glassily staring in front of her, great grey pools. Her mouth sagged slackly.

'What's wrong?' he whispered urgently. 'What's the matter?'

It was as if he hadn't spoken. Her head continued its motions of denial. The hands pushed further from her body. A slick of sweat ran from her neck and trickled under his fingers. The power of his own dream faded.

What did she see?

The wide eyes stared ahead, into the far distance.

'Come on,' he urged, louder this time, shaking her quickly. 'Wake up, Lorna.'

She gave a violent start, hauling back against the headboard. A pillow flopped to the floor. Under his fingers, the trembling died instantly. Her mouth closed with a snap and she blinked twice, very quickly, and he heard her breath come out in a long shudder.

'What is it?' he said, now more unnerved than he had been in the depths of his own nightmare. 'What's wrong?'

She turned, as if only just aware of his presence. She blinked again, then her eyes widened, huge and limpid. A tear spilled from a corner and traced a path of light down her cheek.

Her mouth opened, closed again, then she fell towards him. He caught her in his arms and held her tight, smoothing her hair as if she was a child.

'Tell me,' he finally said.

It had taken a long time to heal. A long time for all of them.

In a precursive parallel to the dream he would have, Jack had come awake, drowsily struggling against the anaesthetic. The drugs helped, but not enough to completely dull the pain of the mending. His head throbbed and a warm raw crater, or so it felt, burned into his cheek. It was sore to breathe, each inhalation bringing a stab in the ribs, front and back. His left leg was stiff and numb, with only a dull gripe in his ankle to tell him he still had a leg.

Recollection came back slowly, individual scenes following on one after the other like ripples in a pond. He could see them, like an outsider, an impassive observer watching the thing flit from girder to beam, seeing Davy hung on the wall, the whiteness of Lorna's bared breasts. It was happening to somebody else. Even the memory brought nothing, no emotion, no fear.

'Must be good stuff they serve here,' he thought to himself, and without warning, a laugh bubbled up from inside. He went into a brief choking spasm and the sudden movement unleashed a rip of pain in his ribs. He coughed, searing himself on his right side, painful enough to make his eyes water.

'Only when I laugh,' he said when it all subsided, remembering a line from some long-forgotten joke.

A young nurse, blonde and pretty in a rosy-cheeked way, came bustling through the swing door of the room. She moved to the clutter of instruments beside the bed and jerked back when Jack spoke.

'Can I have some water?' he asked.

In three minutes Jack had his water, crystal clear and rattling with a stack of ice. It was the best drink he could ever remember. While he sipped it, a middle-aged doctor with craggy grey eyebrows ran through the damage as if reading off a provisions list.

'We've had to put a pin in your ankle,' he said. 'You've a pretty nasty break, but I don't think it's anything to worry about. You'll be walking in six weeks. The ribs were the worst. You'd punctured a lung. We had to drain it and get the old balloon inflated again. It's working fine now, but you'll get a twinge every now and again for a while.'

The doctor leaned over and without preamble, pulled Jack's eyelid down.

'The cheek will heal on its own,' he went on. 'Nasty break on your maxillary, but no point in digging in there. You'll probably find your eye will water for a week or two until the pressure on the lachrymal duct eases off, and you'll have a bit of a dent there, but unless you've ambitions to film stardom, it should be fine. I can get you fixed up at Keltyburn for some reconstruction if you feel the need.'

560

Jack shook his head and instantly regretted it when the ache thumped in his skull. He didn't feel the need for anything yet, except sleep, and the need to know how Davy was.

'Bruises all over the body, and some internal, I shouldn't wonder,' the other man went on, lifting the heavy eyebrows with what looked like considerable effort. 'You've been in the wars, my boy.'

'How long?' he asked, voice rasping over a tender throat.

'As I said, about six weeks.'

'No, how long have I been here?'

'Since last night. You've a good constitution. We had to put you under to get the lung back up and fiddle about with the ribs, but it'll soon wear off. If the pain gets too much, just ring for the nurse. We're real dope fiends here.'

Jack smiled tiredly. He knew about pain.

'And the boy? My nephew?'

'Oh, he'll be fine. Strong young fellow. Nasty wound on his back, and we're a bit concerned about infection. He's still under, I'm afraid, but he'll certainly play football again. How'd it happen?'

'Long story,' he said. 'Too long.'

'Well, there's a whole corridor of people who want to speak to you. I can hold them back until you feel up to it.'

'No. I have to.' The doctor nodded. He turned to go. Jack held up his hand with some difficulty. It felt weighted with lead.

'Is one of them a girl? Name's Breck.'

The other man lifted his eyebrows again.

'Reddish hair? Pretty thing?'

Jack risked another nod, though he took it slowly.

'I need to see her first,' he said. The man went out and there was some noise outside the door. Voices were raised. The doctor said something loud but unintelligible through the swung-shut door. It eased open and Lorna came in, face pallid and dirt-streaked. She was still wearing the long coat Jack had wrapped around her and it scraped the floor at her heels. She quietly closed the door behind her, and came slowly forward. He patted the side of the bed casually, though the movement knifed him in the ribs. He coughed, screwing his face up against the sharp corkscrew in his side, and her eyes widened in alarm, instinctively reaching for him.

561

He took her hand and drew her forward until she sat down.

'Well, Miss fortune teller, did we beat the bastard or what?'

She nodded, hardly a movement, face still solemn.

'Is it bad?'

'Hurts like hell.' He gave her a grin, the first one he could remember in what seemed like a long time. She almost responded. 'Big boys don't cry. They say Davy's fine and I'll be out of here in no time.'

She looked as if she was going to say something, backed off, seemed to make up her mind.

'I was so scared,' she blurted. 'I thought you were dead.'

'You and me both. Sure cured my love of heights, I can tell you,' he said, trying to keep it light. 'I should keep you as a good luck charm.'

'It wasn't luck,' she said. 'It was meant. I know it.'

'I'll have to take your word for it. You've been right so far.' He squeezed her hand. 'Have you been here all night?'

She inclined her head, grey eyes glistening.

'I thought you might die.'

'You mean you didn't see it in the runes? It takes more than that to kill the likes of me.'

The tears swimming in swelling crescent broke over and ran freely down under her eyes, trickling to the corner of her mouth.

'Oh, come on. We beat the bastard, you and me. We make a great team. Once I'm out of here, I want to take you to Hobnobs for a coffee and start over again.'

Lorna squeezed his fingers. The tears continued and he wished they would stop. Her soft grey eyes searched his battered face then fixed themselves on his as if she was afraid he would disappear, and the encompassing, insistent gaze bored its way into a part of him he thought he had closed off forever. An almost forgotten emotion stirred again in there. He pulled her gently towards him and she simply toppled against his chest. A grind of pain growled in his side and he let out a gasp. She hauled back, immediately concerned and contrite.

'Oh, be gentle with me,' he groaned, as a sudden wave of warm tiredness washed over him. She held tight to him for several minutes before she realised he had fallen asleep again. Alone with him, knowing he was safe, she began to cry softly, leaning into his arms.

The next few days were a maelstrom. It wasn't until he woke the second time, to find himself alone and aching all over, that he discovered Julia had been hurt. He refused to see anybody else until he was satisfied her injury – so serious it had taken three hours of surgery to repair the damage to her intestines and abdominal muscles and remove a hard spike of wood that had broken off inside her – was healing, and until he got a promise that he could see both her and Davy later in the day.

Robbie Cattanach slipped into the room before the rest of the crowd.

'Thought I'd be giving you the once over,' he said, grinning boyishly. 'Might have been interesting to find out what makes you tick.'

'Sorry to disappoint,' Jack said drily. He took a gulp of water and swallowed down the cough that threatened to send it back up again. 'You won't get another chance, I can promise.'

'You'll live,' Robbie said. His face went serious for a moment. 'Christ alone knows what you've been up to. Want to tell me what it was?'

'It was just as you described. Like nothing in the natural history books. It was a fucking monster. Remember that Ridley Scott film you were telling me about? It was worse than that.'

'And you killed it?'

'I hope to Christ I have. I don't want to go through that again.'

Ralph Slater came in with Hector Nairn, the divisional commander who had insisted Jack was reassigned to the case.

'Are you up to a statement?'

'I'll give it my best shot,' Jack told his senior officer.

'Miss Breck has declined to make any comment until we've spoken to you. Any reason for that?'

'She's had a tough time. Where's O'Day?'

'We had to take him to the head injuries unit in Glasgow. You nearly killed him.'

'Nearly isn't good enough. Is he under guard?'

'Not necessary. He's in a coma which he may not survive. I'm afraid this might cause us a bit of a problem.'

'No problem to me. Listen, I don't care what happens, but he is not to be left unguarded, even for a moment. And there must be at least two people at all times. With the lights on at all times. Is that clear?'

Jack reached forward and took Hector Nairn by the sleeve of his coat. The man pulled back, narrowing his eyes warily.

'Sure, Jack,' Ralph butted in, taking the heat out of the situation. 'I'll put John McColl onto it right away. He'll make sure.'

Jack sank back against the pillow, breathing a slow sigh after the sudden effort of his outburst.

'How did he get the injury?' the commander asked.

'I hit him across the head with a scaffolding bar.'

'Was that necessary? According to the doctors the man was emaciated to the point of death. He looked as if a breeze might knock him down.'

'Aye, that may be. But he tried to kill me, and would have done it too. Me and Lorna Breck and my nephew. That's what we've been hunting all along.'

'I think there will be a few folk who might find it hard to believe.'

'That's fine by me. But as long as you put a guard on O'Day and keep the lights on him, the killings are at an end. It's finished. We've got it.'

'It?'

'Whatever.'

It took three days to get the statements from both of them and while that was going on, the public inquiries began into the deaths of all of the victims, starting with Marta Herkik. The fiscal recorded five verdicts of suicide and one case, that of Jock Toner, of death by misadventure. Timmy Doyle, Kelly Campbell and the others, with the exception of old George Wilkie, who was still posted missing, and including the McCann children and their father who died in the fire in Murroch Road, were found to have been unlawfully killed by person or persons yet unknown.

The storm blew itself out on the morning after Jack and Lorna staggered out of the deserted shipyard, carrying Davy between them, and a fresh day dawned in Levenford. It took several weeks, despite Blair Bryden's clarion headlines in the *Gazette*, before people actually believed the murders had stopped and that the killer he had dubbed the Shrike was in custody.

Michael O'Day was in intensive care for four weeks while doctors tube-fed him the nourishment his wasted body needed.

John McColl was as good as Ralph's word. There were two officers on guard at all times. There was no need to bother with Jack's injunction about the lights, for in intensive care, they are never off. The man was comatose for another two weeks and finally began to stir under the sheet, still emaciated and pallid, but not as corpselike as he had been. A shallow concave depression reached from his ear to the back of the skull, showing where Jack had smashed him with the bar.

Several doctors, including two consultant neurologists, put him under a battery of examinations. O'Day was awake, but as they say, though the lights were on, there was nobody home. He was unable to speak properly, only managing a few grunted vowels. He had to be taught how to eat and for hours at a time, he would go into a kind of fugue, sitting with his head cocked to the side, mouth slack and drooling, as if listening to far-off voices. His self-appointed lawyers took the medical reports on his assessed brain damage and went hammer and tongs for Jack.

By this time, he was walking, though slowly, and with a stick. Julia had been allowed out of hospital after two weeks, when the infection in her abdomen had finally cleared. Jack had relearned how to use the washing machine and iron clothes, making the house tidy for her return. Davy remembered little about the incident, though he had a repetitive nightmare for several weeks, in which something came for him in the dark. Jack cuddled him until his breath smoothed out and he fell asleep. He saw Lorna Breck every day.

Internal affairs hauled Jack through the mill, and while he couldn't care less, the thought of Ronald Cowie's smirking face helped him defend himself against an accusation of dereliction of duty – in not arresting O'Day in the first place – and grievous bodily harm. The senior officer from another force, having heard the extent of his injuries, and having read Jack's daily reports, requests for extra men, and uncanny predilection for being right, dismissed the allegations. He remained off duty for a further two months until the court case.

Michael O'Day appeared in a wheelchair at the High Court charged only with the murder of Gordon Pirie, the young policeman, attempted murder of David Forest and the killing of Marta Herkik, although the evidence in that was circumstantial and his unwitnessed admission that he had been in Cairn House that night was inadmissible. His lawyers once again claimed police brutality, but they were fighting in the face of the certain knowledge that since O'Day's capture, there had been not a single killing in Levenford.

The accused sat hunched in the dock, barely visible over the wooden handbar. Jack sat with Lorna in the public gallery, both of them mesmerised by the slack-eyed thing which drooled between the two court officers. It took less than a day for the solemn court pronouncement that he was insane and unfit to plead. The Judge, furnished by the prosecution with a full dossier on the atrocity that had spawned in Levenford with the killing of Marta Herkik, decided that as a matter of public safety, he should be confined to the state mental hospital at Dalmoak without limit of time. O'Day passed from the court's jurisdiction into other hands.

Lorna waited with Jack outside the courthouse when it was over. She stayed close. Finally O'Day was wheeled out of the back door towards the waiting secure transporter. The two policemen pushing the wheelchair stopped and turned it to lift it into the van. Lorna turned away, not wanting to look again at the man who had crawled out from under the dark stairwell, but Jack could not avert his eyes.

As O'Day was lifted inside, the vacant expression flicked off. He blinked, focused, then hooked his eyes on Jack's. For several eerie, unnerving seconds, he found himself locked with the other man. Lively, malevolent intelligence danced in O'Day's burning glare. He sat there, hunched like an old and crippled man, white hair awry and patchy, yet his eyes were full of life of a kind. He stared at Jack, mirthlessly challenging, then a creepy smile altered his vapid face. The smile widened, became a grimace which showed two blackened teeth. In that instant, Jack got a flash of a wide, amphibious mouth set with rows of needle shards. O'Day lifted a skinny grey hand and pointed at him. The small movement carried a dreadful menace. Jack felt himself suddenly unmanned. Lorna felt him shudder and looked up at him, saw his eyes fixed on O'Day and turned round quickly.

As soon as she did, the malevolent light flashed out. O'Day's hand fell to his lap. His mouth opened and a trickle of saliva edged down his chin. The officers hauled him into the van and the door closed.

'It's over now,' Lorna said.

Jack looked down at her, clamped his arm across her shoulder and pulled her against him.

'Over and done.'

40

Dalmoak State Mental Hospital is a sprawling cluster of outhouses dominated by a large, square building with a quaintly church-like little belltower. Its whitewashed walls stand in contrast to the surrounding greenery of the countryside close to the river snaking between Lochend and Levenford.

Passers-by on train and in car may catch a glimpse of the innocuous-seeming building, which, in some respects, was built on the same lines as the old seminary in Arden, now rebuilt after the disastrous fire of several years past. From the road, it is sheltered by a line of chestnut trees, then a small conifer plantation which hides the double perimeter fence, the nearest one leaning inwards and topped by lines of taut braided cable connected to insulating saucers and carrying three thousand volts. The chain-link barrier furthest from the building, paralleling the outer, leans outwards, making it difficult to climb. The spirals of razor wire braided along the top, sixteen feet from the ground, add to the discouragement.

Dalmoak State Mental Hospital is one of the three most secure units for the criminally insane in the country. The second fence was constructed after two of the inmates escaped and bludgeoned a passing motorcycle patrolman to death with a single blow of a garden spade which took his head off cleanly under his helmet and batted it forty feet into the stand of chestnuts.

It is here, that some of the most notorious madmen have been locked away, without limit of time. Behind the whitewashed walls, in a barred room, sits Agnes McPhail, the child minder who one day got fed up with the job and let go the six children she was looking after. She did this by dropping them from the thirteenth floor of the tower-block apartment, holding them by the ankles, then watching them dwindle to become red smears on the concrete. Agnes sits and counts up to six on her fingers and dreams of falling bodies. She eats when told and masturbates constantly, hauling up her light cotton gown to rub frantically between her legs. Her pupils have shrunk down to mere pin-points and she will never, ever, get out of Dalmoak.

There are others too. Tom Muir, the Arden butcher who filleted his wife Eadie and offered her as cutlets in his shop window during the mayhem summer that's already part of local history. James Collins, who starved his wife to death in the cellar of their home while he watched pornographic videos in the living room. Annabel Monkton, who stuck a knitting needle through her old mother's ear and into her brain because she was fed up with the clicking sound the old woman made when she knitted scarves. She was well enough, between bouts of morbid depression, to take part in handicrafts, but they never let her handle anything sharp since the day she tried to put a needle into the eye of a frail old woman who had been in Dalmoak since before the war for feeding her husband and her family to the pigs on their farm.

O'Day was brought here and the assessment team took over. They poked and prodded, tried him on barbiturates, electro-convulsive therapy and all manner of things, because in a place like Dalmoak, the inmates are lost to the world. They have ceased to be considered as human beings.

Despite it all, the man remained catatonic. He sat still as stone in his chair, or on his bed, not moving unless moved, speaking to no one, eyes glazed and unfocused. After the initial burst of activity over a newcomer, they assigned him to a room of his own, watered, fed and cleaned him down when needed. He was a model, if uncooperative patient.

In the August of the following year the consultant psychiatrist retired and after an internal upward shuffle, a new resident joined the team. Derek Whiteford was three years out of medical school, had interned in Glasgow, and was delighted not only with the substantial increase in salary which allowed him enough to treat himself to a convertible BMW, but also the chance to work with what he considered the cream of mental patients.

Derek was young and enthusiastic. He had dealt with trauma, schizophrenia, depression and nervous breakdowns. Here, however, were the real psychopaths, people whose brains worked in different ways from the rest of the population, people who heard messages from God, from creatures under the stairs, or from whatever being they believed in. People to whom the knowledge of good and evil had been denied.

Up in the top corner of C Wing, he met Michael O'Day. The notorious *Shrike* sat staring at the wall, giving not a flicker of awareness. Derek talked to him, studying the man's eyes for any hint of perception, but found none. He spent a fortnight, arranging a battery of tests, trying to find a way in, until the lack of response made him give up, disappointed, to seek fresh ground.

It was a year to the day of Marta Herkik's death, with the nights drawn in to early dark, that O'Day said his first word. A winter storm was brewing over the Cardross Hills, flickering the sky green-purple in sporadic flashes. Walter McGowan, a heavy-set nurse with a short crop of iron hair and steroid-abuser's bull neck, had pushed the frail little man back onto the bed. With one practised twist, he'd pulled down the front of the one-piece hospital gown, exposing a ribbed and crinkled chest.

'Washtime, Mickey,' he said, jovially enough. The patient was no trouble. As long as he was slunged down regularly, he didn't smell, and that was fine for Walter. The thin old man didn't care whether his cot was wet or dry, so there was no need to bother with the rubber sheet. It would dry, eventually.

The nurse stripped O'Day quickly until he lay prone and white, then dipped the sponge into the plastic bucket and drew it down the man's body.

'Hot,' O'Day said.

'What's that, Mickey?' Walter asked automatically, before he realised what had happened.

'Too hot,' the man said, voice little more than a cackle.

Walter might have had a weightlifter's body, but he was not stupid. He had a good paying job here, and he wanted to keep it. The new doctor had given them all specific instructions about any changes in patients' condition or behaviour. They had to be reported immediately. He slung the sponge back in the pail, lifted the bucket and backed out of the room, closing the door behind him and locking it with a quick twist.

Dr Whiteford had taken off his immaculate work-coat and was heading for the door as Walter came round the corner.

'Something's happened,' the nurse told him.

570

The young man snatched his hand up to look at his watch.

'I've just finished,' he said irritably.

'But you wanted to know. That's why I came right away.'

Derek Whiteford sighed. 'All right, what is it?'

'It's O'Day. Up in C3.'

'Go on,' the new resident said, taking a step towards the door.

'He just said something to me. He spoke.'

Derek took another step then stopped and spun on his heel.

'What do you mean "spoke"?'

'He just told me his wash water was too hot. Clear as day. It's the first time I've ever heard him say anything. I thought you should know.'

The doctor's expression changed.

'You haven't told anyone else, have you?'

'No. I've just come down.'

'Fine. Let's keep it to ourselves. Don't want to be precipitate, do we?' If O'Day had spoken, then it was a sign he could be coming out of the fugue. And if that was true, there was a certain paper in the first psychiatric examination of the notorious Shrike.

'Won't say a word, Doc,' Walter assured him. Whiteford patted him on the shoulder, a patronising gesture, though Walter was ten years older than he.

'Good man.' He went back to his office, took off his jacket, and got back into the hospital whites.

O'Day was completely naked, sitting on the bed. Water trickled over his ribs. He was staring blankly at the wall, and at first the doctor assumed Walter had been wrong.

'What's this, Mr O'Day? You should be in bed by now.'

The man turned to him, and the vacant look vanished. Whiteford felt a surge of ambitious delight.

'Not tired,' he said, vaguely, then more strongly. 'No need to sleep.'

'Welcome back, Michael. We'd given you up for lost.'

'Lost? Lost souls, hot lost souls, burn forever.'

'No doubt they do, Michael, no doubt they do,' Whiteford replied gleefully.

He told none of the other two psychiatrists about what had happened. The following morning, he visited O'Day again, before seeing any of the other patients. The man was sitting in the same position, as if he hadn't moved. As soon as the doctor stepped into the room, his eyes snapped open.

'Ah, the headshrinker,' O'Day said slowly, his voice totally accentless. 'Come to look in my head.'

'Come to have a chat, and an examination too.' He brought out his stethoscope and without a word, placed it against the man's chest, then against the vein in his neck. The blood hissed pneumatically. Under the beat, Whiteford heard the faint gurgle of turbulence which spoke of valve damage. How serious, he could not say. He would have to call in a specialist. He let the stethoscope dangle at his neck and drew out the pressure meter, quickly rolling the sleeve around the man's skinny arm and pumping the bulb until it bit tight, then listened again. The systolic reading was high. He lowered the pressure, waiting for the diastolic. It was way up, over the hundred. The heartbeat was raised too, and under the pressure of the sleeve, the wheeze of cardiovascular damage was unmistakable. The man was hypertensive, heading maybe slowly, but surely, for a brain haemorrhage. The resident ground his teeth, wondering whether to call the general physician for a further examination.

'Not long, I think,' O'Day said quietly in his ear, so unexpectedly that the doctor drew back.

'What?'

'Weak body. Not long.' He turned to Whiteford. 'And so much to know.'

Whiteford made up his mind.

'I want to ask you some questions.'

'Ask and it shall be yours. Seek and ye shall find. All manner of things.'

He turned to the doctor and held his scrawny hand up.

'But later. I tire in this light. Come later and you shall know everything.' He stared straight into the young man's eyes. Finally, and for some reason he could not fathom, the psychiatrist nodded. He undid the pressure sleeve, slung it and the stethoscope back in his bag and left the room. He closed the door, and when it was locked, he reached and inexplicably rocked the light-switch to off.

At eight in the evening, when the consultant was out to dinner and the senior psychiatrist was on a night off, Whiteford went back to C Wing and opened the heavy door to O'Day's room. He did not put the light on.

This time the man was sitting, naked as before, on his bed, but instead of being hunched over listlessly, he was ramrod straight, his legs folded, hands on his knees.

'Ah, the seeker of knowledge. The digger into the soul.'

'More the mind, actually,' the doctor responded, taken aback.

'Mind, soul, self. There is nothing but the dark.'

'You like the dark?'

'It is all,' O'Day said in that strange flat voice. His white body was a thin ghost in the dim light.

'I want to ask you a few questions.'

'And I will answer, but I need an answer too.'

'Go on.'

'Will you share with me?'

'I don't know what you mean.'

'Will you join me?'

'Of course I will,' the young man said, baffled. He was so keen to start the real file on O'Day that he would have said anything.

'But you must invite me in,' the wizened man said. His voice sounded sly. 'You must ask me to join you.'

Whiteford shrugged. 'Very well. I would be most grateful if you would join me. Please do.'

O'Day lifted his hands from his knees and reached forward, taking the resident's hands in his own, a movement so smooth and so quick it was done before the other man had time to react. The hands were cold, bloodless. He drew the other forward.

A trickle of alarm ran through the doctor, then evaporated. There was no harm in this emaciated little man. Even if he decided to get violent, there was little he could achieve.

'Will you be one with me?' O'Day wheedled insistently.

'Of course, if that's what you want. But first I need. . . .'

'Then join me,' the white figure said. He leaned close to the young doctor, eyes like pits in the dark. They opened and gleamed yellow. Whiteford tried to draw back, tried to pull away, but the eyes had snagged him. They grew wider, whirling yellow orange, mesmeric circles in the dark. He stopped pulling away, found himself leaning forward, began to fall towards the sick yellow.

Something changed.

Hot hunger sparked in his mind. The smell of blood was in his nose and the taste of it in the back of his throat. A coldness welled inside him and he thought of Walter, the big nurse, lying on the floor of the pharmacy room, writhing in pain, his belly slit from groin to sternum, slathered in blood. He saw the consultant, flash Harry McLeish, driving back from his dinner appointment, bloated and warm. Outside the room, through the frosted glass, the lightning pulsed in three sizzling stabs. He turned away from the light, feeling it sear his skin.

The scent of blood was in his nose and his mind was hot and sparking with the sudden urgent *need*.

In front of him, the skeletal man sat still. He reached for him, very gently, feeling the pulse of ailing life. He took the wrinkled head in his hands, savouring the touch, delighting in the surge of appetite.

With one sudden flex, he pushed the man backwards so fast that his head hit against the tiled wall with the sound of an apple trodden underfoot. The air filled with the damp metal scent, and something dripped in the dark.

At nine o'clock, Walter was coming out of the pharmacy, carrying a box of rubber gloves for the nightly shit-and-shovel run on D Wing, when the light went out. He thought a bulb had blown, and had turned to put the box down on the nearest surface when something hit him from behind. He spun round and a cold slick ran across his belly.

'Wha . . .' he started to say, then he was lifted by a colossal power right off his feet. He felt himself forced backwards against the wall. There was a thud and a popping sound as a sharp protrusion went straight through his neck. At that moment, he felt the slippery wetness tumble from his abdomen, hot softness against his legs, then a vast emptiness just under his ribs, as the gloom in the room turned to darkness, to blackness and faded to nothing.

Dr McLeish, the consultant who had succeeded to the job only three months before, came driving up from the security gatehouse in his new Jaguar. He spun the wheel, tyres crunching on the gravel, killed the lights and stepped out.

He never saw what hit him. A dark shape lunged behind an

574

azalea bush and snatched him off his feet. He felt himself tumble through the air. A sharp obstruction snagged at his foot, pulled free and he catapulted onwards. He landed on the high-voltage wires and died instantly, his body dancing in death like a puppet. Instantly the klaxons blared and one by one the outside lights came on. Overhead, thunder exploded as a jagged fork of lightning stabbed down at the chestnut trees and hailstones the size of marbles began to bounce off the gravel.

41

Her mouth opened, closed again, then she fell towards him. He caught her in his arms and held her tight, smoothing her hair as if she was a child.

'Tell me,' he finally said.

She pulled back from him, body singing like a violin string, her face a mask of anguish.

'It's come back,' she said, her voice a dread whisper.

'What has?' he asked, though he didn't have to.

'It's come back again. It's all going to start over.'

'Where?'

'I don't know yet. I saw it, and it saw me. It knows where I am. It knows where *we* are.'

He took her shoulders with both hands, gripping too tight. A dreadful surge of certainty clenched in the pit of his stomach as he looked into her eyes and saw the truth of it.

He stayed like that, locked with her for a long time until finally he relaxed, and drew her back down on him, thinking. He had too many people to protect. And he'd found Lorna Breck. It might have brought them together, this *Shrike*, but he would never let it pull them apart.

'Well, we won't wait for it this time,' he said.